The Nights of Labor

THE WORKERS' DREAM IN
NINETEENTH-CENTURY FRANCE

JACQUES RANCIÈRE

The Nights of Labor

The Workers' Dream in Nineteenth-Century France

Translated from the French
by John Drury
With an Introduction by Donald Reid

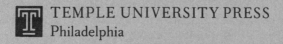 TEMPLE UNIVERSITY PRESS
Philadelphia

La nuit des prolétaires by Jacques Rancière was originally
published by Librairie Arthème Fayard (Paris) © 1981.

Temple University Press, Philadelphia 19122
Copyright © 1989 by Temple University. All rights reserved
Published 1989
Printed in the United States of America

The paper used in this publication meets the minimum
requirements of American National Standard for
Information Sciences—Permanence of Paper for
Printed Library Materials,
ANSI Z39.48-1984

Library of Congress Cataloging-in-Publication Data
Rancière, Jacques.
    [Nuit des prolétaires. English]
    The nights of labor : the workers' dream in nineteenth-
    century France / Jacques Rancière; translated from the
    French by John Drury.
        p.   cm.
    Translation of: La nuit des prolétaires.
    Bibliography: p.
    ISBN 0-87722-625-3 (alk. paper)
    1. Labor and laboring classes—France—History—19th
century.   2. France—Social conditions—19th century.
3. Laboring class writings, French—History and criticism.
4. Proletariat in literature.   I. Title.
HD8429.R3613   1989
305.5'6—dc19   88-32629   CIP

Contents

Author's Preface   vii

Acknowledgments   xiii

Introduction by Donald Reid   xv

PART I: THE MAN IN THE LEATHER APRON

1. The Gate of Hell   3

2. The Gate of Heaven   24

3. The New Babylon   49

4. Circuit Rounds and Spirals   68

5. The Morning Star   99

PART II: THE BROKEN PLANE

6. The Army of Work   137

7. The Lovers of Humanity   164

8. The Hammer and the Anvil   192

9. The Holes of the Temple   230

PART III: THE CHRISTIAN HERCULES

10. The Interrupted Banquet   257

v

11. The Republic of Work   303

12. The Journey of Icarus   349

EPILOGUE: The Night of October   419

Outline Chronology   433

Author's Preface

READERS SHOULD NOT LOOK FOR ANY METAPHORS in my title. I am not going to call up the pains of manufacture's slaves, the unhealthiness of working-class slums, or the wretchedness of bodies worn out by untrammeled exploitation. There will be no exposition of all that here, except through the glances and the words, the dreams and the nightmares, of the characters who will occupy our attention.

Who are they? A few dozen or hundred laborers in their twenties around 1830, who decided, each for himself, just about that time that they would no longer tolerate the intolerable. What they found intolerable was not exactly the poverty, the low wages, the uncomfortable housing, or the ever-present specter of hunger. It was something more basic: the anguish of time shot every day working up wood or iron, sewing clothes, or stitching footwear, for no other purpose than to maintain indefinitely the forces of servitude with those of domination; the humiliating absurdity of having to go out begging, day after day, for this labor in which one's life was lost. There was the oppressive weight of other people as well: the workshop crew with their strut as barroom he-men or their obsequious pose as conscientious workers; the workers waiting outside for a position one would be only too glad to turn over to them; and, finally, the people passing by in carriages and casting disdainful glances at this blighted patch of humanity.

To finish with that, to know why one had not yet finished with it, to change one's life: turning the world upside down begins around the evening hour when normal workers should be tasting the peaceful sleep of people whose work scarcely calls for thinking. This particular evening in October 1839, for example—at 8:00 P.M. to be exact—our characters would be meeting at tailor Martin Rose's place to start a workers' journal.

Vinçard, maker of measures, composes songs for the little party (*goguette*).[1] He has invited Gauny the joiner, whose taciturn disposition prefers to express itself in vengeful couplets. Ponty the cesspool-cleaner, a poet too, would definitely not be there. That bohemian has deliberately chosen to work at night. But the joiner can inform him of the results in one of those letters of his that he recopies around midnight after several rough drafts— letters in which he writes of their ravaged childhood years and their lost lives, of plebeian fevers and those other forms of existence beyond death, which may be beginning at this very moment in the attempt to put off as long as possible the entry into sleep, which will repair the powers of the servile machine.

The topic of this book is, first of all, the history of those nights snatched from the normal round of work and repose. A harmless and imperceptible interruption of the normal round, one might say, in which our characters prepare and dream and already live the impossible: the suspension of the ancestral hierarchy subordinating those dedicated to manual labor to those who have been given the privilege of thinking. Nights of studying, nights of boozing. Long days of hard labor prolonged to hear the message of the apostles or lessons from the instructors of the people, to learn or dream or debate or write. Sunday mornings anticipated, to head out into the country together and catch the break of day. Such follies some will survive well enough, ending up as entrepreneurs or senators for life, and not necessarily traitors. Others will die of them. They will endure the suicide of impossible aspirations, the languor of assassinated revolutions, the consumptive mists of exile in the north, the plagues of that Egypt where they will seek the "female messiah," or the malaria of that Texas where they will try to build Icaria. Most of them, however, will spend their lives in anonymity, out of which will emerge an occasional name: a worker–poet or a strike leader, the organizer of an ephemeral association or the editor of a journal that quickly disappeared.

What do they represent? asks the historian. What are they by comparison with the anonymous masses of the mills or the innumerable militants of the workers' movement? What weight can be attributed to the verses of their poems or even the prose of their "workers' journals" by comparison with the multiple array of daily practices, oppressions, resistances, murmurings, and clashes of workshop and city? Here we have a method-

---

1. *Translator's note:* More formally, the *goguettes* were singing societies that met weekly in cabarets, quasi-institutions that served as locales for the circulation of certain political themes and not just for merrymaking. A participant was a *goguettier*.

ological question that would marry guile to its "naïveté" by identifying the statistical exigencies of science with political principles which state that only the masses make history and which enjoin those who would speak in their name to represent them faithfully.

But perhaps those very "masses" have already given us their answer. Why, in 1833 and 1840, did the striking tailors of Paris want their leader to be André Troncin, a man who divided his free time between the student cafés and his reading of the great thinkers? Why, in 1848, did the working-class painters seek an organizational plan from their bizarre colleague Confais the café-keeper, who ordinarily bored them to death with his Fourierist harmonies and his phrenological experiments? Why did the battling hatmakers seek out the former seminarian Philippe Monnier, whose sister went off to play the "free woman" in Egypt and whose brother-in-law would die in pursuit of his American utopia? Clearly such figures, whose sermons on worker dignity and whose evangelical devotion were studiously shunned, did not represent the ordinary round of their daily labors and angry grievances.

But it is precisely because such figures were "different" that the workers would seek them out when they had something to show the bourgeois classes: proprietors, politicians, or magistrates. It was not simply that such figures knew how to speak better. Something had to be shown, pointed out, to the bourgeoisie, something that went beyond wages, work hours, and the countless little grievances of the wage-earners. It was basically what the foolish nights of their spokesmen already proved: that is, that the proletarian workers should be treated as beings to whom several lives were owed. If the protests of the workshop crew were to find a voice, if the emancipation of the worker was to offer a face to contemplate, if the manual laborers were to exist as subjects of a collective discourse that would give meaning to their manifold meetings and clashes, then their strange spokesmen already had to have made themselves "different": doubly and irremediably excluded for living as workers did and speaking as bourgeois people did.

So we find the history of a solitary word and an impossible identification right at the start of the classic discourses of the revolutionary and labor movement that propose to tell us the word of the laboring collectivity. A history of ghostly doubles and shadow images that the devotees of the masses (Marxist theoreticians, social historians, etc.) have sought to hide again and again behind accepted images of the "worker movement," "popular culture," and the like. Some have fixed in sepia brown the history of the worker movement on the eve of its marriage with proletarian theory, transforming it into a family photo album. Others have mixed those dark browns with the variegated colors of daily life and popular mentalities. Solemn admiration for the unknown soldiers of the working-class army has come to be mixed with tender curiosity about the lives of anonymous workers and with passionate nostalgia for the accomplished feats of artisans or the vigor of popular songs and celebrations. All these forms of homage are unanimous in assuring us that the closer those laborers stick to their collective identity, the more admirable they are; that they become suspect when they choose to live other than as legions and legionnaires, to claim for themselves the errant ways of individuality reserved for the egotistical "petty bourgeois" gentleman or the fanciful "ideologist."

My little story of odd proletarian nights would like to question precisely this jealous concern to preserve popular, plebeian, or proletarian purity. Why does scholarly or militant thought always have to find a wicked third party—petty bourgeoisie, ideologist, or master thinker—and blame on it the shadows and opacities that obscure the harmonious fit between its own self-awareness and the self-identity of its object, the "people?" Is it possible that the wicked witch is conveniently fabricated to exorcise an even greater threat: that is, the sight of our nighttime philosophers invading the terrain of serious thinking? Perhaps scholars and militants would have us believe they find something in the old saw that lay behind Plato's denunciation of the sophist, his little fantasy about philosophy being devastated by "a mass of humans not destined for it by nature, their bodies ruined by manual crafts and their souls broken and crushed by their status as laborers."[2] Or is it possible that the question of dignity starts from the other end? Perhaps scholarly thinking must go overboard on the positivity of the lowly people in order to sharpen the contrast with the illusory shadows of the ideologist and thus make it quite clear that its own dignity is very different from that of mere membership in a wage-earning category.

My questions are not the prelude to trial proceedings, but they do explain why I make no excuse for disregarding the majesty of the masses and the positivity of their practices and concentrating on the words and fantasies of a few dozen "nonrepresentative" individuals. In the labyrinth of their real and imaginary wanderings, I have tried to follow the Ariadne's thread of questions: How is it that our deserters, yearning to break away from the constraints of proletarian life, circuitously and paradoxically forged the image and discourse of worker identity? What new forms of misreading will affect this contradiction when the discourse of laborers

2. Plato, *Republic*, VI, 495, d–e.

in love with the night of intellectuals encounters the discourse of intellectuals in love with the toilsome and glorious days of the laboring people? The question is addressed to us, but it has also been lived up to now in the contradictory relations of such nighttime laborers with the prophets of the new world, whether the latter be Saint-Simonians, Icarians, or others.

It is indeed true that the word of the "bourgeois" apostles is what provokes or deepens the fissure in the workaday round through which our laborers are swept into the spiral of another life. The problem begins, however, when the preachers try to turn that spiral into the straight line leading to the mornings of the "new work," when they try to pin down their faithful to their solid identity as soldiers of the great militant army and prototypes of the worker of the future. As they delight in listening to the message of love, won't the Saint-Simonian workers lose a little more of their identity as robust laborers, which is what the apostolate of the new industry calls for? And, on the other hand, how could the Icarian workers find that identity again in any way that would not be prejudicial to the paternal education of their master?

Here we glimpse missed encounters, the impasses of utopian education, about which edifying thought will not be able to flatter itself for long, imagining them as clearing the ground for the self-emancipation of a scientifically informed working class. The twisted reasonings of the first great workers' journal "put out by workers themselves," *L'Atelier*, already give us a glimpse of the truth. It will later be verified by the astonished inspectors who have the task of overseeing the worker associations resulting from this crooked course. It turns out, you see, that the worker, master of the instruments and products of his labor, cannot be persuaded that he is working "for his own thing."

This paradox should not prompt anyone to rejoice too quickly in the recognition of the futility of emancipation's byways. We would do better to go back and see in it the insistent nature of the initial question: What exactly is this "his own thing" about which the worker should be excited but cannot bring himself to be? What exactly is at stake in this strange effort to reconstruct the world around a center that its inhabitants dream only of fleeing? And isn't it "a different thing" that is gained on these byways that lead nowhere, in this tension of maintaining a basic "no" to the way things are amid all the constraints of proletarian existence? No one today will find comforting reasons for his or her own disillusionment and rancor in following the course of our workers from July 1830, when they vowed that nothing would ever be the same as before, and seeing the contradiction in their relations with the intellectual friends of the people.

Indeed, the lesson of this tale would be the opposite of the one that some like to draw from popular wisdom: that is, a certain measure of the impossible, a rejection of the existing order maintained in the very death of utopia.

Leaving the field open, for once, to the thinking of those not "destined" to think, we may come to see that the relationship between the order of things and the desires of those subjugated to it is a bit more complicated than scholarly treatises realize. Perhaps that may help us to acquire a certain modesty in wielding big words and expressing large sentiments. Who knows?

In any case, those who are venturing into this labyrinth should be honestly forewarned that no answers will be provided them.

Acknowledgments

I WANT TO THANK ALL THOSE who have encouraged me in my labors in this field. A special word of thanks goes to Jean Toussaint Desanti, who guided my doctoral research into the subject. The group engaged in *Révoltes logiques* ("Logical Rebellions") drew my research out of its solitude. Jean Borreil followed the development of this book and meticulously corrected my manuscript. Finally, I would like to thank Danielle, who has been my associate throughout the journey, and my mother, who made it all possible.

Introduction

BY DONALD REID

> Take July 1830: in the imagination of a worker generation, it plays
> exactly the same role as May 1968. It is the moment when they
> decided that "nothing would be as before."
>
> —Jacques Rancière[1]

FOR ITS ONE-HUNDREDTH ISSUE in 1977, *Le Mouvement social,* the leading
organ of social history in France, asked the collective of a new social
history journal, *Les Révoltes logiques,* to give its opinion of *Le Mouvement
social.* The *Révoltes logiques* collective responded with a spirited challenge
to what it saw as the positivism of *Le Mouvement social.* The project of
Le Mouvement social was to know more about what we already know; the
collective declared that it wanted to know *"something else."* "What interests
us," *Les Révoltes logiques* concluded, is "that archives be discourses, that
'ideas' be events, that history be at all times a break, to be interrogated
[*questionnable*] only *here,* only politically."[2]

No individual had been more identified with *Les Révoltes logiques* since
its inception in 1975 than the philosopher Jacques Rancière. His intellectual and political development since the early 1960s provides the key to

---

I first wrote about Jacques Rancière in "The Night of the Proletarians: Decon-
struction and Social History," *Radical History Review* 28–30 (Fall 1984). I have
recycled portions of that essay in this Introduction. These are used with the per-
mission of MARHO: The Radical Historians Organization, Inc. I would like to thank
readers of that essay and of this one, Lloyd Kramer, Sara Maza, Pat O'Brien,
William Reddy, Holly Russell, Joan Scott, and Steve Vincent.

1. "Jacques Rancière," in *Entretiens avec "Le Monde" 1: Philosophie,* ed. Christian
Delacampagne (Paris: La Découverte, 1984), p. 165.

2. Collectif of *Les Révoltes logiques,* "Deux ou trois choses que l'historien social
ne veut pas savoir," *Le Mouvement social* 100 (July–Sept. 1977): 30.

understanding the cryptic battle cry of *Les Révoltes logiques* and the effort
to remain faithful to it in *La nuit des prolétaires: Archives du rêve ouvrier* (1981).

THE YOUNG ALTHUSSERIAN

Rancière first made his mark on the French intellectual scene while
a student at the prestigious Ecole Normale Supérieure on the rue d'Ulm in
Paris in the early- to mid-1960s. There he became one of the star pupils of
the Marxist philosopher Louis Althusser at just the time when Althusser's
attack on Marxist humanism was making him a major intellectual figure.[3]
In 1965 Rancière contributed an essay to Althusser's path-breaking *Lire
"le Capital" I*.[4] Althusser located the break in Marx's writings from a concern with man (ideology) to a focus on modes of production (science) in
1845 (although Marx had never fully thought out the implications of this
shift, a task assumed by Althusser and his students). Rancière pursued
this model with such loyalty that later commentators often use his essay
to illustrate the limits to which Althusser's thought could be taken.[5]

Althusser became a leading intellectual in the Parti Communiste Français (PCF) in the late 1960s by maintaining the distinction between "science," the province of intellectuals, and politics, the Party's responsibility.
But whereas Althusser sustained his balancing act with respect to the
Party—offering the requisite *autocritique* when necessary—his students did
not. They conceived of Althusserianism as offering the chance for "real
participation, *as intellectuals,* in the transformation of the world."[6] This will
to act led them to identify themselves as "pro-Chinese." Such a stance
was antithetical to the neo-Stalinists who headed up the PCF. Not surpris-
ingly, the Althusserian Maoists of the Cercle d'Ulm were kicked out of the
Union des Etudiants Communistes. Galvinized by news of the Cultural
Revolution in China, they founded the Union de la Jeunesse Communiste

3. Robert Geerlandt, *Garaudy et Althusser: Le débat sur l'humanisme dans le Parti
communiste français et son enjeu* (Paris: Presses Universitaires de France, 1978),
places this debate within the context of PCF politics.

4. Jacques Rancière, "Le concept de critique et la critique de l'économie politique: Des 'Manuscrits' de 1844 au *Capital*," in *Lire "le Capital" I* (Paris: Maspero,
1965), pp. 93–210. After Rancière's break with Althusser, this essay was reprinted
separately as *Lire "le Capital" III* (Paris: Maspero, 1973).

5. Mark Poster, *Existential Marxism in Postwar France* (Princeton: Princeton University Press, 1975), pp. 346–47; Tony Judt, *Marxism and the French Left* (New
York: Oxford University Press, 1986), pp. 224–25. Geerlandt, *Garaudy et Althusser*,
pp. 69, 124, notes that Rancière's denial of any creative role to "man" constitutes
an "extreme" formulation of Althusser's position (p. 124).

6. Jacques Rancière, *La leçon d'Althusser* (Paris: Gallimard, 1974), p. 89.

(marxiste–léniniste) late in 1966. Althusser remained a loyal PCF member, but the UJC(m–l) hesitated to attack its mentor directly.

The student uprising of May 1968, followed by the largest general strike in French history, took most *gauchistes*—as those left of the PCF were known—by surprise. While many groups sought to provide leadership to the movement, the UJC(m–l) initially held back. It interpreted the student rebellion culminating in pitched battles with the police on the "Night of the Barricades" as a manifestation of the students' petty bourgeois ideology. Only after workers went on strike did the UJC(m–l) join in, seeking to forge an alliance with the sole true revolutionary force, the proletariat. The Althusserian Maoists of the UJC(m–l) thus came late to the world-turned-upside-down of May 1968. They waited until the entry of the working class righted that world and made correct political practice possible. Like other *gauchiste* currents, the UJC(m–l) blamed the PCF for attempting to restrain the revolutionary impulses shown by striking workers. UJC(m–l) militants placed particular hopes in the rebellious young workers they met in late May and early June.

After May, the UJC(m–l) split. One faction joined with other currents that had come to the fore during the "events" to form the Gauche Prolétarienne (GP), a small but influential Maoist group. Rancière associated with this movement, whose slogan—"On a raison de se révolter"—summed up its impatience with arid theorizing in a time of action. The GP attracted the sympathy of many prominent intellectuals, including Michel Foucault, Maurice Clavel, and Jean-Paul Sartre. The *groupuscule* was well known for its efforts to break down the division between radical intellectuals and workers in order to allow intellectuals "to serve the people," rather than lead them like a Leninist vanguard. To this end, the GP promoted the clandestine "establishment" of intellectuals (mostly students) as workers—*établis*—throughout France.

May 1968 was a turning point for Althusserian Maoists like Rancière. Althusser's critiques of the student movement forced them to come to grips with the thought of their one-time master. For Rancière, the May revolt became inseparable from a revolt against Althusserianism. Taken together, these two revolts acted as a catalyst for Rancière's extended reflection on the radical intelligentsia and its efforts to create a knowledge of society that would not, however subtly, establish new norms and hierarchies, even while promoting social rebellion to overthrow the old.

Beginning with a trenchant critique of Althusser written in July 1969 and continuing in essays written in 1973–74, Rancière argued that May 1968 revealed that Althusserian thought "was a philosophy of order, all of whose principles separated us from the movement of revolt which shook the bourgeois order."[7] He attacked the ujc(m–l) for having carried within it "the uncriticized despotism of 'the science.'" It was this which had placed the ujc(m–l) in "the camp of the mandarins" in May.[8] Ironically, those very students in France who were most vocal in their support of the Cultural Revolution in China had ended up by a ruse of science opposing its analogue in their own country.

ON THE WAY TO LOGICAL REBELLIONS

State repression and popular indifference to the message of the GP contributed to the group's 1973 decision to disband. Equally important, however, was a realization that the locus of popular conflict had shifted from the GP to groups like the Lip watchmakers in Besançon, who had responded to their employer's decision to shut down by occupying their factory and starting up production. It was from this perspective that Rancière criticized the GP for not having extirpated its roots in the Cercle d'Ulm and Althusserian philosophy.

The GP had failed to think out the implications of its centralized structure and in particular the insidious logic of "representation": "the discourse of the universal held in the name of the masses."[9] Intellectual *établis* who took on a proletarian identity "represented" proletarians to other intellectuals, and used the authority their dual identity conferred on them to reestablish the authority of proletarian ideology (for which they were the interpreters) over the supposed petty bourgeois deviations of their non-*établi* peers.[10] The "new forms of expression" emerging in numerous localized struggles threw into question these "discours totalisateurs" of GP militants.[11] Participants in movements like Lip "presented a coherent discourse on their practice, not the words, the cries of indignation or exemplary phrases which *gauchiste* practice clipped from the discourse of revolt to reinscribe in the discourse of the spokespersons of the proletarian universal."[12]

Rancière sketched out this critique of the GP early in 1974. He returned to it a few years later after the sensational emergence onto the French

7. Ibid., p. 9.
8. Ibid., p. 105.
9. Ibid., p. 222.
10. Ibid., pp. 222–25.
11. Ibid., pp. 217, 219.
12. Ibid., p. 220.

intellectual scene of a group of one-time *gauchistes* as spokespersons for a
"New Philosophy" that condemned all "totalizing discourses": the philosophical premises of Marxism led directly to the Soviet concentration
camps. Foucault's exposure in the mid-seventies of the myriad strategies
of power operational throughout society provided the New Philosophers
with an analytical framework. The people, in Maoist terms, or the plebs/
plebeian character ("de la plèbe")—to use the expression of Foucault
and New Philosophers like André Glucksmann—for whom the New Philosophers spoke, was the locus of non-power, suffering, and rebellion.
Knowledge and power were indissolubly linked; all sciences were modes
of repression. The plebs could be known only through its practice. Efforts
to explain its sufferings (for example, in terms of capitalism or building
socialism) were implicit rationalizations of the plebeian plight. The New
Philosophers attacked the state while lauding the often hidden plebeian
micro-resistances. They opposed these to the revolutionary macro-
resistance of the "proletariat," whose political struggles destroyed plebeian culture, thereby leading to the ultimate triumph of the state regard-
less of the apparent outcome of the revolutionary struggle.

There was much in the New Philosophy with which Rancière agreed.
However, he also saw in it a renewed effort to "enthrone a new intelligentsia," which developed out of the theory and practice of the GP. This
interpretation was quite controversial. Rancière's article on the subject
was to have appeared in a special number of *Les Temps modernes*, but was
turned down by the journal's editorial board because of the connections it
drew between the GP and the New Philosophy.[13] (Benny Lévy, former GP
leader, sat on the editorial board.)

From its inception, Rancière wrote, the GP had condemned intellectuals for trying to appropriate and direct spontaneous popular struggles. In
the early seventies, however, the people's reluctance to reveal its inherent rebelliousness gave credence to the theory of the intellectual–*militant*.
Through popular tribunals which tried class enemies, the intellectual–*militant* would create the conditions for the people to express itself; as *militants*,
intellectuals edged back into their accustomed role of spokespersons for

13. Collectif des *Révoltes logiques*, "Les lauriers de mai ou les chemins du pouvoir (1968–1978)," *Les Révoltes logiques* (Feb. 1978): 6. For analysis of the New
Philosophers, see Jacques Rancière, "La bergère au Goulag," *Les Révoltes logiques*
1 (Winter 1975): 96–111; Danielle and Jacques Rancière, "La légende des philosophes (Les intellectuels et la traversée du gauchisme)," *Les Révoltes logiques* (Feb.
1978): 7–25. (On the conflict with *Les Temps modernes*, see the note on page 2 of
this issue of *Les Révoltes logiques*.)

the people. The New Philosophers inherited the legacy of these *militants*. Their identification of truth in the plebs subtly reversed the Althusserian/Leninist/Kautskyite mission of producing a truth (science) and bringing it to the working class, but maintained its conception of the innocence of the missionaries and the truth they conveyed.

What the New Philosophers ignored in their selective reading of Foucault was his recognition that there were no pure discourses of non-power. The people were themselves necessarily involved in a variety of forms of exclusion and oppression. Every act of resistance involved the mobilization of existing expressions of power to oppose others. In the mid-seventies, Rancière concluded, the New Philosophers mobilized a certain interpretation of Foucault against a certain interpretation of Marx to reestablish the radical intellectual's accustomed role as mouthpiece for the people.

Rancière went in another direction, toward Foucault and toward Sartre, Althusser's Marxist alter ego and the GP's staunchest ally in the intellectual world. (In his critique of Althusser's *Réponse à John Lewis*, Rancière pointed out that in a game of textual *cache-cache*, Althusser was using his attack on the obscure British Communist Lewis as a means of getting at Sartre.)[14] The confrontation with Marxist theory and Communist politics has been the crucial experience for French intellectuals in the twentieth century. Having rejected Althusser's symbiotic relationship with the Party and seen the *gauchiste* movement fall apart, young radical intellectuals like Rancière recognized the pertinence of Sartre's extended inquiry into the political situation of intellectuals outside the Party who sought at once to speak the truth and to make revolution.

In the mid-seventies Sartre became involved in a projected television series, "The Meaning of Revolt in the Twentieth Century." Rancière worked on a team with Simone de Beauvoir, one-time GP leaders Lévy and Philippe Gavi, and former *gauchiste*/future New Philosopher Glucksmann that recruited nearly eighty scholars and historians for the enterprise.[15] Although the project was never realized, it helped nurture the Centre de Recherches sur les Idéologies de la Révolte, a group composed mostly of former Maoists. The title was itself a reflection on the members' past: a valorization of the "ideologies" Althusser had denigrated; an echo of the *gauchiste* credo "On a raison de se révolter." Rancière was the leading figure in the Center, which began in 1975 to publish *Les Révoltes logiques*. The journal took its title from lines in Arthur Rimbaud's poem "Démoc-

14. Rancière, *La leçon*, pp. 46–47.
15. Annie Cohen-Solal, *Sartre: A Life*, trans. Anna Cancogni (New York: Pantheon Books, 1987), pp. 504–5.

ratie," a bitterly ironic commentary on the colonialist enterprise: " 'In the cities we will feed the most cynical whoring. We will massacre the logical revolts.' "[16] *Les Révoltes logiques* dedicated itself to the creation of "an alternative historical memory"—not that of the Academy or parties—based on "thought that comes from below."

FROM THE STUDY OF MARX TO THE STUDY OF WORKERS

Rancière first took up labor history in 1972–1973, when the GP was beginning to fall apart and he was returning to his attack on Althusser. Faced, as he said later, with "the impasses of the great idea of the years 1968–1970: the union of intellectual contestation and worker struggle," he looked for guidance to the July Monarchy, when Marx had grafted theory upon workers' protest.[17] For Rancière, completing his critique of Althusser necessarily involved a confrontation with his own contribution to *Lire "le Capital" I*. To accomplish this, Rancière required a new way to read Marx. The nature of class struggle should not be determined by reference to a Marxist science, but read in the contradictions present within Marxist texts themselves. What Rancière the Althusserian had once disdained as unscientific, he now saw as "the *mots d'ordre* of the proletarians' struggle."[18]

The caesura in Marx's work was not the result of an epistemological revolution in 1845, but of his disappointment with the failure of the workers' revolution three years later.[19] This break was marked by repression of the knowledge that artisanal workers opposed to the spread of large industry had formulated the idea of workers' emancipation. Marx (and Engels) came instead to place their hopes for a new revolutionary

16. Rimbaud used quotation marks in "Démocratie" to distance himself from the savage ways in which Western nations sack and plunder non-Western lands, destroying their culturé ("le tambour") and crushing indigenous efforts to combat this exploitation ("les révoltes logiques"). "But," notes Albert Py, "behind the rhythm of their setting-off song, and in the ferocious irony of Rimbaud, one perceives the echoes of another march, to progress, to equality, to peace, a call for a veritable democracy." Rancière and his colleagues on *Les Révoltes logiques* were fascinated by precisely such expeditions, in which the languages of liberation and domination co-mingled. Arthur Rimbaud, *Illuminations*, ed. Albert Py (Geneva: Librairie Droz, 1967), p. 225.

17. "Jacques Rancière," p. 158.

18. Jacques Rancière, "Mode d'emploi pour une réédition de Lire 'le Capital,'" *Les Temps modernes* 328 (Nov. 1973): 796.

19. Ibid., p. 800.

order in the factory proletariat to come, which would be molded by the discipline of large industry.[20] With this development, the proletariat left the realm of social experience to become a normative category consecrated by a certain Marxist "science." Deviations from the Marxist revolutionary project were attributed to "petty bourgeois socialism"; it was the revolutionary intellectuals' job to correct them. This was as true in 1968 as in the past: "history shows us that the workers have never ceased to act like these 'petty bourgeois.'"[21] Marx's ambivalent relationship to Parisian workers—impatience with their moralizing and associations, and admiration for their pitched street battles—was thus codified into a science, of which Althusser was only the latest apostle.

It was time, then, to put aside Marx's writings for those of his worker contemporaries. Rancière had begun his intellectual career in Althusser's crusade against "Marxist humanism" and its legitimation through reference to Marx's early "humanist" writings. It is not surprising that this question would also provide Rancière's *entrée* into the new body of literature. As Rancière pondered the lives and writings of workers in the 1830s, he saw that they generally conceived of affairs in terms of particular trades. When they did speak of workers as a group, however, it was in reaction to bourgeois writers' pejorative moral analyses of the mass of workers. The basic demand of those workers of the July Monarchy who broke with the hermetic discourse of the *compagnonnages* was for the status of "men." They denied the bourgeoisie the right to describe or define them, whether as savages, like the social investigators; as children, like the paternalistic employers; as productive units, like the economists; or as insurrectionaries, like the police. In each case, "the workers' discourse addressed itself first to the bourgeois" who attempted to define the workers' identity in such a way as to deny their right to independence and equality.[22] If anyone failed to merit the title of "man," workers argued, it was the egotistic, materialistic bourgeois of the July Monarchy.

What was Rancière to make of this irruption of "humanism" into worker discourse? He refused the Althusserian technique of interpreting it as "the necessary subordination of the suppressed to the dominant ideology."[23] On the contrary, he initially saw in it that autonomous workers'

20. Ibid., pp. 797–98, n. 2. Alain Faure and Jacques Rancière (eds.), *La parole ouvrière* (Paris: Union Générale d'Editions, 1976), pp. 22–23. (References to this collection are to Rancière's introductions.)

21. "Jacques Rancière," p. 163.

22. Faure and Rancière (eds.), *La parole ouvrière*, p. 14.

23. Ibid., p. 19.

ideology that Althusser had denied and the GP had travestied. For Parisian tailors in 1833 as for the Lip watchmakers, he wrote in 1973–74, " 'Man' is not at all a mask which would turn aside struggle, but a watch-word for moving from practices of workers' control of labor to practices of the appropriation of the means of production."[24] Yet Rancière began to question this reinsertion of the logic of representation almost immediately. Was the audience so clearly the bourgeoisie, and could it be so thoroughly evacuated from the text?

Rancière explored these issues in *La parole ouvrière,* a collection of documents written by workers between 1830 and 1851, which he edited with Alain Faure. In their introductions, Rancière and Faure sketched out a history of the development of working-class thought through the interplay of the revolutionary tradition, embodied in the Revolution of 1830, the transformation and decline of the ethos and organization of the *compagnonnage,* and the development of the idea of workers' emancipation through association. To this extent, *La parole ouvrière* resembles William Sewell's pathbreaking search for the origins of a workers' socialism in "the language of labor."[25]

However, in his commentary Rancière also addressed the "historical ruses of proletarian ideology" that would characterize the doctrines and practices of twentieth-century labor organizations. He found an early instance of such "ruses" in the Christian Socialists of *L'Atelier,* staunch defenders of a working-class ideal against all perceived bourgeois intrusions. The working-class elite of *L'Atelier* "is more concerned with summoning their brothers to instruction and morality that will render them worthy of dealing with bourgeois as equals than with giving reign to the multiple and contradictory modes of expression of worker revolt."[26] The demand to be treated as "men" was therefore at once a gesture of defiance and refusal aimed at the bourgeois and the core of a repressive discourse of working-class morality directed at other workers.

Pondering the importance of "man" first in Marx's writings and then in those of his worker contemporaries led Rancière to the problematic that underpins *The Nights of Labor.* Knowledge of the "working class" was born not of unmediated reflection on an economic structure or cultural matrix, but in conversation and confrontation with an apparent bourgeois "other." The identifications and representations that resulted became in

24. Rancière, *La leçon,* p. 169.
25. William Sewell, Jr., *Work and Revolution in France: The Language of Labor from the Old Regime to 1848* (Cambridge: Cambridge University Press, 1980).
26. Faure and Rancière (eds.), *La parole ouvrière,* p. 209.

turn the sites of ceaseless rounds of exclusion, inclusion, and differentiation that periodically produced confident assertions about *the* proletariat,
the people, *the* plebs. With this, Rancière jettisoned the faith expressed
in *La leçon d'Althusser* that there was an "autonomous path" to socialism
and revolution leading from July Monarchy workers' calls for producers'
associations to the Lip watchmakers' takeover of their factory.[27] What, he
was led to ask, were the implications of other ways of conceptualizing the
history of "*la pensée ouvrière*" in France?

THE DIALOGUE WITH LABOR HISTORY

In the 1970s, labor historians in France and elsewhere were expressing disillusionment with an established Marxist historiography and seeking to incorporate the social and cultural rebellions of the previous decade
into their work. Rancière was tempted by the new developments in labor
history, but ultimately rejected each with a similar "new historicist"–style
argument. Elements in and out of the workers' ranks, he explained, had
erected certain conceptions of skill, resistance, and culture into norms by
which to define and pass judgment on perpetually recalcitrant laborers.
"It is always in the heart of the worker aristocracy that a hegemonic fraction forms, presenting itself as *the* proletariat and affirming the proletarian
capacity to organize another social order, starting with the skills [*compé-
tences*] and values formed in its work and its struggle."[28] Historians, often
quite unconsciously, ratified these developments in their championing of
one mode of interpreting labor or another.

Surveying the field of labor history, Rancière argued that its practitioners widely accepted a sociological determinism which correlated skill
and pride in work to the rise and fall of certain forms of labor activism:
"Technical ability and pride in work thus created the basis for early labor
militancy and it was the Taylorist revolution that spelled the end of this
militancy by imposing massive and bureaucratic forms, which led to the
creation of a new working population lacking professional skills, collective traditions, and interest in their work."[29] Rancière argued that this
conception was false—relatively unskilled workers with little overt pride

27. Jacques Rancière, "Le prolétaire et son double ou le philosophe inconnu,"
Les Révoltes logiques 13 (Winter 1980–81): 6.
28. Jacques Rancière, "Les maillons de la chaîne (Prolétaires et dictatures),"
Les Révoltes logiques 2 (Spring–Summer 1976): 5.
29. Jacques Rancière, "The Myth of the Artisan," *International Labor and Working Class History* 24 (Fall 1983): 1.

or intellectual commitment to their work and skilled workers deeply ambivalent about manual labor had played prominent roles in the workers'
movement. "Militant activity is perhaps inversely proportional to the organic cohesion of the trade, the strength of the organization and the ideology of the group";[30] "the men who are loudest in singing the glory of
Work are those who have most intensely experienced the degeneration of
that ideal."[31] The myth of a genuine artisanal worker socialism was born
in retrospect, as a defense by labor spokesmen against new currents of
political socialism in the late nineteenth and twentieth centuries.

With this in mind, Rancière explored how pre-1914 syndicalism, and
its inversion by the Communists, could lead from a vision of workers'
self-emancipation to state socialism. Why did once anti-statist syndicalists
like Alphonse Merrheim and Gaston Monmousseau preach acceptance of
the state—capitalist or Communist—after World War I? Why did former
anarcho-syndicalists like Georges Dumoulin embrace the ideology of the
Vichy regime?[32] The answer was to be found not in these committed syndicalists' treachery, but in their loyalty to an ideal of the working class
that the mass of workers continually betrayed by putting their immediate
egotistical material interests ahead of what should have been their true
class interest. Non-Communists pointed to labor's abandonment of the
corporatist traditions imputed to artisanal skilled workers; Communists
lamented the failure of assembly-line workers to apply the disciplinary
logic said to characterize their workplace to their attitude to the party.
Discouraged worker leaders promoted the participation of organized labor
in a state apparatus that alone could bring refractory workers to fulfill
their class mission.[33] At the root of this syndicalist tradition was the unar-

---

30. Ibid., p. 4.
31. Ibid., p. 6. William Sewell, Jr., and Christopher Johnson have written brief
responses to Rancière's essay. Sewell agreed that the skill/militancy paradigm
needed to be questioned, but suggested that Rancière's blanket inversion required
qualification: while working-class thought may have been produced by workers
who rejected work, its greatest appeal was to workers who did have pride in their
skills. Johnson argued that tailors took an active role in the Icarian movement not
because of pride or lack of pride in their trade, but because of the specific economic
situation created by changes in production and the market. See Sewell, "Response
to J. Rancière, 'The Myth of the Artisan,' " *International Labor and Working Class
History* 24 (Fall 1983): 17–20, and Johnson, "Response to J. Rancière, 'Le Mythe
de l'Artisan,' " ibid., pp. 21–25.
32. Rancière, "Les maillons," pp. 3–18; "De Pelloutier à Hitler: Syndicalisme
et collaboration," *Les Révoltes logiques* 4 (Winter 1977): 23–61.
33. Rancière, "The Myth of the Artisan," pp. 11–13.

ticulated premise that an outside moralizing force—whether the "neutral" republic, the Vichy regime, or the dictatorship of the proletariat—was necessary to resolve the contradictions inherent in the syndicalist aspirations for the working class.

Rancière was particularly intrigued by the Vichy syndicalists' conception of themselves as heirs to the tradition of militant workers of the pre-Marxist 1830s and 1840s, who had demanded dignity, autonomy, and treatment as equals with masters without having to resort to degrading street demonstrations. Vichy syndicalists championed this idea of "collaboration" in their publications, the most important of which bore the title *L'Atelier*.[34] Rancière concluded from this study that the language of labor was potentially a language of oppression unless infiltrated with practices that undermined it, as happened in France during the years of the Occupation, between the times when class-conscious workers were expected to know how to end a strike and to fight a battle of production:

> Faced with hymns to liberating work, resistance relearns the subversive virtues of working just enough to live, and also those of anti-production, work poorly done and sabotage. . . . The history of worker collaboration and resistance brings to the surface characteristics often poorly discernible in the "normal" course of worker history: that it requires little for the themes that fuel struggle to identify themselves with those that feed submission; that the thought of class must always be traversed by something else, for it not to be the thought of class collaboration.[35]

The French Left, and especially the Communists, Rancière noted in a companion piece, had devoted their historiographic efforts to establishing themselves as the rightful heirs to the tradition of the French Revolution, rather than to a native tradition of workers' culture. They had in the early twentieth century surrendered this terrain to others: civil servants in the Ministry of Labor, Durkheimian sociologists, and militants from older, "workerist" traditions that posited the existence of an independent labor culture compatible with republicanism and set against the revolutionary projects of the Socialists and anarcho-syndicalists, which they saw as imposed from outside upon the working class. In the interwar years, the Socialists and the reformist trade unionists assimilated this workerist tra-

34. Rancière, "De Pelloutier à Hitler," p. 33.
35. Ibid., pp. 60–61.

dition in their campaign against the "alien" PCF, and the same tradition was in turn grafted onto the Vichy regime's efforts to call upon a native tradition of *corporations* and workers' culture free of political impurities. Repudiated after the war, the study of labor culture was taken up again seriously only in the 1960s.[36] In contrast to Third Republic studies which had shown the compatibility of an autonomous labor culture and the state, post-1968 researchers defined their project as a history of workers' culture focused on conflict and struggle.

This approach had its roots in *gauchisme* and the incorporation of Foucault's thought into social history. Some Foucauldians accepted a little too docilely employers' understandings of their disciplinary strategies, simply reformulating them as accusations.[37] Alain Cottereau broke with this approach in his provocative essay on the republican employer Denis Poulot's *Le sublime* (1870). (Poulot took his title from the Parisian argot for the most refractory, hardest-drinking workers.) In Cottereau's hands, Poulot's effort to order and repress Parisian workers in the text is made to elicit examples of workers' ironic sensibility and deeply subversive culture in the workplace, the café, the family, and politics.[38]

Rancière had himself followed a similar strategy in a 1975 paper on worker repudiation of the disciplinary, productivist elements of utopian socialist doctrine,[39] and in an article published the same year that analyzed Second Empire workers' opposition to employers' practices, particularly the hiring of married women: worker–delegates to the 1867 Paris Exposition had argued that working-class women could not achieve equality with men in the workplace; they could do so only by controlling the home and making it a bastion against capitalist encroachment.[40] Only later did

36. Jacques Rancière, "'*Le Social*': The Lost Tradition in French Labour History," in *People's History and Socialist Theory*, ed. Raphael Samuel (London: Routledge & Kegan Paul, 1980), pp. 267–72.

37. Danielle Rancière provides a good critique of this tendency in "Le philanthrope et sa famille," *Les Révoltes logiques* 8–9 (Winter 1979): 99–115. See also Jacques Rancière, "Une femme encombrante," ibid., pp. 116–22.

38. Alain Cottereau, "Etude préalable" to Denis Poulot, *Le sublime* (Paris: Maspero, 1980), pp. 7–102. Cottereau's excellent essay is now available in translation in *Voices of the People*, ed. Adrian Rifkin and Roger Thomas (London: Routledge & Kegan Paul, 1988), pp. 97–177.

39. Jacques Rancière, "Utopistes, bourgeois et prolétaires," in *Le discours utopique*, ed. Maurice de Gandillac and Catherine Piron (Paris: Union Générale d'Éditions, 1978), pp. 69–82.

40. Jacques Rancière and Patrick Vauday, "Going to the Expo: The Worker, His Wife and Machines," in Rifkin and Thomas (eds.), *Voices of the People*, pp. 23–

Rancière decide that the workers' *femme au foyer* anticapitalism should also be interpreted as another manifestation of the mixture of resistance and repression that characterized proletarian ideologies like that of *L'Atelier,* this time directed against women rather than other male workers.[41]

In a published conversation with Cottereau, Rancière and the *Révoltes logiques* collective pointed out the danger that he was (unintentionally) endowing *Le sublime* with the false coherence of a single, inverse truth by interpreting every element in the text in terms of the pure negativity of "worker resistance" and ignoring forms of power that workers themselves might exercise over colleagues, apprentices, or wives.[42] As he had in confronting the New Philosophers, Rancière rejected the "worker resistance" mode of interpretation as a subtle means of confirming the division between the intellectual as thinker and the worker as doer.

Rancière found popular culture no more reliable as a guide for identifying a radical working-class essence than theories of workers' control and workers' resistance. He criticized exponents of a popular culture whose supposed impermeability to outside influence was interpreted as a threat to a hegemonic dominant culture. Was this popular culture as free from contact with dominant culture as suggested, and, more importantly, did its subversive nature derive from its purity? No, Rancière replied. The true threat to the existing order comes when the cultural event challenges the boundaries between labor and leisure, producer and consumer, worker and bourgeois. He drew upon the example of what might be called the audience "performance" at Paris theaters in the first half of the nineteenth century, when bourgeois and workers attended the same playhouses.[43]

Rancière developed this view in an iconoclastic reading of the worker–poets of the July Monarchy. The worker's very decision to write—"la transgression poétique"—created a break with the rhythms of the workplace and popular sociability. "The poetry of the workers was not at first the echo of popular speech but the imitation of the sacred language, the

---

44. This article appeared originally as "En allant à l'expo: L'ouvrier, sa femme et les machines," *Les Révoltes logiques* 1 (Winter 1975): 5–22.

41. Rancière, "Le prolétaire et son double," pp. 5–6.

42. Ibid., p. 10. "Au sublime ouvrier: Entretien avec Alain Cottereau, "*Les Révoltes logiques* 12 (Summer 1980): 31–45.

43. Jacques Rancière, "Good Times or Pleasures at the Barriers," in Rifkin and Thomas (eds.), *Voices of the People*, pp. 51–58. This essay appeared originally as "Le bon temps ou la barrière des plaisirs," *Les Révoltes logiques* 7 (Spring–Summer 1978): 25–66.

forbidden and fascinating language of others."[44] This was all the more so for worker authors who spurned the advice of their literary patrons to write about what they knew (or were supposed to know)—the world of work:

> A worker who had never learned how to write and yet tried to compose verses to suit the taste of his times was perhaps more of a danger to the prevailing ideological order than a worker who performed revolutionary songs. . . . Perhaps the truly dangerous classes are not so much the uncivilised ones thought to undermine society from below, but rather the migrants who move at the borders between classes, individuals and groups who develop capabilities within themselves which are useless for the improvement of their material lives and which in fact are liable to make them despise material concerns."[45]

Such individuals, Rancière argued, performed the truly radical act of breaking down the time-honored barrier separating those who carried out useful labor from those who pondered aesthetics.

Rancière took note not only of the predictable bourgeois dismissal of workers who had wandered outside their station, but that by worker leaders as well, who, as they inveighed against the infiltration of egotistical bourgeois decadence into working-class culture, created a new social status for themselves as "representatives" of a class ideal. Neither worker nor bourgeois, these spokesmen were socially analogous to the popular wineshop singers they criticized. It was only a step, Rancière suggested, to those worker leaders who would turn to the state to maintain the morality and autonomy of workers' culture.[46]

When editing *La parole ouvrière*, Rancière had thought, "No matter how far back one goes in worker history, one sees revolt guided by a judgment that is based on a codification of practices and acceptable or intolerable discourses."[47] After critiquing efforts to represent the working class in terms of the "workerist" tradition of the labor movement, the negativity of workers' counter-strategies, and the positivity of popular culture, Ran-

44. Jacques Rancière, "Ronds de fumée (Les poètes ouvriers dans la France de Louis-Philippe)," *Revue des sciences humaines* 61 (April–June 1983): 37, 33.
45. Rancière, "Good Times," p. 50.
46. Ibid., pp. 82–90.
47. Faure and Rancière (eds.), *La parole ouvrière*, p. 9.

cière was no longer so sure. He came to see that his conflict was with the project of social history itself. Although a new generation of social historians might reject the old Marxist delimitations of the working class, they would necessarily seek to find another working-class essence reflected in workers' organizations, life-styles, patterns of sociability, culture, actions, and so on: "by the bias of an anthropology or a discriminating sociology, we will always be sent back to a . . . workers' ethos, . . . canceling out that which is singular in that production of meaning, in that expression which captures the encounter with the impossible."[48]

Even the best social historians do not encompass this encounter with the impossible in their work. Rancière found much to admire, for example, in E. P. Thompson's *The Making of the English Working Class*.[49] He pointed out to an interviewer that "the notion of class is only ever the product of a bundle of identifications. Thompson showed that 'the formation of the working class' in England was the product of a certain number of procedures [*démarches*], recognitions, discourses. As to the material reality that supports these identifications, it rightly differs from the usual sociological and ethnological objectifications."[50] Yet Rancière's underlying epistemology differentiates him radically from both traditional Marxist historians of labor and their culturalist successors. These historians' efforts to develop genealogies of working-class consciousness and socialist thought, he argues, mask the contradictions inherent in such entities. Rancière's goal is, he frankly admits, "impossible": "knowledge that can be neither the science finally saying the truth about State and Revolution, the proletariat, socialism and the Gulag; nor the voice in person of the excluded and the voiceless; at the very least [a knowledge that is] the maintenance of an irony, of a distance of knowledge from itself that echoes that which does not come to be represented, [a knowledge that] at least prevents the smothering of all that is now insupportable."[51]

48. Rancière, "Le prolétaire et son double," p. 10.

49. E. P. Thompson, *The Making of the English Working Class* (New York: Vintage Books, 1963). For his part, Thompson took note of Rancière's "Maoist freakout" in *La leçon d'Althusser*: see *The Poverty of Theory* (New York: Monthly Review Press, 1978), p. 202, n. 134.

50. François Ewald, "Qu'est-ce que la classe ouvrière?" *Magazine littéraire* 175 (July–Aug. 1981): 64 (an interview with Rancière).

51. Jacques Rancière, "La révolution impensable," *Les Révoltes logiques* 14–15 (Summer 1980): 88.

THE NIGHTS OF LABOR

The Nights of Labor marks an initial summation of Rancière's intellectual career from his Althusserian youth through his Maoist years and the assertion of his own distinct voice in *Les Révoltes logiques*. In settling accounts with Althusser in the early 1970s, Rancière developed a critique of Marx's understanding of the working class. In the second half of the decade he pursued this project with respect to the images of the working class presented by both the labor movement and labor historians. Workers were valorized most, he argued, when they fitted a norm; their "difference" made them suspect. Rancière rooted these images of the working class in past defeats within the labor movement and a contemporary self-doubt among radical intellectuals. In the years following the collapse of *gauchisme,* these intellectuals had sought a certainty in the working-class "other." This fostered "the honest concern to preserve the autonomy of working-class struggle, popular culture, and plebeian wisdom from our own uncertainties and illusions" (p. 14).

Yet, Rancière argued, there was a danger in simply ratifying a knowledge of what constituted the working class which had itself been created by workers disappointed with the moral and political failings of fellow workers and deceived in their own aspirations for another kind of life. Whether studying *L'Atelier,* syndicalists in Vichy, or workers' culture in the Third Republic, Rancière came to the same conclusion. "The troublesome thing was that this worker discourse never functioned so well as when it was doing so in the logic of others or for their profit."[52]

This paradox brought Rancière back to his critique of the process of representation whose doubling always hid a repressed difference. He described his enterprise in *The Nights of Labor* as "an order of discourse that marks the nonconciliation, the difference from itself, of social 'objects.' "[53] Faced with images of the worker as militant, *sublime,* or embodiment of a culture, Rancière declared, "We are not going to scratch images to bring truth to the surface; we are going to shove them aside so that other figures may come together and decompose there" (p. 10). Such a project marked a settling of accounts with the *gauchistes'* preoccupation with their status as intellectuals (as well as the labor history tradition Thompson incarnated). "I took the inverse of the great *gauchiste* theme: the relations of intellectual labor and manual labor. It is not a question here of reeducating intellec-

---

52. Rancière, "Le prolétaire et son double," p. 6.
53. "Jacques Rancière," p. 165.

tuals, but on the contrary of the irruption of negativity, of thought, in the social category always defined by the positivity of its 'making.' "[54]

Rancière conceives of texts not as passive objects to be deciphered and categorized, but as active, constantly posing questions to the would-be interpreter. In the interpreter's quest for a working-class essence, the voices in which workers speak of their existence and aspirations are distorted, amplified, censored, and pushed aside to confirm "the already known." Rancière asks historians, "What exactly is the meaning of this evasion that tends to disqualify the verbiage of every proffered message in favor of the mute eloquence of one who is not heard?" (p. 11). Yet once historians engage with this "verbiage," they can never declare the truth revealed, the working class represented.

Rancière's method in *The Nights of Labor* shares a common strategy with the deconstructionist technique of locating points in the text that reveal contradictions engendered by the suppression of "writing." Rancière latches on to the "interruptions" and "suspensions" of working life that occur when workers try to appropriate for themselves the power reserved for the "other." The element that has traditionally dominated the text— "speech" for deconstructionists; in this case the proletarian as laborer— is deconstructed to reveal the repressed "writing," or the proletarian as thinker. The seeming conformity of workers' lives to sociological constructs gives way under a deconstructionist reading of "interruptions" in these lives. Rancière endows neither literary nor sociological evidence with primacy. Both are unstable texts to be deconstructed; each serves as a context for rather than a reflection of the other.

Each of the three parts of *The Nights of Labor* problematizes a relationship in the conceptualization of the working class: work to the worker; the worker–*militant* to the worker; class consciousness to the worker. In Part I, Rancière reiterates his rejection of efforts to represent the working class in terms of socio-economic criteria or of a complex of gestures and actions. He describes the workers of July Monarchy Paris less in terms of sheer physical exploitation or membership in a corporate community, than as caught up in the perpetual anxiety of fighting to get and keep jobs characterized by moral degradation and mental tedium as much as corporeal hardship. It is not perhaps the working conditions per se that threaten workers with brutishness, but the never-ending need to ferret out the means to assure their sustenance. Categorization by skill, *corpora-*

54. Ewald, "Qu'est-ce que la classe ouvrière?" p. 65.

tion, or workshop organization obscures the complicated, shifting world of subcontracting and de-skilling.

> What defines the personnages of my book as proletarians is not their identification with a job, nor their popular roots; it is the aleatory character of a situation daily put into question, the illusory or transitory character of apparently prestigious qualifications and trades. The condition described today as that of the unstable worker [*travailleur précaire*] is perhaps the fundamental reality of the proletariat. And the modes of existence of workers in 1830 are quite close to those of our temporary workers.[55]

The central figure of Part I is the joiner/floor-layer Gabriel Gauny, who decided to make this precariousness a source of liberation—to conquer the tyranny of the animalistic need to consume through his "cenobitic economy." Gauny took from his experience with bourgeois Saint-Simonians not the project of making work the basis of a new moral order, but the desire to live the contradiction of a manual laborer who philosophizes.[56] Yet Gauny is more than the inversion of the GP *établi*. He is also Rancière's alter ego, the individual who can visit the prison–panopticon and see beyond Foucault's carcereal world to the lesson that work well done can lead to tyranny. It is Gauny who is able, in however incoherent, iconoclastic, and unsustainable a fashion, to preach not the rational reordering of this world, but "the revelation of a different world and the initiation of a new kind of relationship between beings" (p. 116).

Rancière works backward in *The Nights of Labor* from reflections on Gauny to reconsideration in Part II of his earlier work on the interaction of radical intellectuals and workers, itself the decisive event in Gauny's life. In the 1830s, tailors and typographers had formulated the demand to be treated as "men," not because they were highly skilled, were in short supply, or possessed a developed, insular corporate idiom. On the contrary, they had little to protect from other workers and their trades brought them into frequent relations with the bourgeois and their language of liberty and equality. In fact it was not insularity, but contact with elements in the dominant culture that suggested to workers the possibility of a break in their seemingly preordained working lives.

55. Ibid., pp. 64–65.
56. Rancière has assembled and edited a collection of Gauny's writings: *Le philosophe plébéien* (Paris: La Découverte/Maspero, 1983).

No one needs to tell workers that they are exploited; this they already know. What is news to workers is the idea that they may be destined for something other than exploitation. Workers got from encounters with the "other" not a particular doctrine, but the hint of another world, of a reason to revolt other than egotism and materialism. Such meetings of bourgeois and workers, far from anecdotal, are of central importance in the history of "the working class":

> [Workers seek] to appropriate for themselves the night of those who can stay awake, the language of those who do not have to beg, and the image of those who do not need to be flattered. . . . We must examine the mixed scene in which some workers, with the complicity of intellectuals who have gone out to meet them and perhaps wish to expropriate their role, replay and shift the old myth about who has the right to speak for others by trying their hand at words and theories from on high. (pp. 22–23)

Worker recruits and their new Saint-Simonian friends talked past one another. Each concentrated on possibilities inherent in the others' material situation while ignoring their interlocutors' dreams. Some workers saw the Saint-Simonians as a source of work; the most committed were entranced by the opportunities to philosophize—to do "unuseful labor"—in a community of love that the Saint-Simonian students, freed from the necessity of manual labor, could inspire. They were attracted to Saint-Simonianism by the glimpse of a new world, not the improvement of their own.

The privileged Saint-Simonian youths created an image of the worker drawn from their own belief in the positive nature of work, and some—distant forerunners of GP *établis*?—even set out to live a life of manual labor. They were disappointed by workers' rejection of their efforts to organize them into an army of labor. Equally important for Rancière are the disappointed worker recruits. "For these Saint-Simonian missionaries whom it is convenient to picture as students 'in service to the people' [the Maoist credo], were in fact workers or former workers whose whole tragedy was to be sent by their apostolate toward these egotistical workers they had fled in making themselves Saint-Simonians."[57]

The "tragedy" of individuals who had seen another world and become forever different from and disenchanted with the untouched masses sets

57. Rancière, "Le prolétaire et son double," p. 8.

the stage for Part III of *The Nights of Labor*. In this section Rancière discusses the Christian Socialists of *L'Atelier* and their debates with other
worker groups, the cooperatives founded with the assistance of the Second Republic after the June Days in 1848, and Icarian communities in the
United States during the second half of the century. These movements
sought to confirm as the essence of the working class a morality built
upon labor and to guard this working class against bourgeois contamina-
tion (including the oneiric perversions and materialist fantasies instilled by
Saint-Simonians and Fourierists). *L'Atelier*'s plans for association and the
Communists' efforts to build Icaria were at once calls for liberation and
repressive discourses of order. These ideologies of labor and the projects
they inspired were characterized by irresolvable conflicts in which the
virtues of sacrifice and solidarity were found to be one with the "other's"
vices of egotism and materialism. The workers' movement was born of a
contradiction: "The very same word, *emancipation,* is used to denote the
advancement of the individual worker who sets up on his own and the
deliverance of the oppressed proletariat" (p. 32).

Whether in Paris or in Icaria, workers refused to live up to the class
mission conferred on them; they were perpetually false. This resulting deception and disappointment became enshrined in the idea of the working
class that forever beckons to workers with enticing messages of rebellion
and pride, discipline and order. The logic of representation is such that
the "representatives" of the workers would always be different from the
workers themselves and would develop representations of workers that
repressed this difference. "The ruse of reason led dreaming workers on
the true paths of the future, those of disciplines—and dictatorships—of
king work."[58]

Yet *The Nights of Labor* is not a pessimistic book; Rancière's analysis admits of no such conclusiveness. He leaves the reader with a look at letters
written in 1890 by an aging worker–*militante* to the Fourierist intellectual
who had been her lover, in which she tells him that she has never forgotten
her introduction a half-century earlier to the possibility of living another
life. The politics of *The Nights of Labor* is thus not an "allegory of despair," Rancière explains, "but on the contrary an invincible resoluteness
to maintain, in a life devoted to the constraints of the *demande prolétarienne*
and to the hazards of political repression, the initial non-consent; at once
the death of utopia and the refusal of the real."[59]

58. "Jacques Rancière," p. 165.
59. Ibid.

CONCLUSION

As Rancière surveyed the field of social history in the 1970s, he came to believe that its practitioners were simply writing more about what they already knew—that every institution has its basis in class, that the oppressed find the resources within their culture to resist, and so on. It was not that these findings were not "true." But they had become verities: the very certitude of their "truth" seemed to obscure something else— a resistance in the text of history to the historian's project. Two options suggested themselves. The first was to reassert or revivify the old paradigms; the second—Rancière's choice—was to question these paradigms and ask why social historians found them so appealing. With this goal in mind, Rancière deconstructs "the working class" (or "the proletariat") in *The Nights of Labor* to reveal its contradictions and strategies of containment. The book presents the "genealogy" of a concept, but it refuses the historian's standard gambit of identifying once and for all *the* forerunners or *the* chronological markers in an evolutionary process. *The Nights of Labor* exemplifies a diachronic history in which reflection on the past necessarily entails reflection on the discursive production of its own categories, methods and ambitions. The very effort to identify and explain the working class as "other" (or "unity") ultimately questions the identity of the analyst.

The Nights of Labor is an extended *plaidoyer* for social historians to rethink what they study and how they study it. Rancière challenges the literary and sociological canons of the best and most innovative recent social history (represented, for instance, by Sewell's *Work and Revolution in France*). He reads worker-run newspapers less for the programmatic statements they contain than for the contradictory and conflictual stories and letters that continually challenge the coherence of such statements. When Rancière discusses worker–poets, it is for the sake of the uncertainties and questionings in their lives and texts, not their celebrations of labor.[60]

Marx and Sewell respectively suggest that the essence of the nineteenth-century working class is to be found in the factory labor force and the craft organization. Rancière reorients this vision, asking us to examine workers outside these groups—the kinds of people attracted to Saint-Simonianism —and to interpret them neither as Marx and Engels' reviled lumpenproletarians nor as Foucauldian *exclus:* "this aleatory population, in every sense

60. However, Rancière does not fetishize obscure texts. His *Le Philosophe et ses pauvres* (Paris: Fayard, 1983) addresses "major" thinkers, including Plato, Marx, Sartre, and Bourdieu.

of the word, represents less the army of the marginal or declassed than
the proletariat in its very essence that is concealed under the wretched
or glorious image of the factory damned or the pioneers of mechanics"
(p. 147).

Whereas Sewell finds the socialist aspirations of mid-nineteenth-century
Parisian workers rooted in their rethinking of a corporate past, Rancière
remains true to Althusser—or really to Gaston Bachelard, Althusser's
teacher—in conceiving revolutionary socialist ideology as born of a radical "break" with the present (and the ideology of the labor movement as
the ultimately futile effort to interpret workers in light of that break). As
for radical intellectuals, Rancière neither deemphasizes their role in the
formation of socialist ideology, as does Sewell, nor makes them Leninist "guides"; they are the necessary, disturbing presence of an apparent
"other," but they cannot control how their presence will be interpreted.

Rancière proposes a social history self-conscious and self-critical of its
own categories of analysis. Far from inhibiting historians, such a project
should stimulate them, by questioning "presentist" impulses even as it
queries efforts to establish an independent "truth" in the past or future.
The goal is to develop a history that will eschew the patronizing—to use a
metaphor shared by historians of gender and class—approach to the past
that the authority of interpretation threatens to bestow.[61]

Some will worry that the type of post-structuralist interrogation *The
Nights of Labor* exemplifies is yet another variant of Althusser's class struggle in theory or—to paraphrase Sartre—of making Billancourt despair.
This need not be. At a time when intellectuals in France and the West have
estranged themselves from labor movements that themselves rest uneasily
on a changing workforce—itself incompletely grasped in the current repertoire of the images of labor—Rancière's ironic inquiry suggests ways
of meeting the need to think imaginatively about how things are different
from what we "know" them to be.

61. Holly Russell suggested this wording to me.

Part I

The Man in the Leather Apron

It seems to me that I have not found my vocation in hammering iron, although there certainly is nothing ignoble about that calling. Far from it! From the anvil come the warrior's sword that defends the liberty of peoples and the plowshare that feeds them. Great artists have caught the ample, manly poetry of our bronzed faces and our robust limbs, sometimes rendering it with great felicity and energy: our illustrious Charlet, above all, when he sets the leather apron alongside the grenadier's uniform and tells us: "The common people *are* the army."

—Jérôme-Pierre Gilland

CHAPTER 1

The Gate of Hell

You ask me what my life is like right now. It's pretty much the same as always. At the moment I look at myself and weep. Forgive me this bout of puerile vanity. It seems to me that I have not found my vocation in hammering iron.[1]

IN THIS MONTH OF SEPTEMBER 1841, *La Ruche populaire* presents its usual face. The article on apprenticeship, bizarrely titled in Gothic letters, offers us another sigh of complaint rather than a documented study. That approach certainly fits in with the stated aim of a monthly that proposes to be "the mirror of this person's thoughts and that person's feelings, with no literary consistency or coherence; a modest album of the poor and a simple review of the needs and realities of the workshop."[2] It may have succeeded only too well in that effort. The publishers of *L'Atelier*, a rival organ of the "moral and material interests" of workers, saw in this vaunted "hive" of the laborer a noisy Babel of vain murmurings and groans and dreams without substance or consistency.

This time around, however, we might well have had reason to expect something different. The article is signed "Gilland, *worker locksmith,*" and we are surprised right away to find such a complaint issuing from a member of the privileged corporation that stretches from the ancient nobility of smiths to the modern aristocracy of metal fitters. Moreover, Jérôme-Pierre Gilland is not one of those occasional writers who bequeathed to

1. J.-P. Gilland, "De l'apprentissage: Fragment d'une correspondance intime," *La Ruche populaire*, Sept. 1841, pp. 2–3.
2. E. Varin, "A tous," *La Ruche populaire*, Nov. 1839, p. 4. *Translator's Note:* This piece is reprinted in Alain Faure and Jacques Rancière (eds.), *La parole ouvrière: 1830/1851* (Paris: Union Générale d'Éditions, 1976), pp. 219–25. This citation is on p. 220.

posterity only a few pieces of verse or a few summary thoughts, thus testifying to an impotent desire to swap their work tools for the writer's pen. A worker–writer for whom George Sand wrote a preface and a deputy in the Second Republic, Gilland symbolizes the entrance of working-class representatives into the realms of politics and culture and their continuing loyalty to their fellow workers. This son-in-law of a weaver–poet who spent his whole life at his craft will make it a point of personal honor, after Louis Napoleon's coup d'état of December 2, 1851, to pick up his locksmith's tools again and go back to earning his living as a laborer.

Should we attribute much importance to the youthful disclosure of a man who would soon play the role of a worker Cincinnatus? He is not speaking here in his own name, after all; and in such "fragments of private correspondence," which we come across in *La Ruche* and even the austere *Fraternité*, we find a common practice. After the writer has given way to the vagabond thoughts of his double or his demon, the worker–moralist takes over to affirm the virtues of work and the dignity of the worker. Our imaginary correspondent in this case is no different:

> It seems to me that I have not found my vocation in hammering
> iron, although there certainly is nothing ignoble about that calling.
> Far from it! From the anvil come the warrior's sword that defends
> the liberty of peoples and the plowshare that feeds them. Great
> artists have caught the ample, manly poetry of our bronzed faces
> and our robust limbs, sometimes rendering it with great felicity and
> energy: our illustrious Charlet, above all, when he sets the leather
> apron alongside the grenadier's uniform and tells us: "The common
> people *are* the army."
>
> As you can see, I know how to appreciate my craft . . .[3]

So everything is put right again. The depicted virtues of forged metal would quickly return the straying fancies of laborers to their assigned furrows as workers or soldiers in the national ideology. But how certain is the value of the image designed to keep the smith at his anvil if it must unsettle the order of the Platonic Republic, which subordinates the skill of the smith to that of the soldier only by excluding the illusionists who paint bridles, bits, and smiths without knowing anything about either of the two crafts?

The risk is not where we might first fear it to be: that is, in the arrogance

3. Gilland, "De l'apprentissage," pp. 2–3.

aroused by such heroic images of the worker's strength. What worker, especially one a bit enamored of engravings, would openly brag of his robust limbs or his bronzed face in an age when delicacy of joint and whiteness of complexion defined the ideal of the beloved maiden or the envied poet? Moreover, the martial image cannot hide from our locksmith the physical misery of workshop people. A few lines later he shows us that these vaunted physical qualities are simply a varnished reflection of the work and its constraints. Parents eager to thrust their children into the hell of the workshop, for example, know exactly what to say: "If the work is rough, they say the kid is very strong. If it is delicate, on the other hand, they say he is artful. They make him a Hercules or an artist as the case requires."[4] And when the vigor of his limbs is not a fake, for the locksmith it is a curse that excludes him from the realm of images in which he acts as model. A few years later, Pierre Vinçard will point up, in his fate, the extreme example of the alienation that causes the worker suffering, less from the loss of his object than from the loss of his image:

> The severe pose of the metal worker provides for some admirable studies. The Flemish and Dutch schools have shown us how it might be used to good advantage by a Rembrandt or a Van Ostade. But we cannot forget that the workers who served as models for those admirable paintings lost the use of their eyes at a fairly early age, and that fact ruins some of the pleasure we experience when we contemplate the works of those great masters.[5]

The painter's lie brings us back from the illusory sovereignty of the hand to the real sovereignty of the eyes. The ample, manly poetry depicted on workers' faces by the painters of tempered steel is not simply the mask of worker misery. It is the price paid for the abandonment of a dream: that is, another place in the world of images. Behind the pictures depicting their glory lies the shadow side: the lost glory of pictures that they themselves have not made, that they are doomed never to make, as they well know. "As you can see, I know how to appreciate my craft, and yet I would have liked to have been a painter."[6]

It is the dream of moving to the other side of the canvas. But not to represent the people–army symbolized in the hammer and leather apron

---

4. Ibid.
5. Pierre Vinçard, *Les ouvriers de Paris*, Paris, 1851, p. 122.
6. Gilland, "De l'apprentissage," pp. 2–3.

of the smith. Rather, to paint another image of the army of the people: for example, the gold-studded cavalry officer with tricolor plume whose white steed stands out against the Oriental bodies, the fallen horses, and the Egyptian backdrop of desert, sky, and palm tree. It is Gilland himself, in a letter to George Sand, who rates the painter of the proletarian marshall Murat among the painters who have set him dreaming: "I would have liked to have been a painter. Delivering my messages, I could not help but stop and go into ecstasy before the shops with pictures and engravings. You cannot imagine how many blows Gérard, Gros, Bellangé, and Horace Vernet have cost me."[7]

Over against this imperial dream, however, the moralists of the day set very different images of the painter. The pretensions of the scribbler, the debaucheries of the artist, and the miseries of the genius bring us back to the same model: the man who commits suicide pursuing the chimera of glory, in the realm of those shadows whose existence hangs on the whim of the powerful. This fate, we know, does not spare the most illustrious. A few years earlier, the waters of the Seine had swallowed up the despair of Baron Gros. Strangely enough, however, this curse on the artist now comes to envelop the modest existence of the common worker painter, the painter of buildings or signboards. And the working-class moralists are as zealous as the bourgeois moralists in warning about these dangers. We are surprised to find the old editor of *L'Atelier*, Leneveux the printer, placing the trade of painter way down in the hierarchy of occupations offered to adolescents. He ranks it just above the deadly dangerous jobs of the cesspool-cleaner and the ceruse-maker.[8] Neither the comparative mortality rate nor the wage statistics justify such ostracism of the painter's trade. We get a better picture of the thinking underlying such practical advice when we look at the promotional committee for worker associations and see Corbon, Leneveux's colleague, sharing the concern expressed in the question posed by the reporter about an association of worker painters: "The speaker would like to know if the members of the association are married." The peril of the trade is primarily moral, and one cannot "fail to appreciate the influence of marriage on habits of order and economy."[9]

But why are the worker painters the only ones to be scrutinized in terms

7. J.-P. Gilland, *Les conteurs ouvriers*, Paris, 1849, p. xii. Gros's painting of Murat at the battle of Aboukir is in the Versailles Museum. Murat was the son of a cooper. He rose to lead Napoleon's cavalry.

8. Henri Leneveux, *Manuel de l'apprentissage*, Paris, 1855.

9. *Procès-verbaux du Conseil d'encouragement pour les associations ouvrières publiés par Octave Festy*, Paris, 1917, p. 52.

of this general norm, given the hundreds of dossiers under scrutiny? Is it, perhaps, that their immorality exceeds the norm in seduced girls and downed glasses? That theirs is the worst sort of perversion, in that it turns a worker's occupation into the means to flee the condition of the man in the leather apron? That is the temptation from which the "people's priest," Father François-Auguste Ledreuille, would like to save the endangered workers through his Sunday sermons. But the hack writer in him cannot help but give way to the charm of it all, as he imagines the words of a shoemaker who has resolved to give up his own trade for that of painter:

> I will make you woods that aren't there, letters that you would not know how to read, pictures for which the models have never existed. Always in the air like the birds, intoxicated with the sun, chattering, singing to all the echoes of empty rooms, passing from luxurious mansion to attic garret, from countryside to city, not knowing today where one will be working tomorrow. Always new companions and new figures, welcomes at every streetcorner, tables spread at every town gateway, acquaintances at every stage and level, and a good day's work always.[10]

Of course, there must be a sad end for paradisiac temptations to a vagabond life and an airy trade. Ledreuille's painter would end up a consumptive in the town hospital: proof enough that a bird in the hand is worth two in the bush, and that a good trade is better than a bad one.

For Ledreuille's listeners and for those who refuse to listen to him, however, the problem is knowing what exactly is a good trade. Where do you find one that is not subject to accidents, illness, unemployment, salary cuts, off-seasons, and boredom? Ledreuille assures them that such jobs abound in the countryside. Whether he is being ingenuous or cynical, we do not know; but he urges all those driven by poverty to the city to head right back and look for the treasure buried in their father's field.

Less scatterbrained than our preacher and his painter, the former shepherd Gilland knows from experience that the relationship between the nurturing countryside and the illusionary city is a bit more complex. In one of his stories he might well attribute the apprenticeship trials of his double, "little William," to the illusions propagated by a worker boasting about the charms of Parisian life. But he also knows very well that the

10. F.-A. Ledreuille, *Discours prononcés aux réunions des ouvriers de la Société de Saint-François-Xavier à Paris et en province par M. l'abbé François-Auguste Ledreuille, recueillis et publiés par M. l'abbé Faudet,* Paris, 1861, p. 277.

heavenly contemplations of the little shepherd were not feeding his five brothers, that his fall was steep to the bottom of the stone quarry, and that the boy would have to reascend the muddy pathways with his back bent under the weight of his basket.[11] Besides, Gilland himself refused to go back to the pastoral servitude to whose charms he returns his hero. He knows also that the good workers end up in the hospital just as the others do and that, of his first two loves, it was not the woman of ill repute but the respectable seamstress who died of consumption. Poverty is not defined in the relationship of idleness to work but in the impossibility of choosing one's fatigue: "I would have liked to have been a painter. But poverty enjoys no privileges, not even that of choosing this or that fatigue for a living."

What is at stake here is not the right to idleness but the dream of another kind of work: that is, a gentle movement of the hand, slowly following the eyes, on a polished surface. It is also a matter of producing something other than the wrought objects in which the philosophy of the future sees the essence of man-the-producer being realized, at the price of losing some time in the ownership of capital. Our "friend of the workers," Ledreuille, was on target: "woods that aren't there, letters you would not know how to read, pictures for which the models have never existed." They would be so many hieroglyphs of the anticommodity, products of a worker know-how that retains the creative and destructive dream of those proletarian children who seek to exorcise their inexorable future as useful workers. Writes the biographer of a tailor–poet: "In his long breaks he took special delight in executing little products of fantasy that were good for nothing. . . . Thousands of pieces of wood endured the whims of his childlike imagination and were turned into essentially hieroglyphic shapes by his hatchet or his plane."[12]

For these laborers secretly in love with useless things, the image of the worker–soldier could be more dangerous than the evil it sought to cure. For it reconciles the worker to his state only at the cost of giving prime place to the party excluded from the city of workers and soldiers. Behind the depicted glory of the worker lay the falsehood of the image. Behind the falsehood of the image lay the power of the painter, heir to the dream produced by the epic of those proletarian cavaliers whose image he fixed while retaining sovereignty for himself. The reconciling image gets

11. J.-P. Gilland, "Les aventures du petit Guillaume du Mont-Cel," in *Les conteurs ouvriers.*

12. Alphonse Viollet, *Les poètes du peuple au XIXe siècle,* Paris, 1846, p. 2.

its virtues from the very sources producing the separation between the worker's vocation and his state.

To keep the worker in his place, the real-life hierarchy must have its double in an imaginary hierarchy, the latter undermining the former not so much by offering emblems of popular power as by introducing duplicity into the very core of the worker's activity in his place. If the counter-image proposed to the pious workers of the Saint Francis Xavier Society is the image of the sign painter, the reason is that the latter image best manifests the lie in the self-satisfaction of the worker who is happy with his work, the flight of production toward the principle of antiproduction and disorder in the city: not only imitation, but imitation without a model. As it decomposes, the "useful" representation of the happy smith reveals the logic of desertion that will be expressed by the poet to come, the one who will be the first to decipher the "letters that you would not know how to read," the new hieroglyphics of the duplicity of the illiterate: idiotic paintings, doortop decorations, ornamental paintings, tumbler canvases, billboards, popular prints, voyages of discovery of which one has no accounts, republics without histories, the invented color of vowels, a mosque to finish instead of a factory. . . (Rimbaud's "alchimie du verbe" in *Une saison en enfer*).

Are these sophisticated subtleties played on a little confidence that personalizes a great and modest claim of labor? Looking at the mosaic of "fragments of private correspondence," "letters of a nephew to his uncle in the countryside," "indiscretions," "opinions," and invocations that make up *La Ruche populaire*, we may realize, perhaps, that there is more sophistication here than is ordinarily admitted. Behind the lithography of the illustrious Charlet, as under those paintings several times overlaid, we may find traces of many sketchy or corrected images, many landscapes glimpsed or dreamed of.

It is an age, remember, when the growth of court accounts offers an endless harvest of images of the common people to the imagery of the melodrama, as well as to right-minded people and their rhetoric; an age when the revolutionary technique of stereotyping is being enlisted in the educational aims of the *Magasin pittoresque* and the social typing of "physiologies." In such an age there is no worker's claim that does not set the true portrait of the worker over against the commonplace scenes invoked against him by his enemies. But neither is there any true portrait of the worker that does not immediately disappear, by virtue of the power conferred on the identifying image, into the spiral ranging from the meaninglessness of children's hieroglyphics to adult dreams of another life. A question of identity, of image, of the relationship of Self and Other, both involving and concealing the question of maintaining or transgressing the barrier that separates those who think from those who work with their hands.

Here one would like to produce a simple effect: to budge this image of the worker–soldier. One would like first to show off the Parisian sketches, the country watercolors, the Oriental charcoals, and the historical tableaux that lie concealed in the portrait of the man in the leather apron: news items gleaned in the daily round of domination, poverty, and crime; trees or birds glimpsed in the patch of sky that slices the high window of the workshop; vast horizons embraced in laying floors, painting walls, or molding the cornices of an affluent home; blossoming girls and vine branches laden with the fruits of their romancing; souvenirs of the era when Napoleon, the "Man–People," paraded the triumphant commoner through "all the capitals of the civilized world";[13] cavalcades of conquered Algeria, sands of deserts dreamed of, prairies of promised America; harmonies in the June night coming from the Saint-Simonian choirs on the lawn of Ménilmontant. One would like to measure the gap between these hidden images or broken dreams and adherence to the emblems of anvil, plowshare, and sword, to grasp the logic of the identification process wherein those scenes can be covered over, effaced, and recombined, even into the hagiographic and threatened image of the man in the leather apron.

I am not talking exactly about scratching the images in the accustomed ways. I am not talking about the old political approach that unmasks the painful reality underneath the flattering surface. Nor am I talking about the modesty of the historian and the new-look politics that invites us to look under the varnish of heroic paintings and see the circulating blood of a life that is simultaneously more savage and more tranquil. We are not going to scratch images to bring truth to the surface; we are going to shove them aside so that other figures may come together and decompose there. We do not hold for the affectation of those who denounce the tyranny of truth. Rather, insofar as we scrape and clean and take off the varnish, we are surprised to find again and always the pattern of our illustrious Charlet.

To be sure, the characters have changed since his day; and in the accelerated rotation of picture books, we have more than once seen the chosen

13. "Napoléon ou l'Homme–Peuple," Saint-Simonian flysheet, Paris, 1832.

assume the role of the damned and the devils assume the halo of saints. So we have watched the parade of images depicting the grandeur and decadence of the worker myth: nostalgic artisans, proud of their fine work and defending a culture of worker's brain and brawn against the big industry that enslaves and frees; militants brought up in the school of the factory, conscious of their rights and obligations as workers; savage breakers of machines or deserters from the industrial order, later planed by the new disciplines into waxen figures on whose natural wrinkles are inscribed the thoughts of their masters about labor, hygiene, and family; "sublime" workers turning their very adroitness into the instrument of their resistance to factory discipline; and ordinary workers caught in the daily round of their labors, conflicts, and domestic lives.

True enough, this course of changes has some grounds for presenting itself as the path of progress. A shift from the great frescoes of labor misery and struggle to the fruitful austerity of the historian's rule: not words, deeds; not heroism, the daily round; not impressions, numbers; not images, the real thing. The method seems to be recommended by a heartfelt love for science and for the common people. And isn't that what first motivated the present work: to look at craft activities, workshop murmurs, work displacements, and factory forms and regulations and grasp therein the interplay of subjugation and resistance that explains both the materiality of class relations and the ideality of a culture of resistance? It was apparently justifiable to seek out the autonomy of worker word and practice above and beyond the interpretations of intellectuals and the lies of politicians. And it was not surprising to find at the outset that this quest for the muffled truth had to wade through so much babbling: the many professions of faith mimicking politicians, verses in the style of the great poets, moral declamations based on bourgeois norms, and screen representations that had to be scratched off.

But when one does proceed to scrape the varnish off those too civilized savages and those too bourgeois proletarian laborers, there comes a moment when one asks oneself: Is it possible that the quest for the true word compels us to shush so many people? What exactly is the meaning of this evasion that tends to disqualify the verbiage of every proffered message in favor of the mute eloquence of one who is not heard? Isn't there some sort of dodge in this fascination with the mute truth of the popular body, in these evocations of a different culture that the workers—the masses, the people, the plebs—practice with enough contentment to leave to others the lacerations of conscience and the mirages of representation? Hasn't the historian's modesty shared in the benefits of the curious exchange that has occurred since the existence of the worker was proffered as the living refutation of hinterworlds, since the path of descent into hell was presented as the royal road for correcting the vision problems caused by looking too much at the heaven of ideas, since the class once judged by the philosopher's *Republic* to be too ignoble to raise its eyes to heaven has come to be endowed with the supreme nobility of truth incarnate?

Both Marxist science and its denouncers say that here we find the gate of hell and true science, where all the reverie of the ideologist and all the vanity of the master thinker are to be wiped out. It lies in the den of Capital, where the labor of theory must equal the suffering that inscribes on proletarian bodies the truth concealed by the daily religion of commodity exchange and word exchange. It lies in the hell of the damned, where honest, undeceived thinking must recognize the plebeian truth and its denunciation of the science of the masters in the bruises on the people's flesh and their tattoos of revolt. In the modern thinker, then, we find this strange fascination for the truth of the popular body; a long-declared war on all those "unclassed intellectuals," "petty bourgeois ideologists," "master thinkers," who pervert the native truth of it with their rationalizing certitudes; tears of compassion; accusing fingers; and even contrite confessions of having taken part in the work of perversion. But isn't all that just another way of ensuring a share in the division, giving the thinker his dignity by virtue of the bias of his fault-finding?

The modern "reversal" of truth, you see, is really a matter of dividing in two. It has not done away with the old scholarly discourse that excludes the artisan locked in the circle of material needs and labors. It has simply doubled it with a discourse of truth, incarnating the latter in the very same subject who can know neither it nor himself but who cannot help but manifest it in his words and his actions. Thus, mastery ensures a replacement for itself. Sometimes it affirms the inability of the worker to recognize and transform his state without the help of its scholarly science. Sometimes it pays homage to the suffering truth of the popular body and pours shame on the false science that adulterates it: the better to reserve for itself, at the cost of asking forgiveness, the share of semblance that doubles as the lining for science even as ignorance does for the truth. Once upon a time it said: ours is the "lightning flash of thought" that will fructify the "naïve popular terrain." Later it said: theirs is the touchstone of palpable truth, the look of undeceived eyes, the naked cry of anger, the rough discipline that will change the world, the true culture, the sense of festivity, or the smile of plebeian derision; ours, alas, are the pangs of petty bourgeois conscience, the sophistications of empty thinking, and complicity with the science of the masters.

It suffices that the division of shares leaves each in his place, you see, and there are two ways to make sure of that. There is the age-old authoritative franchise. Its conservative version says that if the shoemakers meddle in lawmaking, the city will only end up with bad laws and no more shoes. Its revolutionary version says that if the workers choose to elaborate their own philosophy of worker emancipation, they will simply reproduce the thinking that was expressly designed to blind them and block their road to emancipation. The second approach is the tack of modern flattery, which also has two ways of assuring us that the place of the worker is the royal place; that the actions, murmurs, and struggles of the workshop, the cries and festivities of the common people, enact culture and bear witness to the truth far more than does the vain science of ideologists.

So we have two ways of repeating the same injunction to the suspect population of deserters who are enticed by the semblances of knowledge and imitations of poetry; artisans seduced by the higher profits of philosophy, Plato would say; worker–poets who, in the 1840s, addressed the fruits of their sleepless nights to well-established poets. The gifts were an embarrassment, to judge from the responses of their recipients. Victor Hugo, for example, offers this encouragement to the poetic beginnings of that child given to hieroglyphics who has become a worker tailor: "In your fine verse there is something more than fine verse. There is a strong soul, a lofty heart, a noble and robust spirit. Carry on. Always be what you are: poet and worker. That is to say, thinker and worker." [14]

A great poet does not mince words. It is not too much to say that the fine verses are more than fine verses and to bestow a great future on this "robust" worker poetry in order to pass along the advice that the worker stay in his present place, on the pretense that his place can be divided in two. Unfortunately, experience clearly teaches those who have not read the *Republic* that it simply is not possible to be both poet and worker, thinker and common laborer, at the same time:

> M. Victor Hugo knows very well that a person who performs his task as worker, which is already the work of two since half of the world lives in idleness, cannot carry out his apostolate as poet. [15]

But the inconsistency of the great poet may well have a logic of its own:

14. Constant Hilbey, *Vénalité des journaux*, Paris, 1845, p. 33.
15. Constant Hilbey, *Réponse à tous mes critiques*, Paris, 1846, p. 44.

> Jesus Christ said to the fishermen: Leave your nets and I will make
> you fishers of men. You others, you tell them: Don't leave your
> nets, continue to catch fish for our table, for we are the apostles of
> gluttony and our kingdom is a cooking pot. And our only cry on
> earth is: What shall we eat? What shall we drink? What shall we
> clothe ourselves with?[16]

Here the causticity of the tailor undoubtedly exaggerates the materialism of the writer. Our writer is more concerned about the rarity of his
verse than about the opulence of his table. Another writer, shoemaker–
poet Savinien Lapointe, is a member of a guild that has an old score to
settle with the philosophers and the artists, so he is more sensitive to
the way the discourse on classes slides in and out. His response to the
poet–peer of France, who now invests himself with the title "worker of
thought," gives a better indication of the give-and-take and the polite exchanges that are the price of maintaining the hierarchy of thinkers and
workers. It is not enough for thinkers to ensure their wardrobe by forbidding shoemakers to judge the work of a painter above the shoes. To keep
their place and keep the shoemaker in his, they must pay a cautionary
visit to the workshop, even if it means giving up a little of their usual
comfort: "Certain folks go down into workshops in wooden clogs, for fear
of seeing the common people go up to their homes, even in pumps."[17]

The disguise is surely a bit too worn to revitalize the old representation of the body and the soul. To make more convincing use of the fable
that assigns everyone his proper place, one will have to redistribute the
scenes of order and subversion as well as the qualities of the characters.
It will then be possible to link it in good faith with the honest concern
to preserve the autonomy of working-class struggle, popular culture, and
plebeian wisdom from our own uncertainties and illusions. Our desire that
everyone stay in his place will be more subtle and less riddled with anxiety.
And we will voice it more discreetly, insisting, as occasion warrants, that
the actions of workers are so much more cultivated than their speeches,
their discipline more revolutionary than their outbursts, their smiles more
rebellious than their demands, and their festivities more subversive than
their riots. In short, the more taciturn their speech, the more eloquent we
shall find it; and their subversion will be all the more radical insofar as

16. Hilbey, *Vénalité des journaux*, p. 38.
17. Savinien Lapointe, "Lettre à M. Victor Hugo, pair de France," *L'Union*,
May–June 1846. Reprinted in Faure and Rancière (eds.), *La parole ouvrière*, pp.
259–67. This citation is on p. 266.

it barely makes a ripple on the surface of the day-to-day order. At that price the gods are in the kitchen, the workers are our masters, and truth inhabits the spirit of simple people: "The common people *are* the army."

Seeing these placards show up on the road that was said to lead to the hidden truth of the workshop, I had the urge to make an about-face and go back in the company of those whom I had come across first: those who were traveling the road in the opposite direction, deserting what was said to be their culture and their truth to go toward our shadows. I mean those worker dreamers, prattlers, versifiers, reasoners, and indulgers in sophistry whose notebooks serve as a replacement screen in the mirror of reality granted and appearance withheld and whose falsetto voice creates dissonance in the duet of mute truth and contrite illusion. Perverted proletarians whose discourse is made up of borrowed words. And one knows that these people, so highly praised for keeping an exact account of their dues and debts, almost always give back the borrowed words in a strangely made-up way, with a droll pronunciation of their own. Vinçard notices it in a young Saint-Simonian engraver, "a small young man talking all the time, pretensions to devotion, but far more knowing than all that. He has a surprising daintiness in his pronunciation, so that he is quite boring."[18] The slight young man, too delicate to wear the illustrious Charlet's apron, will die soon after. But not the hardy race of those contraband intellectuals, like the cumbersome German tailor recruited by an illiterate Saint-Simonian missionary: "A hazy, argumentative talker losing himself in a host of hypotheses seasoned with old philosophical citations. There's a guy who is really boring. . . . I like him all the same; but more when he listens, which he does not do very often."[19]

One certainly does hear them with more pleasure when they keep silent. The proletarian pastor Vinçard, who indulges in these reactions against two sheep of the Saint-Simonian flock, will learn this at his own expense when he writes his *Histoire du travail et des travailleurs en France*. It will be his turn to hear that workers contribute much better to the cultural riches of humanity with their work during the day than with the fruit of their sleepless nights, that they have everything to gain by abandoning their "lucubrations," the word used by professional writers and thinkers to write off the work of those who write in the short space of time intervening between the constraint of work and the constraint of sleep.

But their solicitude is in vain when they try to warn these workers

18. Vinçard to Enfantin, April 22, 1837, Fonds Enfantin, Bibliothèque de l'Arsenal, Ms. 7627.
    19. Ibid.

against those who would like to wrest from them the well-earned quietude of their night. If they speak, it is to say that they don't have any
night of their own because night belongs to those who order the labors of
the day. They speak to win the night of their desires: not *their* night, the
"brutalizing night of sleep" that joiner Gauny sees approaching,[20] but *our*
night, the kingdom of shadows and appearances reserved for those who
can stay awake instead of sleeping. The good critic of the *Revue des deux
mondes* watches at the end of the day as "the worker with strong arms and
broad shoulders, his gait slowed by fatigue, returns to the lodgings where
he will again find his evening repast and sleep," and he vainly praises
"the distributive equity of Providence, which has decreed that for him
all upsets and vexations should end with the work of the day."[21] In vain
will others try to teach them that their true culture is in the workshop,
the street, or the cabaret. The gods may be in the kitchen, but they don't
want to go there, any more than does the seamstress who desires to ply
her talent in the house of the fine Saint-Simonian ladies. Her directress in
Saint-Simonism, Eugénie Niboyet, states: "Mme. Guindorff would like to
devote one day a week to the needlework being done on Rue Monsigny.
I think it would not do for Mme. Guindorff to dine in the kitchen."[22] We
do not know where Madame Guindorff finally took her meal. But we do
know what happened to her daughter, Reine (was it proper for a republican mechanic to give a name like "Queen" to a daughter destined for the
trade of seamstress?). Reine was to die of that vanity, victim of her sinful
love for a man of letters. The man drew enough profit from the lesson,
at least, to join Father Ledreuille's battle against the "doctors of the day"
who were perverting the true joys and simple sorrows of working-class
life.[23]

Certainly a foolish vanity: wanting to exchange the true toil and fatigue
of the common laborer for the illusory languors of the bourgeoisie. But
what if the most painful of those fatigues was precisely the fact that they

20. Gauny to Ponty, Jan. 23, 1838, Fonds Gauny, Bibliothèque municipale de
Saint-Denis, Ms. 168. *Translator's Note:* A useful selection of Gauny's writings
and letters is now available in the anthology compiled by the author. See Jacques
Rancière (ed.), *Louis Gabriel Gauny: Le philosophe plébéien* (Paris: La Découverte/
Maspéro, 1983), hereafter cited as *Le philosophe plébéien*. The present letter can be
found on pp. 167–69. This citation is on p. 168.

21. Lerminier, "De la littérature des ouvriers," *Revue des Deux Mondes*, Dec. 15,
1841.

22. Report of Oct. 1, 1831, Fonds Enfantin, Ms. 7815.

23. Raymond Brucker, *Les docteurs du jour devant la famille*, Paris, 1844.

left no time for such languors; what if the truest sorrow lay in not being able to enjoy the false ones? At the gate of hell, the apportionment of true and false, the calculus of pleasures and pains, may well be a bit more subtle than we generally imagine it to be in the case of simple souls:

> There are misfortunes so noble and so well sung that they glitter in the sky of the imagination like apocalyptic stars, their glow causing us to forget our mean sorrows, which, lost in the gullies of this world, seem to be no more than deceptive specks. Childe Harold, Obermann, René, confess to us the fragrance of your agonies. Answer. Were you not happy in your glorious fits of melancholy? For we know that they crown your souls like haloes with the genius of your lamentations and the amplitude of their radiation. Your celebrated pains have their own mysterious recompense, which again corroborates the futility of complaints. Sublime unfortunates! You did not know the sorrow of sorrows, the vulgar sorrow of the lion caught in a trap, of the commoner subjected to horrible sessions in the workshop, the penitentiary expedient gnawing away at spirit and body with boredom and the folly of long labor. Ah, Dante, you old devil, you never traveled to the real hell, the hell without poetry! Adieu![24]

Is that the farewell of a laborer aware of the real sufferings of the work-day to poets who know hell only in their imagination, and to sons of good family who suffer only in their heads? But then again, aren't the worst of true sufferings precisely those of thought? Gauny the joiner goes on to say: "Now our chagrin has reached its peak because it is a reasoned and considered thing."[25] The supreme sorrow of the laborer is to know in truth the misfortune of René, whose parents left him unprotected in life; of Obermann, who could not come to a decision about a career; of Childe Harold, whose passions were too large for the place assigned him by the world. The laborer's hell is not the suffering of the true that leaves all vanity at the door. It is the most radical vanity, of which the other is only the shadow. Those who know only the shadow of hell are actually those who live the true life, and the days of the workshop laborers are merely a dream by comparison. The joiner who bids farewell to old Dante is the

24. Louis Gabriel Gauny, "Opinions," *La Ruche populaire*, April 1841; in Ran-cière (ed.), *Le philosophe plébéien*, p. 37.
25. Ibid.

same fellow who had been urged not long ago, by a floor-tiler friend, to bid farewell to the old world and join him in sharing the true life of the Saint-Simonian community:

> Soon you will leave this world, where I say no more than what you also say with Victor Hugo: "My days vanish from dream to dream." Who better than we can understand all the sorrow in that line of verse: we who have so often tried to step out into the day without wherewithal or success; we who know of all the pleasures God has lavished on the earth but have tasted them only in imagination; we who have some feel for our dignity but have always seen it go unappreciated; we, in short, who have hoped and despaired time and again?[26]

The untruth of the poet does not lie in being unaware of the laborer's sorrows but in voicing them without realizing it. So it has nothing to do with the dialectical lacerations of thinking and being, of certitude and truth, which are to be reconciled in a thought process aware of plebeian sufferings or in proletarian action equipped with the weapons of theory. If the laborer alone experiences the truth of what the poet says, he recognizes only his own nothingness in that truth. Neither one, in his knowledge or his life, holds the truth of which the other produces the semblance, or the knowledge of what the other suffers. Far from the man in the leather apron, the laborer cannot, in the poet's image, recognize any self-identity.

In this exchange of vanities uttered in the manner of Epimenides, which steals away the subject who could attest to the truth about the untruth, the result is not skepticism but a certain kind of knowledge. It is an empty knowledge, if you will, promising no mastery. Something, however, akin to the transgression that prompted a tasting of the fruits of the tree of knowledge: an unknown relish, a bite from which there can be no recovery, an unsettling in which sensible reality itself seems to vacillate and reel. Such was the fever that seized Gauny and his friends one Sunday morning in the country, in May, while they were engaged in their metaphysical chats: "The earth was sinking down and out or we were ascending into empty space, because we saw creations unfolding that are not of here."[27]

26. Bergier to Gauny, May 1832, Fonds Gauny, Ms. 166; in Rancière (ed.), *Le philosophe plébéien*, pp. 156–57.

27. Gauny to Bergier, May 14, 1832, ibid.; in Rancière (ed.), *Le philosophe plébéien*, p. 152.

What relationship is there between the Sunday extravagances of these "artisans" and "petty bourgeois" men on the one hand, and the solid realities of exploitation and class struggle on the other? As with every vertigo and every Sunday, it is one of everything and nothing. Monday they will begin again the monotony of work or the vagrancy of unemployment. The world remains unchanged when the young seamstress leaves the Saint-Simonian preaching session, to which she had gone "to find a bit of droll amusement" and from which she returned "filled with admiration and astonishment for the grandeur of the ideas and the unselfishness of the apostles."[28] Nothing has changed, but nothing will ever be the same as before, either. Fifty years later, when many of the apostles will have forgotten or disavowed it, our seamstress and our joiner will still proudly bear the marks of the bite. For it is in the moments when the real world wavers and seems to reel into mere appearance, more than in the slow accumulation of day-to-day experiences, that it becomes possible to form a judgment about the world.

That is why those other worlds, which supposedly anesthetize the sufferings of the workers, can actually be the thing that sharpens their awareness of such sufferings. That is why those metaphysical problems, said to be good for bishops who find their supper ready and waiting for them, are even more essential for those who set out every morning to find the work on which their evening meal will depend. Who is better suited than those who hire out their bodies day after day to give meaning to dissertations on the distinction between body and soul, time and eternity, or on the origin of humanity and its destiny? Asks L'Atelier: "Can one explore any issue whatever without going back to first causes?"[29] Like the sham passions of poetry, the hinterworlds of metaphysics are simultaneously the supreme luxury and the supreme necessity for the common laborers. Despite his farewell to Dante, Gauny the joiner explains to a ragpicker friend of his the necessity of another world, be it the chimera of believers or that of poets, for the struggle here:

Plunge into terrible readings. That will awaken passions in your wretched existence, and the laborer needs them to stand tall in the face of that which is ready to devour him. So, from the *Imitation* to *Lélia*, explore the enigma of the mysterious and formidable chagrin at work in those with sublime concepts.[30]

28. Désirée Véret to Enfantin, Sept. 11, 1831, Fonds Enfantin, Ms. 7608.
29. "La revue synthétique contre L'Atelier," L'Atelier, June 1843, p. 88.
30. Gauny to Ponty, May 12, 1842, Fonds Gauny, Ms. 168.

So the initial relationship must be reversed. It is the secret of others that the worker needs to define the meaning of his own life and struggle. Not the "secret of the commodity"—isn't every bit of that as clear as day? It is not day but night that is involved here, not the property of others but their "chagrin," their invented sorrow that contains all real sorrows. It is not knowledge of exploitation that the worker needs in order "to stand tall in the face of that which is ready to devour him." What he lacks and needs is a knowledge of self that reveals to him a being dedicated to something else besides exploitation, a revelation of self that comes circuitously by way of the secret of others: that is, those intellectuals and bourgeois people with whom they will later say, and we in turn will repeat, they want to have nothing to do—and especially not with any distinction between the good ones and the bad ones.

But how can we not be struck by the gratitude shown for the love offered by the Saint-Simonian preachers, by the interest shown in the plans of all those who assured them that they had found the remedy for the ills of society in general and the poor classes in particular, by the love lavished on the great poets and popular novelists? The world of the bourgeoisie, like that of the worker, divides in two. There are those who live a vegetative existence, the rich people so persistently depicted as stretched out indolently on their sofas or feather beds, responding only to the fragrance of their own interests and incapable of experiencing the passions of those whose lives entail love, suffering, risk, and dedication. The image may not embody anger over their laziness so much as contempt for such an animal existence. But there are also those others who desert the domestic cult of Baal to set out in search of the unknown: the inventors, the poets, the lovers of the people and the Republic, the organizers of the cities of the future, and the apostles of new religions. The worker needs all of these people, not to gain scientific or scholarly knowledge of his condition, but to entertain and maintain his passions and desires for another world. Otherwise the constraints of labor will level them down to the mere instinct for survival and subsistence, turning the worker brutalized by work and sleep into the servant and accomplice of the rich people bloated with egotism and idleness.

Thus, between the smith and his image, between the image that recalls him to his place and the image that invites him to revolt, we get a slight twist: unexpected meetings and fleeting conversations between our marginal workers who want to learn the secret of noble passions and the marginal intellectuals who want to minister to the sorrows of labor. They are difficult meetings resembling the ones granted by our somber joiner Gauny to the blond preacher who calls himself Moses and dreams of new labors in Egypt: "I am not master of my time, so I cannot go to your place tomorrow. But if you happen to be at Exchange Square between 2:00 and 2:30, we shall see each other as do the wretched shades on the margins of hell."[31]

It is a difficult meeting. Not of poor man and rich man: the "bourgeois" Retouret would even have to borrow money from the "proletarian" Gauny against possible income from his writings. The meeting is difficult because it is a meeting of two worlds that do not run on the same time. Their relationship will be reversed soon enough, to be sure. The frail "pilgrim of eternity" will go off to die under the Algerian sun, leaving the somber joiner half a century to draw profit from the new message. Proclaiming the new order ("classification according to capabilities" and "retribution according to works") but positing love as its origin and basis, this message revives the semblances and contradictions of the old myth in the *Republic*, which said that the mixture of gold, silver, or iron in their souls determined the place allotted to philosopher–kings, warriors, and artisans.[32] The important thing, in any case, is not the content of the doctrines about the new hierarchy of the industrial city but the initial disorder of the picture that marks their enunciation: the meeting of the margins of hell, the mingling of base and precious metals, the visionary alliance or alloy of gold and iron against the dominations and servitudes of the kingdom of silver, the flight established at the heart of the worker's recognition of his image.

Is it really worthwhile to tarry over those encounters? Haven't some been long denouncing the delusions of those who want to straddle two worlds? Haven't they dismissed the false images for the inescapable realities of class struggle that rule out deception at a glance? Haven't others followed suit and described the movement of images as the work of a puppeteer (philanthropist, state, or master thinker), transforming the rigors of the new disciplinary order into a beguiling dream? The poor joiner, the former will say, is going to let himself be taken in by talk about love that seeks to make him forget the struggle. Look, say the latter, at the price in mirages he pays for his entry into the disciplinary universe of the pioneers of the modern industrial order.

But where did they get the idea that workers cannot simultaneously

31. Gauny to Retouret, Oct. 12, 1833, Fonds Gauny, Ms. 165.
32. Plato, *Republic*, III, 415.

love bourgeois people and do battle with them, indulge in Saint-Simonian love for the Father, the East, or the Woman, and flee its railroad empire? Writes one of the faithful: "I marveled at their teachings and preachings. But I was a bit disturbed by the outcome of their efforts and what they hoped and expected to see in the way of loftiness and grandeur in the governmental state."[33] What justifies our claim to see the realm of representation neatly divided between manipulators and manipulated, to see the laboring class as necessarily duped by what it believes? What makes this strange domain an "illusion," by very definition excusing one from trying to say something about it that is at least likely, even if not necessarily true? Isn't it a fact that all talk about illusion—at the cost of some redistributing of knowledge and truth—is designed to suppress the prior question expressed in the myth of the three souls and the three metals, a myth that it is "impossible to make people believe"?

That prior question has to do with the unjustifiable and inescapable frontier separating those whom the deity destines for thinking from those whom he destines for shoemaking. Not the partition that fixes the boundary of the reason by separating it from its other—that is, its margins or its un-thought-out version—but rather the inner frontier dignifying this thinking that makes the weaver its model and, at the same time, the one excluded from it. Perhaps, then, there is something at stake in our effort to mark the digression that intervenes between the old partitions of knowledge and the new apportionments that range thoughts, discourses, and images in the twofold registers of class struggle, science and ideology, power and resistance, mastery and dissidence. Perhaps there is a real point in letting the scene unfold as weavers and shoemakers, joiners or smiths, ask themselves about their identity and their right to speak, carried along by the very logic of the disjunction that prompts recognition of one only at the expense of the other. Such is their venture as they seek to appropriate for themselves the night of those who can stay awake, the language of those who do not have to beg, and the image of those who do not need to be flattered. We must take this detour on the supposedly direct road from exploitation to class message, from worker identity to its collective expression. We must examine the mixed scene in which some workers, with the complicity of intellectuals who have gone out to meet them and perhaps wish to expropriate their role, replay and shift the old myth about

33. Pierre Vinçard, *Mémoires épisodiques d'un vieux chansonnier saint-simonien*, Paris, 1879, pp. 57–58.

who has the right to speak for others by trying their hand at words and theories from on high. Perhaps it is through a few singular passions, a few chance encounters, and a few discussions of the sex of God and the origin of the world that we may see the image of the great labor community take visible shape and hear its voice sound out.

CHAPTER 2

The Gate of Heaven

ONE DIVIDES INTO TWO. But how are we to understand this division of day and night, this split affecting the image of the robust worker? Shall we follow the columnist of the Saint-Simonian *Globe* who, one October evening in 1831, mingled with the crowd of laboring men, women, and apprentices in the Salle des Funambules? If our columnist found Deburau's pantomime special, the reason was that it was precisely the spectacle that the people offered to themselves:

> That man is their actor, their second self. It is the people on stage, and it is the real people. Away with the insignificant medley of secondary performers who dress up as the people and stand behind the stars of the theater. . . . In the farces of that man there is an indefinable touch of bitterness and sadness. The laugh he provokes, issuing so freely and fully from the chest, turns into an ache in the end. After having entertained us so well in countless ways with his drollness and originality, we see poor Deburau—or, rather, the poor people—fall back with his full weight into the state of submissiveness, abasement, and servitude in which we found him at the start, and from which he escaped momentarily to give us so much delight. Farewell, Pierrot! Farewell, Gilles! Farewell, Deburau! Farewell, people! See you tomorrow! Tomorrow you will return to us: still poor and mocking; still awkward, clumsy, and ignorant; still the butt of derision by the idler you feed! There you have your life, your drama, every single moment and always![1]

1. "Spectacles populaires," *Le Globe*, Oct. 28, 1831.

24

Our Saint-Simonian columnist has fully grasped the lesson of his leader, Enfantin: it is in the theater, the new temple of popular aspirations, that one can see the laboring class living its true life. In the relationship of the common people to the stage and in the metamorphoses of their double, our columnist sought out the secret of the people's duplicity. But his choice of spectacle and the interpretation given to the truth of this popular panto-mime—a mute truth once again—takes the revelation of the new theater back to a metaphor that is not so new. On the stage of the Funambules, the *Globe* columnist saw a comic replay of the dramatic days of enthusiasm in July 1830 and their bitter aftermath. In the flights and falls of Deburau he saw an illustration of the major theme of Saint-Simonian propaganda: the people of Paris fought for nothing, or, rather, for the dream of some-thing that they must now try to possess in reality. After their three days of glory, they fell back into an even worse state of wretchedness. They will get out of it only when they are willing to apply to the peaceful armies of labor the dreams of glory that enchant their evening parties and the energy they waste in their days of insurrection with no future.

The fable goes beyond the mere calculus of inventions designed to transform the rebellious energy of the barricades into a production force. Beyond, for example, the "peaceful riots" in which, the first Sunday of every month, rioters and national guardsmen would be asked to bring to public works "the zeal and ardor they might have invested in disturbing public order or restoring it."[2] The image of the people presented here goes further back and forward than does the Saint-Simonian enterprise. It is a double image in which the figure of an exploited and despised people, victim of the ignorance and awkwardness associated with its dull weight as the productive, food-producing class, unites with the figure of the childlike people who transform the dream of their own emancipation into a game with the powerful and an attitude of self-derision. So we have a people who are accomplices in a subordination that allows them the possibility of imaginary denials and symbolic subversions: the evasions of theater scenes and merry evening get-togethers, days of insurrection whose ephemeral victories seem to repeat the function of carnivals and charivaris—to provide the momentary reversal of roles needed to restore equilibrium between rulers and ruled.

In the diverse programs designed to make available the energy lost in popular revolts and festivals, and in the images they project of popular

2. Charles Béranger, "L'émeute," *Le Travail*, June 9, 1832.

ignorance and fickleness, we find a constant. It is the picture of a proletarian people whose consciousness is always being contaminated by the
vestiges of the past or by the societal intermediaries of the present: a working class "in formation," still marked by the cyclical rhythms that govern
the labors, festivals, and "emotions" of country folk; town and city proletarians caught up in the symbolic game played with the royal authorities
by the "preindustrial urban crowds"; the fundamental class contaminated
by the illusions and irresolute forms of action peculiar to their intermediaries—petty bourgeois people, artisans, and shopkeepers—who insinuate
themselves into all the pores of the popular tissue; thus, a working people
who must be given the awareness befitting their social positivity and the
forms of action suited to ensuring their real-life emancipation.

It is at this point that the misunderstanding or mistake intervenes between the interpretation of the actors and the criticism of the theoretician
spectators. The lack of harmony applies, first of all, to the way in which
the action is understood and its results are determined. Such is the case
with the "futile" insurrection of July. It is indeed true that the business
depression after the Revolution brought unemployment or underemploy-
ment to workers who had been doing well, and that it brought ruin to
many initiatives and projects. The awareness that it produced in the interested parties, however, was not simply bitterness over a victory profiting
the bourgeois class alone. It was more akin to a feel for the material sacrifices that must be made to pay for effective social advances: titles of
nobility bought at a high price, or enterprises that will later repay the
expense in pain and trouble.

This disharmony between the order of economic profits and that of social advances marks the recitals of proletarian workers who lived through
the dark years of the Restoration: "The years following the Restoration
were very painful for the workers."[3] In support of this judgment Suzanne
Voilquin does not offer any data that might specifically contradict the
science of economics or its graphs, which assure us that those painful
years were actually favorable to industry and workers. And her brother in
Saint-Simonism, Louis Vinçard, reminds us that the flourishing advance
of business compelled his father, a maker of linear measures, to hire new
workers. But the words of Suzanne Voilquin show us what made up the
wretchedness of those years: the time spent in the servitude of those who
have nothing to do but work as they sift the memory of a few scenes:

3. Suzanne Voilquin, *Souvenirs d'une fille du peuple* (Paris: F. Maspéro, 1978),
p. 68.

the futile defense of a betrayed city, the humiliation of the occupation, the morgue of ghosts. The victory festival of others was enough to turn the prosperous years of business into years of humiliation for the workers. The new employees of flourishing industry did not find their dreams of social advancement satisfied by the security of their condition or the designation of their tasks as skilled.

Such was the case with Jean Marchand, who was hired by the senior Vinçard but valued only "those things that exercise and enlarge the mind."[4] Not included in such things were the fabrication of linear measures and the scientific and industrial spaces in which it operated: that realm of invention and technical intelligence which the progressive bourgeoisie envisioned as effecting the intellectual and material emancipation of the proletariat. For Marchand at least, these matters were not as pertinent as grammar, the manuals of which he constantly perused, and music, which he learned on his own before tackling versification and giving the son of the family rhyming exercises. At the end of that road, when Vinçard the son had learned to express himself better in verse than in prose, lay the *goguettes,* where the aspiration to be recognized as an artist would link up with "love for our national glories and public liberties." This nighttime socialization of individual vanities paved the way for the three glorious days, which were followed by the nights without food or fuel in the winter of 1830–1831. That was the price to be paid for the recognition of worker identity in modern society. But it may also have been a result of the inability of the actors to sustain the glare of that advance, to respond to the question of identity that was brutally asserted in broad daylight. Writes a heroine of July: "Why is it that the brilliant image of those brief instants appears to be merely a fleeting vision in the dark labyrinth where we have come to stray? . . . The reason is that we, like those condemned to the mines, accustomed to the darkness like them, could not sustain the glare of such a bright light."[5]

The metaphor takes us beyond images of the clumsy heaviness of the productive people or the frivolous lightness of the bantering people. Seamstress Julie Fanfernot lets us glimpse something else in the relapse of July, something akin to a penalty for an abortive initiation into the final rite or test. But the journey in the labyrinth of today and the comparison with the light of yesterday rightly reveal a social identity that is more complicated

4. Pierre Vinçard, *Mémoires épisodiques d'un vieux chansonnier saint-simonien,* Paris, 1879, p. 20.

5. Julie Fanfernot, *L'étincelle,* Paris, 1833.

than the marriage of the productive people with the childlike people. In vain will songs and manifestoes hammer out the refrain about the fundamental class, the nurturing source and suffering bottomland of the social body. In an age when philanthropists and utopians, enlightened bourgeoisie and self-taught workers, traditional and revolutionary educators, gave Fénelon's *Télémaque* as a text to proletarians awakening to the intellectual life, how could the latter misread or mistake the lesson of the reform undertaken in the kingdom of Salente, where superfluous craftsmen in the towns, whose trades served only "to disorder morals," were shipped out to rural areas that had an insufficient supply of laborers? Who would believe that these tailors, cabinetmakers, founders, chiselers, lacemakers, ornament-makers, fan-makers, and so on, who live solely off the consumption of luxuries by the affluent classes, could typify the food-producing class of society?

Thus, the crossing of paths on the way to the working-class city and the heights and depths attained there suggest that the ebb and flow of popular movements reflect something other than the versatility of "pre-industrial urban crowds," the strong influence of the petty bourgeoisie, or the imbalances of a class "in formation." Being always in the process of taking shape could be a permanent characteristic of the working class. At every stage it might look like a transit point, so that the eye of the expert gets lost in trying to differentiate the true proletarian laborer from the belated artisan or the disqualified member of the tertiary sector. Our focus here, then, is, and has been for some years, a place of passage and meeting where the sons of peasants who were set on the road to the cities by revolutionary enthusiasms cross paths with high-born people reduced to the proletarian level by some recent political disgrace, with workers who had been temporarily turned into businessmen by *assignat* fever and then returned to their original state, or with soldiers who were forced in 1815 to take to the unknown or forgotten byways of the workshops.

On this thoroughfare they meet: a weaver, son of a linen merchant who was ruined by the vanity that prompted him to purchase a title of nobility on the eve of 1789; the son of a winegrower–cooper who had the good fortune to be able to pursue studies and the bad fortune to see the family assets lost in a lawsuit, thus ending up a typographical worker; an adolescent wool-carder, son of a bankrupt proprietor, who survived childhood by collecting bones from slaughterhouses and mercury from urinals; and the little country boy who has become a tailor because a turner's apprenticeship was beyond his parents' means. They join the anomalous and provisional assemblage of younger sons who have set out to seek, from the uncertain work of their own hands and the unpredictable vicissitudes of industry, a subsistence, a fortune perhaps, that cannot be guaranteed to all by industry or their paternal soil.

Undoubtedly, the Revolution abolished the juridical rigors of the law of primogeniture, which had kept the grandfather of silk-weaver Sébastien Commissaire and the father of embroiderer Suzanne Voilquin from the education and assets reserved for the firstborn of those large families. But even if the younger sons of families with twenty children now tend to have no more than ten, half of whom die rather quickly, they still do not have the means to pay for the apprenticeship of all in some vocational trade (état). All the more, suggest the children now and then, because their fathers were marked by the age of great upheavals, are more taken up with planning castles in Spain for their offspring than positions with a future, and go rolling around in search of fortune like stones that gather no moss. Along with the reality of economic constraint and the aberrations of fancy, family tradition and emotional caprice combine to subject the younger sons of the last generation to the hazards of a lottery in which one loses at every turn.

By opposite roads, then, silk-weaver Commissaire and tailor Troncin would suffer the identical effects of a typical situation: the premature death of one parent and the remarriage of the other. The firstborn child of his father's second marriage, Sébastien Commissaire suffered from his role as an intruder. He was soon put to work by his father (weaver, dyer, and peddler), whose gypsy temperament did not stray from principles of authority and who did not want to be reproached for letting the children of his second marriage eat the hard-earned bread of his older children. But when this unstable father, after settling in Lyons for a time, set out again with one of his elder sons on the road marked by dreams of fortune and aberrations of the heart, young Sébastien found himself, at the age of fourteen, head of the family and fixed in the career of silk-weaver.[6] On the other hand, André Troncin, the second son of the first marriage of a fairly comfortable wood merchant in Besançon, had to endure the antipathy of his stepmother. His elder brother, taken in by an uncle, received training that enabled him to occupy "an honorable place in the commerce of Paris."[7] André, on the other hand, was placed with a tailor—the apprenticeship of the poor—before going to Paris to swell the ranks of the craft with the highest rate of unemployment.

6. Sébastien Commissaire, *Mémoires et souvenirs*, Lyon, 1888.

7. J.-P. Gilland, "Biographie des hommes obscurs: André Troncin," *La Feuille du village*, Nov. 28, 1850.

To be sure, the constraints sending one to Paris and abandoning another in Lyons could be complicated by a more or less deliberate choice. Joiner Agricol Perdiguier could very well have followed his father, who practiced his craft in Morières. His oldest brother, the "educated" one, and his second brother had chosen to work the family land. But Agricol did not want, any more than his brothers did, to work under his father's authority while waiting to be his own master. When he got to Paris, he would not even accept the offer of his aunt to set him up in Avignon. Like his neighbor, locksmith Gilland, he preferred to celebrate from afar the virtues of his birthplace and to contemplate images of evangelical and patriarchal communism in the countryside. There was his grandfather, after all, who took what he wanted from the vineyards of others and recognized the right of everyone else to enter his own and pick the fruits that belonged to no one but God.[8]

In like manner, the proletarian fabulist Lachambeaudie delighted in recalling the fraternal banquets at his village school, at which rich and poor shared the contents of their baskets.[9] But he and Perdiguier chose the solitude of the city and the hazards of competition, an existence on the edge of two worlds imaged in the room that Perdiguier has Gilland visit:

> Agricol Perdiguier lived at 104 Faubourg Saint-Antoine, in a frightful hovel masked on the outside by a superb pastry shop. . . . Almost everything around Agricol Perdiguier was odious and repulsive, but once inside his quarters you found yourself in another world. The room did indeed have bad flooring. Like country shacks, it had large, dark beams on the ceiling. But the room had an alcove and was decorated with a brightly painted paper that gave it an air of gaiety. There were two windows with muslin curtains, through which you could see stirring the foliage of the twining plants that the working-class women of Paris dearly love to cultivate.
>
> The furniture consisted of a very meager bed, several chairs, a walnut chest of drawers, a large square worktable, and an oaken bookcase stocked with good books on every shelf. Over the mantelpiece there was a little mirror in a mahogany frame, attached to the wall by a gilded nail. In front of it there was a glass globe in

8. Agricol Perdiguier, *Mémoires d'un compagnon*, Paris, 1914, pp. 8–9.
9. P. Lachambeaudie, "Le déjeuner à l'école," in *Cent fables*, Paris, 1864, p. 75.

which an artificial bouquet of flowers bloomed on its silken moss. On either side of the mirror hung dainty cushions of dark velvet, festooned with a family medallion and a silver watch—the only jewels in poor households. All of that was neat, shiny, polished, and arranged with the exquisite care that a woman of orderliness and taste lavishes on her surroundings.[10]

It is an emblematic décor. The twining plants visible through the muslin curtains and the artificial flowers blooming in a porcelain basket under glass are both a substitute for, and a farewell to, the lodger's native countryside. Amid the dark beams of the ceiling and the bright wallpaper, the walnut chest of drawers and the mahogany frame, the meager bed and the massive table, the dainty cushions and the stocked bookcase, the mirror over the mantelpiece reflects quite another tale than that of the joiner junkily furnished. It is something along the lines of the multifaceted grandeur and decadence of this ambiguous character, trying hard to transform the rustic frame of his worker existence by decorating it with tokens of bourgeois civilization. The *orderliness* and *taste* of Lise Perdiguier—an exquisite taste found only in big cities, Gilland assures us—bear witness to a way of being social very different from the one imagined in the dreams of philanthropists or in the poetic effusions of Michelet in *The People* (Paris, 1846), although they might employ very similar terms. In the muslin of the curtains, the silk of the artificial flowers, and the gaiety of bright wallpaper, they would have us see the beneficent work of feminine grace, helping to keep the worker within his home and workplace and away from cabarets by creating the charm of a comfort suited to his modest measure. More clear-eyed, perhaps, reactionaries detect here the perilous expectation associated with the unstable position of these former villagers, who cannot find stability except by denying themselves, by going all the way down the road that, they have been foolishly led to believe, should lead workers to bourgeois status by a combination of diligent application to work and enterprising effort.

The misfortune of the worker's condition and the consequent danger for bourgeois order do not lie so much in the unbridled fury of poverty as in the Brownian movements that constantly affect precarious and transitory forms of existence. Eugénie Niboyet visits the home of lacemaker

10. J.-P. Gilland, "Biographie des hommes illustres: Agricol Perdiguier," *La Feuille du village*, April 3, 1851.

Voinier and notes: "They must have been comfortable because their little household is very nice."[11] But the slightest turn of chance, added to the irregularity of work and long off-seasons—three to seven months, depending on the trade—is enough to ruin these fragile positions. In this case it was Voinier's wife who took sick. To take care of her, he had to eat his savings and then quit work. The possessions of the little household, one by one, found their way to the pawnshop, an institution whose operation also embodies the ambiguity of worker misery. For alongside those who go there with their jewels, their linen, or their dowry assets in order to get through the bad months, we find those who utilize this process to procure the first capital assets of an enterprise at a cheaper cost. Thus, the pathways that lead to mastership can be intermingled and confused with the pathways of worker life plain and simple.

For these beings between two worlds, mastership is the normal endpoint, which in no way implies any will to go over to the side of the exploiters. The very same word, *emancipation,* is used to denote the advancement of the individual worker who sets up on his own and the deliverance of the oppressed proletariat. It is this identity of individual and group courses that shows up in the projects that mechanic Claude David tirelessly presents to the capitalists of the Restoration and then the governments of the Second Republic:

> I felt that God did not create us to be the slaves of our brothers, and I bent all my effort to extricate myself from the grip that was choking poor workers. . . . At the age of twenty-three I felt strong enough to effect my deliverance, sensing that the burden I bore was too heavy on me. . . . At that point I had invented a new type of loom that permitted me to manufacture the most beautiful fabrics (shawls). I had enlisted a collaborator to handle the equipment setup. He was a young man who suffered as I did, and who also desired greatly to emancipate himself. . . . We realized that the sufferings we shared were those of our brothers, the common laborers, as well. And I, for my part, had dreams of emancipating a certain number of them with us.[12]

There was scarcely any worker among the most revolutionary ones who did not dream, at some point or another, of becoming a master. More

11. Fonds Enfantin, Bibliothèque de l'Arsenal, Ms. 7815.
12. Claude David, *Organisation du travail*, Paris, 1848, pp. 63–64.

than one achieved that dream. The notion of worker association itself was not inconsistent with the bourgeois science of Poor Richard. Witness the astonishing enterprise set up at the worst point in 1848 by four workers, last-makers, all of them known for their "anarchic" opinions:

> One day four guys met. The national workshops, last refuge against hunger, had been dissolved.
> What to do? The sum total of their combined assets was two francs. . . .
> What can you put together with two francs? asks the millionaire, who spends that amount a hundred times a day.
> Well, what you can do is:
> Buy a log.
> And then?
> Work up that log, get a few shapes out of it, and sell them.
> Then what?
> Buy two logs. All this time you eat little or not at all. You work. And then?
> You create the largest commercial enterprise of its sort, which has seventy associates and does 80,000 francs in transactions per year.[13]

To dream of socialism hardly means to forget the virtues of enterprise. But it is precisely that fact that nullifies paternal exhortations to today's good workers, exhortations promising them the happy fate of those modest workers of the 1820s whose efforts now enable them to enjoy the fine fortune of manufacturers. Today's good workers, you see, quickly came to the same sort of idea on their own. On their own as individuals or in conjunction with a few buddies, they too invested their savings in some enterprise designed to liberate them from their condition as mere laborers. But they soon came to see that the class struggle did not exactly follow the line of division between masters and laborers. Those who had urged them yesterday to get rich by their own efforts now were not so happy to see them take the advice seriously and compete with established positions.

Undoubtedly, the collapse of many transient masters was due to their presumption. They failed to realize that being an adroit worker was not enough to penetrate the mystery of net cost or to know how to judge the solvency of clients. But the impact of knowledge on success was no

13. Émile Jay, "Visite aux associations," *Le Bien-être universel*, Aug. 3, 1851.

less assured than that of hard work and honesty. The science of Pierre-Joseph Proudhon (1809–1865), accountant for a barge line, may have had "a terrible effect"[14] on his employer's competitors and ruined them. But it was of no positive help to him on the day when he, "worn out by the precarious and miserable lot of a worker," set himself up as a printer along with one of his colleagues: "The scanty savings of the two friends were pooled, and all the assets of their families went into this lottery. The treacherous game of business betrayed our hopes. Order, work, economy: nothing was of any use."[15] Aside from the hazards of the industrial lottery, every trade now faced the added menace of being overrun by the faceless enemy that was prowling for prey everywhere. It was the "errant capital, without profession or specific purpose,"[16] denounced in 1848 by the cabinetmakers, masters and workers jointly.

In these circumstances the positions of master and worker are quite often equalized or reversed, giving worker individuality the uncertain hybrid color noted in a group of workers that one Saint-Simonian propagandist is supposed to indoctrinate:

> In this neighborhood there are a large number of men situated somewhere between master and worker. That is to say, they are something of both because they work for a master and are treated as workers by those men, but they in turn are treated as masters by the workers they employ. And since everyone knows everybody else and this neighborhood is partially made up of these political hybrids (for they are greatly occupied with politics), it would be good if our journal got to them and made them a bit knowledgeable about our politics.[17]

This hybrid character typifies the labor population encountered by propagandists of every stripe, not just the worker–masters of the ninth ward just described. And it is quite true that it is what necessitates a search in the political arena for an identity that is not adequately provided by the uncertain lines of division between mastership and wage earning. But it does not follow that this identity itself is uncertain. It is quite true, for example, that the master tailors are all former workers. But that is pre-

14. Proudhon to Ackermann, Sept. 20, 1843, in *Correspondance*, Paris, 1875, II, 10.
15. Proudhon to MM. de l'Académie de Besançon, May 31, 1837, ibid., I, 30.
16. Petition of the cabinetmakers, Archives nationales (A.N.), F 12/4636.
17. Report of Achille Leroux, Fonds Enfantin, Ms. 7816.

cisely why their workers deem it right to demand that the master–worker relationship be that of one bourgeois person to another. If journeymen tailors must show up for hiring in a frock coat, it is only right that, in return, their masters take off their hats upon entering the workshop. This equality in the realm of appearances and conventions expresses the new and paradoxical dignity of the worker by virtue of his participation in the hazards and risks of mastership.

The precariousness of a work menaced not only by the lordly caprices of affluent consumers but also by the speculations of errant capital gives a new cast to the worker dignity arising out of the forced marriage of worker liberty to master liberty. It is no longer the old division of the journeymen guilds (*compagnonnages*) between the season of the masters and that of the workers. Rather, it is a claim to share rightfully in the reality of the risk taken, as the old hierarchies founded on outlay expenses converge with the new justifications of profit. Still domestic, the relationship between the free journeyman and the bourgeois master who needs him tends now to shatter in favor of an imaginary hierarchy in which risk itself, rather than any competence possessed, is the thing that commands recognition. The place commanding respect in this hierarchy is defined in terms of the abjection of the one occupying the bottom rung: the kid in servant's livery on whom the apprentices of the next-door workshop heap their sarcasms; the adult domestic servant whom striking workers say they would never want to become.

The hierarchy certainly has some objective grounds. The domestic is the person for whom parents could not pay any apprenticeship, even that of tailor. At the age of eight or nine they place him in some house so that he might bring in money to them, or at least spare their money more quickly. But this social hierarchy is also asserted insofar as it is the consequence of a radical choice. Domestics are those who, at the age of fifteen, were afraid of the worker's life, "seeing only its bad side, the wretched poverty." This dread of poverty seals their fate. Theirs will be a life coiled in an undivided time and confined to the animal sphere of needs, their masters' and their own: "So then it is all over. Their lot is to serve until they become stewards and (as they say) hold a good position. Possessors of a modest comfort, they can return to their native region and finish up an existence that they have traversed without glory and without being able to claim to have done anything but live."[18]

But what else but living can one claim, except dying? No need of any

18. A. Bertaut, "Au peuple," *La Ruche populaire*, Feb. 1841.

philosopher to teach tailor Bertaut, whose contempt underlines the two words *serve* and *live*, the relationship of servitude to dread of death. Only, this genealogy of servitude does not take us back to the side of mastership but to that third position that would like to be the absence of a bond: *independence.* This is the word commonly used to sum up the ideal of that ambiguous state hauled between the two poles of mastership and servitude. Its superiority over the one and its conflict with the other takes its definition, not from the positivity of competence, but from the choice of its precariousness and the knowledge, or rather semiknowledge, of its suffering. In the short time, says Bertaut, that one can attend formal instruction, or in the schooling provided by the city and by occupational stints all over France, the worker acquires the "semi-instruction" that offers him a certain advantage: "The ability to take cognizance of what is going on in society through his reading of the journals and other writings published to teach the people that they have rights, an advantage often costing them a high price and many a sigh."

The advantage of a sigh! In the comparison of our worker tailor, there is nothing left of what had been classically regarded as the superiority of the laborer's work over the work of the domestic servant: the skillful turn of the hand, the irreplaceable competence that would fashion the worker's pride and prompt the master to compromise. The paradox, you see, is that one can never find enough people for the simple role of domestic servant, but there are always too many workers for a given skilled craft, no matter how lofty it may be. A young typographer of twenty may feel an "immense pleasure" as he stands before his composing stick, the instrument and symbol of his liberty, and says to himself: "I have a craft. I can go anywhere. I need no one."[19] But there is also a more cynical lesson about the way things stand, which the pressman of the *Globe* teaches to a Saint-Simonian typographer. In the industrial anarchy of the day, his skill as such is worth no more than a lottery ticket:

> Since I had no job, Father Chevalier wrote to M. Everat that he
> would like to see me employed at the *Globe*. M. Everat, whom I
> had seen in the parlor, promised to get me in shortly, especially
> since he was unhappy with several compositors. No one was to be
> dismissed illegitimately or hurt. This approach satisfied me, but it
> all went very differently. He wrote to me to come at once and fill

19. Proudhon, *De la justice dans la révolution et dans l'eglise*, Brussels, 1868, II, 348.

the position in question. I thought it vacant, but it wasn't at all. He takes me by the hand and goes up to the newspaper office. He asks for the names of all the compositors working on the paper, writes them on pieces of paper, and puts them in a hat, saying: "Gentlemen, the first name to come out of the hat will be dismissed, and M. Mallard will take his place. And if you gentlemen don't like this procedure, you all can get out too."[20]

Even less than the typographer Mallard can the colleagues of tailor Bertaut succumb to the illusion of noble work. There are worker tailors everywhere: in the workshops, in garrets, in porter's lodges, and on the streets of Paris. There are so many you hardly know the exact count anymore: 22,500 in 1848, according to the statistics of the chamber of commerce; 40,000, according to the estimates of Pierre Vinçard.[21] Nor can anyone say who complains more: the youthful tailors in workshops, squeezed against each other as they sit on the floor, their legs crossed and their chests bent over benches that are always very narrow; or the piece-workers in their garrets, trying to attract a personal clientele for the work they do so cheaply for contractors. No workers are less irreplaceable than the tailors. Yet everyone will tell you: no guild is more sensitive, more solicitous of the respect that is its due, more ready to drag the whole mass of workers into its revolts.

The fact is that the worker dignity of which they pose as the prime representatives has nothing to do with the dignity of one's craft or pride in it. In the worker's world, in fact, that is more a divisive factor, one that can eventuate in a fight to the death. In the 1850s one could still come across corpses of shoemakers here and there. They were the victims of the hatred stirred up in the whole guild of journeymen by the royal craft of carpenters, a hatred of their base and stinking craft, which was usurping the dignity of *compagnonnage*. Nor is the sensitivity of the tailors akin to the aristocratic indignation of the chiselers, which they expressed to the manager of the Gaiety to show their displeasure with a stage piece that depicted them in dress beneath their dignity:

So your actors have never seen chiseler workers, eh? They do not know that the profession of chiseler is a luxury one? They imagine us in dress that is absolutely ridiculous. Let them be good enough

20. Mallard to Lambert, May 1832, Fonds Enfantin, Ms. 7757.
21. Pierre Vinçard, "Les ouvriers tailleurs," *Le Travail affranchi*, Jan. 7, 1849.

to change their costumes or we will go and hiss them. You should know, gentlemen, that we are neither masons nor roofers. It's fine for those fellows to wear costumes like those of your actors![22]

Reprinted in the workers' press, the letter of the chiselers was roundly condemned. But it was precisely those papers whose tone was set by typographers and tailors that raised a hue and cry against this false conception of worker honor. The masons, for their part, did not respond— for three reasons that come down to one, if we can believe the chapter devoted to them by Pierre Vinçard: first, the masons do not read the newspapers; second, they do not go to the theater; third, they do not have any vanity in their dress. All those things cost a lot and would distract them from the only path that matters to them, according to Vinçard: the path that leads from their craft to its essential goal, the purchase of land in the countryside. The mason is the man who applies all his intelligence to the perfection of his craft alone, who astonishes the contractor by the ease with which he can decipher the most complicated plans of men of art. But that does not mean the mason is thereby placed at the peak of the hierarchy. Instead, he is quite low in a certain hierarchy of worker dignity, very close to the borderline separating manual workers from domestic servants. The masons share with the latter a fixation on land and a taste for savings. Is that why their profession so vividly reproduces within itself the tensions of domesticity, the conflicts of those who know only the two social relations of serving and commanding?

> It is a sad thing to see men united by work and danger . . . having no other relationship than that of master to domestic servant. . . . The ambition of the servant boy being to get to be a worker, he views with an envious eye the salary and consideration enjoyed by the journeyman. His mind and his energy concentrate solely on that. So if his master happens to go away for a moment and he himself can leave the mortar mixer, he ascends quickly to grab the trowel and goes to work feverishly. His indolence becomes a feverish activity; the desire to command in his turn and the lure of higher earnings mean that he quickly familiarizes himself with the tools. After some periods of study of this sort, he ordinarily manages to become a worker. But if he succeeds, he, like the

22. *L'Artisan*, Oct. 1842.

freedman of ancient societies, may well be more pitiless than people were toward him.[23]

This look focused on the masons by the former jewel-engraver joins up again with the look cast on domestic servants by the tailor–satirical songwriter of *La Ruche populaire*. The hierarchy undergirding them does not have to do with competency or dress. It has to do with a sensitivity to spectacles that leave those peasant workers unmoved: the marvels—forbidden to their producers—that line the shopwindows of jewelers, furniture merchants, and bronzers; the beautiful arrangement and rich ornamentation of city monuments; the laughs of vaudeville and the tears of melodrama; the passions of politics and the theater. In short, it has to do with everything that causes these workers to live their lives now, not just in the complementarity of craft and firm or even in a conflict-ridden relationship with their masters, but also in the respiration of that entity so difficult to pinpoint but increasingly pregnant even in its cunning effects: public opinion.

Over against the bourgeois vanity of the chiselers and the peasant greediness of the masons, it is this that grounds the specific worker dignity of these tailors, who have come to seek compensation, in their residence in the capital city, for the misery, bad luck, or injustice that their derisory craft has reserved for them. Is it the strategic position of their workshops, cheap hotel rooms, and garrets—between the Chaussée-d'Antin of the royal bourgeoisie and the Tuileries of bourgeois royalty—that gives them, along with the typographers, the privilege of being the first to be in tune with public opinion? Or is it rather the fact that they work in the fashion industry, which is so close to the fashioning of opinion, and in which the marks of social differentiation are made up?

That undoubtedly is the source of the particular nature of the rights they claim in their radicalism. On October 20, 1833, the most progressive of the republican journals, *Le Bon Sens*, informs us with a hint of contempt about the enormous increase in tobacco consumption among the "fashionable young gentlemen." A few days later, it must report a strike by worker tailors over the right to smoke in the workshops. The tailors do not take themselves for "fashionable" people, however, even though they may sometimes dress up as such when they serve as paid applauders at the theater. In its own way the journal *La Fashion* points up the logic

23. Pierre Vinçard, *Les Ouvriers de Paris*, Paris, 1851, p. 48.

that injects questions of decorum into professional exigencies and wage disputes:

> The mason, the carpenter, the painter, and the locksmith do not need luxurious dress for their workdays. A pair of cloth pants, a blouse, and a cap are all they need to lay out money for. A worker tailor does not need really elegant clothes either. Nevertheless, he still must have a dress coat or a frock coat, boots, and a hat. For if he presents himself at a master's place in short jacket and cap, he will not be received. Since he has greater needs, less savings, and less chance for permanent work, he is more unhappy. That is understandable. The simplest way for him to extricate himself from his unfortunate position, in his mind, is to earn more. Hence their coalition against the masters.[24]

In his first attempt at analysis, Augustin Canneva, master tailor and writer of the article, picks up the classic argument of bourgeois people and philanthropists, who see good conduct by the worker as the only solution to the social question. But as he proceeds in further articles on the subject, Canneva's analysis shifts its direction. For Augustin Canneva is not just a representative of all the worker tailors who have become master tailors by diligent effort. He is one of those deviant new masters who are not content to run a business, who are also trying to introduce the mathematical and social sciences into their craft. The group would include master tailor Barde, friend of Saint-Simonians and Fourierists; the proletarian Saint-Simonian Delas, inventor of a machine for taking measurements; and the fierce republican Suireau, one of the leaders of the 1840 strike. Like them, Canneva is a pioneer promoter of the "geometric cut" that has evoked sarcasm from "real" tailors, the latter being incensed at the swagger of these new "cutting professors" or "paper cutters," who have more "students than clients."[25]

Canneva, too, is looking for solutions to a crisis that sets masters and workers in opposition against the backdrop of a common fate they both face: membership in a profession that threatens to be "delivered over to the capitalists" in eight or ten years.[26] In the circle of expenses and demands for rights, he would have us see more than the result of mere

24. *La Fashion*, Dec. 1841.
25. Couannon, *Le Parfait Tailleur*, Paris, 1852, and *Journal des Marchands Tailleurs*, July 1837 and Jan. 1838.
26. *La Fashion*, Aug. 20, 1842.

misconduct by youthful apprentice tailors. He points to the vicious circle
typifying an industry based on fashion and now menaced by the capitalist
rationality of ready-made clothes.

Canneva admits that these young tailors are not reasonable. But isn't
that typical of young people? And who but they could adapt to a trade
that, by virtue of the rhythm of fashionable life, condemns them to five
months of inactivity on the one hand and, during the busy season, to a
work schedule that is incompatible with any family life at all? Today the
craft is not really menaced so much by the young madcaps who want to
earn enough in the seven months of the work season to spend the five
months of the off-season in a pleasurable way. It is threatened much more
by the good spouses and fathers of families who, during the off-season,
hire out their hands for a song to the producers of ready-made clothes,
whose products will hit the market just as work is starting up again in the
regular tailor shops.

Canneva sees the solution to the crisis in an entente between masters
and workers, a united front against their common enemy, which is to
be implemented through equal representation on the arbitration boards
known as the *conseils des prud'hommes*. In 1848 other proprietors will see
owner–worker associations as the only safeguard for a trade in which
market pressure has reduced mastership to a mere illusion of power and
authority. Asks a Bordeaux proprietor in the preamble to his proposed
plan for such an association:

> What really is a proprietor in an individualized industry? Is he any-
> thing more than the sliding slope between producer and consumer,
> the groove along which the metal rolls day after day? What remains
> to him except his oppression by the strong and the dependence of
> the weak upon him?[27]

It is precisely on the sharing of this *remainder,* however, that the battle
is joined. The striking worker tailors echo the affirmation of solidarity and
the proposal for parity in the two demands embodied in the third point
of the program espoused by the Paris strikers of 1833: "relations of independence and equality with the masters." Three specific demands are
covered in the general formula: the right to smoke tobacco, some time
to read newspapers, and the requirement that masters take off their hats
upon entering the workshop. That may be the source behind the 1848

27. Deluc, *Projet d'association des tailleurs de Bordeaux,* A.N., F 12/4631.

shibboleth: "Off with your hat before my cap!" Many will allow themselves to be caught up in this pantomime, but it might well have had
another function: perhaps this recognition of the royalty of the producers
was designed to exorcise the more upsetting strains underlying the bizarre
formula "relations of independence and equality with the masters."

Surely it was a stupid wager for the most easily replaceable worker: not
to be dependent on the person on whom one depends. But in the normal
course of things, these stupid wagers make the most dangerous daredevils.
It is not that they would take their revenge by sabotaging their work.
The very masters who criticize their misconduct generally tend to pay
homage to the care and precision they put into their work. The hygienists,
however, have already pointed up the link between one and the other,
denouncing the subversive effects of a docility that keeps them seated all
the time, pressed up against each other and oblivious to the "time for
eating and sleeping"[28] when the workload is pressing:

> Wherever you find a gathering of idle men, by which I mean men
> who are not applying themselves to muscular effort or whose
> minds are not usefully occupied, there you will find the imagination
> swept into dangerous byways. And since the tailors stay in one
> place, they are condemned to almost complete inactivity.[29]

Misconduct, however, is not the most dangerous effect of this lack of
differentiation between work and rest. It is the more formidable vanity
associated, not with the feeling of being irreplaceable partners by virtue
of their dexterity, knowledge, or quick eye, but rather with the knowledge
that they are *in excess*. All the more so since they chose as their leader, in
the big strikes of 1833 and 1840, a man whose personality was the best
possible expression of the social and imaginary stake in their struggle.
André Troncin was a child in excess from the very start: born in Besançon
in 1802, reduced to a tailor's apprenticeship by a jealous stepmother, and
finding his way to Paris to improve himself in "the elegant, pure, and
exacting taste of cities."[30] Gilland tells us that Troncin "did not despise
the bourgeoisie as a power but detested it as a caste." The bourgeoisie

28. A. Decoux, *Jean-Jacques compris par les tailleurs; ou: Bonheur de tout ce qui peut
coudre, aidé par la philanthropie*, Paris, 1835, p. 15.

29. Monneret, "Hygiène des tailleurs," in Augustin Canneva, *Livre du tailleur*,
Paris, 1838, p. 190.

30. Gilland, "Biographie des hommes obscurs: André Troncin," *La Feuille du
village*, Nov. 28, 1850.

returned him the same divided sentiments. When the caste of masters was not making him spend time in prison, individual masters employing him would assure him earnings of 2,000 to 2,400 francs a year and readily entrust the management of their workshops to a man who cast such a spell on their workers. In the last prison he would enter, which the government of the bourgeois caste would let him leave only as a dying man, he would again ask his wife to send him "the illustrated Gospels my boss gave me as a present that fortnight when I went to so much trouble for his big order."[31]

That privileged relationship certainly put him in the best position to lead the battle for the recognition of those workers without anything to offer in the struggle except the risk of combat itself. He was the best one to lead the collective fight of individuals with none of the mutual ties that made other guilds strong:

> The workers in other crafts are better at acting in concert. . . . The journeymen help each other on their travels. They get each other resources, credit, and work. They bolster each other's morale. Among the worker tailors, on the other hand, we find an unfortunate egotism. No fraternal bond unites them. They meet: good morning! They part: good night! That's it.[32]

The only thing to add is that these workers who merely cross each other's path— a worker tailor rarely remaining three months with the same master—are united only in their relationship to the other party: that is, the bourgeois people whose egotistical lifestyle they mimic, whom they must visit in a frock coat, and from whom they demand a code of conventions in which their right to strike will balance the other party's right to lay them off. "Let the insolent master be deprived of our working arms until he has admitted his wrongs! But let us be fair as well, permitting him to discharge the worker who no longer suits him in a fitting way."[33] The new strikes pioneered by these individualists can no longer beat a retreat

31. Ibid., Dec. 12, 1850.

32. *La Fashion*, April 20, 1842.

33. Grignon, *Réflexions d'un ouvrier tailleur sur la misère des ouvriers en général, la durée des journées de travail, le taux des salaires, les rapports actuellement établis entre les ouvriers et les maîtres d'atelier, la nécessité des associations d'ouvriers comme moyen d'améliorer leur condition*, Paris, 1833, p. 4. Reprinted in Alain Faure and Jacques Rancière (eds.), *La parole ouvrière: 1830/1851* (Paris: Union Général d'Éditions, 1976), pp. 74–81; this citation is on p. 80.

to the Aventine Hill as did the *compagnonnage* damnations of yesterday. But they compensate for this with a game that produces its effect on the enemy in the determination of risk and expense. The feeling of being in excess gives rise to two things. First, it prompts demands for rights from these people who are too many, and who therefore find their dignity in the risk of poverty they have assumed. Second, it prompts collective revolt against a situation that makes each worker one individual too many: that is, against the competition that produces a surplus of laborers.

The game of expense is thus more complicated than we are given to believe by the platitudes of philanthropists, who blame poverty and coalitions on the thoughtless expenditures of pleasure-seeking workers. It is also more complicated than it is interpreted to be by those who oppose the nakedness of the poverty and the seriousness of the fight to the illusory phantasm of such raptures, or who, on the other hand, contrast the savage annals of popular orgy with the homely or militant morality of the worker ant. Even though it is contrasted with the joyous immorality of the worker dandy, the morality of militant dedication has to do with the same point of honor: the refusal to save money as the criterion that establishes the social superiority of the worker's state over that of the domestic servant. This is borne out by the constant diatribes of moralists in *L'Atelier* against the ideology and practice of savings banks. Even more noteworthy is the way they slide between two arguments. One argument denounces any attempt to convert workers to egotism and ruin their solidary action. The other maintains that their living conditions do not permit workers to save. Only domestics save; workers do not. The statement could not possibly be contradicted by statistics showing a constant growth in worker deposits after an initial period of suspicion. It is in the nature of a philosophical *a priori* and a criterion of social dignity.

This refusal to save money does not merely define an abstract unity between the recklessness of the precarious worker and the solicitude of the apostle. It is also to be the basis for a new social recognition, the intermediary that will enable the workers' struggle and solidarity to move from the particularism of specific crafts and the reign of material force to a universality affirming the worker's right to a new apportionment. It is a matter of moving beyond the atomization that accounts for the present situation: "The class does not exist; there are only individuals."[34] But this must be done without turning union into a constraint that would cause a

34. Jules Leroux, *Aux ouvriers typographes*, Paris, 1833, p. 11.

relapse into the reign of force and the power of castes, where the ideal of *compagnonnage* liberty was lost. For the weapons that the old journeymen *compagnons* and their guilds used against their masters were the very same ones that divided them from each other. The force they put into their economic struggle was also the underlying source of their social abasement: "Lacking respect for each other, making war on each other, devouring each other in rivalries, the workers lost their position, their liberty, and their well-being."[35] The reconquest of their lost social rank must come by way of qualitatively new solidarity: not just their rediscovered power as a group imposing its law on the masters, but also a newly achieved universality entailing its recognition and establishing proper social relations that will sanction the place of workers in the kingdom of reason and civilization.

This sort of worker dignity implies a break with those who want to base worker dignity on physical expenditure or manual skill. The discourse presented in *L'Atelier* on behalf of the working class is a discourse of semiworkers: not robust enough or well enough versed in geometry to suit the carpenters; not skillful enough to suit the chiselers. Visiting the printing office, some would judge them to be fake workers: "The foreman was once a lawyer . . . the *homme de conscience* had studied medicine; the compositors included a teacher, a former ship's doctor who had lived for ten years among the Indian tribes of South America, and a Spaniard who had been a captain in the army of Don Miguel."[36]

The description is undoubtedly a bit forced. The old typographers offering it clearly want to come up to the classic image of picturesque physiologies that depict the world of typographers as a "hotel" providing refuge for "abortive vocations, unattained destinations, overturned positions, and disappointed hopes."[37] But even the parties in question must have been somewhat aware of being newcomers in the worker hierarchy because the first editor of *L'Atelier* returns to this question of titles thirty years later:

> We also contributed to the newspaper *L'Atelier* to prove to the workers of all crafts who were there that a tailor using his nee-

35. Perdiguier, *Mémoires d'un compagnon*, p. 243.

36. Décembre and Alonnier, *Typographes et gens de lettres*, Paris, 1862, p. 70. Note that the *homme de conscience* was paid by the day for jobs whose nature did not easily allow for a piecework rate.

37. Jules Ladimir, "Le compositeur typographe," in *Les Français peints par eux-mêmes*, Paris, 1840, I, 266.

dle and a typographer arranging his type characters merit the
respectable title of worker as much as a baker, a cabinetmaker, or
a tanner.[38]

The talk begun in the name of the working class presupposes an internal revolution, an overturning of the older hierarchies based on strength
and skill. For those hierarchies, ultimately rooted in the hazards of birth
or the arbitrary nature of social distinctions, embody the law of castes
that fixes the worker's subordinate position and implant it in the very
midst of the worker's world itself. That accounts for the privileged role
of the curious vanguard made up of those who handle needles and type
characters. They are workers without power or any illusions about their
qualifications. In vain do they pretend to take seriously the basic standards
of qualification and competence that they use to oppose the opening of a
woman's printing office. However rare literate women may be, there are
certainly enough of them to replace all the male typographers.

These haphazard, fugitive workers get their importance from their position on the frontier: close to the bourgeois people, providing them with the
ornaments of social distinction and the material revetments of their thinking, sensitive to the revolutions from above effected through the ascendant
powers of fashion and the press. They are almost bourgeois, in a sense.
They are the ones best situated to borrow bourgeois dress and language,
and hence to point up the signs of disparity. In dress, for example, it might
be a trifling touch of eccentricity or slovenliness, the mockery of the artist
blending with the bad taste of the parvenu: "Something amiss, something
jarring, something grating, something that breaks the harmony and gives
a bad impression, hinting at the worker under the lion's garb."[39]

Above all, these workers are the best situated to reevaluate the bent to
mastership inherent in the transitory worker state, to confront it with the
new conditions of class domination and the reign of capital. They shape a
class discourse with the help of the bookkeepers and shop clerks to whom
L'Atelier accords the right to speak in the name of workers, a right denied
to any manual laborer who grows rich on the work of others. This class
discourse has a precise function. For the worker stopped at the barrier
of mastership and for manual laborers victimized by aristocratic prejudices, it creates a new ideal. The impossibility of escaping their condition
is transformed into a positive refusal: a renunciation of servitudes from

38. Henri Leneveux, *Le travail manuel en France*, Paris, n.d., p. 166.
39. Ladimir, "Le compositeur typographe," p. 271.

above that are savored by the ephemeral proprietor and seen close up by the foreman, the clerk, and the bookkeeper; a substitute claim for a social place that is won in the battle for "equality" with the masters; a class ideal of becoming completely like bourgeois people in order to better point up the difference and affirm the refusal entitling workers to be recognized as their equals. On the one hand, in order to acquire citizenship in bourgeois civilization, they must wipe out the signs of worker specificity hearkening back to the naturalness of castes and the rule of force. On the other hand, they must denounce the bourgeois blemishes of egotism and exploitation in their own behavior. The fight for recognition entails this twofold movement: a transition from the feudal reign of force to the bourgeois reign of reason, and an aristocratic challenge to the bourgeois norms of saving money and getting rich.

It is the dream of a state of equilibrium, a state where the individual whims of bourgeois fortune or aristocratic dignity are whittled down to the definition of a collective identity. It is, for example, the return to the ranks of the young typographer who had first been dazzled by the pomp of the city of kings: "He wanted fashionable clothes, scented linen, gems on his fingers. . . . For company he sought out young people above his station."[40] Then he saw the "dedication and many sacrifices" of his comrades in the struggle and converted his aristocratic taste for spending into his own participation in the democratic struggle of the workers.

This exchange is also the source of a new hierarchy, however. At the worker-degree meeting of Saint-Simonians on December 18, 1831, tapestry-worker Julien Gallé is presented to the assembly after being called to direct propaganda work in one of the four Paris sectors. The young man, whose bearing suggests the bourgeois man as well as the worker, announces the two sacrifices he is going to make for his apostolate. He is going to give the Saint-Simonian family the fruit of his savings; and to serve that family, he is going to give up the position of chief clerk that destined him to succeed his proprietor. But his talk is of gratitude rather than of sacrifice: "Born of proletarian parents and having attained the highest point in commerce that a common worker can attain by his own capabilities alone, I would never have been able to surmount the social barriers between myself and those privileged by birth. I was in despair. You have called me and restored my hope."[41] It is not Julien Gallé's fault that the

40. J.-P. Gilland, "Biographie des hommes obscurs: Adolphe Boyer," *La Feuille du village*, Feb. 13, 1851.
41. *Le Globe*, Dec. 23, 1831.

future would see him end up as a capitalist and philanthropist instead of confirming his choice and his hope. The priests of the new life abandoned him, and so he had to bend all his efforts to "refurbishing the reputation as a hard worker" that he had "tarnished a bit."[42]

But a few decades of commercial success and social action would not suffice to erase the memory of that fleeting moment and that singular dream: the finding of that plenitude and fulfillment that had been sought by complementing the work of the day with evening *goguettes,* the humiliations of fifteen years with three-day revolutions, the bitterness of labor with the successes of one's craft. That was the privileged point of equilibrium between the precariousness of "independent" work and the new servitudes into which one again falls as soon as one rises above it: an undivided time without off-seasons, entailing an activity in which service —without servitude—to others is rewarded with the pleasure of being one's own master instead of having to sell oneself. An individual adventure hung in the imagination of this strange collective destiny: a bourgeois civilization without exploiters, a chivalry without lords, a mastery without masters or servants. In short: the emancipation of the workers.

42. Gallé to Reboul, 1833, Fonds Enfantin, Ms. 7728.

CHAPTER 3

The New Babylon

MUST WE GO BACK FARTHER? "As a boy he got a very lively impression of passionate [church] music and dreamed of being a country priest living in the midst of his cherished flock."[1] The sequel in this case could be pictured too easily: from choirboy dreams to the worker apostolate. For shoemaker Charles Pennekère and his peers, however, the question is more whether they ever had a childhood that was "lovable, heroic, fabulous, worth writing on gold leaf" (Rimbaud, "Matin," *Une saison en enfer*).

Some seem to remember such a childhood. Not the heedlessness of infancy or the robust paradise of childhood games but rather that supplement of childhood, denied to the domestic, between the stage of unreflecting consciousness and that of service—a lost time, the pleasure of which lay not so much in playing as in wandering off by oneself, dreaming, or learning:

> I was always impetuous, but at that age I was so with gentle, dreamy conceptions that strayed into mellow reveries under the shade of trees. . . . Their childish, affectionate poetry and its intoxicating spell became identified with the ambiguous projections of the evening sunlight, the vagabond enthusiasm of the wind as it swirled leaves, the virginal awakening of morning, the oscillating air of night.[2]

1. Report of Delaporte on shoemaker Charles Pennekère, Oct. 22, 1831, Fonds Enfantin, Bibliothèque de l'Arsenal, Ms. 7816.
2. Gauny to Retouret, July 24, 1832, Fonds Gauny, Bibliothèque municipale de Saint-Denis, Ms. 165; reprinted in Jacques Rancière (ed.), *Louis Gabriel Gauny: Le philosophe plébéien* (Paris: La Découverte/Maspéro, 1983), p. 161.

But a chance discovery has already fixed the dreams of this boy in love with vagrancy and botany on a particular obsession. It all began one day when his play with a chance companion was interrupted by the latter's mother, who wanted to ask her son about the pagination of a legend entitled *La Chapelle de saint Léonard*. Our future joiner never got around to reading that piece, but that very day he gave up childhood games and dedicated himself to building up a library for himself. For the sons of poor proletarians living in the Saint-Marcel district, however, libraries were built only a page at a time. Even those one might appropriate from the daily food supply were rarely intact:

> It was agreed that my mother would save for me the sacks holding the nourishing grains that she bought. How great was my enthusiasm that evening back home as I explored those treasures of fragmentary discourse and annal remnants. How irritated and impatient I was when I got to the torn end of a page and could not pursue the narration. There was no follow-up to the first delivery of sacks and wrappings, even though she was urged to buy all her lentils from the same merchant.[3]

Jeanne Deroin, lingerie-maker, apparently did not experience this sort of cutting in childhood. Her style is not the chaotic one characteristic of proletarians who found access to the great book of knowledge only in the torn pages of lentil sacks:

> I was never familiar with the joys of infancy or the games of early childhood. From the time I learned to read, reading became my sole occupation and the charm of my every moment. I felt a vague desire to experience and know everything. God and religion had aroused my attention most of all, but the mobility of my ideas kept me from focusing my attention on one object for a long time. Weary of searching without understanding, I compared and related what was said to me or what was taught me by books to fairy tales. Still too young to appreciate my social position, I was happy. The future seemed bright and gracious. I saw myself rich with the treasures of learning.[4]

3. Gabriel to Louis, Fonds Gauny, Ms. 112. See Rancière (ed.), *Le philosophe plébéien*, p. 28, n. 1.
4. Jeanne Deroin, Profession of faith, Fonds Enfantin, Ms. 7608.

How exactly did this woman learn her humanities, she whose analysis sifted the philosophical contradictions of Saint-Simonism and whose marvelously legible writing contrasts sharply with the scrawl of so much correspondence from the top? We are surprised to learn that for a long time she was refused her teaching certificate, until closer scrutiny evokes suspicion about her legible writing. She undoubtedly learned to read from printed books, and her way of writing reveals an unfinished apprenticeship in adapting printed characters to the proper strokes of school penmanship.

Each one found his or her own way to penetrate the secret of those blackened white pages. The little chimney-sweep and showman, Claude Genoux, found a fragment of paper on the ground and had it deciphered by a passing schoolboy. The latter recognized the two verses of *Athalie* that promise food for body and soul to fledgling birds and lost children. It was at the Foundling Hospital that the little Savoyard would soon get the chance to learn to read and write, along with a sure meal and a bed of his own. With these rudiments under his belt, he would head off along the roads to glean haphazardly the elements of geography, Latin, and Roman history that were missing in his classical education.[5]

This taste for Latin was not unanimously shared. Durand the joiner fulfilled the dream of his unruly schoolboy days when he plunged his hands and head into the waters of the Tiber; but Drevet the mechanic blamed his village school for having taught him to read only the Latin prayers that were chanted at Vespers. Even the teaching of the Roman Church allowed for straying, however. In her convent school and the learning of a brother, a former seminarian, Suzanne Voilquin found the means to read not only Roman history but also all the romances that set young girls dreaming, effecting the poisonous reading of them to her pious mother.[6]

Others got the rudiments at home. Louis Vinçard, for example, was taught the art of reading by his mother. There would be nothing extraordinary about that, except that his almost illiterate mother taught her son what she herself really did not know. This maieutics without guile, of a supposedly ignorant teacher, may well have predisposed the child later to hear and understand a religion that based the education of the future on the revelation of the "Mother." But actually his mother, without realizing

5. Claude Genoux, *Mémoires d'un enfant de la Savoie*, Paris, 1844.

6. Suzanne Voilquin, *Souvenirs d'une fille du peuple* (Paris: F. Maspéro, 1978). Jean-Pierre Drevet, *Le socialisme pratique*, Paris, 1850; excerpts in Alain Faure and Jacques Rancière (eds.), *La parole ouvrière: 1830/1851* (Paris: Union Général d'Éditions, 1976), pp. 396–426. Alphonse Viollet, *Les poètes du peuple au XIXe siècle*, Paris, 1846, on Durand.

it, was merely applying the method of "intellectual emancipation" pioneered by Joseph Jacotot. With the sole addition of a *Télémaque*, Jacotot
promised any commoner aware of his place and role in the social order
"the means of self-instruction without a teacher, hence the means to teach
others what you yourself do not know, in accordance with the principle
of intellectual equality."[7]

For this reason the wife of typographer Orrit went straight to Jacotot himself with her seven-year-old son, who had learned to read on his
own but felt desperate about his inability to write verses. Asked by the
father of "universal education" what he wanted to learn, the boy replied
simply: *everything.*[8] The grand principle of the Jacotot method was "learn
something and relate everything else to it." It obviously clicked with the
real-life experience of people who had picked up fragments of peerless
learning behind sequestered walls or along the byways, from good mon-
archist nuns or a regicidal herbalist: detached articles of a strange but
precious encyclopedia, one of no use except to offer "false notions about
real life"[9]—or, perhaps, true notions about the falsity of this life.

This contradiction brings us to the second and decisive rupture in the
childhood of commoners. The choice to accept the worker's fate and its
hazards rather than the quietude of the domestic servant meets up again
with the fate undergone and rejected: that is, the fate linking the possibility of cultivating one's soul and the necessity of selling one's body with
accidents of birth. Jeanne Deroin bears witness to it: "I saw myself rich
with the treasures of learning, the unique object of my prayers. These
gratifying dreams soon faded away. The necessity of working made me
realize that I, without wealth, would have to give up learning, give up
happiness. I resigned myself."[10] While she resigned herself, hoping to find
other ways to the realm of learning, Gauny did not: "When I became an
adolescent, circumstances plunged me into a world turned upside down.
Tormented by the convulsion, my heart was seized with regular fits of
rage. . . . I came to know vengeance as I underwent the miseries and humiliations of a monotonous novitiate. I was in revolt. My flesh trembled,
my eyes were wild. I was ferocious."[11]

---

7. *Manuel de l'émancipation intellectuelle*, Paris, 1841, p. 4. See Jacques Rancière,
Le Maître ignorant (Paris: Fayard, 1987).

8. Viollet, *Les poètes du peuple*, on Eugène Orrit.

9. Voilquin, *Souvenirs d'une fille du peuple*, p. 65.

10. Deroin, Profession of faith.

11. Gauny to Retouret, July 24, 1832, Fonds Gauny, Ms. 165; in Rancière (ed.),
Le philosophe plébéien, p. 162.

Even more than the encounter with exploitation, the violence of apprenticeship is an internal affair. Deriving from the old reign of force, it unites
workers only in and through the crushing of the weak. It is an initiation
rite wherein the adult workers, already biased against these kids who are
preparing to take away their own livelihoods, take on the additional task
of teaching the kids to renounce the dreams that they themselves have
already had to give up. The desire to make others pay for the sorrow
of being there and the fear of being dislodged by them come together
in words of ridicule and invective that pretend to correct the lazy little
scamps:

> In winter you forbid him to approach the fire on the pretext that he
> is trying to amuse himself around it. When he picks up the hammer
> and smashes his fingers with his first blow from a numb and unsure
> hand, you do not feel sorry for him, you laugh. Instead of helping
> him, you make fun of him. You must pick up the hammer with
> two hands, suggests one worker. He was looking in the air, says
> another. Pay no attention to him, says a third, he did it deliberately
> so that he wouldn't have to do anything today.[12]

Seen from the inside, the relationship between worker life and servitude
shifts. The choice between liberty or death takes on new and more radical
shapes:

> I have seen some poor children, feeling completely desperate and
> accursed, who preferred death to such an existence. They gave
> themselves to it readily and departed this life without regret at the
> very age when it should have been so beautiful. Some have perished
> from all sorts of abusive treatment. Fear of the punishments to
> which they were subjected every day absorbed their thinking even
> in the delirium of fever. . . . Others turned into thieves . . . yes,
> thieves! Not because of the lure of larceny or the need to survive, as
> everyone is tempted to believe, but simply to escape the harshness
> of their plight. And the thing that condemns those who reduced
> them to that state and allows them no justification is the fact
> that those children, locked up like vagrants and treated as such,
> preferred prison to the workshop even when promised pardon and
> indulgence in the future.[13]

12. J.-P. Gilland, *Les conteurs ouvriers*, Paris, 1849.
13. J.-P. Gilland, "De l'apprentissage: Fragment d'une correspondance intime,"
La Ruche populaire, Sept. 1841, pp. 4–5.

The workshop could be worse than prison—now, there was an opinion that undoubtedly justified all the discourses and little stories of clerical and lay moralists addressed to lower-class youths. They described the almost bourgeois dignity of a person with a good line of work and the wretchedness of the little errand boys, the match vendors, and the employees of the other little businesses of Pointe Saint-Eustache who were destined for destitution and the shame of prison.[14]

Perhaps overly sensitive natures tend to exaggerate the suffering involved in the rites of initiation into adult life. The majority of apprentices, after all, did not live in a world of torturers. But what if the evil was even more radical? What if the very entrance into the world of work itself was what defined Gauny's world turned upside down? What if the hazards of selling one's labor power day after day, which elevated the worker above the domestic who had sold it once and for all and thereby alienated his life, was the very source and wellspring of an unremitting anguish associated not with working conditions or pay but with the very necessity of working itself?

Writes Gauny: "The worst of all my ills as a worker is the brutalizing nature of the work. It suffocates me."[15] Is it just the morbid nature of our worker–poet that prompts him to contradict what we have heard from so many sources: that is, the pleasure of the artisan or skilled worker in seeing or holding the fruit of his creative labor, a pleasure marred only by the sorrow of seeing it escape him to fill the treasury of his exploiters? Must we label as trash all the odes glorifying creative labor, the skilled hand, the familiar tool, and the marvelous product? We certainly understand the detachment of tailor–poet Hilbey toward the shameful craft that provides him with a living: "I did not say that I was reduced to sewing children's clothes. I said that I adopted that specialty because it demands less care and intelligence. Let those who want nicely stitched and fashioned clothes make them for themselves, if they like. I, for my part, intend to brutalize myself as little as possible."[16]

But we are surprised to find, on the other hand, that the "people's priest," Ledreuille, must devote so much of his teaching to explaining the necessity of diligent work to the workers in the Saint Francis Xavier Society. If they are willing to dedicate a good portion of the only day of rest

14. Maurice Le Prevost, *Almanach de l'apprenti*, Paris, 1851–1855, and *Les jeunes ouvriers*, Paris, 1862.
15. Gauny to Retouret, Feb. 2, 1834, Fonds Gauny, Ms. 165; in Rancière (ed.), *Le philosophe plébéien*, p. 166.
16. Constant Hilbey, *Réponse à tous mes critiques*, Paris, 1846, p. 51.

recognized by their masters to hearing Ledreuille's sermons as well as
Mass, the reason is that they have nothing to do with those lazy fellows
who are at that very moment getting drunk in bars and preparing to celebrate Holy Monday with new libations. Yet it is precisely to the former
that Ledreuille addresses himself this particular Sunday. He expatiates on
"work without impetuosity or interruption" and regrets to find that "there
are many Babylonians among us."[17] And it is for them that he leads up to
a solemn oath on another Sunday:

> The whole week belongs to work, brethren. Are we resolved to
> work with courage and perseverance, each as best he can, the
> whole week, Monday as well as the other days? This resolution is
> worthy of men of heart. Will you make that resolution? Will you
> do it? (Applause) Yes, I shall repeat in turn . . . to work! From
> tomorrow at break of day, and God grant that work will not be
> lacking for anyone.[18]

Must one do all that if one wants, on Monday morning, to differentiate
the good workers who spent their Sunday in church from the carousers
who spent it in bars? Were the Babylonians really to be found at every
level of the hierarchy that Denis Poulot would establish twenty-five years
later: from the irreproachable "true worker" to the irretrievable "sublimest
of the sublime"?[19]

Ledreuille tells his listeners: "There are plenty of Babylonians among
us, men who work hard for a few days in order to rest and drink and
enjoy themselves the rest of the time."[20] It is a comforting division. But
what if the real mark of the Babylonian is something very different and far
more dangerous? Not preferring drunkenness to work, or even working
harder to get more intoxicated, but rather treating work itself as a form
of intoxication—seeing it as a time of brutishness when the body absents
itself, not by not working, but rather by overworking to the limits of one's
strength in order to procure some free time for oneself. The sober Catholic worker belongs to the race of the Babylonians when he, with the good

17. F.-A. Ledreuille, *Discours prononcés aux réunions des ouvriers de la Société de
Saint-François-Xavier à Paris et en province par M. l'abbé François-Auguste Ledreuille,
recueillis et publiés par M. l'abbé Faudet*, Paris, 1861, p. 66.

18. Ibid., p. 39.

19. See Denis Poulot, *Le sublime; ou: Le travailleur comme il est en 1870 et ce qu'il
peut être* (reprint ed., Paris: A. Cottereau, 1980).

20. Ledreuille, *Discours*, p. 66.

week he has just finished for himself and his master under his belt, robs the latter on Monday of the two francs he would have "saved" out of the four the worker's day of labor produces. And the worker does this with a clean conscience, if we are to judge by the sham questions that come to Ledreuille: "What will happen in the master's case? He will not pay for that day, says the inconstant worker, seeing his honor safe, his integrity intact, and himself free and clear. But that is not the case, my friend. You have lost ten hours of work and wronged him to the tune of two francs, which he will lose for your lack of diligence."[21]

This very Christian idea of the fair price which the preacher stumbles onto, and in which one readily recognizes the rightful claim of the producer aware of the value of his work, is just as much a principle of devaluation: fixing a maximum to work as well as a minimum to its price and establishing the finality of production at the level of an exchange, at best fair, between the interests of the master and the needs of the worker. As Drevet points out: "When we go to the workshop, it is not to do a whole lot of work; it is for the sum that the proprietor has agreed to give us."[22] The relations of independence and equality with the master come down in this case to a complicity of interests. The disinvestment of worker attention harmonizes with the profitability of owner investment only at the expense of the third party whose rights Ledreuille must constantly recall to his listeners: the client, the bourgeois class, the nation's production. "We have not yet invested in industry that point of national honor which serves us so well where it does exist."[23]

Again we have a transfer of energy that does not take place: from the place where the soul has put its treasure to the place where the body produces riches. This energy deficit is estimated at 80 percent of worker capacity by Corbon, the great thinker of *L'Atelier*. It has a very specific character. It is not a refusal to work or any repugnance at the physical expenditure, but a withdrawal of intelligent force: "It seems that this is the problem posed: to spend the least possible amount of intelligent force for the best possible wage."[24] And how could the people's priest frontally attack this principle, the impoverishment of one's tasks, which is the very essence of the Babylonian perversion, without himself running into the scoffing remarks of poet–tailor Hilbey: "Jesus Christ said to the fishermen:

21. Ibid., p. 69.
22. Drevet, *Le socialisme pratique*, p. 55; in Faure and Rancière (eds.), *La parole ouvrière*, p. 416.
23. Ledreuille, *Discours*, p. 71.
24. C. A. Corbon, *De l'enseignement professionnel*, Paris, 1859, p. 59.

Leave your nets and I will make you fishers of men. You others, you tell them: Don't leave your nets, continue to catch fish for our table"?[25]

Can one exhort workers to apply all the strength of their intelligence to work without telling them that there is no other world, no life of the soul apart from the body, and that it is in worker toil and combat that the human being realizes, loses, and must recapture its human essence? Posterity will denounce the effects of this doctrine, evidenced in bondage to work and the supposed power of the workers, but people of that day could only picture it as inciting workers to orgy. It is impossible to escape a circle here, the rigorousness of which is best seen by the editors of *L'Atelier*, good Christians like Ledreuille but also workers: the morality that commands work forbids one to give any positive reasons for it. Giving reasons for working, however high-minded they may be, means sooner or later proposing the image of attractive work. And proposing that image means quickly provoking disgust for work as it presently is. So there is no pleasure to be found in the constraint of work except the constraint itself interiorized as duty: "There is only one single attraction in work— the moral feeling of satisfaction that a man experiences in carrying out his duty."[26]

Now this reduction of the usefulness and pleasure of working to the abstraction of duty may be necessary if the activity of the typographer or tailor is to be recognized as equivalent in social value to that of the tanner or cabinetmaker. But there are not just typographers and tailors at *L'Atelier*, and the typographers are not necessarily typographers only. Consider the man who was the principal inspiration behind the newspaper, Claude Anthime Corbon. The one-time little threader subsequently became a sign-painter, appraiser, typographer, wood and marble sculptor, deputy of the Second Republic, and senator of the Third Republic. For some, he was the model of the worker–craftsman, perfectly embodying the union of manual skill and technical intelligence, author of a work on vocational training, and sometimes hailed as the inspiration behind Marxian "polytechnic" education. And does this archetype of the intelligent worker–artist have nothing to tell us about the labor that gives form and life to wood and marble except the same old story of original sin?

Yes, the fact is that the most polyvalent of workers and the most tireless defender of the duty and dignity of work never speaks to us about what he does. There really is only one thing to say about it, you see. Another

25. See p. 14 in this volume.
26. "Le travail attrayant," *L'Atelier*, June 1842, p. 80.

woodworker, Gauny, is exceptional in that he does give us an hour-by-hour description of his workday. And in it we find the use of a single, sustained metaphor:

> This worker, abandoned to the antinatural activities of our civilization, gets up at 5:00 A.M. to be at the workshop door at 6:00 A.M. As he journeys there, his craft faculties are already functioning. For woodworking, a fatiguing and complicated craft, torments the body and distresses the mind with incessant preoccupations. So our worker feels impatience and chagrin as he contemplates the ten hours of work that loom ahead to devour his soul and stuff his mouth with their meager gain.[27]

The chronicle of our agnostic who curses the calamity of work tells us, first of all, the very same thing that we are told by the normative discourse that extols its necessity. The quality or nature of work is not its crucial feature. The crucial feature is its abstraction: that is, the obligation of the time spent every day in order to procure the means of subsistence for oneself. The double relationship of abstract and concrete, of means and ends, could bring this chronicle of a world turned upside down back to a dialectic concerning the human essence of production, if it were not for one thing that was taken for granted right at the start of the workday —the distinction between body and soul. No one had ever heard it said that the soul could find its full and complete essence in productive work. It is not from that quarter that the original inversion of means and ends can be reversed; and the skilled nature of the labor, the enrichment of the task involving the human spirit as well as the body, cannot compensate for the pain of working for a living. Indeed, it intensifies that pain insofar as it means that the time of necessary servitude will eat into the time for possible liberty.

That is why the most hateful thing about the workday and its every hour may well be the anticipation of it all: "As he heads for his workplace, this man has a singular mien. Anger hatches in his glance. As he bounds along like a rebel slave, one would think he was hastening to sign a pact to wipe out his oppressor."[28] But our rebel slave is hurrying only to be on

27. Louis Gabriel Gauny, "Le travail à la journée," Fonds Gauny, Ms. 126. This text was published in extract form in *Le Tocsin des travailleurs*, June 16, 1848. *Translator's Note:* Page citations here are from the extract reprinted in Rancière (ed.), *Le philosophe plébéien*, pp. 39–43. This citation is on p. 39.

28. Ibid.

time at his place of bondage. The first hour of the workday will see him applying his rebel energy to conscientious work, moving from hatred for the oppressor to the struggle and toil of work:

> When he arrives at the place, the battle begins. First, his poor musculature, somewhat rested from sleep, is focused relentlessly on the task. Giving way to habit and overflowing with solidarity, the worker conscientiously applies himself to doing the job right. Given over momentarily to the inner satisfaction of useful work, he forgets his surroundings. His arms work, some craft detail is done pleasingly, he keeps going. An hour slips by.[29]

In the course of hours marked by the driving rhythm of his arms and pulsations of revolt or reverie, his conscientious forgetfulness of his surroundings takes on the form of an intoxication: "he works violently to achieve the intoxication of oblivion. For a moment he manages to distance himself from the resentful feelings of his implacable memory. He works furiously. A living machine, he gains for the profit of his proprietor what he loses at the expense of his own strength."[30]

In the sober resolution of the first hour and in the delirium of the fifth hour, the one in which the worker takes up the logic of the drunkard and works to forget that he is obliged to work, one might be tempted to see the Saint-Simonian dream of "peaceful riots" already achieved in the daily life of the workshop. But the passing hours reveal the radical deficit in this transfer of energy, which is effectuated only under the twofold image of obliviousness and struggle. The rage becomes productive energy only insofar as thinking deserts the producing body to reproduce the distance of denial. It is work compounded of intoxication and obliviousness, not the fine harmony of attentive intelligence served by a skilled hand. It is another picture of the Babylonian frenzy, in this case not sharing out the hours of work and the hours of orgy, but rather dividing up each hour with the syncopations of anticipation and reminiscence, of productive oblivion and unproductive reverie.

Thus the insurgent slave is indeed an inhabitant of Babylon, but not the one pictured by that curious Christian whose whole interest was focused on the opposition between Belshazzar and Cyrus in the Book of Daniel: that is, between the ruler of the old world destroyed by orgy and the

29. Ibid., p. 40.
30. Ibid., p. 41.

sober organizer of the disciplined armies of the new world. Is it because Gauny, worker and unbeliever, saw his life marked by the passage of an apostle named Moses that he can show us the true place of the worker, even though he would not set foot inside a church to witness the religious marriage of a friend? Is that why he can point up the place of the worker as that of the Hebrew in captivity, victim of oppression by another race and, even more, symbol of the soul held captive by bodily needs and its tasks?

This first exile of the soul accounts for the peculiar cast of the relations of intermingled collaboration and hatred with the master, who represents a more fundamental tyranny. The gulf of exploitation between the two parties is merely the consequence of the upside-down world in which the soul is imprisoned: "These two human beasts, animalizing the topsy-turvy state of things and ulcerating mistrust and hate, bare their fangs at the unequal parts of their prey. But they do not attack, one held back by his chain, the other by ominous presentiments."[31]

Here we have a confrontation between two parties in which hatred is as accidental as love is impossible, and conflict is as inexpiable as it is fortuitous. But it is also a contradiction whose impossible resolution, far from implying the eternity of domination, conjures up a liberation that is to come less from the insurrection of the captives than from the crumbling of the kingdom of captivity. The master of that kingdom, seized with "ominous presentiments," would in that case read his "Mene, Tekel, Peres" (Dan. 5:25–28) in the hateful looks, and even in the docile acts, of his slaves.

This is the starting point for the rhythm that punctuates the ten hours of every workday, each a repetition of the seventy years of Hebrew captivity in Babylon. It is not an accumulation that would cause the awareness of exploitation to explode, or an oscillation between discipline and resistance in their varied forms. Rather, it is the varying tensions of a dialogue, of a play and interplay put on by soul and body. If, in the first hour, it takes the respectable form of recommendations made by a moralist soul to an applied body, it soon becomes involved in the games of forgetfulness and resentment, irritation and reminiscence. As early as the second hour, for example, the nice song serving as a stimulus to useful work reveals its duplicity. The machinery of the moralized body skids on the sounds punctuating its toil and slips into a very different refrain and lesson:

31. Ibid., p. 39.

Sometimes, in an untimely fit of gaiety, he hums an old beloved air that his father sang. Gradually going astray in the caprices of the sounds, which pervert his first memory, the measure of his joy undergoes a bizarre change. He is murmuring a song of rebellion that simulates a fusillade.[32]

This impromptu murmur of the body is the first sign of straying, the first *contretemps* or syncopation. Slipping from remembrance of distant childhood to remembrance of July, it will bring the soul back to its pains by way of its pleasures:

> But an hour remains to be used up before the rest hour arrives. The worker grows irritated. Reveries await him with a display of the riches promised by the wonders of a good organization. Benumbed by the comings and goings of the entrepreneur or his foreman, he is forced to reach an understanding with one of them about plans that weary attention. Dry observations meet with parsimonious responses. And their looks exchange dissatisfactions that drive an even deeper separation between the two men.[33]

This first appearance of the master has nothing in common with the distant and reassuring image of the idle exploiter. He does not drag himself from sofa to feather bed, as in the texts. This master moves his head and legs far too much. He comes on the scene less as the enemy than as the intruder. His comings and goings are intolerable. They would remind one of the jailer's round if he were simply content to observe the prisoners. But the master intends to curb the spirit of the worker, forcing him to apply his intelligence to his task. In the upside-down world he takes for his kingdom, the master is first a noisy footstep tearing the soul away from its dream of the promised land and dragging it back to its captivity. He is the spoilsport who rules out peaceful dreaming about the enjoyments of good organization where it has no place.

So the third hour goes by. It is time for a meal that could not possibly offer food for the soul. Mealtime merely revives the basic constraint: the body must be nourished so that it can continue an activity that has no purpose but its nourishment. So our worker's first meal will be marked

32. Ibid., p. 40.
33. Ibid.

by a vain effort to evade those sensations that prolong or anticipate the constraint of work:

> The worker's stomach, with an appetite whetted by turbulent work, is not nourished in accordance with the rules of hygiene. It is filled with the more or less watered-down vittles of a wicked restaurant-keeper. . . . The foul air takes the edge off his senses. And even though his imagination, independent of time and place, invents a harmonious existence for itself, it soon is brought down to the garbage of the real world.
>
> The worker absolutely wants a bit of happiness. He eats hurriedly to be his own man for a little while, to wander for twenty minutes in the depths of some vague hope. But his attentive ear remains on the alert, nevertheless, because the bell will soon sound; and its sound importunes him in advance by arousing dangerous comparisons with those who live off the work of others.[34]

These comparisons are dangerous, first of all, for those who make them. The irritation, the convulsions, the bodily contractions, and the looks of rage evoked by the anticipated sound of the bell really define the servile malady of the victims of the upside-down world. They do not suggest any form of consciousness-raising that would lead to the realization of a fraternal society in which the soul could recognize the abode of which it preserves a remembrance. Once again the "thought of insurrection" evoked by the bell leads only to the work that is to be begun again: "When he gets back to the workshop, duty sustains him. He is armed with resolutions in the face of the seven inevitable and monotonous hours whose yoke he must bear to feed his body." Is it to win pardon that his body becomes a willing accomplice and offers the distraction of work to his spirit, which is subjected to the yoke of the workshop for the body's sake? "Often a job difficulty skillfully overcome distracts him a bit and breaks up the long stretch of time."

A bit of reassurance, then, is in order for those who would like the worker to find intellectual satisfaction in his work. Work, in fact, does sometimes offer a distraction from its own pains. But it soon becomes clear that this pleasure is not the kind philosophy would present as distinguishing the true good of the soul from the good commonly coveted by emperors and kings. It is not a pleasure that can be shared: "He applauds

34. Ibid., pp. 40–41.

himself over his success and would like to share with his fellow worker the good technique he figured out and used. But the other worker, less rebellious or more desperately in need, responds only furtively. For he notices the hated eye of the master, who is constantly on the lookout as he prowls among his workers."[35]

This is the first time that the other worker enters our picture, and he does so as one who refuses communication. The happy relationship of the worker to his work shatters on the only thing that might make it purposeful for him: a fraternal relationship with another worker. If combat is not the way for the captive soul, neither is work as an attractive thing. His hope for a different relationship with his work is ruined by the looks of complicity binding the other workers to their master. Anticipation of the master's glance throws the dream of attractive, fraternal work back to another stage—the productive frenzy of the insurgent slave:

> This damned worker is indignant over the inquisition conducted by the master's glance. A burst of hatred stirs him right down to the bone. When this commotion finally subsides, he works violently to achieve the intoxication of oblivion. For a moment he manages to distance himself from the resentful feelings of his implacable memory. He works furiously. A living machine, he gains for the profit of his proprietor what he loses at the expense of his own strength.[36]

But it is not awareness of exploitation that will halt the producing machine. Once someone knows his existence has been sold, what is the point of simply caviling at the buyer's profits? It is not the rebelliousness of the exploited worker but the anger of a thought surrendered that will curb bodily movement by asserting its own rights. But this right of a soul quickly turns in a new direction, insofar as the workshop enclosure and its high window offer no view of freedom except that of flying birds and fluttering leaves. It becomes a dream of vegetative life that would annihilate sorrow, or of an animal life in which free flight embodies self-forgetfulness:

> Above the nearby roofs the joiner glimpses the top of a poplar tree balancing in the air. He covets the vegetative existence of the tree

35. Ibid., p. 41.
36. Ibid.

and would gladly bury himself in its bark to avoid further suffering. A few ravens are just passing. He dreams of the vast perspective which they command and of which he is deprived. He sees the beautiful countryside toward which they are flying. In his delirium he envies those free birds living by the laws of God and would like to descend from human being to animal.[37]

Even before his soul has recovered conscious awareness of its destiny, the warning of a comrade, again merely an intermediary between him and the master's glance, brings him back to reality. He comes back to the wood and tackles it once more; back to the comparisons he makes "in spite of himself"; back to the torture of his body suffocating from the dust of wood shavings, and the curses it evokes from him; back to the cramped, narrow space between workbenches and the curses it prompts. "Everything becomes hateful to him: his master and everything else! The second third of the day is gone through with feelings of abhorrence and disgust."[38]

In the second work break, this mood will give rise to a force that is something quite different from convulsion. His whole description contrasts sharply with that of the first meal break, which was dominated by the impatience of hunger and anticipation of the clock. Need is quickly taken care of: "Impatient and fiery, he quickly satisfies his hunger." The rebellion he propagates now is no longer associated with the irritation and rage of insurgent slaves but with an apostolate establishing the laws of a world put right again:

> He unleashes his popular passions instantly. He reveals to his comrades the extent of their rights and the exact sum of their duties. His inspiration rouses those brutalized outcasts. Tireless apostle of rebellion, he draws them into a corner and denounces the taxes of body and soul that they must pay to a society that disinherits them. Then the conspirators swear an oath to revolt against the bridle that is choking them.[39]

Between the seventh and eighth work hour something happens. It is in the nature of a fragile union of two contradictory images: apostolate and

37. Ibid.
38. Ibid., p. 42.
39. Ibid.

conspiracy. But the conspiracy involved is not that of a contemporary song revealing the clear visage of a union of conscious workers conspiring in broad daylight.[40] Thanks to the voice of the apostle, who at the moment is more a passing stranger than a comrade in work and therefore in brutalization, it is the breath of the spirit penetrating the walls of the workshop for a moment and then heading out, where it wills, to arouse other outcasts. It is a conspiracy without face or temporal bounds, entailing neither the revolt of the eighth hour nor the organization of liberation's stages. But neither is this momentary reversal of complicities, which unite the community with the master against each individual worker during the hours of work, akin to the ephemeral symbolic reversals of power that punctuate the time of domination. In the intervals of work it prefigures, along with transformed relationships between individuals, the coming of a new age, the temporal nature of which, when the bell sounds, will be shown by this change: its arrival will surprise them rather than making them suffer in anticipation of it.

Before long, however, the bell brings the communion of the apostle back to the solitude of the worker and the fever of the rebel to whom everything and everyone are hostile. His suffering in the workshop is now redoubled by thoughts of a world outside—not the place of escape, but a place where the encirclement of work by a working-class society turns the position he would like to flee into a position to be defended: "For at the door of the workshop, workers are waiting for a position to become vacant. This surplus of common people in civilization puts them at the mercy of the one who sacrifices workers to work."[41]

This priest of a false god, as we know, is himself merely the privileged hostage of an order he does not rule. That is why the overturning of the upside-down world does not occur by means of his overthrow but rather entails the reestablishment of a fraternal relationship with him: a meeting of equals face to face or a mutual avowal of love. It is this establishment of a human relationship with his boss that haunts the two hours after his rest period. He feels ashamed of his subordination as tangibly as he feels aware of his exploitation in this search for fraternity: "He is ashamed of the conventions established between them, which keep him at a distance and always at an inferior level. . . . Not wanting to despair completely,

40. Charles Gille, "L'union des camarades," in P. Brochon, *Le pamphlet du pauvre*, Paris, 1957, p. 149.

41. Gauny, "Le travail à la journée," in Rancière (ed.), *Le philosophe plébéien*, p. 42.

he looks for friendly faces because fraternity is his first passion. Making a superhuman effort, he tries to love his boss."[42]

His first passion, however, is incapable of undoing the effects of its frustration, which have hardened into the features of a body docile to work but indocile to love. These are the stigmata of a world in which the status of every individual is so defined that every object of love is a subject of exploitation:

> His looks, though sanctified by a religious feeling, are too settled to allay the antipathy. It is too late. Hate is scorching hot. That is the way the displacements of our society have willed it to be. He still perseveres, looking as gently as possible at the wife and children of his master. But in them he sees only present and future exploiters. The wife is only a ruinous surcharge, her frivolous expenditures evoking the severe exactions he must endure.[43]

The circle closes again. In the displacements of society, the very thing that would make the master human is the thing prompting the inhumanity of his exploitation. It is what brings the two parties face to face: on the one hand, the one who works to provide a family of workers with food and the possibility of reproduction, and who is compromised by the very excess of that reproduction; on the other hand, the one who exploits to feed his family of exploiters, and who thus consecrates all his capacity for love to the maintenance of exploitation.

It is in this circle that the workshop hours orbit until the last hour. That hour drags out unduly, thanks to the same factor that shortened the rest period—expectant waiting:

> It is the most terrible hour, summing up all the others. Expectant waiting exaggerates its duration tenfold. Weary boredom, the horrible occupation of producers condemned to labors whose long duration evokes disgust, torments the limbs and spirit of the worker. The bodily positions required by his craft irritate him. Everything within him yearns to escape from him and head out for some unknown that is desired as happiness and good fortune. Evening falls, and his soul wears itself out counting the minutes.[44]

42. Ibid.
43. Ibid., pp. 42–43.
44. Ibid., p. 43.

The bell finally sounds, permitting our captive to abandon his "out-house of servitude." Unfortunately it does not return him to freedom but to the suffering of a new anticipation. The off-season of winter awaits him. Then, either the hunger of his children or the work found to feed them will deprive him of the only good thing that remains for the common laborer—his night, the lengthening of which is the only advantage of the winter dead season:

> This coming winter, if he does not work, his children will wake up to ask him for food. If he finds a bit of work in that hard season, he can already anticipate his apprehensiveness about the odious evenings before bedtime. His soul, obstinately fixed on the pleasures of study, will want to abstract itself from industrial preoccupations and devote the night to the pleasure of learning and the charm of producing. It will be in despair if fate refuses it the exercise of this indefeasible right.[45]

To be sure, our rebel joiner has exaggerated the dilemma a bit in his own case to more closely identify his own workday with that of the "countless unfortunates who, like him, live off a work ravaged by the old world." He himself has no children to feed. But this situation puts him in a position to radicalize the problem. How can one establish, in the intervals of servitude, the new time of liberation: not the insurrection of slaves but the advent of a new sociability between individuals who have already, each on his own, thrown off the servile passions that are indefinitely reproduced by the rhythm of work hours, the cycles of activity and rest, and the alternations of employment and unemployment? A society of free workers, you see. Viewed up close, the project might well exceed the already unprecedented demand for "relations of equality" with the masters. The principle is easy enough to formulate, of course: "Let us hasten to associate ourselves and bring to the same table the fruits of our common harvest."[46] But the pathways of this hastening are not exactly quick or straight. The obstacle in this case does not come from the masters–jailers. It is a matter of knowing which way these pathways of liberty go, pathways that can be traveled only by individuals who have already been liberated.

45. Ibid.
46. Ibid.

CHAPTER 4

Circuit Rounds and Spirals

ANOTHER FEVER, ANOTHER EXILE. This printer has gone back out the door he just entered: "On the fifth day we got the sinister message—nothing more to do!"[1]

These mishaps are frequent in the typographer's trade, one marked by the singular fact that a day *at* work is not necessarily a day *of* work: "It is pretty much only in the printshop that one is permitted the revolting and wicked abuse of hiring people and keeping them behind bars or under lock and key, without feeling obliged to give them any work or remuneration."[2] That is the lot of the slip compositors (*paquetiers*) who populate the book printshops. The foresight of the masters prompts them to hire people all the more lavishly insofar as that costs them nothing. The workers are present in the shop from morning on but paid on a piecework basis, so they simply wait for the contingencies of work to offer them a few hours of remunerative activity.

But even that sort of patchy workday can become a privilege when a crisis hits the printshop. Then the typographer, chased from the paradise of the aristocratic journal compositors on the Right Bank, begins his descent on the road that will first lead him to the proletarian bookwork compositors on the Left Bank and then sweep him into the spiral that winds out from the first circle of printshops administratively tolerated in the quarters (Montrouge, Vaugirard, Montmarte, Belleville . . .) to the distant wreath of establishments set up by modern entrepreneurs farther and farther away from the taxes and troubles of the capital (Sèvres, Saint-Germain, Lagny, Corbeil . . .).

1. Supernant, "Révélations d'un coeur malade," *La Ruche populaire*, Feb. 1840, p. 26.
2. Coutant, *Du salaire des ouvriers compositeurs*, Paris, 1861, p. 13.

Our fictional printer has traversed the spiral from the heart of Paris to the heart of hell, driven by some ill whose causes our storyteller deems it irrelevant to analyze right now: "As everyone knows, a noxious influence has battened on industry in general and the printing trade in particular. But this is neither the place nor the time to investigate the cause of this influence, which has been disastrously progressive for some years."[3] A noxious influence, an epidemic, an external ill invading what would be the normal life of the social body: such images may be essential to a perception that refuses to separate the science of doctors from the devotion of lifesavers and the starts of sick people. This convergence itself pinpoints well enough the one and only source of all social ills: the fundamental ill that economics calls competition and morality calls egotism.

It is another and different malady. It is no longer the joiner's feverish anticipation, but in the slow agony of a life "begged from God minute by minute" and in the round of knocking on the doors of workshops that are closed, deserted, or dormant, it is the same perduring exchange between sufferings of the soul and sufferings of the body. It is another exile, but this one does not take the form of imprisoning the captive soul in the needs of the body and the walls of the workshop. The kingdom of our printer is of this world: not in the clouds of our rebellious joiner, but in the streets, sights, and sounds of the city:

> For a long time I had no family, since I lost my mother quite young. So I had created a new family for myself out of the immense population that gravitates around the bosom of the city every day. I loved it as my second mother, still alive after the other one had died. Alive in its patchwork houses and motley buildings, its sky, and its sounds, which I had seen and heard from the moment I was granted sight and hearing. Sitting on a sidewalk stone like a baby in its cradle, I recognized a brother in every passing creature, a familiar toy in every monument, a friendly call in every one of the myriad sounds that assaulted my ears.[4]

Upon entering the workplace, the orphan who had re-created a family out of the harlequin city was not suddenly and irremediably separated from the pathways of his childhood. The world of our printer–*goguettier* was not cut in two, as was that of our joiner–poet. And so his exile, before

3. Supernant, "Révélations d'un coeur malade," *La Ruche populaire*, p. 23.
4. Ibid.

becoming a geographic exodus toward the printshops of the periphery, takes the form of a loss of reality, of a hallucination that robs him of his maternal space:

> When the time came that I found myself, at the corner of every crossroad and the threshold of every thoroughfare, a young man already weary of real life and trying to summon up again the illusions of a happy childhood to make of them a pillow on which I might dream, if not sleep, during my long nights of insomnia, and every time found myself anticipated by the filthy and insatiable Harpy called Poverty, the specter that I kept fleeing everywhere and always and that kept pursuing me everywhere and always, I was forced to keep going straight ahead and farther until it had lost my track.[5]

In these rhetorical figures, borrowed from the models of the day, we sense here more than the effort of our apprentice writer to turn the prose of everyday life into poetry: a certain insistence on using metaphor to move reality into the realm of fiction. That very same year Villermé had taught bourgeois curiosity and compassion to recognize the haunts and scars of poverty. Here it is as if that poverty were entitled to literal and literary existence only in the extenuated form of a spectral destiny pursuing the errant soul—as if the reality of unemployment and poverty were not so much the raw manifestation of the social ill as the hallucination produced by the fundamental sickness of a life dedicated to seeking something it does not desire.

Through the pride of some or the repugnance of others, however, work did seem to present a virtue that was acknowledged by all. It was the means to independence: that is, to a life exempted from the servitude of seeking. But how is one now to describe the life that hangs on the search for work? That life functions as no more than the substitute for its own ideal, a remedy for or a mere derivative of its own illness. In the work our errant printer finally gets, he will find repair for the energies that had been impaired, not so much by hunger as by the anticipation of it, by the constraint of *finding* some work:

> After the incredible surprise of being employed immediately after my arrival, I had again set about . . . rebuilding my future from day

5. Ibid.

to day, the only one on which we could rely, we other workers. . . . For me work was then the repairer of the many breaches that long inaction had just made in my position, which was already precarious even in less wretched times. It was a potent topic to set over against the anxious question of *how to stay alive,* that terrible leprosy that decimates one-third of the population. They pose this question in the morning as a system to beat, but find it still unresolved when evening comes.[6]

After those four days of freedom from the anxiety of the puzzle and the obstacle course came the verdict of the fifth day, "nothing more to do," which a voice from somewhere else prompted him to complete with: "except die."

That is why he is now riveted on the Corbeil Bridge, right where a framework of crossbeams takes the place of the railing that had been destroyed at the time of the foreign invasion. He is not entirely alone, because the storyteller has placed him under the virtual gaze of travelers; they may go by too quickly to pay attention to him, but it is on consideration of them that his gaze at the river hangs:

> What would they say, those people passing down there in that coach, heading speedily for Paris on the road that hugs the right bank of the Seine, if I were to reveal to them the idea that absorbs me. . . .
>
> If they knew why I chose to lean on this barred wooden railing, through which I gaze eagerly at the flowing water, rather than on the stone railing that would prevent me from seeing it; if they recognized the wretched hope that fixes my gaze on the crest of each wave and forces it to follow that wave doggedly until my weary sight loses it in the confusion of all the waves vanishing on the horizon. . . . The hope is this: that giddiness will carry me away, and the waves as well, toward Paris—unperturbed, gently lulled to sleep like those people in their coach.[7]

A desire to let himself go without asking for anything more, but also a desire to return from his place of exile, by the most direct route, to his childhood home, his maternal city. "Rivers are roads that move and take

6. Ibid.
7. Ibid.

you where you want to go." What we have here is not a decision but an impatience, not any real giddiness but the yearning for it. How could the hasty look of the travelers discern what is at issue here? That night of the laborer by which alone he can match the day of the rich person: a journey without detour or shock, its pomp defining an equality exactly the opposite of that with which the preachers make the rich fear a death as destitute as the life of the poor. Their questions and counsels would necessarily bypass the problem: "What would they say? Perhaps this: he's mad—does one die for that?"

The question is obviously put badly. One does not die *for* that, one simply dies *of* it. It is not a final solution whose excess in proportion to its cause could be denounced. Rather, it is the final end of an illness, of a slow divestment of the real: the advance of empty time on full time, expanding the latter's intermissions; the leprosy of "how to stay alive"; the erosion of being by nothingness; the limit of that relationship of dependence that makes up "a life begged from God minute by minute." How could these rich questioners comprehend this complicated identity of ill and deliverance? For people of their class, death has the coarse features of the absolute Other. That is why they clearly differentiate the illnesses or violences to which one succumbs from the reasons for which one may yearn to die. It does not work the same way in the class of men with robust limbs and bronzed faces. The proximity of death is not manifested solely in and through the familiar forms: familiarity with violent relationships (brawls between journeymen guilds or others) that makes the hazardous life weigh less heavily on riot days; the bruising and wearing down of the body by work accidents and illnesses that curtail the hope of life and the calculations associated with it; the morbidity of the common people's city, which circulates the miasmas of cholera and insurrection at the same speed. There is also that sensitive frailty that tradition more readily attributes to the languors of the idle. When the warden of the Belle-Ile penitentiary gets the humanitarian idea of having the political prisoners bathe in the sea, you witness this strange episode. The model soldier of the people's army, silkweaver–sergeant–deputy Sébastien Commissaire, whose body as a child had been hardened in the icy waters of the Doubs River, faints; he cannot bear the smell of sea water. The very experience of prison brings out in militant workers a propensity of the soul to amplify the sufferings of the body and of the body to waste away from the wounds of the soul. How many die in a few weeks or a few months from the injustice of a sentence or the abandonment of those for whom they have submitted to it, from the stigma of time spent among thieves and convicts or the opposite rigors of isolation in a cell!

But one need not personally experience prison to die of the fatigues and lacerations of the apostolate. So died ivory-turner Desmartin, languishing away on the morrow of June 1848, and composer Saumont, driven to despair by the splitup of the typographical society. These political languors are close to the exhaustion of those who succumbed to the impossible task of leading a double life: for example, printer Eugène Orrit, whom the bilingual *Télémaque* left by Jacotot could not get through his double duties as laborer by day and encyclopedist by night. At the borderline these instances of decay produce a strangely ambiguous image of the exemplary death, a confused intermingling of the effects of hunger and the effects of discouragement, of vanquished resistance to disease and the decision to have done with it, of the price of presumption and the bitter wages of devotion. Every time a worker, often a printer, suffers for what he has said or written—when Hégésippe Moreau dies in the hospital or Adolphe Boyer commits suicide—two legendary deaths are evoked: the people's poets, Gilbert and Malfilâtre. But no one really knows anymore what exactly they died of: hunger, illness, suicide, or madness. And even at the obsequies for Adolphe Boyer, killed by the failure of his book, the eulogy of printer Vannostal has difficulty characterizing his end. While Vannostal stigmatizes "this epidemic mania of suicide," he asks God to excuse Boyer for having fallen "into a weakness so common in irreligious ages like our own; for He would be unjust if He were to punish the worker who falls, worn out by fatigue."[8] The suicide of the discouraged militant —the failed writer, say wagging tongues—is the very same as the fatigue of the one who worked too much. And many proletarian deaths have the quality marking the legendary deaths of children of the common people who wanted to break through the barrier: abandon, in both senses of the word—loneliness and giddiness. They are very gentle deaths, which look like a simple letting-oneself-go to the natural elements. The models of our illustrious Charlet do not kill themselves with the sword at all. Like Jules Mercier and Reine Guindorff, they let themselves go in the waters of the Seine; or, like Claire Demar and Adolphe Boyer, they calmly stretch out after having stuffed their stove and blocked up all the openings through which the heat might escape.

Supernant, however, does not let his fictional character succumb to gid-

8. *La Ruche populaire* and *L'Atelier*, Oct. 1841.

diness. This is, without doubt, in his interest as an author—he has no other character. But the sequel of the story will show us precisely that the latter makes sense only by virtue of his other: the double toward whose house he now hastens on the rain-soaked road without giving in to the temptation to let himself fall. Another and the same character, the printer whose time has holes in it, on the one hand, and, on the other, the proletarian of thought, the worker whose time has no measure and who is promised no salary for the order and regularity that the visitor observes in his cold, empty room: "I glanced at his table. Papers and books were arranged on it the way he used to arrange them when he foresaw that he had to tackle a work of some importance. The start of a rough draft lay in front of his one and only chair."[9] Let us spare ourselves the time spent by our hero in detecting, in the dampness of the accumulated ashes and the drying up of the ink, the signs of long abandonment. He then goes over and draws the curtains of the bed on which his friend lies—dead, of course, not from having nothing to print up but probably from having too many texts still waiting to be printed up. The narrator does not tell us exactly. He postpones the sequel and the moral to a subsequent issue.

But there will be no sequel—in all likelihood because our author is one of the militant printers who, in the autumn of 1840, tired of doing literature on worker miseries in *La Ruche*, will rejoin comrades at *L'Atelier* who have decided to propose positive solutions and to awaken the moral energies that will give workers mastery over their destiny. So it is up to us to draw the lessons of the fable, which are not so obvious as they might seem. The suspended ending may illustrate the sermons that point up the danger of literary pretensions to haughty proletarians. But the body of the story has already destroyed the antithetical image of the good trade that offers a living to the honest, industrious laborer. At the common boundary of work and nonwork, of hand-work and thought-work, one and the same malady renders the destinies of laborer and writer equally deadly. And if the printer who cannot sell the use of his hands resists the cold of the off-season better than the writer who cannot sell the fruit of his thinking, the main reason is this: the nobler the function attained, the crueler the malady.

The principal danger, which will turn the hierarchy of functions upside down, lies elsewhere: not in dying of one's thought-work but in living by it. That is the lesson of another little tale in *La Ruche* about a "lost

9. Supernant, "Révélations d'un coeur malade," *La Ruche populaire*.

life."[10] The author, Pierre Vinçard, brings us back to the scene of a joinery workshop that seems to know nothing of the printshop's dead periods. There, too, hiring took place at good moments in the dismal decade of the twenties, and it was not always done with discernment. The master sets out to make the rounds of the asylums and lets the orphanage authorities palm off on him young Georges, a boy with neither the taste nor skill for work. In despair that he will make nothing out of him, he entrusts Georges's apprenticeship to Urbain, a worker who is remarkable for his competence and, even more, for the dignity he gets from his mother, "a woman of superior intelligence and a loving, sensitive soul." Those kinds of superiority give perilous kinds of pedagogy. Urbain turns Georges into a passable worker, but the main thing is that he lends him books. The books are read so avidly that one day the young man declares to his mentor that he can no longer remain a worker, because he has come to realize that "material work was incompatible with serious studies; because if an inspiration comes to you during the workday, you must wait until evening to take advantage of it; and by that very fact it very often escapes you." The work of thinking cannot be done on a part-time basis. In vain will Urbain remind his pupil that Plautus turned the grindstone and that Jean-Jacques Rousseau copied music. In vain will he try to hold him back from the road to disgrace when Georges, having lived off a young working girl, plans to abandon her when she becomes pregnant because his vocation cannot tolerate any obstacle. Georges will pursue his course to the final scene: Urbain, seeking new lodgings, accidentally comes across the room where Georges is dying, not of hunger but of moral destitution.

The key scene of the story is the one where Urbain comes to remind Georges of his duties as lover and father and finds him in the company of the absolute Other, the man who lives no more by his own thinking than by his own hands but rather by the thinking of others: the *feuilletoniste,* who in this case has come with cigar and cane to pressure Georges into discrediting the work of an author who displeases his masters. Georges, who had intended to praise the author, would settle for not saying anything good about the author's work. Nothing doing! The *feuilletoniste* is a creature devoid of the reserve that allows the joiner to give himself to his master only for his money, to invest in the same action the zeal that acquits him of his work and the rage that liberates his thinking. The man who lives by the work of his hands can play off his arms against the

10. Pierre Vinçard, "Une vie perdue," *La Ruche populaire,* June 1841.

thinking of his master, or play off his thinking against the materiality of his work. But the man who lives by his thinking can no longer use guile on the account books of work well done/rightly done. He must always do more, unreservedly alienating the most precious possession he has. A proletarian of thought is a contradiction in terms, which can be resolved only in death or servitude. The course from proletarian to apostle is unthinkable in terms of a career. And so *La Ruche populaire* does not allow as collaborators "people whose material existence depends on their way of thinking and writing."[11] It admits only the proletarians who have reached the same conclusion as Urbain: "I prefer to plane my boards, it is less humiliating."

Less humiliating, undoubtedly, especially since Agricol Perdiguier and George Sand have given the trade its literary dignity. It is again by a trick of literature that the antithesis of the lost worker is to be a joiner–philosopher. The very same chiseler who mocks the mason's trowel is always ready to exalt the music of "his" plane; but the authentic joiner Gauny, who already mistrusted the spiritedness of Saint-Simonian choirs, does not find satisfaction or recompense in this industrious music. The man who planes his boards does not sell his thoughts to a master, but it is still necessary that the continual practice of this operation leave him a thought; that the noise of the plane, the mechanical use of his arms, and the fatigue of his brain not turn the independence of the journeyman vis-à-vis the master into a mere alibi for his bondage to work.

Now there we have a formidable ordeal every day: hiring out one's body without alienating one's thinking, "stealing a few scraps of leisure" from time's "frenzy of tyrannical activity."[12] The "cancer that gnaws the soul of the day-laborer"[13] harnessed to his bench bears the same name as the fatal malady that seizes printer–poet Hégésippe Moreau coming out of the printshop—even though he has made the wise resolve to be "a worker by trade and a poet by fancy," making his work for a living the daytime drug that he must prolong with opium to escape the agony of nights and Sundays.[14] The malady is called boredom: the mutual numbness of body

11. Pierre Vinçard, "Réponse au journal *Le Globe*," *La Ruche populaire*, 1841, p. 17.

12. Gauny to Ponty, Fonds Gauny, Bibliothèque municipale de Saint-Denis, Ms. 168, Jan. 22, 1838; in Jacques Rancière (ed.), *Louis Gabriel Gauny: Le philosophe plébéien* (Paris: La Découverte/Maspéro, 1983), p. 167.

13. Gauny, "Le travail à la tâche," Fonds Gauny, Ms. 134; in Rancière (ed.), *Le philosophe plébéien*, p. 45.

14. Letter cited by G. Benoît-Guyod, *La vie maudite de Hégésippe Moreau*, Paris, 1945, p. 228.

and soul, from which the latter dies more nobly but no less surely than it does from its fall into venality. In the apportionment of labors of body and labors of thought, of daytime occupations and nighttime occupations, of exigencies of body and exigencies of soul, the balancing point presupposes a more subtle geometry than that which presides over journeyman masterpieces.

That geometry could not possibly reside, for example, in the simple reversal effected by Gauny's friend and contradictor, Louis-Marie Ponty, whose childhood was one of rebellion against school and whose adolescence was one of rebellion against apprenticeship in any and every trade. Determined never to worry about knowing "the time indicated on the clock by the hand of our industrious chain gangs," Ponty solved the problem by making night his workday and daytime his night.[15] Ragpicker, then cesspool-cleaner, he reserves the daytime for himself, to write in the sunlight, dream, and build up his library at the second-hand bookdealers along the river. It is an inversion of time, but also of the relations that classically link worker liberty to the nobility of his task and tool. It is choosing crap as the price of liberty, which he justifies in an ode to a colleague:

> Laisse-les donc t'insulter dans la rue,
> Vrai lazzarone aussi libre que l'air,
> Va! tout outil est un poignard qui tue
> La liberté, de nos biens le plus cher.[16]

To Gauny this liberty is merely the worst of servitudes: the kind that corrupts the night of the soul with the obligations of a task doomed to dejection, accompanied by gross remarks and, under its vagabond appearances, subject to constraining relations with authority. So he will not give up until he has led this bohemian of thirty-five to take up again, as an apprentice, the workshop route that he himself detests:

> If you, with your love of fine things and your passion for liberty, were to recoil today from the vexations that other habits always produce in us, you would be a coward. If you were to return to

15. Letters of Gabriel to Louis and Louis to Gabriel; in Rancière (ed.), *Le philosophe plébéien*, pp. 179–94.

16. "Galerie des chansonniers: Ponty," *La Chanson*, Dec. 26, 1880. "Let them insult you in the street / true beggar free as the air / every tool is a dagger that kills / liberty, of our possessions the most dear."

your former occupations—degrading by virtue of the illegitimate forced labors demanded by their exploiters—and again brutalize yourself in your stupefying and fetid nights, you would destroy in your spirit the developmental part that the Great All placed in each of its manifestations so that they might rise, with all their might, above the snares of fate. . . .

Have courage, and flee abasement, vile degradation, the shameful subordination that your masters will increasingly demand as the years diminish your physical resources—the only supports, untrustworthy ones, that linger in the worker's old age.[17]

So one must go by way of the drastic conditions of a true trade. It is in the workday and one's relationship with a tool, not alongside those things, that liberty has to set up its margins. Though it is an instrument of servitude, the tool is the minimal precondition if the proletarian is to have any independence. Gauny, then, will turn himself into a marginal insider, a floor-layer on a piecework basis, working his own hours in houses without master, overseer, or colleagues. The freedom of the jobber is earned with difficulty, to be sure, because the competition is rough and the price is high:

He is overwhelmed with indifference and unproductive matters. He is the one that the entrepreneur sacrifices to his day-laborers. Before anything else the entrepreneur readies work for them and neglects the jobber, whose lost time in no way hurts the entrepreneur. If some unproductive piece of work crops up, he imposes it on the jobber; and it is always the jobber that he satisfies last, enclosing him in the exigencies of a finished task without any concern for the hours and pains he expends on it. But in work where he breathes at his ease and is at home.[18]

Being at home: the ways of realizing this dream have nothing to do with the patriarchal daydreams of those philanthropists who would like to reconstruct the lost unity of work and the family order through the ordered disposition of social palaces, the rural peal of urban factories, or work done at home by little hands/little fairies of the hearth. Being at home

17. Gauny to Ponty, May 4, 1838, Fonds Gauny, Ms. 168; in Rancière (ed.), *Le philosophe plébéien*, p. 169–70.

18. Gauny, "Le travail à la tâche," Fonds Gauny, Ms. 134; in Rancière (ed.), *Le philosophe plébéien*, p. 45.

means fleeing the workshop of the master, but not for the sake of a place more inhabited by human warmth or humanitarian kindness. Fleeing, on the contrary, to that deserted space that is not yet a residence: a vacant place where the masons have finished their work but the owners have not yet installed their belongings—hence, a place where for this brief interval the constraint is broken that wedges the laborer between the entrepreneur, master of work, and the bourgeois man, master of the proprietary order, so that the floor-layer will be able to arrange a staging of his work that will be both the semblance of his ownership and the reality of his liberty.

The semblance of an ownership. It is in shouldering his insecurity that the worker can affirm an ownership of his work that does not reside in the relationship between his instruments (which are his at the master's as much as here) and his product, but primarily in the reversal of his relationship to time:

> The worker, who has not been winded by the exactness of the hour, considers his task for a moment as he prepares to undertake its sound execution. Nothing about his tools repels him; it is with a sort of affection that he handles them. Abandoning himself to the riches of his liberty, he is never made gloomy by his workplaces or the time he must spend there. . . . He does not dread the abhorrent gaze of the master or the time signals that force the other workers to break up their conversation and hurry under the yoke. On the job one effort excites another, the movements follow one another in a straight and spirited way. Lured toward the conclusion of the work, he is taken up by the charm as he kills boredom; that awful cancer that gnaws the soul of the day-laborer. . . .[19]

> Made feverish by action, he finds that the hours roll by quickly. His task, which he fecundates as he accelerates it, is a magnetism that dominates his thinking from morning to evening and ensures that he devours time, whereas the day-laborer is devoured by it.[20]

This curious reversal is yet again enunciated in terms of a physical constraint and a physiological disorder. Like all the workers who gravitate toward utopian circles, Gauny is an adept of parallel medicines: to the cancer of the day-laborer he opposes the magnetism that dominates thinking in order to free it and the homeopathy that cures like with like,

19. Ibid.
20. Ibid., p. 48.

the fever of servile work with the fever of free work. The floor-layer has the same body to feed as does the day-laborer; and his actions to achieve that end should not have any less frenzy. But the mastery of his time and the solitude of his space change the nature of this fever and reverse the relationship of dependence:

> As he gives air to his thinking every day, the floor-layer mortifies his body more and more. He must operate with frenzy because piecework has only laminated recompenses. Many workers, wanting to free themselves, try their hand at this specialty of the joiner's craft and compete with him. The craft bends this man under violent hardships that must be experienced to be appreciated. For it is crawling along on his knees that he lays the floor, tormented by the work, enchanted by the liberty! He mortifies his body to give flight to his soul; all unawares, this jobber is linked to the fathers of the desert by his renunciations![21]

The desert, i.e., the infinite given in broad daylight to the solitary gaze of the floor-layer: that is what separates the asceticism of the floor-layer from the mortifications, kindred at first glance, that grounded the daytime liberty of cesspool-cleaner Ponty or the evening pride of a Claude Genoux as he took up his pen again, after having spent the workday at the jobs of mason's laborer and shoeblack. Argues Genoux:

> Those paltry trades, which many people find debasing, abject, and unworthy of a thinking person—for the simple reason that they themselves do not think—seemed on the contrary to raise me in my own estimation. Not unaware of my own worth and perhaps exaggerating my merit, I was proud to be able to bend to every sort of toil, proud of my thousand francs and the verses I penciled on every wall. I would have bet a hundred to one that I was the top *goujat* [mason's boy] in the world.[22]

This sort of mortification is at once too glorified and too vile. It is not a matter of paying with crap work for the right to fly off to the poetic heaven. There is no elevation of thought where the body lives in ugliness

21. Ibid., p. 45.
22. Claude Genoux, *Mémoires d'un enfant de la Savoie*, Paris, 1844, p. 167.

and degradation. The sanctification of the soul comes about by way of the sanctification of the senses: of one's ear, liberated from the grossness of talk in workshop and street as well as from the imperious ringing of the bell; of one's gaze, liberated from the monotone gray of the workshop and the hatred aroused by the master's gaze. "Better than a mirror," the soul of the floor-layer reflects the sights around him. He cannot earn the purity of his night by debasing the purity of his workday. It is the harmony stolen from this place, from which he will soon be excluded, that makes him feel at home: "Believing himself at home, he loves the arrangement of a room so long as he has not finished laying the floor. If the window opens out on a garden or commands a view of a picturesque horizon, he stops his arms a moment and glides in imagination toward the spacious view to enjoy it better than the possessors of the neighboring residences."[23]

The view encompassed is undoubtedly more ample than the tops of the poplars glimpsed through the workshop window. But don't these possessions presented to the worker's gaze call to mind those "palaces of ideas" built, says Feuerbach, by philosophers living in thatched cottages? To tell the truth, even this portion is more than the "plebeian philosopher" seems to expect for his old age. Writing to his favorite contradictor, he will soon call to mind the common lot that awaits them: going to die at the old-age refuge and asylum of Bicêtre and "not having a shack of decent size in which to live and die freely in one's final days, in the company of friends who love us, be it book or engraving, tool or piece of furniture, animals or people . . . and not being able to live with our books until death."[24]

So he is not unaware of the fact that at the end of his "free" course he will have neither château nor cottage, or even those palaces of ideas that adorn the want of them. Apparently it is not on the side of the robust hands and productive work that one must call for the dissipation of illusion: because work, the worker's possession of his work, is the very heart of the illusion, and also because, at the same time, there is no illusion in the sense meant by philosophers and politicians—that is, something opposed to conscious awareness of a destiny endured or of the right conditions for transforming it. For this "illusion" is completely transparent. It is not unaware of anything about its causes or effects and seals no pact with the enemy it serves:

23. Gauny, "Le travail à la tâche," in Rancière (ed.), *Le philosophe plébéien*, pp. 45–46.

24. Gauny to Ponty, April 4, 1856, Fonds Gauny, Ms. 168, in Rancière (ed.), *Le philosophe plébéien*, p. 176.

This man is made tranquil by the ownership of his arms, which he appreciates better than the day-laborer, because no look of a master precipitates their movements. He believes that his powers are his own when no will but his own activates them. He also knows that the entrepreneur is hardly upset by the time he spends at his work, provided that the execution of it is irreproachable. He is less aware of exploitation than the day-laborer. He believes he is obeying only the necessity of things, so much does his emancipation delude him. But the old society is there to treacherously sink its horrible scorpion claws into his being and ruin him before his time, deluding him about the excitement of the courage that he uses for the benefit of his enemy.

But this worker draws secret pleasure from the very uncertainty of his occupation.[25]

Possession of self through which loss of self is reproduced; an illusion profitable to exploitation that rests on the reality of emancipation. This complementarity does not imprison illusion in the circle of a nonrecognition or even a complicity. The movement here is that of a spiral that, in the very resemblance of the circles in which the same energy is consumed for the benefit of the enemy, achieves a real ascent toward a different mode of social existence. Because a different society presupposes the production of a different humanity, not a destructive confrontation with the master or the bourgeois class, because the healing of the ill entails the singular asceticism of rebellion and its apostolic propagation, the illusion of emancipation is not a nonrecognition reproducing domination but the twisted path whose circle comes as close as possible to this reproduction, but with an already crucial swerve or digression. That the bell no longer makes itself heard or, above all, heeded, that the master is dispossessed of the sovereignty of his gaze and is no more than the accountant of social exploitation: these two little differences cannot be reduced to a trick permitting the productive investment of rebellious energy. The absence of the master from the time and space of productive work turns this exploited work into something more: not just a bargain promising the master a better return in exchange for the freedom of the worker's movements but the formation of a type of worker belonging to a different history than that of mastery. So there is no paradox in the fact that the path of emancipation

25. Gauny, "Le travail à la tâche," in Rancière (ed.), *Le philosophe plébéien*, pp. 46–47.

is first the path whereon one is liberated from that hatred of the master experienced by the rebel slave. Servility and hatred are two characteristics of the very same world, two manifestations of the very same malady. The fact that the freedman no longer deals with the master but with the "old society" defines not only a forward step in the awareness of exploitation but also an ascent in the hierarchy of beings and social forms. The rebel is still another worker; the emancipated worker cannot not be a rebel. The voluptuousness of emancipation is a fever from which one cannot be cured and which one cannot help but communicate. Attachment to the doctrine of palingenesis and the philosophy of the "ordeal" (*L'Épreuve*) propagated by Pierre-Simon Ballanche may be peculiar to Gauny, but not this vision that inscribes militant teaching and example in a spiral of the hierarchy of the forms of being.

This initiation establishes a division of time that is the antithesis of the one describing the descent of the printer into hell: a positive presence of nonbeing—absence, illusion, future—in being, where it is no longer death but rebirth that is anticipated. And so the dead time of unemployment is no longer the slow erosion of life, dispossession of the environment, flight pursued by fate. On the contrary, it is the march of a conqueror through the streets of the city, intoxicated with his liberty and receiving from the multitude of slaves the respects due to a superior type of humanity:

> This worker draws secret pleasure from the very uncertainty of his occupation, subject more than any other to unemployment. If he is without a bit of work, he looks for it without fearing the torment of diligence. He sets out on the track of work with consciousness of his liberty, sure of encountering among the poor day-laborers, whom he sometimes questions in his explorations, the look of covetousness they send to this worker, whose vigorous retort is a revolt against their existence in chains and whose flame is a probe passed over their slavish miseries. For this man of rebellion is a passionate advocate of propaganda. If his inquiring efforts are fruitless, he puts off his pursuit of work to the next day and walks for a long time to satisfy his need for action and to enjoy, as a plebeian philosopher, the ravishing nonchalance of liberty, which is filled to overflowing with serenity and energy by the pomp of the sun, the breath of the wind, and his own thoughts in line with the impetuosities of nature.[26]

26. Ibid., p. 47.

Our floor-layer's account (dream) of this suspended time of unemployment, then, will be a point-by-point contradiction of the story of the printer. The latter described "a slow, anguished, intolerable agony of progressive reductions in well-being or in habits that have reached the point of privation of the most absolute necessities."[27] The floor-layer, by contrast, "batters in his savings and, ready to exhaust his last resources, surpasses himself in expedients to husband the little he has, macerating himself to hire himself out."[28]

To the destiny of privations endured is opposed the maceration that also has the playful aspect of a calculation designed to prevent the joiner from falling back into the circle of need and day-work. Such an important stake could not possibly be handled solely by the expedients indicated by necessity. A science is needed, and the singular genius of the floor-layer creates it and gives it a name—*cenobitic economy;* a modern transposition of the rule of Pythagoras's companions, a science of the ways to manage the budget of rebels, making the restriction of their needs the way to purchase the maximum of liberty at the best price. The preamble of this new science explains its principle forthrightly: it is necessary to break the circle linking claims to the chances of consumption, to turn around the game of a political economy that preaches the virtues of saving to the poor but subjugates them by means of consumption. But it is also necessary to refute the ironic argument of his friend the cesspool-cleaner, who is quick to see in this science of asceticism an unexpected support for the defenders of the existing governmental system, which has its own way of compelling workers to carry out, willy-nilly, "the Pythagorean alimentary system."[29] The cenobite, then, intends to spell out at once his science's "goal of emancipation":

> Moderation is far from helping the tyrant to subject the worker to the smallness of his wages. The saving that the latter is to make is an intelligent and scorching weapon that cuts the other to the quick. The one who produces must work when and as he feels like it, profiting from the entire gain of his work; and he must

27. Supernant, "Révélations d'un coeur malade," *La Ruche populaire*, Feb. 1840, p. 24.

28. Gauny, "Le travail à la tâche," in Rancière (ed.), *Le philosophe plébéien*, p. 47.

29. Letters of Gabriel to Louis and Louis to Gabriel; in Rancière (ed.), *Le philosophe plébéien*, pp. 179–94.

legitimately earn a great deal to purchase a great deal of existence and liberty.[30]

Cenobitic economy is not the "spiritual point of honor" of political economy. In the order of consumption as in the order of production, the problem is not to possess "one's own" object but to possess oneself, to develop strengths that can no longer be satisfied by any of the bribes that exploitation offers to servility. There again the marvels of illusory possession are not allowed to stand in the way of the "objective" transformation of the conditions of exploitation. The kingdom of Baal will be toppled only by the army of deserters who have learned to put their hearts where their treasure is: elsewhere, nowhere, everywhere. It is not just the search for work that sets the cenobite walking. It is a law of cenobitic economy that links the development of his liberty to this exercise: "When one disposes of oneself in absolute independence, one must walk from morning to night."[31] That law also increases the expenditures for this practice: in the cenobite's budget, footwear represents 7 percent of the total expenditures. And so the necessary and useless meanderings from workshop to workshop that tortured the printer here take on the form of a tracking game or a hunting party, no longer punctuated by the anxiety of seeking work but pointed toward everything in the stage-décor of the city or the physiognomy of its actors that suggests to the hunter a prey to be captured, to the marginal person a place for his liberty to be lodged.

> He imagines, plans, makes suggestions to himself. He pries into every possible corner, traverses the streets, the alleys, and the crossroads. As he scrutinizes the structures of the most sumptuous neighborhoods or strays off on the loneliest circuit rounds, his gaze has the keenness of a bird of prey without food. Finally, he runs into a comrade, a kind of strange cynic made up in sarcasms and a great wine taster.[32]

A genre scene in the form of animal comedy. The meeting of the bird of prey and the made-up cynic is not accidental. The travels of the rebel

---

30. Gauny, " Économie cénobitique," Fonds Gauny, Ms. 151; extracts in Rancière (ed.), *Le philosophe plébéien*, pp. 99–111.
31. Ibid., p. 106.
32. Gauny, "Le travail à la tâche," in Rancière (ed.), *Le philosophe plébéien*, p. 47.

necessarily cross, or instinctively follow, the paths of the societally en-
franchised intermediaries—and parasites—who make up the mixed, inter-
loping population of freedmen let loose on the shifting frontier between
the world of slaves and the world of masters: petty contractors and sub-
contractors, journeymen who try to undertake jobs on their own, worker–
innkeepers or wine merchants, foremen who engage in hiring. It is with
one of these rakish characters, whose powers are seated and negotiated in
a cabaret, that the ascetic will have to reach an agreement—in an exchange
of libations where virtue, in order to seduce vice, pays it the opposite
homage of its hypocrisy:

> he runs into a comrade, a kind of strange cynic made up in sarcasms
> and a great wine taster. Since this fellow has under contract a fairly
> sizable number of jobs, he must hire in spite of himself. Lost in the
> corruption of society, he cannot and will not master his vile habits.
> Matter is his aim; he reverences Gargantua in pampering his body.
> Our floor-layer without work, who knows his concrete tastes,
> proposes to this favorite of work that they go to a cabaret. Talking
> shop there, they empty a bottle together, then another if necessary,
> and our worker manages to persuade this little Machiavelli, who
> cannot do without a mate, to choose him as an assistant, leaving
> him with the tacit hope that he will repeatedly shell out for libations
> according to the duration of the jobs. Moving from one thing to
> another, and despite their opposite habits, the two men end up
> spending the day drinking. By evening inebriation is giving them
> hallucinations. They recount stories, the conclusion of which seems
> to be a conspiratorial end for some passer-by. But what does it
> matter to the one? The wine excites him; perhaps he is boasting.
> As for the other, he would listen to parricides in order to live free.[33]

So long as the old society imposes its law, the margins of liberty are
also the margins of exploitation; and the rebel hunter of shadows there is
obliged to pull some of the strings of those workers and employers whom
the worker-turned-employer Denis Poulot will call "sublime," thinking
that he is being ironic. In the tropes of language that qualify the ambiguous world of the intermediary freedmen, however, Gauny would have us
see instead the optical illusion that threatens the hunter's quest. The sublime worker is the one who lets go of the shadow for the sake of the prey,

33. Ibid., pp. 47–48.

taking the intoxication of wine for that of liberty and turning his riotous independence into a new way of renewing the pact of exploitation. The ascending road of the rebel passes through this confrontation with his double, but without relapsing into the "debauchery" that moralists see as necessarily sinking the independence of the jobber: "Those moralists are wrong, or, rather, wrong us. Although this independence has its days of orgy, it adds to the extensiveness of thinking and lavishes around its adept a fluid of dignity that compensates a hundredfold for the aberrations it must endure."[34] The enjoyment of independence would not be capable of fixing the rebel in the compromise with the old society that leaves him so many secret pleasures. For he is the man whose gaze never ceases to command his arms and all his senses. Before being someone who suffers and protests in the face of the situation imposed on him, he is a man who sees the intolerable. When he reascends to his realm of attractive work, it is always the window that attracts him—and those vast perspectives where two blots of shadow suddenly appear. The two blots are two of the buildings that the spirit of enterprise and the spirit of reform have succeeded in erecting in these years: the factory and the cellular prison.

> With a circular glance he has taken in everything: the monuments and the prisons, the tumultuous city and its ramparts, the wisps of umbrage beyond the walls and the venturesome clouds in the infinite atmosphere. He goes back to work. But his soul reflects the things going on outside better than a mirror, because it passes through the stones; he perceives the abominations they hide. The prisoners in their stifling cells and the hirelings consumed by factories sweep him into humanitarian fits of rage in which their indignation, accusing society, makes him forget the splendors of space and suffer from the evil he has seen.[35]

So the free worker can no longer detach his gaze from those two shadows on the horizon of his empire: the factory, where the hirelings suffer, deprived of the means or the strength to emancipate themselves; the prison, enclosing those who lost their way on the pathways of liberty. But the gazes he directs toward the two edifices cannot be identical. Except for its size, the factory is a place similar to the one he has deserted. It encloses only those who give their consent. So it is natural that the

34. Ibid., p. 49.
35. Ibid., p. 46.

rebellious worker would be more interested in the place that has the privation of liberty for its rationale and that encloses, out of principle, those
who chose to shake themselves free of the common discipline. And the
worker in the building trade quite naturally asks himself questions about
this architectural novelty of the late 1830s, the cellular prison. "Quite
naturally" is perhaps saying too much. His colleagues do not seem to ask
themselves any questions about these new buildings and these new works.
That certainly won't hobble the curiosity of the rebel. He wants to know
what is on the other side of the walls that blacken his horizon. His curiosity reaching the pitch of a fixed idea or obsession, he has come to prowl
around one of these model prisons—La Roquette, undoubtedly—and has
settled down in his customary place for dealing with the agents of the old
world, the cabaret, at the hour when they are most easily snared in their
own corruption—dinnertime: "When the hour arrived, he caught sight of
a master-journeyman mason with a narrow forehead, concupiscent nose,
flabby cheeks, and gluttonous mouth—the typical animal glutton yielding
to seduction."[36] Lavater's science of physiognomy rarely fails the hunter
of liberty: an inquiry made about an imaginary comrade, a glass of wine
offered, and the work boss of the model prison is in the power of his
curiosity:

> The one expresses his desire to get to know the new system
> of detention. The other, ensconcing himself in the vanity of his
> authority, anticipates him and offers to escort him inside the
> prison as a new employee. The latter wanted to make his kindness
> profitable for his stomach but did not know how to state his
> speculation in an acceptable way. The former, guessing this, spared
> the materialist embarrassment by inviting him to dine after the
> painful exploration. This offer was accepted. Then they entered the
> compartments of the immense tomb.[37]

And so the visitor got to see the "mirage of torments" displayed at the
"panoptic center of the abyss," where one can turn completely around
and see "all the spokes of this wheel of torture": means of torture with
which he was already familiar, but with which one could play tricks in the

---

36. Gauny, "Aux ouvriers constructeurs de prisons cellulaires," Fonds Gauny,
Ms. 116; in Rancière (ed.), *Le philosophe plébéien*, pp. 65–85. This citation is on
p. 72.
   37. Ibid., pp. 72–73.

master's workshop. First, there is the impossibility of a spoken word that might find a response, or even an echo:

> No break in the walls, nothing filters through, everything gets lost. One senses there that tidiness and regularity are deadly. The air, circulating comfortably there, reeks of the base tyranny in the divisibility of its powers. One walks without calling up any echoes. Before the jailers, the objects make signs to keep silent and give the order to suffer.[38]

> The outside oxygen . . . is sanctimoniously replaced by an air-intake setup that, through the arrangement of its flow, loses the voice of the prisoner if he attempts to communicate into his aperture. The latrine area in each cell is also built according to this method of deafness, which buries voice and life without killing them.[39]

Above all, there is the irremediable subjection of the prisoner to the eye of the jailer, the permanent anticipation of a gaze that is not seen, the absence of night. The doors of the cell

> are pierced with a five-centimeter hole furnished with glass and covered with an opaque disk, which disappears into the thickness of the wood at the discretion of the watcher in order to spy furtively into the inside of the cell. This eye of the door, blind and seeing at the same time, pries unawares into the actions of the prisoner who, convulsed by boredom and restlessness, feels entangled in the chain of this hated gaze.[40]

> At night a gas jet lights up the damned. Troubled in his sleep by this torturous flame, he curses his fate even more and, unable to acclimate himself to his hell, peruses his peephole box, fearing to find there the treacherous eye of the jailer moving in the hole of the door.[41]

The panoptic setup is designed not so much to ensure that the penitentiary apparatus can keep tabs on the prisoner's deeds and gestures as

38. Ibid., p. 73.
39. Ibid., p. 75.
40. Ibid., p. 74.
41. Ibid., p. 75.

it is to strip them of anything that escapes knowing, anything that allows them to exist elsewhere or otherwise than in the gaze of the master.

To modern theories (e.g., those of Foucault) that oppose penitentiary knowledge of the individual and rehabilitation of the delinquent soul to the ancient shiver of torture, the gaze of the building-trade worker throws back another image in which surveillance has no function but that of torture. The person under surveillance is not a man you observe and correct; he is a hostage you wall in. The cellular architecture effects this new torture: a prison where the nooks and crannies offer no shadows, where no obscurity permits meditation to escape, where no complicity is exchanged or purchased, where no chance allows for the enjoyment, even the futile enjoyment, of hope—a world without fissures or interstices through which liberty, or merely the dream of it, could pass:

> The stones are of the best quality and meticulously installed. Their joints fit together as tightly as possible.[42]

> Astonishing precautions are taken to prevent escape. The coping of the circuit round and the exterior angle of the walls are rounded off so that even the wiriest hand could not clamp onto it. Iron bars, doors, lights, Judas holes, guards, and radiating perspectives threaten, spy, line up, and keep a lookout on the prisoners.[43]

A prison from which one cannot escape. It seems to be the most natural thing in the world. But at this point in time it is a novelty that gives reason for shock and indignation. It so happens that people *do* escape from the ancient prisons that chance has adapted to modern forms of detention: Sainte-Pélagie, Madelonettes, la Force. That is in the nature of things. The criminal—or insurgent—has chosen the way of chance and luck. He is entitled to a prison where escape is chancy but not completely impossible. How is it that those who build these flawless structures are not conscious of the fact that they are building a tomb for their brothers?

> Every layer of stone they lay is an outrage against humanity, one more weight thrown on the deafness of their conscience. They build these hideous cells against themselves, for it is their race that feeds the monster. The inequality of conditions, long-

42. Ibid., p. 73.
43. Ibid., p. 76.

term unemployment, the repugnance aroused by a job that is too exploitative or against our tastes, the absence of education, an extortion, a comparison, a vertigo: sometimes these things make the weakest and the strongest of the common people wage war against the society that disinherits them in their mother's womb and forbids them to live in the full employment of their faculties.[44]

The weakest and the strongest: those who do not have the resources to resist fatality and those who have too much energy not to defy it. The detailed catalogue of the factors that sweep the proletarian into the path leading to prison is immediately denied by this division, which refers the etiology of common crime back to the two extremes of decadence and transgression. The privileged relationship of the proletarian to the criminal passes through this twofold rejection. The disgust and revolt regularly expressed by strikers condemned to endure the abject promiscuity of the degenerate population in the central prisons leave no room for recognition of the convict as an unfortunate proletarian. And, on the opposite end, the mythical relationship of the people to the criminal they see mounting the scaffold exceeds any justification or compassion for the victim of poverty. The overall relationship of the condemned criminal (revealer, mirror, hostage, challenge) to the society that judges and executes him counts more than the etiology of crime or the pathology of decadence. Although worker chronicles quite frequently evoke the spectacle of the guillotine and the figure of the criminal, only rarely do they offer us either real or fictional genealogies of the crime.

The criminal represents not so much a particular victim of the lack of social foresight as the singular agent of an overall protest against that lack. He represents the people less in his suffering than in his hatred, in the excess that denounces a society in which destinies are not in proportion to vocations:

> The poor person is born with an ardent soul that he needs to exalt, to lavish on all that surrounds him. But no, he is not born for that! And in the midst of all that, you want hatred not to spring up in his heart, you want him not to envy the lot of his rich neighbor when he is surrounded by all the hideous trappings of poverty.[45]

44. Ibid., pp. 67–68.
45. Marie-Reine Guindorff, "De la peine de mort," *Tribune des femmes*, Dec. 1833, p. 81.

The genealogy of crime provided by Marie-Reine Guindorff in these sentences is exemplary. What matters first and foremost is not the neediness caused by poverty or even the covetousness aroused by the spectacle of wealth. At the source we find not a lack but an excess: the impossibility imposed on the proletarian of existing to the full extent of his abilities, and in accordance with his need for expansion, causes the hatred that the environment of poverty turns into covetousness, into greed for the things possessed by those human beings who prevent him from existing.

This economy of repressed power, popularized by the Saint-Simonians and the Fourierists, gives the criminal his heroic literary referent. Just before the Guindorff plea, in the same issue of the *Tribune des femmes*, Pauline Roland offers "A Word on Byron." In the crimes of his heroes she points to "an energetic protest against the order of things in the milieu where they lived, where everything was arranged and leveled in such a way that qualities beyond the ordinary measure could not regularly find a place there."[46] Under the two figures—the hero out of place in the *juste milieu* ("golden mean") of social values, and the criminal whose transgression reveals the repression of the popular soul—one and the same theme recurs obsessively: the theme of the "strong nature." It was an enigma that both repelled and fascinated the men who were trying to think about both the future forms of social reciprocity and the forces capable of inducing the transformation.

Even among those who most energetically reject the militant worker's twisting of strict morality, the question always ends up returning in the form of repentance or an admitted misjudgment. Even the most intractable of the critics putting out *L'Atelier*, Corbon, will himself end up making a full apology in *Le secret du peuple de Paris* (1863). His rival at *La Ruche populaire*, Vinçard, had been invited thirty years earlier to this sort of reconsideration. Through others, Enfantin had approached him in 1832 on behalf of his companion in prison, the painter Bouzelin, who had been condemned to death for the Saint-Merri insurrection. Vinçard was asked to help get his sentence commuted by providing him with testimonials of good citizenship. And indeed, when Bouzelin was not drinking, beating his wife, or quarreling with his neighbors, he was distinguished by his zeal in fighting fires and pursuing robbers. So Vinçard will provide testimonials for this "naughty rogue . . . drunkard, debauchee, duelist, brawler,"[47] but all the more grudgingly because the last "robber" stopped and sabered

46. Pauline Roland, "Un mot sur Byron," ibid., pp. 73–74.
47. Pierre Vinçard, *Mémoires épisodiques d'un vieux chansonnier saint-simonien*, Paris, 1879, p. 143.

by the heroic Bouzelin was merely a lover fleeing the noisy wrath of his mistress. Bouzelin does get his sentence commuted, and soon the good luck of a fire in the prison permits him to show off his prowess and win his liberty. But the freed Bouzelin will not escape the fate of those whose rages exceed the social norm. Getting into an argument with his wife, who is reproaching him for his ingratitude toward a benefactor, in a paroxysm of rage Bouzelin will grab a knife and plunge it into his own body: the savage end of a strong nature in the image of a working-class generation that is still poorly civilized.

In the next generation, the alliance of militant devotion and crime will take up more refined figures. The most singular will be Emmanuel Barthélemy, the young mechanic condemned to hard labor for the murder of a policeman: black-gloved commandant of the formidable barricade of Faubourg du Temple during the June days of revolt, escaped prisoner and then exile in London, cultivated member of Louis Blanc's London salon, a man with seductively good manners. He will drop his reserve to kill one of his June comrades in arms in a duel before committing another murder—crime of passion or political provocation?—and ending up on the London scaffold.[48]

For the moment, however, the strong natures are still of a cruder stuff, and recognition of this enigma leads Vinçard to a fairly clear conclusion:

> After the incidents I have just related, I had to fight with all my strength against my habitual tendency to reject everything that seemed to me to deviate from the norm of strict obligations laid down by society. . . .
>
> These facts relating to the unfortunate Bouzelin, whose life was compounded of so many vices and acts of generous dedication, forced me to reflect deeply on the readiness with which we anathematize these exceptional natures, sometimes the most interesting ones from a general point of view.[49]

Adhering to sound Saint-Simonian orthodoxy, Vinçard suggests that the solution is a matter of opening careers to these "energetic and passionate" human beings whose sentimental disposition triggers great dedication and great crimes.

On this subject, too, his friend and junior Gauny cannot hold to the

48. Malwida von Meysenbug, *Mémoires d'une idéaliste*, Paris, 1900, II, 20–21, 50–64.

49. Vinçard, *Mémoires épisodiques*, pp. 148–49.

single principle of optimizing energies. He may share the common ideal of reeducation—involving the passions if need be—for a convict who is more ill than culpable, but the look he gives "the Attilas of private property" cannot be satisfied with anticipating outlets for people with overflowing energies. The convict is not simply a savage rebelling against the norms of the honest artisan; he also represents the perversion of rebel energy that could destroy the proprietary order. The convict belongs to the family of the rebel, and the latter admits to having in him "the irons of an assassin." But the assassin belongs to the rebel's family as his negative image: a recovery of the rebel impulse, the devastations of which do not stir up the flames of revolt but rather represent a relapse into the fever of consumption through which Capital keeps its victims in chains and prevents them from intensifying their powers of independence, which would spell its ruin if they were to develop. The banalized vandalism of these Attilas, then, is caught in the trap that offers the shadow of the prey in place of the prey of the shadow. By contrast, the Tantalus/Spartacus of rebellion withdraws the infiniteness of his desire from the normal mechanisms of need and gratification. With his power of refusal, he uses sublimation to intensify his radical nonadaptation to the existing economic order: the lure of rebel virtue that liberates surplus energy from the vices consistent with the lure of mercantile attraction:

> Before he has the capital that is to pay for his gratification, he contemplates the object of his legitimate covetousness, sniffs it as his prey, admires it with shivers of desire, carries away its shadow. . . . This Tantalus becomes virtuous in his austerity, ingenious in his cleverness. His spirit entertains new studies, extraordinary emotions, and passions that enliven him a hundred times. If he has had only four hundred francs a year of income or salary, he prolongs the service of his footwear by mortifying himself a little, or, rather, by familiarizing himself with the rigidity of the ground. He does the same with other needs and manages to overcome the thing desired by having emancipated his reason and his independence.[50]

The moral lesson given to the hoarder points to a different economy in which it is no longer a matter simply of transferring energies and goods but of changing their nature. The thief remains this side of it, a would-be

50. Gauny, "Économie cénobitique," Fonds Gauny, Ms. 151.

rebel who failed, a hostage of the old world. So there is nothing shocking in the fact that he is caught in the shabbiness of his desire. But the new torture of the cellular prison changes the very import of his punishment, transforming the degenerate accomplice of proprietary passion into the exemplary victim of despotism. For it is only liberty that it represses in his case. So one is not absolving the thief or the criminal when one sees in the cellular prison the absolute crime, the crime with one sole aim: that of killing liberty. And below these criminals who have gotten lost in the realms of liberty one must place those who renounced beforehand any and all exploration outside the pathways marked out by the ruse of wages: the beast-men, machine-men, who build cellular prisons.

> In their dazed and liberty-killing stupidity, these subordinate members lend themselves to the shameful cruelties of the inventors, following their plan and all its horrors line by line. These human machines are neither for nor against what they are building. They work like beasts to earn their measure of pay without critically examining their task: ready to demolish what they have so solidly built; ready to forge iron collars for all at the risk of injuring themselves; and amenable to any odious work that ensures them a wage. They pile stone on stone, pump air into the lungs of the prisoners, repudiate justice by perfecting the impossibilities of escape, cut off outside space from view, and complicate the inquisition that comes to life in the stone, the iron, and the wood that conceal and watch over the torments of the prisoners. They complete this prison and its blind cavities of a burning court without singeing their souls in this work of the damned.[51]

The fact is that it is not customary for a mason to wonder about what he is building, a locksmith to wonder about what he is forging, or a joiner to wonder about what he is assembling. At the height of anarcho-syndicalism, a meeting of the Building Trade Federation will reject the question by turning it around: in capitalist society, what building is not conceived by the enemies of the workers and used in the service of the ruling class?

Perhaps, to take the question seriously, one must start with the hierarchy of the forms of existence rather than with class divisions. The cellu-

51. Gauny, "Aux ouvriers constructeurs de prisons cellulaires," in Rancière (ed.), *Le philosophe plébéien*, pp. 69–70.

lar prison lays hold of the normal order of wage work at the point where
its hirelings are constructing the last circle of hell for their brothers. But
it is at this point, nevertheless, that they could best register their power to
say no. If an inspiring orator could persuade them to stop their work, you
would see this curious spectacle: the architects and all the organizers of
the cell system trying by themselves to put their hellish dream on its feet.
The important thing is not so much that they would be clumsy at it. It
is, rather, that the fantastic forms born of their awkward blunders would
reveal, in all their purity, the delirious schemes of tyranny that the perfection of working-class labor conceals in the finish of the final product. In
other words, it is the worker's work that, in the twofold morality of work
well done and work for a living, banalizes the insanity of the despotic
authority. This accounts for the exemplary value that the "work" would
have taken on if it had been left to the care of the conceivers and planners
of the cell system:

> Wanting to erect their project high in the air, they would have
> shaped the most incredible Babel in the world. A misshapen ruin
> pierced with a crushing amalgam of torture crypts. A rough outline
> in iron and stone of an abominable idea, in which the frenzy and
> rage of the prisoners would have been guessed ahead of time. A
> slaughterhouse constructed with so little balance that the people,
> gazing at this new Moloch, would have feared being buried under
> its fall; and its hideous and revolting appearance would have
> forcibly informed them of the strength of their peaceable resistance
> while handing over the authors of this murderous extravagance to
> scathing denunciations.[52]

In a single glance, perhaps the first and certainly the most powerful of
the images that will make up the myth of the general strike—certainly
not the poor and boastful imagery that pictures the rich as incapable of
providing for their needs on their own. Gauny and his brothers are paid
to know that one has no need of a special vocation where necessity is in
command. The idea of the indispensable proletarian here takes on a completely different luster. In a contradictory image we are presented with the
strength of the two parties and a denunciation of their alliance: Moloch–
Babel, the monstrous and tottering edifice of a power compelled to carry

52. Ibid., pp. 70–71.

out the details of its designs by itself because of the desertion of the slaves of Babylon.

An impossible dream, discouraged by the unconsciousness of these workers who know nothing about any work except the abstraction of the wage it promises? But isn't unconsciousness a simple negation? Wouldn't it suffice if once someone were to make clear the sufferings of the immured prisoners to these builders who always withdraw from a place before it is inhabited? "If the workers were to form a council before accepting a work of repression, the remark of a single one of them about its detestable side would suffice for it to be condemned by all. Logic is a light that rises high as it illuminates multitudes."[53] A spark is all that is needed. Where might it come from to propagate the light of awareness and the fire of revolt? "Perhaps a famous orator, addressing these assistant jailers without feelings, would have been able to touch their hearts."[54]

Our floor-layer, unfortunately, is not an orator. How could he be, when the solitude where he nurtures his rebellion simultaneously deprives him of all conversation that would exercise his eloquence? "The more he exercises his reflection inside himself to seek out the joint of our sorrows, the more his desire imagines common domains for future populations, the less his spoken word feels capable of expressing his utopias."[55] But, as a matter of fact, it isn't necessary for him to go and speak to the crowds. It is enough that he traverses the city at his usual pace, talking to himself, only a little louder than usual. For he knows very well the flaw that is dreaded by the masters: the Paris worker is a gawking boob. Making a spectacle of oneself is setting the trap in which to catch his good conscience as a worker: "The democrat traverses the city, talking to himself. The sentences of his monologue capture the curiosity of passers-by. Each one grasps some truth in it. Without stopping, he touches the wound of their existence that impoverishes the master's interest. . . . at these remarks tossed into the air, the crowd surrounds the revolutionary, who, without addressing himself to anyone, seems to be haranguing a multitude."[56] The wind blows where it wills, and surely some building-trade workers will be found who will hear and understand the description of the cellular hell. There is little chance of success with the masons, of course; they do not

---

53. Ibid., p. 85.
54. Ibid., p. 70.
55. Gauny, "Le travail à la tâche," ibid., p. 46.
56. Gauny, "Les manufactures," Fonds Gauny, Ms. 130.

permit themselves to be distracted from their work, and they often return home to their lodgings in gangs. But a joiner, a locksmith, perhaps, and the flame will be lit.

The workshops are going to close, the yards are going to come to a standstill. The cenobite begins his evening walk. He now calls himself by a different name: the Philadelphian.

CHAPTER 5

The Morning Star

"WHEN WE CONSIDER the depravities of the world, a misanthropy often takes hold of our hearts, a need for solitude makes us long for desert places; but there is no one to save in the deserts."[1] Let us leave it to the platitude of the time to ask why one must save others and to suspect that the will to power lies concealed behind this self-sacrificing devotion. After all, the same air had already reached the ears of the ill-fated Boyer: "People treated him as a fool, as an ambitious man who wanted to become famous and popular by upsetting society because he yearned for domination."[2] The conjecture is frivolous, first of all, quite aside from being spiteful and, in Boyer's case, lethal. One who has gone into the desert enters a relationship with salvation and the law—old or new—in which the caprice of his desires plays little part. One who has had the revelation of another world finds himself in a strange relationship of obligation vis-à-vis his brothers—a persecuted people but also a rabble that worships the golden calf and the fatted ox. To grasp it, we do better to give up the old evident certainties that contrast the condescension of the philanthropist or the intellectual toward ills they themselves do not suffer with the militant worker's realization of the need to transform a situation whose daily suffering he shares with his comrades. Classic images confront solidarities from below with calculated liberalities from above, the scales of justice with the arbitrariness of charity, the gains of combat with the small profits of petition. But perhaps the passwords of the battle have blurred the visage and motives of the combatants. Before judges on the lookout for the beast lusting to seize and possess the enjoyments of the rich, to our eyes seeking the tangled network of solidarity in all its forms, the

1. Louis Gabriel Gauny, "Opinions," *La Ruche populaire*, April 1841.
2. *La Ruche populaire*, Oct. 1841.

egalitarian militant presents himself instead in the classic posture of the person who does right by others: he opens his purse to the needy and dedicates his waking hours to trying to alleviate the physical and moral miseries of the people. So appeared the jeweler Page, one of the founders of *L'Humanitaire,* when he came before the magistrates entrusted with the task of condemning the most scandalous of the communist journals: "He often took into his place workers who were completely destitute. Although he earned his money from the sweat of his brow, he never hesitated to offer them advances and even gave them clothes. And although he had often been badly recompensed, that did not stop him from doing it all over again."[3]

What makes the dedication of the communist apostle singular is not his preferring the clenched fists and locked arms of combat to the open hand of charity. It is a peculiar course, a certain detour winding between the offerings of individual generosity and the rules of social justice, and readily passing through the pathways of metaphysics. "I always found him very curious to learn about the points of transcendental philosophy," notes the same witness cited above, a doctor engaged by the patient's peculiar questions for the man of science. "He often asked me about social questions, but only from the scientific standpoint. For example, one day he asked me if social equality could be established as an absolute proposition. I told him that, scientifically, social inequality necessarily followed from the inequality of our organs."[4] A disappointing response. But precisely these disappointments are the lot of the egalitarian militant, ever shuttling him from the ingratitude of dedication to the lost illusions of science. If the philosophy of *Community* has the role of a compensation, it is not one in the trivial sense of cupidity, of greed for the wealth of the well-to-do. Nor is it meant to serve as an illusion that goes beyond the quickly reached limits of proletarian philanthropy or makes up for the neglected weapons of worker organization and combat.

What first sets a limit to the proletarian apostolate is not so much the feebleness of its resources as the ingratitude with which it is paid. But that very thing gives it a new impetus: "Although he had often been badly recompensed, that did not stop him from doing it all over again." Although . . . Because? The egalitarian apostolate is different from philanthropic offerings in this respect above all: it all goes on as if it were precisely the ingratitude that gave it its motion. Undoubtedly philanthropic practice

3. Trial of *L'Humanitaire*, court session of Nov. 11, 1841, *Gazette des tribunaux.*
4. Ibid.

itself often shows a deficit on the books of accountants, who would like to see a return in added or surplus values of morality for the advances in provisions, wood, and clothing given to the poor. In any case, it is rare that their debtors do not pay the philanthropists with thanks, which has the threefold advantage of costing the giver nothing, giving pleasure to the receiver no matter what, and already indicating some progress in popular morality. Moreover, how could these respectable people blame the parsimony organizing these semblances when they themselves want to teach the poor precisely the virtues of saving and properly understood individual interest? Where the narrow circle of philanthropic exchange closes somehow or other, the lack of gratitude sweeps the charitable pro-letarian into the endless spiral of the egalitarian militant's disappointments and hopes. Before excluding the charitable exchange of favors and their payment in gratitude and moralization, he himself is excluded: deprived of return like Page, having his fraternal zeal viewed with suspicion like Boyer, or, like Gilland, prevented from meeting men who would set in motion the association for which he dreams and sacrifices his own possible well-being.

Shouldn't these disillusionments bring these concocters of social recipes back to the reality of the struggle and the patience of organization where the solid bonds of worker fraternity are woven? But what if things usually went just the opposite? Let us listen to the story of hosiery worker Zacharie Seigneurgens, who was brought up for trial shortly before the founders of *L'Humanitaire*, in that same October of 1841 when Adolphe Boyer put an end to his life. Like many others, this story begins with the July barricades and the disappointment that, in mid-August 1830, took hold of the working-class combatants as they became quickly aware of the ingratitude of their rich allies of three days.

When his fellow hosiery workers were about to follow the example of the farriers, the locksmiths, and the spinners in expressing their disillu-sionment and mustering their claims by means of "coalition," Seigneur-gens wanted them to avoid the risks of a fight out in the open and without unity. To harmonize individual wills and provide them with "some de-gree of effectiveness," he organized an "operations center to maintain and direct this harmony": the Society of Paris Hosiery Workers. Unfortu-nately, he needed only a little time to discern, in the society born of his solicitude, the same vice underlying bourgeois ingratitude: *egotism*. And it was perhaps all the more formidable in this case, since it could take refuge behind the organizational rules that set forth the common interests of worker solidarity:

Around last February, I proposed to them that we provide some help, from the funds of the society, for a widow with children whose husband had contributed twenty to twenty-five francs to our treasury. The deceased had found himself taken off the membership roll of the association for default of payment; for, due to the poor state of his health, he could barely earn enough to provide bread for his table. These men rejected my proposal. They alleged that the original purpose and destination of the funds could not be changed—the society had been founded in the interests of hosiery workers in general, and so they could not go along with giving help to individuals.

I did not insist; they were within the bounds of legality stipulated by the rules.[5]

More ideologically advanced than their founder, these members already knew how to give preference to the principles of their organization over help in the form of charity to individuals. But why was it enough for Seigneurgens, compromised by the imprudent actions of the leaders of the Society of the Rights of Man, to find himself in prison, for these same men, who were so haughty and picky about the rules of their association, to send the one packing with the other? "They were within the bounds of legality stipulated by the rules." But why did they abolish Article 63 of the same rules? It said: "The dissolution of the society cannot be brought under deliberation. A single member alone has the right to oppose it. A person who would make that proposal would immediately be taken off the rolls of the society, and his exclusion would be pronounced by the assembly." To give the appearance of killing the society legally, they would certainly have begun by annulling this article. What a bitter mockery! The majority reached a decision; the money was taken out; there is nothing more to be said.[6]

At the end of the affair, the accounts made out by the militant republican compel him to again call into question the arithmetic of democracy. Henceforth the realization of worker community will go by way of a privileged relationship: not that of the majority to the rules, but that of principle to the individual who is the exception: the widow he should have helped in spite of the rules, the single individual whose veto is enough

5. Zéphir-Zacharie Seigneurgens, *Lettre sur la formation de la Société des ouvriers bonnetiers de Paris, dite Bourse auxiliaire, adressée à tous ses confrères à l'occasion de sa dissolution*, Paris, n.d., pp. 2–3.

6. Ibid., p. 3.

to prevent the destruction of the law of the association. He has perceived a link between the principle of egotism and the government of majorities, and so this working-class militant and republican will henceforth be a *communist* propagandist: a militant on behalf of a principle, no longer a militant on behalf of a class or a form of government. For "some principle of some sort must be acknowledged *a priori,* and it should be the principle of inequality or that of equality." But it could not possibly be that of the majority. "For we said that the law of majorities was not a principle, because a principle is immutable and the will of majorities could change."[7]

The conclusion of a twofold revolt brought to communism a certain number of the working-class leaders issuing from the Society of the Rights of Man. On the one hand, they had pondered in prison the thoughtlessness of the chiefs—intellectuals and bourgeois politicians—whose carefully kept registers had betrayed them to repression. They had waxed indignant at the privileges granted in detention in accordance with the social status of the revolutionaries, as well as at the lotteries and balls of republican high society, held supposedly for the benefit of poor prisoners. This experience prompted them to set the solidarities of class over against the inequality of political societies. On the other hand, they had also seen their brothers forget this solidarity with regard to them and even take advantage of their absence to let the project they had initiated go to ruin. So it is a different division into "classes" that will ground their egalitarian apostolate, a perception of an exploitation that is displaced by comparison with that which defines the economic power of the master over the worker. Drawing up the final balance sheet on the liquidation of their society, Seigneurgens has the hosiery workers hear the discourse of cabinetmaker Olivier to his colleagues when they met to found their society:

> By comparison, let us separate society into two classes of human beings and say to them: those who live only for themselves are egotists, since they live only to drink, eat, and sleep like brute animals; those who sacrifice their personal interest to that of society are social human beings. And let us say to them: To which of these two classes of human beings do you belong? And so, those who tell us they belong to the latter class, they are the ones we will accept into our ranks. . . . With such elements we will be sure to arrive at our goal. The first Christians who left the heart of Judea

7. *Cour d'assises de la Seine: Audience du 30 oct. 1841—Affaire du Moniteur républicain,* published by Zéphir-Zacharie Seigneurgens, Paris, 1842, pp. 11 and 13.

to preach their doctrine all over the earth were as poor as we are, but they were rich in dedication, animated by a firm and resolute conviction, and guided by an ardent faith. They endured all the torments and tortures imaginable with the greatest resignation. And they managed to change the face of human society at large.[8]

The best is certain, but it comes by way of the worst. The sufferings of the apostle are not a metaphor here for the hazards of the struggle, or an alibi for the power of the chief. Those who belong to the summoned class have much more to lose than their chains: a business, a workshop, a house, a family. Anxious to evoke shame as well as to prove his point, Seigneurgens chooses a witness to impress those who believe only in martyrs:

> Olivier was a cabinetmaker employing three or four workers. . . . Arrested in the demonstration against the planned outposts, he was a defendant in what was known as the "Trial of the Twenty-seven." He was acquitted by the Seine Court of Assize. Arrested again for the affairs of April, he spent several months in the dungeons of la Force. He did not come out again until the month of July, but very sick. During his detention, his children had died of want; his wife had gone mad. Returning home, he found neither benches nor tools, neither his bed nor his other belongings. Debilitated by weakness and illness, he committed himself to the Saint-Antoine Home. After prolonged sufferings, he died around the month of October 1834.[9]

The natural death of the cabinetmaker presents the same symptoms as the "malady of our century" that overcame Boyer. These two victims of "exhaustion" experienced the fulfillment of the same necessity that finds expression in Adolphe Boyer's testament:

> If you want to know why I give myself death, here is the reason. As regards the worker, in the present condition of society, the more egoistic and selfish he is, the happier he is. If he loves his family and seeks its welfare, he endures countless sufferings. But if he

8. Seigneurgens, *Lettre sur la formation de la Société des ouvriers bonnetiers*, p. 14.
9. Ibid., p. 9.

sincerely loves society and his fellow creatures, he must end like
me.[10]

Sincere love, death impulse? In that case, would what separates the
self-sacrificing dedication of the militant from the beneficence of the philanthropist be the profound misanthropy on which it is based and to which
that sincere love unceasingly returns until it dies of it? It is not simply
human ingratitude that is involved here but also and above all a disappointed promise, the difference between the great days of popular generosity and the daily round of competition that bolsters the egotisms that are
fatal to the pioneers of regeneration. The bitter grief at seeing the people
satisfied with their humiliation and indifferent to those who want to draw
them out of it is sustained even by the communion and enthusiasm of the
days when the people are king. This is the twofold sentiment expressed
in the letters of dressmaker Désirée Véret to Father Enfantin. Explaining
the state that she was brought out of by the revelation of the doctrine, she
writes: "I was highly contemptuous of the human species . . . tranquil in
my indifference and self-sufficient. I was not linked to individuals at all
but . . . to the infinite."[11] But when Enfantin was acquitted of the charge
of fraud and applauded by the crowd, the complicity of one day revived
the feeling of a more fundamental communion with the people of July:

> I was happy to see those noble workers crowd around you. . . . I
> am truly of the people because I always commune with them when
> I see them gathered together in the public square, whether they
> have come there sullen and fierce to energetically demand freedom
> and bread or have come to see up close the man that I love among
> all men. My love for them always rises to the point of rapture. My
> tear-filled eyes rest on those masses. . . . They are truly the heart
> of God. Happy the man, happy the woman, who will know how to
> make themselves loved by them.[12]

It is this vision divided in two that grounds the dream of *Association,* a
word that always exceeds the modest appearances under which the ini-

10. *La Ruche populaire,* Oct. 1841.
11. Désirée Véret to Enfantin, Aug. 31, 1832, Fonds Enfantin, Bibliothèque de
l'Arsenal, Ms. 7608.
12. Désirée Véret to Enfantin, Oct. 20, 1832, ibid.

tiators present it to their colleagues: let us unite to stop the depreciation of our wages, to offer ourselves mutual aid, to take care of our sick and aged; better yet, let us pool our savings, our arms, and our tools so that we ourselves can exploit our industry. Even this "better" is ridiculous in comparison with the dream of a different humanity that it mints: little republics of chair-turners, box-makers and packers, file-makers, jewelry-gilders. The apostles soon noticed what was lacking in these soberly ruled meetings based on self-interest: "There is no quarreling. The proceedings are orderly and serious. But it is a communion of interests only, not of sympathy. For the most part, the members are strangers to each other; their action does not extend beyond the outskirts; their association is not long-lasting. In a word, there is no love there."[13]

Association is what is missing in the associations, the thing that would make them the realization of a principle rather than a combination of interests, even of collectivized interests. The communists who criticize the associations and the other schools that promote their realization agree on the distinction as a principle. Some simply regard the paradox as insoluble, whereas others accept the challenge to promote the *sympathetic* association of human beings who have been regenerated by the *egotistical* association of needs and interests: "I have always thought that association would emancipate the workers, and that it alone should be upheld and extolled. I made great sacrifices for it, engaging in concrete experimentation after preaching about it. I lost a great deal with no results, but I persist nonetheless in dreaming of association and calling for it."[14] It is not only the outrages endured by the apostle that confirm the necessity of the regenerative apostolate. In addition, his obstinacy in pursuing a project that always ends up in disappointment is the best proof he can offer of the efficacy of self-sacrificing dedication, the very dedication that association is to put in place of the power of egotism.

This demonstration, in any case, is not a matter of choice. In vain does he try to make his comrades believe that his effort simply actualizes a duty whose necessity any worker can verify in the reality around him and whose common force he can find in the simplicity of his soul. "In this, as in many other things, good will accomplishes all." So speaks the apostle André, in a story by Gilland, to his fellow worker Joseph, who is alert but a bit skeptical. "I doubt it," replies Joseph. "Besides, some well-informed comrades told me that you had some sort of revelation in your

13. "Aux ouvriers par un ouvrier," *Le Globe*, June 4, 1832.
14. J.-P. Gilland, *Les conteurs ouvriers*, Paris, 1849, pp. xix–xx.

childhood."[15] Such things are known in the workshops; the initiates cannot hide the marks of their election. And so it will not take much to get
André to recount the vision of a boy, brother of little William and little
Gilland, who went out to glean for his father and was drawn away from
the perception of real things by the celestial music of nature:

> It is impossible to paint what I saw and felt then. There are no
> words for it. It was a wholly mysterious world full of visions, splen-
> dors, and harmonies; and my spirit towered over the magnificences
> of this sublime creation as the dazzling glories of heaven over the
> primitive, virgin beauties of the unknown world. . . . From that day
> on, I believed I had been initiated into a new life and I no longer
> wanted to live as I had lived before that. . . . From that point on, it
> seemed to me that I was a chosen one of God, and that the vision
> presaged a great destiny for me. I had already read the Bible, and I
> said to myself: David was a shepherd like me, and David killed the
> giant. He was a great king, a great poet, and his glory was equal
> to his omnipotence. Mine is the celestial harp, mine a dazzling and
> radiant future![16]

The dream is shattered, obviously, when the child finds himself again
in the workshop of one of those manufacturers who are not satisfied with
exploiting the feeble powers of children, who also make a point of killing
in them any feeling for another world—anything and everything delicate,
sensitive, poetic, and superior that heaven has put in them:

> I was a fallen angel! I felt it, and the humiliation horrified me. I
> yearned to shake off the muck with which misfortune had covered
> me. . . . And during the night, when excessive fatigue kept me from
> sleeping, I wept for my vanished illusions as the exile weeps for the
> sun of his native land. . . . It is at that time that my life was marked
> by the reserve, coldness, and disdain for my fellows that I made a
> matter of pride and that made me ridiculous in their eyes. . . . The
> chaffing of my comrades brought me back to reason.[17]

Is it the weariness brought on by a long Sunday walk or, more likely,
his own complicity with the "reason" in question that prevents the hon-

15. J.-P. Gilland, "L'incompris," ibid., pp. 73–74.
16. Ibid., pp. 83–84.
17. Ibid., p. 84.

est Joseph from being astonished by such an unlikely conclusion? How can one take seriously this return to reason that is so quick to shift from the suffering of jeers to the good sense of the jeerers and to charitable thoughts for one's persecutors?

> The chaffing of my comrades brought me back to reason. I made up my mind to live in this world where I had thought myself seriously out of place; and instead of turning away in horror from what I called the crimes and unkindnesses of human beings, I now saw around me nothing but unfortunate beings, replete with weaknesses, infirmities, miseries, and mistakes, whom charity enjoined me to aid, feel sorry for, love, encourage, and console.[18]

The opposition between a world of illusions and a world of sane and suffering reality certainly leads to a strange reduction here, so that our Christian worker tends to turn the son of God and descendant of David into the president of a philanthropic society of carpenters. Better to follow the more roundabout course that Gilland retraces for us in a less simplistic autobiography. If the young locksmith changed his relationship to others, it was not so much because of the lesson taught by their chaffing; rather, it was the rebound effect of the awkward generosity of those well-intentioned colleagues who took him off to drown his sorrows in cabaret wine. He did not find intoxication or the assuagement of his miseries there, but a kind of attention different from that of others and thereby perhaps the means to reconcile the destiny of the chosen with that of the pariah:

> I observed and penetrated there the human nature that I would have been inclined to slight or perhaps even despise if I had seen only its coarse surface. More curious about the truth or more attentive than most of my companions, I chose the right moment to get them to open their hearts, to make their confession to me, to show themselves to me as they were and as God sees us all. My experiments proved this to me: that all human beings were unhappy; that, for one reason or another, they all harbored a great sadness inside themselves; that this ill can be discovered even in those who deny it with the utmost obstinacy and feigned indifference; that their moral misery far surpasses their material misery, however great it may be.[19]

18. Ibid.
19. J.-P. Gilland, "Préface," in *Les conteurs ouvriers*, pp. xvii–xviii.

From fallen angel to militant worker the road no longer goes by way of the good sense of laughers but by way of the curiosity of the connoisseur of souls, who finds the same melancholy of the infinite buried in the decadence of cabaret pleasure-seekers. This identification with the divine gaze opens the way for an apostolate that renews ties with the dreams of childhood: "In the Middle Ages, after my first disappointments, I would undoubtedly have become a religious. I would have thrown myself entirely into the ascetic life. In these times of ours, I aimed, if not higher, at least more correctly."[20] But it is not simply a matter of adapting one's dream: the religion of the infinite in which one tries to forget the sorrows of a disappointing humanity can no longer be separated from the new religion that puts the fraternity of human beings at its heart. For anyone who has fallen into the servitude of proletarian existence, the return to the paradise partially opened by the solitary revelation of the boy Gilland or the books of little Jeanne Deroin goes by way of the infinite detour of others. We find that expressed in the itinerary of the young lingerie-maker, who would have liked to limit the detour to its simplest expression: that is, a contract between two parties wherein she would exchange the gifts of her love for those of knowledge:

> The necessity of working made me realize that I, deprived of wealth, had to renounce knowledge, happiness—I resigned myself. A secret hope still delighted me. I said to myself: I will meet a philosopher as poor as I myself in worldly goods but rich in knowledge, ugly as Aesop but loving and virtuous. He will share with me the gifts of knowledge, I will repay him with love and gratitude. Linked by a holy bond, we will console each other for the sorrows of life.[21]

Unfortunately, the holy bonds of matrimony recognize no exchange of obligations between the man, however much of a philosopher he may be, and the most loving woman except the unequal bargain in which one has only the right to obey and the other only the duty to protect, which is to say, command. "One day I opened the law book and I read these words: the husband owes protection to his wife, the wife owes obedience to her husband. I felt vivid indignation. Never, I said to myself, will I purchase happiness at the price of enslavement. I choose to live and suffer alone,

20. Ibid., p. xviii.
21. Jeanne Deroin, Profession of faith, Fonds Enfantin, Ms. 7608.

ignorant, useless, forgotten, but free." No contract of the kind offered by ancient religions or new books of legislation can satisfy the desire for the infinite awakened by the first books of knowledge. For both religion and legislation are there solely to maintain the barriers that keep the proletariat from pursuing their dreams. That, at least, is the conclusion to which our solitary woman is led as she devotes herself to examining the world around her: "The result of my meditations was that all religions were a tissue of absurdities invented to enslave the human race, that laws were a weapon in the hands of the powerful on earth to oppress the weak, and that they served only to legitimize the injustices of the great."[22]

But alongside the enslaving chains forged by the books of civil and religious law there are other ties woven by other books: chronicles of heroic actions, collections of poignant sorrows, albums of delightful emotions. If the bruised soul cannot remain in the solitude of the deserts where it has taken refuge, the reason is not primarily that its ambition lacks souls to save; the reason is that the desert, since the time the footprints of a few solitary walkers left their mark there, is populated with the echo of great civic actions and nostalgia for friendships:

> I felt the need to isolate myself, to breathe a purer air. The most lowly shanty, the hollow of a tree or rock, would have fulfilled all my desires.
>
> But I tried in vain to break the ties that bound me to the world. I always felt the most lively enthusiasm at the recital of a noble action. I felt tender compassion at the sight of the sufferings of my fellow creatures. My heart was broken with regret at not being able to assuage them, and the interest I took in political events showed me that love of country was still all-powerful over my soul.
>
> So I was not at one with myself, and I suffered from this painful situation. I lacked a belief, a goal, an active life. I resolved to review the judgments I had entertained and to seek the truth with ardent zeal.[23]

A new search for truth by a self-examination that wipes out all the opinions accepted up to then. Like her proletarian brothers who are learning the secrets of versification in Racine's *Athalie*, this dreamy woman with a practical spirit has managed to find in the national classics a method that

22. Ibid.
23. Ibid.

will permit her to do without the excessively high price of philosophy professors. But it is also natural that proximity of circumstance should lead her to proceed in the manner of the autodidact apprentice of Geneva rather than that of the student of La Flèche. She will proceed more like Rousseau than Descartes, for she, too, seeks less a body of knowledge than a belief, less the foundations of a new science of the world or society than the first link of a new chain of relations between beings. And so she takes a shortcut between the hypothesis of the malicious genius and the proof from effects, in line with a quest that is more concerned with the origin of good and evil than with the foundations of truth and error. Once assured that there is no effect without a cause, that therefore there is a first cause of the universe, and that this just and intelligent God made the earth "rich in what can make man happy," she concluded: "Evil came from the fact that a certain number had arrogated to themselves exclusively what belongs to all. But I realized that these egotistical people had misconstrued their true interests, for they do not possess happiness, which really consists more in moral perfection, in interior joys and possessions, than in the possession of earthly goods."[24] An intelligent God who assures the universe its rationality; a purely human origin of evil, which is at bottom a misjudgment rather than ill will; a conscience, "the voice of God himself," which grounds the obligation to do good and promises in its own satisfaction the only reward worthy of the effort: these are the necessary and sufficient principles of a militant action that is perhaps less mindful of its effects on the future government of human beings and affairs than of the indefinitely renewed links between the progress of self and the transformation of others.

This shift from the representation of the goal toward the infinity of the course is here expressed in terms of virtue that is prepared for sacrifice: "The active human being, the virtuous human being, is supposed to carry out a sublime mission. His whole life should be a continual battle against the errors and prejudices of his age."[25] But the representation of sacrifice still speaks the language of the old world, reckoning profits and losses according to the logic of contracts that tie the worker to the master or the wife to the husband. In this reckoning, self-satisfaction as recompense for the pains of the apostle is a mere trifle. But what satisfaction, except that of her masters, can serve as recompense for the surplus labor of the lingerie-maker and the wife? And, again, to be understood by a few people means

24. Ibid.
25. Ibid.

a great deal to these overly informed dressmakers who have been reduced to the pleasures of solitude by the egotism of the world: "I had always been envious of the happiness of devotees. At least, I said to myself, they are understood by a few people and are not, like me, thrown into a chaos of contrary opinions akin to that of the Tower of Babel, where each individual seems to have forgotten his natural language in order to speak a private dialect."[26] To speak one's natural language, the language of tomorrow, the language of all: this gift outweighs the pleasures of solitude. The happiness of devotees is not contemplation but conversion. Solitude may well bring with it the desires for the infinite that jostle each other at all the barriers of the physical and moral misery of the workers. But the infinite is no longer something given in the course of contemplation. It must be realized in a certain grouping of sensitive beings. No matter how grievous the vicissitudes of propagation may be, no matter how restricted the circle of the initiates, their realized anticipation of future humanity is henceforth their sole enjoyment, and it makes all others insipid.

This is also the lesson that Pierre Vinçard means to get across when he publishes new "fragments of a private correspondence" in *La Fraternité de 1845*. Once again we meet Urbain the initiator and Georges the unfortunate initiate. This time it is not the workshop that Georges wants to abandon but the struggle and perhaps life: "I am carried away with anger and indignation at my brothers. I accuse them of indifference to everything that should touch them most, and I am beginning to think that their apathy is the sole cause of their poignant miseries. . . . Only a very small number of us want what is good, and the whole of society is in league against us."[27] The persuasive force of Urbain's reply will lie less in his appeal for patience than in his proof that it is impossible to turn back: "What! I took away the veil of ignorance from your mind, initiated you into all our theories of association, and gave you this vitality of heart and spirit without which one would not know how to live, and you would reserve your powers and your activity only for yourself, for yourself alone." This turning away is not just wicked; it is impossible. Georges misses the animal existence he led before the revelation and complains that the light burns as it illuminates. Urbain gives two replies that come down to one: a person who has come to know this light can no longer find any joy outside

26. Désirée Véret to Enfantin, Sept. 11, 1831, Fonds Enfantin, Ms. 7608.

27. Pierre Vinçard, "Fragments d'une correspondance intime," *La Fraternité de 1845*, May 1846, pp. 147–48.

its burn, and he cannot experience it without simultaneously illuminating others:

> And do you expect to find in isolation the tranquility, the peace, for which you are yearning? Don't you know that certain torments are like the skin of Nessus, and that the same goes for our ideas, from which one cannot disengage oneself once one has understood them? . . . Above all, you must realize that our society is so corroded and withered by the evils it conceals in its bosom that it is very difficult to find, outside of our dreams of the future, the ideal happiness that is the illusion of every imagination like yours.[28]

The crooked line of illusion and the imaginary is not allowed to be put in opposition to the straight line of knowledge and action; neither is the duty of the militant allowed to be in opposition to the pleasure of the initiate. The sorrow of exploitation and the pleasure of belonging to the sect of those who are aware of it, the dreams of a happy future and the disappointment of seeing its potential beneficiaries turn away from it, discouragements that make fidelity to the radiant image more necessary, nonsatisfaction that never ceases to beget the same image—it is not without reason that this imaginary correspondence is put under the patronage of those heroes who thought they were expressing only their own sufferings but thereby became the interpreter of the miseries experienced by all: René, Werther, Obermann. Where better than in their "egotistical" accounts can one find in pure form the balancing of exquisite sorrows and mortal joys that serves as the pulse-beat of apostolic activity, of the propaganda for another life that already is the reality of that other life in exact proportion to the disappointment? The austerity of duty, expressed in terms as close as possible to those of the gospel parables (the salt of the earth, the lamp under a bushel), is modulated in accordance with the new joys of imagination, sympathies, and humanitarian passions. "A belief, a goal"—not a theory designed to organize armies of combatants; the principle of a new sociability, a new religion whose content ("faith") and very form of propagation are identical—sympathetic union in the ascending movement of beings.

It is not a matter of self-sacrifice, of curtailing one's pleasures for the good of the cause. The solitaries have already renounced the mixed plea-

28. Ibid.

sures of servitude that are attached to the works and loves of the old world. The principle of propagation is, on the contrary, excess, superabundance of being. And so it is possible only when the heart, which has been dried up by the material and materialistic harshness of the world of exploitation, is irrigated with the new love: "For a long time I listened silently to the message of love that Saint-Simon bequeathed to us. . . . Till now it had fallen into my heart without producing any echo, as water falls on greedy sand, penetrates it, and leaves nothing on the surface. But then, lo and behold, the heart is full, the sand is soaked."[29] Now it is impossible for this heart not to overflow, to pour itself out to other thirsty hearts. The golden-mean milieus, the advocates and mentalities of the just-right middle ground (e.g., the *juste milieu* of Louis Philippe's regime), waste their energy in denouncing the excesses of these humanitarian religions, for it is excess that founds these new families. The new love cannot be the familial exchange of services whose very closure fixes the inequality, condemning the naïveté of the wife who would exchange her love for learning. Love is exchanged only for love, which makes the exchange only by giving itself without reckoning: an overflowing current, a whirlwind, a giddiness; a community of excess beyond the disappointments of contract and gratitude. At the very time that the Saint-Simonian priests are proposing the priestly couple of the Father and the Woman as the principle of the religion of the future, it is another couple that sublimates the desires of the proletarian initiates: the complicity of friendship, the resonance of like to like, the openness to the universal conspiration of harmonies rather than the complementarity of qualities and services attributed to each of the two sexes.

This is the virginal dawn celebrated by joiner Gauny and bookkeeper Thierry in the dead of the winter of 1831. To his new friend, who thanks him for having regenerated him, Gauny returns the homage of the flower to the dew: "When you shed your dawn on my face, when the dew of your life fell on my tempest-tossed soil, no, I was no longer from here. Having escaped the revolts of my being . . . I became a flower, a loving and solitary flower crumpled by your breath as it picked my petals, scented for you alone."[30] But dew would not know how to fall for one being alone, or a flower how to conceal its perfume from others, or a plant how to refrain from healing pains. In their "pensive twoness," or in their "unitive

29. Hippolyte Pennekère, Profession of faith, Fonds Enfantin, Ms. 7794.

30. Gauny to Thierry, "Offertoire," Fonds Gauny, Bibliothèque municipale de Saint-Denis, Ms. 172.

threeness" when they make shoemaker Boileau a partner in the emotions of their dawn, the two young men will not be able to drink in the new religion of fraternity without spreading it abroad on their dreamy strolls. It is the mission of dew, flower, or plant, one with the fulfillment of their being: "I have told you twenty times that our actions have a purpose, that each scene of our life is another link Providence is adding to the humanitarian chain. Nothing is sterile, everything from the atom to the human being bears its fruit, each has its mission in time and space to reach the kingdom of truth."[31]

The mission of the three friends is no different from the universal conspiration in which the poets of the time sense the gestation of the new world. Thence derives the peculiar form of their Sunday propagandizing. It is very different from the forms that are organized rationally by the Saint-Simonian polytechnicians or the republican students of law and medicine. The latter frequent the cabarets where workers get together, pinpoint those whose powers of persuasion win them a hearing from their fellows, and get to know the lodgings where a certain brochure would set off a spark; the former draw up lists of addresses for the use of their missionaries, who in return select for them the hierarchized public for their teachings. But on this particular Sunday in May 1832, our three proletarians (Gauny, Thierry, and Boileau) did not undertake a mission to recruit workers. They set off to unfurl their own liberty, a liberty that is degraded every wage-earning day. They have no addresses, just a completely natural direction: to follow the bend of the rivers back toward their source. They set out "incomplete in causality, rich in memories, happy with the future . . . taking joy in one and the same thought but plunged into solitude." From the banks of the Seine to the banks of the Marne, submissive to the echoes of nature and their own emotions and enjoying the shades "where the wind slips its youthful delirium," they have been able to expand their souls, saturate their hearts with love, and put their ideas "at ease." And so they now can exchange them at a village inn:

> Then, in a room with visible joists and thick walls without papering, we opened up to each other in all our intensity. Our countless apprehensions could find expression only in sighs, many ardent emotions, hypotheses raised and shot down, poetry, metaphysical

31. Bergier to Gauny, May 1832, Fonds Gauny, Ms. 166; in Jacques Rancière (ed.), *Louis Gabriel Gauny: Le philosophe plébéien* (Paris: La Découverte/Maspero, 1983), pp. 154–58. This citation is on p. 154.

obscurity, vehemence, reticence, vestiges of the ideal, Byronism.
. . . The earth was sinking down and out or we were ascending into
empty space, because we saw creations unfolding that are not of
here.[32]

These closet deliriums are also preparations for hunting. Our strollers
of the faith can now tackle the other clients of the inn, but their chance
propagandizing is also selective. Whereas the orator addresses himself to
everyone present, the expansive soul seeks its peers and finds them, in line
with the science of physiognomy so dear to our joiner, in the faces of fellow diners: "Since we were not the only guests in the place, we scrutinized
them closely to judge their character in Lavater's way. About a dozen of
them were at a table close to ours. We liked four of them, but we invited
all to fraternize." Four for three—the progression is reasonable. For the
reckoning is also a choice in which each soul senses a potential sympathy
close to his own. The delicate shoemaker Boileau takes "a young blond
gardener, well-built and candid as a smile of innocence." The dialectician
Thierry takes charge of "a vinedresser who was an artilleryman not long
ago, and a clearly reflective cooper who seeks only the chance to love."
Gauny "fastens onto a butcher."

> Then Boileau, Thierry, and myself were a tempest of thinking,
> whirling up into our holy transports the transports of those around
> us. We made these men, still fierce or restricted, understand God,
> immortality, what we mean by a soul, by virtue. We excised more
> than one corrosion, put out more than one fire, got down to
> talking as familiar friends, banished license, and made them almost
> Saint-Simonians.[33]

Undoubtedly these "almost Saint-Simonians" did not learn much about
classification according to capacities, remuneration according to works,
and other principles of the doctrine. But the essence is certainly there:
corrosions excised, fires put out, balm poured on the ulcerations of the
old world to revive the capacity for loving; the revelation of a different
world and the initiation of a new kind of relationship between beings. It is
less a matter of proving to this butcher, for example, the superiority of the

32. Gauny to Bergier, May 14, 1832, Fonds Gauny, Ms. 166; in Rancière (ed.),
Le philosophe plébéien, pp. 151–54. This citation is on p. 152.
33. Ibid., p. 153.

Saint-Simonian way of organizing work than of changing right now and
henceforth his way of living, of extirpating the brutality of feeling produced by the brutal acts of his daily office. This sympathetic persuasion
logically goes by way of homeopathy:

> Enchained to the carnivore with a terrible face, I immediately
> raised my voice to the pitch of his anger. Rummaging his lost soul,
> I found a strong will, a frenzy that is only the lunacy of virtuality.
> I believe I staunched the venom coating it a bit, because he was at
> ease with me. I made myself almost him to understand him better.
> He admitted his furies to me, tasted several of our opinions, and
> promised me that when he disemboweled his sheep, he would no
> longer be hellish in this necessary atrocity.[34]

The new love knows how to choose its prey. On this Sunday, when
the old believers are gathered around their pastor to consume the flesh
and blood of the divine Lamb, these strollers are teaching a cooper, a
vinedresser, and a butcher to soften the furies of wine, blood, and flesh,
to divest the act that kills the sheep of its sacrificial fury. The new love
is, by rights, a religion without sacrifice: devotion to a Virgin who, like
Angélique in a story by Gilland, initiates the children of the people into
celestial loves only to die of weakness before the age of marriage; a religion without a Golgotha, whose propagation from the banks of the Jordan
and the Sermon on the Mount needs no redeemer's blood to spread to
the streets of Jerusalem and the roadways of the world. For there is no
redemption or message other than the transformation of the deeds and
thoughts of those who follow the little band: a religion of friendship, a
society of wayfarers on the road to perfection who reject models based
on murder and fraternities based on consumption. It is not at the inn table
but on the road back that the little band will see their work of seduction
triumph and the communion of souls turn into a reality:

> In the soft pallors of evening, the men were more tender. . . .
> We were about to part company. Boileau was eloquent, Thierry
> captivating, all religiously moved when the four proposed to
> accompany us for a distance. We rushed out, one with the other,
> walking along together. An indefinable, intoxicating air swept us

34. Ibid.

along. We parted from each other with an embrace, hoping to see each other soon again and more perfect.[35]

The stroll of the little band offers the most natural image of progress from the twilight of a Sunday in May to the mornings of the new humanity. But how could these Sunday dreams of love withstand the weekday law, the order of work and family? Harassed by his wife and victimized by a father-in-law who sees the Saint-Simonian family mainly as a clientele for his housepainting work, the apostle Bergier will soon take off the habit and again pick up his trade as a floor-tiler. Shoemaker Boileau will return to proletarian anonymity, later to dream of a departure for Icaria that will never be made. Finally, the celestial friendship of Gauny and Thierry will end up a victim of Thierry's conjugal tribulations. The latter had given evidence of his fidelity by giving the names of the dead apostle Moses and his angel friend Gabriel to the child of a wife incestuously named Amélie. But Amélie, it seems, is fanciful and extravagant: meaning that she proves to be incapable of making ends meet with the two francs per day that every economist worthy of the name considers enough to manage an ordinary household in a capable way. So Jules Thierry will take his child away, find a better housekeeper, and ask his friend, compromised in the payment of Amélie's debts, not to disturb with further visits the household peace necessary for the education of little Moses.

"Don't confuse the religion of fraternity with the fanaticism of the family."[36] The futile advice of the joiner to his friend serves as the moral of the story of the little band. We are now at the last day of the autumn of 1840. The fine days of July and after have come to an end. Bourgeois economists are enjoying themselves while worker apostles are worried about the changes evident in worker habits and mentalities. The ideas of comfort and saving, says one group—egotism, says the other—are beginning to filter down from the ruling classes to a fraction of the popular classes. Fanaticism of the family instead of the religion of fraternity.

Undoubtedly there is something excessive in this partition. It is not true that the religiosity of apostolic hearts is giving way purely and simply to material interests. Jules Thierry is enriching his correspondence with citations from the *Imitation of Christ*, and more than one republican is letting himself be convinced by Lamennais or Buchez to identify the cause of

35. Ibid.
36. Gauny to Thierry, Dec. 21, 1840, Fonds Gauny, Ms. 172.

the people with that of the Redeemer. But this religion of the Redeemer certainly can no longer be equated with the pleasures of Sunday strolls and propagandizing. Over against the happy proselytism of little bands is now set the image of the wordbearer–crossbearer. It is a religion of sacrifice whose form (self-sacrificing dedication) is dissociated from the goal pursued: the "moral and material interests of the working classes." Nor is it the case that the progress of humanitarian doctrines is slowing down or yielding. On the contrary, its pace is very fast, too fast for the Sunday strollers who linger to follow the meanderings of the Marne. It no longer maintains the rhythm of friendly walks, of the songs and balls organized by Louis Vinçard for the Saint-Simonian family. Vinçard, for one, bitterly resents the lesson inflicted by his old friend Lenoir the cabinetmaker, who has moved on to the scientific socialism of the day, Fourierism: "From the top of your scientific pulpit you disdain and look down on *goguettes,* sing-along walks, worker balls. . . . All that is rococo. . . . You just keep walking and walking and, as this other fellow says who forgets to sign his letter, let those who have corns on their feet look out."[37] The end time for little bands returns God's strollers to their solitude or forces them to find new relations between their own deliverance and the emancipation of the masses whose idolatrous practices they have fled. They must again shoulder their own marginality or find some point of support in the order of work and family.

Our rebellious floor-layer, Gauny, has chosen the first way, shunning the solidarities of family and guild, the humiliations and rages of the workshop as well as the pursuit of claims based on household budgets. Cenobitic economy has this substitutive function as well: the compression of bodily needs raises the spiritual force of revolt and thereby provides the soul with the superabundance no longer given by the chain of friendship. The latter can then be reconstituted insofar as it is stripped of all particularism. The propagator no longer seeks to reconstitute a small band. As an anonymous and isolated individual, he sets off to share the spark of the spirit of revolt—of the spirit, period—with a crowd capable of catching fire precisely insofar as it is not a gathering of families, societies, classes, or corporations but a pure collection of sensitive individuals: that is, a mass fusing through the energy of its molecules, with which the rebel makes contact at one point in a relationship without reciprocity. "The rebel worker, lost in the immense arena of life, should consider himself

37. Vinçard to Lenoir, May 16, 1836, Fonds Enfantin, Ms. 7627.

a gladiator of independence abandoned by the very people who share his cause. Let him fight without calling for help, without ever asking for mercy."[38]

But this stoic solitude, which forces him to rationalize his own power to resist the order of production and consumption, gives him sovereignty over the urban space that traverses and surrounds the proprietary citadels on all sides. If for him the humanitarian chain no longer has the materiality of the Saint-Simonian apostles' collar, it is not the *flatus vocis* of republican rhetoric either. Rather, it is the collection of encounters and pleasant surprises that makes the stroller quick to seize upon individual members of the working class at their point of fragility, of incandescence: in the dead times of no work, on the roads and squares of the space allotted to the possession of all, in the vagueness of solitary reveries and the emotion of fortuitous gatherings: "And so he goes from individual to individual, unfolding his soul, giving and receiving as he attaches himself to the race rather than to the person, deriving from it a very high appreciation of happiness as he goes along on this journey of friendship."[39] This friendship is all the more lively and contagious in that it is always only a passing encounter because the rebel does not cease to travel between these two places, these two modes of existence and liberty: the desert, where "seditious thinking ferments," and the "extreme crowd," whose density alone, by its speed of propagation, gives it its explosive force.

These voyages of the spirit give the solitary propagandist two models —the man of the city Diogenes, and the man of the desert Saint John the Baptist—who also represent two moments in the formation of rebel consciousness. Diogenes the Cynic incarnates the moment when rebel individuality is formed by the invention of that strange science "of possessing everything without having anything, by attacking ownership with renunciation."[40] An exemplary figure for the modern cenobite who individually breaks away from the reign of exploitation by restraining the consumption of the senses "that is obtained only in exchange for a product wrested from either exploitation or slavery." But this liberty that individually provokes each passer-by to recover "the dignity of his nature" remains limited to the "rectangular reason" of a practical philosophy that is incapable of glimpsing different futures for human liberty and is satisfied to possess "an active morality and an ordinary intelligence that could aug-

38. Gauny, "Économie cénobitique," Fonds Gauny, Ms. 151.
39. Gauny, "Les deux familles," ibid.
40. Gauny, "Diogène et saint Jean le Précurseur," ibid. In Rancière (ed.), *Le philosophe plébéien*, pp. 120–26; this citation is on p. 123.

ment the liberty and happiness of the citizen": a reason to be enjoyed to
the maximum that is permitted by the present relationship of liberty to
slavery, as might have been the reason of the emancipated floor-layer if
he had not alienated his gaze in the fixed idea of the prison.

The Baptist, the man of the desert, takes his stand beyond the balances
of rectified reason. He is a spirit in revolt, in the most immediate sense
of the term: his imagination immersed in those "unions with God, nature,
and beings" in which the heavenly floor-layer gets lost a bit too often (according to the philosophical cesspool-cleaner Ponty), but also "given over
to suffering," his solitary meditation gathering together the sorrows and
hopes of humanity. And so, with the vision of future deliverance, he finds
the strength to make his word heard from the recesses of desert places
—thanks first of all to passers-by, who are already discontented with the
laws ruling the city and who instruct other passers-by, the latter leading an
ever-growing crowd to the monologue-become-sermon of the anchorite.
And, in truth, he teaches them a strange Christianity:

> Announcing the redeemer to them, he commanded them to unite
> against the wicked and march into battle. Then, in one bound,
> he left the earth and showed them the eternity each one of them
> possesses in successive existences, under the laws of motion and
> reproduction. Returning here, he lost them in history by putting
> before them so many miseries and terrors, so many infamies and
> carnages, that the multitude, its spirit in revolt, was straining
> toward an unknown time for getting its revenge. Showing them
> the horizon, he symbolized the uncertainties of it. And the rays of
> evening over the red clouds in the wind gave them indomitable
> desires of ascending and being.[41]

This "revenge" is no longer the wrath of the restive slave but a "divine
insurrection," linking the revolution of cities to the endless march to the
horizon through the deserts, to the ceaseless discovery of new lands.
"Diogenes represented the right of the individual. Saint John embodied
the unchaining of humanity. The one was the expression of the citizen
making himself his own master; the other was the torch of revolutions.
Together they summed up the universal emancipation being engendered
in the world and perpetuated by the disciple and the apostle."[42]

41. Ibid., p. 125.
42. Ibid.

A happy image of an army of humanitarian liberation taking shape in the empty spaces of the old despotisms. But the new despotisms know the roads that lead from the desert to the city. Lying in wait "in all the corners of the soul," they pursue apostles who deliver their thoughts to crowds. The army of propagandists must henceforth be a secret army—not in the sense of those conspiratorial societies ruled by hierarchical discipline but, rather, close to certain anarchistic dreams: an army of combatants whose unforeseeable strength comes from the fact that they do not implement the directive of any center and that each is unaware of what the other is doing:

> Diogenes and the Precursor exist forever. Leaving their age, the
> essence of their life is transfused from rebel to rebel . . . so that
> an army of propagandists, bearing within the sacred flame of
> these two gladiators of thought, patiently brings popular resistance
> to the point of combustion. Not knowing one another, they are
> neither the fanatics of the corporate body nor the victims of
> felony. Rekindling their souls in the phlogiston of their hearts,
> they multiply mysteriously by means of the vitality of the apostolic
> message, which radicalizes individual morality and rationalizes the
> unity of rights.[43]

Neither the victims of felony nor the fanatics of the corporate body; neither the army of the outcasts of exploitation nor the army of producers anticipating the Republic of workers by their organization. Properly speaking, the nonexistent army of men who have already renounced all the benefits and interiorized all the negations of the world of exploitation, who already live the nonbeing of this world. This cobbler whose coarse shirt is not the product of the exploitation of any wage-earner, and whose spirit spares no pains to find the incommensurable in the infinitely small. This wheelwright who has built his cottage himself, its badly built walls nurturing diverse vegetation outside and covered inside with plans and geometric figures whose lines seem to stretch toward the impossible, and who, while dreaming of sounding the depths of the earth and finding the way to realize perpetual motion, invents traction systems to alleviate the pain of horses and curb the excessive speed of the carriages of the rich. This peddler, ever ready to fight and ever ready to settle quarrels, whose movement is agitated by a feel for all the tortures and all the sui-

43. Ibid., p. 126.

cides perpetrated at the same moment. This knife-grinder on the city's outskirts who has rationalized his "nonpossession" to make it an owner-ship of all that he does not have.[44] All these *independents* producing the force of revolution amid the crowd of slaves and operators, insofar as they have already lost their own chains and carry only those of others; messen-gers of a revolutionary time that will be a time of lightning, of meeting, of the instantaneous and uninterrupted propagation of the light.

What will fascinate Gauny in the spring of 1848 will be the multipli-cation of the open-air discussions where dreams of the future society are interchanged. What he will give priority to in the demands proposed to the Club of Workers will be the permanence of clubs. What he will imag-ine most vividly about the coming society will be the density of events, the circulation of discourses, the messages depicted on the houses of cities, the stones of squares, and the posts of crossroads, marking a universe populated with spoken words: public lectures on the "Rights of Man," the "Social Contract," and "Voluntary Servitude"; public bowling greens; the winding streets of the "insurrectional city" with their fascines, their sawhorse barricades, and their arcades; columns in all the boroughs and on all the roads, on which would be inscribed the Rights of Man and the crimes committed against liberty; statues in the immense gardens open to strollers of the city–universe named Libérie; feasts of friendship where the steps of temples will be "covered with chatterers pondering together the most abstruse theses of theology"; monuments put at the disposal of orators who "will draw their zest from the fluids of the assembly"; an infi-nite and infinitely populated world where "no lane and no blind alley will be without episodes," where "every demonstration should have its initia-tor, should produce an act which, at the appointed time, is repeated along the line by degrees"; a city "resplendent with movements" and "endowed with the force of great things." As for social reforms, the orator notes that "they will come in their due season."[45] But what season can be imagined other than the permanence of lightning?

The utopia of the solitary floor-layer and loving stroller, content to know the workers of the workshop and the supporters of the family, the irregulars of work or morality, in the sole time of miracle and the pure

44. Gauny, "Les indépendants," Fonds Gauny, Ms. 115; in Rancière (ed.), *Le philosophe plébéien*, pp. 127–33. This citation is on p. 128.

45. Gauny, "Aux prolétaires," Fonds Gauny, Ms. 93; idem, "A l'amitié," Ms. 139. See also the following by Gauny: "Club des Travailleurs," Ms. 163; "Lacédé-mone et Libérie," Ms. 151; and "La multitude," *Le Tocsin des travailleurs*, June 11, 1848.

space of the encounter between souls. How could all the others be satisfied with that? The secretaries of worker societies, charged to defend the
interests of colleagues who are in no hurry to pay their assessments. The
big-hearted workers who are constantly solicited by the distress of fathers
who are unemployed or mothers whose husbands spend the household
money in cabarets. The pioneers of association, weighed down by members who are more interested in future benefits than in the extra effort
needed to get the enterprise off and running. The worker journalists who
must represent to others—bourgeois people, writers, politicians—a working class whose coarseness they themselves despise. All those who are
forced, by their place in workshop, guild, neighborhood, organization, or
journal, to daily compare their dreams of the absolute with the countless
shabby things in the order of work and family.

The problem is only now and then a matter of what self-image to
project: for example, when the militant must offer to public view a private
life that belies the accusations of an opponent who is quick to impute
subversive opinions to disordered morals. Thus, at the moment when the
trial of *L'Humanitaire* again raises the great phantasm of the community
of women, weaver and communist Sébastien Commissaire breaks off his
liaison with a young woman.[46] But the problem is less often the "debauchery" of the militant, exposed to the pitiless gaze of decent workers, than
his angelism, which separates the morality peculiar to his activity from
the ordinary morality of those decent workers. How to get the apostolic
ideal across to all without placing oneself on a higher plane and nulli-
fying the most effective form of propaganda: example? "If we were to
imagine that we think differently from the rest of men, that our nature
is essentially different from theirs, why and by what right would we tell
them to follow our counsel and example?" To this question, posed by the
sententious Perdiguier to a nephew who is too quickly discouraged with
human beings, the most illustrious of examples responds: "When Jesus
chose to preach to human beings, he became a human being himself and
lived among human beings."[47] The example is an optical illusion, however; it is precisely because he is of a different nature that the Son of God
can endure the afflictions of human beings and drink the chalice to the
dregs in order to save them, without falling into disgrace. But the worker
apostles have no choice but to live with human beings. Not only does

46. Sébastien Commissaire, *Mémoires et souvenirs*, Lyon, 1888, p. 114.
47. Perdiguier to André Alliaud, Feb. 9, 1844, *Correspondance inédite*, published
by Jean Briquet, Paris, 1966, p. 77.

their sacrifice, in and of itself, fail to bring redemption to human beings sunk in their "material interests"; they must also risk their own identity in coming to terms with those interests that no longer leave fishermen or publicans free to abandon their nets, account books, or families in order to follow the new message.

For the power of material interests lies in the fact that they already know how to come to terms with more than one virtue recommended or approved by civil or religious morality. Over against the animal egotism of the dissipated rake, they set the self-sacrificing dedication of the worker, the good family man who in a single act sacrifices his own egotistical pleasures and solidarity with his comrades to the welfare of his family. Didn't Perdiguier himself get the benefit of this moral lesson from a comrade he had come to solicit? His comrade said: "When I get my pay, I set some aside to get through the week. The surplus I put in the savings bank. So I never have anything left for anyone."[48]

And so the apostle must now become a strategist. In his turn he must now define standards of "material interests" and "moral interests" and find a measure common to both the extravagant dedication of the militant and the thrifty dedication of the "true worker." "To go for the goal with the help of the means": this is the problem formulated by typographer Vasbenter when confronted with Flora Tristan's projected universal union of workers. We must "take the elements on which we want to work as they are."[49] It is useless to summon the workers of the bourgeois monarchy to the morality of devotees:

> The public arena is entirely taken up with egotism and shabby tribulations. You hear only a voice speaking to you on behalf of material interests—of well-proven material interests at that. Okay, we must appeal to material interests! So let us make no appeals for dedication—all ears would remain deaf to them. Let us appeal to egotism, and you will see this inert mass stir and start with a thrill. I do not mean to imply that we should renounce regeneration —quite the contrary—but we must conceal the goal so as not to scare away the weak, the strong, or the tremblers. We must do as Epicurus did. When all the philosophical sects of Greece were questing for happiness and inveighing against pleasure, he

48. *Biographie de l'auteur du Livre du Compagnonnage*, Paris, 1846, p. 21.
49. Vasbenter to Flora Tristan, June 11, 1843, in Jules Puech, *La Vie et l'Oeuvre de Flora Tristan*, Paris, 1925, p. 473.

appealed to the younger generation and said that happiness lay in pleasure. They ran to his gardens because he promised pleasure. But they were greatly surprised: Epicurus placed pleasure in the sweet enjoyments of the soul.[50]

Let us not make any mistake about this: the garden of Epicurus that serves as a trap for the pleasure-seekers of the industrial era has nothing to beguile the votaries of *fêtes galantes*. It is a serious organization: a mutual-aid association with headquarters in Paris and committees in all the cities; investing its funds at 4 percent the better to help the sick, the infirm, and workers without work; offering transient workers bed and board at a cheap price, but also allowing fathers of families to go out and buy the food their families need at the going price; finally, maintaining a correspondence between the cities that informs people where the labor is in short supply and where it is overabundant. So much for the promised pleasures. And for the true enjoyments of the soul:

> When one managed to win over a large number of workers, with the pecuniary resources of the association it would be easy to establish libraries and schools where workers would come to refresh themselves and relax from their rugged labors. . . . I think that with such an organization one would have found the means to moralize and instruct workers. Gathered together, knowing themselves, and feeling their strength, these men would change course. The propaganda could be active and captivating. Men of intelligence and heart would find a new means of self-development. Those given over to their own inspirations would get from it things new and unknown to them. In a short time you would see emerging from the ranks of the working class men capable of understanding and guiding the interests of this huge number of pariahs.[51]

A mass of pariahs and a few men capable of understanding and guiding *their* interests: would so much effort be needed to find oneself back at the initial situation, for all practical purposes? Isn't it a shortsighted strategy to seek to pass along the breath of the spirit only in diversions from work, to appeal by way of material interests to this change of course that opens out on unknown inspirations? But perhaps that is putting the question

50. Ibid.
51. Ibid., pp. 475–76.

badly. Perhaps it is not so much a matter of shouldering the regeneration
of the pariahs of the industrial order as of ensuring to "men of intelligence
and heart" the mass of unskilled laborers that will permit them to rise to
power, the future instrument of this regeneration. "Go for the goal with
the help of the means": around 1850 Vasbenter's master, former barge-
line accountant Proudhon, will come to suspect that his first disciple, the
editor of his journal, might be nothing but a Jacobin in disguise.

That is not what disturbs locksmith Gilland or his friends on *L'Atelier*.
The master who recalled them to the truths of the Gospel, Buchez, is also
the author of the *Histoire parlementaire de la Révolution française* that confirmed them in their love for Robespierre. They too feel that the chains
of the world of material interests are too tight to give way to the force
of the apostolic word alone. The apostles must indeed become leaders.
But it would be futile for them to use deceit in this exigency, to lead the
masses in the opposite direction from that proposed first. In choosing to
come to terms with the full unfolding of egotistical interests through the
promise of happiness, they would only lend their support to a movement
that would necessarily go toward the dominant idea of happiness, the one
proposed by the dominant society. Given the current of egotistical happiness, the only way to turn the tide is to organize the counter-current of a
different principle capable of being acknowledged by all. And for that one
must also reject the seductions of a double and doubly dangerous morality
that would either exempt the apostle from the common norms of true
workers or restrict the demanding morality of dedication to the leaders
of men and promise pariahs the collective benefits of social regeneration
without demanding from them an individual effort at moral regeneration.

A counter-current cannot be the solitary effort of swimmers vainly
trying their best to resist. It must be the positivity of another current, a
different force, uniting apostolic energy with that of the mass. This presupposes that each party would be able to recognize itself in the other
party, that the apostle could teach the masses to regard as *their* duty the
devotion he practices out of the expansive necessity of his nature. But
to do that, he himself would have to renounce the roles of fallen angel
and chosen bard, would have to live not only with others but like them,
making his own the motivations and aspirations of the decent worker who
aspires to put in good workdays and have a nice household. He need not
disown his own inspirations, the paradise of his readings and his strolls;
but he must find for his pleasures and his sacrifices some point of identification with the rights and duties whose necessary reciprocity he teaches
to pariahs. In the encounter between what he thought was his disgrace

and what is to ground the rehabilitation of the pariahs, one single principle presents itself to represent simultaneously the preserved dignity of
the apostle and the regained dignity of the masses, to anticipate the glory
they will share tomorrow in the servitudes they share today: work.

Wasn't that the very advice that Urbain gave to Georges? "Come on,
brother . . . instead of bowing your head humbly and murmuring, I am a
pariah, hold it up high instead, with nobility and pride, and say, I am a
worker."[52] Hold your head up high, just as others fall on their knees and
pronounce the words, waiting for faith to come? The advice may be sound,
but it seems out of place. In this "private correspondence," Georges was
not rebelling against the obligation to work but against the apathy of the
workers. But Urbain has not mistaken the point here. It is no longer a
matter of summoning the fallen angel to accept his status as a manual
laborer by evoking Plautus's grindstone or Rousseau's work as a copyist,
or by comparing the servitude of the pen to the independence of the plane.
It is no longer a matter of self-identity but a matter of identifying oneself
with others. And it is for that very reason that one must add on the point
about the nobility of the worker, which is said with too much affectation
for one not to sense in it the voice of the self-made man. There is no
other way but this voluntaristic reversal, a narrow path between cynicism
and despair, that reconciles the solitary with the idolatrous crowd of his
brothers, in image at least. And so Gilland has the fallen child and the
worker moralist engage in dialogue once again, this time in verse:

> Inspiré, je rêvais de splendides lumières
> Le respect des palais et l'amour des chaumières. . . .
> L'illusion n'est plus! Dans mon âme contrainte,
> Du feu pur et sacré la flamme s'est éteinte;
> Revenu pour toujours aux choses positives,
> Je me trouve semblable à ces pauvres captives
> Qui loin du sol natal pleurent de souvenir.[53]

52. P. Vinçard, "Fragments d'une correspondance intime," *La Fraternité de 1845*,
May 1846.

53. J.-P. Gilland, "Une plainte," in *Les conteurs ouvriers*, Paris, 1849, pp. 320–
21. "Inspired, I dreamed of splendid lights / The respect of palaces and the love
of thatched cottages . . . / The illusion is no more! In my constricted heart, / The
flame of the pure, sacred fire has gone out; / Brought back forever to positive
things, / I feel like those poor captives / Who, far from their native sun, weep
from remembering."

But the militant is there to ensure that the voice of the captive soul does not die "forgotten in the desert," to make its vocation the mission of a chosen race, authorizing it at the same time to disdain the clamors of the mob and to announce the redemptive reign of the workers:

> Frère, relève-toi, reprends force et courage,
> Soldat blessé mais fier, cherche encore les combats;
> Nul travail n'avilit, c'est à nous d'être sage,
> Et de mépriser ceux qui ne travaillent pas.
>
> Quand tu sens dan ton coeur bouillonner ta pensée
> Ne la comprime plus car c'est un don sacré;
> Dédaigne les clameurs de la foule insensée,
> Le poète est puissant quand il est inspiré.
>
> Dieu qui mit sur ton front ce signe: Intelligence,
> Te réserve sans doute un glorieux destin;
> Vers le but aspiré, marche, ton jour s'avance,
> Marche, ne vois-tu pas l'étoile du matin?
>
> Ah! si nous faiblissons, nous, la race féconde,
> Nous, travailleurs bénis des mains du créateur,
> Qui donc se dévouera pour le salut du monde?
> L'avenir veut encore le sang d'un rédempteur.[54]

Beyond the simple haggling between the one who scorns work and those who jeer at poets, would identity be rediscovered again in the ample, manly poetry common to foreheads bronzed by the forge and foreheads marked with the sign of Intelligence? Again it is a double negation that is to make the election of the poet the sign of his membership in a chosen

---

54. Ibid., pp. 321–22. "Brother, get up again, again take courage and strength, / Soldier, wounded but proud, seek battles again; / No work is degrading, it's for us to be wise, / And to disregard those who do not do work. / When you feel your thought bubbling inside your heart / Restrain it no longer, for it is a sacred gift; / Disdain the clamors of the senseless mob, / The poet is potent when he is inspired. / God, who put on your forehead this sign: Intelligence, / Surely reserves a glorious destiny for you; / Go forward toward the goal you seek, your day draws nearer, / Go forward, don't you see the morning star? / Ah, if we falter, we, the fertile race, / Workers blessed by the creator's hands, / Who then will sacrifice themselves for the salvation of the world? / The future still wants the blood of a redeemer."

race whose extent remains remarkably ambiguous: as if the worker–poet could not resign himself unreservedly to transferring the redemptive mission of God's chosen ones to the working class. But there lies the logic that gives back to children who have fallen into the coarseness of proletarian ways the legitimacy of a heritage identified with the regenerating mission of the world of workers, which is to be regarded less as a societal class than as a race of humanity. The morning star, happy end to the night of solitaries; painful uprooting from the secret night of the initiates, redeemed by possible identification with the dawn of the miracle. With either the prescience of a poet or the retrospective trick of a writer, the poem, published in 1849, is dated January 1848.

But before the glorious mornings when dreams of the absolute mingle with worker claims and popular outbursts, there are the more modest mornings when this dignity is to be won somewhere between the degradation of work's pariahs and the disgraceful fall of those who try to forget it in the intoxication of barrier-district bars, where the common people can sip duty-free wine outside the gates of Paris and its tolls. Such is this spring Sunday. The once-fallen child, André, is strolling in the woods near the capital with his new friend, Joseph. On this day in May 1842, the two friends are not looking for the sentimental intoxications of their 1832 elders. They are more modestly happy "to be able to get out of the workshop one day a week and come to breathe the pure air of the woods."[55] The pleasures of friendship are tending to shift thoughtlessly from apostolic enthusiasm to worker hygiene. One regret, however, casts a shadow over the country party of the two friends. They were to have been three, but their friend Charles is not with them, undoubtedly snatched away in his fatidic transit through the barrier. For Charles is one of those poets appreciated in the barrier bars, and he does not know how to resist the pleasure of stopping and taking up his station in them: "He knows that his songs give pleasure to the crowd. That is why he always mingles with it, wherever he finds it, in order to get its applause, its praise, and its caresses—as if those cabaret 'bravos!' could touch a truly delicate soul, as if those wine-soaked brains could express anything but the filthy sensations of their Bacchic frenzies."[56]

The fall of the worker–artist is not a new theme. What is new is the form given to this fall: no longer misery, suicide, or alienation into the hands of the powerful, but rather the hell of antipoetry, the society of

55. Gilland, "L'incompris," ibid., p. 64.
56. Ibid., p. 68.

wine-soaked beasts. One who refuses to stoop to devoting himself to the laborer's work can only fall into the subproletarian underworld. And once again it is this fall that will serve to prove *a contrario* the nobility and sanctity of the laborer's work. It is time to have done with the image of the fallen angel. What is at stake is the education of the man of the new generation, the worker Joseph: undoubtedly entering the active life after the great years 1830–1834, more sensible than enthusiastic, more decent than devout, ready to condemn angelic pretensions but also to replace them with the decent "epicureanism" of workers concerned about their duties and open to the delicacies of the soul but also moderately eager and earnest about the future that is to be fashioned. He must be shown that one can study and use one's pen, not to play the barrier bard but to anticipate "the duties that the laboring class will have to fulfill some day in order to defend its rights, interests, and liberty on its own."[57] It must be proved to him that the vigils of the writer and the dedication of the militant are merely extensions of the natural aspiration of the worker who is a good father and family man, without in any way standing in the way of his duties. This explains the current reaction to polemics that disparage the "literature of workers":

> With their bitter irony and cruel sarcasms, they go after those of us who are conscious of our dignity and raise our voices to reclaim our place in the sun, a bit of bread for our large families, a bit of happiness in this world for our poor little children! But I really believe I am one of those who should be forgiven for this eccentricity, as they say, for it does no harm to my everyday work, or to the many duties that my condition imposes on me.[58]

It is the natural solicitude of the father and family man that should credit the disinterested dedication of the militant and the audacity of the worker–writer. The paternal tenderness of the sensitive Gilland is certainly known to us. But can it make us forget the apostolic extravagances that preceded his status as a decent father and family man? Hadn't his first love been for a girl of ill repute whom he wanted to redeem by marrying her? Gilland, it is true, had thought up a way to test the sincerity of his intended wife's repentance. The couple were to adopt an orphan, a child left by an ex-soldier to a poor working girl who had just died. But the young apostle's

57. Ibid., p. 70.
58. Ibid., pp. 71–72.

mother was wise enough to forewarn him against this strange proof of
love:

> She told me that the woman I wanted to make my companion
> would not love me, that she would not comprehend my sacrifice at
> all, that she would abandon me for the first debauched man with
> money, that the world was wicked, and that the child would be
> used against me as a reproach, as the fruit of my own misconduct.
> Mothers are always a bit egotistical in their tender foresight. Mine
> spoke the language of reason.[59]

A little egotism brings us back to a conception of dedication that can
actually be exemplary. The reason of families, which dreads gossip and
harries acts of generosity bringing no return, denounces the paradoxical links between angelism and base acts of venality. In their private life
proletarians of good will are not obligated to assume responsibility for
lost women and foundlings, the very act whereby bourgeois philanthropy
maintains and supports the evil it wants to cure. The marriage of apostles
should not be seen as an act of redemption but rather as the exemplary
establishment of a household.

The matter seems simple: marriage of the decent workingman with the
pure workingwoman. But Gilland's second love, less equivocal but no less
disastrous, proves that it is not simple at all. This time he met his fiancée
in the very heart of the laboring and domestic order. She is a seamstress in
the next shop, which is kept by the wife of his boss. The young workingman redoubles his efforts to buy himself a household, without sacrificing
his nighttime studies to that goal. The young woman also works to get
herself a household—works too hard, unfortunately: "She got sick, grew
weaker, and weaker, and died."[60] The workingwoman, an "ungodly word"
for Michelet, the author of *Le peuple*, a deadly thing for the worker–poet:
to be betrothed to death by toils too difficult for a woman. But this feminine frailty is not determined in those calculations for which Proudhon
will be ridiculed. Here it clearly represents a certain impossibility of being.
The young workingwoman, who was named Angélique, reappears in several of Gilland's poems or stories under different figures, the virgin too
pure for existence tending to overlay and conceal the workingwoman too
fragile for work. In "The White Rose," for example, Angélique becomes

59. Gilland, "Préface," in *Les conteurs ouvriers*, p. xv.
60. Ibid., p. xvi.

the daughter of a factory master, a girl who dies of a fatigue that has nothing to do with physical labor: consumption according to the doctors, homesickness according to the child to whom she tells her visions and recites the verses of Hégésippe Moreau. Continuing the chain of transformations, we would undoubtedly meet the daughter of councillor Crespel, Antonia in the *Tales of Hoffmann*, who died from not being able to stop singing. More fortunate than the poet, the locksmith will find happiness in his third love, with a woman named Félicie. Though the daughter of a weaver–poet, she nevertheless is above all what a workingman needs— not a poetess or even a workingwoman, but a housekeeper:

> The acquaintance I had struck up with the old poet of our village brought me the happiness of possessing an intelligent and sweet companion, the sort that I needed and that few people can boast of having. You know our friends, our home. Our household is the sort one might well wish for many people in our wretched society.[61]

This is the ambiguous happiness that must be presented to the worker Joseph so that he may be led to realize that the apostle's study and activity are accessible to every worker of good will. The conceded normality is to permit the maintenance of the slight deviation, the different aspiration that calls for the working-class army to start moving toward the new heaven. This difference, this other pulse in the shared destiny of work's struggles, is ever threatened. The prosaic Joseph is all too ready to heartily congratulate the man who has renounced the illusions and enthusiasms of poetry. Of what use could that fever be today? It is "more sensible and consoling" for him to renounce this alien malady that causes some to be treated as madmen and others to die of misery, and is cured in the case of some only by prostituting themselves for the powerful. In the face of this prosaic banality, it is necessary to defend the priesthood that denounces the tyrannies of the old world and brings enthusiasm to the heart of the people. And that is why it is necessary to liquidate for good the fallen poet Charles, the man who has fallen to the lowest depths for having wanted to ascend too high. Returning toward the barrier to get back to "their too hard bed, where they always find a peaceful sleep and sometimes dreams of happiness,"[62] Joseph and André will see a man being led away, drunk and disfigured, covered with blood and dirt, his clothes in tatters. It is

61. Ibid., p. xix.
62. Gilland, "L'incompris," ibid., p. 86.

Charles, of course, who had been caught in the mists of wine and a brutish brawl. He is led away to the station house and the company of thieves, drunks, and prostitutes, leaving there only to go to the hospital and die of the blows he had received.

The definitive liquidation of a man who wanted to use poetry to flee the worker's condition: this time not in the solitude of a room where the vitality of the angel is worn out but in the sewer of a population that has gone back to animality. It is no longer simply a death or a suicide; it is a degradation in the military sense of the word. It is the announcement of a different hierarchy, a different honor: that of work. The morning star . . . By 6:00 A.M. the next day, Joseph and André will be at the workshop. In 1848 an old locksmith will say it to Pierre Vinçard: "Our trade is visibly becoming moralized. We have destroyed Monday." And the father of Georges and Urbain will comment: "He was as proud as the disabled soldier who says, I fought at Austerlitz."[63]

A straight line drawn by crooked paths? Apparently it was necessary to go through a few heresies before these new converts could succeed where the priest of the people failed. The final victory of the Galilean, or rather of his disciple of the eleventh hour, the one whose maxim will be inscribed on the front page of L'Atelier: "He who does not want to work should not eat." Finally everything is in order, and we can leave locksmith Gilland, reconciled with his image and his colleagues, to his working Mondays. He surely will have merited the eulogy given by his friend Corbon, who offered him as an example to a turner who was not content with his lot:

> You knew G——, the locksmith of Faubourg. . . . He was not the sort of man who had the least contempt for his craft. He performed it with pleasure even. It is for that reason that he never lacked for work, and always having to do delicate work, he earned his livelihood all the better. . . ; That did not prevent our friend G—— from giving sizable satisfaction to the needs of his spirit after he had applied himself to his daily work. . . . And if he took off from work on Monday, so as not to be all alone at the workshop, it was with his books that he spent the many days that others spend . . . you know where.[64]

He took off from work on Monday! These Christians are bigger liars than the last of the Cretans. We must begin again from the beginning.

63. Pierre Vinçard, Les Ouvriers de Paris, Paris, 1851, pp. 120–21.
64. C. A. Corbon, De l'enseignement professionnel, Paris, 1859, pp. 67–68.

Part II

The Broken Plane

"Soon the plane will be broken for you."
—Bergier to Gauny,
May 1832

CHAPTER 6

The Army of Work

HIS NAME IS ARMAND HENNEQUIN, aged twenty-seven; born in Belgium of a French father, the chief customs collector there. He lived for a long time in Sedan, where he had been a copying clerk in a large cloth mill. Having been a bailiff's clerk and then secretary to the Marchioness Duchillon, he is, like many others, people of pen or tool, "without occupation to his taste and capacity" since the glorious July Revolution (1830) undid the existing order of work and social position.[1] And so from writing work

1. Report of Delaporte, Fonds Enfantin, Bibliothèque de l'Arsenal, Ms. 7816. Unless otherwise indicated, the citations of this chapter refer to the dossiers of *L'Enseignement des ouvriers* that contain the reports of the ward directors and directresses, put in place by the Saint-Simonian hierarchy from July 1831 to the end of November 1831 (the date of the "schism" between Enfantin and Bazard). Carton 7815 contains the reports relating to the first six wards (*arrondissements*): the Right Bank, with the exception of the quarters of Arcis and Quinze-Vingts. Carton 7816 contains materials relating to the other six wards: the two quarters mentioned above, the islands, and the Left Bank. To avoid a mass of notes, I offer the following list. It gives for each ward the directors and directresses whose reports are utilized, followed in parentheses by the names of the workers under their jurisdiction:

First ward: Moroche, Madame Dumont; then first and second wards combined: Clouet, Haspott (Brion, Chapon, Desclos, Dodmond, Grossetête, Knobel, Lebeau, Rossignol).

Third ward: Biard, Madame Biard (Adélaïde Baudelot, Fontaine, Maire, Sarrazin).

Fourth and fifth wards: Botiau, Eugénie Niboyet (Bar, Béranger, Bernard Louis, Brosset, Brousse, Chazeret, Chérot, Colas, Coligny, Conchon, Dagoreau, Delanoë, Feytaud, Guindorff, Jeandin, Lambinet, Fanny Lebert, A. Lenoir, Lhopital-Navarre, Madame Molière, Madame Peiffer, Madame Pierron, Raimbault, Martin Rose, Ruffin, Vedrenne).

Sixth ward: Prévôt, Véturie Espagne (Boissy, Madame Lauzanne, Claudine

he descended to the making of quill pens. But the early symptoms of a new misfortune are added on to the bitter consequence of the people's victory: the merchant who used to supply him with quills can no longer bring them in from the Orient because of cholera. Now Hennequin must purchase them from wholesalers by the case, fifty thousand in each. He cannot, however, borrow the hundred francs he needs to buy a case. He already owes sixty francs to a neighborhood workingwoman, whom he is avoiding as long as he lacks the wherewithal to repay her. So he liquidates his stock of quills by making toothpicks for various merchants. That earns him thirty sous a day. Sick, he has not called in a doctor for fear of having to pay him. His garret in the Saint-Victor quarter is almost entirely stripped of furniture. When he has placed all his toothpicks, he will have to think up other ways to earn a living.

He came to Saint-Simonism on his own. Chancing one day to enter the hall of the Redoute, he was taken with the teaching of Father Jules (Lechevallier). He went to see the oldest of the Doctrine's workers, master tailor Clouet, who sent him to Delaporte, the director in charge of teaching workers of the twelfth ward. Aware of the capabilities of this recruit, Delaporte gave him hope that the Doctrine could perhaps help him: supporting his commercial activities by advancing him a hundred francs, requalifying him by giving him copying work to do. In the meantime Hennequin, whose faith is disinterested, uses his free time to propagate the new religion. Not without difficulties, notes his director: "He is a mixture

---

Mantoux, Mongallet, Madame Pottier, Madame Roubaud, Marie-Élizabeth Savy, Viel).

Seventh ward: Lesbazeilles (Courajout, Dallongeville, Dantard, Delaunay, Dupont, Grincourt, Guéneau, Lebret, Mauhin, Minck, Philippe Monnier, Moreau, Orièvre, Perennez, Prété, Welter).

Eighth ward: Raymond and Sophie Bonheur (Barberot—or Barbaroux, Boblet, Bourguet, Carré, Chassard, Coquerel, Derory, Dudin, Gaigneux, Gallet, Geoffroy, Huguenin, Korsch, Lené, P. Lenoir, Widow Percinet, Platel, Quesnel, Thuillier).

Ninth ward: Achille Leroux (Cailloux).

Tenth ward: Bobin, Dugelay (Boutelet, Ménétrier, Nollet).

Eleventh ward: Parent, Adrienne Mallard (Baron, Bonnefond, Chanon, Delacommune, Grégeur, Henry, Langevin, Vieillard).

Twelfth ward: Delaporte, Félicie Herbault (Bergier, Boileau, Bulloz, Chartier, Confais, Dadon, Delvincourt, Deschamps, Dubut, Elliot, Fausse, Gauny, Hennequin, Jousse, Labbé, Lefoulon, Madame Libert, Sophie Maillet, Alexandre Pennekère, Charles and Hippolyte Pennekère, Mademoiselle Pollonais, Quicherat, Tiers, Augustine Tiers).

of the secretary of Marchioness Duchillon and the peddler of toothpicks that is not yet well formed. You sense that he is ill at ease; he hardly dares to approach his brothers." With the help of faith, however, he has begun the conquest of his neighborhood connections and has led several recruits to the Doctrine.

He began with his neighbor on the same floor, Sophie Maillet, a linen seamstress born in the Jura. We do not know how she found herself in Paris in 1819. But the fact remains that she endured the dreaded fate of girls on their own. Seduced and abandoned by a joiner named Guillou, who now practices his craft in Briare, she is raising her son of nine by herself. She has not, however, rolled on to the slope of melodrama that leads inexorably to prostitution. She has a craft that assures her almost sufficient resources, she owes nothing, her son goes to the mutual school, and her lodgings are well kept. One can even see presiding there "a certain touch of taste and cosiness," in which Delaporte detects "the ability to put a household in order" and perhaps could detect wider aspirations. But this modest comfort is completely precarious. Soon Sophie Maillet will find herself driven to put her boy into an orphanage. Need we be astonished that her difficulties as a proletarian and her harsh experience as a woman should dispose her to listen to the Saint-Simonian message? Her experience with the clergy and hypocrites detached her from Christianity a long time ago. And her "readiness to oblige," which has brought her a great deal of ingratitude, prompts her again to leave the solitude in which she had locked up her disillusionment in order to listen to these men and women who want to alleviate the material and moral miseries of the working class. The "sympathetic tendency" that the apostles try to uncover in the manners of their interlocutors can already be read on her face. Undoubtedly the expression in her blue eyes makes clear that she has "more sweetness and goodness than intellectual power." But Sophie Maillet is not devoid of capabilities: "Her language is passionate, although incorrect, often florid, and almost always clever." And so Félicie Herbault, directress of the twelfth ward, gets her admitted not only to the Sunday afternoon lessons on Rue Taitbout, for which the tickets are freely distributed, but also to a private lesson for women given by one of the favorites of the Saint-Simonian hierarchy: Marie Talon.

No doubt this intellectual curiosity is less vividly shared by Hennequin's other neophytes. First there is the former soldier and cloth finisher, Nicolas Grincourt, whom he must have known in Sedan, which was Grincourt's native place. Coming to Paris, Grincourt also found himself without employment in his craft after July. He even joined the newly created municipal guard, for want of anything better. But his wife, whom people consider more "advanced" than him, feared for the future of their adopted child in these troubled times and made him leave the municipal guard. He finally found a place as a common laborer, for one franc fifty a day, in a hat factory in the Popincourt quarter. Hardly enough to pay for the rent and groceries for three people while repaying debts incurred during the period of unemployment. Most of the furniture and effects of the Grincourt family have gone to the pawnshop. He needs three hundred francs to get them out of there, and the new law obliges clients to do it within six months. He still entertains a modicum of hope about managing to do that: if the gentlemen of the Doctrine are interested, he can furnish them with felt hats at the factory price and thus reclaim part of his property. These utilitarian preoccupations do not prevent Grincourt from understanding and propagating the doctrine: in his own way, of course, which is not that of a marchioness's secretary but that of a man of good sense who learned to love order in the army.

Hennequin then tries the distiller Deschamps and practices his preaching at the latter's liquor shop, 131 Rue Saint-Victor. Deschamps, who is the father of four children, has more good will than learning; and his wife is "not yet moved." But she did tell Delaporte that she listened with pleasure to his "son" Hennequin, and Deschamps himself took a blue ticket to go to Rue Taitbout the next Sunday. A little lower down on Rue Saint-Victor, Hennequin is trying to convert the Tiers family. Papa Tiers would be an interesting recruit because he, in his sixties and a Parisian by birth, works at the chimney-sweeping operation at 75 Rue Saint-Victor and exercises a certain influence over the minds of a throng of little chimney-sweeps. But if Tiers is a man "quick to perceive what is just and useful to society, and ready to contribute his share," his zeal for the doctrine is a bit restricted by his family. He has a blue ticket for Rue Taitbout but hardly ever uses it, being in the habit of visiting his brother on Sundays. And his wife, satisfied with the comfort of the household, does not want to hear any talk of Saint-Simonism. Her daughter, Marie-Augustine, is in a better position to comprehend the doctrine. Separated for several years now from her husband, one M. De Bergue, she could get out of the habits of seclusion and solitude in which marital woes have confined her. But the young woman, who sews very well, finds the idea of association repugnant. She does not see herself in the collectivity of a sewing workshop, and she has told Delaporte of her fear of having to wear a uniform. Delaporte, however, has so reassured her about the voluntary and progressive character of the association that he thinks he has actually convinced her. He has no doubt that "if the time comes when uniform and workshop are necessary, she will be the first to desire them."

A little farther away, near the Rue Saint-Jacques, other convinced people bring their parents, relations, friends, and clients. There is the painter Confais, a native of Switzerland raised in Normandy, who traveled quite a bit before settling down in Paris fifteen years ago. He found himself sympathetic to the doctrine when he read *Le Globe*'s long and comprehensive report, published in February, on anticlerical and antilegitimist riots that included the looting of the archbishop's residence. To the resources of his craft Confais adds the exploitation of a furnished lodging-house at 270 Rue Saint-Jacques; and he has pointed out to the Doctrine the most interesting of his clients, Madame Libert, a workingwoman who is paying dearly for her marriage to a young man of good family, who, disowned by his family, has had to join the army. In the same quarter, the young typographer Alexandre Pennekère has converted his elder brothers: Hippolyte, messenger for a dealer in prints; and Charles, the fellow who had once dreamed of being a country curate and later found himself a shoemaker. Weary of that sedentary craft, Charles has become a clerk in a paper shop, at two francs fifty per day. The modesty of his salary has not prevented him from satisfying the "demon of learning" that inhabits him, and he has put together his own little library of three hundred volumes. His tastes are not thwarted by his young female companion, a mender and stitcher presently without work. The "good little woman," who has just had a little girl given the first name July, is not disturbed by the demon of learning, but she does not mean to remain unacquainted with the sentiments and benevolent acts of her spouse. The Pennekère brothers, still boiling with the ardor of the three revolutionary days of July, have begun to make converts: first their sister Lise, also a stitcher, and their brother-in-law, artist-painter Le Foulon. Lise "by her tone and manners can bear close comparison with most of the ladies of the bourgeoisie"; and her husband is to be presented to the Rue Monsigny salon by Monsieur De la Porte (ennobled for the occasion by Félicie Herbault).

Alexandre Pennekère has also undertaken the conversion of typographer Armand Chartier and the more difficult task of converting his wife. She is a clear-starcher laundress who employs four workingwomen; and if she was converted, she could offer a little work to the Doctrine's unemployed lingerie-makers. Hippolyte Pennekère has indoctrinated Elliot, a printer of copper engravings, who also enjoys a relative degree of comfort and uses it generously; besides his two daughters, one apprenticed to a lingerie-maker and the other to a milliner, he is bringing up the son of his brother, a tinman. Like many men working at the frontier of industry and art, Elliot has gotten culture for himself in his own way: "He has read a good bit, but his readings are disconnected." This is characteristic of the age in which this man, born in 1786, must have learned to read. It was mainly in the *philosophes* of the Enlightenment that he found his "confused bits of learning" and the ideas he would not put together very well. We find the same sort of confusion in the bookbinder Bulloz, who stopped his studies in the fourth year at the Mortain high school and gives evidence of "a metaphysical tendency that, left undeveloped, gives little clarity to his ideas and, above all, his style." There ends the comparison between the modest prosperity of the printer and the ill-starred career of the binder. A supernumerary in the tax department in 1812, then a conscript, in 1814 Bulloz saw his administrative career shattered by his political opinions. He then learned the craft of binding and tried to set up on his own; but success did not follow. Bulloz had to sell his workshop and go out looking for work. Without work for eight months, he owes three hundred francs to friends and has left some of his effects at the pawnshop.

In the Saint-Marcel quarter, it is the former drum major Bergier who presides over recruitment. He now practices the craft of floor-tiler, which yields good days on which he earns four francs but also offers almost six off-season months a year. With the two francs a day earned by his wife as a lingerie-maker, however, he seems to be in a position to pretty nearly meet the needs of his household and his two young children. Delaporte ascertains that the furniture is good enough, the household properly kept up, and the little library very well put together. For Bergier's taste for letters developed during his days as a soldier; and if he earns his living as a floor-tiler, letters alone have his love, and he dreams of devoting himself exclusively to them. He has written without success for the theater, and "what drew his attention to the doctrine is his bruised ability."

And so Bergier, little predisposed to the role of preacher by his unsociable character and a slight stutter, has mainly converted men with whom he already shared the fraternity of the same interests: cabinetmaker Delvincourt, intellectually developed enough to read directly the *Exposition de la doctrine saint-simonienne*; Marcel Fausse (a *motteur*, whose work is to make up clods of peat for burning), a man of great intellectual capacity but victim of a terrible disease that rivets him to a hospital bed and makes him the prey of sufferings that have at times led him to the limits of derangement; shoemaker Boileau, who got his education in the fever of the Revolution and from the age of twelve on served in the armies of the Republic and then of the Empire; and a certain "Gony, joiner," whose identity Delaporte was not able to ascertain very well because the "scornful haughtiness" with which he was received had dissuaded him from asking for the usual information. These elective affinities do not prompt Bergier to neglect the propagandizing of his family. And while his wife is putting up some resistance, in the trifling fear of giving up a religion for which she no longer has any devotion, his father-in-law, painter Dubut, is ready to enter the Saint-Simonian association.

In other quarters propagation follows similar paths: affinities, neighbors, families. Talk of the new religion reached the Widow Percinet on Rue de Charonne. She had raised by herself her son, who died from grief over an unhappy marriage, and then her three grandchildren, and now, at the age of seventy-six, must still work to take care of their needs.

> Wanting to see for herself, as she put it, she came last Sunday to the lesson. Returning home, she gathered around her several neighbors who were used to paying attention to her and curious to know what she was going to tell them. She told them: My children, I am seventy-six years old. I have lived an honorable and irreproachable life, but I must tell you today that I shall die a Saint-Simonian.

These words, according to Raymond Bonheur, "had an immense impact on several people." The young folk, for their part, do more organized propagandizing. Engraver Rossignol, whose parents are the caretakers of a house inhabited by a large number of domestics, often gathers them together in the evening at the lodge to expound the Doctrine to them. Typographer Lené was converted by his aunt, Madame Vincent, an embroiderer whose lean weeks are fed by the hope that the coming winter will bring embroidered cloaks back into fashion; on Fridays he has his fellow workers at the royal printing office come together in her lodgings. The director himself has not missed one of her lessons. Joiner Conchon gives lessons at his place, passes out *Le Globe* to twenty or thirty people, and has converted his whole tenement. Capmaker Dantard and cabinet-maker Lenoir, too, seem to have turned their tenement into a little Saint-Simonian island. On Rue de Bourgogne farrier Boutelet converted his whole workshop by himself; he now wants a copy of *Le Globe* left in his forge or with the wineshop next door, which will permit instruction of customers waiting for work to be done.

In general, however, the pathways of proselytism do not follow the organization of workshop collectivities or craft collectivities. The groups of a quarter often have the anomalous shape of the army of proselytes enlisted for Delaporte and Félicie Herbault by Pennekère, Bergier, Hennequin, and others in the twelfth ward. The catalogue seems to discourage in advance any attempt at classification of capacities and organization into association. On November 26, 1831, the list of "acceptants" who have made their profession of Saint-Simonian faith in the twelfth ward runs as follows: one printer, two type-founders, one floor-tiler, two house-painters, one cotton-spinner, one bookkeeper (employed as a carrier at *Le Globe*), two masons, four shoemakers, one apprentice tapestry-worker, one hosier, three joiners, one day-laborer, one common laborer at the mint, one sawyer, one type-polisher (female), one glover (female), two colorists, one cook (female), seven or eight workingwomen (linen-workers, day-laborers, washerwomen, or burnishers). To which is attached a complementary list: three printing compositors, one artist-painter, one gatherer, one clerk, two stitchers, one laundress, and one shoemaker. This unclassable population is noteworthy mainly for those who are absent from it: there is not a single representative of the conspicuous industry in the twelfth ward, the leather industry dealing in skins and hides. It is not among the curriers, tawers, and tanners—who are nevertheless remarkable for their traditions of solidarity and giving help to the unemployed—that the new religion of association is recruiting its partisans. This situation is not peculiar to the "declassed" of the twelfth ward. The working-class quarters in the east show a similar dispersion. To be sure, the cabinetmakers' group is noticeable in the Faubourg Saint-Antoine; but no more than in the Popincourt quarter, center of the jewelers, goldsmiths, carvers, lace-makers, and tanners of Morocco leather of the Fabrique de Paris, where the cabinetmakers and piano-makers constitute the foundation of the house of association. It is not in the established worker families, in these craft republics whose solidarity goes hand in hand with their exclusivity, that the new religion and the new family can grow and develop; rather, it is in the dispersion of individuals whom no family or territorial law rivets to the place where they reside, whom no tradition or vocation has destined for the craft they exercise.

These groups based on affinities and chance, isolated from the great worker concentrations, are not for that reason collections of marginal people. Undoubtedly, a few shattered fortunes and a few lost military or nobiliary glories contribute their note of nostalgia or eccentricity. Former blacksmith Haspot, director of the first ward, is not unmoved when he runs into a man named Fontaine: former officer in the Grand Army, then director of a mutual school in the Midi, then the victim of reactionary fanaticism, and now reduced to singing in the streets. For her part, Adélaïde Baudelot, a hair-braider whom fifteen years of poverty have reduced almost to a skeleton, evokes memories of a grandfather who had been an adviser to the Parlement. Masson de Coligny, placed in the printshop of the Doctrine, dreams nonetheless of the glory of his family and his past as a guard of Joseph Napoléon. Elsewhere there are old dreams that never manage to resign themselves to labors that, in fact, are not even among the most repugnant. Cabinetmaker Dudin "was born for less material works." Mauhin the tailor, who prides himself on having done work for Terneaux, manufacturer and member of parliament, has composed a work on the heredity of the peerage in his spare moments, of which he unfortunately has no lack. On the morrow of the July days, he also addressed a profession of political faith in verse to Casimir Delavigne. The illustrious author has made him some promises, but he is content to send him some places for his pieces. Elsewhere again one encounters an unappreciated inventor, Chanon the tapestry-worker:

> He is taken up with perfecting the trade he practices. The discoveries he has made in this direction occupy him exclusively. They are his life, his happiness, his whole existence. . . . He wants to have the certainty that the fruit of his labors, of his late-night work, will not be buried in oblivion, that his name will be attached to it. That is his ambition; and present-day society, in which he has found only jealousy, inspires contempt in him. That is why he presents himself to the Saint-Simonian religion.

Chanon does not come with empty hands. He has just invented a window-sash system that allows one to open windows without disturbing the closed curtains. "He is ready to give the results of all his labors to our religion, provided that his name does not perish." Cabinetmaker Thuillier, also a capable man, did not invent anything, but he had a going enterprise. Unfortunately his desire to go too far, too fast, brought on his fall from that flourishing state.

Alongside these too-enterprising men, the missionaries sometimes come across a cenobite who has isolated himself from the fashions and consumptions, if not the ideas, of his time. Thus, hatter Gallet, without work for some months, has sold a piece of property for three thousand francs, using half to give his children a start in life and ready to give the other half to the Doctrine, since he personally has hardly any needs. He showed Raymond Bonheur, director of the eighth ward, a closet filled with completely outmoded clothes that he makes himself from very thick cloth. This attire does not seem to trouble him, any more than does his inseparable umbrella with its circumference of six paces.

Overall, however, this gallery of picturesque portraits makes up a normal population. If one were to make use of very incomplete data to compare the Saint-Simonian rank and file with what the statistics—rough estimates, after all—tell us of the general population, one would find that the former were regular enough. The age of the members is around the average—thirty-three. That will be the average age of those arrested in June 1848, who are more representative of the working-class population in general than of a militant avant-garde, thanks to the arbitrariness of the repression. It is the typical age of the most visible Saint-Simonian workers—for example, those who don the apostolic habit at Ménilmontant: Bergier (thirty-four), Charles Pennekère (thirty-five), and the "butcher" Desloges (thirty-three). This population of average age also reflects the demographic movements of the epoch. Like the overall working-class population of Paris, it is made up for the most part of immigrants, who generally have come to Paris in the course of the last fifteen years. Of sixty workers whose origins are precisely known to us, eighteen were born in Paris, thirty-eight in the provinces, and four abroad. To be sure, the proportion of immigrants in this very limited sample is noticeably higher than that established by Bertillon's statistics for 1833. His figures give an equal division between the indigenous and immigrant populations. But since they are based on the death tables, they inevitably deal with an older population, one essentially prior to the new tide of immigration in the 1820s and 1830s.

On the other hand, the extrapolations we can make here correspond almost exactly to the native–immigrant breakdown (27 percent to 73 percent) of the population arrested in June 1848. If, with all corrections made, the immigrant population remains slightly overrepresented in both cases, we should undoubtedly view this less as the expression of a militant ardor that retained the savage energy of the soil than as the sign of a precarious state of existence, of the absence of the protective milieu (familial, vocational, territorial, sometimes political) that more readily puts these individuals on the roads commonly used by agents of repression, visitors of the poor, and propagandists of whatever doctrine. The "regularity" of the Saint-Simonian people is also confirmed by their geographical distribution. The new Parisians who constitute the majority were almost all born north of the line from La Manche to Ain that marks the boundaries of immigration in the first part of the century. This geographical frontier, people know, doubles with an imaginary frontier. South of the line, which

Baron Dupin's maps trace from Saint-Malo to Geneva, begins a different territory: *France obscure,* where, except for a few enclaves, the highest concentrations of illiteracy are to be found; the other France, where people commit suicide less but murder more, where they respect human beings less but propertied estates more; the land of temporary migrants (natives of the Auvergne or masons from the Creuse) who invest in land the proceeds of their Parisian labors and occasional swindling; the territory of journeymen *compagnonnages* and fanaticisms, where Saint-Simonian missionaries will meet with more than one stone.[2]

Normal, in sum, is the word for these men in their thirties who come from the Eure, Ardennes, Yonne, or Somme, marry women who came to Paris by similar trajectories, and have an average of two children by them. Alongside the guild families of *compagnons* and the old endogamous crafts, this aleatory population, in every sense of the word, represents less the army of the marginal or declassed than the proletariat in its very essence that is concealed under the wretched or glorious images of the factory damned or the pioneers of mechanics. They represent very accurately the aleatory history and geography that bring together those individuals who live, each and every one, in the absolute precariousness of having no trump to play but the availability of their arms and suffering from the day-to-day uncertainty of their employment more than from the exploitation of their product. Of course this aleatory population of precarious workers presents a certain hierarchy of positions. At the top we find a few masters who are fairly comfortable: bootmaker Moreau, capmaker Dantard, tailors Delacommune and Martin Rose. The wives of the latter two men, it seems, have the manners of bourgeois ladies. But the most glittering successes in the Saint-Simonian family remain modest. None of the master tailors or bootmakers of the Doctrine are entitled to the honors of the *Almanach du commerce.* And the successes are often fragile. Combmaker Dupont, besides his six francs a day and the salary of his embroiderer wife, has at his disposal his mother's life-annuity and personal property of a thousand francs; but he has had to go heavily into debt to buy his tools and take care of a sick child. So he has liabilities of 615 francs: 220 francs of back rent, 120 francs of "pressing debts," 60 francs "on loan," and 215 francs worth of property (jewelry, watch, and silverware) at the pawnshop.

Unfortunately positions seem more stable at the bottom of the ladder, where more than one character would figure to advantage in *Les mystères de Paris*: for example, the typographer Raimbault, who goes two or three

2. See Charles Dupin, *Forces productives et commerciales de la France,* Paris, 1827.

days a week without eating and whose mother is dying in the hospital. Another such case would be joiner Cailloux, who has been overwhelmed with misfortunes since birth and incapacitated for his craft by an accident on the job. "Lying on his straw, often without sheets or food," he has vainly sought any sort of employment within his capacity; and he now sells in the marketplace knickknacks that bring him fifteen to twenty sous per day. Stripped of everything, no longer able to borrow without hope of paying back, Cailloux spends most of his days without nourishment, except perhaps a pound or a half-pound of bread for himself and his wife, who must watch over the display and is thus prevented from going out to look for work. Sophie Bonheur, joint director of the eighth ward with her husband, arrives at the home of crystal-cutter Korsch at the same time as the tax clerks who have come to seize property unless payment is made immediately. Fortunately they have not swooped down on the feeble defenses of Madame Korsch and her daughter Julie, who have gone out looking for work; they have fallen upon the master of the house, who has had a year to exhaust all the places he might find employment, and his son, who is also without work. So the clerks decide to put off the seizure until the next time. But the next time there will undoubtedly no longer be anything to seize. The Korsch family, who pay—or are supposed to pay—two hundred and fifty francs for the yearly rent of two small and ugly rooms, have been reduced to selling or pawning the contents of their domicile. They no longer have even a coverlet for their little Rosalie, aged seven, who is afflicted with a brain fever. The money obtained by Sophie Bonheur to redeem the coverlet will, unfortunately, not be enough to save the child. But perhaps Raymond Bonheur, author of a discourse at her grave, will be reminded of her in the Fourierist circles where he will later have the opportunity to meet Eugène Sue, the narrator of the identical misfortunes of gem-cutter Morel.

Between those two extremes lies a gradation of positions in which one would find it very difficult to discover a hierarchy of qualifications. Undoubtedly, the unfortunate Cailloux was never a member of the joiner elite. He tells us himself that he derived little profit from his years of apprenticeship: "I never took a liking to the work for the simple reason that I had been overwhelmed by it and never had the least enjoyment of my age." Former soldier Orièvre had been successively a bookkeeper, a porcelain-worker, and a day-laborer, and now seeks to be a carrier at *Le Globe*; according to the classification of his director, Lesbazeilles, he ranks among the "completely worthless." Even more devoid of capabilities is the common laborer Baron, who at the age of fifty-two earns a few sous a day by running errands. All the directors have the same complaint about the sort of people coming to them: too many "unfortunates" (Clouet), men "entirely devoid of any ability" (Raymond Bonheur), "invalids or incompetents" (Parent). But once these have been pushed aside, there remains a population of workers, often the majority, whose capabilities have no means of expressing themselves and of redressing a situation marked by the accumulation of debts. Cailloux undoubtedly never had a calling to joinery work. Achille Leroux, director of the ninth ward, nonetheless recognizes in him "a man who stands out in the class where he is by the facility with which he does certain things." Cailloux had shown him, for example, "a book of songs, a novel, and architectural wash sketches" that struck Leroux as "very well done." The dancing teacher Henry, who once managed a ballroom, could still give lessons; but he would need the proper clothes to present himself to the clientele. Bootmaker Vedrenne had been a cutter in the foremost shops of Paris and could very well direct an association of workers in his craft. In the meantime, he is without work. His wife is an unemployed doorkeeper and hemmer (she assists her husband when he has work). They live with their four children in a small, unwholesome room that contains only a bed and a table. Turner–mechanic Chazeret excels in the art of turning and does some cabinetmaking. He possesses a working stock that could occupy ten persons of his craft. But at the moment he owes 300 francs to his landlord and 200 to various creditors. To begin paying them, he is waiting for the hypothetical returns of little pieces that he has laid out, for a value of 174 francs, at the Bazar Saint-Honoré. Typographer Delaunay, who owes 128 francs and 75 centimes to his baker alone, has no work in his craft and earns a bit of money by making silk hats. Minck the currier, like his one-time soldier colleagues Grincourt and Orièvre, has been reduced to the status of a day-laborer.

But the paradox is that these disqualified states are no more precarious, and sometimes just as remunerative, as those of qualified or skilled workers paid on a piecework basis or working on their own. Grincourt earns one franc fifty a day as a common laborer in a hat factory. That is as much as lace-maker Maire gets, and he is on the job from 5:00 A.M. to 9:00 P.M.; more than copper-mounter Welter, whose day's wages sometimes do not exceed fifty centimes, or self-employed bootmaker Dallongeville, who for the moment is making five francs a week: almost as much as cabinetmakers Carré, Lenoir, and Platel, whose monthly earnings are between thirty-five and forty-five francs. One must take into account the off-seasons, of course, which vary with the craft, and not mistake for ready cash the earnings declared by the interested parties, anxious to show off their capabilities or their distress, as the case may be. But one thing does seem to be certain in the approximate nature of the figures. Because of competition exacerbated by an employment crisis—jobs have not resumed their normal course since July 1830—we see a certain equalization of revenues and a certain leveling of qualifications at work in different ways: forced disqualification of individuals and a decrease in the work given out on a piecework basis or in the price paid for workmanship. Cabinetmaker Dudin spelled out the matter for Raymond Bonheur: he is paid 12 to 14 francs for making a chest of drawers that will cost the buyer 100 francs; 40 francs of that goes for the material and supplies, and 46 to 48 francs are profit for the wholesaler and retailer.

This leveling down toward an average defined by irregularity of position and earnings is attested to by Lesbazeilles's roster of the acceptants of the seventh ward, to take one example: seven of the acceptants enjoy "assured and sufficient" work; eleven have "irregular and insufficient" work; four are without work. But Lesbazeilles, evidently anxious to show that he has not recruited too many "unfortunates" to weigh down the Doctrine, has faked his roster a bit. Into the first category he put apprentice capmaker Guéneau, an adolescent who is housed and fed by his master, himself a Saint-Simonian, and who obviously has no needs (and hardly more convictions, in all likelihood). Into that category he also put cardboard-maker Courajout, who earns one franc fifty a day in a firm that keeps him out of affection but that will soon be unable to employ him. So we must play up the importance of the intermediate category, where the "irregularity" and "insufficiency" of work quickly reach their limit. Such is the case with wood-sculptor Perennez, who is also retained out of affection in a firm where he earns one franc fifty. With this sum, the former seminarian must feed his female companion, who is apparently unemployed, and his three children. Such is also the case of tailor Mauhin, whose three francs were keeping his wife and three children alive without luxuries but who has not been earning anything for two months. And such is the case of copper-mounter Welter, whose wages, sometimes limited to ten sous, must still nourish two children of the six he has raised.

But these fathers with irregular and insufficient work do not fit the classic image of the improvident poor who are equally incapable of feeding their children and limiting their procreation. Taking into account the quite extraordinary attractions offered by the prospect of Saint-Simonian boarding schools and retirement homes for old workers, the percentage of large families with many children and elderly people seems modest. And the large families in difficulty encountered by the directors do not necessarily bear witness to any unwholesome proliferation engendered by the humus of poverty. The admission of painter-decorator Chérot and his wife, burdened with six children, to the "preparatory degree" of bourgeois neophytes shows their cultural and social level. Like him, joiner Labbé and tailor Desclos, with five and six children respectively, have had the means to raise their large families. Undoubtedly the most comfortable of Lesbazeilles's proselytes are those who were wise enough to practice restraint. Capmaker Dantard can extend to the amelioriation of the poor the generosity he had been extending to ungrateful nephews since his own household has no children. His tenement neighbor, bootmaker Moreau, waited until he was past thirty to wed a woman thirteen years younger, by whom he has a little girl put out to be nursed. But it is not evident, for all that, that those who choose to marry young, and who have two or sometimes three children between their twentieth and thirtieth birthdays, are acting out of the brutish lack of foresight that economists ascribe to the poor. In a world where retirement does not exist and where one's labor power is used up quickly, the ways of foresight are not so clear-cut. And a number of indicators tend to show that these fathers lack neither prudence nor solicitude: the fairly general spread of births, which the general statistics of the era show to be sensitive as well to fluctuations in the economic outlook; the rarity of cases of infant mortality reported by the Saint-Simonian visitors; and the care given to the education of children. The average parents, to be sure, are far removed from the affectation with which Caroline Béranger raises her little Sophie, whom Madame Bonheur found to be "intelligent but pretentious," and who would be quite pleased to see Father Enfantin correcting her letters while he was in prison. The attention given to the education of children is also verified by more than one sign. Cabinetmaker Carré splits half of his income between his rent and this education. Nollet the gilder asks for a Saint-Simonian to instruct his children, "desiring to take them out of a school where they are not learning anything." Chair-maker Lebeau even holds up his profession of faith until the promised opening of a "boarding school" so as not to have his children prematurely lose the benefit of the instruction given them by an uncle who is a priest and a sister who is a nun. Generally, these children are then placed in some apprenticeship, only rarely in charitable institutions. And they do not seem to be abandoned to the good will of their masters: bookbinder Jousse does not hesitate to withdraw his son from the hands of a master who is maltreating him.

Thus the levels of foresight and qualification seem to be equally unsuited to defining the normal irregularity of the Saint-Simonian worker population and to explaining the differentiation it presents. Through the difference of trades and family situations, the resources of the majority always seem to revolve around the very same figures. One example attesting to this fact involves the projected house of association for the eighth ward. The Bonheur couple meet with the hesitations of cabinetmaker Lenoir and his colleagues. The latter fear that the association will be "a clever way to exploit them," making them support the upkeep of the families of wallpaper workers, who are less skilled, are more prolific, and work in the factories of the periphery. Say the cabinetmakers: "For a man who earns a good day's wage, it would not be very logical to join up with a man who cannot or does not know how to earn as much." But the ten to fifteen francs per week presently earned by Lenoir and his buddies suggest that the hierarchy they uphold is far more cultural and social than economic. And the projected budget of the house seems to indicate that the factory workers, fathers of large families, do not necessarily need to have the burden of their offspring supported by others. It is alarming, of course, to find that of the twenty-two children in the care of an anticipated association between eight couples, one widower, two bachelors, and four old people, six belong to Boblet alone (Charles, Brutus), a wallpaper printer. But Boblet, with the very slight earnings of his two eldest children and his dressmaker wife, takes in a total of 160 francs a month: that is, 20 francs a head, which corresponds almost exactly to the overall average of 950 francs for forty-five people. To be sure, it is less than the income of copper-founder Derory, whose daily wages of 5 francs assure a monthly revenue of 120 francs to a family of four; and less than the income of cabinetmaker Dudin, who, thanks to the hard work of a laundress wife, takes in the same revenue of 120 francs for four. But it is as much as, or more than, the incomes of his fellow printers, Chassard (80 francs for four persons) and Barberot (95 francs for five); of mattress-carder Huguenin (70 francs for four); and above all, of the cabinetmakers with "good daily wages" Platel (50 to 60 francs for three) and Carré (50 francs for three). The fluctuation of the figures gives a sort of average minimum living wage of 20 francs per person a month, in which differentiated social needs are neutralized. This minimum living wage of the churlish wallpaper-printer and the elegant cabinetmaker will also be that of the artist–apostle. When Raymond and Sophie Bonheur, too occupied with their apostolate to exercise their already fairly unremunerative arts as painter and musician, ask the Doctrine to take care of their family, the budget estimated for them and their four children will come to the same 20 francs a head: 24 francs for bread, 15 francs for lunch, 30 for dinner, 4 for beer, 30 for rent, 15 for wet-nurse expenses, and 10 for laundering—120 francs for the upkeep of six people.

This minimum living wage, around which revolve the revenues of the Saint-Simonian proletarians, is obviously a bit higher than the figures used by philanthropists to establish the *comfort* threshold for working-class households. In the early thirties, Bigot de Morogues has a family of five living comfortably in Paris on annual income of 860 francs.[3] Ten years later, Gérando will have the same family living on 840 francs and 15 centimes (scientific accuracy obliges).[4] In 1831 Raymond Bonheur and his followers, on the other hand, needed 1,200 francs simply to keep five people alive. It is true that the philanthropists, who do not haggle about workers' consumption of bread, are more stingy about their consumption of meat and vegetables—not to mention liquor, of course, which they can hardly limit too much; that a kilo of bread costs them 27 to 34 centimes "on the average," whereas Voinier apparently pays 42 centimes for it, admittedly in a year of bad harvests; that 19 francs and 95 centimes suffice Bigot de Morogues for the cost of furniture, tobacco, and other frivolous things; and that Gérando in 1841 is still paying only 50 francs rent that already in 1831 costs Madame Vincent and gas-man Brousse 100 francs, Welter and Raimbault 120 francs, tailor Bernard and Dallongeville 140 francs, Voinier and gilder Bourguet 200 francs, porcelain-painter Bazin 240 francs, and Korsch and Dupont 250 francs. These latter figures are undoubtedly a bit high. In 1841 mechanic Schachérer, refuting Gérando, will put at only 115 francs the rent of a family that is "among the lowest-paid." But their rents indicate precisely that Korsch, Voinier, and their comrades have not always been in their current wretched position, that their destiny is not an inexorable distress but a day-to-day balancing of income and expenses that is menaced by the least mishap and that can be undone by the mere addition of some unforeseen circumstances to the contingencies of work: a wife's sickness for Voinier; that of a child for Dupont; the care of invalid parents for joiner Gaignieux; the death of a spouse for cabinetmaker Carré or for Madame Moret, directress of a sizable laundry business; the accident of joiner Cailloux; the debt not paid to dancing teacher Henry; the cutoff of quill supplies for Hennequin; and so forth.

A minuscule event could likewise ruin any of those minuscule enter-

3. Bigot de Morogues, *De la misère des ouvriers et de la marche à suivre pour y remédier*, Paris, 1832, pp. 53–54.
4. Gérando, cited by Schachérer, "Budget des travailleurs," *La Ruche populaire*, Aug. 1841.

prises that combine the hazards of pay with those of capital and that function, like the big enterprises, only on the uncertainties of credit. One example is the business of last-maker Prété, who is used to making advances of 300 or 400 francs and paying, depending on the returns, the 200 or 300 francs of back rent he owes his landlord. Or that of tailor Chapon, whose wife keeps up a table for the workers and who has 1,000 francs of credit and 700 francs of debit. The cancellation of an order for forms counted upon by the one, unemployment hitting the clients of the other, can at any time be added to a dubious credit, causing them to relapse into the situation in which so many of their fellows flounder: the bill that grows longer at the baker's (the 128-franc debt of typographer Delaunay represents almost six months' worth of bread for a family); the increasingly exorbitant weight of rents that were in proportion to income not so long ago; the pawnshop, where one finds the external signs of differentiated riches that are rendered equal by bankruptcy—the gold watch of bootmaker Bar at 30 francs and the gold watch of Dupont the combmaker at 130 francs.

How could these men, whose displacements around the threshold of the minimum mimic bourgeois rises and falls, believe speeches affirming the material and moral omnipotence of work? If the Saint-Simonian message can make itself heard, is it not to the extent that it, in being directed to people who live the universe of work as that of chance, does not separate the question of industriousness from that of providence? Isn't it that it touches to the quick of their personal experience these workers for whom being an artisan on one's own, a day-laborer in a factory, a correspondence clerk, a dealer in knickknacks, or an actor in little theaters is a matter of happenstance? It is not the marginality but the very experience of the proletarian condition, the awareness of work in the abstract, that is expressed in the job applications, indifferent to permutations of qualifications, that simultaneously accept the declassing of the common laborer and aspire to the dignity of bourgeois occupations and considerations. Such is that of lace-maker Voinier, the man whose nice "little household" was ruined by his wife's illness. Voinier, who is "intelligent and able-bodied" according to Eugénie Niboyet, is willing to serve as "a common laborer, domestic servant, messenger, in order to earn bread for his wife." But this situation of seeking work and this acceptance of domestic servitude only reinforces his irritability at seeing, on Rue Taitbout, the proletarians pushed out of the empty seats reserved for bourgeois people who are late: a republicanism dovetailing with a professional vocation that is not in lace-making or the handling of goods but in written accounts of a certain kind. Disagreeing with Enfantin's line, Voinier will find in the Society of the Rights of Man secretarial work that is more in line with his own convictions and capabilities, but only moderately remunerative (eighty francs per month) and equally exposed to a precariousness that in this case will take on the visage of prison.

A political identification closer to a social identity that brings out the abstraction of work at the core of the fluctuating good and bad fortunes of the proletarians. This is well expressed in the letter where "bookseller–stallkeeper" Ruffin gracefully accepts the fact that the coveted position of carrier on *Le Globe* has been given to a "good brother," chair-maker Dagoreau, but also recommends himself for any and every other opportunity: "I would remind you that no sort of work in line with my physical and moral powers as well as my capabilities (is repugnant to me), according to the fundamental principles of our Doctrine; and that, if need be, I could wear blouse, short jacket, and cap . . . or don broadcloth coat and pants."[5] It is first in the clothes that he wears that the work of the tailor is to disappear. The encounter of pen and tool takes place quite naturally at this point of indifference, produced by the normal irregularity of proletarian destinies, where the blouse is interchanged with the coat. So it is and it is not by chance that this dealer in second-hand books is chosen by Enfantin to play the great scene of the kiss for the proletarian.

Blouse or coat—they exemplify an average condition and paradoxical principle of differentiation for a population in which the hierarchies are as sharply shown up as they are ill-founded. The questions of differentiation in dress surely have their place there; the alleged professional superiority of the cabinetmakers in the eighth ward over the wallpaper-printers may well be mainly a question of appearance; the latter, notes Raymond Bonheur, are "less sensitive about their dress." But what grounds the superiority of the Saint-Simonian worker elite is perhaps not so much the neutral elegance of their dress as their cognizance of the equivalence between blouse and coat, of this abstraction of work that marks proletarian identity more than does swarthiness of forehead, robustness of limb, or callousness of hand.

The coming of the missionaries of this new philanthropy, which seeks to alleviate proletarian woes while suppressing charitable almsgiving and inheritance, plays the role of analyst with respect to this mixed working-class population. It sends off in the same direction those comfortable workers who are satisfied with their craft or confident about the promo-

5. Ruffin to Michel Chevalier, Fonds Enfantin, Ms. 7606.

tional virtues of work, and those unfortunates who regard the Doctrine as an employment agency or a charitable institution. But it brings together in the idea and practical perspective of *association* workers differing in qualifications, resources, and lifestyles but united by the same feeling of precariousness and by the same will to try a pattern of social relationships offering both an individual outlet and the example of a solution that might be offered for collective precariousness. In the Bonne-Nouvelle quarter, which serves as a middle ground between the Chaussée-d'Antin and the working-class quarters to the east, Eugénie Niboyet quickly perceives the necessity of forming not one but two associations, "because of the development of some and the brutish degradation of others." The "advanced" ones, who are asking to be associated with each other, for the moment belong almost to two different worlds. Tailor Martin Rose is comfortable and his wife "seems rather to belong to the comfortable class than the poor class by virtue of her manners." The family of mechanic Guindorff has personal property of 3,000 francs; his wife and daughters sew to perfection; but they are even more remarkable for the intellectual capabilities that give them direct access to the bourgeois preparatory degree. The same holds true for the wife of tailor Colas; and clockmaker Charles Béranger, who has exchanged his tools for the pen of the journalist, claims to be satisfied with his salary. By contrast, painter Chérot and chair-maker Dagoreau are without work; so are Voinier and bootmaker Vedrenne, whose distress is well known. What brings them together is perhaps, first of all, the fact that the talk and manners of the latter four men still indicate a more favored position once upon a time, and the fact that the first four are aware of the precariousness of their privileges. Madame Guindorff "says she has large resources and the certainty of an inheritance"; she nevertheless is without work for the moment and has 600 francs of debit against 400 francs of credit. Béranger will truly need his expected inheritance of 1,200 francs to pay back his 900-franc debt. This sort of personal experience of the neutralization of conditions is suited to arousing an interest in the doctrine akin to that expressed by printer Giot in his profession of faith: "It isn't either wealth or poverty that engages me in this matter."[6] What engages them all in this venture, besides the recognized limitations of the promotional powers of work, is the limit deliberately set on the hopes placed in it: an attitude perfectly expressed by the man who would be the first soldier of "the peaceable army of workers," Desloges, who has been "a saddler, coach-maker, tailor, *chef de départ,* cook, clerk, cartridge-

---

6. Giot, Profession of faith, Fonds Enfantin, Ms. 7794.

maker, plater, digger, blacksmith, mason, under the appearance of many other crafts and always with a different expectation [i.e., of a new life]."[7] That expectation has made them all look for some way besides work to lift themselves out of the misery of their proletarian lives by linking their own destiny to others: the "society of beneficent men," which Chérot had entered as a young man before being undeceived by its doings;[8] the political fever of Voinier and Dagoreau for the liberty of July or Poland the martyr; the yearning of Reine Guindorff for the learning that was denied to women and that she would have her sisters benefit from.

This different expectation equalizes the desire of the very capable and too well informed seamstress and that of the illiterate and unskilled worker tailor, Delas, "feeble companion, working little and badly, hence earning and living on next to nothing, with no thought of the morrow," who has the same reply for all advice given him to improve his skills: "Bah, that will not last. Have I been made to sew little stitches forever?"[9] A few years later, however, when he has nothing better to do, Delas will take sufficient interest in sewing to invent a machine for taking measurements and establish the General Association of Tailors, Delas and Company. And if he considers his vocation to be something other than needlework, he will still manage to play his role in the modern and mute version of the Sermon on the Mount delivered to the population assembled on the hill overlooking Montereau by the soldier–missionaries of the peaceable army of workers —he will be religiously occupied in fraternally sewing the pants and red vest of the tailor.[10] It is true that disdain for the shabby details of one's craft can accompany an abstract love of work. The somewhat condescending eulogy of the tailor–apostle in Vinçard's memoirs is accompanied by a frank affirmation of the gap separating love of work from relish for one's craft: "They say that it is good to make children start work at a tender age, that it makes them better practitioners. I am not a very convincing example of this, because I, for all my good will, have never been anything but a very mediocre worker. Be that as it may, I did pick up the habit, or, better, the love of work, which is certainly something."[11] Yes, that is certainly something, but nothing definite and precise. Hence the possibility of passing off as a correction of words what is really a substitution

7. Desloges to Ollivier, Fonds Enfantin, Ms. 7714.

8. Chérot, Profession of faith, Ms. 7794.

9. Pierre Vinçard, *Mémoires épisodiques d'un vieux chansonnier saint-simonien*, Paris, 1879, p. 95.

10. *Livre des Actes*, Paris, 1833, p. 33.

11. Vinçard, *Mémoires épisodiques*, p. 10.

between two words that are so often put in opposition by the tongue: habit–love. A marriage of reason and convenience in which the routine of work is deemed to offer the means of escaping the servile condition: in the framework of a society divided into classes, "it is fortunate that work is indispensable, because if it were not, the poor would live completely at the discretion of the rich, who would be masters of their lives or deaths by giving or refusing them the primary necessities of existence."[12]

The apparent absurdity of this reasoning points up the sore point and the most intolerable contradiction of the relationship of exploitation— the transformation of the instrument of liberty into an instrument of ser- vility, the process of applying for work in which one finds oneself face to face with those one feeds. Says one of the comrades of the fellow cited above: "I held servitude in horror. But often, in spite of myself, I had to work for masters who, having drunk deeply of my sweat, still thought they were doing me a charitable favor in giving me my pay."[13] Hence the two seemingly contradictory shapes assumed by the rejection of servility: the "diligent and continuous work" (i.e., not subject to the constraints of demand) that Giot hopes for;[14] and the freedom that Guérineau says he has quite often paid for with privations. Hence, also, the constant slip- page between the discourse of the Saint-Simonian propagators and the discourse to be found in the professions of faith made by the workers. The Saint-Simonian propagators hammer out in every key the opposition between the *workers* who produce wealth and the *idlers* who seize it as their possession, whereas in their professions of faith the workers constantly come back from that economic opposition to the social opposition be- tween *the rich* who give work and *the poor* who are forced to beg for it. This social distribution, this fixation on the dual relationship of demand, hardly authorizes anyone to conceive the notion that the producers could save themselves. This salvation requires not so much the collectivization of the instruments of production as a rupture in the process of social domina- tion. To the struggle that the workers, by joining together in association, can wage against a perilous chance whose real name is competition must be added the miracle of a split in the process reproducing the ruling class. And that is exactly what is represented by this new society of young poly- technicians, lawyers, doctors, and other young men of good family who,

12. Cochareau, Profession of faith, Fonds Enfantin, Ms. 7794.
13. Guérineau, Profession of faith, Ms. 7794.
14. Giot, Profession of faith, Ms. 7794.

in a practical way, are again pointing an accusing finger at the chance of birth and the system of egotism, and giving up ready-made business careers and preferments to dedicate their abilities to improving the material and moral condition of the laboring class. The professions of faith made by the worker neophytes bear witness to this miraculous reversal of the logic of the system, which surpasses any and all philanthropy: "I could not imagine that people so unselfish existed. . . . I set foot on a land unknown to me. . . . I thought it was a dream appearing to me. . . . I approach closer, and imagine my astonishment when I became convinced that your assembly was made up of but a single family."[15]

For these human beings suspended between work and assistance, constantly thrown back from the feeling of fatality to the fight against oppression, this new family represents, more than the rationality of an organization of work, a different space for their lives as workers: a helping milieu for the weakness of the disinherited, whose act of work is constantly pushed back again toward the act of demanding it, as if toward its limit; a chosen milieu restoring these human beings to the dignity of their nature, which is sunk in the twofold servitude of work and the quest for it: "Before you, we were merely the springs of an immense machine that operated only on need; now that your voice has spoken and your doctrine has been understood, we are, or at least we are becoming, human beings."[16] Painter Laurent Ortion and his colleagues have no need of Latin to grasp the great principle of Saint-Simonian philology: a new *religion*, that is, a new *tie* or *link* (Latin *re-ligare*) between human beings. The organization of work is really the institution of the family of workers. The word that attracts these men to the Doctrine, far more than the words *work* and *association,* is the word *love.* Delaporte's sharp eye sees clear evidence of this fact in Mademoiselle Pollonais, colorer of engravings, whose family was of old linked to that of Beaumarchais and whose early years were "surrounded by *philosophes*":

> She has not yet attained a very lofty social viewpoint. What seems to have prompted her adherence is not so much the broad and immense goal of association and universal transformation, which she likes but finds hard to embrace in its full compass, as the happiness of having around her a family of her own choice to love

15. Professions of faith by Guérineau, Madame Nollet, and Colas.
16. Laurent Ortion, Profession of faith.

and be loved by. But from the standpoint where her organization and education have placed her, she is attached to us by the most indissoluble tie—by the love she has for us and expects from us.

A family of her own choice to love and be loved by: an undefined relationship on the boundary between fraternal friendship and the need for protection by relatives, between egotistical intimacy and the tenderness of self-sacrificing attachments; a decent love that imperceptibly displaces the rules of social reproduction. One in the image of those couples whose good understanding and exemplary morality are the paradoxical fruit of a conjugal irregularity: the "wife" of Charles Pennekère, so well matched with her husband, whose dark, loving eyes, smile, and confident air touch Delaporte's heart and whose manners breathe "a pure and gracious modesty devoid of prudery," did not make any stop at city hall, because Charles once entered an unfortunate marriage there; the Feytaud woman, a laundress remarkable for her intellectual development and her "capacity for sympathy," isn't any more married to Feytaud the typographer. Where could one find a more perfect morality than that of Feytaud's young woman, who helps to care for the needs of her mother with the modest earnings of the household and still manages to put some savings into the bank? Yet Father Feytaud is opposed to the marriage, which he undoubtedly regards as disadvantageous for his talented son. The latter, in any case, was able to find the right words to assure his pregnant companion about her future and wept sincere tears over the dead baby. Even more meritorious is the attitude of plumber Coquerel, known for being a worker "who has conducted his affairs honorably"; he treats as his own the four children of his companion, separated from a "dissolute" husband who is "unworthy of her." Other irregularities may be due to poverty: weaver Quesnel, former foreman and exemplary worker, victim of all sorts of misfortunes, does not have the thirty francs needed to get married. Former seminarian Perennez may have more ideological reasons for living in a free union with the mother of his three children. As for the unfortunate Henry, he finds consolation for his social fall and his wife's infidelities in his young female companion and his child.

So these relations have nothing to do with the moral effronteries theorized by Father Enfantin. Living in concubinage, Feytaud will not hesitate to denounce them, even at the risk of losing his job at *Le Globe*. The model serving as the norm for these modest deviations is always that of the family, but of a slightly displaced family using the law of affinities to correct the wrongdoings of chance, those of paternal authority, and the economic calculations that also preside over working-class marriages. That is why these "irregulars" can enter into complicity with the representatives of a conjugal order that allows room for some transgression of the family order. Typographer Langevin boasts, to be sure, of "the most tender of mothers," who worked hard to raise him, and of the "perfect" spouse that God has granted him. But he has a tough battle to wage with that tender mother, who is not at all inclined to forget that the perfect spouse did not wait for her son to become a mother. Charles Mallard did not have to defy any authority; but in order to wed and protect—too much, undoubtedly—an embroiderer of sixteen, deprived of a dead mother and of a father who went off to repair a situation in ruins, he rejected the advantageous offer of a father who wanted to "sell" his daughter to him.[17] Former blacksmith Haspott, on the other hand, married against the will of his father. His dedicated human heart had already sensed, on a trip where he met the adolescent girl who was busy taking care of her eleven brothers and sisters, that she would be linked to his existence. And when he came across her again in Paris, in the terrible, solitary situation of the Monnier sisters and Sophie Maillet, he conceived and executed the plan of marrying her in the face of all opposition. His protective love was apparently more fortunate than that of the ill-starred Charles Mallard, who was abandoned by his Adrienne, but not completely unlike that of Mallard's sister-in-law, Suzanne, who forgot her wound as a seduced daughter of the common people in the task of making a man out of the gallant and queer Voilquin and in the hope, ever disappointed, of maternity.

These experiences are also close to the destiny of those solitaries who have expanded their own disappointed affections or maternal feelings into humanitarian passions. Such are the two heroines of July who have come to find in the loving calm of the apostolic family what they had vainly sought in the fever of the barricades: midwife Marie-Louise Rondet and seamstress Julie Fanfernot. Orphaned at an early age, Rondet soon separated from her husband. After some studies in surgery, she decided to try her luck in Argentina. Shipwreck landed her in Africa, where she took care of smallpox victims for a time. She returned to France and was decorated for her actions in July, but she was not able to win recognition for her surgical inventions and break down "the envy that ordinarily is directed at women who have the courage to rise above their sex."[18]

As for Julie Fanfernot, she had experienced something even harder than

17. Mallard to Lambert, June 1832, Fonds Enfantin, Ms. 7757.
18. *Le Globe*, Dec. 17, 1831.

the fate of being an orphan. Throwing her out of their home and heart, her parents had said to her: "In giving you life, we gave you more than we ever intended."[19] From the age of fourteen on, she kept several families alive with the work of her hands and her industrious intelligence. But instead of honors and the joys of marriage, she came to know the distress of mothers who are in danger of losing their child because they can no longer pay for its nursing expenses. Incapable of finding, in the absence of her son, the energy needed to buy him back, Julie traveled a hundred miles on foot to see him again. "She did more. She settled down near him, far from all the practices of her trade. She worked there as a reaper gathering in the harvest. For a long time she earned twelve sous a day and finally managed to get her son back." A heroine of the barricades, later arrested for coming to the defense of an old man mistreated by the authorities, Julie had always refused to go scraping and bowing in the antechambers of the new monarchy in order to solicit a decoration. But for this child of hers, reborn of work that dried up her hands and bent her forehead toward the soil, she accepted the ministerial favor of a school uniform and a scholarship that would permit him to be brought up with the "privileged elite."

The sufferings of childhoods that chance or the harshness of the old order stripped of love; adolescences brutally thrown into the misery of work or the perils of seduction; the rejection of patriarchal authority and marriages of convenience; the self-sacrificing dedication of eldest sons; the tender affection of protective spouses for the fragility of working girls; motherhood dearly won or painfully vanished: all these sentimental trajectories, normal affections, and minute deviations divert the energies that work consumes—rarely enough for their well-being, but often too much for their taste—toward these places where conjugal irregularities and elective affinities can expand into humanitarian passions. Such is the case in these halls where Enfantin, Barrault, Baud, or Retouret, surrounded by young apostles of imposing majesty and young women of charming modesty, get across the impassioned accents of the new love; where Claire Bazard asks her "children" to draw near in order to get them to admit the grief that blurs their glances with tears. In this maternal look at the griefs of the children of the people perhaps something is at work that will justify the protest and retreat of this too attentive mother. Not the ordinary disorders or ridiculous dodges of fickle tailor Brion: "Something is bugging me, and I must wait for it to get off my back." His colleague

19. *Oeuvres de Saint-Simon et d'Enfantin*, Paris, 1865, V, 154.

Colas saw through the futility of that clearly enough: "There are secrets that penetrate and always reach the heart of a tender mother."[20] Rather, there is a more upsetting secret on the faces of these women to whom the mother of workers simply does not know how to speak. It cannot be out of simple prudery that she will soon denounce the immoral apostle of the joint emancipation of women and workers. It is, perhaps, from some presentiment of a more hidden immorality that she stops at the edge of the road at whose end, eight years later, two years after the suicide of Reine Guindorff, daughter of the common people Suzanne Voilquin will bid farewell to her father, friend, and lover Enfantin. In the glances blurred with tears of joy that express the fraternal communion of the proletarians and the bourgeois, that virtuous spouse may have glimpsed the discreet flame of an unknown adultery.

20. Professions of faith by Brion and Colas, Ms. 7794.

CHAPTER 7

The Lovers of Humanity

Thrown on this earth by parents whose whole heritage was nothing but the misfortune granted at all times to the laboring classes. . . . Without parents on this earth, without resources, left to myself and abandoned in the midst of a world little concerned about my weakness and misery. . . . Thrown into the world at the age of fourteen without props or education. . . . I believed myself deprived forever of maternal kindness. . . . I was longing for something that I did not know, that I could not yet know, since I had not yet heard those words that should reverberate in the depths of every heart. Before I heard them, those consoling words . . . I often regretted that my parents had given birth to me so that I could see suffering and suffer myself.[1]

UNDOUBTEDLY PAINTER LAURENT ORTION, tailor Lenz, Madame Nollet, and dressmaker Antonia Chollet did not go very far to find the terms that serve as beads in their long plaints about their disinherited childhoods, their orphan existences, and their faceless loves. The models are furnished by texts written by two sons of the common people who have attained the dignity of apostles. "I was hurled into the midst of a humanity that my heart tried hard to find loving . . .": that is how it is put in the profession of faith by painter Machereau, the son of a porter.[2] And in his article and pamphlet we find former blacksmith Haspott describing the abandonment

---

1. Professions of faith by Laurent Ortion, Lenz, Madame Nollet, Antonia Chollet; Fonds Enfantin, Bibliothèque de l'Arsenal, Ms. 7794. Most of the professions of faith cited in this chapter come from this carton; the reference will not be repeated when that is the case.
2. Machereau, Profession of faith, *L'Organisateur*, March 5, 1831.

of working-class sons, "left to themselves without advice or support."[3] These models for the use of proletarians, in turn, echo the more aristocratic complaints of the orphaned René, who was delivered into the hands of strangers and forced to set out all alone on the stormy ocean of a world whose harbors and reefs were equally unknown to him.

There is no reason to doubt the truth of these proletarian miseries just because the narrative account of them is modeled on the recital of those immaterial sorrows. Listening to and learning by heart, reading and recopying, decomposing and recomposing the few texts that one has managed to expropriate from the patrimony of the literate: that is the natural way in which those who have not been educated in schools can simultaneously express the sorrows of their condition and take their first steps in the territory of their own emancipation. It is in accordance with this method of "intellectual emancipation" that Joseph Jacotot would have every proletarian conscious of the dignity of his or her being open the *Télémaque* to the chapter on the lamentations of Calypso and there learn the secret of learning everything and expressing everything. How would it not be easier still to learn, in the confessions of the orphans of the century, how to read and speak all the sufferings of these proletarians that society brings into existence only so that there can be too many of them? The common derelictions of the proletarians can be reduced to the form of a family romance and the reckoning of an elementary arithmetic: "Son of a family of five children, of which two were cherished and the other three were victims of the first two": that is how the fate of the unfortunate René is summed up. Joiner Cailloux is more verbose in denouncing the absence of maternal love that is at the root of his umpteen misfortunes:

> Born of a pitiless mother unworthy of the name mother, and losing my father at the age of five months, I was taken by an uncle who raised me until I was ten. Up to that point I was very well. But my uncle, lacking resources, sent me to Paris to his sister's, my aunt. There I found a very different life. This aunt sent me to school. But from 5:00 A.M. I had been up with needle in hand until the very hour for school to open. With a little morsel of bread put in my hand, I headed off to school until it closed, after which I took up the needle again until 11:00 P.M. At the age of twelve I made my First Communion and I was put into apprenticeship. And morning

3. Haspott, "Aux ouvriers par un ouvrier," *L'Organisateur*, June 4, 1831; also published in pamphlet form.

and evening, even at mealtime, I always had needle in hand and was very often overwhelmed with mistreatment, which gave me a terrible disposition. Worst of all, I could not learn to work for want of tools. I collected some tips to get them for myself, which earned me a lot of reproaches and even blows, for that did not cost my aunt anything. I will point out that at the time she was fairly comfortable. Yet she gave me so little to eat that by 6:00 A.M. it was all eaten; and if it had not been for the generosity of my bourgeois [master], I would have gone without eating most of the time. Often, too, I was compelled to force down spoiled grub. In the end, thanks to this sort of treatment, I never took a liking to the work for the simple reason that I had been overwhelmed by it and never had the least enjoyment of my age. With my apprenticeship finished and no possibility of earning my living, my aunt sent me back to my mother. She sent me into the woods. Not bringing her back big enough bundles of sticks, I was again overwhelmed by her mistreatment, so much so that I resolved to head for Paris and beg rather than stay there any longer.[4]

Three years of bondage to a restaurant-keeper, hard labor as a journeyman wine merchant to earn enough to pick up the craft of a joiner once again, a marriage handicapped by the trickery of a mother-in-law, a terrible and ruinous childbirth, the loss of the child at six months, and two accidents on the job that disable him for the practice of his craft will lead Cailloux, again aided by the good heart of his bourgeois master, to go looking for his mother's protection one last time. When it is refused him once again, Cailloux, overwhelmed with suffering, hunger, and despair, will seek refuge in the new family: "I said that I wanted to lay down my crushing burden in the bosom of a true mother and so here it is."

It is entirely logical for Cailloux to ask the Saint-Simonian family for the assistance and affection that he never got from his own mother and aunt but sometimes got from his "bourgeois" masters. More frequent, however, is a course that runs from one's own little family, too quickly undone by the harsh stepmother of society, to a little family reconstituted by a precocious marriage and then again affected adversely by grief or disappointment, and thence to the big family of the Saint-Simonian association. Only "the heavy weight of every sort of misery" compelled the parents of lace-maker Jumentier to abandon their son "to the mercy of all those who

4. Cailloux to Achille Leroux, Fonds Enfantin, Ms. 7816.

clearly chose to take pity on [his] position." Only the death of his own family, "under the weight of sorrows," threw tailor Lenz into life on his own at the age of eight. The caresses of the little family generally form the only cell of protection and love in the face of the harshness of the world of work. "They love each other and seem to be happy": this is something often noted by the directors, who are partly moved and partly irritated by the somewhat exclusivist tenderness of these homes, where, in the interval between the great days of popular rising, people invest the essentials of the ever bruised dream of a society of love. Such was the case with Madame Nollet, thrown into a hostile world too young but lucky enough to find there a loving husband. Before the "surprise" of July and the Saint-Simonian "dream," she had confined all her hopes within the universe of her family: "I no longer wanted to be involved in any society other than that of my husband and children." Sometimes there is a direct path from this broken society to the Saint-Simonian family. So it was in the case of upholsterer Duviquet, who was reduced to poverty by the post-July unemployment and the illness of his young wife, who died carrying the fruit of their love: "Left to myself, yes, my fathers, it is in your arms, in your family, that I shall find true happiness again." More often, however, the path goes by way of the shooting pains of a melancholy born of societal disappointments and humiliations, for which family tenderness often serves as a remedy.

For every misery of proletarian life is doubly intensified by a relationship of humiliation vis-à-vis the rich man who "gives" work and whose gaze continually disqualifies material poverty as moral vileness. Voinier uses contrast to spell out the advantages of the Saint-Simonian future:

> We will no longer see the old septuagenarian dragging his sorry life from door to door, begging for the bread that is often refused him by the rich millionaires who live in mansions, often in debauchery and idleness. . . . In short, we will no longer see, as we have been seeing for more than a year, workers without work, without bread, in rags and misery, lacking the bare necessities, falling over from weakness and need at every streetcorner, while at the same instant one of those people whose hearts are hardened by money and idleness is going by and saying disdainfully: a drunken worker.

On the conventional theme of the opposition between the homeless producer and the mansions of idleness, these texts compose a tiny variation, in which the vigilance of the directors should recognize a sentiment

to be extirpated from hearts not entirely cured of the republican fever—
bitterness, a way of insisting too much not only on the misery of the worker
and the idleness of the rich man', but also, and even more, on the humiliations of the former and the insensitivity of the latter; in short, a way of
transforming social inequality into a debt of honor, of declaring the debt
inextinguishable and reconciliation impossible between the offender and
the offended. This is the sentiment evident, for example, in the profession
of faith of the unappreciated Bergier, stifled in all his attempts to soar beyond his own sphere: "Twenty times I attempted the prodigy and twenty
times I was driven back by the barrier of considerations and privileges."
But others have no need of his vanity as an offended author to recognize
his description of the oppressive social machine:

> Here it is credulity victimized by horrible speculations; there it is
> the humble voice of merit stifled by the insidious voice of intrigue.
> At this point it is egotism with its greedy eye, ready to break all
> social ties to augment the wealth it already possesses to superfluity.
> Farther on, it is the rights of the weak trampled underfoot by the
> colossus of considerations and prerogatives.

Egotism and intrigue, considerations and prerogatives: they have suffered from them without even wanting to surmount any barrier. There
are the humiliations and vengeances endured by the former soldiers of
the Grand Army upon their return to civilian life: finisher Bois, "fallen
. . . by the course of events after 1814 into Fortune's disfavor"; or gilder
Lhoumeaux, "for a long time now bruised by the injustice, jealousy, and
egotism of people, of which I have been the victim since I left military
service in 1815." It may be a more intimate bruise suffered through contact
with the barrier of privileges: a service not recognized by a dignitary of
the Empire that determined Charles Pennekère's hatred unto death of the
rich; a friendship betrayed, in the case of the sensitive Caroline Béranger: "betrayed from childhood in my affections, spurned by a girlfriend
whose heart was changed by good fortune, I cursed the human species
and considered myself disengaged from all friendship."

The seduction of Suzanne Voilquin by a young man from a respectable family; the 120 francs not paid back to Henry by a leading citizen
of ample means; the inventions not recognized; the help not offered; the
sensitivity bruised; the annuities or medals owed but denied; the simple
looks of indifference or acts of scorn: all multiply the debts too deeply inscribed in the flesh and the heart to be paid off later with wage increases.

For these resentments can no longer absolve the rich except at the cost of a misanthropy embracing the whole species: "In all the actions of human beings you see nothing but egotism, mistrust, and bad faith. . . . Almost always betrayed by those in whom I put my trust, my heart was filled with bitterness. . . . Always betrayed, always bruised, always spurned, never understood, I had learned to doubt that sentiments of generosity still existed anywhere."[5] They do not even need to explain how they have been bruised. It is the fate of all those men and women who wanted to take a new look at their condition and learned how to suffer not only their own ills but all the sorrows and humiliations that make up their daily spectacle. The multitude of these clashes with the social order readily link up with the experience of those who have traveled far in the territories of injustice. Soldiers like Bois, for example, who have experienced not only the horrors of war but also the monotony of oppression: "I traversed a portion of Europe in the wake of armies, and everywhere I have seen the weak oppressed by the strong, not only in the most general human relations, but even in the most minute family ties." Or sailors, like occasional lace-seller Maire, who have verified the universal enslavement of man by man from the banks of the Thames to the banks of the Ganges:

> Several parts of the globe that I have traversed have provided me, on a thousand different points, with the opportunity to convert to a half-Christian, half-liberal morality creatures whom the rapacious European blights and brutalizes instead of enlightening. Ha! Had I been a Saint-Simonian, then the echo would have reverberated with the name of Saint-Simon, and I would have experienced some solace for the sorrow I felt at the sight of the tortures merited scarcely or not at all but nevertheless inflicted on old people, pregnant women, and children. . . . You have portrayed the plight of proletarians as almost as wretched as that of blacks. Alas, you have told us the truth. I myself and many others are proof of it. We all know that if, elsewhere, the education of blacks is carried out with whip, torture, and dissoluteness, here the education of proletarians is carried out with sword and bayonet, infamy and immorality.

Savagery is everywhere, in fact: in Poland the martyr, where the over-excited imagination of Dagoreau calls up the "noble victims of despotism

5. Professions of faith by Armand, Martin, and Eugénie Tétard.

whose last cry has reached us"; on the plain of Grenelle, where engraver Rossignol saw a soldier executed for the murder of one of his companions.

To these humiliations felt, miseries observed, and cries of pain heard is added the impossibility of finding fraternal souls with whom to share the suffering:

> In a labyrinth of calamities I was searching vainly for a tie that would bind a few friends to me and thus permit my soul to pour out the sorrows with which it was saturated. A vain hope, because the divided world of opinions and interests, this world completely split up by virtue of the heterogeneous education given to every individual, could not accord me the frank, pure friendship I so ardently desired.

One and the same cause determines the countless forms of oppression and prevents sensitive souls from finding sisterly souls with whom to share their suffering. Guérineau can sum up in a formula the long periodic sentences of Armand: "I looked for human beings but I found only egotism and unfortunates." Insofar as human beings go, he found only authors and victims of human misfortunes. One must look elsewhere for the principles of fraternity: in the solitude where printer Meunier, "distressed at seeing the ills of society, the sufferings of the poor people, the ingratitude and egotism of the rich," will commune with the heroes of humanitarian religion:

> Everywhere I looked for friends with whom I might be able to share my distress. All spurned me. Then I became melancholic; sadness had charms for me. I immersed myself in solitude, and there, to console myself, I read the books of humanity's benefactors. I liked to remind myself of their sublime actions. I experienced a kind of pleasure in these dreams of happiness. No, I said to myself, humanity is not destined to be eternally oppressed. There will be some generous human being who will come to free it, to give it back a new life.

It is without affectation that printer Meunier, whose morbid timidity is pointed out to us by Parent, recomposes the description of his solitary reveries from the text of a former apprentice engraver. The language of Jean-Jacques Rousseau comes naturally to the pen of these sons of artisans to whom nature has given too sensitive a heart, or their earliest education too vivid an imagination, for them to tolerate the workshop hazings of the herd gentlemen, the Messieurs Ducommun, or to share the amusements of their apprentices. The same thing can be detected in the dejections and enthusiasms of chiseler Roussel:

> The only pleasure I tasted now and then was that of being alone in the midst of a wood. There I seemed to be surrounded by the magnificence of the divinity, which I contemplated with love, and also with admiration. There I soared above the depravities of human beings that I bemoaned, but without bitterness, in my reveries. O God of goodness, you alone penetrated my heart in that moment of ecstasy; you alone had my love!

In this language of natural religion, the young people marked by the pantheism of the Romantic generation can communicate with the people who had been raised in the civil and military tumults of the French Revolution and the Napoleonic Empire and were more or less confusedly nourished by the principles of the *philosophes,* civic feasts, and the cult of the Supreme Being. Some, admittedly, had succumbed to skepticism and said: "We are now rid of false notions. We too wanted to improve the lot of human beings. We thought them good. We know them better than you do, and we have paid dearly for this sad experience." But others have kept their faith, such as the fellow from Dole in his seventies who informs the editors of *Le Globe* of the plan for a civic cult that he had put together at a time when dechristianization was reviving pure morality in the hearts of the people.[6]

A privileged moment: the old believers in God the clockmaker, the freethinkers of natural morality, and those whose spirits are inflamed with Romantic palingenesis of all sorts can still join together to celebrate a deity tangible in the starry heavens and the human heart, whose cult reconciles hatred of priests with the need for faith, bitter experience of an egotistical world with the sentiment of human communion. Amid this diffuse religiosity the Saint-Simonian proclamation proposes to be recognized as a new religion. But such recognition does not come easily: "I admit it. I shrank from the word 'religion.' . . . A new religion in the nineteenth century? . . . The word . . . repelled me."[7] The most convinced

6. Letter of Perrenet to *Le Globe*, Fonds Enfantin, Ms. 7606.
7. Professions of faith by Bois (Ms. 7794), Jeanne Deroin (Ms. 7608), and Bazin (*Le Globe*, Jan. 21, 1832).

adherents shared such reservations at first. In the proclamations of the doctrine Vinçard first saw a Jesuitical scheme.[8] Désirée Véret first entered Taitbout Hall "to find a subject for humorous talk."[9] And painter Bazin, future "sacristan" in the Temple of Ménilmontant, went there "to add banter and effrontery to his immorality."[10] But more than one unbeliever was "amazed to find a tear moistening his eyelid," and vainly tried to defend himself against it. Thus, the new convert Bazin "accused his emotion of cowardice and said of you: they are learned men but they are hypocrites." A feeble defense where the issue is not the threat posed by sanctimonious hypocrites to bourgeois fortunes and households but the seductive allure of words of love descending to the men and women of the common people. They would and would not like to taste the dangerous charm of those words, at the risk of being just another number in the catalogue of seduced girls and enrolled proletarians: "I was eager for such words. . . . The habit of being betrayed. . . . I felt the need to love again"[11] A third love after the betrayals of friendship and the temporary quietude of the household. A second Church after the church they loved for its pomp and hymns before they came to despise its priests and dogmas; a Church whose priests, sacrificing career and fortune to improve the plight of the poor, for once bring their actions in line with the divine words of love.

So they will be believers in the new religion, at first out of hatred for the old religion. Undoubtedly, its criticism of original sin and its affirmation of a God whose kingdom is of this world and whose children bring peace rather than the sword are seductive for these progressive human beings. But over against a historical philosophy of revelation, which assigns each religion and party its rationale in the march of progress, the bitterness of these bruised hearts sets a metaphysics of good and evil, of light and darkness, in which the original truth has been dissembled by the dark ministers of double truth:

> Raised in the beliefs of Christianity, it did not take me long to see
> that religion had been perverted . . . that instead of enlightening
> human beings so that they could break their chains, people spoke
> a language to them that they could not understand, making use

8. Vinçard, *Mémoires épisodiques d'un vieux chansonnier saint-simonien*, Paris, 1879, p. 35.

9. Désirée Véret to Enfantin, Sept. 11, 1831, Ms. 7608.

10. Bazin, "Pensées religieuses," *Le Globe*, Jan. 21, 1832.

11. Professions of faith by Madame Nollet, Eugénie Tétard, and Caroline Béranger.

of their ignorance and profiting from it to leave them in complete brutishness. I saw that religion was merely trafficking, that the favors shown to us as heavenly were sold after long debates as one sells beasts in the market. . . . Having witnessed intolerable abuses, I distanced myself from every nuance of the Roman Catholic religion. The mere sight of a priest and I was beside myself.

The intolerance of Guérineau is echoed in the disgust of Chérot, of type-founder Foulon, and of ex-soldier Coligny: "The egotism and bad faith of its priestly ministers . . . of men who call themselves ministers of God and deny His laws every day. . . . these men, most if not all, hid a black soul under their priestly dress." It was at a school run by Brothers that Laurent Ortion learned atheism: "They wanted to inspire terror in me; the hell they painted before my eyes was terrible; I was not afraid of it. They wanted me to feel in my heart the happiness of heaven, but I did not grasp it. And so I was plunged into the deepest atheism."

This atheism is not experienced as a liberation of thought but as a sickness of the soul and a numbing of sensitivity. In the disarray of their hearts, all these people again found the lesson taught by Rousseau's Savoyard vicar to a young man, an apprentice without work and a traveler without compass: "This state is hardly endurable; it is distressing and painful. It is only the interest of vice or laziness of soul that leaves us in it."[12] And it may even be that joiner Conchon reread his model before spelling out his own foolish meanderings on the sea of opinions in his profession of faith:

> Like a mariner on a stormy sea who keeps sailing in search of a port where he might land, I did not, in fact, profess atheism, because in and around me I sensed something supernatural that spoke to me of a God, a sovereign and invisible being making this sublime universe move in an orderly way. . . . Despite the admirable harmony that reigns over the earth, I nevertheless noticed that there was something wrong in society that was causing an ongoing uneasiness. But not knowing at all where it came from or what route I should take to be happy, I continued to meander here and there.

To land in port, it is not enough to have a belief recognizing the divine harmony in the physical universe. More is needed: a religion that reme-

12. *Émile; ou: De l'éducation*, The Hague, 1762, III, 25.

dies the gap between that harmony and the disorder of social inequalities, injustices, and humiliations, a religion that simultaneously recalls the children of the common people to the dignity of their being and establishes not only the principle of social harmony—the principle, recognizable by all, of a tie or communion between sentient beings—but also the table of another law, a remuneration for human actions other than the profits of the world of exploitation or the distinctions of the world of oppression. It is in that quest that Chérot entered freemasonry, that Guérineau went out to hear Reformed preaching, and that Labonni chose to familiarize himself with the Jewish and Protestant religions: infidels rather than atheists, men of errant belief looking for some communion to which to attach it. How could they find the principle of their emancipation in the irreligion of materialism? For them materialism is not a doctrine but a state: the religion of what is, the reality of the world of egotism that causes them to suffer doubly—from the oppression of the rich and from the impossibility of uniting against it. The vacuum of celestial religion can only be the omnipotence of terrestrial domination:

> To the extent that the human being breaks loose from its duties, its heart cannot remain empty. It soon feels the need for a new love and imperceptibly turns gold into the object of its most precious affections. As in the days of fetishism, its treasure is the God of its family. . . . Is a father marrying off his children? The church ceremony is no more than a trifle, the civil ceremony an empty obeisance to laws; the real sacrament takes place at the notary's. It is there that everyone is calm and reflective. There only one sentiment speaks to the heart: cupidity, the love of gold, the love of their God.

The sentiment of "artist" Baret is also very much that of the workers whom he will meet now and then on the stage of theater productions in the city's outskirts: materialism is the philosophy of the bourgeoisie, the straightforward consecration of the existing order. The only ones to take delight in it are the "interest of vice or laziness of soul," the avidity of men of property or the discouragement of proletarians plunged into the "numbness" where Laurent Ortion had been cast by his distaste for the education offered by the Brothers, into the "drowsiness of misery and disorder" where Bois had been cast by his vain struggle against the humiliations of poverty. This drowsiness, this monotonous functioning of the machine of needs, can find its adequate expression in the materialist image of a world produced by chance or abandoned to itself. But anyone who wants to be awake needs a religion: "The mere sight of a priest and I was beside myself. But I must admit that I was not happy, that without religion each and every human being would become like a brute beast. I lacked something I could not define." It is not to please the Saint-Simonian priests that the very radical Guérineau affirms the militant necessity of a religion. A few months later, when he has returned to the republican ranks, he will speak a language just as religious to his section members:

> We, too, have a religion. It is that of Christians, but not as ex-pounded by those priests who, to satisfy their own vile cupidity, took care to distort everything conducive to liberty. We are Christians in accordance with Jesus of Nazareth, for Jesus was nothing but a virtuous republican who was inspired by the supreme Being to reveal a new law, the bases of which lay in putting all human beings on the same level.[13]

The "classification according to capacities" of the Saint-Simonian priests and the "same level" of the republican Christ go back to the same idea, which equates with the bonds of a religion the principles for overturn-ing the material disorder of social positions. Only the word *religion* seems capable of naming the principle that brings together a personal morality, a militant obligation, and an organizational project to bring the social order back into harmony with the cosmological order.

An ambiguous religion, earthly and heavenly at the same time. It fixes its object here: the reorganization of ties between human beings. It grounds the source and principle of its obligation elsewhere. Or, rather, it lets itself be divided between the transcendence of its faith and the immanence of its virtue. What these people find, what they hope for, believe, and sometimes pretend to find, in Saint-Simonism is this religion that would not be one, whose represented transcendence would have no other object than that of making tangible the obligation of natural morality: "I felt a desire to become a Saint-Simonian because I recognized that it was the morality of the upright human being, which does not lie in intolerance, superstition, and fanaticism, but whose essence is to love one's fellow creature, to help him with all one's might, to defend him at the risk of one's life, to do good

13. Guérineau, *Pourquoi nous sommes républicains et ce que nous voulons*, Paris, 1832.

and avoid evil." This reduction of the Saint-Simonian mystique to natural morality, which takes on the allure of a plain uprightness for Foulon, for Jeanne Deroin becomes the occasion for a radical reflection on the relations between the representation of the deity and the principles of militant obligation. She, for her part, takes seriously the central dogma of the new religion: the *rehabilitation of matter* as opposed to the dogma of the fall. Original sin turned the earth into a place of exile and put the kingdom of God in the hereafter. The new dogma affirms the immanence of the deity in the universe, the historical progress of its revelation, and the necessity of building its kingdom in the here and now of industrious works and human association. Its whole logic operates in the supposed equivalence between a historical teleology of perfectibility and a pantheistic religion of the here below. But this supposed coherence is the impossible marriage of two contradictory principles:

> To reconcile two opposed opinions, the Saint-Simonians have chosen to take the middle ground, the *juste milieu,* between spiritualism and materialism. But it seems that the latter system is the consequence of their doctrine.
>
> According to them, the universe in its entirety forms only a single being endowed with intelligence and will, power and beauty. Isn't that precisely what the partisans of atheism call nature?
>
> The intelligence of this being amounts to sensing its existence; it is instinctive. Its will is the necessity of being; or, to put it better, it does not have any; if it is not free to cease to be, it is impotent; hence it is not God.[14]

Undoubtedly Jeanne Deroin drew on pamphlets of the Buchez camp denouncing the "pantheistic" deviation imposed on Saint-Simonism by Enfantin.[15] But her rejection of a God incapable of ceasing to be expresses well the perception of those proletarians tempted more than once to tear themselves away by death from the inexorable necessity of the needs-machine. This instinctive repugnance for a deity incapable of ending the necessity that commands its being lies behind the logical exposition of the dilemma inherent in Saint-Simonian pantheism:

> If the universe is all that is, if the human being is a modification of this great All, then such a belief is not a religion and cannot give

14. Jeanne Deroin, Profession of faith, Fonds Enfantin, Ms. 7608.

15. See *Lettre d'un disciple de la Science nouvelle aux religionnaires prétendus saint-simoniens de l'*Organisateur *et du* Globe, Paris, 1831.

rise to any cult. For the human being, as an intimate and necessary part of this great Being, should not render it any homage. . . . The love, the innate thought of conservation, the providential law of progress, that are the attributes of this great Being—are they not an effect of the necessity of being? So it is pointless to honor it. It is not an intelligent cause but a perfectly organized machine, with necessity ruling all its movements.

The contradiction is clear, but its solution gives rise to ambiguity. One could read here a criticism of religious representation, bringing the communion of beings and the law of progress back from their speculative alienation to their sensible reality; an appeal for a consistent materialism that would strip earthly exigency of its last theological cover. But the course undertaken here runs exactly counter to one that links the possibility of transforming action to a critique of representation. It is religious distance, the divine *strangeness*, that permits a critique of earth, a way out of the reign of necessity. In this quarrel of religion, it is not simply a matter of giving an interpretation of the world that fixes its principle on transforming social action. The conception of the deity also provides the model, the *analogon*, of this action. Moreover, that is the way the Saint-Simonian religion understands it. It does not mean to be a simple faith in the progressiveness of revelation, encouraging human efforts toward a future of indefinite progress. Its "pantheism" literally grounds militant *enthusiasm* on the representation of a communion of individuals in the deity of the All. It is the way in which these young bourgeois people theoretically ground the end of a system of chance identified with the privilege of birth. Reacting against social apportionments tied to the arbitrariness of birth and the atomization of individuals, they inscribe their dedication to the poor classes in the ontological necessity of a sympathetic community of all that is. Jeanne Deroin undoubtedly offers an excessively mechanistic interpretation of that moral pantheism. But she also speaks of a margin where the necessity immanent in the great All evokes less the universal communion of beings than the inhuman springs of the needs-machine. The critique of the "chance of birth" divides in two. To theoretically ground its destruction in practice, it is not enough to turn the universe into the kingdom of the deity and history into the process of its revelation. It is also necessary that the rationality of that universe and that history go back to a free causality and betoken the preeminence of the active spirit over passive matter.

This reversal of perspectives translates into an insistence on pointing up the ontological hierarchy of the two principles: "Spirit is pure, matter is corruptible. Spirit is intelligent, matter is inert. . . . Spirit is indivisible, matter is infinitely divisible. How could one assume that spirit is inherent in matter? One might just as well say that movement is inherent in the pendulum of a clock." The ontological hierarchy of the predicates is equally the opposition of two moral and political principles. And the classic clockmaker analogy makes clear the militant import of this deism: its rejection of those models of equilibrium that see in the movement of humanity no image but that of the adjustment of material interests. Such, for example, is the *Système des compensations* that the celebrated Pierre Azaïs (1766–1845) spells out for the Society of Civilization, now and then interrupted by the objection of a worker: "Your system derives from fatalism. Fatalism leads to resignation, and absolute resignation produces tyranny. Therefore, you profess tyranny."[16]

To this thought focusing on compensations, which provides the various politics of the *juste milieu* with their theoretical consecration, the Saint-Simonians oppose the law of progress, which again picks up the theory of material interests for the benefit of the disinherited. But a religion of progress is still only a contradictory *juste milieu* if, in affirming the movement, it lets stand in its basic principle the pair, chance and necessity. If one wants to bring together the scattered atoms of the egotistical world in a harmonious social whole, one must destroy in principle any and every mechanistic representation of the world, any and every idea of a necessity immanent in the movement of the atoms. In going around the difficulty, the Saint-Simonian religion is divided between two contradictory principles: "To say that everything in the universe is ultimately God, that it is at once spirit and matter . . . is implicitly to deny the existence of God. To recognize and proclaim the law of progress is to admit a beginning, to recognize a prior cause."

But perhaps this contradiction in the Saint-Simonian religion goes back to its very status as a "political system covered with a religious veil to satisfy human weakness":

> After he had conceived a vast political system with the aim of making human beings better and happier, Saint-Simon recognized the impossibility of reconstructing afresh the social edifice in the presence of existing religions, which are continually at war with enlightenment and civilization and want to drag society into a retrograde movement. . . .

16. Cited by E. Souvestre, "Les penseurs inconnus," *La Revue de Paris*, March 1839, p. 246.

He did not want to recognize a purely spiritual God, because he felt it necessary to bring humanity back to positive ideas and attach it to earthly things.

He did not want to admit materialism in an explicit way, because he recognized the influence of religious ideas on the human spirit, because he deemed religious enthusiasm necessary for the propagation of his doctrine.

The end of the analysis contradicts its beginning. The form, religion, is not a means of coming to terms with the existing religions. That means would be ill-advised. And the enthusiasm necessary for propagating the doctrine is not in the order of means; it is inherent in the transcendence of this belief that elevates love of one's fellow creatures to the rank of love of God. The contradiction of politics and religion, of materialism and spiritualism, is not the result of an inconsistency or a trick. The antinomy of the learned dogma is not unrelated to the contradiction felt by the young lingerie-maker when she was trying to isolate herself from the world of oppression but found herself unable to break the ties with humanity forged by her admiration for great actions and her compassion for every sort of suffering: "I was not at one with myself. . . . I lacked a belief, a goal, an active life." Found at last, belief offers "a few absolute truths" to ground some action, but it does not get rid of the contradiction that continually recurs between a "materialism" that links the enterprise of social transformation to hatred of the hawkers of paradise, and a "spiritualism" that must look outside the servitude of the material world for the faith necessary for its transformation. The deism of the faithful is simultaneously antinomic and complementary to the pantheism of the "priests." The contradictions of the Saint-Simonian religion do not mean that it goes no place. On the contrary, they make it the possible place for a grateful avowal in the very form of the misunderstanding. Jeanne Deroin may still have her reservations. But her brothers and sisters, like the incredulous Bazin, can unite republican faith with providentialist dogma and head off to preach "God the good [male], God the good [female], and the infiniteness of intelligence" to golden-mean milieus that profess "God the seed, God the necessary, and ultimately, by degrees, God the nothing."[17] To resolve the dilemma is really to remain in the contradiction. The "religion" has no content other than politics. But this politics can break off compromises with the forces of egotism only by means of the transcendence

17. Bazin to Enfantin, March 25, 1833, Ms. 7647.

of a religion that typifies a world order in the image of its ends or offers the model of an action freed from the chain of necessity. At the undefined boundaries of "simple reason," the republican cult of virtue and the mysticism of the living universe meet in this transcendent religion of fraternity that alone can ground a politics of association among human beings.

So this ambiguous religion organizes the encounter between the barricade people of the egalitarian Republic and the apostles of hierarchical association. But the practical conjunction is more difficult to effect than is the syncretism of religions. Henri Fournel, entrusted (along with Claire Bazard) with the task of teaching workers, bluntly spells out their very strict conception of their mission vis-à-vis the proletarians of July:

> Of all those men of the old world we have made new men. They had faith in violence, and today they have faith only in the power of your peaceable word to improve their lot. They were unbelievers because they saw themselves abandoned by God, and they have come to recognize the envoys of God himself in the people who lavish the treasures of your love upon them. They used to murmur against all authority, but they have learned to bless yours and take glory in becoming your sons. They were impatient for a quick emancipation, but they have come to realize that only by long effort can this emancipation, peacefully won, be complete.[18]

Fournel's report parades an optimum situation. In practice the directors have a bit more difficulty in destroying sentiments of republicanism and antihierarchical liberalism among their catechumens. This is particularly true for Delaporte as he grapples with the hardheads of Faubourg Saint-Jacques and Faubourg Saint-Marcel: Gauny, who sees in the very rigor of Delaporte's reasoning only the despotic manifestation of the privilege of his education; Charles Pennekère, who cannot be induced to give up his hatred of the rich even by the offer of a district directorship; his brother Alexandre, who retains "a slight ferment of republican passions"; Confais, whose participation in a street demonstration on behalf of Poland is reported by an obliging neighbor, and to whom Delaporte must "make clear how much impropriety there was in that." In the face of the real threat of European war over the issue of Poland, Hippolyte Pennekère is all set to take up arms in order to repel the invader. To calm him down, Delaporte must employ all the resources of his dialectics: "I made him understand

18. *Oeuvres de Saint-Simon et d'Enfantin*, Paris, 1865, III, 208.

that our duty and our mission were, first and foremost, to proclaim the good news; then, that if invasion took place, it would only be because God willed it, and He would permit it only to help progress along."

The opposition seems absolute: the patriotic ardor of the soldiers of the new Year II versus the devout providentialism of the doctrinaire. But it is worth noting that the latter has only a risky improvisation on a too hastily learned lesson to oppose to the certitude of faith in the republican trinity. For the issue of Poland is precisely the one that places the metaphysics of the doctrine in contradiction with its morality. The preaching of Barrault and Laurent on "intervention" refrains from entrusting the fate of the Poles to divine providence; and even the future supremacy of the peaceful association of peoples is subordinated by them to criticism of the "egotism" that serves as the basis for *juste-milieu* opposition of all sorts to French intervention.[19] Alfred Voilquin, too, manages to draw out the logic of an interpretation in which universal association is not the negation but the continuation of the civil barricades and the liberative wars of revolutionary France: "My heart thrilled, and still does, at the memory of your manly accents invoking, under our glorious banner, the support we owe to our brothers in Poland." To be sure, these ambiguities are heightened by the personality of the preachers: the former Carbonaro Laurent, and Barrault, future manager of the *Tocsin des travailleurs*. But it is no accident that the Saint-Simonian hierarchy entrusted these two members, the closest to "liberalism," rather than doctrine men, with the main responsibility for sermons designed to make the *religious* import of the doctrine clear to a public that has come partly out of republican passion for the enfranchisement of workers and partly to indulge in Voltairean mockery of the new priests. Only for the moment does the enthusiasm of liberty, equality, and fraternity conceal the religious energy capable of turning the forms and dogmas of the new apostolate into the founding principle and source of a living reality.

In the model profession of faith by the artist son of the common people, it is the July Revolution that acts as the good news, the revelation of the redemptive religion:

> On that day, and only on that day in my past life, did I glimpse, in the midst of the people revolting as a single human being, the future that I find today. I felt myself alive with the life of those around me when my hand, covered with the muck of the

19. "L'intervention," ibid., XLIII, 339f.

heroic street, shook the honorably callused hand of the worker, the smooth white hand of the student, and even the hand of the bourgeois idler; it was always a human being moved by my fears and my hopes. A secret flame, a divine voice, revealed a UNIVERSAL ASSOCIATION to me. O my fathers, of all the news I yearned for, what good news it brought me! That instantaneous movement that brought me closer to a human being and worked its effect in the two of us as in every being, that feeling which invited me to gently reveal secrets to a human being whose name and life I had no need to know in order to confide in him, said to me: No, human beings are not born to hate, they are born to love; yes, association and love are their needs. Ah, I no longer miss that paradise promised to the mere spirituality of my being alone. Henceforth I will touch and hear and see loving beings who are alive with my life.[20]

It is to the artist, the prototype of a social reconciliation diametrically opposed to that of the *juste milieu,* the just-right middle ground, that there recurred this figuration of the fraternal street—no longer a weapon against an existing enemy but a connecting link, a matter of equal exchange between soft, smooth hands and callused hands. July, then, represents the unanimous revolution, the insurrection of love prefiguring the peaceful association to come. It is simply a matter of converting the fighting people to a true awareness of its power: not violence or numbers, but the association of human beings governed by the hierarchy of the most captivating hearts. The simple opposition of sterile violence and fruitful association thus gives way to the tension peculiar to the proletarian experience of July: the disappointed hope for a political change and the solemn manifestation of the united power of the people, the tangible birth certificate of the religion of progress. And so we find the former guard of Joseph Napoléon and the joiner who nostalgically pines for the great man each in his own way managing to take up the Saint-Simonian interpretation of the three days in July:

> Only one fruit remains to us from that revolution: the holy work of our master, the improvement of the moral, intellectual, and physical lot of the most numerous class. . . [:] this fine institution, perhaps the only benefit of the three days, since such an institution, as holy as it is pure, has been established and, under the fallen system, was

20. Machereau, Profession of faith, *L'Organisateur*, March 5, 1831.

lacking to us, who were forced to keep hidden in our hearts the most precious thing man has: liberty.

If Dagoreau, Coligny, and their brothers can recognize the heritage of July in a new Church, the reason is that the revelation of the three days has more to do with a certain existential suffering than with the question of a political regime. That is also why they find it easy to weave the threads of their own personal experience on the woof provided by the apostles:

> I continued to wander here and there. . . . No, I said to myself, there will never be any happiness for us. . . . Until the solemn day when an astonished world was informed of the overthrow of the legitimist regime in France. . . . July appeared to me as a halo of happiness. I was going to be free, I said to myself. . . . I will not detail for you the part I played in it. I would simply have you know that no king's palace ever saw me except on July 29. . . .
>
> Well, then, what came of all that? . . . I fought for liberty, I was wounded, I became more miserable than I had been, and I saw people still more miserable! . . . The three memorable days presaged happiness for me, but I soon saw to my sorrow that some wanted to cover them with a veil to make us forget them. . . . The men of the old aristocracy had disappeared, those of the new aristocracy replaced them.[21]

Those days of glory followed by days of bitterness confirm the Saint-Simonian analysis of the power of the people as revealed and then led astray. They serve as the bases for conversions that describe the very same process evident in the revelation of July: "listlessness" again taking hold of bodies and spirits before the closed horizon of an interminable unhappiness; the surprise—announced by a neighbor, a visitor, or public rumor—of the providential happening that lifts up heads bowed down under material and moral misery; headlong involvement in the new alliance of smooth hands and callused hands, in the open confrontation of two worlds, at the end of which appears a future of fraternal liberty:

> I was immersed in reflections that I would always be unhappy when my Saint-Simonian neighbors came looking for me. They asked why I was fretting. I told them. They induced me to go with

21. Professions of faith by Conchon, Madame Nollet, Bois, and Labonni.

them to the preaching session. Oh, what joy took hold of my heart when I heard the message of Saint-Simon from your lips! The talk is only of the happiness of the most numerous and poorest class, where all human beings call each other by name and say to each other: we are all brothers and sisters, and we make up one single family. It will no longer be as it was in the religion of my fathers, where I had been raised in ignorance, since I do not know how to read or write.

A family religion of love, an education that brings the children of the common people out of the misery and poverty of their parents: the remarks dictated by the illiterate Guissard, "obliged to work as a poor wretch" from his tender years, aptly sum up the two great themes elaborated with rhetorical flourishes by such educated workers as printers Meunier and Langevin, painter Laurent Ortion, and tailor Calvet. For both the most unpolished and the most educated, the Saint-Simonian future unfolds on two levels: mystical communion of a society of brothers, and empirical organization of protection for the weak, this being practiced mainly at the two extremes of life that work cannot support—childhood and old age. The utilitarians seeking assistance and the idealists dreaming of a people brought up under the sun of reason join hands in this slight warping of the doctrine that puts more stress on egalitarian treatment of future and former workers than on the hierarchical organization of active workers, on the formation of capabilities than on their classification by the Saint-Simonian priests. "Improving the plight of the poorest and most numerous class" and "education for our children": those are the two phrases that Madame Nollet first retained from the preaching session to which a brother had brought her to assuage her sadness. And they are echoed in Chérot's resolution favoring "this doctrine that is so much in sympathy with the thinking of my whole life, which has always been that people be admitted without distinction to the benefits of education, that science, the arts, and industry be the lot of those human beings judged to be the most capable."

Thus, Chérot and his brothers do not oppose their republican convictions to the hierarchical classification of capacities. The biggest leveler among them, Guérineau, will still acknowledge the distinction of virtues and talents before his section members. But the organization that attracts them is the one that will give each person the opportunity to train his capabilities and profit from them rather than the one promising to classify them equitably. They recognize the canonical articles of faith: "classification according to capabilities, retribution according to works." But their

picture of the Saint-Simonian future readily leaves the modalities of classification and retribution hazy and stresses the education that is simultaneously to eliminate the hazard of birth and uproot the sentiment of egotism.
Entrusted with the task of refuting those who denounce that future in
the name of liberty, Langevin prefers to argue from the opposite end by
pointing up the servitude of the "free" proletarian. And when, for the
benefit of the incredulous, he enumerates the advantages of the doctrine,
he simply overlooks the benefits of classification: "You shudder, fathers,
at the thought that your son will not inherit. But think about it. In the
Saint-Simonians he will find a family that will give him a moral, physical,
intellectual, and vocational education, and retirement after his work." The
profession of faith by his colleague Meunier is just as reserved about the
interval between education and retirement. He certainly includes classification among the articles of faith of which his spiritual "regeneration"
makes him an adherent. But his grand fresco of the future skillfully evades
the issue amid the benefits of vocational education and the patriarchal
wisdom of the hierarchy of love:

> All, without distinction, will get a general or moral education that
> will develop their sympathies and teach them to love the function
> they will exercise in society, and then the special or vocational
> education that will teach them the trade to which they will be
> called by their ability. . . . All will have a retirement after they have
> worked. . . . The most loving will be called upon to govern the
> universal family and will see to it that humanity makes as much
> progress as possible.

This young man may not have learned how to read in *Télémaque*, but
the social education and family government he outlines evoke the beard
of Mentor more than that of the Saint-Simonian priest–engineers. This
mixture of patriarchal utopia and educational republicanism is not simply
a way of getting around the promise of an ecclesiastical and industrial
hierarchy of classifiers. It also reflects the ambiguity of the request for
protection associated with the proletarian feeling of abandonment and
chance. This request oscillates between projected plans for some social
security for workers and the endless quest for love; between the tranquil
perspective of a general and vocational education leading to a working life
without unemployment and ultimately to the comfort of retirement, and
the fresco of a fraternal humanity brought to communion in the cult of
Virtue by their priests and fathers.

The two visions are not contradictory, of course. The organization of work and social security is meant to dispel the "uncertainty about their future" that makes men egotistical, to create the state without either wealth or poverty that will permit workers to open themselves to the disinterested joys of love. And the suppression of inheritance, combined with retirement for the aged, will regenerate the family ties that serve as a model for the future ties of universal association: "In our old age we will be assured of our children's love. Unlike today, they will not wait impatiently for the last moment of our lives in order to inherit our wealth or, if we are indigent, to be free and clear of us."

But is it really this assurance of a peaceful old age embellished with an unknown filial love that alleviates the bitterness of the veterans of the republican or imperial dream and the melancholy of young people born too late in an orphan century? Isn't it just as much the possible break right now with the world of egotism and humiliation, the materially indiscernible but crucial change that cabinetmaker Boissy invites his Toulouse brothers to make from "tears extorted by misfortune and suffering" to "tears that one likes to shed"—gentle tears of a happiness already fully present in the message of promise and the exchange of love?

> Stand up in the midst of the unfortunate workers, your friends and comrades, and say to them: Leave, leave this society for which you do everything and which does nothing for you, this society in which those who do everything have nothing and those who do nothing have everything. . . . A new world is offered to you. Throw yourselves into the arms of the generous people who come to announce it to you, and soon you will be happy.

Starting with the future happiness promised to associated humanity, we note a twofold slippage taking place. Those who flee the old world to hear the good news enter, by that very fact alone, a new world prefigured better by words and acts of love than by any plan of social organization. But that prefigured future may be less that of the larger society than that of the little family realizing within its precincts the life of love that is rejected by a world addicted to the religion of gold:

> Ah, my brothers, I ask you: Isn't it time to put an end to such disorder, or to participate in it no longer? Let us separate ourselves from a world where honor is no more than a word, love a piece of folly, friendship a chimera. Let us all join hands. In our circle a person will love his wife for the qualities of her heart and respect

her for her virtues, and honor will exist for all human beings. Your children will cherish you and take watchful care of your old age.

For artist Baret, the happiness of a circle that will make decent family love possible. For the unfortunate Henry, the happiness of communing soon at the fraternal table of the house of association: "See, the moment is approaching when we are going to gather together, to live together around one and the same table, seeing ourselves as one single family, united by the bonds of fraternity and friendship." For a tailor enjoying comfort and a typographer dying of hunger, the happiness of already being infinitely far away from the world of egotism, humiliation, and hatred: "You have taken me away from the public pillory to admit me to an abode of delights. . . . You have taken me out of darkness to call me to your association. You have delivered me from all fraud and dissimulation; you have snatched me away from that egotistical people."[22]

It may not have been necessary for Claire Bazard, upset at having nothing concrete to offer her catechumens, to urge them not to despise the sweet consolations of love.[23] Some of them already have too much of a tendency to overlook the militant future of propagandizing and the hard-working future of association in favor of the sweetness of maternal caresses and the fraternal effusions that the tender Meunier evokes with more lyricism than he devotes to the future organization of work:

O you sensitive hearts that love virtue, come with us to taste its inexpressible charms! In the world it is persecuted and crowned with thorns, but among us it is loved and respected and crowned with flowers. And you who have been beaten down and made sorrowful by misfortune, come and unload your sorrows in the bosom of our fathers; come to our place; you will find friends to console you, and gaiety will be reborn in your hearts.

The lesson of love may have won over these republican hearts only too well: the opposition between the violence of the old world and the fraternal peace of the new world tends to become an opposition between the outside world one is fleeing and the haven of peace one has found in the closed space of the Saint-Simonian Family.

A trap in which orthodoxy is caught, or a trick without malice of the

22. Professions of faith by Colas and Raimbault.
23. Lesson of Claire Bazard, *L'Organisateur*, June 18, 1831.

orthodox? In preaching the new love too much and combining deed with word only too well, isn't the Doctrine separating from the world of misery and combat the very people it is proposing to send into it as missionaries? Isn't it becoming, for the very workers for whom it is supposed to be organizing hard-working weekdays, the festive Sunday, the day off that would like to last forever? "You know it. Our workdays are long and painful. Ah, how many times we long for Sunday. . . . You alone know how many ills your gentle words make tolerable for us. You alone can appreciate how sweet are these moments of religious fraternity presided over by you."[24] You alone know: but in contrast to the dual relationship of this confidence, which slips from a disciple deprived of his Sunday love-fest by the closing of Taitbout Hall, stand the descriptions of family happiness concluding with the propagandizing required to summon the whole of humanity to the communion table. Yet how could those afflicted hearts, which have finally found the warmth of friendship, return to the cold world of exterior darkness? It still chills the heart of the melancholic Roussel: "When I am surrounded by people you have reared, I find there a warm friendship that warms me up again; but when necessity compels me to approach the outside world, I again meet with ice in the human heart." Even cabinetmaker Lenoir, the most orthodox of Saint-Simonian workers before becoming the most dogmatic of Fourierist workers, must try twice before he can attempt to speak to his brothers of Toulouse: "It is a tough thing for someone who has been abandoned by the whole of society to come to bear witness to that society of all his love for it and to ask in exchange that it love us as well."[25]

But this love returned to a society that has done nothing for them is also the only way in which they might be able to recompense the love given them by those apostles who owe them nothing. Like the caresses that the scrupulous Léné accuses himself of stealing once upon a time, before paying for them with weekly propaganda work, the pleasures of family love would become culpable if their beneficiaries did not settle the debt contracted with the young bourgeois people who have dedicated their bodies and resources to improving the lot of the poor. It is no longer love but exploitation or bondage, where one gives and the other receives. Egalitarianism does not mean rejecting good turns but finding the proper measure for paying them back. Voinier was upset in Taitbout Hall when he saw proletarians pushed back from empty seats reserved for bourgeois people.

24. Letter of Bernard, *Le Globe*, Feb. 2, 1832.
25. Speech of Lenoir to the Church of Toulouse, *Le Globe*, Feb. 3, 1832.

But his dignity is not offended when he spells out the problem of the social debt imposed by nature in terms of gratitude: "And it is to you, my fathers and mothers, that we owe this future of happiness, you who have sacrificed everything for the moral, intellectual, and physical betterment of the poorest and most numerous class. How, my brothers and sisters, will we be able to demonstrate sufficient gratitude to our fathers and mothers for so many benefits?" In the situation of dependence in which the Saint-Simonian proletarians find themselves, active gratitude, recompense for benefits received, is the only way to safeguard egalitarian principles.

This obviously is easier said than done. More than one of these people who have no wealth to sacrifice to the Doctrine express concern about the role they can play in its success. Madame Perronet regrets that "the loss of her fortune prevents her today from associating herself with your fine actions." The sentiment is echoed in the scruples of Conchon and tailor Barbez:

> I would come more readily and with more enthusiasm if my social position had put me in a better position to do something for the society in the way of more direct and bigger aid. Otherwise, it seems to me that I am going to be a bother, so to speak. . . . I would be receiving without giving anything. I am poor, but I do not want something for nothing.

Colas has the solution for this problem, however:

> Erase from the profession of faith I gave you those words that suggest I could never help you in your labors. . . . You, my brothers, who feel the same way, let us not imagine ourselves insolvent debtors. Let us pay back with nightly labors those that our fathers perform for us. Our combined ideas should beget wonders. Let us not forget that there were days when the blood of one was to conserve that of the other, and that so much sympathy must forge indissoluble ties. Reunited now under the same banner, let us close ranks to keep indifference out. Let us march with a quicker step toward the dwellers in darkness. Let us take as our guide the torch that our fathers have handed over to us.

The "Chant du Départ," the torch of our fathers, the parade of Enlightenment, the "military faith" dreamed of by Labonni, that of Year II, the Grand Army, or the days of July: if the republican was willing to give up his bitterness so as to come and enjoy the taste of peace and love, the Saint-Simonian will pay off his debt of propagandizing only by rediscovering the accents and rhythms of the Republic marching toward the destruction of tyrants. "Let us unite, I say for my part, and under the spell of the Saint-Simonian religion I also exclaim: Come to us, friends, relatives, compatriots! Let a new and truly holy alliance unite us! Then we shall teach these hereditary despots that kings are made for their peoples, not peoples for kings." Voilquin's bold language is exceptional. This architect declassed by the Saint-Simonian leadership to the degree of worker is obviously claiming a right to the passion accorded the artist. The most excited proletarians put it other ways. Despite his emotion, Dagoreau agrees to return from Poland to France and from republican heresy to an orthodoxy that preserves the movement of the revolutionary army on the march, but he also manages to find a new trinity to replace the trinity of liberty, equality, and fraternity:

> Ah, my dear brothers, sorrow bewilders me, but I return to you. Is it true that the same fate has been reserved for us? Is it true that the despots want to tear our liberty away from us? Let us close ranks around our supreme fathers. Let us fix our gaze on the liberating banner that Saint-Simon unfolded before us. And let us show all the peoples blinded by despotism this indelible inscription: the Association, Union, and Power of all the peoples of the earth.

Between the religion of the Republic and the mystique of progress, between the violence of the democratic army and the peace of the hierarchical association, it is always the very same compromise that finds expression in the vision of universal association: the grand march of peoples brandishing the banner of liberty that puts despots to flight and breaks the chains of bondage. The fullest and most complete figuration of it comes, naturally enough, to the most religious of anticlerical republicans, the young engraver Rossignol:

> Glory to you, Father and Mother, who summon into your temples this magnanimous and generous people, conqueror of the barricades . . . this heroic people that broke its irons to escape bondage and reconquer the independence of its homeland but up to now has found no recompense except poverty, privations, and horrible sufferings. . . . In the future the peoples will line up under the

protective standard to form an indissoluble and inviolable alliance. . . . We see them breaking the chains of bondage, ascending the high mountains, and moving with quick, majestic step toward grand Universal Association, holding in one hand the olive branch of peace, in the other the banner of Immortal Liberty on which is imprinted: To the lovers of humanity—love, union, liberty.

CHAPTER 8

The Hammer and the Anvil

CHRISTMAS ON EARTH: the singing choirs of heaven, the march of peoples moving beyond sandy shores and mountains to hail the flight of tyrants and the birth of the new work. All of it, lies: well-learned lessons intermingled with more ancient refrains and rewarded in advance at a discount with jobs as typographers or carriers on *Le Globe*, porters at the house of association, or domestics on Rue Monsigny; with orders for suits or hats, chair repairs, painting work, rent advances, redemption of personal effects from the pawnshop, and so forth. "They would profess any dogma, provided that they had something to eat."[1] Though it may be a bit supercilious, the judgment of artist Raymond Bonheur is more than confirmed by worker Parent:

> I divide the workers who have approached the Saint-Simonian religion into four classes:
> 1. Those who have grasped all or some of its principles and have adopted it out of conviction.
> 2. Those who, being employed directly or indirectly by the Saint-Simonian society, have adopted our religion so as not to lose their material position.
> 3. Those who have come to us believing that we could get them work.
> 4. Those who have failed to understand us, think that we give out charity, and come to us to get it.
> The first group is not the largest one, methinks.

1. Report of Raymond Bonheur, Fonds Enfantin, Bibliothèque de l'Arsenal, Ms. 7816. I shall not repeat the references for reports of the district directors cited in this chapter. Readers are referred to the listing given in note 1 of Chapter 6.

Parent has some reason to be bitter as he makes up what he says will be his first and last report. It is 4:00 A.M., Sunday, November 27, 1831. If he follows the same schedule as his colleague in the twelfth district, he will have begun his apostolic workday before 7:00 A.M. on the previous day. Such is Delaporte's schedule. On Tuesdays, Thursdays, and Saturdays, he receives workers from 7:00 A.M. on. He also receives them on Monday and Wednesday evenings, and Saturday evening after the lesson at the Athenaeum, which brings together the faithful of the three quarters on the Left Bank. The rest of the time he goes to visit Saint-Simonian workers whom he must prepare morally for association and possible converts called to his attention by his faithful or by the central office for propaganda work. If these people work outside their home all day, then he must pay them a visit before his morning office hours.

It is true that Parent devotes less time than Delaporte to receiving workers and propagating the doctrine. But there is a very specific reason for this: he is not remunerated by the Doctrine and continues to practice his trade to earn a living. For these directors to whom Claire Bazard and Henri Fournel have entrusted the task of morally converting and materially classifying workers, with the aim of creating associations, are not well-off young people sensitive to the people's cause. They do not come from the same world as the members of the higher degrees of the hierarchy: polytechnicians, engineers, writers, scholars, or lawyers. These latter people, like Fournel himself, have often given up their career and dedicated part of their inheritance and all of their time to the Doctrine. But that does not mean that they do door-to-door work in the neighborhoods of the common people. They put out *Le Globe*, do preaching and teaching at headquarters, and travel from Brest to Lyon, and from Toulouse to Brussels, to preach missions and set up churches. The district directors, on the other hand, are recruited in the "preparatory degree." By virtue of their trade, their past, or their material situation, they are generally close to the proletarian condition. Haspott is a former smith. Botiau was an upholstery worker and then a clerk for a wool-finisher. Several are in the printing trade: typographers Achille and Jules Leroux, proofreader Biard, and perhaps Parent as well. Clouet is a worker tailor who became a master. Prévôt has a haberdashery business at Saint Martin's Market. The Saint-Simonian apostolate of Lesbazeilles is an extension of his work as a doctor for the poor. Only Delaporte, whose craft is unknown to us, could be considered a dilettante sensitive to the suffering of the common people. As for artist Raymond Bonheur, he does not live off his paintings but off his drawing lessons, which are as rare as the piano lessons given by his wife. To those whose apostolate is full-time, the Doctrine gives monthly pay ranging from eighty to a hundred francs, which does not leave them much in the way of savings. When the moment of Saint-Simonian bankruptcy occurs, the appeals of Botiau and Haspott reveal a distress at least equal to that of the people they are assisting right now.

The women associated with the direction of each district often have a higher social rank. Not only is it more difficult for proletarian women to emancipate themselves, but the function of the female directors is different as well. Whereas the "industrials"—Clouet, Haspott, Botiau, and Parent—are there by reason of their familiarity with proletarian language and situation, Eugénie Niboyet, Félicie Herbault, Madame Dumont, and Véturie Espagne come to make concrete in the daily lives and homes of proletarians the sympathy of the bourgeois apostles. In their double role as women and bourgeois people, they are there to develop the *sympathetic* tendency of the proletarians and to smooth over at times the roughness of their relations with the "fathers," who are a bit too close to their condition for their counsels not to evoke some irritability. An assistant who does not have "the easy manner and open air indispensable for speaking to workers" is even advised to "seek out more regular contact with Saint-Simonian ladies to achieve the fullest possible measure of Saint-Simonian polish." But in day-to-day practice, involving the assuagement of misery and bitterness and the overcoming of resistance, the task of work classification and that of maternal moralization tend to become identical, just as differences in perception between those discovering the materiality of popular sufferings and those trying to escape all that tend to be erased. Worker Parent and bourgeois lady Eugénie Niboyet, former workers now serving as officials of the Doctrine such as Haspott and Botiau, Doctor Lesbazeilles and artists Raymond and Sophie Bonheur, share one and the same militant discourse certifying the exact same thing: the interminable task of improving the physical and moral condition of the laboring class, the endless contradiction whereby this task incessantly reproduces the conditions it seeks to wipe out—those of the egotism of the old world.

An interminable task that has to do with assuaging the misery of the people—*not,* stresses Delaporte, the "general misery that is infinitely moving but does not prompt people to do much," the misery that Charles Duveyrier, in charge of the preparatory degree, embellishes with his "elegant improvisations," but the "individual, here and now" misery "that breaks our hearts every day." Delaporte makes clear, of course, that these individual miseries are palpable to him only because of their social character. Such, for example, are the sufferings of the wife battered by a husband who leaves her no more than two sous for her daily subsistence: "All the details of those countless sufferings I have stored in me and felt in the keenest manner because they have a general character. But it is not so with individual sufferings as such. Thus, I would have passed by a woman on whom a beam had fallen without picking her up, without paying any attention, because that misfortune would be merely individual."[2] The radicalness of that statement will earn Delaporte a reprimand from Enfantin. But the distinction is, in truth, wholly a distinction of reason. It is known that pieces of wood tend to fall mainly on battered wives or on joiners unloved by their mothers. And when the latter get up again, as was the case with Cailloux, it is always with a wound preventing them from practicing the craft they had learned and condemning them to the "social" misery of chance employment. The case of day-laborer Baron is more prosaic than that of the unloved joiner but just as indicative: if he fell under the weight of his load in the factory where he had just been hired, the reason was that all summer he had been eating nothing but potatoes boiled in water. There is no chance in the lives of those whose whole existence is doomed to chance. Every visitor who comes knocking at the door of the directors, every room the directors visit on the upper floors of the Popincourt quarter, Quinze-Vingts, Arcis, or Faubourg Saint-Marcel, conceals an individual misery that is simultaneously a social misery. But, by the same token, every heart that opens to recount its material woes reveals the moral misery produced by an existence condemned to mere survival that no longer permits a person to imagine the possibility of another life.

That is how the time and passion of the apostles are divided up. First of all, from hour to hour and door to door, there are the "poignant sorrows caused by the spectacle of so much suffering whose remedy is not in hand": the destitution of Raimbault, who has sold all his possessions one by one and now has nothing left but his sorrow; of Madame Bar, who does not even have a straw mattress or sheets for her imminent delivery of a baby; of tailor Bonnefond, unemployed, spouse of a deranged wife and constantly driven out of lodgings he cannot pay for; of Henry, who did not come to last Sunday's lesson for lack of shoes; of Madame Peiffer, without news of a baby whose wet-nurse she has not been able to pay for ten months; of little Rosalie Korsch, who is dying of cold as her parents' furniture is seized by tax agents. But the pain of this interminable journey to the land of poverty is soon aggravated by the weariness of these failed encounters: one was looking for apostles and finds only beggars.

2. *Oeuvres de Saint-Simon et d'Enfantin*, Paris, 1865, XVI, 230–31.

August 20, 1831: "Delanoë believes that changing religion means putting out one's hand where one expects to receive money." October 15, 1831: "Delanoë is asking for clothes, etc. He is always asking for something. Delanoë works, keeps a young flirt of a working girl, and drinks a bit. Madame Molière is also asking for things and does not understand a word of doctrine. To tell the truth, it would be advisable to give some instruction to those who tend to recommend such people."

Perhaps Eugénie Niboyet will manage to make herself understood. But the diary of Véturie Espagne suggests that the matter is hopeless. Madame Lauzanne "considers the Doctrine as a huge house of commerce where all the members, kind hearts and good people, try to help the poor class out of difficulty by having them work for them and paying them in accordance with this work." Claudine Mantoux, whose husband disappeared at the moment of his enlistment fourteen years ago and who works in a hat factory, "believes that the Society was set up to give work to workers without it. . . . She would like to be a member, provided that she is not obliged to change her religion, can go to Mass, and can continue to live alone as she has been doing for the past fourteen years." Marie-Élizabeth Savy, bringing up by herself the child born of her liaison with a man above her station, is mainly interested in the projected schools that she calls "*les petits collèges.*" She wants to know whether her son will be able to make his First Communion if he is placed in one of these "little schools." Madame Pottier, confectioner and pensioned widow of a July combatant, had heard talk of the association that always runs the same way: "Workers in misery and without work will be helped and given employment." Madame Mongallet, whose joiner husband is looking for a position in the Popincourt house of association, says "that she will be a Saint-Simonian when someone gives her money and that she will be peaceful in her room. She expects to inherit from her father a sum of around 2,500 francs and then she will leave the Doctrine." If nothing is to be expected from these women too wrapped up in self-interest, hardly more is to be expected from the disinterestedness that takes the form of polite indifference in the case of certain bachelors. Tinman Dodmond, for example, has "gentle and steady ways" and keeps his place neat and tidy: "He has no work. He is thinking of going to eat his money, as he puts it, with one of his brothers. He is quite cool to the Doctrine. It is not that there is anything he cannot understand. But, like so many workers, he does not see in it a career suited to his activity. The association, which we said a couple of words about, was well received by him; but always with the air of a man who judges something to be good for others."

And so the interminable task of the visitor to the poor is doubled, is contradicted by the explanation, to be repeated over and over again, of a doctrine that proposes precisely to eliminate both the poor and their visitors, to break the circle of demand that its course reproduces indefinitely. Each time it is the work of an hour and a half, according to Delaporte's reports of his mission work with Madame Tiers or penmanship-teacher Dadon: "I nonetheless spelled out the Saint-Simonian religion for her and her family for an hour and a half. . . . a catechism session of an hour and a half that I gave him brought more progress than a month of lessons for the general public." Returning from these sermons, the directors ritually assert that they have left behind them a "completely transformed" person, only to find out soon enough, as did the directors of blacksmith Knobel, that the door had shut behind them on the closed little world of the egotistical proletarian: "When we speak to him of the Doctrine, he seems to warm to it very much; but scarcely are we gone when he falls backs into his indifference and egotism." So the lesson must be picked up again the next week, and one might also want to look more attentively at the setup of the home to glimpse some truth not offered by the face or talk of one's interlocutor. That inspection may be the quick, comprehensive glance of Eugénie Niboyet: "We were quite satisfied with her home. . . . They must have been comfortable because their little household is very nice." Or it may be marked by Delaporte's attention to detail, combining the precision of a doctor's eye ("she rocks and swaddles her baby") with a fascination for the unusual: "There are three clocks in his bedroom. I propose to ask him about that." But another visit to Dadon's place, to pierce the secret of his three clocks, would teach Delaporte nothing further.

For Parent, the puzzle of these encounters that fail in the case of the apostles and sometimes succeed only too well in the case of their hosts can be read openly in the first principles of the doctrine: "The first group is not the largest one, methinks. You proclaim everywhere that you come to raise the poorest class, to draw it out of the state of ignorance in which it finds itself. But in saying that, we are saying that this class cannot understand us." You proclaim—we are saying—this class cannot: a relationship dual and triangular at the same time, embodying the overall impossibility of the educational mission and the untenable position of those who, once they have understood, no longer belong to the world to which they must nevertheless continually return as workers or as apostles. The religious form of the doctrine should permit these people, who have abandoned their fishing nets to become fishers of men, to turn the learned message into the object of a popular faith. Instead, the religious analogy points

up the limitations of the new religion, which, paradoxically enough, are
bound up with its superiority:

> Jesus laid down the principles of his religion without drawing out
> their consequences. From the very first, the disciples of Saint-
> Simon have drawn all the possible conclusions of their doctrine.
> The common people could follow Jesus, who offered them only
> principles within the grasp of their minds. The common people do
> not understand us, because we, so as not to deceive them, chose to
> make clear to them all the consequences of the principles that our
> Master had proclaimed, to show them the final goal toward which
> we were heading with humanity.

This explanation is flattering but a bit counterfeit. Does the failure to
understand really derive from the fact that the goal is too far away and the
road too steep? Isn't it, rather, that the object of this religion is too near for
the heavenly rewards of faith and the earthly advantages of charity not to
be confused? A religion that seeks to improve the lot of the poorest class:
how could a person not mistake one for the other? "I live in the quarter
where most of the members of the Society of Saint Joseph are recruited
and . . . I am pained to see that workers confuse us with that Jesuit institution." Parent should have begun by informing his faithful, as did Eugénie
Niboyet and Botiau from August 13 on, that "they should not expect alms
from the Doctrine, which has come to abolish them." Only association
can eliminate the exploitation of work and the humiliation of asking for
it. And association means, first of all, the struggle of each individual—
proletarian or bourgeois—against egotism. But how could human beings
"immersed in the battles of egotism"—that is, in the daily struggle to find
the means to stay alive—rise to the level of humanitarian sympathy if
the example did not come from those who could do it at less cost? In his
situation of unemployment and absolute poverty, how could bootmaker
Bar, dedicated but still influenced by "the outside world and especially the
habits of the industrial class," find the heart to propagate the doctrine if
its emissaries looked on indifferently as his wife prepares to deliver her
baby on the bare floor of their room? And so Eugénie Niboyet will give
Madame Bar clothes for the baby, five francs to take baths, a straw mattress, a cushion, two pairs of sheets, a blanket, a pillow, two pillowcases,
and four nightgowns. Raimbault could be driven to extreme measures by
despair; he should be given a few errands to run until something better turns up. And wouldn't it be advisable to give a few sewing jobs to

Madame Langevin, a midwife without assignments who is trying to convert a husband as devoted as he is devoid of means? Says Parent: "We know that alms demoralize people, but at the moment we have no other means to help the unfortunates who come to us."

Of course, these offerings of help claim to be not so much charity as an advance on the social usefulness of individuals capable of working for the Doctrine only if someone loosens the grip of misery that is paralyzing their zeal. And there is constant reaffirmation of the principle of discarding those whose position permits one to conjecture that they can find some material self-interest in the Doctrine. Thus Raymond Bonheur delays accepting hatter Geoffrey: "I do not know well enough whether, despite my observations, he may not be attracted to some extent by overly personal motives (he is without work)." But how can one ever know? Is the authenticity of a person's faith ordinarily to be judged in terms of the sacrifice of material interests? Then what about those who have nothing to sacrifice? Whether "advanced" or "brutalized," able workers or beggars, men of heart or men of the belly, almost all are or will be without work at some point or other. The teaching of workers began with the slack season of summer; autumn has brought no resurgence of jobs, which have been in decline since the July Revolution. And so the list of names in Eugénie Niboyet's notebook grows longer: Dagoreau would like to be a carrier on *Le Globe*, Fanny Lebert and Mademoiselle Pierron would like to be folders there, and Colas would like to be employed in correspondence. Voinier would like someone "to take an interest in him and try to help him earn a little money." His brother would like to have a joinery workshop with Conchon in the house of association on Rue de La Tour d'Auvergne. Bar and Vedrenne would like a shoe store there, Madame Lambinet a position as porter, Madame Henry a position as cook; and the senior Lambinet is offering to run errands for some small compensation.

The whole project of association, then, is trapped, not only by circumstance, but also by its very definition of the social solution to proletarian miseries. No matter how it is presented and how much stress is laid on the religious nature of its principle, doesn't association always come down to promising proletarians a future well-being to be achieved with less trouble? Notes Raymond Bonheur: "People present themselves who are wholly devoid of ability but who, in the name of association, are all the more disposed to join it insofar as they are old or without a lucrative calling." But even some real workers who have no paying position, such as locksmith Ménétrier, do not avoid this deviation that sees in the association a future equated more with the calm of retirement than with the ardor of combined work. Reports Dugelay: "He asked me if the Doctrine would take care of him when he is old and beyond working. I told him that since the Doctrine was busy founding houses of education, as it grew larger it would also form houses to provide rest for the aged, but that one had to beware of adopting the Doctrine out of self-interest."

This egotism of the people given assistance is a heavy burden on the Family; and it also has the effect, according to Parent, of driving away those who could offer it their ability and dedication. He has seen "capable workers who share our ideas refusing to associate with us because we have in our midst too many people who are lazy, disabled, or incompetent." The former secretary of a mutual-aid society is clearly quite ready, in the face of the people sent to him continually by the incompetent Baron, to adopt as his own the viewpoint of those solid workers. To attract the latter, he proposes to organize a "material test" designed to pinpoint workers "belonging to one of the last three classes" (see p. 192) by having them do some sort of work, by placing them with masters devoted to the Doctrine, or, better yet, by organizing them according to craft so that they can "get to know each other in a tangible way." But doesn't that approach mean adopting the egotism of the "true workers" as opposed to that of those getting aid or that of Denis Poulot's "sublime" workers? Thus the idea of "association" is constantly shuttled between the egotistical pole of assistance and the egotistical pole of enterprise. To anyone who wants to serve and use the proletariat in its twofold character as the "suffering worker," it shows up really in its contradictory and doubly disappointing identity as a chronic recipient of aid and a potential master.

Is it not time, then, to approach the battle against egotism on both fronts with redoubled energy? In his weekly program, shouldn't Raymond Bonheur add a new lesson on the religious character of the Doctrine and Association? But it is precisely the opposite approach that is adopted, this second week of August, by the very same apostle who, a month earlier, served as "herald" in the solemn ceremony of the "general communion of the Saint-Simonian family." He devotes his lesson to pointing up "its advantages from the individual standpoint, leaving the religious aspect as a stepping stone for subsequent gatherings." Here we have the prudence of the missionary getting to know his world but also his presentiment that the question of egotism is not reducible to a matter of morality, that this new Christianity seeking to be the religion of the industrial era is not, for all that, necessarily contemporaneous with the proletarian era:

> How can we do otherwise with people most painfully tempered and
> exposed in the battles of egotism? It is somehow under the Jewish

aspect that they must be linked to make their way in harmony toward the promised land, and in truth they are situated vis-à-vis the rich people who exploit them as the Jews vis-à-vis the Egyptians. While we threaten the powerful with incessant plagues, they, irritated, make their slaves feel the fear of abandonment and the desert and threaten to dismiss them if they talk doctrine. But from day to day the evil mounts. The latter see the price of their hard labor decrease, their particular position worsen; most of them are in debt, and this can only grow.

The "egotism" of proletarians is not a vice to be uprooted by preaching but a social situation that can be transformed only by contradicting its principle. The "Jewish question" is not about the religion of gold but the reality of bondage, a reality harsher still since God's envoys arrived to proclaim the journey to the promised land—the only differences being that today the desert is the threat of the Egyptians rather than the road to Canaan, and that the masters no longer avenge themselves on those who talk of leaving them by overloading them with work but rather by depriving them of work. That, you see, is how they try—everywhere, to some extent—to silence the rumor of the promised land. "Lenoir was talking too much in the workshop," and his fellow cabinetmaker Platel "has been forbidden by his bourgeois master to talk doctrine." Type-founder Vieillard "suffers a great deal for our doctrines in the foundry of M. Appert, who does not allow anyone to concern himself with our principles in the workshop." Locksmith Viel comes to undertake work in a shop where he had already made a deal, finds himself forbidden entry, and learns from comrades working inside that the master "has also threatened them with dismissal if they continue to hang around him." The master must also have warned his colleagues, because several others have adopted the same measures with regard to the Saint-Simonian. It is also forbidden "to talk doctrine" in the workshops of the Mint. They do talk about the doctrine at the workshop of Froment, a dresser of merino wool, where Botiau once worked; but they speak ill of it, and worker Jeandin was unmasked and discharged when he tried to respond to the calumnies. Grégeur, who worked in a brandy distillery in Montrouge that seemed to know nothing of the Lord's Day, took off one Sunday to attend the lesson. He was dismissed, "the master having noticed that the undertaking went just as well with one less man." But one need not be a day-laborer to be reminded of one's fate as a man in excess. Those who work for themselves are as dependent as the factory slaves on the good will of the wealthy class, and they risk seeing their clientele disappear if they reveal themselves openly as Saint-

Simonians. This explains the great difficulty of the houses of association if they must lodge workers still dependent on the old world: "The communal houses have the disadvantage of causing those who will come to them to lose business; since they often have relations with hostile people, they must use their intelligence to get wages out of them without offending them in any way."

So proletarian egotism again brings up the question of debt and sacrifice. Aren't these requests for jobs and positions that besiege the Doctrine the counterpart of the risks taken for it by people whose bondage lies in lack of work rather than too much of it? After a letter from Conchon protesting against giving jobs to a master outside the Doctrine, Botiau points up the generality of the situation: "Soon, they say, we will have to provide for ourselves or hide our religious opinions. For already in several areas where we are known, people say to you—the Society of which you are a member could well get it for you since it purportedly seeks to improve your plight; we have barely any for ourselves." Isn't it the Doctrine itself that confronts its faithful with this dilemma: either to look for their bread in the world of egotism, at the risk of conforming to its principles, or to ask it of the religion of association, at the risk of being accused of egotism? Doesn't Raymond Bonheur himself ask the Doctrine to take charge of his family to permit it to savor, instead of the "bread of the Christian passion," the "sweeter bread of love's transfiguration"? How can one explain the fact that proletarians cannot ask for their share of the sweet bread of this religion of love without being accused of Jewish egotism? When the order is given to the directors to recruit no more poor people to be cared for by the Doctrine, the unhappy Baron returns his reproach to Parent and his peers, reminding them that even his job as a messenger at three sous has suffered because of his faith:

> It was a matter of taking the poorest and most numerous class
> out of the bondage to which they found themselves reduced.
> Then, suddenly, we are made to see that to be delivered from the
> misfortunes hovering over our heads we must have a little wealth;
> or, without it, nothing changes, always miseries for the poor. . . .
> When I called myself a Christian, I had only three sous a day to
> live on, since I could not earn more, but still I could get that always.
> And what is the situation now that I have declared myself a Saint-
> Simonian? I have lost the confidence of the people who enabled me
> to earn that little income and now find myself abandoned on every
> side.

Despite his distress, Baron is determined to show slanderers that he will not profess any dogma other than that of Saint-Simon in order to get food, and that he will die of hunger rather than ask help of parish priests. "In the end I can always tell myself, as I deliver up my soul: I leave this earth inhabited by only a very few just human beings in order to hand myself over to God, my master, to obtain a sweet and happy life that will make me forget the toils and sufferings I was forced to endure in this world."

But the proof of truth and death is two-edged. To show that the material interest of the worker is an imposed condition and that he nevertheless is capable of sacrificing it will undoubtedly rehabilitate him morally; but it does not prove his social ability to transform his situation as a hostage to egotism. In rejecting a moral interpretation of proletarian egotism, the parable of Raymond Bonheur and the "testament" of Baron may only radicalize the problem. If egotism is not the mere absence of self-sacrificing dedication but the positivity of a world, then giving proof, even the supreme proof, of one's disinterestedness will not suffice to destroy it. By dying of hunger rather than renouncing his faith, Baron will again merely confirm his inability to participate as a worker in the apostolic work of the association. The proletarians have already proved that they know how to renounce the egotism of survival and confront death for their own dignity or the liberty of all. But this negation remains formal and impotent. It is no longer in death from combat or sacrifice but in a life of work and wage earning that workers are to prove their ability to overcome egotism. The transformation of their suffering into apostolic dedication does not entail merely an excess of sacrifice. The very quality of that suffering must be changed. Apostolic suffering is fundamentally the suffering of the Other. One must *know* how to suffer, how to exchange one's own suffering with that of the Other, in order to make it a real and effective apostolic virtue. It is this twofold suffering that characterizes the directors, former proletarians who have experienced the miseries they encounter, persons of bourgeois status whose hearts are broken by the spectacle of unknown sufferings. They all suffer simultaneously from the pains that bourgeois egotism forces the proletarians to undergo and from the disappointments caused them by proletarian egotism; from not being able to effectively assuage the ills of the workers because of the heedlessness of the Family, and from being prevented by the solicitations of the workers from enjoying the Family's life of love.

But their double suffering does not equally tackle and overcome the egotism of proletarians and that of bourgeois Saint-Simonians. The latter egotism can be corrected easily. It is true that the "preparatory degree" for bourgeois people is, in Delaporte's judgment, "cold and indifferent"; but that defect has to do mainly with the personality of its director, the scribbler Duveyrier, who discourses elegantly on the misery of the common people in general. If he were replaced with a man well situated to know the sufferings of individuals—Doctor Léon Simon—one could transform the overly distant sympathy of bourgeois members for the people's condition and teach them how to suffer from proletarian suffering and develop an active apostolic love in that interchange. But is the converse true for the Saint-Simonian proletarians, Jews in Egypt to whom the Doctrine can offer only fine words and various forms of assistance while stipulating that they are to give up republican eloquence and the servile resources of alms? Does their double relationship to Pharaoh and Moses permit a symmetrical conversion of their suffering into apostolic love? To be sure, they can offer the bourgeois members of the Family "love for love." But quite aside from the fact that love is always impure when it is given to priests of a doctrine that assures material benefits for workers today, or promises them for tomorrow, it remains an inadequate form of apostolic exchange. Proletarians would have to be able to suffer from the suffering of *the others,* the rich people—about whom, however, Raymond Bonheur surmises that they will not yield "except in the midst of trumpets, bloodshed, and cries of hunger and despair." Charles Pennekère is certainly willing to acknowledge the egotism involved in sacrificing himself for the good of his brothers alone: "I was not religious. I loved the proletarians because I loved myself in them." So at the session of December 25, 1831, he declares that he is renouncing the egotism of proletarian fraternity that fed his hatred for the bourgeoisie; to ratify his conversion, he embraces one of those people whom he had vowed to loathe for life. But this effusion of a Christmas Day seems negligible compared with the effusions and hates of the three days in July. Charles Pennekère himself makes clear the purely arithmetic character of this circumstantial love. It is merely an excess of gratitude toward the Saint-Simonian priests over his bitterness toward the privileged. On the preceding Sunday Pennekère had said: "I feel that I love you even more than I hate them. I love everyone and you can count on me."[3]

"I love everyone": a way of not looking too closely at the faces of those whom one should try especially hard to love. It is obviously easier for proletarians to play the great scene of callused hands shaking smooth hands than to understand the sufferings of the privileged. When they do make

3. *Enseignement des ouvriers,* session of Dec. 25, 1831; *Le Globe,* Dec. 30, 1831.

this effort at sympathy, curiously enough they manage to see only one misfortune for the rich—their insensitivity: "They end their days without knowing true happiness as we do, because the gold they have accumulated has not helped them to alleviate want; whereas, in our case, the simple workday does not belong to us, it belongs to all those who, like us, suffer from poverty."[4] Right off, it would be illogical to ask proletarians to feel an unhappiness that lies precisely in insensitivity. But this "poverty" of the rich class is not a mere being of reason, the simple difference between their insensitivity and the generosity of the common people. It is also the very source and principle of the egotism that causes suffering to the proletarians: "I pondered the fact that rich people glutted with gold will see unfortunates dying of hunger and cold at their doors without offering them a helping hand." In the "unhappiness" of the rich there is nothing for proletarians to recognize but the source and principle of their own oppression; and the only sentiment of understanding they could feel with respect to it is that sentiment of *bitterness* that forms the very core of "liberal" or republican passion.

So the problem is not limited to the "last three classes" specified by Parent: the beggars, clients, or permanent wards of the Doctrine who are incapable of feeling and suffering anything beyond their own misery and individual ways of reproducing it or surmounting it. More radically still, the problem concerns Parent's first class: those people who are intellectually capable of understanding the doctrine and morally prepared to work for the good of all. These people can feel a suffering that is not limited to their own individual misery. But their excess of suffering can only take the form of bitterness toward the rich and powerful. Their theoretical intelligence and their practical good will are incapable of making them conceive of a *suffering of the Other* that their imagination has no way of representing to them. Their mind and heart can be Saint-Simonian; their imagination necessarily remains republican. Entering the doorway pointed out by Bergier as that of his friend Gauny, Delaporte instantly experienced the joys and discouragements of his colleagues who use up their weeks purging people of their republican passions—the very same people they had left "entirely transformed" the week before. Along with his admiration for Gauny's "lofty capacity," Delaporte has also sensed the defiance of his "horribly ulcerated noble heart" and the value of such a conversion: "If I manage to rescue him from it, I will feel joy for the rest of my days, because he suffers well and will be of mighty service to the

4. Lebret, Profession of faith.

religion." But the simple arithmetic that would turn Gauny's fine suffering into apostolic ability by subtracting his liberal defiance is once again misleading and false. The liberalism that is superfluous for the apostolate soon proves to be so consubstantial with the perfection of his suffering that the subtraction has all the appearances of an Eleatic paradox:

> His liberal defiance is so heightened that he even fought against the conviction that I was instilling in his heart, as if it would have been a fatal influence on his liberty and an abuse of my facility in expressing myself. And I dare not believe that I managed to make him realize that my only superiority over him was the superiority of the Saint-Simonian conception over the philosophical or liberal conception, and that he would take up his place above me again once he came to acknowledge our conception.

"The philosophical or liberal conception": Delaporte is used to the solidarity of the two terms. It is the "metaphysical tendency" of his faithful that grounds their exclusivist passions for the Republic, the enfranchisement of workers, or Poland the martyr. This is not the simple sequence leading from a philosophy of enlightenment to a revolutionary politics. The metaphysical tendency of the proletarians is to absolutize the oppositions between true and false, good and evil, liberty and servitude. It is this absolutization that blocks a dialectical view of the relationship between social progress and political authority, enfranchisement and hierarchy. And it rests on the "liberal" view of the world, a representation contracted around the dual relationship of inequality: the bitter picture of the poor person dying at the doorway of those living in mansions, but also the humiliation of the autodidact on whom the rhetoric of the apostles tries to force conviction. Liberalism is a representation of the bourgeois person before being a politics with respect to him, a relationship to the talk of the other before being a doctrine. This accounts for the circle in which Delaporte finds himself trapped in trying to convince Gauny that the hierarchy of the two interlocutors is merely the superiority of one teaching over the other, when the whole process of convincing him proves the contrary and confirms the position of his adversary. This also accounts for the sensitivities about rank, perhaps the desires for advancement, that characterize these republican passions. The neophytes leave the preaching sessions "moved" and "enthused" by the message of love that equalizes rich and poor, educator and pupil; but they find all their "liberal defiance" once again in their dual relationship with their directors. And also the sensitivities that, in the face of bourgeois teaching, cling to the dignity of republican proletarians and claim, in the hierarchy of the bourgeois family, the promotions that rightfully belong to those who ask for neither jobs nor charitable assistance.

Thus there is a doubly twisted relationship between liberal defiance toward the teaching of the doctrine and republican enthusiasm for the preaching of it, between reserve toward the hierarchy of classifiers and desire for promotion in the Family. Anxious to stay on practical ground, Parent only brings out the dilemma more clearly by proposing a solution designed to "establish love more quickly by relying on already existing relations": that is, the organization of Saint-Simonian workers, no longer by neighborhoods, but rather by trades. This reorganization would certainly have two advantages: it would provide knowledge of the material capacity of the aspirants and thereby eliminate those whose inability to earn a living by their trade would only bring potential recipients of aid to the Doctrine; and it would make use of the diversity of customs and traditions that the epoch of guilds had bequeathed to the working class.

One could thereby eliminate the obstacle whose nature Parent had come to know well in the mutual-aid society he had been running since 1817. His efforts to expand its framework by appealing "to enlightened people and the protection of more eminent men" had run aground, not so much on any general class hostility as on the relationship of humiliation inherent in dialogue between bourgeois people and proletarians:

> In the presence of people from the privileged class, workers cannot speak freely; they lose their spontaneity. This is your fault to some extent. The human being cannot be perfect. If the learned man knows generalities better, the worker usually knows the details better. But when he tells you privileged people that you are mistaken, the poor unfortunate is often repulsed with a disdainful smile, which he returns to you with interest, I admit.

If one wants to convert that usurious exchange of disdain into reciprocal love, then the obstacle must be turned into an instrument; somehow the workers must be loosed from the Saint-Simonian hierarchy. Isn't that the very thing that Enfantin has just done for the women, taking them out of positions fixed by the male hierarchy and restoring them to an equality that might facilitate the revelation of the Woman? Won't the spontaneous tendency toward association bound up with the very organization of worker crafts make it easier for this reversal to take place, making it possible for the apostles to abandon their illusory privilege as learned doctors and instead learn, derive inspiration, from the revelations that the proletarians, like the women, will then offer them without constraint?

> In the new industrial organization I think it would be advisable to leave the workers in a state of liberty where they could tell you everything they think, suffer, hope for. For they are like the Woman. They have many revelations to make to you. For you to be able to come to know them and profit from them, your hand must be felt less at their meetings. Or, rather, they must have meetings where your hand is not felt at all, so that the spark of life in them may develop and serve all.

But can the new life of love truly develop in meetings patterned after the model of the guild associations, hence locked up in the collective egotism homologous to the individual egotism of people "of gentle and decent ways"? Doesn't the economical desire to establish love "more quickly" by relying on "already existing" relations represent a return to the shabbiness of those decent relations between associated workers that was denounced in Haspott's pamphlet? As he put it: "There is no quarreling. The proceedings are orderly and serious. But it is a communion of interests only, not of sympathy. . . . In a word, there is no love there." And so we are confronted with a paradox. The power of love could not develop outside the clashes of dual relationship and hierarchy. And "liberalism" could not lend itself to a "liberation" of proletarians and women that looses them from the formal rules of hierarchy so as to better set in motion the classic division of sensibility and understanding, of the (feminine or proletarian) science of "details" and the (masculine or bourgeois) science of generalities. From the women's side, it is Eugénie Niboyet who protests when the destruction of the feminine hierarchy results in her demotion from her post as directress, leaving her with the "free" function of associate. She refuses to be thus confined to the detail work of going door to door to individuals while losing the authority to teach and preach to the masses:

> It is by the mouth of a woman that the Saint-Simonian message should be taught and preached to workers, I think. To take away this faculty from us is to take away our life! Doing propagation work to individuals is undoubtedly a great deal, but not enough activity for me. I like to work on the masses because it is there that

I feel all my power! I am an apostle. I have received much. I have much to give. . . . I am conscious of the activity I desire to expend on workers because I love them. When I offer them a lesson, I feel I am completely on fire, and I recover from the pains entailed in propagandizing individuals.

Is this the protest of a bourgeois lady anxious to recover, as an apostle, the social superiority whose normal exercise she has renounced? No doubt it is; but the logic of debt, sacrifice, and vocation that sustains it is very close to that of her catechumens.

They, too, react against the sleight of hand involved in the "rehabilitation of the flesh" proclaimed by Enfantin under the three images of "industry," "worship," and "women." The only effect of this rehabilitation is to maintain its beneficiaries in the subordinate and inferior "liberty" and "equality" of the *matter* in which the apostles read revelation and from which they draw their inspiration. Like the bourgeois lady, proletarians want a recognized place in the hierarchy of the Family instead of this imaginary promotion: a place to which they are entitled by reason of the sacrifices they too have made for the Doctrine and by reason of their vocation as propagandizers that is determined by their very debt. So they lay a claim to entrance into the hierarchy of the Family by virtue of admittance to the "preparatory degree." After their profession of faith, Botiau's faithful "want to know the point of this formality, since they are not part of the Family, not being in the degree of initiation." And the same Parent who wants to rely on the autonomous organization of the workers underlines this second "delicate question," which goes counter to the first: the same people who don't like the idea of bourgeois people discussing their affairs want to participate in their life and be classed among them.

Some workers . . . are complaining that they are not being treated any better in the Saint-Simonian society than in the society outside, that they have no way of advancing in the hierarchy. [Parent had already asked the person in charge of propagandizing] what would be done with workers when they had received all the Saint-Simonian moral instruction that anyone is capable of getting. The active human being needs to have someone point out a goal for his activity. What will be the motive force behind this emulation in the new organization you are preparing? Don't overlook this question. It is vital because without emulation our society will be, for workers, nothing more than a society of sluggards.

A society of sluggards: the impatience of the apostles confronted with workers who are concerned solely with the torpors of retirement is unexpectedly turned back on themselves. Those who are not slumbering in dreams of a future without fatigue are asking for a society in which it is possible for them to advance, to be something besides interchangeable workers locked into the "details" of their industrial task. Dedicated or not, the proletarians necessarily have "the individual point of view." Where profit is not the thing guiding them, it is the hope of gaining access to another mode of social existence. The contradiction of the Saint-Simonian worker does not lie where it might seem to at first: in the opposition between the earthiness of requests for work or assistance and the declarations of heavenly love of Rossignol, Colas, Roussel, Meunier, and Martin. Their love letters are not insincere. Better-off than their brother workers or more heedless of material contingencies, these writers often belong, or come very close to belonging, to the aristocracy of the preparatory degree; they have no higher interest in the doctrine than that of exchanging love. Tailor Colas gets a good living from his craft; jeweler Roussel is without work but refuses association precisely so as not to be a burden to the Doctrine; printer Meunier asks only that he be allowed to enjoy the Saint-Simonian message in peace; the "Saint-Simonian engravings" of Rossignol do not seem to be very marketable; and grocer Martin will write off the few hundred francs owed to him by the Family. Thus the "individual point of view" of these proletarians has nothing to do with material self-interest. For that very reason, however, it points up a more radical difficulty: the inability of proletarians to participate as *workers* in the apostolate of work.

The Doctrine does not have to face up to the simple contradiction between proletarian words and proletarian practices but rather to the splitting in two of this suffering worker whose miseries it would like to assuage and whose "industrious" capability it would like to promote. In place of the suffering worker appear two characters: the egotistical worker and the loving proletarian. And while the former can address himself to the Doctrine only in the form of a request, the pure love of the latter is no longer that of a worker. Thus the differentiated behavior of the Saint-Simonian proletarians does not contradict their professions of faith. Rather, it confirms the paradox therein: they were Saint-Simonians insofar as they were republicans; likewise, they can love the religion announcing the glorious kingdom of work only insofar as they are something other than workers. The worker is necessarily locked up in the egotistical circle of demand. As for the proletarian, he can return "love for love" because he is both more and less than a worker. But this love remains unproductive: by increasing the number of proselytes through the obligation of propagandizing, it can only augment the already excessive population of dreamers or aid recipients who are good for nothing but their own multiplication. It is in the form of work that proletarians should pay the apostles back for the love the latter bring to their sufferings. But the whole thing is impossible. It is not just that the Doctrine is not an industrial enterprise, that it can put the workers to work only under the conditions of the old philanthropy. Even more importantly, work is not a gift that the proletarian could contribute in an exchange of love. Work, properly speaking, is his alienation, not something he divests himself of but something that comes to him from outside: the bourgeois people are the ones who *give* work. And the relationship to be had with them as *workers* is always that of asking for work, whether it be humble or sullen, individual or collective. Love is necessarily beyond this obligatory relationship between work and the request for it.

So the conversion of the worker of the old world into a Saint-Simonian worker seems to be impossible: insofar as he is a worker, he cannot be a Saint-Simonian; insofar as he is a Saint-Simonian, he is no longer a productive worker ("When, in the midst of my work, I ponder the beauties of Saint-Simonism, my hand stops").[5] And the work of Bazin is not even the sort that spoils the hands and brutalizes the spirit. The porcelain-painter is aware of belonging to an "aristocratic industry." Later placed as guardian of the "Temple" of Ménilmontant, he will agree, out of love for the Father, to compromise his material interests and risk persecution by wearing the apostolic habit; but he will not push his zeal to the point of maintaining the buildings and garden. Whether egotistical or disinterested, the proletarian proves to be equally unclassable, out of place with regard to all the positions that the doctrine can assign to him and incapable of participating as a worker in the apostolic work that is supposed to effect the deliverance of his class.

This is perfectly exemplified in the case of Gauny. Among Delaporte's affiliates, he is the one who knows best how to suffer; he is also the most disinterested, since he does not ask for work or position in the preparatory degree and even shuns the promotion that Bergier offers him into the bosom of the Family. This radical disinterestedness takes the form of an aspiration for the infinite that exceeds not only the work of the "machine" one "hires out" eleven hours a day but also the honors of the republi-

5. Bazin to Enfantin, Fonds Enfantin, Ms. 7624.

can career and the caresses of the loving family—an absolute that, in its
very principle, contradicts the progress one sees represented in it. From
his very first visit, Delaporte is confronted with this metaphysical antinomy that transforms the "subtraction" of Gauny's liberal defiance into
an Eleatic paradox:

> He conceives of morality as an absolute and invariable standard,
> and the human being as able to take a passionate interest in it for
> its own sake, for its abstract beauty. Asked to specify the limit he
> would place on morality, he said to me: infinite goodness.
>
> I hope I convinced him of the inconsistency of presenting the
> infinite as a determined standard, since the idea of the infinite
> always assumes something beyond what we know . . . that for us
> love could not be a sheer abstraction but a desire for a determined
> object; that we undoubtedly love only objects to which we feel tied,
> which we feel or know to be in relation to us; that our knowledge
> is progressive, hence also our love and then our morality.

The philosophy lesson is irreproachable, but incapable of moving the
joiner–metaphysician out of the antinomy of the determined infinite that
prevents him from conceiving the determinations of knowledge and the
stages of the strategy. It is not simply an appearance of reason or an
illusion of sensibility that engenders these contradictory images of the
republican imagination and these antinomies of liberal metaphysics. The
paradox of the infinite focuses the impossible movement of the proletarian to break away from an intolerable and insurmountable servitude. It is
his very position as a proletarian that produces, in this least egotistical
of proselytes, the splitting of consciousness that rules out the apostolic
communion of the worker.

Even when he comes to find, in the friendship of Moses Retouret, a
force more suited than Delaporte's teaching to "crush" this "liberal defiance," which he himself calls his "vengeance," Gauny will experience
the very same impossibility of transforming his love from afar into active
communion:

> Two inconsistencies come together in me. The one comes by way
> of electric impulses. It is a virile will, a primordial force to act,
> to advance in perfection, to love without constraint or restriction,
> and to crush the hydra that imprisons me. The other is a solitary,
> sophistic, horrible impulse. I see and love your harmony, and do

not see any harmony in myself. I would like to mingle my voice with the modulations of your hymns. My mouth is nailed shut. I cannot launch my prayer into the flames of your prayers. I cannot pray. A nightmarish impediment makes my life an infernal delirium and the quivering idea of an improbable dream. . . .

I shall always be loyal to your cause, but shall turn aside and keep away from the joys of those who come to share your works on the days of assembly.[6]

Do these two inconsistencies, which are not just the quirks of one character, attest to the contradiction of a generation involved in the transition from the old to the new world? "Two worlds live in us, one in the agony of its death throes, the other struggling with the joys of infancy."[7] But the constraints of proletarian space contrast with the dialectical hopes of the time, as the tortures of prison contrast with the joyous pangs of childbirth: "To the right and left of us, before and behind us, is work. . . . work with its inquisitional demands . . . holds me stuck in the glue pot of its cloaca."[8] To the dialectical optimism of the "rehabilitation of the flesh" that heralds the kingdom of the New Work along with its organization of industry, Gauny's "sophistry" opposes the metaphysical pessimism of the Son of Earth and friend of Ideas: that is, himself as the contradictory unity and embodiment of the distinction made by Plato in the *Parmenides*. Industry and the flesh are the very things from which he despairs of being redeemed: the daily-recurring constraint of selling his liberty with his labor power. In vain does Enfantin pretend to attribute to bourgeois meanness and hypocrisy the accusations of materialism he foresees being made against the new morality: "To combat us, they will all turn themselves into Christians, exclaiming that we have fallen from heaven and come crashing down on this filthy earth of wages, because they are unaware of the glory of emancipated industry."[9] Proletarian Gauny, however, does not have to turn himself into a Christian. He already knows he is fallen from another world, stuck in the glue pot on the filthy earth of wages, doomed to a hope that lies solely in another existence beyond all

6. Gauny to Retouret, July 24, 1832, Fonds Gauny, Bibliothèque municipale de Saint-Denis, Ms. 165; reprinted in Jacques Rancière (ed.), *Louis Gabriel Gauny: Le philosophe plébéien* (Paris: La Découverte/Maspéro, 1983), pp. 162–63.
7. Thierry to Gauny, Dec. 2, 1832, Fonds Gauny, Ms. 172.
8. Gauny to Retouret, Oct. 27, 1833, Fonds Gauny, Ms. 165.
9. *Oeuvres de Saint-Simon et d'Enfantin*, XIV, 73.

the kingdoms of work. The rehabilitation of the proletarian can only be his emancipation from the flesh.

As we range from those waiting only for retirement to this proletarian who yearns only for the infinite, with those dreaming of the march of peoples somewhere in between, we are forced to see one and the same thing: the worker of the new world is nowhere to be found. And one cannot see how he could possibly emerge from the base depths of the "suffering worker" or the proud heights of the "loving proletarian." A new human being must be invented: the "loving worker." That is the task spelled out by Enfantin on the morrow of the schism provoked by the re-habilitation of the flesh, when he announces its practical realization under three aspects: the organization of industry, the establishment of cultic worship, and the emancipation of the woman. His decision to transform a labor of "savants" (*docteurs*) into a labor of "apostles," to move from the propagation of dogma to the implementation of cult and industry, implies criticism of the still-Christian outlook and still-philanthropic practice that were bent upon assuaging the sufferings of the workers while teaching them how to fight against egotism:

> Up to now we have been for them merely *philanthropist*–savants. We have not enabled them to live our Saint-Simonian life. . . .
>
> Yes, the work we are performing today is a work of *matter,* a work of *industry*. It is the *flesh* we are rehabilitating [and] sanctifying. But remember what Eugène[10] said: "The sacred fire of enthusiasm is not lit at the feeble hearth of philanthropy." . . .
>
> Yes, we have done well in entering the worker's chamber, taking him out of it, and associating him with his brothers. We also do well in establishing workshops, watching over the moral, intellectual, and physical betterment of the children who come to us. But we would be abdicating the mission that *Saint-Simon* gave us, and we would deserve the accusations hurled at us, if we were to reduce the new temple to the shabby proportions of a barracks, or, rather, a hospice. Those are not the forms of aid that the poorest and most numerous class expects from the sons of Saint-Simon. It wants an *entirely new life,* a life of religion and poetry. It needs greatness, glory, artists who exalt and captivate it. The laborer wants festivals.[11]

10. Eugène Rodriguès, author of *Lettres sur la religion et la politique*, Paris, 1831.
11. *Oeuvres de Saint-Simon et d'Enfantin*, XIV, 73–74.

"An entirely new life": here the contradictory relationship between pro-letarian "individualism" and Saint-Simonian communion finds an opti-mistic solution. It was only the philanthropic, dualistic character of the love shown to the proletarians that thwarted the growth of their love, which was wedged between the narrow confines of shopkeeper demand and the excesses of liberal passion. It is because the would-be apostles were still only philanthropic savants that they attracted a population that always fell short of the ideal of the "religious" worker or went too far beyond it. That would include not only the "incompetents" and "invalids" ready to profess any dogma for food but also the worker "savants" more interested in the cloudy reaches of the dogma of love than in the reli-gion of productive work: "It is easy to see that the vast majority of those who have come to us are worker savants rather than rugged, vigorous workers."[12] It is by way of art, prefiguration of the religion and work of the future and paradigm of the new social individuality, that the contra-dictions of egotism and association, of work and love, can be surmounted. Work will be religion only if religion becomes theater: "The new Church is founded, and it is also a new theater. The Christian churches are de-serted, the playhouses are filled with the faithful, the actor is replacing the priest. . . . The fulminations of the Vatican slide over the theater. There is no way they could reduce it to ashes, because the poorest and most numerous class is there *en masse; it lives* only there."[13]

The communion of the theater in place of the lacerations of suffering? The imaginary unity of a representation that soon reveals a new duality: "the laborer wants festivals," but the apostles barely give him one. And it is a strange festival indeed, literally designed to lay the temple foundations of the festivals of the future. On July 1, 1832, in the garden of Ménil-montant where they are on retreat, the apostles have invited the workers of Paris to the "opening of the Temple constructions." It is a festival of work, then, a Labor Day celebration. But the performance, punctuated by the words of Barrault and the music of Félicien David, does not offer any particularly esthetic intensity:

> The shovelers fill the wheelbarrows. The wheelbarrowers set off
> in file, preceded by the fillers walking two by two and followed by
> four additional fillers as reserves. . . . The wheelbarrowers come
> four by four to take on a load. They go to the excavation by the

12. Ibid., XVI, 92.
13. Ibid., XIV, 123.

left road and return by the right road, thus circling the upper part
of the lawn.[14]

The official chronicler of the ceremony shows us that the crowd of visitors is not gripped by the rapturous intoxication of this new theater but by
an approving curiosity that leaves it at a respectful distance from the spectacle. If the spectacle does make an impression on it, it does so because it is
in the nature of a moral demonstration. The crowd looks "with a mixture
of astonishment and respect on these young men, bareheaded in the hot
sun, devoting themselves to hard work and thus preparing themselves for
the wearying life of the apostle." The crowd of workers is offered simply
work as a spectacle; but this work is elevated to a religious stature, which
they themselves could never give it, not so much by the accompanying
song as by the nature of those doing the work. This work, consecrated
in the abstraction of fatigue before being so in the finality of the undertaking, is the work of bourgeois men "inoculating themselves" with the
proletarian nature.

In reality, however, the spectacle divides in two. Each group of shovel-
ers, wheelbarrowers, and fillers is composed equally of "members of the
Family" and "men of Paris." The latter come to offer their Sunday as
workers to apostles whose "every day is for the people."[15] So we have a
double sacrifice of men submitting religiously to the same discipline. But
it is clearly not an equal match. In offering their surplus labor for free,
the "men of Paris" demonstrate not so much their own apostolic ability
as that of the bourgeois men capable of organizing them religiously to the
extent that they themselves lay down their savant's pen for the worker's
tool. Similar though the discipline of the two parties may be, it is not of
the same nature. The apostles are going through the classic apprenticeship
of command, which involves a stint of obedience; the workers are demon-
strating the already present capability of this command. In the peaceable
army of workers, as in any army, the important thing is not the recruiting of soldiers but the training of officers. The "proletarians" who have
to be trained are the officers of the army of work. But these proletarians
officers of the future cannot be people who were made proletarians by
the accident of birth. They can only be people who have chosen to become so: an inverted image of the revolutionary and imperial army taken
as the model of the peaceable army of workers. The worker of the new

14. Ibid., VII, 145–46.
15. Ibid., VII, 137.

world, the smith of the army of the people, cannot be the old proletarian regenerated but rather the young apostle transfigured. Barrault's excitement prompts him to express it in terms more brutal than he may actually intend: "The apostle is the hammer, but the people are the anvil."[16]

As a matter of theater, an exercise in military training. Enfantin was right to correct himself when he denounced the shabbiness of an association of workers reduced to the proportions of a barracks "*or, rather, a hospice.*" For it is indeed an army that must be put together to resolve the contradictions in the organization of workers by attacking their material basis. If one no longer wants to deal with savants or recipients of aid, one must no longer proffer fine words or little jobs to proletarians, but a real industrial project. To do that, one must appeal to bankers, proposing to them an apostolic undertaking that is at the same time a profitable industrial enterprise: "The reform of some branch of the workings of the *Globe* or some new and major step forward in *communications* between human beings."[17] The sound execution of this plan would be guaranteed by the industrial worth of the Saint-Simonian engineers, but also by their ability to transform the soldiers of riot into soldiers of work. The houses of association on Rue Popincourt and Rue de La Tour d'Auvergne, which are nothing in the way of an "industrial" effort and house semi-idlers whose monthly earnings do not even cover the cost of their food, already bear witness to this moral effort that seems to be far removed from the pageantry of the theater. "They have given us a life of love," attests cabinetmaker Boissy in paying homage to the directors of the Popincourt house.[18] But the "communion" that the apostles should have with proletarians now takes on a very different import. The kind word or caress of the savant–philanthropist should now become the practical education of the apostle–commander:

> Your affection for them is still merely *theoretical*. It is necessary that it become *practical*, mingling with your blood and your flesh. . . . To command *workers*, you must first know *the worker*, have his lifestyle, *commune* intimately not only in the depths of your heart but also in raw practice with *the poorest and most numerous class*. God has providentially brought the rudiments of this *peaceable army* to you; He has sent us our *workers*. So begin your industrial education with

16. Ibid., VII, 139.
17. Ibid., XVI, 80.
18. *Enseignement des ouvriers*, session of Dec. 25, 1831; *Le Globe*, Dec. 30, 1831.

them. Of course, you will fall short of sharing their labors, of being at work with them, of living their life completely; but at least you can mingle your bourgeois life a bit with that of the proletarian.[19]

The new communion shows up as the opposite of the savant's educational relationship. The educators need to be educated, and the workers must instruct the bourgeois members in the realities of proletarian life. But in so doing, the workers are merely educating their own masters, of course. In this task they are merely anonymous representatives of the class whose material and moral characteristics must be completely familiar to the future commanders of the peaceable army if the latter are to be equipped for their task, which is first of all a task of selection:

> So *communicate* with them and see which of them are ready to respond when we make our big appeal to the *engineers* and *bankers*. Seek out especially their industrial worth, not, as we have done so far, their intellectual ability. . . . We have given medical doctors to our *workers* and we certainly have done well. But in this medical effort what have we done in the way of hygiene? Nothing. Isn't that one proof that we have looked on them more as sick people than as healthy, robust beings? . . . Today the *worker* is bound to expect more of us. Let us make every effort to discover the needs and desires of the robust people, full of health and life.[20]

Thus, among the suffering workers and the savant workers the apostles have nothing more to do than to select and command the robust workers. In the game that will be played henceforth between "the Proletarian" to come, the officer of the army of work, and his solid recruits, what place remains for the chance proletarians whom the Doctrine had attracted earlier? To the workers responsible for the four propaganda centers, which have replaced the district directorates, Stéphane Flachat offers directives that one would readily assume had been designed to discourage them or their visitors:

> Before speaking to them of the *political economy* and the *politics* we have taught to the world, you will develop for them the new morality taught us by our Father Enfantin. . . . You will also say

19. *Oeuvres de Saint-Simon et d'Enfantin*, XVI, 89–91.
20. Ibid., XVI, 91–93.

whether your new industry is *attractive* to you. . . . You will say what you feel about the pleasures and the glory of your apostolate. You will tell them how you accept its *fatigues,* love its hopes, bless its joys. . . . Don't forget that in your propagandizing work among the workers you are to keep in the background what you might know of our Supreme Father's plans for industrial implementation.[21]

It is indeed a radical way to put off petitioners. But one can appreciate the difficulties of the newly promoted Vinçard in trying to argue for the prescribed "developments." Clearly, neither he nor his colleagues are being relied on to command or serve in the army of workers. At most they might wield a pickaxe and regulate the drill in the Festivals of Work; or, better, be counted on to compose hymns bearing witness, alongside the manual apprenticeship of the savants, to the intellectual and spiritual ability acquired by Saint-Simonian proletarians.

Men for representation, in other words. Hence the declassed architect Voilquin will be offbase in his comments at the time of the community retreat at Ménilmontant. He is mistaken in denouncing the mediocre work of the Doctrine's common laborers and the attitude of proletarians who are more concerned about finding an elusive rhyme than helping the apostles who are being initiated into proletarian labors:

> In my excursions around Ménilmontant, who were among the most intense workers that I saw? Some of those fathers whose social position in the outside world should have rendered them the most unfit for hard, material work; while some of their sons, brimming with youthfulness and health, were lazing on the lawn and searching for the measure or caesura of a verse that would not come. Others, proletarians not long ago, should have been setting an example but were retiring gravely to their chamber to meditate on ways to harmonize worship with industry: incapable of being disturbed in their reveries by any call except the call to meals.[22]

The allusion is without a doubt directed first and foremost at the giant Bergier. Besides Desloges and Charles Pennekère, he was the only proletarian to participate in the retreat. But the point is that Bergier is not

21. *Le Globe,* Feb. 27, 1832.
22. Voilquin to Enfantin, Fonds Enfantin, Ms. 7627.

at Ménilmontant to prove that he knows how to work with his hands. While explicitly denouncing this bad apostle, Charles Mallard indirectly justifies his behavior with the question he poses to "Father" Lambert: "Is the proletarian, who has experienced each and every misfortune of a badly organized society, called to the apostolate? And what good can he do for humanity by becoming an apostle?"[23] In any case, it is clear that proletarian Bergier has not been called to an apostolate involving initiation into the proletariat:

> Getting up at 5:00 A.M. to the sound of a horn; devoting oneself to the full range of domestic labors; wielding wheelbarrow and trowel; gardening, digging, weeding; donning full dress at 5:00 P.M., dining, conversing, singing, exercising, sleeping on a hammock, and observing a religious celibacy: all that curiously hardens young men. . . . Soon the proletarian will be in our midst.[24]

True enough, Chevalier does not rule out the possibility that this proletarian–poet of the future may come from the ranks of the empirical proletarians who come to Ménilmontant on Sundays. For example, there is that joiner introduced to him one Sunday in May by his friend Bergier: "Perhaps this bard is among the proletarians around us already! We see some remarkable ones indeed. Last Sunday I chatted with a joiner brimming with a great future."[25] Exactly what the future of this joiner might consist of, Enfantin's lieutenant does not say. But Bergier, for one, has a very definite idea as to what it is not to be: "Soon the plane will be broken for you."[26] No future in joinery work, then. But is it really a question of the future? In any case, it is nothing resembling the long apostolic marches for which the Ménilmontant exercise is a preparation; rather, it is the suspended time of vacation, a souvenir or presentiment of other existences. The workday Bergier invites Gauny to come and share with him resembles that of apostle Chevalier about as little as the country party of the proletarian resembles the initiation of the bourgeois to the labors of earth:

23. Mallard to Lambert, ibid., Ms. 7757.
24. Chevalier to Brisbane, *Oeuvres de Saint-Simon et d'Enfantin*, VII, 37.
25. Ibid.
26. Bergier to Gauny, May 1832, Fonds Gauny, Ms. 166; in Rancière (ed.), *Le philosophe plébéien*, p. 155.

Day has broken. The morning wind balances on the treetops. The bird chanting the return of day brings such emotion to my heart that I fear bewilderment. . . . I cannot tell you all the charm this life has for me in comparison with my life a year ago. There are the works, the exercises, the games. On the lawn in the evening there are the various little stories. Last evening, for example, Cavel told us of the conversation he had had with two May beetles, whom he had expiring of love.[27]

Bergier is not inviting his friend to days of idleness, however, and he is not unmindful of fraternal labor even though he may put particular stress on the music lessons. But the glance he gives to the disposition of labors and tools evokes more the trappings and games of vacations at the country manor than the rough apprenticeship of the apostolate:

On one side the spade, the rake, the watering can, for gardening work; then the axe for chopping down trees. On another side the mason's hammer for smashing and the joiner's hammer. On still another side the painter's brush and the brush to polish rooms. Finally, all these jobs, presented under their natural face (i.e., the welfare of humanity), are performed with unflinching zeal; they do not tire us. Their purpose dominates all our thoughts, and our hearts are also stimulated by the chants of some, the presence of our supreme father, and the puns of Father Lambert.[28]

A variety of natural labors that love for humanity enables one to perform painlessly—would the defect of the bad apostle be not so much fearing fatigue as not finding it? In the description of these children's games, there is always the same foreshortening from the domestic and sentimental economy of the small family to the great maneuvers of universal association, the same confusion that retains and remembers, of the laborious work of the apostles, only the sweetness of loving relations: "gentle embraces . . . words of love and dedication to humanity . . . you heard only sighs . . . how sweet this emotion is." Bergier certainly has not forgotten that the emancipation already won by him commits him to

27. Bergier to Gauny, May 1832, Fonds Gauny, Ms. 166; in Rancière (ed.), *Le philosophe plébéien*, pp. 147 and 150.
28. Ibid., p. 149.

the rough task of emancipating all his brothers, of stopping for them the chariot of misfortune "at the risk of falling under its wheels." But the ideal of natural work he describes today and prefigures for tomorrow, rendered alluring by humanitarian love, is itself suspect. Enfantin takes pains to offer a reminder to one disciple attracted by the Fourierist craze: the retreat at Ménilmontant is not made to attempt an experience of attractive work by means of fraternal love. In short, it is not an attempt to realize Fourierism by Christian means: "It is not *work done* we are supposed to show the world today so that it may know us and, above all, love us. And so I am little concerned with regulating *fixed* and *variable functions,* with establishing the *occupations* and *pleasures,* the *work* and *leisure,* of a peaceable workshop that might make us known. . . . For, in truth, I am thinking only of having us *loved, respected, glorified.*"[29] Ménilmontant is not a phalanstery imaging the future organization of work ("here there are neither druids nor hordes [as in Fourier's theory] for the drains of our family"), but neither is it a simple initiation into manual work for generous savants anxious to serve the people. It is the laboratory for training an apostolic body—a new type of human being who possesses both the "gift of tongues" (i.e., the art of speaking to the common people) and the ability to train his body to any and all conditions:

> The apostolic nature must be formed. For that, we first had to leave our Monsigny shell, in which we were suffocating. Then we had to leave behind our habits of mastery and idleness, shape our bodies to work and exercise, our voices to chants, our ears to harmony. . . . Before all else, apostles must be (don't laugh) *good bedfellows,* good children trained to a common life that is quite up to date. They must know themselves from the tops of their heads to the tips of their toes. We need characters that live everywhere, off everything, and with everyone. We need human beings who have been ground down by daily poverty yet are so full of life that they get up again always, and always greater.

Here we have something very different from bourgeois savants educated in proletarian labors and sufferings. In his couplets for the inauguration of the Temple construction, Barrault described them as "*neither* masters *nor* servants / *neither* common people *nor* bourgeois." The new human being

29. Enfantin to Capella, April 30, 1832, *Oeuvres de Saint-Simon et d'Enfantin,* VII, 15–26.

has not only left the shell of the bourgeois savants, whose hierarchy had "smooth white skin." He has also shed the weakness of those "worker savants" whom mothers swaddled and rocked in their cradles and whom the privations of an undernourished childhood and the rages of an adolescence condemned to accursed work have rendered too frail or vindictive to proudly wear the leather apron of the illustrious Charlet. The new human being steps in to make up for the impossible identification of the proletarian with his image: a hierarchy with bronzed skin and callused hands, men no longer with leather apron but rather with leather skin.

So the apostles of the new work have managed to slip between the proletarians of the old world and their image. It is a substitution without too much violence: the proletarians are cheated of the promised delights of fraternal association, but exempted from the rough maneuvers of the new work. Seizing from them an image that was too heavy for them to bear, the new human beings leave them in exchange the envied power of simulacra: the hymns of Vinçard, Bergier, and Jules Mercier; the promenades with song and the impromptu choruses in the theatrical performances organized by Julien Gallé; the exhibition offered on the Montereau hillside—apostles sewing the apostolic habit of Delas; for Bazin, guarding the temple of Ménilmontant and Enfantin's habit. To makers of measures who love "work" more than their own craft, tailors weary of sewing little stitches, overqualified tapestry workers who recoil from a future of enrichment, painters who sleep during the "sermon on self-interest"[30] and like to promenade their faith with their industry, the new human beings propose this exchange: instead of the Promised Land, they give them the task of guarding the Temple of faith and bygone loves. They leave in their care, along with the function of choristers, the singing of those couplets for various occasions in which posterity will be quick to see the hymn of the artisan happy with his work, when they may well be only a well-understood misunderstanding set to music: the glory of the new work modulated by the obsolete rhythm of their dreams of love.

But it is also the only theater that will issue from the epic of the new human beings who set out to raise the peaceable army of workers throughout France and then effect the marriage of East and West in Egypt. Quickly, indeed, does the theatrical dream of Enfantin and Michel Chevalier vanish: the contagion of the apostles going to every city and town and fanning out to every inn and post office, becoming ferrymen and postilions to recruit and send everywhere, by land and sea, new detachments

30. Bazin to Enfantin, Dec. 1832, Fonds Enfantin, Ms. 7647.

of the soldiers of work, with proud chests wearing belt and red beret, the "cockade of the party of workers";[31] the medallion of the Father and the collar of the apostles, the captivating singing of the "Appel" or the "Salut au Père," the new dramas and the Festivals of the People. Vanishes as well the revelation of the apostolic body in the very midst of forges, mines, and workyards, the spectacle of the Word-made-flesh presented by these artists, engineers, and officers turning the wheel or bearing the burden of manual labor. Far from Ménilmontant, the fatigue of the apostles represents nothing more than the phraseless, aimless work of the proletarian:

> I write to you with hands blackened by iron filings and oil. . . . In the capacity of a manual laborer turning the wheel, I have given proofs of courage, strength, and perseverance. I have known what it is to eat bread moistened by the sweat of monotonous labor. . . . We thought our behavior would be such as to impress the least impressionable. It has been nothing of the sort.[32]

The letters of musician Rogé and military engineers Hoart and Bruneau bear witness to a double failure: the failure to forge a body of apostles who would transfigure the sufferings and routines of the proletarian body; and the futility of the sacrifice itself, to which the demonstration of the missionaries was then reduced.

True enough, even this lack of success offers to the dialectics some material in return: if the sermons and living examples of the apostolate have failed to hatch the seeds of the future, the reason may be that they are already present someplace where the old ratiocinating and philanthropic habits of savants do not permit the apostles to recognize them. This is the revelation offered to Captain Hoart at the workyards of Grenoble. There Captain Hoart, while keeping his apostle's uniform, has again taken his normal place as a leader of men. The surrounding world, admittedly, is too "cold and glazed for any labor of words," for any political, religious, or military enthusiasm. But this very void surrounding work not commanded by the enthusiasm of any humanitarian project and not given rhythm by the music of any festival lets appear the seed of the future that can only

31. Michel Chevalier to Rousseau and Biard; in H. R. d'Allemagne, *Les Saint-Simoniens (1827–1837)*, Paris, 1930, p. 326.
32. Letters of Hoart, Rogé, and Bruneau to Enfantin, Feb.–April 1833, Fonds Enfantin, Ms. 7647.

sprout in a place where production is the only activity and consumption its only end:

> In the workyards there begins to sprout the idea of work as a point of honor. A worker who has acquired a reputation for courage and strength that is validated by the foremen and his fellow workers in the yard would regard himself as disgraced if he shrank from difficulties. Is there a perilous passage to be cleared for a wagon? The leader walks ahead and the passage is cleared.
>
> All these phenomena of life are still quite undeveloped, but all make clear that the future lies there. At the moment, the stimuli for this life are *hunger* and *orgy*. The human word has little power to command work. Hunger drives people to it; but today it is *orgy*, especially, that develops their forces, multiplies them a hundredfold. The worker moved by the desire to avoid hunger applies himself to the day's work. But the worker who is driven by a desire for great consumption works wonders; he applies himself to the task.[33]

The whole balance of the system has seesawed on one and the same representation: the petty appetites of a worker moved only by the desire to "avoid hunger." No longer is it a thirst for justice and love that stands over against the hunger of the self-interested worker, but rather an even bigger hunger. In the workyards where no altruistic dedication or dream of the Promised Land steps in to stay the worker's arm, where there is nothing else to do but produce more so as to consume more, the solution to classification according to capacities and retribution according to works thrusts itself upon us. It is the intensity of the worker's desire to consume that grounds a hierarchy of capacities and retributions self-evident to all: "The Justice of the workyard is recompense according to one's works. In this connection the worker has such scrupulousness that he can detect the smallest mistake made in the matter. He loves the person who carries out this justice, even when that involves curtness or even harshness." This effectuation of Justice does not represent the perfection of industrial association to come, of course: "Enthusiasm for *production* is ready to blossom, but only ready. The workers have only a vague awareness of production from a general point of view. They do not yet sense clearly its political value." But even that opens the way to a future as remote from the dreams

---

33. Hoart to Enfantin, August 1833, Fonds Enfantin, Ms. 7733.

of assured retirement as it is from the restful strains of that love which
performed fraternal works without fatigue:

> It is in these vast workyards that we come to see how much we
> must transform the language we once addressed to workers. We felt
> sorry for their *sufferings*. As an El Dorado we offered them a future
> of *muscular repose,* of *work without fatigue;* we showed them *machines*
> producing everything and demanding little material activity. All
> that was still bound up with *Christianity*. They were philanthropic
> jeremiads that could penetrate the hearts of men of *theory* only.
> Good workers want *fatiguing labors* because they love *glory,* because
> *work* is their *life*. You cannot hold them back for long without
> employing their powers. They would sooner destroy houses or give
> themselves over to debauchery, to orgy. . . . Wanting to bemoan
> the *sufferings* of *work* is like pitying the *savant* because his *head* is
> fatigued by the elaboration of *ideas*. We will not see the *sorrows*
> steadily diminishing. Rather, we will see the *joys* coming more and
> more into harmony with the sufferings. The time separating fatigue
> from recompense, from *pleasure,* will become increasingly shorter.[34]

Is this the solution to the "Jewish question" of Raymond Bonheur?
Shortening the arid interval between pain and enjoyment was the project
that brought together the tangled contradictions of the apostolate of work
between the impatiences of egotism and the infinities of love. In moving
beyond the moral formulation of the problem, which sought to link merit
to disinterestedness, Hoart does not yet move out of the paradoxes of the
infinitely small: "To the greatest fatigues, to the greatest sorrows, will correspond ever more immediately the greatest pleasures, the most delightful
rests. . . . There is difficulty because the interval separating suffering from
its reward is not infinitely small."[35] But how could the immediate know of
degrees, and division to infinity cease to separate enjoyment from suffering? Fortunately, the solution surfaces at the same time. *Intensity,* perfect
Jack-of-all-trades and Promised Land of dialectics, comes along to resolve
the antinomies of quantity and quality, work and pleasure, egotism and
unselfish dedication: the ongoing intensity of a labor whose intoxication
(i.e., "glory") anticipates pleasurable enjoyment, and of a pleasurable enjoyment that is not rest but consumption (i.e., destruction). In this identity

34. Ibid.
35. Hoart to Decaen, August 1833, Fonds Enfantin, Ms. 7733.

of the intensity of creative expenditure and the intensity of destructive expenditure, the progress of industrial work participates in the progress of divine work, and the life of the worker is in the image of God's life:

> God is the greatest producer and the greatest consumer. The many creatures consumed and produced all at once! The countless meta- morphoses in an instant! But let us not forget that this immense consumption tends unceasingly toward an ever greater develop- ment of all that is, toward an ever more complete production. God never stops consuming and producing. That is His life. . . . Producing and consuming: that is the life of the people, the life of God.[36]

No more need of festivals of work or of common people for this new divine mystery that the well-informed self-interest of the manufacturers celebrates every day without knowing it: "The leaders of industry instinc- tively know this fact because, in their practice, in order to achieve great results they offer a great deal of money or provide wine and meat."[37]

Remember Parent's proposed solution: to "establish love more quickly by relying on already existing relations" (see p. 207). Might it be enough to shift one's place and travel a bit along the roads and railways and workyards of the future to find already at work the new worker whom preaching sought in vain to forge in the common people made up of shoe- makers and tailors, in the city of workshops and stores of egotism, of fleshes and theaters of love? But wasn't it first necessary to change one's skin, to incarnate the word of the savant in proletarian flesh, in order to be able to recognize the elect of God in this beast of work marching to stick and carrot, producing to consume and consuming to produce?

The new worker has been found, and he bears a curious resemblance to the slave of old. And so they will go looking for him a little farther away, to the East, in Egypt, the new Promised Land that the Jews deserted and that is to be the place where the work of the future will be accomplished: "To us outsiders . . . men from the liberal nations where the human being no longer marches in dense masses to the stick, a workyard of 40,000 men seems to be a dream out of *A Thousand and One Nights*. It is an or- dinary thing here, where 300,000 men dug the Mamoudieh canal and left fifteen to twenty thousand dead on the battlefield . . . where the traveler

36. Ibid.
37. Ibid.

beds under the stars and lives on a few beans."[38] A modest orgy, cut to
the measure of the sham direction exercised over this work, on a canal
that will not be made, by apostles serving as "voluntary engineers" who
have no authority over the troops of *fellahs* marching to the tune of fife,
tarabouk, and reed flute other than the authority accorded them by their
dream: one more time, one last time for the apostle become proletarian,
the illusion of a command and the reality of a sacrifice. On the banks of
the Nile, only the plague awaits Captain Hoart, the new man, who "first
among the privileged delivered up his body to the harshest sufferings of
work in order to incarnate in the temple a new life of hope and love."[39]

What is taking shape between the metropolis in the West and the desert
in the East is not so much the industrial command of the future as its
ghostly double, the staging of a piece in which the old image of the happy
smith is divided up among the three partners in a new game of doubles: in
the marches of the East, the engineer apostle of industrial religion, bourgeois reborn as proletarian, sometimes commanding the labor of the new
slaves but more often forging its heavenly image; facing him, the beast of
work consecrated as the worker for glory, unwitting pioneer of the new
work; in the metropolis of the West, the choir of old-world proletarians,
tailors and shoemakers and joiners and painters and floor-layers, their
loyal and distant homage celebrating the new work in which they have no
part except to recognize in it, or pretend to recognize, their own dreams
as loving children: illusion, lie, truth—who knows?—on the banks of a
different river, the Lethe. Such is the souvenir of love wherein the guardian of the abandoned temple of Ménilmontant evokes the joy of an August
night between the release of the Father from prison and his departure for
the East:

> Often, in private among ourselves or to visitors, we talk about the
> delightful month of August 1833: the release of our Father, the
> nighttime entry, the star of our Mother, the handshake to the old
> man, the first visit to my Adèle, our emotion. And our eyes are
> moist—that's with happiness, Father, and that, Father, is like the
> first love, it cannot be forgotten. . . . The sky is blue in Paris at this
> moment. Shall I see that of the East one day? Are the minarets of
> Cairo impressive? Shall I trample underfoot the sand of the desert?

38. Enfantin to Hoart and Bruneau, March 1834, *Oeuvres de Saint-Simon et
d'Enfantin*, IX, 208–9.
39. Hoart to Suzanne Voilquin, Feb. 1834, Fonds Enfantin, Ms. 7733.

Shall I share the sufferings of those peoples? . . . Father, count on us always. Your devoted son in this life and the next. If the beautiful mythological fiction, the river Lethe, is not a fable, on the other side, Father, when caterpillar will be butterfly, all God's and the Father's.[40]

40. Bazin to Enfantin, May 4, 1834, Fonds Enfantin, Ms. 7795.

CHAPTER 9

The Holes of the Temple

FROM CATERPILLAR TO BUTTERFLY, from the banks of the Seine to the banks
of the Lethe: the route of the chrysalis will not pass by the banks of the
Nile. In vain does the apostle Moses, who has decided to go and find his
"Mother" again in the new Promised Land, urge his friend, joiner Gauny,
to follow his example:

> I have already resolved, and given my word to others, that at the
> Father's signal I shall go with the workers and women to Egypt:
> the Egypt that today calls back the People of God in the name of
> liberty, with the promise of justice and the hope of abundance; the
> Egypt where the Daughter of the Pharaoh is to definitively declare
> herself the Mother of life's abandoned children and restore every
> infant to its mother's breast.
>   Gauny, think about it!
>   Soon, very soon, Gabriel, I shall be on my way. And you, what
> about you, my Brother?
>   You helped me to sense it, something said it to you the other
> day through me: "I swear by the immense, by the eternal, we will
> not always be enchained, wretched,"[1] Gauny . . . go seek it:
>   West into East, the Proletarian of France fertilizing the Arab's
> desert and liberty; the free woman of Europe tearing away the
> veils that envelop the beauty of her sister of Asia like a cloud
> and converting the ancient despot to the gentle sweetness of an
> unknown kiss!
>   Seek yet again: the streaming voluptuousness of labor's sweat

1. Citation of an earlier letter (Jan. 24, 1834) from Gauny to Retouret.

and toil, the well-beloved land, jealous and throbbing with love, the ravished and radiant heavens!

Gabriel, don't you see our place in this great battle of the powers of goodness establishing their empire, to the envy of the fading powers of evil?

O my brother, Gabriel, stout worker! Will you deprive me of your robust strength and your bold courage, you, my dark-eyed brother?[2]

The blond preacher surely knows his answer already. What joiner would travel so far to seek the streaming sweat and toil that he found long ago without ever having yearned for them? What liberty could he ever expect from the "robust strength"—just another name for necessity—that daily obliges him to hire out his body to the enemy? And how might he identify with those companions of Moses whose "ordeal" he is invited by his friend to share? His daily-renewed misery identifies much more with the journey of the Wandering Jew, *Ahasvérus,* whose story Edgar Quinet (1803–1875) has just retold in a prose poem that borrows Herder's and Ballanche's ideas about palingenesis. And the attributes of glorious work, in whose name Moses summons his brother of the proletarian tribe, are nothing but the stigmata of forced labor:

The streaming voluptuousness of labor's sweat and toil? How would you know about them, since you have never worked? . . .

Moses mine, I am not a stout worker. I am, for myself, a fatal, necessary worker. . . . My robust strength is simply nervous energy, my bold courage is galvanizing courage, and my dark eye is a fool's eye.[3]

To correct the inversion that turns the marks of the proletarian's bondage into his glory is also to return to the "free" space of the eastern desert the meaning that Enlightenment thought gave it. The very same necessity that forges in the worker's body its illusory power puts into the proletarian soul the "liberal" anguish that prevents it from finding, in the classic

2. Retouret to Gauny, Jan. 30, 1834, Fonds d'Eichthal, Bibliothèque Thiers; reprinted in Jacques Rancière (ed.), *Louis Gabriel Gauny: Le philosophe plébéien* (Paris: La Découverte/Maspero, 1983), pp. 164–65.

3. Gauny to Retouret, Feb. 2, 1834, Fonds Gauny, Bibliothèque municipale de Saint-Denis, Ms. 165; in Rancière (ed.), *Le philosophe plébéien,* p. 166.

space of despotism, the unity of a grain of sand. "What would I be in the face of the Arab and his desert and his liberty, I who pulse all over with agonies? What a grain of sand is in the face of the pyramids; and besides, for ancient and modern despots my thinking has all the looks of Brutus's dagger."[4]

Once upon a time the religion of progress had managed to transmute revolutionary energies into the power of love. The new exodus sends proletarians back to the insurmountable reality of their exile and splits the faith in progress into the divided state of a consciousness constrained to live on two levels: in the *here and now* of forced labor accompanied by all sorts of republican bitterness and sporadic hope; and in the presentiment of a hereafter or beyond more closely linked to the mysteries of Orpheus, rejuvenated by Ballanche's palingenesis, than to the Promised Land or the Kingdom of the Son. From one to the other, the journey—the ordeal—of the proletarian cannot be redeemed by the march of any industrial army or transfigured by any project in time:

> I have already told you: I no longer have faith in time. I no longer believe in its organic missions. My existence is too twisted by its subversions.
>
> For me liberty, love, the collective action of my duration, my social necessity: it's something beyond the skies. . . .
>
> Did you get me right when you quoted me? I take myself as the authority: for us the immense, the eternal, are in the realm of futurations.
>
> My place is where my presence will be more useful than my absence. I will be a nothing in Egypt. In France I will help sustain infectious days.[5]

So his choice has been made: here and elsewhere, but not down there on the great highways of the industrial future. Only destitution will be able to push him, much later than some of his co-religionists, to try a stint in those workyards of the future. At the peak of the 1846–1847 crisis, he, like them, will have to resort to Enfantin's patronage to get a small post in the railroad administration. It is not the work of the railroad pioneers that attracts them but the hoped-for quiet of a little job in the shadow of the offices and warehouses of the vast railway enterprise. More for-

4. Ibid.
5. Ibid., pp. 165–66.

tunate than switchman Charles Pennekère and overseer Desloges, who have been thrown out into all the material perils and disciplinary rigors of the new Moloch, Gauny will glean a job as a railyard watchman from the very special patronage of a Father he persists in addressing as "Citizen." There, for four years, besides "fine leisure activities" and plenty of open air for both "the lungs and propaganda work," he will have an opportunity to find both the calmness of solitude and a multitude to be inflamed with his rebel energy.[6] But there he will also apprehend the full extent of the slavery and the new feudalism embellished by images of the peaceful army of workers. There he will observe the four circles of the model industrial hell, where machine improvements are refining the despotic tortures of the cellular prison into instruments of a production serfdom.

It is, first of all, the Temple of the machine, transformed into "sanctuaries of penance" by the "numbered forges, the alignment of stations and lathes, the monotonous hum of the motor." There "matter, obedient accomplice of the inventor's conceptions, . . . exercises command without pity and sits on its throne amid its servants, demeaning their dexterity and their thinking with its inert comprehension."[7] Sacrificed to the reign of things, these human beings are parked in their places, locked up henceforth in the perfection of a single detail and obsessed anew with the peril of gears that neither hear nor heed when a human being howls with pain.

Hell is also in the vast rotundas of traction where the locomotives are repaired and stoked up. In this second circle of tortures, "there is no lack of room and yet air is wanting."[8] For the masters had gotten wind of the subversion that used to circulate in workshops through the tiniest of sighs or gestures, and so they had the genius of architects build them armed citadels against this new peril: "They have borrowed what they could from the system of cellular prisons, constructing their workshops on the panoptic model so that, from a central point that branches out into divergent mirages akin to radiating threads of a spider's web, the foreman can see the most private acts and relations of his subordinates."[9]

In truth, however, no peculiar architecture is needed to stamp the omnipresence of mastery and servitude on the body of the workers. On the lines and landing platforms as well as in the depots, the satraps of Capital

6. Gauny to Enfantin, 1851, Fonds Enfantin, Bibliothèque de l'Arsenal, Ms. 7630; in Rancière (ed.), *Le philosophe plébéien*, pp. 174–75.

7. Gauny, "Les chemins de fer," Fonds Gauny, Ms. 119; in Rancière (ed.), *Le philosophe plébéien*, p. 51.

8. Ibid., p. 53.

9. Ibid.

do it by obliging their subordinates to wear the livery that vainly tries to pass for the "uniform" of the peaceable army of workers. This "traitorous linguistics" is denounced by the lesions and contusions that inscribe the arbitrariness of Capital's power on the body of "the damned." If it is his whim, won't one or another of these satraps order the worker to get a crew cut, or to trim a beard whose fullness outrages the strict mustache of the officers of the railroad army?

But that is not yet the last circle of hell. It is there in the signal towers and excavations where the switchmen and roadsmen, harassed by the dreaded spying of their foremen as well as by their anxious wait for trains, "bestialize themselves in order to endure their lot as automatons"[10] and in order to escape the schizophrenia of a spirit "filled with thoughts in ruins, thoughts scattered and broken into an expanse of shadowy fragments seeking vainly to reunite":[11] the animal kingdom, the return of spirit to matter—there where the epic of the new human being was presaged. In the final analysis, then, to the egotism of the Jews of Egypt and the lacerations of republican Protestantism, the light of the East and the hierarchy of the future offer only a return to the archaic realms of the human dialectic: the immediacy of feudal servitudes or animal religions—the serfdom of the worker chained to his specialty, the panoptic wheel of torture, the livery of domestic service, and ultimate return to the beast. Such, in minted coin, is the materialized dream of the new human being, of the kingdom of God on earth.

From this reckoning up of the new world, Gauny does not draw any resignation to the familiar fatality of the old world but rather the idea that the course must be run in the opposite direction. The kingdom of God, heaven on earth, can only be the reign of Baal, reserving for proletarians the role of "crucified" along the way. The course of their liberation must run in the opposite direction, from earth to heaven; and it can commend itself to only one hero–engineer, borrowed not from the "new Christianity" but from ancient paganism: Icarus. Over against the hellish industry of the railroads, which devastate the earth and rivet the chains of slavery on the body of human beings, he sets the great hope of a celestial science and industry—aerostatics:

> These aerial transports, admirable in their economy and wondrous in their flight, will soar over the sky like flocks of gigantic birds,

10. Ibid., p. 60.
11. Ibid.

covering the sun only with their fleeting shadow and not ravaging it. Then agriculture, clearing away the ruins of the railroads, will give the world back its sites and its forests, its grace and its emancipation, employing workers brutalized by the terrible locomotives in the regenerative work offered by a cultivation that is in the form of a national association. As for the aeronauts, they will organize themselves in accordance with the fraternal pact that will rule society. All will share in the common benefits in accordance with the time they have put in, and so each will feel his own good fortune grow with the good fortune of others. Then the rail lines, ripped up and covered with vegetation, after a few years will leave behind only the distant memory of their speculations and catastrophes.[12]

A coherent industrial myth withdrawing the philosophy of progress from the "necessity" of a new feudalism and serfdom that is supposedly to end with the radiant dawn of the workers. Only Icarian industry will make association possible, and the latter is to reign simultaneously on earth and in heaven. But this myth reconciling the *here* and the *elsewhere* of the faith in progress still does not eliminate the duality: the worker of the future will remain a double being—man of earth and son of sky.

For the time being, however, the days of the pariahs are more modestly divided between "this life of struggle, this individual life . . . the transient sorrows of the positive life," found again by the unfortunate Bazin, who has been chased out of the now sold estate of Ménilmontant, and "the peaceful dream, the angelic fiction of the faith, the ideal happiness of the life to come" that serve as interludes.[13] He is "always with another expectation," like "the first soldier of the peaceable army of workers," the man of a thousand trades, Desloges, whom caring for an aged mother, a wife, and three children has kept far away from the apostles who were summoning him to Egypt. This hope has to be strong to chase away the bitterness of the former missionary's current labors. Desloges, who has taken back from his rival Bazin the lodge at Ménilmontant, is filling up the holes in the Temple's foundation for the benefit of the new purchaser, a man of the old nobility. Desloges needs "a truly religious strength to live under such management. There is no sense in trying to express it in words. One has to live the experience."[14] But what does the master's personality matter,

12. Ibid., p. 64.
13. Bazin to Enfantin, May 24, 1835, Fonds Enfantin, Ms. 7624.
14. Desloges to Ollivier, Fonds Enfantin, Ms. 7714.

after all? From now on, can the worker for whom the plane has not been broken do anything else but fill up daily, with the work of his own hands, the holes of the temple of hope?

"Is the proletarian, who has experienced each and every misfortune of a badly organized society, called to the apostolate?" The man who asked that question, Charles Mallard, has already paid with his life for his attempt to answer it. Emigrating to establish a fraternal colony in America, he managed to experience the egotism and duplicity of his supposed brothers before dying of cholera.[15] But his sister-in-law, Suzanne Voilquin, will take up the challenge again upon her return from Egypt: what is impossible for the proletarian man may not be for the proletarian woman. After being trained in obstetrics and homeopathy and getting certified as a midwife, the former embroiderer means to turn her profession into an apostolate, forming the woman of the future while taking care of her present ills, delivering the future humanity as well as the babies of proletarians: "I sought certification as a midwife only to use it as a means. I said to myself: let us heal, let us embellish the flesh, and the spirit will be with us and the heart will love us."[16] Of course, her destitution compels her to "turn this fine profession into a trade, but as seldom as possible." But she has in mind something very different from a modest livelihood in exchange for offering medical services to poor women:

> With my profession and my free, independent position, I plan to establish a center of major influence that will later produce great good, not only with respect to motherhood but also with respect to all the sentiments that go to make up life. I have no desire to see pale copies of the Sister of Charity reproduced around me. My focus is woman, whom I want to see elevated in all the beauty of her nature.[17]

And thus it will be possible for the proletarian, midwife and healer of her sisters, to reconcile concern for the material with a humanitarian priesthood, to help a type of future humanity blossom both materially and spiritually. But the mischances of proletarian existence are never long in hitting, especially for those who expose themselves to protect others from them. Soon the dedication of Suzanne's brother to the cause of his fellow

15. See Voilquin to Lambert, Fonds Enfantin, Ms. 7791.
16. Suzanne Voilquin to Enfantin, Jan. 23, 1838, Fonds Enfantin, Ms. 7627.
17. Ibid.

hatters will lead him to prison, from which he will emerge innocent but felled by a fatal languor. Suzanne will then have to take in charge her niece as well as her aged father, who has not garnered any wealth from forty years of business ventures. Responsible for supporting a family, she will have to give up her independence as a priestess and again separate her exchange of material services from the apostolate of the future:

> That requires more than a month of routine, something counter to my habit that is more difficult to get into. It means turning my profession, which I would like to link to the priestly service of the future, into a matter of speculation and money. That wearies me, displeases me, puts me in a bad mood. Then I look around me and say to myself: that is the way it must be since your existence tripled a month ago. You are a midwife of 1838, not a priestess of the future. I immediately resign myself and quite simply start trying to drum up a clientele as others do.[18]

The arithmetic of social contradictions is strict: an existence tripled is a life reduced to one-third of itself. To gain an "independent existence" that will benefit her father and niece, the priestess will have to abandon her "social and religious life." To fulfill her duties to her own relatives, she will have to travel far from them, "drumming up a clientele" in Saint Petersburg (Russia), in the East of cold work as opposed to both the Egypt of the prophets and the America of utopias: "From that moment I became part of the world in order to get a decent, independent livelihood from it through my work and let you and my aged father enjoy it. Forced to sell all my time, talk, and exterior life, I had to suppress my own heart and will, retaining only my freedom of thought."[19]

Another exile in the realms of phraseless work is that of Désirée Véret in the England of machines. There she has nothing to do but work instead of serve, and look for pleasure instead of love:

> The work is so unappealing that I would prefer to be in the galleys. We must work from 7:00 A.M. until midnight (at the earliest) . . . and we are subjected to the varying caprices of the stock market. Oh, what a stupid business it is, this civilized industry! . . . You

18. Suzanne Voilquin to Enfantin, May 13, 1838, ibid.
19. Suzanne Voilquin, *Souvenirs d'une fille du peuple* (Paris: F. Maspéro, 1978), p. 402.

expect, my dear M. Fourier, that love will come along to distract
me, the love of an Englishman, is that what you're thinking? In
that they are the same as they are in mechanics. They can only
handle the material side or a fanciful love that exists only in the
imagination. . . . Never shall I have the sort of love I properly need.
I have made my decision about it and settle for pleasure.[20]

Such is the decision of exiled women who settle for the material reality
of duties and pleasures while dreaming, after midnight, of the phalanstery
or the future humanity. By its very radicalness, their decision denounces
the compromise by which their brothers try to overlook their own exile
between the daily round of jobs—which, on the whole, are more plentiful
than they were in 1831—and the happy reunions of anniversary festivals:
dances in the Barrière des Amandiers, get-togethers on the Île Seguin or
the Île Saint-Denis to celebrate the Father's birthday or the inauguration
of the Temple works. But isn't that to reduce the temple of the future
to the shabby dimensions of something that is no longer even the hospice offered to poverty by philanthropic generosity, though perhaps its
equivalent in terms of worker aspirations: the Sunday islands of love or
the *goguettes* of Saturday evening? A return to the sources or a withdrawal
to the ordinary round of proletarian amusements.

True enough, this withdrawal can appeal to the rules of strategy and
the exigencies of propaganda. For the good cause Vinçard, for example,
tries to express the new faith in the old idiom of republican epicureanism.
To get himself admitted as a "demon of hell" to the *goguette* of the "Hell-
raisers" (*Infernaux*), he borrows the air of "Ran Tan Plan" to affirm the
transition from the table of Bacchus to the holy table:

Lubriques ou bacchiques	Impatient I am
Je suis impatient	For orders satanic,
Des ordres sataniques	Wanton or Bacchic,
Et d'être officiant	And to officiate
A l'immonde table.	At the table unclean.
Je viens en béat	I come all devout
Me donner au diable	To give to the devil
En votre Sabbat	Myself at your Sabbath.

20. Désirée Véret to Fourier, Aug. 14, 1833, Archives nationales (A.N.), 10
As 42.

A ma grasse encolure
A mon air libertin
On voit que par nature
Je suis un peu Mandrin.
Je ne tairai guère
Qu'en vrai Belzébuth
L'humaine matière
Fut souvent mon but.

. . . Vous avez souvenance
Des endiablés exploits
Qu'en notre indépendance
Nous fîmes autrefois,
Fessant d'étrivières,
Gendarmes, mouchards.
J'ai vu leur derrière
Au feu des pétards

. . . Si l'infernal Empire
Accepte mon bilan,
Ne faut qu'il ignore
Que ces jours bruyants
Pour moi sont encore
Petits jeux d'enfants.

Oui, glacés d'épouvante,
Démons, frémissez tous!
Celui qui se présente
Est plus diable que vous

. . . Apprenez qu'en mon âme
Un diabolique feu
Me fit croire en la femme
Comme l'on croit en Dieu

. . . Je crois qu'au plus digne
Appartient le pouvoir,
Mais de la naissance,
En diable enragé,
Je hais la puissance
Et les préjugés

From my fatty appearance
And my air libertine
You can see that by nature
I'm a bit of Mandrin.
I'll not hide the fact that
As a true Beelzebub,
Human material
Was often my butt.

. . . You do recollect
The devilish exploits
We used to perform
In our independence:
Spanking the butts off
Cops and stool pigeons,
I saw their behind
By firecracker light.

. . . If the infernal Empire
Accepts my life's reckoning,
It surely must know
That those noisy days
For me are no more
Than games children play.

Yes, freeze in your terror,
Demons, tremble you all!
He who presents himself
Is more devilish than you.

. . . Know that in my soul
A diabolical fire
Makes me believe in the
    woman
As one believes in God.

To the worthiest, I believe,
Belongs authority;
But as devil determined,
I have hated the power
And prejudices of birth.

Puisqu'il faut tout vous dire,	For I must tell all,
Garnements de l'Enfer,	You young scamps of hell:
La grand poêle à frire	The big frying pan
M'attend chez Lucifer.	Awaits me at Lucifer's.
Soit dit sans mystère	Be it said without mystery,
Sachez donc enfin	And know in the end,
Que le nouveau frère	That your new brother
Est saint-simonien.[21]	Is a Saint-Simonian.

A nice copying exercise, but what exactly is to be expected from this marriage of heaven and earth, this parody of a witches' sabbath, which consecrates the murky wine of *goguettes* as the blood of the new covenant in order to raise the votaries of republican Bacchus to the communion of Universal Association? It certainly must be admitted that this faith is a bit corroded by worldly skepticism: "All that is song, just song; but it helps one to live, and one who lives will see."[22] But it is not from the camp of Saint-Simonian integrism that this impiousness will be denounced. After all, these prosaic wedding feasts of Cana merely pick up again, on the proletarian side, the use of symbolic acts and religious language anticipating, in the realm of representation, the transformation of an as yet unchanged reality. In the image of those metamorphoses that had a bourgeois man in rolled-up shirtsleeves being taken for a proletarian, an embrace for the reconciliation of classes, and a few holes in a suburban garden for the temple of the future humanity, the proletarian family can certainly present their fraternal collects as apostolic acts and a *goguette* refrain as the canticle of the new age. Criticism of these sacramental parodies, then, will come from another quarter. Cabinetmaker Lenoir, who has moved on to Fourierism, will be the one to recall Vinçard to the serious substance of the religious promise: it is not a matter of rebaptizing the good works and bad couplets of the past, of conceptually changing the wine of the *goguette* into the wine of communion; the table of daily bread must be transformed in reality into the table of Universal Communion. It is no longer a matter of giving new names to ancient practices but of producing new *social deeds*:

> You pride yourself on deeds that you have criticized in the philanthropists and that you do not even have the merit of having

21. Pierre Vinçard, "Aux Infernaux," in a letter to Enfantin, March 12, 1838, Fonds Enfantin, Ms. 7627.

22. Vinçard to Enfantin, ibid.

invented. Thus, you remind me that we helped this person or that person. I know it. I was there. Not being able to do better, we did good. But all that cannot be put down in the books as a social deed . . . unless you find a big difference in it because you did it for the sake of Religion, which would change something for the ear but nothing for the intellect. It would be merely a more resonant word; the deed would be exactly the same. . . . So long as you have performed only deeds like that, deeds put forward in *goguettes,* you have no right to think you have done any work of good will more powerful than money. But when you have abolished the exploitation of the poor by the rich for some portion of humanity by bringing their respective self-interests into harmony, when you have managed to emancipate women from the authority of the husband, when you have preserved these same women from the horrors of prostitution by effecting their material emancipation, without which any other is impossible, when you have placed children in an environment where they can grow integrally and freely according to their capabilities, and when you have established a genuine solidarity for this whole portion of the human family, then you will be able to say: We have done something social. . . . C'mon, old boy, agree that our song-filled walks and philanthropic balls—or religious balls, if you will—which were the feasible manifestations of our good will, are not deeds of such a nature as to save the world.[23]

To "save the world," the religion of the future must turn aside from miracles that flatter the illusions of the senses and turn toward those that give the common people the body's bread along with that of the soul. Saint-Simonism merely reenacts the wedding feast of Cana; Fourierism offers the science of the multiplication of the loaves and fishes, which alone is capable of getting beyond the oppositions between egotism and selfless dedication, conflicting material interests and the imaginary enjoyments of fraternity. Later, Lenoir will take it upon himself to offer the same sort of reminder to his Saint-Simonian colleagues on *La Ruche populaire.* It is in the triteness of social cookery that the holy table of Universal Communion is prepared, and it is disdain for the "shabby" realities of matter that is delaying the fulfillment of the Promise:

23. Lenoir to Vinçard, May 15, 1836, Fonds Enfantin, Ms. 7755.

> You should realize that cries of sublime enthusiasm will issue
> from every human breast, that tears of unprecedented joy will
> fill every eye, the day they can say to each other: Brothers, want
> has disappeared from our world; the table is now set for the
> whole earth; no more workingmen or workingwomen, old folks or
> children, suffering from hunger; all are summoned to the universal
> banquet, and all are coming to quench their thirst. . . .
>
> You should also realize that if our human race is still sunk in
> poverty, ignorance, and brutishness after almost seven thousand
> years of existence, this is the natural, logical consequence of its
> disdain for those labors that, in every age, have been deemed
> unworthy of the attention of the well-bred human being and good
> only for occupying the rabble, be it composed of slaves, serfs, or
> proletarians. It is the consequence of the stupid pride that, even
> today, deems trivial such products as ONIONS and POTATOES. Oh,
> the silliness of human beings—trivial things indeed! They are the
> works of God![24]

The rehabilitation of matter is not a question of apostolic ceremonies
that fill up, by way of imagination, the gap between material labors and celestial harmonies. It is the work of union effected by scientific knowledge
between providential calculations and household accounts. Over against
the parodies of qualitative transformation are set the true miracles of quantity. Enfantin's outlook must be reversed in order to keep the promises of
Saint-Simonism. To oppose the great work of the industrial apostolate to
the paltry realities of homely beef broth is to devote oneself to the imaginary campaigns of armies that are nowhere to be found. It is the *science*
of housekeeping that is to provide the bases of what is promised in vain
by the representations of the industrial religion. On this point the gastro-
nomic fancies that Lenoir shares with his master, Fourier—and Lenoir's
wife is, admittedly, a cook—link up again with the experience that had led
the female pioneers of the women's apostolate to societal science: it is not
the free Woman who should preside over the project of Universal Association; rather, industrial and domestic association, by taking the place
of the parceling-out evident in the family, will lay the material bases for
the liberation of women and men. By 1833 Reine Guindorff had already
turned back on the Saint-Simonians the argument about "formal" liberty

24. Lenoir, "Ce qui est et ce qui n'est pas progrès," *La Ruche populaire*, Feb.
1840.

they had used against republicans: "If you say to women who are begging for a remedy for their own sufferings and those of their children . . . 'reclaim your moral liberty,' aren't you like those who say to the common people suffering from hunger, 'reclaim your political rights,' as if those rights could satisfy it and organize work differently?"[25] The best way for women to acquire their liberty, then, is for them "to preach in order to hasten the realization of a new social order in which association is to replace isolation, and in which all jobs are organized in such a way that there will be room for us in all those we are able to perform."[26]

So there is a double exigency. On the one hand, women must be assured the means of an independent existence, without which they will always be the *slaves* of men, for "the man who gives us our material life can always demand in exchange that we submit to his desires."[27] But this independence cannot simply be the effect on private life of a new organization of the production sphere. It also implies the industrialization of the private sphere, where the woman is a slave in a second way—prevented by household chores from devoting herself to all the careers she is capable of handling: "When its organization is *based on association,* it will employ only a meager portion of women, only those whose inclination is in that direction; then other women will be able to turn to anything and everything else that suits them."[28] The representation of *moral* emancipation must be replaced by propaganda efforts for the experimental realization of the *material* emancipation that serves as the basis for *social* emancipation. That is the only way to give all the people their daily bread while satisfying the thirst of those men and women who are held back by the obligations of family attachments and the inability of the civilized order to give free rein to their aspirations.

So the phalanstery has a double advantage over the industrial religion. It begins at the beginning, with the material basis of emancipation. But this materiality is not merely an intoxication with production in which the calculations of some and the reveries of others are supposed to get lost. In place of the paradoxes of a doctrine arrested by the interval between work and enjoyment, the Fourierist science puts the calculus of attractions that socializes self-interests and makes desires for the infinite productive. To the impossible fabrication of the new human being it opposes a distribu-

25. Reine Guindorff, "Aux femmes," *Tribune des femmes*, première année, p. 205.
26. Ibid.
27. Ibid.
28. Ibid.

tion of differences that shapes the harmonious order with the elements of civilized anarchy. It is the latter aspect, in particular, that maintains a hold on the mobile Désirée Véret. Her encounter with Enfantin had drawn her out of the egotistical quietude of her infinite and created in her "a veritable anarchy, a living image of society."[29] This anarchy does not enable her to figure out how exactly she might contribute to the phalanstery she eagerly awaits: "It is not that I have any hope of going there, because I often ask myself what I would be good for in a phalanstery. My nature has been broken and twisted by civilization. There is in me a chaos I cannot clarify; the longer I live, the more incomprehensible I find myself."[30] But the incoherence that prevents her from finding her place in the harmonious order is, for the man of science, a tool for giving definition to her: "I give my pen free rein, certain that nothing is lost on you and that, amid the complaints of this poor civilized creature, you will find a few seeds that will make a happy and harmonious creature out of her."[31] Unlike Gauny, then, whose absence of "harmony" kept him far away from the harmony of Saint-Simonian choirs, she will be able, thanks to Fourier's *discovery,* to see "faces brimming with openness and happiness" in place of the "cold, arid figures" of proletarian exile; and she will be able to abandon herself to her natural bent "without fear of bruising those around her or being bruised by them."[32]

The powerlessness of good will, the power of science, to satisfy the needs of the workers as it reconciles the divided nature of proletarians. By the same token, however, the conditions for this reconciliation fall outside their power. They are dependent on science, which calculates both attractions and the material resources needed for the experiment. The proletarians wait and look for the work of the savant. The savant, in turn, waits and looks for the money of capitalists, to whom he tries to prove that doubling the enjoyments of the proletarians will quadruple the product of their labor. Unfortunately, such lines of reasoning attract only the limited resources and scarcely enlightened good will of leftist philanthropists. At Condé-sur-Vesgre and Cîteaux, and later in Texas, only caricatures of a phalanstery will ever emerge: simple communities of impotent good wills, rebaptized rather than transformed by the associative theory. Even these failures, of course, can be used as evidence by the savants. Of the abortive

29. Désirée Véret to Enfantin, Aug. 31, 1832, Fonds Enfantin, Ms. 7608.
30. Désirée Véret to Fourier, Aug. 14, 1833, A.N., 10 As 42.
31. Ibid.
32. Ibid.

project in Texas, Considérant will later say that it had been productive precisely insofar as it had been invested with theory. Where savants can always find confirmation *a contrario* of the power of *science* and *money,* aren't proletarians led to verify the powerlessness of "material conditions" that exclude their own power? Having come to Condé-sur-Vesgre to find the solution to the contradictions facing a proletarian woman divided between maternal passions and duties on the one hand and the will for societal involvement on the other, Julie Fanfernot soon discerns the flaw in an organization that claims that "the phalanstery would be an abortive endeavor if sentiment were to take the place of money."[33]

So far as reconciliation goes, the community of attractive work simply leads the double life of the proletarian back to a unity like that of English mechanics or bloodless Russian work in the cold: "Their organization was only a mass of machines, without movement and riddled with impotence. . . . They want to regenerate society, yet remain enslaved to all that is most ignorant and stupid about society."[34] What the phalanstery lacks, quite plainly, is the power of the common people, a paradoxical power consisting in the very *division* that the Fourierist associative science, on the heels of the industrial religion, sought to suppress: the contradictory unity of egotistical needs and unlimited acts of dedication, of ambiguous submissions and unexpected uprisings; the power of songs or sentiments without object that put distance between the proletarian and the very order they embellish; the ignored efficacy of the illusion that has the inhabitants of shanties sojourning in the palaces of ideas. On one day only, the Fourierists of Condé saw the dreariness of their community enlivened—by the songs of a passing Saint-Simonian. To the Maecenas of the place, who discovers in the songs of Vinçard the *heartiness* lacking in his community, the pastor–musician of the laboring "family" can point up the contradiction of Fourierist materialism:

> You mean you don't have people and hours for pleasure, musicians to set people dancing, a few joyous refrains on Sunday to put heart into work? In that case you will fight in vain against the old world, which dispenses pleasures to the idle to the point of satiety and offers none of that to workers.[35]

33. Julie Fanfernot to Vinçard; quoted in Pierre Vinçard, *Mémoires épisodiques d'un vieux chansonnier saint-simonien,* Paris, 1879, p. 161.
34. Ibid.
35. Vincard, *Mémoires épisodiques,* pp. 159–60.

"To put heart into work": this heartiness is possible only if one leaves the definition of work sufficiently vague. The power of "another expectation" denounces the mirage of attractive work. The heart can go "to work" with the same energy of song that drove it yesterday, or will drive it tomorrow, to temple reveries, barricade gunshots, or the collective suspension of work. Lenoir may mockingly contrast the twin powers of science and money with the mere good will of fraternal sentiments and the futility of song-filled promenades, but Vinçard can turn the argument back on him. First of all, the cabinetmaker who expatiates so well on the "power of silver" possesses it no more than does his debating foe. Moreover and more important, that power is real only as a power of exploitation: "With the power of silver they have made social slippers that chase us drolly. Don't you agree? The hide they employ is a little less supple than the fur that adorns their own slippers. It isn't of deerskin, either; the feet are not too comfortable in it."[36]

Of the two "powers" advocated by Lenoir, one—money—is, and cannot help but be, the power of what is, the power of privilege and exploitation. The other—intelligence—is in actuality too accommodating to the first power for one to be able to pinpoint among its children those who are legitimate: "The fact is that it has the larger family, and it evidently plays the prostitute because you see too many bastards strutting around with its name when they have no right to it: for example, intrigue, guile, caviling, contradiction, chicanery, pettifogging, bathos, and real bloopers."[37] These travesties of an intelligence that has prostituted itself to the power of money are more terrible than the illusions of sentiment. Lenoir had written ironically of differences between philanthropic practices and apostolic acts that are differences "for the ear" alone. Vinçard returns the auditory metaphor: "You talk of logic, but reasoning is a noise that often lacks even an echo. It is the surging surf that bellows and dashes but cannot touch the sky. It is a death rattle, a noise without effect and often without a cause."[38]

Over against this noise without cause, effect, or echo Vinçard sets the only power capable of rising from earth to heaven: a power that manifests itself in "the throbbings of the heart," is a present from a God "who gives Himself completely," and has been placed "in the heart of the common people and woman." It is not the mere illusion of grand sentiments

36. Vinçard to Lenoir, May 16, 1836, Fonds Enfantin, Ms. 7627.
37. Ibid.
38. Ibid.

and high-sounding words rebaptizing the charities of philanthropy and the *ran-tan-plan* tunes of the cabaret. For the fraternal help doled out among Saint-Simonians was not aimed at misfortune but at the *social value* of individuals capable of returning a hundredfold to the general project: "The philanthropists do nothing. . . . We were making human beings, and we actually did that. With the factitious power *money*, we make the power *heart* blossom. . . . Do philanthropists concern themselves with that?"[39] As for *goguettes*, song-filled walks, and "philanthropic balls—or religious balls, if you will," which the cabinetmaker deems "rococo" from atop his "scientific chair," they have shown recently that they were the locus of a religious sentiment capable of making the established powers tremble. "Perhaps the temple of the people is not positively there at present, but, my friend, it wasn't so long ago that holy and religious things were being done there. Remember its high priest, Béranger."[40] Those holy and religious things certainly paved the way for the glorious revolution that, under the bright sun of July, proved to all the idolatrous worshipers of material or scientific powers that the power of the heart, the power of the common people, was not that of impulses and refrains without consequence.

More than ever, then, the Fourierist provocation leads the most orthodox member of the Saint-Simonian faithful back to the unimpeachable model of any and all popular emancipation: no other way for the common people except the one in which they manifest *their* power, the power revealed in that suspended time of July. The conflict here does not have to do with opposing interpretations of the three July days in terms of violence versus fraternity, success versus failure. It is between those who recognize in them the start of a new era—the era of the common people's power—and those who do not. This recognition should lead not only to an overthrow of the relations established by ancient and modern wisdom between the illusion of popular impulses and the reality of material conditions, but also to a redistribution of the old hierarchy sustaining the order of that city closed to illusion-makers: the ancient Platonic city of *nous* ("mind, intelligence"), *thumos* ("heartfelt feeling, courage"), and *epithumia* ("material desire"). The utopians have been vainly employing these years of reflection in defining the new measures and proportions of the trinitarian hierarchy. The trivial conspiring of print merchants and singing workers has already foiled the calculations of their science. From the warriors—or

39. Ibid.
40. Ibid. Pierre-Jean de Béranger (1780–1857) was an enormously popular lyric poet of republican and Bonapartist sentiments.

from their image—the proletarians stole the power of the heart that they today oppose to the complicities of science and material interests.

Thus, the opposition between morality and material efficacy is turned around. Deprived of the power of the people, social science can only be the science of exploitation; and the only progress it can propose to proletarians is that which would turn them into a bourgeois people: that is, into animals enslaved to their bellies. A monstrous dream, if it were not unrealizable; but also, perhaps, unrealizable because monstrous, because in contradiction to the power of the people, which never works so well for the material development of progress as when it turns its back on the calculations of the science of material interests. Thus, the people's action of 1830 practically inaugurated the era of the withering-away of exploitation by transforming it from "social practice suffered" into "calamity confessed by the greatest number." It is this slow but inescapable progress of principle penetrating the thought and action of the masses that the "quick-witted" mind of the social doctors wants to lock up in the mechanical movements of its parallelograms of forces.

In *La Ruche populaire*, it is quite naturally a former director of worker education, Gustave Biard, who offers the following retort and lesson to apprentice doctor Lenoir:

> Reality, judge of last and supreme resort of every theory begotten by the mind, makes short shrift of the integralities or organized systems of all these professors of social grammar. When you get right down to it, human beings and things operate as ordained by the infinite economy. And of all the proposed programs, it is ever and always moral thoughts alone (i.e., universal thoughts) that serve as a beacon to the people (i.e., the mass of human beings) in finding the main road amid the multitude of shortcuts into which the mob of quick-witted minds, with good or bad intent, tries to lead them astray. For these quick-witted minds are ready to take a rule for a gospel, an expanse of one hundred square *toises* [1 *toise* = 1.949 meters] dotted with farms for a world, a few railway lines for a fusion of all interests, and a communal restaurant for an association.[41]

A rule, a hundred square *toises*, a few railway lines, a communal restaurant: this denunciation of the Fourierist parallelogram reminds us a bit of

41. Gustave Biard, "Vues sur l'école des intérêts matériels," *La Ruche populaire*, March 1840.

the four circles of hell described by Gauny. For this critique of Fourierism has a specific function: it allows the Saint-Simonian proletarians to pursue their dream by exorcising images of the worker as machine and the bestialized proletarian. It must be made clear that the Fourierist primacy of material conditions has no model other than that furnished by those privileged by fortune, "whose belly is their god" and whose head

> typifies that of an ostrich in relation to the carnal mass, atop which it sits like a marabou stork on an elephant. . . . When you say that the first and most important thing is to establish domestic associations where all are plentifully supplied with the basics of food, clothing, and shelter, and you do not enact any parallel program to be carried out as a moral project, you are failing to notice that you are tending to turn society into an ostrich: that is, an animal whose belly is bigger than its heart, all egotism and totally devoid of self-sacrificing dedication.[42]

If the article of the typographer–savant had not put an end to the fraternal debate, the quibbling cabinetmaker would undoubtedly have asked for some explanation concerning the slippage of metaphor, whereby the heart is put in place of the head so as to more easily subsume the question of science under the classic opposition of egotism and self-sacrificing dedication: a steady slippage from logical possibility to material possibility, and from material possibility to moral acceptability. Because three terms, not two, are needed to establish the *practical* privilege of dedication. Why appeal to self-sacrificing dedication, ask the Fourierists, if you can establish the common welfare without having recourse to this badly shared out virtue? Replies Biard:

> Why dedication? Because your fine programs of association are merely programs and do not end up being realized in any way. Because the people, with all that, remain what they are: exploited by the schemers who put to good use and personal profit the time spent by the system-makers in babbling. Because those schemers would soon vanish if, instead of preaching what cannot be even partially turned into reality, we all labored to perfect and complete our collective sovereignty.[43]

42. Ibid.
43. Ibid.

The Fourierist friends of Lenoir might ask in reply: Doesn't that mean letting the people die of hunger while they wait for the "perfecting" of that sovereignty? Let them set to work, then, replies Biard, but that material test presupposes a moral preamble: How can people work when the source of all the people's work, dedication, has been dried up? The incarnation of the monster, a people without self-sacrificing dedication, is happily arrested at its source and principle by the contradiction involved:

> The first task is to give people the wherewithal to live. Okay, show us your power to materialize the miracle of the five loaves and two fishes . . . and then you can chat to us after that. But, again, you don't accomplish anything. And it's a good thing, too, because if you were able to organize things without moral duties or dedication, you would turn the common people into what oligarchies have been in every age: a collection of imposters enjoying a carefree life, chatting about morality, justice, and public order with their backs to the fireplace and their bellies at the table, and wholly in the grip of the cunning appetites of an incurable egotism.[44]

The former Companion of the Woman and his worker proselytes feel the same way that the intellectual laborers of Brook Farm will later feel: "The experiment, so far as its original projectors were concerned, proved long ago a failure, first lapsing into Fourierism, and dying, as it well deserved, for this infidelity to its own higher spirit."[45] To them the Fourierist fare represents another relapse of the angelic dream, the animalization of the humanitarian religion. But now, in this year 1840, a morose tenth anniversary, the classical and distant image of the religion of castes—immediate, animal, and Oriental—takes on an unexpected and close-up shape: that is, a proletarian class transformed into a flock of petty bourgeois, wearing Jérôme Paturot's cotton cap and spouting the opinions of Joseph Prudhomme, the petty bourgeois cartoon-character created by Henri Monnier. The image of a new political animal extolled by economists and philanthropists: the worker won over to the proprietary instincts of saving and the seductions of cheap comfort, and hence dispossessed of the illusory and real power of the people, the "heart power" that is the

44. Ibid.
45. Nathaniel Hawthorne, *The Blithedale Romance* (1852), Norton Critical Edition (New York: Norton, 1978), p. 226.

source of uncalculated dedication and incalculable subversion. How could the companions of the apostle Vinçard, who has just opened a little optical business in Saucède Lane and now finds himself "a shopkeeper . . . all but bourgeois,"[46] how could those apostles turned back to an individual use of their capabilities by the absence of work, remain insensible to "the diabolic winds that are blowing from God knows where and, instead of fanning the divine fire of great affairs, lifting away, chasing, and extinguishing even the last tiny sparks of enthusiasm"?[47] How could they not dread the reigning atmosphere of shabbiness fomented both by the preaching of the official economists on the virtue of savings banks and by the bookkeeping of an opposition busy analyzing budgets and endowments? "Everything is wasting away, shrinking. Everything is paltry and mean. . . . We are being crammed with *brioche* rolls [light, fluffy rolls that are very rich] of all sorts: monarchical, liberal, constitutional. That does not cramp animal life at all. It kills the spirit and the heart, but so what? Just as long as one can live comfortably—that's the essential thing."[48]

In the apologies for cheap comfort, as in the discourses of a liberalism that itself has passed over into the regime of *brioche* rolls, the proletarian faithful read a real menace:

> If among the people every individual could call himself bourgeois and proprietor, that would be the end of all glory, all nationality, for the people. What future might be expected of a people composed of petty bourgeois individuals? Of a people wherein each individual would make himself the center, would have to defend his own little property, his own little store, his own little workshop, his own little political rights, because everything would then be infinitely little?[49]

This future rejected by tailor Desplanches resembles, stroke for stroke, the destiny evoked by Biard: a people consisting of Fourierist imposters chatting about morality, justice, and public order with their backs to the fireplace and their bellies at the table. To the lost children of Saint-Simonism, who had been attracted for a moment by the new hope, the Fourierist gastrosophy now seems to be the mere point of honor of a world consecrated to the religion of the belly, the savant's version of the cult of Baal.

46. Vinçard to Enfantin, Aug. 8, 1838, Fonds Enfantin, Ms. 7627.
47. Vinçard, "Sur la réforme électorale," *La Ruche populaire*, March 1840.
48. Ibid.
49. Desplanches, "Un mot à la bourgeoisie," *La Ruche populaire*, July 1841.

But isn't this furious attack on the animal caricature of their religion the interment of their own faith as well? We cannot help but be struck by the words now being employed by the apostles of love and the heart's power: "that would be the end of all nationality. . . . a people wherein each individual would make himself the center. . . . to perfect and complete our collective sovereignty. . . . it is up to each generation to work for the benefit of the next generation." This is no longer the mystical and sensuous prose of the Saint-Simonian priests; but neither are these the words and expressions with which the proletarian faithful tried to effect some reconciliation between the former and the reveries of natural religion or the fevers of republican passion. If the vocabulary is different, the reason is that the imaginary universe of the worker apostles has changed— perhaps even more quickly than the people's living conditions. You don't come across many workers chatting about morality, justice, and public order with their backs to the fireplace and their bellies at the table, but the image of the holy table is now shattered. Now you have on one side the evangelical and democratic altar of sacrifice; on the other, the oligarchic banquet table where the pigs grow fat. On one side the simple morality of duty and fraternity where each and every child of the common people can commune with the sacrifice ordained by divine providence; on the other, the aristocratic morality of pleasure and enjoyment, extolled for their own benefit by the oligarchic castes of all times and degraded by their needs into handouts of bread and circuses designed to consolidate the bondage of the common people. But what about these principles now being used by the last squad of Saint-Simonian proletarians to beat down the Fourierist beast? It was ten years earlier that Philippe Buchez, a former Carbonaro and former disciple of Saint-Simon, who has now returned to the religion of his Christian childhood, began to forge them, not *for* Saint-Simonism but *against* it. The present "Saint-Simonian" criticism of Fourierism merely picks up the themes advocated ten years earlier by Buchez and his disciples of the "New Science" in their indictment of Enfantin's version of Saint-Simonism. It was back in 1829 that Buchez saw, in the mystical form given to the "New Christianity" by Enfantin and Eugène Rodriguès, the absolute evil, the pantheistic beast; and he immediately set out to refute it. On the theoretical level, first of all, he showed that their doctrine, which turned spirit and matter into two finite aspects of the divine infinite, entailed a theory of necessity that deprived moral action and human progress of the two preconditions making them possible: a free spontaneity and a resistant matter. Then, on the practical level, he denounced Enfantin's "rehabilitation" of the flesh as a mere sublimation of the worship of the belly and the nighttime depravities of the "banal flesh of the crossroads," proposing only "to plunge human beings once again into the privileges of castes, the promiscuity of beasts, and the orgies of the cult of Pan."[50] From there Buchez went on to construct patiently, in opposition to the new religions and utopias, the solid edifice of a few principles valid for all: the only religion that can ensure the moral redemption and material well-being of the people's children is the religion of fraternity announced by Jesus Christ; but the bonds of that fraternal religion had to be loosed from the equivocal entwinements of the new eucharists.

The true religion of the people can be recognized in four attributes. First, it is *Catholic,* that is, democratic: the religion of a salvation by and for the collectivity, opposed to the privileges—Jewish, Protestant, or what have you—of individual faith and individual salvation. Second, it is a *moral* religion, sending out an appeal to every individual, not in terms of enjoyment promised or even right recognized, but rather in terms of a duty imposed. And so its gospel hero is the centurion who knows that he is not worthy to receive the Lord but believes that the latter's word will heal his servant just as surely as he knows that his own orders ought to be obeyed.[51] Third, this religion is also *social* in both its means and its ends. It promises each individual his or her modest share in the collective happiness, but only to the extent that he or she has sacrificed a proportionate share of egotistical happiness. Fourth and perhaps most important of all, this religion is *national,* linking the specific duty of workers and that of all citizens to the ends pursued by a French nation that is the eldest daughter, not of the Church but of the Gospel itself. The whole destiny of that nation is actually inscribed on its birth certificate. It took shape, at the time of Clovis, in the struggle against the barbarian propagators of the Arian heresy. That heresy had a very precise import that makes it the very model of the religions of egotism: it separated the person of the Son from the divinity of the Father only to make His morality optional for people with power who are unwilling to sacrifice their privileges to the divine message of fraternity. The apostles of the battle against egotism must try to "perfect and complete . . . collective sovereignty," which in turn has a national mission to carry out against the egotism championed by the Protestant nations. It must subject the egotisms of castes

50. *Lettre d'un disciple de la Science nouvelle aux religionnaires prétendus saint-simoniens de l'*Organisateur *et du* Globe, Paris, 1831, p. 37. And "De la nationalité," *L'Européen,* 1832, p. 146.

51. Matthew 8:5–13. "Introduction à la lecture des Saints Évangiles," *L'Européen,* 1837, p. 74.

to the reign of fraternity, completing this project that has been carried on through the antifeudal centralizations of monarchical France and the liberating conquests of republican France.

This belated settling of accounts between Saint-Simonian and Fourierist workers reveals the following new scene. Over against the Saint-Simonian communion—promiscuity—of hearts, sexes, and classes, and over against the Fourierist science of attractions—of interests—a new religion has been forged under the cover of a return to the ancient one. It is a democratic, moral, social, and national religion, unraveling the ambiguities of proletarian "liberalism" for the benefit of workers and militants of good will. No longer an ambiguous religion of Working, it is an unequivocal religion of works. Not a religion for workers, a religion for all. But something more real and effective for the future advances or submissions of work than the cults organized in work's name: that is, the source and principle of a reversal that proclaims the same morality of self-sacrificing dedication for all but specifies its measure and prototype in the class of people who have no way of escaping the law of sacrifice—the proletarians constrained in the ordinary round of their days to go out looking for their family's bread in work, and in exceptional times to go out and defend the soil of their homeland. For proletarians it is no longer a matter of appropriating to themselves the night of bourgeois apostles and poets but of constructing a world wherein the bourgeoisie will know in truth, no longer in sham images, the workday of the worker.

In vain, then, did the Saint-Simonian proletarians of *La Ruche populaire* ("The People's Beehive") believe that they could still use the "association of hearts" as a "lever" to found "with all the thoughts that occupy the world, a new social and truly patriotic party that might continue, embrace, and unite in sublime concert all the lost voices in this great Babel."[52] The new social party, the workers' party, needs more rigid levers and less buzzing lodgings. It needs a doctrine that has the potential to be the law of the coming world. Soon some editors of *La Ruche populaire* will leave to found a journal designed to oppose the unitary and anonymous voice of a single principle to the concert of Babelian polyphony. It will be called *L'Atelier* ("The Workshop").

52. "Réponse au Journal du Peuple," *La Ruche populaire*, Dec. 1839.

Part III

The Christian Hercules

"Work is the Christian Hercules."
—Chevé, *Catholicisme et Démocratie;
ou: Le règne du Christ*

CHAPTER 10

The Interrupted Banquet

"HOW MANY OUT OF TEN ARE MARRIED?" The question raised by the "Inquiry About Work and Workers by the Workers Themselves" is not incongruous; it is simply pointless. For Citizen Cabet has already anticipated the answer in the form of a subsidiary question: "Why so few?" The answer to this second question is no mystery; and it, too, is provided in advance under the heading "workers' vices." The militant investigators will have no trouble finding that the percentage of married workers is in inverse proportion to the percentage of subjects addicted to familiar vices: alcoholism, barrier districts, cafés, gambling, fancy dress, dances, neighborhood bars, debauchery, carnival.[1]

Such are the banalities of the 1840s, the clichés used by the "friend of the workers," Baron Dupin, to embroider his interminable lessons on the regenerating virtue of savings banks. Is it really so surprising that we find them reiterated by his most radical adversary, the pontiff of communism, Étienne Cabet (1788–1856)? For when it comes to workers, Cabet does not really know any except the few respectable, well-dressed gentlemen whom he teaches on Sunday mornings in his salon on Rue Jean-Jacques Rousseau: for example, tailor Favard, mason Nadaud, baker Robillard, and jeweler Prudent. It is this complicity that marks the novelty of the decade just beginning. Right after the uprising of 1830, the orators of the people of July needed only a stroke of the pen to brush away the allegations, more frightened than bold, of men of property on the defensive: allegations comparing the common people of the city's outskirts to the barbarians of an earlier day who were camped at the gates of the Roman Empire. Then there was no lack of images of the people's reality to refute such sem-

1. "Enquête sur le travail et les travailleurs par les travailleurs eux-mêmes," Cabet Archives, International Institute of Social History, Amsterdam.

blances of reasoning, and to remind those with smooth, white hands that under the rude manners and plain clothes of the men with callused hands beat a heart for "great things."

It is precisely this clear relationship between appearance and being that has now been lost. Here in the 1840s it is not a question of extolling the heart that beats under plain clothes. Everyone agrees, in any case, that the clothes are not as plain as they used to be: a benefit of machines, say the economists, which have brought both cheap fabrics and homely comfort to the worker; a growth of superficial needs, say the worker publicists, needs of appearance that are being satisfied at the expense of basic necessities. There is also less talk of callused hands and bronzed foreheads, almost as if the worker's body were losing the signs of its distinctiveness as the apparel of poverty grew more sophisticated, as if it were losing the hallmarks of liberty that distinguished the worker from the slave, even the slave in revolt. The interplay of being and appearance, reversing ideally the submission of working-class misery to the paneled rooms of idleness, has been succeeded by this mixed spectacle intermingling the stigmata of poverty and the stigmata of pleasure to shape the figure of an animalized people. And indignant replies to bourgeois descriptions have given way to a certain shared view of the spectacle of degradation. The monotonous bourgeois enumeration of worker vices is matched by the obsessive visions that haunt the journals of every stripe put out by informed workers dedicated to defending the interests of their own class. There is no point here in trying to separate out the Catholic invectives of *L'Atelier*, the Saint-Simonian dislikes of *L'Union*, or the communist indignations of *La Fraternité* when confronted with the coarseness of popular amusements:

> We have finally gotten through those degrading days that bring back to life in our cities the obstinate traditions of the first savages. Yes, everything tends toward the beast during those days. Pasteboard faces, snouts, enormous beaks, and mugs hide the noble lineaments of the human being. Bodies are covered with bumps and lumps; heads with manes, horns, and scales. Everything is disguised in brutish form. . . . Walk around during these festivals. Listen to the deafening screams and the dissonant sounds of the instruments. And if, amid these infamies, you see the savage woman devouring raw flesh, you may wonder whether you are in a civilized country or among barbarians. . . . The voices are alike and no longer have anything human about them: something screechy, fluty, and shrill, like the cries uttered by wild creatures in the

forest. Then, when the pack is satiated and the spirituous drinks are fermenting in their empty brains . . . there are such shrieks of delirium and frenzy that pity grips your heart.[2]

The degradation of carnival lasts for only a few days each year, fortunately, but every week has a Sunday and a Monday for those leisure-time activities of workers that become, in the "filthy sewer called the barrier district," identified with the work of debauchery.[3] And the confusion of the barriers tends to spill over into the streets of the working-class outskirts or suburbs:

> We reach Rue Sainte-Marguerite, a veritable sewer of demoralization and impurities. It is narrow, dingy, dirty . . . repellent.
> . . . All sexes and ages are thrown together pellmell: prostitutes without work, strolling singers, organ-grinders who sleep there for two sous, sidewalk jugglers, fortune tellers . . . the whole medley swarming and crawling around, shouting curses or singing obscenities, and shamelessly indulging in acts of the most revolting cynicism.[4]

A vision borrowed from the bourgeois, one in which social rejection of the Other contaminates moral categories to the point where the effects of poverty are immediately identified with the hallmarks of vice, and the unemployment of a prostitute is offered as a further manifestation of her depravity? But the bourgeois gentleman, you see, does not need to prove that this terrible medley of vice and lewdness belongs to a different race than his own; to stress so obligingly the signs of animality that differentiate the flock of debauchery from the working-class people; or to denounce in his columns the adulterated wine of the barriers, a "melange of logwood and litharge,"[5] in order to make clear that the barrier alcoholic is not just another drunken worker but the consumer of an orgiastic brew that has nothing to do with the invigorating beverage of the worker. A bourgeois

2. "Le carnaval," *La Fraternité*, March 1842, p. 43. "Des plaisirs grossiers que le gouvernement donne ou laisse prendre au peuple," *L'Union*, Jan. 1845. "Le carnaval," *L'Atelier*, March 1844, p. 95.
3. Démocrite Laloupe, "Variétés: La barrière Mont-Parnasse," *L'Imprimerie*, Jan. 14, 1840.
4. "Variétés: Le faubourg Saint-Antoine," *L'Atelier*, April 1843, p. 64; reproduced under J.-P. Gilland's signature in *L'Almanach du travail*, Paris, 1851.
5. Laloupe, "Variétés: La barrière Mont-Parnasse."

gentleman can overlook these distinctions, but not locksmith Gilland, poet and militant of the Faubourg Saint-Antoine; the more precarious he finds the borderline, the more anxious he is to point up the division between the two populations:

> But let no one think that there we have the people of the [Saint-Antoine] district. Those who think so are seriously mistaken, taking the froth for the wave, the less for the liquor. . . . It is at their work that the people must be estimated. It is in the workshops, and nowhere else, that you find them. If you go there, you will see a human being of rough and ready labors, not a human being of laziness or debauchery. So let no one go looking for them where they aren't, or pretend to see them where they have never been.[6]

But everyone knows that in these difficult times the vivifying sojourn in the workshops is the lot of the privileged, that the common people are often where they ought not and would rather not be: in the streets of the outlying district or at that Pointe Saint-Eustache where the workers out walking and the unemployed making the rounds of the workshops on the Right Bank meet up with the *commissionnaires* in search of assignments and the itinerant dealers to hum the songs played by the organist of the sewer—*Le Mariage à la mode*, *La Lorette*, *Les Amours d'aujourd'hui*, and *Le Dimanche d'un ouvrier*. And, above all, by what strange metamorphosis is the workshop, the temple of popular morality, becoming the school of depravity for the worker's wife and children? "The workshops are infested with a gang of dirty creatures differing from brute animals only in the fact that they use their reason to sink to a level even lower than the animals."[7] Granted that these dirty creatures are few in number, why is it that the decent workers seem to be powerless against their influence? Everywhere the froth is corrupting the wave and the lees are denaturing the liquor. In the very place where the people should present themselves truly, there appears the character shaped by the gaze of the bourgeois gentleman. Mask, dress, and ribald refrain alter the physiognomy and voice of the worker. And all the distinctions between true and false people, appearance and reality, are powerless against this confusion, this loss of the identity that had been achieved by the people of July. Ten years later, it is again in

6. "Variétés: Le faubourg Saint-Antoine."
7. "Des apprentis," *L'Atelier*, Aug. 1842, p. 85.

the look or representation of the Other that the working-class people find their identity:

> When a worker appears on the stage, he is drunk, coarse, or ridiculous. Lack of manners, stupid ideas, vile expressions, and obscene gestures: he has them all. What hurts us deeply is seeing workers remain impassive in the face of these daily insults and sometimes even applauding them as if they were the true, spiritual depiction of their morals and ways.[8]

It is futile, then, for *L'Atelier* to maintain that the popular types in the songs of the *goguettiers* are "without models among us," that they are merely "hideous phantoms peopling delirious imaginings."[9] If those delirious imaginings are understood and then picked up by other workers on their own, that is enough to give them verisimilitude, in the eyes of the bourgeois person, as a depiction of the popular body:

> Among our adversaries today there are men who have an interest in believing that these monstrous personifications are our true portraits. There are people for whom these infamies are a stroke of good luck. They retail and spread them around, saying: "*What do you expect from the common people! There you have their own self-portrait!*" It is against all that that our protest is directed. It is with a view to the evil that may come of it that we contemptuously denounce the blockheads of our class who, out of blindness or vanity, unwittingly turn themselves into accomplices of our enemies.[10]

Types without models, delirious imaginings, products of brains "deformed by the excesses of nighttime orgy" (so the orgy is real, then?), people who have an interest in believing personifications taken for portraits, unwitting blockhead accomplices of an evil that may come of it—in this tale of drunken creators, blind actors, and malevolent spectators, the visible matter is fully produced, and continually reproduced, for the representation that confiscates the identity of the working class in the upper-class view of the dangerous class:

8. "De l'enseignement fait au peuple par la presse, les feuilletons, les romans, etc.," *L'Atelier*, Nov. 1843, p. 27.
9. "Variétés: Les goguettes, deuxième article," ibid., Aug. 1844, p. 175.
10. Ibid.

> Look, there you see this people that is claiming its rights and
> complaining about its poverty. . . . Look at it indulging in its
> natural instincts and passions. . . . Once upon a time, at public
> festivals, one gave it fodder as one would feed a dog, and it was not
> indignant. It is always the same. . . . Don't we see it every Sunday
> when we pass through one or another barrier district on the way to
> our countryside! [11]

This view does not simply justify the authority of the dominant class; it constitutes the dominated class as such. For it is not the mechanical necessity of the mode of production that puts the working class in its inferior place. It is the judgment of the dominant class that condemns the working class to incessant work by denying it the attributes of a free human being capable of using its leisure for some activity other than the orgy of the slave:

> Remember what M. Guizot said: that incessant work, keeping the
> worker without respite in order to guarantee tomorrow's bread, was
> the indispensable condition for protecting society. . . . M. Guizot
> is no ignoramus or crusty bigot. He is an inflexible logician. For
> him there are two species of human beings: the upper class, the
> bourgeoisie destined for command and all the benefits it reaps; and
> the lower classes, destined to obedience and exploitation. [12]

The working class is, first of all, a caste constituted by the decision of its masters, as every caste is. And it is kept in its servitude by their gaze, which, like that of the ancient master at his slaves, sees the hallmarks of their membership in an inferior race in the materiality of their labors and the coarseness of their pleasures, in the emptiness of their thinking and the brand on their flesh. At a time when the great concentrations of industry and finance are imposing the theme of the "new feudalism," there is a heightening of the complementary fear of the "fatal road" to "industrial serfdom." It would take the workers back to the abject condition of the ancient slave, which consists precisely in the lack of differentiation between material poverty and moral decadence:

11. "Variétés: Les chansons des rues," *L'Atelier*, Aug. 1843, p. 107; and "De l'ivrognerie," ibid., Jan. 1844, p. 62.
12. "Le phalanstérien et le radical," *L'Atelier*, Nov. 1843, p. 21.

There is one thing that does not seem to have gotten through effectively enough to the working classes in general. . . . That it is absolutely impossible for those classes to remain in their present position for long. They must either sink back lower than they have ever been or rise to the level of the other classes. If they let themselves be carried down the "fatal road" toward which the industrial regime is pushing them all the time, they will soon arrive at the state of abjection and shameful misery to which the working-class population of England has fallen, perhaps never to rise again. . . . We shall be like abject herds of slaves, our anger or revolt no cause for fear to those in power since they will know that we have been greatly enfeebled by distress of body and corruption of spirit.[13]

The battle to be fought, then, is not one of revolt. The slave revolts, tries to throw off his yoke; but his only standpoint is the material interest of his caste. Neither is it simply a clash between the producing class and the idle class; the opposition between work and pleasure is secondary in the constitution of classes. The master's decision first separates those to whom has fallen the function of the Universal from those who are condemned to serve the needs of others by their inability to rise above their own needs. And the fact that the master falls short in the vocation he has arrogated to himself does not affect the validity of the principle he usurps, or of the gaze that sets it to work. To win their emancipation, the popular classes must, in the very eyes of the bourgeoisie that defends nothing but its own interests, prove that they are "something other than a productive force, a brute force that must be driven and contained by the intelligent will of the educated classes."[14] And to prove that, they must be able to suppress themselves as social classes defending their own particular interests. If July once established the dignity of the producer class, the reason was that for three days it had served only the cause of liberty and the nation, while production, its clash of interests, and the related purchase of pleasures were suspended. It was neither violence nor fraternity that had advanced the people's cause, but their identification with the general cause. This legitimacy was then lost in a decade of insurrections, plots, and surprise attacks of an increasingly minority nature. They brought the violence of July 1830 back to the mere manifestation of a

13. "Introduction à la troisième année," *L'Atelier*, Sept. 1842, p. 1.
14. "Introduction à la cinquième année," *L'Atelier*, Oct. 1844, p. 1.

brute force, homologous to the degradation of the productive force. Hence the decision and solemn appeal that is echoed and reechoed in the early 1840s by the communists of *La Fraternité* and *Le Populaire* as well as by the Neo-Catholics of *L'Atelier*: to exchange the gun, weapon of a combat that has become obscure to everyone and to itself, for the pen, instrument of the "conspiracy in broad daylight" that propaganda is, establishing the legitimacy of the common people's claims in the manifestation of their intellectual and moral dignity.

But this choice of "reform" immediately runs up against the cutting edge of its own contradiction: the way of peace alone can wrest the common people from their fall into disgrace, but the only cause of this fall into disgrace is the "peace" itself. The battle has lost its meaningfulness and sunk into the murkiness of brute force because it has become alien to a people whose energy has fallen back again into the twofold brutality of productive force and material appetites. And it is here that the relationship between the abjection of the people and the gaze of the ruling class takes on a twist. For the relapse of the people is something more than the normal fate of a "peace" that is always the "peace" of the oppressors, something more than the old peace strategy of bread and circuses. The caste put in power by the July uprising is novel in this respect: it is the first not to justify itself in terms of some service, not to legitimate itself in terms of any principle other than that of egotism. And this is evident in Baron Dupin's phrase that sums up and serves as the motto for the regime: "everyone at home in his own place, everyone for himself" (*chacun chez soi, chacun pour soi*). The approximations of the age-old corruption have been replaced by the rigor of the system of material interests, a "vast system of corruption and brutalization" whose logic is "to divert the people from social and political questions by stimulating in them the attraction of gain and the desire for accumulation, a passion that excludes all others and completely demoralizes the individual who succumbs to it."[15] The gross debauchery that serves as an argument for the bourgeois gentleman as he passes through the barrier district is the common people's application of his own principles. But the whole business of corruption goes deeper than that: in correcting the grossness of popular pleasure, the bourgeoisie offers to initiate the people into the secret of its own pleasure. The great remedy offered by economists and philanthropists to moralize the lower classes is *saving,* which teaches people to postpone pleasure in order to multiply it and to exchange every particular pleasure for the fundamental

15. "Des Caisses d'Épargne," *L'Atelier,* Jan. 1844, p. 51.

pleasure of profit or gain. And the heroines of this initiation, celebrated by the inevitable Dupin, are those women cooks who, "in those critical but respectable years between forty and fifty, found in thrifty saving the means to marry young men enticed by their savings."[16]

To be sure, the menace of corruption is still quite localized in this instance. The caste of workers so taken by the passion for gain as to marry those enticing cooks does not represent the working people any more than does the teeming, servile mob on Rue Sainte-Marguerite. The radical perversion, the one that "moralizes" proletarian pleasure into pleasure postponed (i.e., into an exploitative force), is exercised mainly on the enlightened fraction of the working class, on those who reject the bondage of incessant production and brutish consumption. That is how *L'Atelier* interprets the plan proposed by Émile de Girardin's *La Presse*, the most enlightened organ of the "material interests." It would transform the militant avant-garde into a working-class aristocracy at the disposal of the rulers:

> There are intelligent, capable men among the workers. Society does not give them much consideration. Seeing that they are not classed as they should be, they enter into conflict with society and lead the masses to plunder the rich. The only way for society to defend itself against this proletarian invasion is to create a credit bank for loans administered by the government. It would provide workers possessing intelligence, good behavior, and love for work . . . with the means to establish themselves.[17]

Such is the picture of one world: between the blind depravity of the barrier districts and the circumspect corruption of saving lies the daily routine of production and reproduction that turns each individual worker into the enemy of all and makes him the servant of his own egotism. In this system the course of "reform" is singularly exacting. It is not enough to go the people's own way and simply replace this gun by means of which they serve as so much cannon-fodder in battles benefiting others. The way or course must be that of a different principle, and the latter cannot be the simple, classically celebrated dignity of hands fashioning the object that serves to give pleasure to the idle. The forced practice of

16. Ibid.
17. "Les grands journaux et l'organisation du travail," *L'Atelier*, Oct. 1842, p. 15.

work has no value in itself, any more than do the two aims it pursues: the wage that feeds the worker and the product that serves the pleasure of the rich. The emancipation of the worker can only be the disappearance of the working class as such: that is, the sovereignty of the people. But the latter must be the sovereignty of a principle that transcends peoples even as it suppresses classes: that is, the principle of morality presiding over the forward march of societies. Over against the egotistical reign of the bourgeoisie, the "right and proper" way of the working class is the way of universality, the way of morality.

And so the unanimous watchword of the avant-garde of the people's movement is: a *return to morality*! Such a return will prove to the bourgeoisie that workers are not what it pretends they are, and it will also purify workers of bourgeois vices. The exploited worker is doubly the victim of the *demoralization* of a society that, in order to exploit him more surely, disarms his revolt by fashioning in him the soul of an exploiter. He can emancipate himself only by a surplus of morality that would transpose the material constraint of the double workday in order to reverse it. He can redeem himself from his depravation only by redeeming that of the exploiter as well. To the surplus of material labor imposed by proprietary profit he must oppose the surplus of moral work known as selfless dedication. The latter, then, is something more than the solidarity of workers engaged in a struggle; slaves are solidary in revolt, and even egotists stick together as long as their interests dovetail. Selfless dedication is the counterweight to the system linking the worker's surplus labor to his moral inferiority. The working class must prove itself to be "at least equal in intelligence and superior in morality" to its rival, not just to answer bourgeois slurs but to win its equality. To reestablish the proper balance, it must become the worker of the moral reign of humanity, by its surplus dedication linking up with the surplus of providence that creates and preserves the harmony of the world.

Identity seems to reign, then, both in the diagnosis of the malady and the prescribed remedy. The Catholics of *L'Atelier* could readily sign the invocation directed by the communists of *La Fraternité* against the timid offensive of the materialists of *L'Humanitaire*:

> For ten years now the materialist system has triumphed, with the
> Guizots, the Humanns, and all the enthusiasts of material interest
> and the *fait accompli*. And what have been the results? Egotism,
> isolation, war, competition, poverty, and hunger. . . . And what has

become of friendship, patriotism, disinterestedness, abnegation? All such virtues have been relegated to the rank of prejudices!

Ah, let us get back to healthy morality! It's about time! No, the human being does not exist for itself! No, the human being is not the brutish and unintelligent result of games of chance, the combination of a few molecules. The human body is merely a garment concealing an intelligence, the latter being the child of a higher, eternal, working intelligence that creates and preserves the world.[18]

Isn't that a Credo that could be professed by all who belong to what *L'Atelier* calls the "purely popular party": that is, the party of those who seek the emancipation of the people by their own works—excluding the "pure revolutionaries," who take it back to a political upheaval, and the materialists or Fourierists, who promise it to them as a result of their science? The workers of *L'Atelier* are perpetual republicans and former nonbelievers whom the eloquence of Lamennais and the logic of Buchez have brought back to a Catholicism now identified with republican duty. Shouldn't they subscribe to this creed that is suitable for uniting all the forms and variations of the republican and socialist religion? The moral religion of fraternity actually does integrate the two fundamental aspects. The first is the egalitarian cult of human unity, heir of the fraternal banquet whose genealogy is traced by Pierre Leroux from the laws of Minos to the eucharistic table, and from the disappointments of Christianity to the coming kingdom of God–Humanity. The second is the aristocratic morality of the Philadelphians, already practicing today the virtues of the "Republic of God," the realization of which is proposed by Constantin Pecqueur to all those who know "only one theory, love; only one praxis, love; only one politics, equality; only one duty, renunciation of the miseries, follies, and infamies of egotism; only one goal and faith, God; and only one means, dedication or sacrifice."[19] What better to oppose to egotism's hierarchy of pleasures than this community of artisans of the moral reign of God, the theory of which is formulated in a verse of the Epistle to the Romans: "We, though many, are one body in Jesus Christ, and we are all members one of another"?[20] Corresponding to the abstractness of

18. "Critique de l'Humanitaire," *La Fraternité*, Aug. 1841.
19. C. Pecqueur, *De la République de Dieu*, Paris, 1844, p. ii.
20. Romans 12:5; cited by P. Leroux, *De l'Humanité*, Paris, 1840, II, 374.

the principle is the clear lesson to be drawn from the favorite symbol of socialist writings of the day: the cluster of grapes carried by one believer to a recluse in the Thebaid region, carried by that recluse to his nearest recluse neighbor, and so gradually making its way around the Thebaid and returning, sanctified by fraternity, to its starting point.

A beautiful image to adorn the standard of the battle against egotism. But can that standard be adorned with an image without contradicting its principle, without proposing, in place of the coarse allure of material pleasures, the more venomous charm of the image itself? If there is one thing that the workers of *L'Atelier* should have learned in Buchez's school, it is certainly this: to ferret out egotism in all its folds and forms; to check out every image in terms of its social value and every association of individuals in terms of the "aim of its activity," the only thing permitting one to form a judgment about its moral character. But in the last analysis, there are only two aims of activity, the egotistical satisfaction of appetites or the dedicated performance of duty; only two types of association, communities of work or groupings of self-interest; and only two types of images, those which represent to the human spirit the majesty of social labor or those which seek to please the eye with arbitrary subjects of fantasy in capricious tones and chiaroscuros—that is, those which stimulate dedication or those which call up pleasure. Thus, one must press the fraternal cluster of grapes to see what comes out: the beverage of the worker or the liquor of orgy. And the intention of virtuous devotees of eucharistic images has no bearing on the matter: "Human egotism is so subtle! It knows so well how to blend into everything, even under highly respectable appearances, friends, that we must be as wary of it as we would be of our most dangerous enemy. Let us go down into ourselves and ask what flatters us in the appeals that are made to us every day."[21]

"Let us go down into ourselves": it is worth pausing over this invocation, this summons to an entirely new journey. Up to now, workers summoning their brothers to moral reform have offered them a simple either–or choice: Did they want to remain sunk in the mire of exploitation and ignorance or rise to the intellectual and moral dignity of human beings? It is still in those terms that *La Fraternité de 1845* summons workers to the holy work of study required for their emancipation:

> Workers, how many things must be reformed in us! Let each
> individual undertake a serious examination of conscience. Let him

21. "Aux ouvriers communistes," *L'Atelier*, June 1841, p. 74.

ask himself what needs reforming in his tastes, his pleasures, his relationships, and the use of his time. Let us cut back on the idleness, uselessness, or viciousness in our present way of life and dedicate the results to the life of the mind. . . . Are you resigned to living eternally the brutalizing life that the present-day world offers you? Are you going to say no to the complete development of your being? . . . Wise up, at last, and lift yourselves out of your intellectual lethargy, your shameful degradation.[22]

The division is clear: the heights or the depths, matter or spirit, sleep or wakefulness. So what possible purpose can be served by this other movement, this *descent into oneself,* into which the editors of *L'Atelier* are transforming the examination of conscience and the value judgment proposed by their colleagues of *La Fraternité?* If they tried that descent into self, what would those colleagues find to say about the attraction exercised on them by the cluster of grapes? What might be the response of shoemaker Savary or bronze-worker Malarmet, the most respected spokesmen of the communist workers; of the former Saint-Simonian Voinier, who had revolted in disgust at Enfantin's moral heresy; of typographer Stévenot, colleague and companion in arms regarded highly enough by the republican typographers of *L'Atelier* to have been given a seat on the first committee of their paper; of locksmith Narcy, a disciple of Pecqueur; and of all their comrades of *La Fraternité* whose communist apostolate is underwritten by what they can contribute from their meager wages and their short supply of leisure time? Surely they would say that in the symbol they see only fraternal happiness based on material sacrifice. And to their testimony of persecutions endured as the price of their lives of dedication, they would add all those who attest to the evangelical legitimacy of their ideal: the bread and wine of the eucharistic sacrifice; the vineyard where workers of the eleventh hour receive the same pay as those of the first hour; the community of the first Christians and the punishment meted out to Ananias; the long series of homilies preached against individual possession, inequality, and usury by all the pastors of the ancient Church—Saint Clement, Saint Ambrose, Saint John Chrysostom, Saint Augustine; and then Saint Gregory of Nyssa, Lactantius, Origen, Tertullian, Saint Benedict of Nursia, and a hundred others who turned community of goods into the only mode of material life measuring up to the purity of evangelical morals.

22. "Aux ouvriers: Sur la nécessité de l'étude comme moyen d'affranchissement," *La Fraternité de 1845,* May 1845, pp. 46–47.

But the new Christians of *L'Atelier* have nothing to do with Fathers of the Church. Never do they reply to any argument based on patristic authority. The letter kills, the spirit alone gives life. And the spirit of Christianity is this one question: What is your aim of activity? What is it that flatters you in this image? The answer surely is in the question itself: if the image flatters, the reason is that it is flattering. In the edifying journey of the cluster of grapes one cannot help but see, under the trappings of sacrifice, the same vice that sullies "moral reform" as understood by *La Fraternité*: that is, reform of worker *tastes, pleasures, relationships,* and *use of time*. There really is no need to go down very far into oneself; a slightly more attentive rereading of self will do. In that pretty thought there is not a word about duty; there is only a calculus of pleasures, a refinement of enjoyment. And in the circuit of the grape cluster there are actually only two attractions: that of being received gratuitously, undoubtedly from the hands of some philanthropist, in the manner of the day, who had gotten it from the work of others; and that of being given gratuitously, without any obligation—hence out of caprice. For there is no other word to use for this love of neighbor that is not governed by the law of any authority and the safekeeping of any collectivity. The fraternity of these "men of good desire"[23] has no principle except the caprice of the idle; through it, therefore, the standard of egotism is again introduced into the ranks of the popular party to divide and corrupt it. However austere the language of the communists and however long the list of their patristic references, the aim they propose to themselves as a task, and to others as a state, can be summed up in one word: happiness—that is to say, the egotistical satisfaction of individual appetites.

But why jump to that last conclusion? The communists, after all, make a point of proving the contrary: that is, that the happiness promised by fraternity cannot look to any model in the realm of egotism, since for each individual it consists only in participation in the common happiness. So let their opponents have done with their stupid imagery of Procrustes' bed, partition, pillage, and orgy:

> The common happiness. For our detractors this expression is the equivalent of an alarm bell, signaling the dissolution of all societal elements. . . . But what does this formidable expression really mean? . . . A social situation resulting in the fusion of sentiments, unity, harmony of wills and interests, the complete development of

23. "Morale," *La Fraternité de 1845*, Dec. 1845.

people's abilities in terms of each one's function in society. . . . This principle, based on reciprocity, brings all human beings together, unites them, and immerses them in one and the same communion of sentiment and action. How could it be a solvent, or detach them from common duties?[24]

The answer is easy. One can always twist the meaning of words for the benefit of philologists, and take away the color of standards to prove that they are colorless. In this case, however, the standard of the "common happiness" is not unfurled before philologists but before the popular masses crushed by poverty and prone to hallucinations of hunger. And the words have a meaning consecrated by usage—that is, by the personal experience that human beings inscribe in them and the dreams they project into them. This is true of the French language, at least. For there are languages that are less solidly "fixed," in which the words slide over each other to the point of erasing the contrast between active and passive, being and nothingness, desire and duty. That, according to Buchez, is the character of the still-immature language of the Germans: a floating and drifting that pushes words toward identity and sanctions confusions as well as all the twists of dialectics.[25]

The editors of *La Fraternité* have allowed themselves to be contaminated by this Germanic virus. With their use of language, they attack the benchmarks offered to morality by common experience. One need only look at the space taken up in their columns by quotes from the *Junge Generation* and the latest developments beyond the Rhine in the Neo-Hegelian critique of religion. One also has to translate into everyday language their "big words" and their "sentences that put you out of breath," subjecting them to the rule of usage that holds the same place in the order of interpretation as does the primacy of practice in the order of certitude. And usage establishes well enough that by "happiness" people mean a satisfaction of needs that knows nothing of the common rule or equitable sharing: "Should you take it into your head to ask the authors or propagators of those publications the question, What is happiness? some will tell you right out that it is eating when you're hungry, drinking when you're thirsty, sleeping when you feel like it, procreating when you want

24. "Moralité de la doctrine communiste," *La Fraternité de 1841*, May 1842, pp. 53–54.

25. Philippe Buchez, *Essai d'un traité complet de philosophie, du point de vue du Catholicisme et du progrès*, Paris, 1838–1840, II, 346f.

to, and working as little as possible."[26] But that is not what the workers of *La Fraternité* say. Month after month they persist in trying to make their adversaries realize that for them the satisfaction of material needs is not happiness but merely the elimination of the material preoccupations that prevent individuals from pursuing the supreme happiness—the harmony of souls:

> We call for an order of things that will satisfy all necessities and thus eliminate all the causes of degradation associated with the defects of social institutions. Yes, we seek for our unfortunate brothers the bread of the body they often lack, and at the same time we seek for all the bread of the mind that present-day Society distributes so stingily. . . . We are communists, finally, because we want to raise our brothers up from the moral degradation, the coarse materialism, that blights their soul. That, in the future, public foresight will be such that the human being need no longer worry about the satisfaction of his needs any more than he worries about the air he breathes: such is the extent of our desires. So what is immoral about them?[27]

What is immoral about them? Quite simply that they do away with the distinctive feature by which every mind aware of the meaning of words and uncorrupted by the sophisms of the time recognizes morality: constraint. To set up an opposition between a material world of necessity left in the care of social foresight and an immaterial world of love and dedication is the most subtle way to justify egotism. For it eliminates the very precondition for sacrifice: the *material* opposition of duty to pleasure. The communists of *La Fraternité* do not summon the masses to pleasures of the flesh, of course. More crafty, they say that this satisfaction of appetites *is not* pleasure, and they turn the accusation of materialism back on *L'Atelier*:

> Would you have human pleasure on earth consist of eating and drinking? One would think so when one sees the inscription on the masthead of your paper: whoever does not want to work should not eat! Which means . . . if you do right, your reward will be to eat; if you do wrong, your punishment will be not to eat! A doctrine made for the belly of beasts, not for human hearts.[28]

26. "Discussion sur le communisme," *L'Atelier*, Sept. 1845, p. 180.
27. "Moralité de la doctrine communiste," p. 54.
28. *La Fraternité de 1841*, June 1841.

To this brutish happiness the communists of *La Fraternité* oppose the true pleasure of fraternal dedication, "which is wholly of the moral order and never practiced for the business of material life."[29] A sliding of words —from sacrifice to duty to dedication to fraternity to happiness—down the slope toward the total collapse of the morality meant for the artisans of God's kingdom. So thinks *L'Atelier*:

> Does it take much reflection to see where that leads? When you have put in the minds of all humans that they have been made for happiness, no one will want to fulfill their social duties, because every duty is a pain. No one will want to submit to moral prohibitions, because such prohibitions are obstacles to our pleasures. And let no group of people come along and tell us that by happiness they mean the pleasure of dedicating themselves to each other. . . . Dedication is an act of sacrifice, and in no language have sacrifice and happiness designated the same thing.[30]

"In no language": apparently these self-taught workers and Catholics of recent vintage do not understand the Latin of their Mass. Common experience, on the other hand, is there with its evident truths to confirm the law that makes pure obligation the only possible motive force of moral action:

> We know very well that the communists say that there is very real moral happiness in dedication and self-sacrifice. That is not the way we see it. True, there is great moral satisfaction in having performed an act of self-sacrifice, but the pain almost always wins out over the pleasure. For dedication and self-sacrifice, there must be a more powerful motive than that of moral happiness. The proof is that opportunities abound today for people to procure that happiness for themselves, and those opportunities do not decrease because very few people are tempted to taste and enjoy that happiness.[31]

If dedication is to cease being the exception, it is as evident as any first truth that it must become the rule. The fatal slide of fraternity toward plea-

29. "À l'Atelier: Ce que les communistes entendent par le mot *bonheur*," *La Fraternité de 1845*, Aug. 1845, p. 68.
30. "Aux ouvriers communistes," *L'Atelier*, June 1841, p. 74.
31. Ibid.

sure must be countered by a movement in the opposite direction: from the dedication of people of heart to the constraint of duty. And this identification can be established only *a contrario*. Dedication should be defined not as an attraction, but as a resistance, as "man's battle against his instinct for self-preservation and his desires for pleasure";[32] and its moral sway is established by a negation that reduces all happiness to the positive enjoyment of material pleasures. If each person is to be "thoroughly convinced" of the necessity of self-sacrificing dedication, no depiction of pleasure, even of the most ethereal sort, should be part of his idea of dedication.

Such is the circle in which the "sophisms" of the communists must be enclosed: it is impossible to conceive of a happiness different from mere material satisfaction; impossible, therefore, to call upon workers of the world of material interests to work for a "social arrangement" that is supposed to provide future generations with an inconceivable happiness. Doesn't the very frame of mind of the editors of *La Fraternité* prove this? Those men, for whom prison has often been the price of their dedication, admit that they themselves are too corrupted to turn their ideal into reality. And they criticize the initiatives of community-founders: with people perverted by the world of egotism, such efforts end up in failure and thereby compromise the communist cause. First there must be a new education to shape the pioneers of the new world.

But it is obvious that this remedy merely pushes the problem further back and radicalizes it. Who will these educators be? The problem is not exactly that of knowing who will educate them. There really is no lack of educators, of people who feel sure that they can bring to the masses brutalized by ignorance and egotism the education that will alter their instincts and turn them toward the city of harmony; that they can deliver them from habits that prevent them from finding satisfaction as individuals in the collective arrangement. But right there, says *L'Atelier*, we can see the immutable principle of the science of "educators": the calculus of pleasures, the science of the Fourierist beast. So far as harmony goes, this science can offer only a refinement of the egotistical corruption whose effect is both the depravity of the individual and the division of the community:

> Look where that leads! By the most elementary logic one would be forced to end up in Fourierism, which excites and promises satisfaction of all the appetites, even the most shameful ones. . . .
> There will always be division in the community. . . . But, you say,

32. "Variétés: le travail attrayant," *L'Atelier*, June 1842, p. 80.

education will forestall those divisions. Well now, who will do the educating? Those who want marriage or those who don't? If the whole community is called upon to express its view, then whatever its decision may be, there will be malcontents who will break away and found a rival community. Who could rightly prevent them from doing that? They are seeking their own happiness. And if they find it—pardon this gross thought—in sodomy or bestiality. . . . Wouldn't you recoil, comrades, if you were on the slope leading down to those infamous practices?[33]

Of course they would recoil! At a distance of forty years their brother in communism, Sébastien Commissaire, will still remember the disgust he felt as a boy on discovering the pleasures of a young shepherd with his goats.[34] But their disgust has a very specific cast: to them the pleasures of shepherds are loutish country games. They, too, have fled to civilized metropolises to escape the coarseness of rustic labors and delights. But the editors of L'Atelier, convinced, more by Buchez than by their own personal experience, of the native purity of country ways, mean to show the communists of La Fraternité that those are, in fact, the civilized pleasures of their ancient models: "The Romans were sophisticates in matters of pleasure. They were given an education in happiness, and they gave themselves over to the squalid pleasures we have just mentioned."[35]

But notice the shift in meaning embodied in this Roman example. No longer are we dealing with the pleasures of slaves in which their masters detect the inferior race. Here we have the pleasures of the masters: the orgies of Juvenal or the mixed pleasures of bacchanalia intermingling masters and slaves. This shift of scene is crucial. No longer is it a matter of justifying, under the master's contemptuous gaze, the rising above hard labors and coarse pleasures with which the people's militant avant-garde summon their brothers to begin their emancipation. Along the pathway to this emancipation comes a different gaze to alter the meaning of moral work. It is the gaze of the working people, which, spontaneously or at the instigation of interested polemicists, identifies the noble ideal of the communists or other reformers with the depravities of sloth, orgy, or the community of women—ultimately, then, with the pleasures of the idle. Now this superficial gaze from below, like its equivalent from above, sees

33. "Aux ouvriers communistes," L'Atelier, June 1841, p. 74; and Sept. 1841, p. 3.
34. Sébastien Commissaire, Mémoires et souvenirs, Lyon, 1888, p. 54.
35. See note 33.

rightly. The communists would be wrong to charge calumny. Here again appearance cannot be separated from being. However far removed they may be from the depravities imputed to them, the communists are incapable of putting a stop to the representation of them. For, on another level, to be brought out by the double register of reasoned argumentation, their theory is merely the philosophical form of those perversions. In all its pairings of words, the very austere language of *La Fraternité* makes clear that the core of its thesis dovetails with the common perception of it as a revival of the vices of Sodom and Gomorrah:

> Doesn't the human being find itself again, whole and entire, in the human being? Doesn't it see its own intelligence glitter there, its own passions reign there? Doesn't it hear the voice of its own affections and inclinations there . . . ? Haven't individual weakness and the sympathetic attraction of like for like fashioned an imperious law of association? And is it really so far from the manifold, profound relations and incessant intermingling between diverse intelligences effected by the needs of human nature to sharing in common the things produced by those intelligences?[36]

In vain does the communist doctrine seek to establish its evangelical legitimacy. Each of its metaphors and circumlocutions betrays the fact that the love for one's fellow creature that serves as the basis for its community of property does not derive from the preaching of Jesus but from the discourse of Pausanius. Instead of being the fulfillment of divine law, this love means to be its very principle: immediate relationship of the One to the Other, providential attraction of Like for Like, which, under the pretext of laying the basis for dedication, reduces it to the passivity of a universal harmony "sweeping hearts and spirits willy-nilly toward the great goal of humanity—that is, impelling them to mingle all their efforts and movements in the mysterious scheme of universal activity."[37] So we get a confused jumbling of the great Whole, which, in order to blend communist fraternity into the harmony of the celestial spheres, identifies the human work of association with the instinctive finality of animal unions. In this "voice of one and the same affections and propensities,"

36. "Du principe communiste et de ses détracteurs," *La Fraternité*, Aug. 1842, p. 77.
37. "À l'Atelier," *La Fraternité de 1845*, Oct. 1845, p. 89.

this "sympathetic attraction," this "incessant medley," how can one fail to recognize the language of the beast slain by Buchez, the teacher of those associated with *L'Atelier*? It preaches the fusion of souls and the republic of the pure instead of the rehabilitation of the flesh and women's liberation. But it is ever the same principle, the "pantheistic" philosophy that grounds the vices of sodomy, bestiality, and incest in the order of universal reason by eliminating the three preconditions for moral work: the opposition between active and passive, the separation between the animal kingdom and humanity, and the difference between generations that measures the distance from performed work to its product, from law to pleasurable enjoyment.

There is no point in retorting that this is the pleasure of mere representation. For it is the representation itself that destroys the principle of dedication by rendering present its outcome. It is an anticipation of the One, a presuming of the Whole, that encloses communist fraternity in an insurmountable dilemma: either it proposes to the masses the motive of happiness and thereby destroys any and every moral tie between individuals; or else it teaches them the incomprehensible ideal of a happiness alien to everything they invest in that word. Instead of a common obligation, then, it would lay the basis for the reserved knowledge and secret loves of the republic of the pure. The orgy promised to the masses and the unperformable ideal of the Society of Philadelphians freed from the brutality of popular appetites have the same effect. They both ruin the preconditions for the only truly realizable unity: that of individuals associated in one and the same *community of work*. The bad faith of the people that accuses the communists both of wanting community sharing of women and of paving the way for the generalization of monastic life is not mistaken: "Society as a whole is not so witless that it does not know very well . . . where the application of your theories would lead it."[38] Not to the community sharing of women or to the monastery, actually, but simply nowhere: to the unresolvable flux of a love indefinitely shuttled between the promiscuity of the common Venus's orgies and the elitism of the celestial Venus's pleasures; to the confusion in which the pure fraternity and love of Philadelphians and monks display the same ferment of dissolution as a commonplace orgy—that is, the overturning of the dualist principle that grounds the social bond and the real work of dedication. By either aggravating or denying the opposition of spirit to matter, they likewise

38. "Aux ouvriers communistes," *L'Atelier*, Sept. 1841, p. 2.

reduce the activity of the one to the passivity of the other. The principle of pantheism in all its forms is always the same: immobility, absence of performed work.

Thus, the duplicity of popular reasoning sanctions the truth of dualism. Communism is unrealizable for two reasons that come down to one: it is impossible because immoral, immoral because impossible. It is a mere hallucination, in other words, that must necessarily be dissolved by practice. But to leave it to practice to do this dissolving is, on the other hand, to let it do its work as a dissolvent. There is no mere representation for the theory that makes morality the *criterion* of certitude. Image effects are always real effects, and every representation involves an identity. There is a real menace represented by the ambiguous images of fraternity, the Republic of God, humanitarianism, fusionism, and the countless other masks of the pantheist beast, and it must be repulsed by theory under pain of corrupting practice. The menace is the loss of popular identity by the very ones who were claiming to liberate it from the bourgeois view: that is, the militants of the "people's party." The question of identity governing the emancipation of the people has now been shifted and placed inside the party made up of those "more active and energetic" than the mass:

> That portion of the people in whom all the revolutionary energy of our time is summed up and in whom the memory of the great victory of July feeds a burning round of activity. . . . That mass of human beings betrayed in their political hopes, violated in their national sentiments, and humiliated in their situation as wage-earners. . . . Those people naturally provoked, exposed to the most urgent solicitations of all sorts, excited by everything that can humble the senses [and] flatter the spirit—in a word, by everything said and done around and above them.[39]

It is among the élite of those dedicated to the fight against class and the power of egotism that pantheist immorality, enjoyment anticipated, takes on its importance as a social issue. For there was an element of bad faith in Buchez's argument against the Saint-Simonian apostles. The young preachers of that doctrine did not need to proclaim the rehabilitation of matter and women's liberation in order to win a large share of material pleasures and good fortune, whether aristocratic or common. Their social position was enough to assure them of such things. Such is not the case

39. Ibid.

with the decent workers and courageous combatants of the Republic, who, without realizing it or choosing it, succumbed to seduction and wanted to taste the voluptuousness they preached: that is, the intellectual pleasure of knowing the nullity of the principles governing the social order and commonplace thinking; the moral pleasure of tasting, under no constraint except that of enlightened reason, the pure happiness of dedication; in short, the key to the city in the "republic of revealers" that raises its Babel right in the ranks of the people's party.[40] In these new loves of Poros ("Wealth") and Penia ("Poverty") that ground illusions of the fraternal banquet, Poros is now the seducer. The enlightened *philosophes* and the young bourgeois in love with the people have inoculated their proletarian disciples with the poison of a corruption that, under the flattering appearances of the intellectual happiness of sages and the moral happiness of saints, simply makes them desire the "free" activity and "pure" enjoyment of the idle.

Egotism is a crafty devil, working its most radical effects at the very heart of the dedication of dedicated human beings. It comes along and takes up its place in the *surplus,* the intellectual and moral *excess,* that is indispensable for proletarian emancipation. To foil its stratagems, one must oppose to every other motivation the pure exigency of a duty whose sole representable effect is not *the good* but *the lesser evil*. But at the same time, one must somehow lessen the importance of this duty, stripping it of the aristocratic presumptuousness that still clings to representations of rational legislation and the realm of ends, bringing it back down to the common condition of work and the obligation deriving not only from the law but also from the condemnation. We must never forget: "That we have been made to work, to work always, and that the only thing we might be able to demand is sufficiency of life—that is, sufficient well-being for us to carry out our function suitably. Anything beyond that is absurd and dangerous."[41]

Only the dogma of the fall of man can give morality to the work of emancipation. We must have done with the old Saint-Simonian sophism that still fetters the apostles of natural religion and republican virtue. It simply is not true that the dogma of original sin entails the slavery of the worker. Quite the contrary is true. By grounding the obligation of work in the universality of the human condition, that dogma shatters the

40. "Fin de la discussion entre La Fraternité et l'Atelier," *L'Atelier,* Feb. 1846, p. 263.
41. "Aux ouvriers communistes," *L'Atelier,* Sept. 1841, p. 3.

system that made labor the lot reserved to the lower caste. We must also have done with word games involving the equivocal use of "fraternity" and "communion." If Christianity can be the religion of the republican trinity, the reason lies not in the fraternity of the eucharistic meal but in the equality of the fall. The Christian idea of sacrifice must be stripped of everything that, through the representation of shared bread and wine, goes back to the pagan games of transubstantiation: confusion of bodies and sexes at the banquet of Pausanias and Aristophanes; confusion of classes at the nighttime nuptials of Poros and Penia and in the animal disguises of the mixed bacchanalia wherein the historical tradition sees prefigured the egalitarianism of the Christian community. The Christian religion will be the religion of emancipation only if it says goodbye to all those images that make bad apostles glow, to all those representations of sacrifice as the here-and-now communion of the fraternal banquet. So, no bread and wine that is transformed into anything else but the power of life-giving work; no divine flesh and blood offered on the table of any meal; no members mingled in the body of the God–Man; no Epistle to the Romans, incurable in any case; no need to learn Greek or to know anything of Paul's message except the clear rule opposed to both the insatiable appetites and the uncontrolled generosities of the Thessalonians: "Whoever does not want to work should not eat." And it really does not matter that, in order to restore to the Son of God's sacrifice its strict meaning as family dedication, we must paradoxically return to the animal figures of paganism:

> There is a touching symbol that the ancient world has bequeathed to modern societies and that should always be present in your memory as the most beautiful of examples: it is a bird who is tearing away at its own chest to give life to its offspring, and who will die after performing this sublime sacrifice. Don't forget this symbol, people. Be generous to the point of giving all your blood for your own. Don't fear death. You can overcome, and you would not know how to succumb. Eternal life is yours through the veneration of those who will follow, and for you the future holds a baptism of eternity, the approbation of future ages.[42]

A strange figure replacing the crucified Christ, whose body and blood nurture fraternal communion: Christ the pelican—father, not brother—

---

42. "De l'enseignement fait au peuple par la presse, les feuilletons, les romans, etc.," *L'Atelier*, Nov. 1843, p. 27.

whose last sacrifice for his children prolongs the daily dedication of life-nurturing labor. The convergence between the learned critique of pantheism and the judgments of the crowd expresses the preconditions for the covenant that is indispensable for the people's work. To realize the Christian law of progress, "summoning all to the performance of free sacrifice,"[43] the excess of sacrifice must be brought back to the intensification of the workers' dedication to family, which already finds its model in their supreme dedication to the national cause. To make sure that dedication's pure forgetfulness of self, which is a battle against the instinct for self-preservation, does not lose itself in the pantheistic indifference between life and death, pleasure and suicide, to make sure that it becomes the progressive heritage of generations, a twofold principle of conservation must be interposed between the negation of sacrifice and the infinity of lesser-evil work: *the family* of paternal authority and life-nurturing labor; and *the nation,* whose community gives to labor its collective sense of work. The religion of workers can be fraternal and cosmopolitan only in the androgynous reveries of intellectuals who are "friends of the people" and of workers who are victims of their seduction, of that intermediary people that takes its borderline position in the order of caste-barriers for an avant-garde position in the emancipation of the people and humanity. The work of popular dedication must be paternal and filial before being fraternal, national before being humanitarian. To take morality as the criterion of certitude is to make its rationale that of the masses, to abdicate its own proper name and its particular standard in the collective identity of an actual people, of a work community already in existence. To bring the multitude to the moral reform that will make it worthy of political and social reform, the party must first reform itself, must again find in the ways and reasons of the multitude the principles of real dedication, the manifestation of which is blocked by its own profligacy of ideas or habits:

> Communists, none of the ideas you have taught as new mark any progress over the old French ideas. Have you found any formula more perfect than the national formula of liberty, equality, fraternity, unity? No? Well, then, what is the point of fashioning particular communities in the great community? . . . In our opinion, the mass of the people has not left the path of progress. If it does not proceed more quickly, the fault lies with us all or, rather, with all those who have divided and misled us on the pretext of making

43. "De la morale," *L'Européen*, 1832, p. 246.

us move forward. . . . Workers! Let us discipline ourselves! Let us get back into the ranks! We do not call you to gather around us, because we are neither a person nor a party. We are the multitude. Be the multitude as we are![44]

Get back into the ranks, then. To make these words of advice more effective, their authors are modest enough to make clear that they are merely proposing the way that enabled them to be the first to leave the pathways of error:

> We can admit it. We too have had our moments of doubt and falling away. . . . We have all been more or less tormented by the ideas that now torment you. We have been led to social conclusions like yours. We were wont to use the same language as you, and we also thought we were among the most advanced. Today we have returned to different sentiments. We follow the ordinary course among the multitude, step by step. It is not for us to decide whether you too will abandon the theories that divert you from works to be performed right now and thus make you the terror of society.[45]

But the honest editors of L'Atelier strive in vain to convince us that this rude discipline by itself holds back their appetite for debauchery: "As for ourselves, if we had not returned purely and simply to Christianity, we would have become materialists and concerned ourselves solely with satisfying our instincts."[46] No one is fooled by the argument. The main heresy threatening L'Atelier is not to be found in the lure of *outside* things. On the contrary, it is to be found *inside,* at the very heart of its militant orthodoxy, in the nihilism of sacrifice, which, beyond the opposition of instinct and duty, links up again with the pantheist principle and its communist effects. If the battle against heresy is interminable, we can be sure that heresy is in place and that it even identifies with the Grand Inquisitor. In the redaction of L'Atelier, that role is played by the most implacable nemesis of the false prophets of love, the former comrade in arms of Catholic Poland the martyr, the friend of Dominicans who once thought that he might don their habit: bookkeeper Chevé. We cannot help but recognize the ineradicable pantheist heresy in the mystical language used by this

44. "Aux ouvriers communistes," *L'Atelier*, June 1841, pp. 74–75.
45. "Aux ouvriers communistes," *L'Atelier*, Sept. 1841, p. 2.
46. "Discussion sur la certitude morale et religieuse," *L'Atelier*, May 1843, p. 83.

"economist" of *L'Atelier* to communicate with the most virtuous and hence most insidious of the false prophets, Pecqueur, author of *De la République de Dieu* (*God's Republic*, 1844):

> We are in God and God is in us only through sacrifice. There is your faith and ours, and some day it should be that of all humanity.
>
> So we all have only one religion, sacrifice, because God manifests himself to the world only in and through sacrifice.
>
> So let us really sacrifice in spirit and in truth. Let us sacrifice all our own sentiments, thoughts, wills. Let us sacrifice them not only vis-à-vis our brothers but also vis-à-vis ourselves [and] God. In a word, let us all die to ourselves in all things so that God may live in us and we in God. There is our morality, our dogma, our worship. . . .
>
> No sentiment, thought, will, of our own, except universal Love, Unity, and sacrifice: that is universal Communion. God in us and we in God, each in all and all in each: that is creation, immortality, and life. The finite is transformed into the infinite, multiplicity into unity, the contingent into the absolute. We die as humanity to rise again as God.[47]

To this profession of faith we can apply the infallible criterion of Buchez: "Since the assertion that all things are identical, that opposites are the same and identical, is the essential constituent of pantheism, the system must be brought back to this question and judged in terms of it."[48] Here the case is quickly judged. There is not a single phrase in Chevé's letter that does not ruin ten years of Buchez's teaching, that does not take the supposedly rediscovered faith of their grandfathers and reduce it to modern heresies: over against the egotism of Protestant individualism, the heresy of Spinoza the Jew, transmitted by Lessing to Eugène Rodriguès and, through the latter, to Enfantin, and making the finite a modality of the infinite and each individual a part of the divine Whole; over against the brutal language of exploitation and animalization in the British vein, the refinements of the German language, which reduces opposites to identity. The dualistic morality of Christianity and France now sees the mediation of sacrifice being reduced to the direct, immediate pleasure or enjoyment of

47. Chevé to Pecqueur, Jan. 10, 1843, Pecqueur Archives, International Institute of Social History, Amsterdam.
48. Buchez, *Essai d'un traité complet de philosophie*, II, 334.

the One. In the pantheist night where the human equals the divine, the absolute alienation of dedication joins up again with the absolute of egotistical pleasure: pure consumption or consummation of self, the identity of sacrifice and egotism is called suicide.

So one must face up to the logic of two suicides: the "extreme consequence" of Saint-Simonian pantheism as pointed out back in 1831 by the "disciple of the New Science,"[49] and the end promised ten years later to victims of dedication by the testament of another editor of L'Atelier, Adolphe Boyer. Wrote Boyer:

> If you want to know the cause of my death, here it is. As regards the worker, in the present condition of society, the more egoistic and selfish he is, the happier he is. If he loves his family and seeks its welfare, he endures countless sufferings. But if he sincerely loves society and his fellow creatures, he must end like me.[50]

It is no easy matter to qualify the "egotism" that drove to suicide the ill-starred author of a work on the condition of workers and how it might be improved by the organization of work: De l'état des ouvriers et de son amélioration par l'organisation du travail. For the bourgeois press has already seized on the incident and is using it to kill two birds with one stone—to denounce once again the presumption that prompts workers to abandon their own tools for the writer's pen, and to liken the dedication and projects of the reformer workers to the egotistical desire to rise above the common people's condition that has already killed people like Gilbert, Malfilâtre, and Hégésippe Moreau. And so L'Atelier must first vindicate the memory of its collaborator against a journalist of Les Débats, who has contrasted the fatal vanity of the worker publicist with the assured happiness of the hard-working, economical laborer.[51] But to stick with this opposition between dedication and thrift is to sanction an even more pernicious version of Boyer's act. Someone has already vouched for Boyer's unselfishness —the patron who had found him a place at Paul Dupont's, the executor attentive to the letter of his testament, but also a perfect example of those seducers of the people blamed for all the perversions of the popular party in the same issue of L'Atelier: the Saint-Simonian Isaac Péreire. The latter

49. Lettre d'un disciple de la Science nouvelle aux religionnaires prétendus saint-simoniens de l'Organisateur et du Globe, Paris, 1831, pp. 27f.

50. La Ruche populaire, Oct. 1841.

51. "Sur les réflexions du Globe et des Débats à propos du suicide de Boyer," L'Atelier, Nov. 1841, pp. 19–20.

depicts Boyer as the victim, not of his own presumption, but of working-class incomprehension. He presents the case in his own peculiar terms, of course, contrasting the worker anxious for serious, peaceful reforms with a mass led by demagogues to understand only the language of revolution.[52] But once one has refuted the old Saint-Simonian stereotype, one finds oneself at the heart of the problem. If it is not revolutionary frenzy that makes the masses deaf to reformist writings, mustn't it be the opposite: their apathy, their inability to understand the language of dedication in general? "People saw him as a fool, a man of ambition who wanted to make himself famous and popular by overthrowing society."[53] What reply is *L'Atelier* to make to the funeral eulogy given, it so happens, by a Saint-Simonian typographer who prefers to set aside the great theses and focus on the bare facts? Notes typographer Vannostal:

> Boyer had contracted obligations that he could not meet when they fell due. To this embarrassment was added his sorrow at seeing that the majority of the working class did not yet appreciate its full power and looked with apathy and indifference on everything that could contribute to its emancipation.
>
> Their slowness in signing a petition to the city council of Paris against the *prud'hommes* [joint management and labor arbitration boards] . . . put the finishing touch to his discouragement. He ended up in doubt, that fatal malady of our century, and he put an end to his life.[54]

The typographers of *L'Atelier* refrain from responding to this speech by their colleague Vannostal. They simply cut it in two. They stoutly approve his condemnation of the fatal malady and refute the argument about working-class "apathy" elsewhere: 1,067 signatures from the typography craft alone on the famous petition are enough to prove that the working class is not indifferent to its enfranchisement. The cause of the malady fatal to Boyer must be sought elsewhere: not in the ambition concealed under his dedication but in the confusion that caused the latter to take the shape of the former. The anonymous letters of workers accusing Boyer of wanting to make a name for himself bring out clearly the contradiction in signing one's name to an act of self-sacrificing dedication. The

52. *Le Moniteur parisien*, Oct. 28, 1841.
53. *La Ruche populaire*, Oct. 1841.
54. Ibid.

idlers are the ones who want their generosity to be repaid with thanks: for example, the benefactors of the Petit-Bourg orphanage whose philanthropy is rewarded with little plaques on the headboards of their protégés' beds.[55] In choosing to sign his name, a dedicated worker loses his right to the only identity that can legitimate his message: the people's collective identity. It is to merit that identity that the editors of *L'Atelier* insist upon strict anonymity for their articles, thereby opposing the "Babelian" principle of the worker–writers of *La Ruche populaire*. The book of the people must be one in its appearance as well as in its doctrine, unshaken by the signatures of proper names and particular theories. The vicissitudes of reality and the judgments of common sense confirm the accord between the commandments of morality and the rules of political action:

> It is less a matter of giving luster to proper names than of giving luster to the collective name of the People. Besides, rarely can a worker compose a book on his own, and even more rarely can he make the sacrifices needed to publish it. . . . It is because he wanted to walk alone and speak in his own name that one of our unfortunate comrades was led to surrender himself to death.[56]

The haughty pride of gratuitous dedication, the desire for individual recognition, the sin of egotism. Having put down the *feuilletonistes* of work and thrift, *L'Atelier* must now pick up their judgments insofar as they are also the judgments of Boyer's anonymous correspondents, representatives in their own way of the "public opinion" that, in practice, exercises the theoretical sovereignty of morality. Boyer's dedication had been contaminated by the teachings of "educators," and his militant force had been diminished by a youth of debauchery. This ill-starred man must be assigned a place among "the second-rate capacities, the badly governed imaginations . . . that legion of suffering spirits who feel but do not do," those "feeble combatants" doomed to the exemplary fate of the failed authors Escousse and Lebas, who were saved from oblivion by their joint suicide and a poem by Béranger:

> And you too, Boyer, did you not disregard the power of a holy and fraternal union on the day your hands lit the fatal furnace? Shall we call to mind the pale Pleiad of all those lost children without

55. "Colonie de Petit-Bourg," *L'Atelier*, Aug. 1845, p. 172.
56. "Si les ouvriers doivent se permettre d'écrire," *L'Atelier*, March 1843, p. 56.

friends or mother, of those pitiful muses, Gilbert and Malfilâtre, whose miserable death was their only fortune. . . . No, let us leave their ashes in peace. But let us say to adolescent vocations that the moral tale of the fabulist is ever true, and that there is something in the world weaker than infancy: haughty isolation.[57]

This condemnation must be put back in its context, to be sure. The writer is trying to refute the bourgeois argument that every worker who concerns himself with something besides his craft necessarily becomes a declassed outcast harmful to society and himself. The Association of Workers for Intellectual Works is the third way to escape the dilemma of incessant work or perdition. But it presupposes a transformation of the ideal opposing the gratuitous surplus of moral work to industrial servitude, a discreet acquiescence to the ministers and *feuilletonistes* of the existing order. The primary opposition now is no longer between the dedicated ones and the egotists, or even between workers and pleasure-seekers; the opposition is between the preserving social principle and the corrupting social principle. And this latter corruption is no longer equated so much with the order of the Guizots and the Humanns, with a system that commonly produces the drunks of barrier districts and the fanatics of thrift, as with the presence of an alien, mixed element that confuses the barriers between the sexes, the classes, and morality. For the worker's *association* to display its full force, which constituted the majesty of *parlements,* learned societies, the university, and the Roman Senate, it must be led back out of the pathways into which it has been misled by Fourier or the "so-called disciples of Saint-Simon"[58]—the pathways that serve as the meetingplace between bourgeois pretending to be proletarians and laborers pretending to be philanthropists and writers. The root evil lies in this realm of mixed loves and misconstrued devotions where workers try to lay hold of the acme, the *ne plus ultra,* of aristocratic pleasure: not the mansions of wealth, but its leisure, the *otium* that is even more pernicious as the principle of devotion than as the principle of otioseness.

A conversion in outlook, a change in the arithmetic. People had to do more, but the evil lies in excess: love overflowing into debauchery, nights made feverish by the chimera of the Golden Age and the mania of sacrifice. In a way, the minister of material interests and incessant labor is right: the moral principle preserving society should be identical to the material

57. "De l'association dans les travaux intellectuels," *L'Atelier*, Dec. 1843, p. 40.
58. Ibid., p. 39.

principle preserving individuals. Dedication had first been presented as man's battle against "his instinct for self-preservation and his desires for pleasure." Now it is time for those "who are not philosophers" to recognize in morality "the best means of individual and societal preservation."[59] This is the mathematical demonstration performed by Supernant, repentant *goguettier* and former editor of *La Ruche populaire,* as he concludes his diatribe against *goguettes:*

> If you consider the smallness of wages today, if you realize that only with stubborn perseverance and dogged employment of his time, his sole and precious capital, can the laborer satisfy his most basic needs, then you can readily appreciate the serious upsets produced in the lives of those people whose minds are continually preoccupied with anything and everything but their work. . . . Application without respite is a matter of life and death for the worker.[60]

If the evil lies wholly in the leisure time that serves as the basis for the perverse pleasures of "intellectual happiness" and "moral happiness," then the most effective and radical way to uproot it is to deny the very existence of leisure for any worker who is anxious to make a living for himself and his family from his work. But while that denies existence to the perversions of dedication, doesn't it also deny the very possibility of dedication itself? Mustn't one find some place for the activity of the militant in this employment of time that condemns to disgrace and death those who want to do something besides their work?

> Among the workers there are men of energy and conviction. To attend to the improvements and reforms demanded immediately and imperiously by the position forced on the laboring classes in our day, these men generously sacrifice a few hours out of their workday and nobly face the crises they must endure for interrupting their daily work. But what an enormous difference there is between such men, who deduct a few moments from their thirteen hours of fatigue and devote them to the lofty point of view of the well-being and enfranchisement of all workers, and the jackasses whose

59. "Discussion sur la certitude morale et religieuse," *L'Atelier,* May 1843, p. 84.
60. "Variétés: les goguettes," *L'Atelier,* Oct. 1844; attributed to Supernant by *La Chanson,* Dec. 1879, p. 153.

diversions have no aim but the satisfaction of their own egotistical and sterile vanity. In a situation where application to work without respite is a matter of life or death for the worker, so to speak, the moral preoccupations of the former are those of dedication; the preoccupations of the latter are suicide.[61]

The opposition of dedication to egotism is clear, but the opposition of sacrifice to suicide is much less clear. How can the "enormous difference" in quality between "the lofty point of view" of enfranchisement and the satisfaction of egotistical vanity alter the simple arithmetic indicating that any quantity subtracted from the vital minimum has to result in the killing of life? The only way to separate Boyer's dedication from Escousse's suicide is to say that the subtraction in the former case is not a subtraction. This solution is effected imaginarily in the argumentation and projected really into the future of association: the hours of dedication, deducted not from the time of work but from the *time of fatigue,* are counted as hours of work, so they can be added to the other hours of work as homogeneous quantities. If the time taken from work for dedication is not suicidal, the reason is that it is really not taken, that the work of dedication is interchangeable with labor. By the same token, this means that labor, the material exercise of strength serving the reproduction of life, is immediately and directly equivalent to the work of dedication. The labor and the work must be interchangeable. For that to be possible, however, the two must have a common element. That common element can only be *obligation,* which must be felt to be "immediate and imperious" in both cases. The fatigues of devotion and the fatigues of life-nurturing labor can be interchanged or added to each other in the calculation of common work because and insofar as they are products of one and the same effort to obey constraint or compulsion.

This is a curious equality indeed, which can provide a foundation for the work of popular dedication only by turning it upside down. In the image of their leaders, working-class people were to do *more* to reestablish equality, to disprove the bourgeois view that saw the hallmarks of their degradation as so many signs of their condemnation to incessant work and, at the same time, saw this incessant work as the only way to prevent that degradation from turning into the dissolution of the societal bond. In the course of this battle, however, those involved encountered the communist heresy and the hapless victims of dedication. This encounter has

61. Ibid.

forced them to go back over their arithmetic, to link corruption with the
excess of leisure and morality with the impossibility of leisure. Here we
have the generalization of a whole category of "impossibles" already encountered when the view and strategy of those in power had to be denied.
It was *impossible* that the animal creatures crawling around the sewer of
Rue Sainte-Marguerite were workers, because the latter were in the workshops. It was *impossible* that the bourgeoisie, in line with the scheme of *La
Presse*, might buy off with credit the workers who had the confidence of
their comrades, because workers are suspicious by nature and trust only
those who earn their trust and more. It was *impossible* that the working-
class people would let themselves be corrupted by savings, because they
did not earn enough to satisfy their immediate needs. They had no time for
loitering in the streets, not enough money, no trust. A simple arithmetic
of lack was always there to exorcise the image of corruption and bolster
the common wisdom that idleness—that is, excess time—was the source
and principle of all the vices. Thus, the "wholly beneficent" influence of
almost all women in the ranks of the common people does not signify
any "status grace" attached to commoner identity: "It merely signifies that
their situation, in line with the precept dictating that each person should
live by his or her work, does not allow them those obligatory periods of
leisure time that give rise to all the proclivities of egotism; their position
forces them, as it were, to employ in the service of society an activity that
our fashionable ladies think should be expended in the opposite way."[62]

It is here that the argument making a virtue of necessity comes to take
its place at the core of the militant ethics of dedication, that the obligation
to do more in this line, in order to move from the material realm to the
moral realm, is reduced to the impossibility of excess's opening the way
to immorality. The time to do more can only be the time for corruption
or suicide. Just as there is no happiness other than physical happiness, so
dedication cannot be defined in any terms other than those of constrained
or compelled work. The surplus of dedication is an evanescent quantity
that must be identified with the fatigue of the worker's effort if it is not to
be confused with the time of corruption that condemns to death misconstrued dedication as well as the vanity of the *goguettier* and the depravity
of orgies.

In vain does *L'Atelier* try to oppose "free will" to the law of progress
as understood by *La Fraternité*, the latter reducing liberty to cognizance

62. "Les dames du grand monde," *L'Atelier*, May 1844, p. 122.

of the laws of social harmony.[63] This free will, true principle of progress and morality, is never exercised so well as when it is strictly compelled by material obligation! Once again the identicalness of free morality and material necessity surfaces at the core of emancipation; and work takes its place at the center of God's moral kingdom, thanks not to the grandeur attached to productive work, but rather to the *lack* that removes time from immorality and preserves dedication from suicide. So those who furnish the model of moral work are those who cannot do otherwise. To be sure, *L'Atelier* denies having succumbed to a "narrow and exclusivist sentiment" in its definition of the word "worker": "We declare once and for all that, in general terms, we recognize as workers all those human beings who, by whatever sort of labor, participate in the societal task; and we regard as unworthy of this designation only those who do not give to society at least as much as they receive from it."[64] This definition makes room for the surplus value of dedication as well as that of material labor. But *L'Atelier* must quickly return from the confusion of such "vague generalities" to the usage of "ordinary language": "We give the name 'workers' to that class of laborers who are obliged, in order to live, to hire out their arms to someone wanting to employ them."[65] Now, who is unaware of the fact that the very precondition of this hiring-out is that the worker is always compelled to give more than he receives? And no foresight that comes down to charity, no mere whiff of instruction, no nonexistent political rights, can make up for this subtraction, to which are added the sacrifices made to beget new workers and the blood shed unequally for the cause of the nation. So doesn't it turn out, by simple arithmetic, that the "egotistical" workers, whose labor generally has no aim other than the reproduction of their labor power, are in fact the workers *par excellence,* the artisans of the kingdom of God in the social order?

Well, yes and no. In becoming identified with the surplus value of labor, thanks to the constraint of time and measure, the excess of dedication cannot stop being its contrary. It is only in the writings of professor Buchez or student-professor Ott that idle identity eaten away by corruption meets its opposite in the simple and robust dualist principle of working spirit and resistant matter (metal to be forged *and* instinct to be mastered). For the organ of the moral *and* material interests of the workers, *L'Atelier,* the

63. "Discussion sur le communisme," *L'Atelier*, Nov. 1845, pp. 211–12.
64. "Réponse à quelques objections," *L'Atelier*, Nov. 1840, p. 19.
65. Ibid., p. 20.

whole problem lies in this conjunction whereby the division of the One into two and the identity of opposites end up besieging the royalty of work at its very birth: the identity of the life of morality and the death of sacrifice, of the death of egotism and the life of societal preservation. The reign of associated workers both will and will not be that of the hard-working multitude that is supposedly more advanced than the dedicated avant-garde:

> Now you will ask us what association will change. We, in turn, will ask you what it will *not* change. . . . Replacing a worker bowed under wage humiliation and his master's disdain, induced into self-contempt by other people's contempt for him, and often led thereby to the brutish self-degradation of vice, will be a free and honored worker, now bound only by the laws of association to which he has freely consented, regaining his complete dignity as a human being and taking full cognizance of his moral worth, prompted by the respect of others to respect, rehabilitate, and ennoble himself by practicing the virtues.[66]

Here is a reasonable ideal of a worker for the future, combining the nobility of militant obligation with the respectability of the good worker. But in this prospective picture, which is supposed to prove to communists and skeptics that worker association is something other than a form of collective egotism for workers, heresy is never far away. The anonymous article on the "organization of work" soon betrays the hand of our enthusiast, Chevé: "All were necessarily bitter adversaries. One worker would try to supplant his rival by an even more base submissiveness to the master's wishes, by acceptance of an even more degrading wage, by treachery even. And behold, now they are as one, the interest of each has become the interest of all; they are as one and the same body, and someone who wrongs one wrongs the others."[67]

"One and the same body": the dream of a society of "equal exchange" that this as yet unconfessed disciple of Proudhon would like to found on a single little article of the Code (the suppression of the *rente*); a world of "nonexploitation" in which the work of each is passed along to all and that of all is passed along to each, like "the circulation of blood in the human

66. "Organisation du travail," *L'Atelier*, Oct. 1843, p. 12.
67. Ibid.

body" or the "fertilization of the earth by the great arteries of our rivers",[68] a "holy communion" quick to lay claim once again to the all too celebrated lineage of the despisers of usury and wealth—Saint Ambrose, Saint John Chrysostom, Saint Basil, Saint Gregory of Nyssa, and all those Fathers of the Church whose writings leave them defenseless against those who would transform them into Fathers of the Community.

It is the chronic pantheist error of the mystical bookkeeper, but it is only a momentary lapse of vigilance by the screening committee for articles. One looks in vain for the follow-up article promised for the next issue of *L'Atelier*. In its place the committee, though hardly infatuated with workshop "versifiers," inserted a satire of several hundred Alexandrines against fraudulent merchants. Better to let the heretical Inquisitor celebrate, in his own writings and at his own risk, this new deity wedding the pagan idol to the Son of the true God:

> Woe to anyone who rejects work as an abasement, for it is the only title of nobility that traverses time and is even inscribed in the book of eternity. It is the throne where the human being displays its full royal majesty and moves toward the Eternal One to receive from his hands the crown of glory. . . .
>
> Work is the Christian Hercules. In his left hand he holds out two swords, one for subduing the earth and the other for subduing his own passions. In his right hand he waves two torches, the torch of genius and the torch of liberty. Science is his strength, charity his triumph.
>
> Idleness is the adulterous Venus. Vice is born of her, and ignorance is her child. She is life devouring itself, the crossroads prostitute selling her flesh to death and her soul to Satan.[69]

Right on! with regard to the adulterous Venus; but the militants of association wouldn't get much of a grip on the workers' future if they encumbered their hands with two swords of negation and two torches of affirmation. The kingdom of associated workers must be announced in more modest terms:

68. Chevé, *Catholicisme et démocratie; ou: Le règne du Christ*, Paris, 1842, pp. 119f. See idem, *Le dernier mot du socialisme par un catholique*, Paris, 1849.
69. Chevé, *Catholicisme et démocratie*, pp. 113–14.

We foresee a time when money will no longer bear interest, but that day is still far away. . . . No one will take that to mean the absence of power. . . . In our contract the former or present master is replaced by the manager; this word is more suitable, but the directive function is the same. . . . To repeat, it takes many qualities to make a good associate: . . . lowly dedication at all hours . . . the spirit of discipline . . . the virtue of voluntarily submitting to the yoke, which is so necessary. . . . Here we have ten workers who borrow 10,000 francs to start a business. Their labor fertilizes the borrowed capital, and within five years, more or less, the capital is paid back and the instrument of work is the property of the association. In our system, and at the end of an obligatory contract, this property would not be divisible among the associates in its totality. There would be a reserve fund that would accumulate indefinitely out of a specified portion of the profits—one-fourth or one-fifth. . . . There lies the start of the indivisible capital, the impersonal property, that will ensure the indefinite growth of the association. Suppose this reserve capital is 5,000 francs today. So we enlarge our operations, take in five new associates if we can, and in a year the reserve capital will be 10,000 francs instead of 5,000. With it we shall then emancipate ten exploited workers.

So there is our snowball. The bigger it grows, the more hands will be needed to roll it. And these emancipated hands will bring in others down the line. . . .

We agree that this is small potatoes, but everything begins that way in the world.[70]

But the problem is not that the snowball of association rolls slowly. The problem is knowing what exactly makes it roll. For the obvious dichotomies governing moral work become curiously compounded when such work translates into the organization of labor. The initial demonstration, which had been entrusted to Chevé, seemed clear enough. The aim was to unite contraries and thus get beyond the opposition of two systems: the "free competition of exclusively individual property or ownership" and the doctrine "that starts off with the societal unit, denies the individual, and

70. *L'Atelier*: "Opinions de la presse sur l'organisation du travail," Nov. 1842, p. 21; "Réforme industrielle: du régime des corporations," April 1842, p. 62; "Organisation du travail: nouvelle série, 5ᵉ article," Aug. 1845, p. 162; "Organisation du travail: nouvelle série, 4ᵉ article," May 1845, p. 119.

wants everything to be communal, both production and distribution."[71] This union of contraries is not effected in the German style: identity. It is done in the French style, which the writer for *L'Atelier* has quite obviously borrowed, though he does not breathe a word about it, from a recent work (*What Is Property?*) by a printer–philosopher from Besançon (Pierre-Joseph Proudhon). Each of the opposing principles is assigned its place on the balance scale. In the realm of *production,* collective appropriation of the means of production is supposed to put an end to the exploitation rooted in individual expropriation. In the realm of *distribution,* one must challenge the communists, who deny all ownership and promise an optimal satisfaction of needs. In opposition to them one must propose individual ownership of consumable riches that are the fruits of labor. "The problem of distribution can thus be formulated as follows: to find a combination that reconciles, unites, and coordinates these two apparently contradictory principles—(1) equality in the satisfaction of all needs, in accordance with their nature, proportion, and intensity; (2) equality for each member of the social body in production value and value received."[72]

Obviously, this equality is possible only through collective possession of the means of production, which frees labor from the tithe expropriated by idleness. But it also presupposes that between the two realms (production and distribution) there exists a principle of equality—the remuneration of work. In the absence of such a principle, the communists are caught in an unresolvable dilemma. Either they promise the satisfaction of every need, but without the means to provide it, or else they ensure that satisfaction, but using a compulsion that eliminates the most precious pleasure they dangle before the worker: that is, the freedom to work or relax when one feels like it, to shift from one place to another at will, or even to take those trips around the world that editors of *L'Humanitaire* promise five or six times in a lifetime to those who will adopt their principles. Notes *L'Atelier*:

> If the community were to grant the liberties we have just mentioned, it would perish; for the number of people who would abuse them would be immense. Thus, the preconditions for its very existence would prevent it from granting such freedom. But if you remunerate work with an exchangeable token, then the human

71. Ibid., "Réforme industrielle: organisation du travail," July 1841, p. 85.
72. Ibid., p. 86.

being is free to work more or work less, to come and go. . . . In worker association, distribution takes place, always equally for each worker, according to the degree and proportion of what he has produced. Then each one, absolute judge of his own desires and needs, is in charge of satisfying them as much as he wants, giving to society a value equal to the riches he desires. This also preserves the ongoing motor of work and progress, which consists mainly in the freedom, desires, and needs of the human personality.[73]

"A value equal to the riches he desires": the equality is simple. This equation of value created and value received, of effort expended and the satisfaction of needs, defines justice. Unfortunately, one of the terms in the equation divides in two. For the value of work cannot be measured in terms of wage exploitation. It should reflect the new social principle being implemented: "In the distribution each performance should be assessed only in terms of the effort and dedication it has cost, not in terms of its intrinsic value."[74] If it is not to degenerate into a shabby collective of petty proprietors, the work of an association of workers cannot disregard this principle of remuneration: "The wage should be based, not on differentiation of skills, but on the dangers and fatigues to which they expose people and on the aversions they evoke. By giving this basis to wages, we believe that equality will find its value reckoned all the better insofar as it goes hand in hand with justice."[75] Except for one thing: it is not the same equality or the same justice; the sum total of aversions overcome, you see, might not add much to the total of riches to be distributed. To be sure, the pleasures desired by the pious Chevé and his comrades are not the sort that call for a surplus of manual labor and productivity. But then one has every right to ask at this point exactly what sort of dedication it is that permits the "free personality," judge of its own desires and needs, to purchase pleasures for itself. Is association simply to be a better way of procuring for oneself the pleasures of egotism, be they refined or not? A better way of producing more to consume more, as our Saint-Simonian apostle and engineer might express it in his logic? A better way of working more to rest more, according to the Babylonian logic denounced by the people's priest?

73. Ibid., "Organisation du travail: nouvelle série, 4ᵉ article," May 1845, p. 121; and "Réforme industrielle: organisation du travail," p. 86.
74. Ibid., "Réforme industrielle: organisation du travail," July 1841.
75. Ibid., "Organisation du travail: nouvelle série, 4ᵉ article," May 1845, p. 120.

So let us abandon this terrain where Proudhon's individualism of means converges with the communist or Saint-Simonian immorality of ends. Let us get back once more to healthy morality: that is, to the twofold viewpoint of a social utility that obligates and an individual resistance that must be overcome:

> We don't think anyone will object to the notion that the mode of remunerating work must seek to stimulate production to the highest possible degree. Present-day societies have immense material needs: real, pressing needs that have not yet been met, that can be satisfied only by labor as immense as the needs themselves. Our farmers lack the most basic necessities of life. In many localities not all of them have bread, wheat, or rye, not by a long shot. Their houses, their shacks rather, do not have paved or inlaid floors. They have no furniture at all, and warm clothes are a great luxury for them. All these things are necessities, and they will have to be produced as soon as political reform places those deprived of them in the ranks of citizens.[76]

This social duty would not be one, of course, if it did not run up against a spontaneous tendency to resist it: "And here we must bow our head under a reproach that applies to all humanity. We refer to the instinctive repugnance that every person has against real, fruitful labor."[77] That is indeed the perfect situation for the exercise of dedication; unfortunately, it is also the situation in which dedication becomes inapplicable as a principle of remuneration. How can we get the immense surplus of riches demanded by the welfare of society with a remuneration that grows in proportion to the worthlessness or unproductiveness of repugnances overcome? And so the sacrosanct principle is discreetly set aside in favor of a realistic comparison of the respective advantages of pay by the workday and piecework pay. The question is quickly decided against the former: "Although the majority perform such work with all possible probity and skill, it nevertheless is true that this work never has the vigor and energy of labor on a piecework basis."[78] From the "natural laziness" that rests content with the routine of work by the day to the lesser social utility of such work, morality here finds its place in negative terms. But the converse is far

76. Ibid., "Des différent modes de rétribution du travail," July 1843, p. 98.
77. Ibid.
78. Ibid.

more difficult to establish. How to ground as morality the incentive of piecework that will enable society to give the inhabitants of rural areas the most basic necessities of life? "Will you accuse us, as some communists have done, of trying to stimulate human beings with the hideous lure of money? In this case the argument is specious, though it has a certain sentimental likelihood that makes it harder to combat."[79] As we would expect of him, the writer of the article does not believe "that useful actions, especially those of the moral order, could in principle have gain for their goal"; and he can only criticize the general who urged his troops on by promising them monetary rewards.[80] Our writer, however, certainly would not have criticized the general for promising his troops medals, or even the simple gratitude of future generations. Well, it is now firmly established that there are not two types of incentives or two types of pleasures. As long as one is counting on incentives, it is better to appeal to the effective desire for money than to the whims of humanitarian glory. And when you consider the matter, don't such accusations of egotism themselves adopt an egotistical viewpoint, putting individual betterment before the common welfare?

> You cannot simply consider the individual, either. You must judge and act in terms of society. Now, in the industrial order, is it good that work make progress in speed and perfection? Not only is that good, it is of the utmost necessity. If we stimulate this progress with the hope of honorary rewards, will we get it? Yes, indeed! If we add to that a monetary recompense, will we get even more progress? No one can doubt that.[81]

This maieutic lesson at a pellmell pace cannot, however, let us forget the grounding principle of the whole edifice: that is, that the preservation or dissolution of societal bonds depends on motives that individuals adopt for themselves. To remove the obstacle, we must go back to the New Testament and read it in the Protestant version—with the Epistle of James amputated. The intractable Chevé loved to remind people that the Epistle of James condemned not only the wicked rich but the rich in general. Now the writer for *L'Atelier* offers this viewpoint:

79. Ibid.
80. Ibid.
81. Ibid.

By stimulating love for money, will society lose in morality what it gains in industrial or agricultural improvement, hence in well-being? We don't think so. Because it is not what one gains that demoralizes, but rather the use that one makes of it. So society, following the gospel precept as closely as possible, should provide recompense in accordance with works. If you thereby become relatively rich, the Gospel is there and the moral law is there to indicate to you the use to which you should put your riches.[82]

To each, then, according to his capabilities and his works. For the hard workers there is the incentive of a relative enrichment; in the same Gospel that sanctifies the earthly recompense of the just man, they can find the way to avoid depravity. For ordinary workers there is the incentive of daily hunger. For those who would like to satisfy that hunger without doing anything, there is the chastisement of forced labor. Finally, for the weakling workers—who are abandoned by the new Christians and left to the process of market selection, say the communists maliciously—there is some labor suited to their capacities. Thus, the ordered kingdom of work takes the form of a new syncretism. Insofar as recompense is concerned, we have a purified Saint-Simonism: by a strict remuneration of dedication in the form of power or money, it takes the aberrations of the hierarchy of love back to the strict original principle of classification according to capabilities and retribution according to works. Insofar as pain and punishment are concerned, we have a Christianity reduced to the dogma of the fall and ultimately resolved to pay the workers of the eleventh hour on a piecework basis.

Here we have an exchange in which the Christian rigor of law and penalty and the Saint-Simonian justice of classification and recompense come along to correct what each religion had left to the arbitrary love of engineer–apostles and philanthropic grape-growers. But in this exchange preeminence tends to be reversed. Now everyone knows that it is the recompense, not the pain or penalty, that prompts individuals to contribute to the progress of society. Discreetly redressing, before openly attacking, Chevé's feverish dreams of new Thebaids, of corporations and workers united in the mystical body of Christ, weaver–typographer–joiner–sculptor and future deputy Corbon can pretend he is expressing only the modest simplicity of the Christian rule and common

82. Ibid.

sense. But over against the mystical dream of universal association, he is actually outlining something else: a republic of merit founded less on the sublimities of dedication or the universality of the law than on the free flight of abilities and emulation of the innovators and workers of progress. A republic that will give everyone his chance, but first those who know how to help themselves; that will patronize the associations, not so much as embryos of the city of communitarian work, but rather as the avant-garde of a movement that is more important than the goal and that must incessantly revolutionize production conditions and human relationships.

Is this the individualism of the pioneers of progress, replacing the Christian and national morality of work? But perhaps this return to "ego-tism" is itself a substitute as well, one designed to avoid losing, in the pro-saic banality of the organization of work, that *other thing* that the morality of work commanded to be sacrificed to the common measure. Despite all their denials, don't the worker–artist Corbon and the mystical bookkeeper Chevé still feel that the rewards and pains of the organization of work will never be more than substitutes for the pleasures and sacrifices forbidden to the working-class people as such, except in brief and chance encoun-ters: the life hidden in God of cenobites and Philadelphians; the great days when they storm Bastilles "in the time it takes a child to play a game of handball," when, "between two settings of the sun," one makes "a revo-lution that changes the face of a whole people";[83] the cause of oppressed nationalities; the work of artists and inventors; and the new epic of those warrior monks and fighting workers who cross the seas to improve the globe and repel barbarism in the desert sands?

And a final paradox of the republic of work envisioned by the editors of *L'Atelier*: it is also to preserve this supplement, which their morality bade them abolish, that this republic's pioneers chose the side they did. Going against the dreams of the worker Left, which wants to give the instruments of work and collective emancipation to worker corporations, they decided to support the party of those curious friends of worker association, lawyer Marie and banker Goudchaux, who have been trying to establish a social base among the worker élite for their future republic of moderation and honesty. When a carpenter from *L'Atelier* came to the republican banker to lay out a plan for organizing his corporation in such a way that he could do without men of money, the banker spelled out his own plan: "We form a society of bankers and take up a subscription among us. When we have put together a capital of 200,000 francs, we shall choose men from

83. Chevé, *Catholicisme et démocratie*, p. 20.

various worker corporations and make them managers in the various associations that offer us the best guarantees."[84] We look in vain in *L'Atelier*
for a mention of that meeting or a denunciation of that plan, though it
seems awfully similar to the corrupting scheme envisioned not long ago
by *La Presse*. Worse still, at a meeting at Marie's, which brought together
representatives of the worker journals and the socialist sects, the representatives of *L'Atelier* were almost the only ones from their class to support
the banker's principle of "partial associations." That was an extreme sort
of rallying around indeed, a restriction of the field of association designed
to correct the restriction of the principle itself. The same measure that reduces dreams and suicidal dedications to the modesty of worker efforts is
also supposed to prevent the paltriness of the organization of labor from
spreading to the dimensions of the societal work. The principle of work/
labor brings individual vanities back to the common condition; the principle of its remuneration brings the constraint of duty back to the morality
of effort, and societal progress back to the deployment of capabilities.

So rather than focusing on the austere façade of the palace of work, one
must keep a sharp lookout for what puts its ordering out of joint. It is not
without reason that the editors of *L'Atelier* found suitable for their mast-
head only the negative recommendation of Saint Paul, an apostle from
whom they certainly could have borrowed more exalting mottoes: "Whoever does not want to work should not eat." It is as if this shabby relationship between labor and subsistence, where the reasons of the avant-garde
try to link up again with those of the masses, were also the locale of a
purely negative and provisional compromise between the contradictions
specific to this avant-garde, one that is divided as to what it should oppose
to the kingdom of idleness: the harmony of the earthly city of Christ or the
adventure of a progress in which the pathways of worker nomadism cross
those of free enterprise. The kingdom of labor and societal duty remains,
decidedly, a simple transit point. In the austere frontispiece borrowed from
the apostle–worker we must see not so much the proclamation of a new
age as a sign of dissolution and a mark of doubt affecting this monarchy
at its very origins:

> The group of workers who took over this plan for the organization
> of work and propagated it as best they could seemed to be aware
> of the impossibility of carrying out a system that demanded so

84. Cited in Auguste Desmoulins, "Le capital et les associations partielles," in
Almanach des corporations nouvelles, Paris, 1852, pp. 114–15.

much abnegation and sustained effort. The proof lies in the fact that they did not make any great effort to preach by example. I know something about the matter. I recall perfectly well what I felt and said out loud more than once: that I would find it very difficult to bow to the exigencies of such an order of things.[85]

Failing to practice oneself, one can always encourage others. Soon the republic of lawyer Marie and banker Goudchaux will name Corbon and Danguy of *L'Atelier* members of the Committee for the Encouragement of Worker Associations. Do they still have faith at the moment the crusade begins? Well, in any case, others certainly have it for them.

85. C. A. Corbon, *Le secret du peuple de Paris*, Paris, 1863, pp. 129–30.

CHAPTER 11

The Republic of Work

The manager of the tailors opened the door of the workshop, calling for a moment of silence and introducing us as friends of all the assembled workers. Almost forty were present—and it was Monday morning, I am delighted to point out right off the bat. The tailors greeted us effusively. A smile of deep satisfaction lit up their faces, which were thin and pale but also frank and intelligent.[1]

THIS DOOR OPENING INTO A SCENE of fraternal association reveals to the eyes of the visiting representatives of the people nothing but a huge room where the associated tailors squat and work from morning to night on the bare floor, a bit harder than they used to do at the shops of their masters. But there are three little lithographs on the wall and, while his colleagues discuss working conditions with the workers, locksmith Gilland, deputy for today but art lover always, goes closer to see what the lithographs are about: "One was the portrait of a heroic man who had his faults, but whom the people pitied, forgave, and worshiped."[2] Alongside this picture of Armand Barbès (1809–1870), dedicated if not enlightened defender of the people, was another image that a very young man, an orphan taken in by the association, offered for the admiration of the visitor: "Another lithograph depicting Jesus crowned with thorns and leaning on two allegorical figures, liberty and equality. In this moving picture the Son of God holds under his bare feet the demon of pride, who is vomiting gold. And the word 'Hope' is inscribed on the shining disk above his head, which is

1. J.-P. Gilland, *Revue anecdotique des associations ouvrières*, Paris, 1850, p. 10.
2. Gilland, *Revue anecdotique*.

all tenderness and meekness."[3] After these two images of sacrifice comes an image of fecundity and fraternal prosperity:

> This time it was the Republic, a strong and gorgeous woman, depicted as happy but a bit austere. She wore a Phrygian cap [symbol of liberty], a wreath of flowers, and a long flowing dress. Her only ornament is a bronze level on her forehead. . . . Behind this figure of the Republic are superb cities whose monuments touch the sky, fields filled with corn, hillsides covered with grapes. She calmly offers one of her hands to be kissed by a colossal lion, who fondles it. With her other hand she is showing a hive of busy bees to a group of studious children at her feet.[4]

Of course the locksmith–poet, who spends his nights polishing his prose and verse, is paid to know that good intentions are not enough to guarantee the artistic worth of an image, or perhaps even its social utility. But how could the worker deputy resist the temptation to read, in the very coarseness of the imagery, the evident sign of a clear-cut antagonism between two worlds?

> At the sight of these poor, dismal little images, bought perhaps for twenty centimes at the streetcorner display of an itinerant dealer, sketches very incorrectly executed but lofty and moral in conception, I could not help but form a mental comparison. The evening before, I had been in the home of people belonging to high society. . . . When I entered their salon, the first thing to attract my attention was two little statues: Leda and the Swan, and Sara the Bather. The latter was undraped and seen from the front on a swing of leaves that made her raise one knee to her face. . . . The relief was indeed superb!
>
> Present-day society as a whole, it seemed to me, could be summed up in these seemingly simple and frivolous things.
>
> On the one hand comfort, sweet leisure, discreet debauchery, petty interests, petty frivolities, petty vices, and ennui: the ennui of a life dull and useless when it is not scandalous and criminal.
>
> On the other hand a profound destitution after strenuous labors,

3. Ibid.
4. Ibid.

a living faith revealed in works, absolute dedication, all wicked passions sacrificed to a generous idea, love of neighbor carried out in the most sublime sacrifices, and, for boon and consolation in the world, only the hope of bequeathing a better future to future generations.[5]

The plain evidence of the little things that are at once the décor of day-to-day activity and the image of the world being forged therein. No confusion, no common measure between two universes. On the one hand the narrow, curved space of idle salons, where the languor of shabby passions coils in the softness of seats and is modeled on the slenderness of statues. On the other hand the rectangular architecture of vast spaces where nudity serves as a stage-effect for sublime self-sacrifices that are imaged in four-penny lithographs. A double universe equally governed by the law of proportion: the world of idleness can be populated only by dwarfish sentiments, and even the self-interest in it is petty; whereas the grandeur of worker self-sacrifice is necessarily proportionate to the intensity of the pains and the depth of the destitution. In the collapse of the realm of material interests, one finds again the virtues of poverty and the clear opposition of two imageries: in the orators of the bourgeoisie, the phantasm world of pillage; in the poets of the laboring people, the geometry of compensations. It is in that respect that the destitution of association can represent the Promised Land: undoing the confusion of images and pleasures, it gives back to the working people images that are theirs alone and the intimacy of family pleasures. In this paradise regained of identity, the actions of work, painful as they may be, are reflected accurately in the heroism of the figures who adorn the bare walls. Once the confusion of the barrier districts is brought to an end, the fraternity of the banquet table will coincide with the morality of labor efforts and festivals. No one thinks that the revolution is a gala dinner. But in barrier-district Pigalle, where the associated cooks are serving the saddlers their first meal; in Saint Joseph's Court, where the association of cabinetmakers is holding a family party to celebrate its medal at the Exposition; and in the suburbs of La Villette, where the carriage joiners detain the visiting representatives of the people for lunch in the workshop itself, the frugal repast of fraternal workers, repeating the miracles of multiplied bread and consecrated wine, again takes on the fragrance of Sundays in the countryside:

5. Ibid.

The luncheon for the saddlers was to have taken place at 11:00 A.M. It was 10:30 before the tables arrived. There were only eight francs left in the cash box, so the payment of the invoice was put off until the afternoon. . . . In an instant trestles were set up. On them were laid new white planks of fir, their cleanliness and fine scent reminding us of country linen. Each worker put down his pittance and his bread. The wine arrived from outside with all the glasses that could be obtained in the vicinity. Still, some people had none. I shared mine with an apprentice of fifteen who had never been at such a feast in his life. Others imitated my example with those next to them. The bread was divided into as many pieces as there were people present. After everyone had received a share, we toasted twice and clinked glasses all around: first to the democratic Republic and then to association and the enfranchisement of workers. . . . There were more than a hundred people around a modestly furnished table. Cordiality stood in for luxury, decency for etiquette. There were speeches glorifying work, offering moral edification to the people, and blessing the Republic, which is truly loved only by the poor. Then everyone sang in turn: the men, the women, the children. It was stately, tender, enthusiastic, or naïve, but always fine. . . . Then the strolling musicians were introduced to the proceedings. Granted the right to have their shrill fiddle or cold-infected harp sound in the ears of the people, they all understood, without having to be reminded, that this was neither the time nor the place for the smutty songs of the barrier districts.[6]

In the eyes of the former shepherd and those of the "exiled" Pauline Roland searching for lost community, association is not just the undertaking of workers liberated from exploitation by a master; it is the center of a reconstituted universe of the people. No degrading spectacle captures the attention of the worker–deputy in the barrier district of La Villette as he makes the rounds of neighborhood associations. In his view Rue Sainte-Marguerite is an alien enclave in the suburb of Saint-Antoine, where even the names of the courts combine village intimacy with evangelical purity: Cour des Deux-Soeurs, Cour du Nom-de-Jésus, Cour du Panier-fleuri, Cour du Saint-Esprit, and Cour de la Bonne-Graine.[7] At the center of this

6. Pauline Roland, "Chronique des associations ouvrières: Les cuisiniers," *La République*, March 31, 1850; and Gilland, *Revue anecdotique*, pp. 45–46, 68.
7. Gilland, *Revue anecdotique*, pp. 62–64.

universe, the fraternity of worker songs and glasses of wine is no longer in opposition to family duties; nor does the egotism of private hearth and home stand in opposition to worker solidarity. Now the identity of laborious effort and moral work takes Gilland back to the paradise lost by the boy who had fallen into the world of work:

> Then everyone sang in turn: the men, the women, the children. . . . Most of the workers now make up songs of their own and lose nothing thereby. . . . The muse, daughter of palaces, descends to the workshop. Soon she will visit the huts of the poor and bring radiance to the brow of manual laborers. A bit more waiting, a bit more instruction, and all human beings will be living the life of the thinking mind, the only kind of life that can help people put up with the pains and miseries of this other life.[8]

Family portraits, snapshots of the revolution like the countless ones taken home by distinguished visitors who are attentive to the gestures and symbols of the new life: the worker who now knows for what and for whom he works, the boss who is boss only because of the love aroused by his selfless and immeasurable dedication, the woman respected at home and in the workshop who has set aside her cooking pot to go and eat with her children at the table of these large families, where one is no longer served by *garçons* but by *citoyens;* the child at last protected, the orphan taken in, the outcasts of education becoming orators or poets; the street musicians and print sellers changing their repertoire or their display. The poet of *L'Atelier* has chosen the better part, and it will not be taken away from him. But his editorial colleagues, typographer Danguy and member of the Assembly Corbon, both of whom have resigned from the Committee for the Encouragement of Worker Associations, know well enough that the Revolution is not a banquet, even a frugal one, and that daguerreotypes of fraternity have nothing to do with the time and constraints involved in the work of association. What is the point of these heroic efforts expended in industries on sufferance, which may possibly revive only at some point in time when the association has ceased to live? It is certainly nice to see workshops packed on Monday morning, but that does not mean that the articles fashioned so diligently in them will find buyers. And before banqueting to celebrate the medal won at the Exposition, it might have been wise for the cabinetmakers to find out what

8. Ibid., p. 68.

buyer would appear, in these troubled times, for their costly bookcase of jacaranda and rosewood.

Worth noting is the fact that the association evoking the least lyrical flights from chronicler Gilland is actually the most exemplary association of all. It is the association of gilt jewelers, which arose in 1834 directly out of Buchez's teachings and which, in its model statutes of 1843, enshrined the great principle of an indivisible reserve fund, removing the product of association work from the profits accruing to worker egotism. That association does not organize eucharistic repasts for visitors; but every Monday morning it holds an hour and a half of evangelical readings before its general assembly meets to discuss measures to be adopted and faults to be corrected for the smooth running of the establishment. Things are running just as smoothly in its four branches, adroitly differentiated in terms of their respective markets: one for costly goods destined for the Parisian market, one for "goods for Germany," and two for exports to the colonies. The Committee for the Encouragement of Worker Associations took no big risk in allocating 25,000 francs to it out of the loan of three million francs that it was to divide up among the various worker associations: "We can say that it is money loaned with full security and that it will return to the taxpayers interest down to the last cent."[9] On the other hand, the committee did not risk a penny of government money on the strenuous labor and touching fraternity of the clothes tailors, the carriage workers, and the piano-makers celebrated so emotionally by our writer–worker. Association, you see, is not the start of a new life; it is a situation in which workers experience their ability to manage their own affairs. Success, not effort, is the acid test. Let the experiment be made under bad conditions, and the counter-propaganda will be directly proportional to the extent of the dedication workers have displayed. From the very first meeting of the Committee for the Encouragement of Worker Associations, its chairman, worker delegate and vice president of the National Assembly Corbon, had stressed the primacy of the principle of efficacy. The committee reporter tells us: "The conditions that seem the most desirable to him are those having to do with the duration and success of the association."[10]

Moreover, the cause at stake involves first and foremost the very principles of L'Atelier. On the Committee for Encouraging Worker Associations, besides two editors of that journal (Corbon and Danguy), are two intellectual disciples of Buchez (Ott and Feugueray) and the attorney of

9. Ibid., p. 88; and Archives nationales (A.N.), F 12/4625.

10. Procès-verbaux du Conseil d'encouragement pour les associations ouvrières, published by Octave Festy, Paris, 1917, p. 10.

the gilt jewelers (delegate Leblond). The attempted test is theirs, first of all. It was on Corbon's initiative that the Assembly, on July 5, 1848, voted a credit of three million francs to encourage worker associations. The vote was unanimous and taken without debate—in other words, without any great concern for the master plan of Buchez, the master thinker behind *L'Atelier*. For on the day after the events of June 1848, the great thought of the party of decent, moderate socialists had all the allure of good insurance at a bargain price: simultaneous balm for the miseries of the workers and for the bad conscience of the republican representatives; satisfaction given to the working-class fraction which, in both street battles and Assembly debates, had stood for republican order over against partisans of the red republic; a fine gesture on behalf of the workers, which should make them less attentive to murmurs and cries for revenge. Three million francs in loans, some of which would certainly be paid back, was not too high a price to pay for all that. In reckoning the average amount of capital per worker to be invested in an industrial enterprise, there was certainly enough, just enough, to encourage one to two thousand workers to take the path of association. But who was unaware that modesty in the early phases—the careful selection of men who possessed, not "fraternal dedication" in general, but the "down-to-earth dedication" of pioneers—was the strict precondition for the morality and success of an association? The modesty of the sum asked for by Corbon was not a concession to the forces of reaction—quite the contrary. It would have been easy enough for him to ask for "a large credit that the National Assembly would not have quibbled over." But then he would have fallen into the trap set by the enemies of worker association:

> The adversaries of association would have eagerly voted an enormous sum to be handed out to all comers, associated workers of every caliber, so that at the end of a certain period of time these adversaries could trumpet victoriously from their rostrum: Mad theoreticians induced workers to believe that they could dispense with masters. . . . The experiment was tried but it was unsuccessful. Wage-earners, then, should resign themselves to remaining wage-earners.[11]

Undoubtedly the logic of the failed provocation could be grounded on something better than hearsay and secret intentions. The crude, provincial

11. "De l'association ouvrière: distribution du crédit des trois millions," *L'Atelier*, Aug. 7, 1848, p. 195.

frankness of prefectorial reports gives a better indication of the prudent compromise with the present state of forces and of the confident cynicism vis-à-vis the future of the experiment undertaken, both of which are part of the picture. Thus, from inquiries undertaken by the prefect of the Rhône for the committee it seems

> that the worker association of velvet-weavers should be nixed as uncertain in its chances for success and disastrous in its consequences. But on the other hand, even though all expectations are against it, and perhaps precisely for that reason, I think one cannot dispense with attempting the crucial experiment that is being demanded.
>
> First of all, the administration should not lose sight of the fact that it is still dependent, in a way, on the circumstances that gave rise to the projected association in question.
>
> Manufacturing workers have been subjected to the influence of reckless preachments. A fairly large number of them have accepted as a truth that they are the victims of capital. They see their future well-being in association, and they seek the cooperation of the government in freeing themselves from what they call industrial servitude.
>
> Such being their state of mind, a refusal would only worsen the problem, and the most logical arguments would not convince them. I think it would be better, even at the cost of some money, to leave it to events to enlighten them about their true interests by demonstrating the inanity of the theories on which they are basing their so-called emancipation.[12]

Actual experience is crucial for all, therefore; and that is why the Buchez clan wants to limit its risks along with its extent. Do less, but do it better. Or, rather, *less* is, in and of itself, the proof of *better*. In the difficult accord to be reached between the morality of association and its chances of success (hence its effectiveness as propaganda), the criterion of the small number quickly becomes decisive. But nothing implies it by right, and it would seem even more moral to entrust the experiment to projects of collective enfranchisement and to men already dedicated to them than to these little groups of workers who put their skills and savings in common to gain access jointly to mastership. At the first meeting the president,

12. Report of the prefect of Rhône, May 5, 1849, A.N., F 12/4620 B.

Corbon, asks "that it be clearly understood that advances will be made only to workers who, at their own peril and risk, have made real efforts to enter upon the path of association."[13]

But choosing would be easy if it were simply a matter of selecting, among the petitioners, the groups or individuals who had not waited for the manna of three million francs to draw up and sometimes try to implement plans of association. Take, for example, those worker painters whose delegates had already discussed and approved the plan for the organization of work that drew its inspiration from a draft of 1838 and was actually prepared by a veteran of associational doctrines: painter–glazier–café-keeper–phrenologist and dealer in daguerreotypes Confais, who had been a Saint-Simonian in 1831 and editor of Fourier's *Nouveau Monde* in 1840. Starting off from a proposal for the organization of the whole corporation, which could be generalized to cover all crafts and trades, Confais had reduced his initial ambition to an association of one hundred members. The latter would form the embryo, without renouncing the principles adopted by the corporation: election of all bosses; establishing, by drawing lots, a rotation that gives an equal number of workdays to all the associates; and a division of earnings into four parts—the first for amortization, the second for aid to the sick and aged, the third to be divided among the members, and the fourth for a reserve fund designed to provide mutual assistance among all industries.[14]

Ensuring a nonviolent shift from private industry to an association of producers is also the thrust of the plan presented as early as May to the work committee by the delegates of the porcelain workers of Limoges. And if one is to believe the prefect of Vienne, this worker population, already "profoundly impacted" by socialism, is better placed than any other to carry out this transition: "Nowhere would the test of association be accepted with more enthusiasm by workers, followed with more attention, carried out with more dedication. . . . I don't think one could find, in any other industry, a group of workers more intelligent, more convinced of the grandeur of the task they carry out, more devoted to its success."[15] Moreover, the fraternal spirit and lofty morality of this asso-

13. *Procès-verbaux du Conseil d'encouragement*, p. 5.
14. *Organisation du Travail proposée par Confais et adoptée par les citoyens membres de la Commission de la corporation des ouvriers peintres*, Paris, 1848, A.N., F 12/4630. See Alain Faure and Jacques Rancière (eds.), *La parole ouvrière 1830/1851* (Paris: Union Générale d'Éditions, 1976), pp. 325–36.
15. Office du Travail, *Les associations professionnelles ouvrières*, Paris, 1903, III, 527 and 530.

ciation is brought out in the extensions it plans to give to its work: a cooperative butcher shop and bakery; vegetable gardens; a teacher for the children and a committee of nine members to oversee their education as well as the manners and language of their parents. The same educational concern also typifies the project conceived around 1837 and spelled out in May 1848 by the Bordeaux tailor Deluc, along with five masters and more than a hundred associates: to the work organization is to be joined an organized common habitat; its dining room "could be converted in the evening after work into a study hall where anyone could, at little cost, pursue elementary courses in letters and the sciences."[16] Children would get a free education there, and as much as possible would be set up in common so that the "tableau of human life" might no longer be "the fact of separation and isolation."

One might well remain skeptical reading the bizarrely constructed phrases of this tailor, who promises to solve "the whole problem of the happiness of the human race." But there are more literate workers who can support their promises with the witness of their sacrifices and their results. Thus the old shoemaker and former editor of the *Nouveau Monde*, Laurent Héronville, who in 1831 had originated a projected association of worker shoemakers, brings with him the experience acquired over eight years by the Workingmen's Association of Shoemakers. This organization sought to go beyond the limits of mutual-aid societies. Instead of simply giving aid to the unemployed, it intended to find them work, either by serving as an employment bureau or by organizing its own workshop for their benefit. It was on the basis of this experience, attested to by its annual balance sheet, that it had already asked the work committee for the monetary resources to transform itself into a production association.[17] As for typographer Parmentier, he had tried another way to involve his brothers in the association route, which was barred by the high prices of a license and printing equipment. He had set up a publishing firm named Fraternal Industry, the profits of which were to enable the associates to purchase a printing establishment. Unfortunately, the terrible years 1846 and 1847 were not propitious for the book trade in general, much less for the sale of works by subscription in workshops. The spring of 1848 was even worse, and Fraternal Industry was on the verge of bankruptcy. But with government help in purchasing a printshop, orders for schoolbooks, and printings for parliamentarians, Parmentier feels quite confident that

16. A.N., F 12/4631.
17. Dossiers Callerot (F 12/4630) and Héronville (F 12/4633), A.N.

among the two thousand typographers of Paris whose delegate he is, he will find as many associates. Thanks to their modest contribution of one franc each, they will be able to support those of their fellow workers who would offer them the example of emancipation.[18]

Then there are the Lyons workshop foremen whose crafts the Fourierist Coignet plans to bring into association; the lace-makers of "Father" Gardèche, a devotee of the fusionist religion and a founding member in 1845 of the United Industries Company; and the iron-founders whose representative, Dumoulin, had created an ephemeral production company back in 1836. Besides them there are the men who, in the eyes of Gilland and many others, are the very image of the fraternal revolution of February. Consider the two thousand tailors who have come from all over—even from Belgium, Germany, and Italy, claim the police—and who now find themselves in the converted premises of Clichy, formerly a debtor's prison. There they make uniforms for the militia. Under the direction of a former ateliériste, Philippe Bérard, they do not actually implement any plan for the organization of work; they are content to practice evangelical fraternity. There are no bosses, simply "delegates for special services."[19] All the members, whatever their qualifications or responsibilities, receive the same sum of two francs a day; and the door is open to all those men and women who need work to escape poverty or dishonor. That holds true even for the women sent by the officials of the twelve wards. They too get their two francs, even though they don't know how to make trousers and the fraternal tailors must undo and redo their work. When they have finished their work for the city of Paris, they plan to devote themselves to a project they hold dear. They want to make clothes for their brother workers, clothes of good quality at a cheap price. Don't they have every right to say, in support of their request, that their practical courage and tested fraternity are the best pledge of success?[20]

But that is not how the morality of association keeps its accounts. No one contests the touching fraternity of the tailors, the exemplary devotion of Parmentier, the eight years of experience gathered by the Workingmen's Association of Shoemakers, or the morality and capability of the porcelain delegates. But that is not the issue. What bothers the committee, and the Buchez clan especially, is the makeup of these associations: indistinct conglomerations of hundreds of associates who may well have

18. A.N., F 12/4635 B.
19. Report of Loyeux, police superintendent, July 27, 1848, A.N., C 933.
20. Dossier Jeanne, A.N., F 12/4633.

suffered and worked together, but who were brought together in the first place by the hazards of unemployment or mere membership in a trade corporation. How can one foresee the success of a workshop of shoemakers where you never find the same workers on the job? How can one see associates in the silent partners of Parmentier who, for a franc a month, will share possession of a printing establishment where they themselves will not work? The prefect of Vienne will be advised to check whether the personnel of the association of porcelain workers is "well composed" and, above all, whether it might not be "too numerous."[21] Because large numbers give these hard-working associations of laborers the same features found in communities of fraternal banqueters; they make them simultaneously impossible and immoral. Castles in Spain, like the grand plans of the Lyons weavers and velvet-weavers. But when these impossible fantasies actually take shape, it is their immorality that strikes Corbon: "One counts only by crafts, just as generals evaluate the force of their army by the number of bayonets. . . . The human being disappears completely. The only concern is the relative size and importance of the production forces."[22]

Large numbers are, in and of themselves. a principle of immorality: that is, of sterility. How else explain the curious logic that unites the criticism of reporter Ott and chairman Corbon against the project of the porcelain workers? One is opposed to an initiative that will take place in a troubled industry where the association will face competition from powerful employer establishments. The other reminds people that associations are not supposed to be "absorbent" in character and suggests that the project be divided up into several small associations. It is difficult to see how such small associations could better withstand the competition from the large firms of Limoges by competing with each other as well. It could only be by virtue of some principle of inverse proportion whereby the numerical increase of an association automatically decreases its morality and the fruitfulness of its efforts. The "grand" association envisioned by the worker corporations in the spring of 1848 is one of those "societies of sleepers" denounced not long ago by a Saint-Simonian worker: a society of brothers in which one shares the black bread of poverty, an association providing aid to the sick and the aged and protection against the vicissitudes of employment. In the eyes of the men of *L'Atelier*, the problem

21. *Procès-verbaux du Conseil d'encouragement*, p. 124.
22. Ibid., pp. 186–87.

lies in this idea spread from the heights of Luxembourg to the grassroots assemblies of workers in the spring, in this fraternity envisioned as refuge or mutual protection against the mischances of industry. Today it is no longer a matter of rescuing each other from the risks of industry but of running those risks to ensure the victory of principle. Of course, those grand associations conceived in the spring had goals of conquest in mind. Even though they begin with a few workers, their avowed aim is gradually to draw in all the workers of a corporation in order to monopolize, for the benefit of the workers, the work whose profits were divided up among the masters of old. But at bottom it is the same thing: the sleep of the Great All that suffocates the energy of pioneers along with the incentives of competition. A no to monopoly and associations of an "absorbent" character. The incessant appeals of Corbon dovetail with the logic of that curious surgery by which *L'Atelier* intended to root out the evil of the pantheist beast: just as the body is divided into "an infinity of members," so the association of each trade should be divided "into an infinite number of partial societies."[23] So that division *ad infinitum* may continue to separate work from pleasure, it must also continue to separate work from itself.

But here the phantasm of the Great All, of the cannibalistic corporation, steps in very nicely to serve the more earthly worries of employers and committee notables who believe that this "immoral" suppression of competition and employer profits is only too possible. And they certainly will not trouble themselves over the philosophical contradiction that prompts them to join the Buchez clan in rejecting big worker associations while backing against them the vast plans for associations between owners and workers that were improvised, as luck would have it, by bankrupt spinning-mill owners. And so the compromise will be worked out. The *Atelier* camp gets the right to dictate the principles—which is the essential thing for them and does not subtract a sou from the fund of three million —and to draw up the model statutes that will impose on all associations the sacrosanct principle of indivisible reserve funds and the obligation, on paper, to turn all their auxiliaries into full-fledged associates. For the rest, there will be a few costly worker–owner "associations" imposed by the right wing and a prudent choice of worker associations whose chief merits are the small number of their members and the modesty of their pretensions. There is 18,000 francs for the eight associates of typographer Prêves, whose activist credentials in association are more obscure than

23. "Organisation du travail," *L'Atelier*, Oct. 1843, p. 9.

those of Parmentier's friends, but who are assured a useful and secure venture from the printing of *L'Écho agricole*.[24] There is 8,000 francs for the twelve associates of painter Esseule, whose morality is not above average for the trade (it will soon come to light that the honest manager has falsified the books a bit, and as for the workers, an inspector will several times drop in to their headquarters to find no one there but the concierge), but who have the advantage over Confais's companions of being far less numerous and clearly less ambitious.[25] There is 16,000 francs for the seven iron-founders gathered into a national workshop by former soldier Colin. In his idle saunterings after returning to civilian life, he had come upon a copy of the *Voyage en Icarie*. Hardly seduced by utopia but attracted by the practical side of the matter, he has undertaken to lead his little world as he might in the army and bring it to the "true Icaria."[26]

Matters could have gone on like that, except for the untimely intervention of printing foreman Remquet. His plan is to make an association out of one of the most celebrated printing houses of Paris, that of Paul Renouard. The venerable establishment on Rue Garancière is one of those that did not withstand the tempest of February. Even before the Revolution, it had been foolish enough to involve itself in the speculations of the book trade. To this was added the publication, done at great expense and just completed, of a ten-volume illustrated work "stripped of any saleability by the political changes."[27] The fact remains that the house is for sale; and its foreman, Remquet, has managed to persuade the printshop's workers to form an association in order to buy the business and run it on their own. At first glance the project might well seem to be a perfect symbol of the February Revolution. Here we have workers, without violence and with the help of the republican government, turned into owners of the instrument of work over which they already possess technical mastery: workers now masters of an enterprise where some of them, at least, have worked for more than a decade to enrich an owner whose ideas and practices were thoroughly monarchical. The image is beautiful, but foreman Remquet has been at his trade for thirty years and is past the age for dreams. The brutality of the terms in the bylaws of Remquet and Company attract the attention of committee-reporter Danguy and chairman

24. *Procès-verbaux du Conseil d'encouragement*, p. 23; and A.N., F 12/4627.

25. *Procès-verbaux du Conseil d'encouragement*, p. 54; and Dossier Canonicat, A.N., F 12/4621.

26. *Procès-verbaux du Conseil d'encouragement*, pp. 29–32; and Émile Jay, "Visite aux associations," *Le Bien-être universel*, Aug. 3, 1851.

27. Dossier Remquet, A.N., F 12/4627 B.

Corbon. They are not bothered by the clear-cut assertion of the manager's powers, which are "all those of a proprietor." They themselves have always set the hierarchy of dedication over against daydreams of equality and maintained that the "directorial function" remains the same, under the "more suitable" title of manager. But are we really talking about dedication in the case of an association that hopes to buy up its instrument of work in ten years by withholding 25 percent of wages paid on a piecework basis? Say the associated workers: "Our aim is not to improve our present position as workers. What we want is to find ourselves, when the society comes to an end, in possession of a sum of capital sizable enough to have a real impact on our position."[28] These shock troops of associated work have dotted their *i*'s and crossed their *t*'s: one should leave fraternity to daydreamers and see in the new morality of association the old principle that grounds the rights of capital on work and savings and promises enjoyment of them to all those who are willing to dedicate themselves exclusively to it. As one of the associates puts it: "However steady and hard-working a worker may be, there isn't one that doesn't waste time coming late, leaving early, loafing a bit in the workshop, reading newspapers, etc., etc."[29] Over against the necessary and adequate morality of the "steady and hard-working" worker, who works for others and loafs for himself, must be set the terribly exacting morality of unremitting effort, of time saved and pleasure deferred, of capital.

That is more than the realistic dreamers of *L'Atelier* can comprehend. Struck by the "egotistical character" of this association, whose workers "must be viewed as petty capitalists," it seems to them, Corbon and Danguy express doubts about the "free and voluntary" nature of the association contracted between the typographers and Remquet, creditor as well as confidential clerk of their former employer. But the right wing, like its model worker and stooge Peupin, watchmaker and delegate, marvels at the lofty morality of the sacrifice made by the associated workers and at their refusal to compromise. It demands backup verification of Danguy's negative report. And so a rather solemn special session is held at the printshop one morning in November. Two members of the committee, printer Guiraudet and foreman Richard, are on hand to test the morality of the ties established between Remquet and his former subordinates. They will serve very sanctimoniously as devil's advocates, translating the austere principles of the *Atelier* faction into simple, paternal terms:

28. Ibid.
29. Ibid.

> M. Guiraudet takes the floor and, in words of the most kindly sort, tries to make the workers present appreciate the seriousness of the commitments they have just reiterated. . . . He points out that withholding one-fourth of their salaries amounts to a considerable sum. . . . He appeals to married men, then to young men who may enter marriage. He urges them to consider whether they may have regrets later, when it is too late. M. Guiraudet goes into specific details about family burdens and expenses. He also adds that there is something else in life besides material needs to be satisfied: when the body has done its work, both it and the spirit need relaxation and diversion.[30]

But the associated workers have deliberately chosen work over family, capital over forms of relaxation. As for their minds and spirits, if the 25 percent withholding leaves them no leisure to read the newspaper in the workplace, it is understood that they will read it when their workday is over.

> Many responses bear witness to the persistence of the associ-
> ates, while also indicating their thanks for the paternal advice of
> M. Guiraudet. . . . M. Richard asks the following questions:
> — Is ten years the term expressly desired by all?
> — Yes, unanimously.
> — Is the withholding of 25 percent of the wages, not something
>   else, the wish of all?
> — Yes, unanimously. . . .
> — Does each of the associates refuse to touch any part of the
>   profits or anything else before the expiration of the society?
> — Yes, unanimously. The division will be made in the books,
>   but nothing will be touched! The associates want not only to
>   become owners of the printshop but to have a little capital on
>   hand for themselves as individuals on the day of liquidation.[31]

That says it all. The perseverance of these workers, attached to their dream of a little capital for themselves, puts an end to the grand dream of *L'Atelier*. The determination of the Renouard workers not only wins the day but also puts an end to the modest strut of Buchez's thought on the

30. Ibid.
31. Ibid.

stage of universal history. The association Remquet and Company will get its 80,000 francs, although it will have to accept the conditions regarding the indivisible reserve funds and the participation of temporary workers in the profits. Corbon and Danguy, along with their theoreticians Ott and Feugueray, will hand in their resignations after having thrown all their forces into this exemplary battle. Between the springtime of the February Revolution and the autumn of the prince–president (Louis Napoleon Bonaparte), the moral republic of *L'Atelier* will complete its season, a season marked by the return to order.[32]

The end of *L'Atelier* dream is not the end of association, however, even though the victorious clique, now free to be more generous to the spinners, also chooses some strange associations. One example is the Finino and Company "National Factory, under the protection of the French Republic," conceived by a bronze employer who does not want to abandon the workers among whom he has lived for thirty-two years without making some gesture on their behalf.[33] Inquiries are made more difficult by the fact that "the workers . . . practice dissimulation with an art all the more treacherous because it is hidden under the appearances of boorishness and naïveté." But the inspector learns soon enough that this manager, who tolerates no remarks from his board of directors and expels the treasurer occupied with drawing up an inventory of the statuary, has simply found a convenient way to help out his treasury. The latter had been in difficulty since the February Revolution stopped exportation of his bronze animals: Newfoundland dogs, poodles, greyhounds, and spaniels; big foxes and little foxes; lions erect and lions recumbent; and other animals in bronze. The association of mechanics, Dautry and Company, has ways of making clear its more authentically working-class character. There are its bizarre accounting practices, which include listing an item purchased for 12,000 francs at 18,000 francs on its books; the reason given is the work involved in setting it up properly. Particularly indicative is the mechanics' resoluteness on the matter of wages. They calmly deduct their five francs a day from the government funds, "in conformity with their bylaws, to be sure, but without any justification in terms of productive work." That seems to be the only point on which the associates agree. Soon the manager will fire the foreman for incompetence and laziness—the same foreman who had been accusing him of incompetence and intemperance. Then the man-

32. For the committee debates on the Remquet affair, see *Procès-verbaux du Conseil d'encouragement*, pp. 154–58 and 175–80.
33. A.N., F 12/4623.

ager himself will be fired for absenteeism, thus benefiting a new manager destined for the same fate.[34] The association of papermakers specializing in account books, Beaugrand and Company, seemed to have gotten off to a better start and to have hit upon a sure thing, since it would supply an article needed by the other associations. But it went overboard in anticipating its promised prosperity, adding substantial "advances" to salaries already higher than those stipulated in the bylaws. The firing (on the grounds of "repeated drunkenness") of three associates opposed to these practices evidently did not improve an already critical situation; and so the accountant and two associates have left, according to the manager's account, to sell wares to those shipping off to find gold in California.[35]

But alongside these dubious associations, which the committee funds have assured transit from the national workshops of 1848 to the great California adventure of 1850, there are enough associations on the committee's registers that are determined to use the government grants to make sure that the spirit of the February Revolution triumphs in the world of industry. They include workers anxious to emancipate themselves from the tutelage of masters or the exploitation of *commissionnaires:* for example, the cabinetmakers, the file-cutters, the makers of musical instruments, the chair-joiners, the typographers of the Desoye association, and the workers in surgical instruments. They also include small proprietors and workers determined to labor on a footing of fraternal equality, such as the saddletree-makers.

And then there are all those whose sincere dedication to the idea is made plain precisely in their decision to do without government aid. Such are the three heroic associations that, with the fraternal tailors, embody the golden legend of association. First we have the chair-turners. In the spring they had dreamed of bringing the whole corporation into an association. In the autumn they united in a group of fifteen, with no contract aside from their pledged word and no capital except 313 francs and their indomitable courage: the courage of a manager who pulls the first cart of purchased wood, slips under the load, and breaks his thumb; and the courage of associates getting through the winter on five francs a week, "ill-fed, shoeless, barely covered by their linen clothes, but not complaining and not flinching at their work any more than would a soldier under fire."[36] Second we have the tin-lampmakers, who followed the chair-turners' ex-

34. Ibid.
35. Ibid., F 12/4620.
36. A. Cochut, *Les Associations ouvrières*, Paris, 1851, p. 82.

ample in January 1849. They had 400 francs' worth of loaned material and 300 francs in shares, which left them with 10 francs after paying for the first installation of equipment. The first transaction of which the association retained a memory involved a lantern worth twelve francs, "a piece of good luck that was not to be repeated for a long time."[37] In March the association found itself reduced to three associates. By cutting their salary to three, two, and one franc per week and going to break the bread of fraternity with workers outside, they managed to get eleven of their comrades to come back and to amass 700 francs of savings in July. The takeoff of this first capital would enable these associates (whose bylaws promise aid to "all those persons with whom the associates will be or will have been closely united in their lifetime by the truest and most sacred ties, the ties of the heart") to experience the solidarity of other pioneers of association. With their help they will finally meet with success.[38]

That would also be true for the third group, the piano-makers. In March they were installed in quarters whose nature and shabbiness Gilland's pen could find no words to describe. To get through two months without work, they had to send to the pawnshop, after their clothes and their beds, "the poor little silver watch so useful to them, the little marriage piece to which they are so attached, the blessed wedding ring of one's spouse."[39] Finally, they found a little work: "The dividend was six francs sixty-one centimes each. Each got five francs on account for wages; the rest was spent on a fraternal meal that brought together their wives and children. Most of them had not drunk wine for a year. The outlay for each household was about thirty-two sous. That is how they celebrated the first success of their association, and the memory of it still fills them with emotion."[40] The first piano, ordered by a philanthropic but thrifty baker, would be paid for in bread, shared out according to need, but the next piano would be paid for in cash. Soon they would be able to have the weekly wages raised to five, ten, and twenty francs, redeem bedding, engagement rings, and family souvenirs from the pawnshop, and set out on the road to prosperity.

So we have something other than illusory images of communion to which were opposed realistic calculations of the work of association. In the spring of 1849, when the democratic electors dismissed Corbon and

37. Ibid., p. 52.
38. Anatole Lemercier, *Études sur les associations ouvrières*, Paris, 1857, pp. 148 and 150.
39. Gilland, *Revue anecdotique*, p. 38.
40. Véron, *Les associations ouvrières de consommation, de crédit et de production en Angleterre, en Allemagne et en France*, Paris, 1865, p. 209.

his friends from the National Assembly but elected the poet Gilland, crowned with the halo of an arbitrary arrest during the worker uprising in June 1848, would the workshop dreamers, faced with the decline of the political republic, initiate the counter-march of the social republic? The chair-joiners of the former conspirator Antoine, the file workers who leave prisoners or dead every day of insurrection, the feverish last-makers, and the impetuous cabinetmakers—would they represent the first detachments of a "barbarian" army quite different from the pillaging hordes conjured up by the order of Louis Philippe or the moderate republic?

> The assembled associates—they are the sovereign people. . . . On the prescribed day the forges are put out, the tools are neatly put away, the workshop is cleaned until it shines. The work stools are set around a long row of benches on which the vises remain fixed in place. In the center is a platform with an armchair and several other chairs for the members of the board. The associates arrive in decent and sometimes rather exquisite attire. Each takes his seat around the row of benches transformed into a council table. As they deliberate with their arms leaning on the vises, do they not remind us of those warriors of Germany and Gaul, those future masters of the modern world who deliberated with their hand on their weapons?[41]

But the file-cutters do not aspire to mastery of the world. They cling to the idea that was "fermenting" in their corporation in the spring of 1848: "Not so much that of increasing wages as that of winning the sort of independence, the sort of intellectual and moral rehabilitation, that is bound to raise the wage-earner to the level of other citizens"; a conjunction of being and seeming faithful to the set purpose of the 1840s. There are neither blouses nor callused hands in this assembly of sovereign work. The soldiers of association deliberate with their hands on their weapons, but in city dress. Politeness of form and language shows up in them at the same time that concern for dress does. For these are the necessary complements of the education that is to make them complete citizens: "There is no longer any worker who does not know how to read, write, and do arithmetic. It is kind of a point of honor among them to know the history of France."[42]

41. Cochut, *Les associations ouvrières*, p. 71.
42. Ibid., p. 74.

As we know already, the moral republic of workers is not exactly identified with the kingdom of productive work. It is not that the workshop rules are less severe than they were in the proprietary order. They avoid annoying measures and leave the matter of applying sanctions to the chosen authorities of the general assembly and the board of directors. But they feel bound to be even more intractable in repressing the same faults: assaults, drunkenness, acts of carelessness, coarse remarks, corruption of apprentices, and so on. The identical rules of the cabinetmakers of Cour Saint-Joseph and the Desoye typographical association set these fines: for drunkenness in the workplace, five francs; for assaults, ten francs; for insults or indecent remarks, one to ten francs; for coarse remarks in the presence of strangers, two to ten francs (all these penalties were combined with a threat of exclusion in the event of repetition); for lack of order, propriety, or economy in one's work, a reprimand followed by a fine of two francs and a threat of exclusion; immediate exclusion for refusing to work; a reprimand followed by exclusion for coarse or obscene remarks to apprentices.[43]

But this very severity raises suspicion: given the daily rate of pay for cabinetmakers, one can hardly see how such fines could be applied strictly. The pay rate of the typographers might well lend itself better to such severity, if the Desoye associates did not have to face the consequences of the judicial fines that rain down on the association for its printing of "demagogic" pamphlets. Their situation is undoubtedly like that of the workers in surgical instruments, whose manager frankly admits that he cannot reestablish order by using rules and penalties "so exaggerated that execution is no longer possible."[44] The associates of Colin retort to their military manager, when he invokes the rules, that it had been "agreed that they would not be followed to the letter."[45] This dodge goes back to a more serious principle: the strictness of the rulebook, which may be inapplicable, goes hand in hand with the degree of equality exhibited. So it is more lax where belief in equality is not the order of the day. In sharp contrast to the Desoye rule is the completely paternal direction of Remquet. Convinced that the workers are "big children," Remquet does not take the trouble to make up a rulebook that reminds them of their duties by reminding them of their dignity as citizens. He handles problems gently, as they come up, inculcating morality by example. When an

43. Dossiers Desoye (F 12/4622) and Rey-Drien (F 12/4627), A.N.
44. Dossier Haan, A.N., F 12/4624.
45. Dossier Colin, A.N., F 12/4621.

inspector presses him to break with this respect for Monday, so contrary
to the good order of his association, Remquet insists on the surer progress
of his own way of moralizing gently by his own personal influence. Notes
the inspector: "In this connection he gave the example of one of his associates who had just recently regularized an illegitimate union by getting
married. He added that in some associates he had even noticed inclinations
to fulfill their religious duties."[46]

Undoubtedly the file-cutters are not hostile to religion and marriage,
even though they scandalize the inspector by taking back, upon his release
from prison, an associate sentenced for adultery. But this way of moralization cannot be that of fraternal associations. For all that, Monday is not
imposed in the association of file-cutters, where every morning one has
an hour to shuffle into the workshop, and each worker himself marks the
time of his arrival on a slate. But each associate also owes the association
99 hours of work over twelve workdays, and the number of extra hours
there is strictly limited. The same holds true for the joiners of Antoine,
where an associate owes 120 hours over fifteen workdays, without being
able to put in more than one extra hour per day. Of course, the free and
fraternal character of these dispositions is all the more appreciated insofar
as the time of full employment, which would make them more coercive,
is still far away. And so long as the crisis lasts, the principle of fraternity
enjoins the hiring of new associates rather than making the old associates
work to their maximum capacity. It is this supplement of fraternity that is
the soul of rulebook equality. If the latter punishes worker assaults and injuries, the former forbids disputes among the associates. "Workers should
love each other and forgive each other the little weaknesses of vanity,"
says the regulation hung in a large frame of blackened tinplate on the
wall of the tinmen.[47] For their part, the chair-turners have put reprimands
above fines, and in their assembly of October 1850 the file-cutters made a
radical decision: "Fines have been abolished. Today the penalty is purely
moral. A worker convicted of a fault sees his name written on a board
with a justified reprimand."[48] There is also such a board in the quarters
of the armchair-joiners, but there they like especially to cite the case of
two associates who came forward on their own to accuse themselves of a
quarrel and ask that their names be written on the board.

Moral republics of worker solidarity, more than republics of egalitarian

46. See note 27.
47. Cochut, *Les associations ouvrières*, p. 59.
48. Dossier Wursthorn, A.N., F 12/4628.

work. The fraternal tailors certainly did not remove from their statutes the principle of spring 1848: From each according to his ability, to each according to his needs. But they add: "Until this principle can be put into practice, thanks to its general acceptance, the inspection committee, at the proposal of the manager, will determine the settlement of the price of workmanship."[49] The practicable and almost necessary equality of a workshop refuge, which lives on official orders and is incapable of classifying by capacity the shifting population of hundreds of workers equally constrained by penury, is no longer such for an association that lives on its own resources and is already shouldering a heavy tribute to fraternity by paying three francs to vestmakers for vests that bring fifteen sous in proprietary industry. For eighteen months they submitted to equality of wages "to consecrate the principle," but the "test is over": "Fraternity does not require sacrificing the good to the bad, the courageous to the lazy. . . . Fraternity wills that each be recompensed according to his merit and classified according to his dedication and ability."[50]

Moral Saint-Simonism, in line with the principles of *L'Atelier*, which corrects for inequality of aptitude by rewarding dedication. The democracy that puts officials paid at the worker rate under the control of the general assembly is combined with the maintained inequality of piecework. Only lack of work or raw materials will sometimes prompt twists in this principle. But the same fraternity that forbids sacrificing the courageous to the lazy also bids the strong help the weak. And so the piecework wage is accompanied by an egalitarian corrective among the chair-turners, the tin-lampmakers, and several other associations. There is a sharing of profits in terms of worktime rather than in terms of earnings: support of the weak by the strong, but also a limitation on the tendency of the "strong" toward a dangerous overproduction and a roundabout form of moralization, giving the diligence of the weak an advantage over the buzzsaw pace of the strong workers, who are divided between the intoxication of production and that of the cabaret. Here again the fraternal principle is all the stronger in that it is inscribed above the written law. Such is the case even with the file-cutters, who happen to be much admired for the rules of their general assemblies. These democrats, so fastidious about the letter of their rules and bylaws, did not include the egalitarian sharing of profits in their written statutes. It belongs, rather, to the unwritten law of fraternity: "The sharing of profits offers a touching scene. They begin

49. Lemercier, *Études sur les associations ouvrières*, p. 141.
50. Gilland, *Revue anecdotique*, p. 26.

by dividing them up unequally in proportion to labor and wages. Once the portions are so made up, each associate is invited to take his share. No one moves. Then the portions are mixed up together. The profits are again placed in common and shared out per head, on the basis of fraternal equality."[51]

Moving as the scene may be, it cannot conceal the paradox: to mitigate the inequality of wages by sharing out profits equally is somehow to place egotism on the side of labor and fraternity on the side of capital. Isn't it the practice of commercial companies, ask the Lyons weavers, to distribute profits to associates without taking into account the greater or lesser energy they have expended in the service of the company?[52] The analogy has a strange ring to it, and it is misleading as well. While capitalists have every interest in seeing an increase in the portion of profits appropriated from salaried labor, the interest of fraternal worker–capitalists is necessarily more ambiguous. And the inspectors assigned to watchdog their associations have great difficulty in trying to evaluate the relationship between their activity as workers and their interests as entrepreneurs.

They are captivated, first of all, despite their prejudices, by their pluck at work, by the skill and inner order of the little workshop republics. The saddletree-makers must deal with their Lorraine competitors' access to raw materials and cheaper manual labor, and so they have imposed on themselves deductions of 10 and then 20 percent from their salaries; but successive reports indicate plenty of activity, regular accounts, a perfect harmony, a strict and promptly executed set of rules, and superior manufacture. Among the cabinetmakers "the fabrication is done with great care; they do not make what is called trash." Among the porcelain-decorators, faced with competition based on the exploitation of children, the inspector is taken with the charm of "this gathering of men, women, and children hard at work and happy with their lot. . . . Some are talented artists. With incredible nimbleness some make little bouquets while others make elegant arabesques with a paintbrush steeped in a brown solution that turns gold in the fire." And, quite naturally, the most fraternal of the supported associations is also the most prosperous: "The association of file-makers, thanks to a firm and capable management, boasts a superior manufacture, diligent work, perfect harmony, regular books, and a quick and easy sale of its products." The fraternal courage invested in enduring the obligatory communism of poverty seems to augur success when business picks up:

51. Émile Jay, "Visite aux associations," *Le Bien-être universel*, Aug. 3, 1851.
52. Dossier Brosse, A.N., F 12/4620.

"The cessation of the harmony that has reigned up to now among the associates could only impede its progress; but there is no good reason to foresee the breakdown of a harmony that the very prosperity of the association should tend to consolidate."[53]

Yet it is here that logic will suffer its first outrages. It soon turns out that inner order and harmony tend to decrease with commercial success: "The dominant qualities of this association's personnel are jealousy and mistrust, and curiously enough this mistrust seems to grow with their commercial success. . . . It is in the heat of activity and work, at the moment when the efforts of each could meet with success, that suspicions invade these restless spirits most of all."[54] Restless spirits, fidgety people, rebellious dispositions: from now on, reports month after month will reiterate such descriptions, which are enough to explain the "jarring vexations" afflicting associations that nevertheless move ahead on the road to success with them, as they supposedly would without them.

There is evidently a strong temptation to impute the source of such dissensions to the undisciplined nature of socialist workers. But empirical observers have learned to mistrust the simple identifications of socialism, laziness, and debauchery that are taken for granted by the "mad dogs" of order. The police superintendent, given the task of investigating the morality of workers in musical instruments, has already drawn a picture that is very inconclusive about the relationship between vocational seriousness, private morality, and political position. One Charles Petit, for example, has lived for a long time at the same address with his wife, his old mother, and a lunatic niece. He is without work and professes advanced political opinions. Nevertheless, he "conducted himself well" in the riots as an officer in the national guard. By contrast, the man named Breton, who employs a worker and an apprentice, had to be disarmed in June because of his revolutionary remarks. With regard to one Charles Haan, an unemployed widower who lives in concubinage with a working-woman by whom he has a child, reports about his morals and politics are all good. M. Roche, who also lives in concubinage, with a woman who does not devote herself to any occupation and is exhausting his resources, is considered a hard-working man. Likewise, François Langer is considered a partisan of socialist doctrines, but his moral conduct does

53. A.N., Dossiers King (F 12/4624), Drien (F 12/4627, May 19, 1850), Duriez (F 12/4623, Dec. 12, 1849), and Wursthorn (F 12/4628, Aug. 16 and Nov. 16, 1849).

54. A.N., Dossiers Mauny (F 12/4626, July 22, 1851) and Colin (F 12/4621, Dec. 1849).

not prompt any unfavorable comment. In all, four of the five workers imbued with socialist principles are "favorably represented" in terms of morals, half of the unemployed are known to be friends of order, and the bachelors are viewed as well as those living in concubinage or the fathers of large families. Only a little later, it is remarked on the inspection reports that Petit, socialist but friend of order, does some business on his own account and directs dissidence in the association together with a man named Albert, who nevertheless "has good behavior and is considered a friend of order."[55]

Such ambiguities should be absent from the legendary association of gilt jewelers, where candidates for admission must solemnly affirm their attachment "to the Catholic principles our society has taught us," their faith that Leroy, Thibault and Company will put them victoriously to work, and their resolve "always to take the Holy Gospels as the rule for [their] judgment and [their] conduct." But a report of November 1850 has us envisaging the "withdrawal" of an associate whose conduct has been "hardly in conformity with the precepts guiding this firm." The exclusion of M. De Cressac for a moral fault seems to take some time, however, and it entails the requested separation of three other associates. In this case the inspector can reverse the usual explanation: he says that these skirmishes are due to the excessive rigorousness of the old Buchez guard that runs the association.[56]

But this simple linking of opposites, of rulebook strictness to the rebelliousness of restless spirits, cannot be applied to the tensions marking the course of the saddletree-makers or the file-cutters. The marvelous harmony of the first days have been followed by the "annoyances" and "cruel trials" endured by the manager of the file-cutters, and by the acts of insubordination that rain down fines on the associated saddletree-makers of M. King: suspension of two women for quarreling in the workshop; a fine of one franc for a commotion in the workshop; a fine of six francs levied on M. Cusin for assaulting a co-worker; M. Russel reprimanded for talk harmful to the company; reprimands to two foremen for lack of supervision; ten centimes deducted for each hour below the weekly minimum of fifty hours; numerous fines for misconduct; reductions for badly done work. The abundance of reports "undoubtedly indicates rebelliousness in the personnel, but at the same time it reveals a management exhausting its

55. Dossier Hubart-Houzé, A.N., F 12/4622, police investigation of Feb. 1849 and inspection report of Nov. 20, 1850.
56. Dossier Leroy-Thibault, A.N., F 12/4625.

energy on the letter of the statutes and rules."[57] Does that simply mean
that the management has become hardened by the "repressive system"
required to run an association "generally made up of difficult and unrea-
sonable people"? Mustn't we see in that a curious ordering among the
tensions of productive energy, the excesses of insubordination, and the
rigors of the law? The report of October 24, 1850, then notes the full-scale
activity of the association, which has had to extend the workday to fifteen
hours, the numerous deliberations of the board of directors, the detailed
examination of accounts, the strict application of fines, and the frequent
changes in management: "All that suggests a restless and unstable population, but one that knows how to restrain itself by strict observance of
the statutes."[58] Clearly this is something different from the pacific vision
of associated work that the promotional pamphlets happily contrast with
the conflicts resulting inevitably from employer arbitrariness and worker
bitterness. Nor is this the utopian vision of a poet of the coming century:
Brecht's great productivity based on great insubordination. Between the
two is a mixed energy in which the tension of productive effort, rebellious energy, and the passion for legalism go back to the same principle,
a principle divided within itself. Perhaps the peculiar makeup of the King
association has something to do with the exacerbation of its conflicts:
"This association, made up of a conglomeration of small employers and
saddletree-makers, undoubtedly owes a large part of the difficulties im-
peding its progress to this union of hostile elements."[59]

But aren't the personnel of associations generally recruited in the midst
of these "political half-breeds," noted in an earlier day by the Saint-
Simonian recruiter Achille Leroux, who is now a colonist in Algeria? They
are not simply ruined or modest owners, or workers who may have lacked
the capital, the commercial ability, the taste for risk or domination, to
become masters. They also include people who have brought to the organization of their brothers or the democratic fight their energy and capacity
for mastership, and who sometimes find in association, along with the
ruin of their fraternal hopes, ways to rise in the social scale. In the workshop of proprietary workers, the excitement, bitterness, and defiance of
emancipated workers happen to overdetermine the tensions and evasions
displacing the productive and rebellious energy of insurgent slaves. And
so the progressive withdrawal of former employers, who take up work on

57. Dossier King, A.N., F 12/4624.
58. Ibid.
59. Ibid.

their own account once the crisis has passed, scarcely modifies the conflict-ridden economy of the association of saddletree-makers. On April 27, 1852,

> the workshop is in full swing. But the work is on a piecework basis, and the manager, regardless of the urgency, cannot get the diligence that the abundance of orders requires. The worker, in this business especially, will not work on Monday at any price. To remarks made to him, he invariably replies that he is *at his pieces*—that if he does not work, he is not paid. You cannot get out of him any effort in the interest of the business.[60]

But when King, grieved by the ingratitude of associates "who have no regard for his efforts and sacrifices," resigns and takes the four best workers with him, that is enough to get the other associates to give up their defense of wages and to wage war, as entrepreneurs, against the new competitor. The report of July 29 observes "the same busyness" (so it was not so feeble, after all), "further stimulated by the withdrawal of M. King, who now has set himself up as a competitor." But this busyness, more stimulated by the present competition of former managers than by their orders of an earlier day, lends itself to an appreciation that is likewise ambiguous. November 25, 1852: "In this workshop the distribution of work has always been difficult. More than once I have pointed up the ungovernable character of this association. The result is delay in deliveries and uneven work." Couldn't the company counter this negative judgment by pointing to the decrease in reports of infractions? But that decrease can be read the other way: it proves that the reins once held on rebelliousness "seem to have noticeably slackened." Yet the report of June 28, 1853, tells us: "Be that as it may, the company is expanding its connections and the "volume of business is increasing." And the report of April 29, 1854, reveals the basis of that success: "The activity prevailing in workshops has always been the best guarantee against internal disorders and upsets." This busyness and activity, the best remedy for the upsets that diminish it, does not preclude a new delay the following month in a delivery to the army: "It is likely that a similar incident would not occur in the workshop of a proprietor, but in an association of workers, curiously enough, you

60. Ibid.

cannot find anyone who is willing to put out an extra effort in the general interest."[61]

There is no point in following, from contradiction to contradiction, the twisted road that leads the association of saddletree-makers to its final undoing, due much more to the conscientious efforts of their former associates and a political weapon (the withdrawal of military orders) than to its own energetic discords. Even more instructive is the near logic governing the course of the file-cutters. Whereas the report of October 1850 announces the suppression of fines in that exemplary association and the report of February 1851 informs us that it holds first place in its specialty, a different tone begins to sound in April. Manager Wursthorn, too, criticizes the ingratitude of associates who show no thanks for his sacrifices (he earns less than his worker associates doing piecework), and he "sees in the collectivity a source of difficulty for worker association." Weary of "factions" and "vexations," he will withdraw in January 1852 from an association whose "superior" manufacture and "diligent" work are henceforth seen with very different eyes by the inspector. July 27, 1852: "I have already said that in this association authority was absent, that the work was irregular and careless." This absence and carelessness seem relative, however, when we see the results indicated by the next month's report. That report also spells out the ill afflicting an association that is nevertheless doing well: "It is deficient basically in internal discipline. At a given moment, the manager cannot get a burst of extra effort. The worker cannot be persuaded that he is working for his own thing. This radical vice will always be an obstacle to the growth that could be realized by an establishment which is otherwise situated in the most favorable circumstances." November 25, 1852: "The ill will of the majority of the members of this association and the vexations experienced by the management impede all growth and result in unproductive work. That is why the company is always in straitened circumstances, even though the merchandise sells, and on a scale that would realize a significant profit in a proprietor's workshop." Hence the seemingly inescapable conclusion in the report of May 26, 1853: "This lack of internal order is superabundant proof that the worker needs an authority imposed on him, since he, on his own, is not willing to apply his efforts in something of personal interest to him."[62] The already twisted logic of this argument takes another twist

61. Ibid.
62. A.N., F 12/4628.

when, with a breath of new-found hope, the report of August 1853 informs us that a needed purge has taken place, and that the establishment still holds first place in Paris. From that we must conclude that it never lost its hold on first place, and that during the whole time that the vexations of rebels impeded all development and the absence of a master caused unproductive work, resulting in a production that would yield significant profits in a master's shop, the establishment never ceased to prevail over establishments governed by employer authority and productivity.

Let us not be too quick to blame the prejudices of inspectors Guyot and Bonnaire. There really is something incomprehensible in the functioning of these establishments where it is always the property owner who responds to remarks addressed to a worker, and the wage-earner who responds to remarks addressed to an employer. Rightly irritated at the makers of gas appliances, who pay themselves a full day's wage despite the falling off of work, the inspectors can only sympathize with the misfortunes of those same associates, who are the victims of their helpers. Obliged by the rigorous terms of the loan contract imposed by the men of *L'Atelier* to pay out profits to temporary co-workers or bring them into the association, they have had to take on as associates Messrs. Leblanc and Errard. These two men set an example of insubordination and disorder, "to the point of playing dice in the workshop." And the associates had to give one of them 500 francs to get him to go play dice elsewhere.[63] Even aside from such extreme cases, it is not so easy to define exactly "the personal interest" or "his own thing" for which the associated worker cannot be persuaded he is working. To be sure, the police superintendent watching over the Lyons associations believes that he can absolve the associated velvet-weavers of any sin of contradiction. The fact is that the associates find themselves facing alternatives that are all too clear:

> Either to earn the highest possible price for their work, which is a real and certain profit, at the risk of causing a loss for the company . . . or to work for the real price of what they make, in the hope of profiting from the earnings of the company if it is successful.
>
> From the standpoint of profit, the surest course is obviously to realize profits on what they make right away, either by raising the figure higher or by making only those articles that are the most profitable for the workers.[64]

63. Dossier Picard, A.N., F 12/4627.
64. Dossier Brosse, A.N., F 12/4620, report of March 11, 1850.

Is this the typical behavior of wage-earners, quickly returned from the grand dreams of the moral rehabilitation of their class to the status quo of the daily wage war, but also profiting as much as possible from the duplicity of their present status: using the relative stability of their employment as owners to optimize the chances for success of the combat weapons they still hold as wage-earners? The explanation recurs in every critical situation. Thus, the associated dyers "have abused their wages"; the workers in surgical instruments, in addition to charging high prices for their work, spend their time asking for "advances" on the basis of an ill-defined set of bylaws; among the makers of musical instruments, the cost of labor "seems to exert too heavy a weight . . . a tendency noticeable in worker association in general." But these assertions are immediately contradicted by reminders about the courageous reductions tolerated by workers in one association or another. As always, the contradiction is given its sharpest edge in reports about the file-cutters. January 29, 1853: "The work cannot be distributed profitably, because here especially the worker tries to get the highest possible salary without the least concern in the world for the interests of the business. Still less would he come in on Monday to finish a job that is impatiently awaited." But another report of Bonnaire evaluates these excessive wages as being of the most modest sort: "In this workshop where everyone works for his own thing, the average daily wage for piecework does not exceed 2.45 francs; whereas in employer shops, these same workers earn 4 to 5 francs. One can only conclude that, curiously enough, the independent worker who is working for himself produces less than he does for a master who makes his authority felt."[65]

A conclusion known in advance: things would not go that way in the shops of employers. The only question Bonnaire forgets to ask himself is this: Isn't it in the shops of employers that the file-cutters learned to take Mondays off and to vary the intensity of their productive energy as they felt like it? Perhaps we must reverse the terms of the problem and say that the strangeness is not where he pretends to see it, and that the contradiction does not lie where it first strikes us. Strictly speaking, one could see how the worker might be shrewd enough to sacrifice the future interests of the business to his own immediate personal interests, and thoughtless enough not to notice that 5 francs are worth more than 2.45 francs; being egotistical is not enough to ensure that one is well-informed about one's

65. Dossier Wursthorn, A.N., F 12/4628, reports of Jan. 29, 1853, and June 22, 1852.

own interests. The thing that is truly strange and hard to understand is this: How can the employer establishments, which have taken some pains to impose their "authority" on this restless corporation of workers, give wages that elude the most active of the houses in their line of work? Isn't what is missing in the association not so much the material exercise of authority as its magical efficacy, not so much productive capacity or even accounting knowledge as the secret alchemy of profit?

There are things that could be learned, to be sure. The manager of the workers in surgical instruments could have learned in the long run how to do costing; that would have kept him from leading the association to ruin through the very expansion his energetic direction produced for its business. The cabinetmakers, so careful yesterday in calculating the profits of exploitative *commissionnaires* and so unskilled today in setting prices, could have learned how to spot the bad payers and thus avoid the constant conversion of monies owed to the firm into losses on the balance sheet. The makers of musical instruments could have avoided the seizure of their saxophones if they had studied the patent legislation and found a shrewder way to counterfeit M. Sax's instrument. On the other hand, the unfortunate umbrella-makers, who had carefully studied their costs and the commercial chances for their articles, were obviously defenseless against the cholera that, in the space of a workday, drove away all the purchasers of the province. The cabinetmakers, the file-cutters, and even the very serious gilt jewelers or porcelain-decorators cannot do much about the uncertain solvency of American buyers, or about local circumstances that close the markets of Germany, Africa, or South America. But perhaps it is no accident that they must go so far to seek out their clients. Some of their compatriots are only too willing to help along the "industrial risks" designed to harden them. The associated saddletree-makers or file-cutters are too uncertain as clients to be allowed to purchase their iron on credit; and the uncertainty of their deliveries will be a weighty argument in persuading the payer government to have more serious establishments supply the cavalry or the schools of arts and crafts. Similarly, the makers of surgical instruments will see the national institute for the disabled closed to them, and the makers of copper instruments will see the regimental band market closed to them. All that is quite aside from political circumstances and their impact: in January 1852, the inspector declares that the Desoye printing shop, whose business is fed mainly by "pamphlets of political discussion and debate," has abruptly lost a sizable portion of its clientele.

Is this the complicity of the risks of business, which now hit the associates both as workers and as owners, with a political order promising fewer and fewer clients to workers who wanted to become masters? But there is also the more secret complicity of business risks with the nomadism, the worker "restlessness," that again takes over and rejects the productive rationality of "extra efforts" in line with the demands of a given moment! The "upsets," "disturbances," "cabals," and "rebellions" that punctuate the life of worker associations can be readily reduced to one fundamental conflict. On the one side is the manager, who represents the rationality of the collective enterprise. He asks for extra efforts to satisfy the clientele brought in by his efforts, proposes that the associates reduce their wages in proportion to their labors, gives priority to the increase of capital over salary increases or the sharing of profits, complains about the shoddy work of the associates, and deplores their ingratitude. On the other side are the worker associates, who question the competence of the manager. They denounce his weakness vis-à-vis *commissionnaires,* his lack of keenness about the solvency of clients, his trips that are rarely profitable for their business but sometimes useful for his own upward mobility, his authoritarianism as an upstart employer, and the unfairness that permits him to notice their absences and drafts of wine, whereas they cannot ask him to account for the time he spends on trips and outings for the association.[66]

The fate of the association of iron-founders offers an exemplary case. Manager and associates have been at odds since August 1849 because the associates, who are "completely illiterate and without any notions of grammar," mean to read newspapers in the workshop. A meeting takes place, presided over by the Committee for the Encouragement of Worker Associations, at which they futilely denounce the authoritarianism of former soldier Colin. They, in turn, are subjected to the "severe remarks of M. Guiraudet" when they request, with misplaced "insistence," that the workshop rule make Monday an exception.[67] The passing of the rule does not stop the conflict from continuing in the very midst of "activity and work," right up to the crisis of January 1850. Colin reproaches the associates for their insubordination, their absences, and their visits to the wine shop. They answer his accusations by attacking a system of fines that "does not seem dignified to them, can harm them substantially, and can make them an object of ridicule." When Colin criticizes poor workmanship, they accuse Colin of accepting prices that are too low. To this accusation their manager can reply

66. *Enquête sur les Sociétés de coopération,* Paris, 1866, p. 169; and Dossier King, A.N., F 12/4624, report of May 28, 1855.
67. Dossier Colin, A.N., F 12/4621, report of Sept. 1849.

that it was not up to him to regulate the price of merchandise; that there are fluctuations in commerce and industry one must follow and endure . . . ; that it would be a shocking injustice to make him responsible for these facts because he cannot close his workshop in such cases, as an owner can. He must follow the daily course and procure work for his associates, trying to fight as best he can against these industrial chances, which are sometimes unfavorable but nevertheless inevitable for him and for many people.[68]

Colin's activity is certainly overwhelming. But couldn't he lighten the heavy load on his shoulders a bit by convening his management board more often, acquainting it with the state of business affairs, and giving them access to the books that do not leave his home? As for his comment on "bad industrial conditions," even associates as unfamiliar with the rules of arithmetic as they are with the rules of grammar detect a bit too much deviousness in it. We learn this from the proceedings of the "extraordinary general assembly" they hold on January 30, where they accuse Colin of slandering the work of the associates to camouflage the profits of the association:

> At the last meeting no one wanted to tell the truth—that Colin's intention was not to pay back the monies that the government loaned us, inasmuch as he told us that the association of earthenware potters was made up of imbeciles for revealing profits, the government having the right to make them reimburse the money it had loaned them. And he says: As for me, I would not be so stupid as to show profits; I have ninety-nine years to pay them back. Actually, he shows us a deficit, and to cover himself he slanders us before the committee, undoubtedly saying that we did not want to work.[69]

At the conclusion of this debate, which goes round in circles, the "extraordinery [sic] general assembly" votes for the dismissal of Colin and the temporary closing of the workshop. Colin has the workshop reopened and replaces the associates with helpers, who hasten to address a respectful plea to the minister: Would he please be good enough to decide to keep in his office a manager whose departure would leave some thirty decent

68. Dossier Colin, A.N., F 12/4621.
69. Ibid.

workers without resources? Following this, Colin will remain associated with himself, not sharing his account books with the inspector any more than he had shared them with his associates.

It is by an even more remarkable route that their neighbors, the "imbecilic" earthenware potters, arrive at the same result. It must be said that the Mauny association had never been one of those "drawing its strength from the letter of statutes and regulations." In November 1849, it still did not have workshop bylaws: "The manager of this association does not distribute the work. He assembles the members and says: Here are the orders I have received. I need that in eight days. You see to it that it is done. And everything is ready on the set date."[70] In February 1851, a reminder about the statutes gets a blunt response: "The establishment is running well. Don't ask for anything more." But it is precisely this smooth running and progress that soon arouse the "jealousy" of the personnel and the bizarre "defiance" that seems to go with commercial success. The associates reach the conclusion that they can ask for a sharing out of the profits that are to be shared. Bonnaire admits that "they are incontestably within their rights." But manager Mauny, "considering the expenses of the business, would regard the commercial future of the association and its very existence as essentially compromised if this distribution took place."[71] Faced with his intransigence, the associates announce their intention to quit the establishment. But first they want their share of the profits and "a compensation of one thousand francs for each, on the pretext that they are leaving an enterprise on the road to prosperity." Meanwhile, "they recognize no authority, work at their pleasure, and try to do mischief." So Mauny must ask the (sane) half of the work force to inspect the work of the other half. Unfortunately, this inspection goes nowhere: "No one paid any attention. When someone did offer a criticism, he found himself the butt of invectives from the person to whom it was addressed. So they chose to say nothing, and things went along as best they might."[72] Mauny agrees to share profits in February 1852. After getting their hands on them, the associates hand in their resignations. Then they return to the workshop and work as wage-earners for their former manager.

Two exemplary stories for the use of those who said that workers could never work for "their own thing," that they would always need a master. Aren't we forced to the same conclusion when we move from the homely

70. Dossier Mauny, A.N., F 12/4626.
71. Ibid.
72. Mauny, letter, Dec. 1851, ibid.

conflicts of the iron-founders and potters of the twelfth ward to the combat with blunted weapons of the typographers of the eleventh ward? Desoye, formerly of *L'Atelier,* undoubtedly means to take the high ground and draw up the moral as well as financial balance sheet of an association whose liquidation he proposes to stubborn associates two months after Louis Napoleon's coup of December 2. First there are the raw results of two years of business: "The work of seventeen associates, working from the first to the last day of the year at five francs a day and giving up their fifth, even in the best year cannot cover the general expenses, the capital interest on the funds advanced by the government, and the costs of inspection."[73] Estimating future expenses, one must include the replacement of "almost worn-out" material and bad debts, "from which even the most meticulous prudence cannot be sheltered." It would be pointless to try to redress the situation by trying to win a "more solid and solvent" clientele that would permit the associates to hire helpers and profit from their work: "A new clientele would have to be sought out in a class where the system of worker associations finds little favor. . . . All things being equal, if you were in competition with another printshop to get some piece of work, you would fail simply because you are a worker association. The truth is . . . that today worker association in theory is viewed as a utopia, and in actual fact is viewed as a club and a seedbed of anarchy." At this juncture we again find the initial tie between the economic question and the social question, the undeniable identity of being and appearing. If association is represented as a seedbed of anarchy, that is, again, what it is. In the trivial sense it is one insofar as the manager, "filled with disgust," can criticize the intrigues of an opposition led by a former foreman soon convicted of unscrupulousness, the debauches of an associate covered up by his comrades, or the absences of another associate whom he vainly tried to dismiss. But it is also one in the deeper sense that what in 1848 appeared to be a moral union of free and voluntary associates once again presents the classic configuration governing proletarian lives and stripping the aggregation of their atoms of any and all morality: that is, theirs is a chance meeting.

> It is not reasoned choice, sympathy, similarity of character, agreement on political and religious matters, or recognition of proven merit that has brought us together from various points, but rather

73. Dossier Desoye, A.N., F 12/4622, note read at the general assembly of Feb. 22, 1852.

chance. We came to know each other only when it was too late for that. Bending our character to that of others was an effort we had not dreamed of. We met each other at angles, hence the antipathies and the mute battles that may have concealed our hates under the semblances of friendship. In brief, there is our story.[74]

A noble conclusion! The cruel games of work and chance, the former governing the course of industry and the latter governing proletarian lives. This twofold rambling would circumscribe the theater where the fate of associations is played out and would suffice to explain the various paths leading to their ruin: bad industrial conditions, overwhelming competition, managerial incompetence, worker insubordination, all too human conflicts between the former equals and the man they had chosen for their boss. Together with the direct and indirect effects of the counter-revolution of December 2, 1851, doesn't all that provide some explanation for the sad fate of almost all the associations? But here we have a first-class witness, the manager of the most prosperous of the surviving associations, mason Cohadon, who does not believe at all in this fine chain of sufficient reasons. The president of the 1865 committee inquiring into cooperative societies is astonished by his skepticism. Didn't most of the associations collapse "because they did not show any profits, because their operations were badly managed or the associates did not get along with each other"? "I don't know about that," replies Cohadon, noting especially the brilliant growth achieved by the former association of potters: "In general, they have had intelligent managers, too intelligent, perhaps; and operations have been managed well."[75]

The rude criticism of the iron-founders was not so far off the mark: there is an intelligent way to manage, to deal with industrial conditions, managerial mistakes, the absence of profits, and the misunderstanding of associates. The "almost worn-out" materiel of the association of Desoye and Company seems restored to new, the discouragement of the manager easily overcome, and the risk of bad debts greatly minimized when the associated printshop, now liquidated, is repurchased by the same Desoye. The stagnation of political publishing after the coup of December 2 permitted him to make the kind of deal that the flourishing market for files and the especially rebellious disposition of his associates denied to Wursthorn, who, as early as August 1851, was thinking of "reorganizing on

74. Ibid.
75. *Enquête sur les Sociétés de coopération*, p. 300.

a new basis" with a "less dependent" administration. This was successfully done, on the other hand, by the working-class administrators of the
Aniche glassworks. It put an end to three years of conflicts with associates who arrived "too late," left "too early," took "twice the coal accorded
by custom," refused jobs ordered by the clientele when they were "less
lucrative" for the worker, and opposed all dismissals because "a worker
doesn't dismiss another worker." When they reorganized "on a new basis"
in January 1852, they had already succeeded in discouraging those associates who could not dismiss workers and making them long passionately
to return to their halcyon days as wage-earners. In 1850 they said: "If we
have achieved good results, it is only by violating the statutes. We have
wielded a high hand. We have dominated, commanded, made ourselves
hated." In reality, comments the subprefect of Douai: "They made themselves employers, and they have replaced the exploitation of man by man
with the exploitation of the worker by a subsidized oligarchy."[76]

The effect of December 2, then, was not so much repression as holding
up a mirror to these little workshop republics so that they might recognize
their new face and giving a final push to any radical decisions that might
result. The events of December 2 did not "for a moment trouble the calm"
of the workers in musical instruments, whose association "today seems
mainly preoccupied with its material interests." The saddletree-makers remained calm "amid the most recent agitations," despite the fine promises
of their manager to representative Victor Hugo, who was finally escorted
by a lone member of the association of last-makers in his nighttime ram-
blings through the barricades. And although the irreducible file-cutters
lost a former delegate of their corporation in the fight, the police superintendent of Faubourg Saint-Antoine went in person to the headquarters of
the cabinetmakers to "congratulate the workers on their behavior during
the recent events."

The page having been quickly turned, some associations prefer to break
up; such is the inglorious finish of the fraternal tailors and the carriage
workers. Some reorganize "on a new basis." Others finally realize, or their
manager decides to make them realize, that their survival depends on the
full and complete restoration of the principle of authority. Imprisoned for
a time in December, the manager of the armchair-joiners, Antoine, re-
membered the lesson. Later he will confess to a German visitor: "Ah, well,
yes, I made my own little coup d'état, just like anyone else. And why not,

76. Dossier Gobbe and Sourd, A.N., F 12/4623, report of the subprefect of
Douai, May 5, 1850.

since coups d'état turn out so well! What we other Frenchmen need in all things is a good and strong authority."[77] The former champion of the social republic breathes the air of the day. For the moment he proclaims the virtues of order and work. Soon we see him deserting the association and fleeing "god knows where, under scarcely edifying circumstances." But that does not prevent the association from continuing to work and make people work: the report of the delegates to the 1862 Exposition will note that with respect to their helpers, these associated workers "practice exploitation on a greater scale than is done anywhere else."[78]

Some resist, to be sure, maintaining their little republic in the midst of imperial order and corruption. Before the 1865 commission of inquiry, the chair-turners express in a minor key the persistence of the ideals, now reduced from the great republican family to the little worker family:

> We are hard-working laborers, living as a family and taking seriously the principle and interests of association. And nothing is more suited to developing the intelligence of the worker, who feels free and assured of his work because he is no longer worried about being dismissed at any moment, as he might be by an employer. We invent work procedures and look for new models; our clientele is very satisfied with our products.[79]

But haven't they all—like the masons of Cohadon, who refuse to take in their old comrade Martin Nadaud for fear of losing official orders— emasculated the ideal to which they avow their loyalty? A man of the younger generation, bronze-setter Perachon, openly raises doubts about the cooperative and fraternal character of associations employing up to two or three hundred helpers. In the association of masons there are "few associates who handle the trowel."[80] But, he is asked, how are they to do without helpers? "You can't refuse to satisfy clients when they offer you work. Otherwise, you lose them." And of course the association of masons wanted to invite their helpers to share in the profits. But it soon saw that such a course "made it the loser" because the helpers want to share the profits but not the risks. The success of independent associations over the subsidized associations is greatly tied up with the fact that they have been able to recruit salaried helpers as they please. The subsidized associations,

77. Véron, *Les associations ouvrières*, p. 196.
78. *Les associations professionnelles ouvrières*, II, 677.
79. *Enquête sur les Sociétés de coopération*, p. 318.
80. Ibid., p. 168.

on the other hand, have been shackled by the fatal Article 25, inherited from the days when the *Atelier* faction reigned. That article obligated them to recruit either new associates or co-workers with a share in the profits, thus putting the "real workers" at the mercy of the "vagabond class of workers"[81] who come looking for profits among the saddletree-makers or wanting to play dice among the makers of gas appliances.

But who is still taken in by these moral justifications? Didn't Desoye himself outwit his associates by clearly summing up the situation for them: for the association to be viable, it would have to find work to occupy not only the seventeen associates but also the helpers, "whose involvement is indispensable if we are to cover our expenses, make good our deficit, and realize profits." The association can make real profits only by taking advantage of helpers. In its very success, the model enterprise of his colleague Remquet offers the counter-proof. To be sure, his associates reach the end of their ten years with assets of close to 150,000 francs to share. But only 56,000 francs of that sum are profits of the organization, which is encumbered by interest payments and the indivisible reserve funds as well as by the infamous Article 25. The remaining 94,000 francs simply represent the sum withheld from associate wages. Now, it is certainly something to have demonstrated the virtues of obligatory saving and converted these workers, who are "big children, real minors who mainly need to be helped and encouraged on the path of goodness."[82] But the ways of saving are not yet those of capital, and the power-wielding capitalists of the Remquet association ultimately find themselves at a disadvantage in comparison with the independent associates of the fraternal association of piano-makers. In their revised statutes of 1852, the piano-makers were very precise in setting the new limits of their fraternity. By a majority of fifteen votes to ten, they rejected the equal sharing of *their* benefits as workers and restricted equality to a very specific area: "The profits realized on the work of helpers are to be shared equally among all the associates."[83]

Those who dreamed of amassing "a little capital" and those who hoped for the "moral rehabilitation" of their class would surely agree in 1865 with the strong statements of the representative of the association of spectacle-makers, which had been lucky enough to be warned as early as 1848 by

81. Dossier King, A.N., F 12/4624, report of May 28, 1855.

82. *À Son Excellence M. le Ministre de l'Agriculture et du Commerce: Société ouvrière Remquet et Cie—Compte rendu 1849–1859*, p. 6. A.N., F 12/4627.

83. *Les associations professionnelles ouvrières*, II, 727.

the man who drew up their statutes. He, banker and republican minister Goudchaux, had acquainted them with this fundamental principle: "Don't forget that capital is the basis of work. There's the whole secret."[84] Today they are flourishing and prosperous. The investment of each associate has been raised to 3,000 and then 5,000 francs as a maximum, and they are careful not to touch their profits. They have managed "to rivet the understanding of each worker on one single point," in a division of labor where each pair of spectacles passes through the hands of fifteen individuals 360 times. They do employ helpers, of course, and they think that they can sum up the moral of seventeen years of experience as follows:

> In 1848 workers misconstrued their business. They thought that labor was everything, and they completely overlooked capital. We have moved away from those ideas. . . . If we have seen such growth, the reason is that we came to realize that capital was necessary for the emancipation of the worker.[85]

Undoubtedly the file-cutters, whose treasurer, former conspirator and former Icarian Montagne, has just died and left his widow "a little fortune of reasonable size that he earned in the association,"[86] would absolutely refuse to say that capital is the basis of work. But since 1848 all have come to realize that work could not be the *whole* whose fraternal kingdom would absorb the egotistical empire of profit. The kingdom of work could not possibly be that of identity, of self-mastery. In the microcosm where one observed the singular experiment of the worker as master of his own thing and self-made product of his own toil, the family quarrels of association have instead revealed in a magnifying glass the rules and ruses, the battles and complicities, that define the game of wages. The world of "industrial chances" could only be the world of this double ground, where there is no mastery except over another; where only Capital can make Work its "own thing"; and where the fight against the parasitism of exploitation is not a reappropriation but a reverse parasitism, the worker regaining his dignity by finding a thousand ways to absent himself from the work he does for another. Isn't it impossible for the family photograph of these little egalitarian oligarchies of worker patrons to hide the troubling lesson of experience—that there may be no citizens in the republic of work,

---

84. *Enquête sur les Sociétés de coopération*, p. 325.
85. Ibid., p. 324.
86. *Le Crédit au travail*, Jan. 27, 1864.

only foreigners: errant capital, laborers gone over to the side of masters, workers absent from their productive work?

Wasn't that to be expected, given the very bases of the experiment? And wasn't that the presentiment of those Proudhonian workers who, as early as 1850, sought to demystify the golden legend of the tailors who were busy trying to make a fraternal profit off the labor of their sister dress-makers and off the price at which they sold to their proletarian brothers? Weren't typographer Duchêne, former member of Fraternal Industry, and tailor Wahry, who resigned from the association of tailors, right in point-ing out that the germ of all exploitation is contained in the simple principle of seeking profit in order to increase the business of the association and open it to a greater number of workers? "Because if one makes a profit, then we have one of two things: either the *producer* has not been *paid enough* or the *consumer* has *paid too much*. . . . And what is normally the status of the consumer supplied by you? That of *proletarian*."[87] How, then, escape from this circle, in which you exploit proletarians in order to better eman-cipate them? You must "abandon all the forms of economic relationship employed up to now, *give up* having company capital *as such* and making a profit off others in order to increase it. Instead, you must create an establishment where the associates "call upon the consumers themselves to make advances to them, give them credit, finance *them*, by purchasing consumption bonds that are always redeemable in products."[88] No more employer capital as such and wage-earner concern for his own interest. Instead, a different world that grounds fraternity not on shared poverty or mutual exploitation, but on the very form of economic relations. A world of reciprocal exchange that is the opposite of the Saint-Simonian engineer's universe of God the producer and consumer: "On the contrary, picture a different world. One in which *each one lends, each one owes; all are debtors, all are lenders*. Oh what harmony will exist among the regular movements of the heavens! . . . *Because nature created humanity only to lend and borrow*."[89]

This is the basis and principle of the "free, fraternal, egalitarian" counter-association of worker tailors, founded by Wahry under the banner

87. Wahry, *La réciprocité: moyen de solution du problème de réforme sociale au point de vue industriel*, Paris, 1850.

88. Wahry, "Des différentes formes de l'association ouvrière," in *Almanach des corporations nouvelles*, Paris, 1852, pp. 121–22; in Faure and Rancière (eds.), *La parole ouvrière*, pp. 435–43.

89. *Pantagruel*, Book III, chap. IV; cited by Wahry, "Des différentes formes," p. 117.

of *Reciprocity*. And the observer in 1865 will certainly be astonished to see that an association founded on a principle so contrary to industrial laws has maintained its modest existence amid the shipwreck of so many associations. He does not know what to admire most: "The perseverance of the associates in an enterprise with no future, or the decency of their clients, which has enabled them to escape for so long the likely consequences of their imprudence."[90] But doesn't this mediocre survival point up what is missing in the rules of this frugal fraternity in order to typify the harmony of celestial movements? And how can we not sense the shabby accounting used by the former seminarian Duchêne to promise, at a cheap price, the heavenly harmony of his companions on the *Voice of the People*, the former communist Wahry and the too Christian Chevé:

> You want to expand your business and give all the work possible to workers? Sell genuine products; no more fraud; sell them cheaply. Don't appropriate anything above the cost price. . . . You will thereby have a large clientele; work will replace usury; and you will arrive at fraternity in one bound through justice, which is better than aspiring to it through monopoly and exploitation.[91]

To be sure, justice is better than exploitation, and the prey better than the shadow. But isn't the relationship between these two inequalities a bit more complicated than it appears in Duchêne's calculations? Is the economic order really the privileged locale of justice? And doesn't the shadow reach farther than the prey? These are the sort of questions that one man comes to ask himself: the great director and loser of the whole story, former representative Corbon. He had gone off to find the reason for the failure as well as *The Secret of the People of Paris*. Gradually he was led to overthrow all the presuppositions underlying the metaphysics of *L'Atelier* and the morality of association. No more perpetual association or indivisible funds; experience had refuted these monkish fantasies. But, above all, no more of the dogma of the fall and of reparation through work, of "drivel" about corrupting individualism and collective rule to curb its capricious aspirations. No more of earthly merit and of unceasing application to moralizing and productive work. The secret of the Babylonian people of Paris is also the secret of progress:

90. Véron, *Les associations ouvrières*, p. 198.
91. *La Voix du peuple*, Jan. 3, 1850.

Once upon a time I had been naïve enough to fall in line with the moralists and scold the worker chap whose vagabond spirit does not want to remain in the earthiness of the workshop and be absorbed in the making of a chair cane, or a hat lining, or a composing slip, or a shoe, or whatever division or subdivision of labor. . . . I had not yet grasped his secret. I was inclined not to appreciate the great and legitimate need for an exterior life that characterizes the worker of Paris. . . . For our worker, daily work is merely the forced labor of each day. And since he generally has no serious, lasting love for his work, he devotes to it only the least portion of his intellectual worth. The products that are the pride of the Parisian workshop are still far from bearing witness to the employment of all the faculties of the worker. Only momentarily, to overcome some difficulty, is he wholly taken up with his work. He works at half-mast, so to speak. Moreover, there are a multitude of jobs that would disgust his spirit if, on his own, he were not marvelously addicted to traveling the world. . . . If this worker could have become what I wanted him to become, he very probably would have done so only by stifling his great aspirations. And he would have dropped down to the third category of the middle class of people, unless he had taken his place in the bourgeoisie—which, from our standpoint, comes down to the same thing. When, by way of exception, the worker chap resolves to get ahead, it is rare that his generous aspirations persist.[92]

But these great aspirations seem quite small in the very earthly attention to wage-earner interests evident in association conflicts, in the narrow perspectives of certain contemporary strikes, or in the insistent dreams of returning to the corporations that mark the start of the 1860s. But isn't this meanness characteristic of a spirit that refuses to invest anything of his aspirations for a different world in workshop matters?

What is at the bottom of his demands is the desire for a guarantee against any eventuality that would force him to look for employment or to wrangle about his wage, and generally against anything that obliges his spirit to expend effort on matters concerning his trade. This need sometimes leads him to join up with schemes that

92. C. A. Corbon, *Le secret du peuple de Paris*, Paris, 1863, pp. 184–85.

would give the dreariest impression of his spirit, if one did not know how generally unfit he is to understand practical affairs.[93]

Hence the failure of these associations whose "earthly heroism" is too much for the simplifying laziness of the worker and too little for the great aspirations he preserves therein. Indeed, the editor of *L'Atelier* had long ago sensed that worker association could not possibly be the end of progress or the kingdom of Christ: "Would Franklin have invented the lightning rod if he had been retained by some typographical association? Would the fishermen who left their nets to follow Christ have won the right to give them up from an association?"[94] But that was still merely the particular truth of an apostle obliged to identify his way with that of the working-class multitude in order to bring back home a people gone astray. Now the former Christian, won over to the virtues of skepticism, turns around the order of his reasons in order to identify them once again with those of a people discovered to be different. The republic of the people could not be that of work. It is a strange sermon, running counter to a time when the dreams of association are ready to crop up again, more lively than ever. But there is also the fact that to the practical and slightly positivist criticism of old illusions there is now linked the intention to exorcise an ever present menace—the fact that in the very exaltation of the republic of producers, the efficacy of illusion again gets lost in the meshes of the system of material interests. Hence the need to set up, term for term, a people even more vagabond that it appears to itself, in opposition to the robust and practical people of not long ago. For the time has also come when it is no longer a matter of setting straight the image of the people, of moralizing the people to summon them to an awareness of their being; now, in the reclaimed separation of being and seeming, it is a matter of interpreting those tendencies, obscure to themselves, that push the people they know not where:

> It is undoubtedly to these peculiar and persistent dispositions that we must attribute the failure of worker associations. . . . Aside from the moment of enthusiasm in 1848, when one offers the Parisian worker this means of emancipating himself in droves, he accepts it with an eagerness that is more apparent than real. It

93. Ibid., pp. 185–86.
94. "Réforme industrielle: De l'association ouvrière," *L'Atelier*, Dec. 1842, p. 29.

seems that an inner voice tells him that he would become capable of practicing association only by losing a capability of another order, a higher order. To be sure, he does not take account of his instinctive repugnance; but we, who are beginning to see better into the depths of his soul, we can explain what is going on inside him better than he can.

. . . He does not want to build his house as he is advised to do it, or on the land that one suggests he acquire. He prefers to camp under his tent, as if he glimpsed vaguely in the distance the object of his ardent aspirations, the radiant city where his ideal of justice reigns. . . .

And since there is, at the heart of present things, a whole revolution to carry out in the innermost conditions of society, and our people are the instinctive force propelling it, his secret is to remain disengaged and available.[95]

How is it that the modern disciples of Saint Paul didn't think of it sooner: the worker apostle was, specifically, a maker of tents!

95. Corbon, *Le secret du peuple de Paris*, pp. 186–88.

CHAPTER 12

The Journey of Icarus

THE DIFFICULTY IS NOT THE ENCAMPING. It is knowing where one camps and where the Promised Land is. Because there is and there isn't a road: "The word *road* I use here does not mean at all what it means in Europe. Here it refers to the way you must necessarily go through, even though there is no line marked out from the point of departure to the point of arrival."[1] It is not just that there are as yet no paths for vehicles through the forests and prairies of Texas. In addition, there are three countries in one: the desert of persecuted believers, the fertile valleys of Icaria, and the virgin lands of the New World. But at the start the travelers have no doubts. Even if the topography of the new country bears little resemblance to the maps Cabet supplied to the soldiers of his vanguard, they know enough about it to recognize it as their destination: "We shall have a climate as mild, a more beautiful sky, a fertile, virgin land covered with stout vegetation and able to provide us with almost all the fruits and animals of our own country."[2] Later on, they will accuse the prospectuses of this curious geographer of having deliberately led them astray. But for the moment they have no trouble recognizing, feature for feature, the description of the Promised Land—at once virgin and fruitful, savage and familiar, forsaken and populated with fraternal beings:

> The air is excellent. The sun is hot, but a fresh breeze blows continually, refreshing the air. . . . The soil is so fertile that one hardly need scratch it to sow it, and it yields much more than in France. . . . The proof is our wheat, which is magnificent. . . . Although we sowed it in the prairie just after having burned the

1. Lévi's diary of the trip, *Le Populaire*, Aug. 20, 1848.
2. *Réalisation de la Communauté d'Icarie*, Paris, 1847, p. 38.

grass, which is very tall, and did not plow or dig, we are astonished to see it so fine and sprouting so quickly. . . . We placed the grains in the bosom of the earth and barely a few days later the plant came out . . . the sources of running water are as common as in France. Here you find some caymans or big crocodiles that go back into the water at the slightest noise. . . . the flesh of this animal is very good to eat. It inspires no fear. . . . There are eighty-pound carp, some fine perch, and a large number of other fishes . . . vine stalks that are thicker than one's leg and climb around the oak trees fifty or sixty feet high, with clusters of grapes of an enormous size. . . . The cows, horses, pigs, and hens cost nothing to feed, not even the trouble of tending them; they are outside day and night and have no stable. The inhabitants live almost without working. They barely sow their maize and build themselves a cabin in which to live. Many Americans and Texans come to see us; they are very kind and honest. People camp and sleep outdoors; they don't lock anything up, and they never steal. We lost a few full sacks and a gun; they informed us of this from a good distance away, and the gun was brought back to us from seven or eight leagues away.[3]

Isn't that what true communists knew: you must not seek the coming of the kingdom of fraternity in shopkeeper schemes of associations; you must go looking for it in the soil of a virgin nature, which alone is capable of truly effecting the multiplication of the fishes and bringing to maturity grapes large enough for the fraternal banquet? The identity of concept and reality here finds its symbol not in some heavenly manna, but in the immaterial dew whose miraculous properties are stressed by all: "The ground is moistened by a plentiful dew that never fails to fall every night; the extraordinary thing is that we slept outdoors and got this dew without anyone's becoming unwell."[4]

But joiner Moity and gardener Champeau are victims of their own precipitancy, as is tailor Boué, who is so happy to have found again the plow of his adolescence in order to be "the first plowman in Icaria." The fertile fields and fish-stocked rivers of Sulphur Prairie are not yet Icaria, merely an outpost on the route of the pioneers. The true Icaria is farther west, where no road leads, beyond forests of brushwood, rivers with no bridge

3. Letters of Moity and Champeau, *Le Populaire*, June 4 and 9, and July 23, 1848.
4. Letter of Moity, ibid., July 9, 1848.

across them, and mosquito-infested marshes; Mother Nature is also the land of dedication, where one must plow to reap and sow to harvest. At the end of this road that is no road, the plateau of Cross Timber undoubtedly again presents all the features of the sought-for land:

> Icaria, our Icaria, is big and beautiful. . . . There are immense prairies, forests, streams of good clear water. . . . The temperature is very mild. . . . Very good and healthy is a breeze that blows continually with plentiful dew in the morning and makes the land fertile. . . . The flowers that are grown with great care in the gardens of Europe are wild here on the prairies. . . . We have vine-trellises a hundred feet high that are filled with grapes. . . . There is very good water and plenty of fish in the rivers. We killed two crocodiles that were six feet long; these animals are very good to eat. . . . There is also plenty of game, such as deer and kid goats, a little rabbit and partridge, and many very large turkeys. . . . On the 30th of last month, I killed one that was twenty pounds. . . . There are no thieves or ferocious beasts. . . . We have been very well received by Americans. . . . Their customs are very simple. Their demonstration of friendship is a handshake; they do not offer food and drink twice.[5]

At first glance the Promised Land again makes itself known. A savage land from which the savagery has been pushed back: "As for the Indians, our countryside is not subject to their incursions. Twenty miles ahead of us is the cordon of troops designed to contain them."[6] And the savagery may only be the unrecognized simplicity of fraternal nature: "The most advanced settlers do not seem to fear them at all. With our principles of peace and fraternity, we will have even less reason to fear them." A paradise where divine providence has gone overboard in removing all malignancy from snakes: "The snakes are not to be feared at all. Even the rattlesnake is not dreaded. . . . You hear the rattlesnake, you have time to take every precaution to kill it, it flees and never attacks."[7]

But if there are no snakes to fear in Icaria, there are no apples to pick either: "As for fruit trees, there are none."[8] The image of an Eden offering

5. Letters of Viardot, Boissonnet, Lévi, Rousset, Guillot, and Therme, ibid., Aug. 13 and 20, 1848.
6. Letter of Rougier, ibid., Aug. 27, 1848.
7. Letter of Therme, ibid., Aug. 20.
8. Letter of Buisson, ibid., Aug. 13.

its plentiful fruits without effort and its miraculous catch of fish is now postponed. The mildness of the climate is no longer evidenced by sensation but demonstrated by a reasoning process that highlights the harshness of the effort: "It must be that the climate here is excellent because if we all had done in Europe what we are doing here, we all would be dead. Imagine trekking all day in the heat, sleeping on the ground at night with a thin coverlet for protection, drinking from all the holes in the ground. . . . Despite all that, my health has not yet undergone the slightest alteration."[9] Apparently there is no more breeze to cool the air, and a moderately clear water in the holes. The healthiness of Icaria's climate is now determined by looking at afflictions endured, and the fertility of its soil is now seen in the future—as a result of work and a promise of industry. Exclaims Boissonnet, who is from Lyons: "Victory! Icaria has been founded in one of the most beautiful lands in the world. . . . It is a fertile land where one can get two harvests a year. Finally, we have everything to fulfill our dreams, to make a model nation." But his fellow townsman Buisson changes the picture a bit even as he confirms Boissonnet's enthusiastic statements:

> Boissonnet is not exaggerating when he tells you that it is the most beautiful country in the world.
> Of fruit trees there are none. What we have in great number are vines and mulberry trees. There are very beautiful vines. We shall make superb plantations of them, and in two years we shall be able to harvest wine.
> The mulberry trees around us are right for silk. We have eaten mulberries in great quantities and we shall be able to make finer plantations than there are in France. . . . I urge all our brothers who are silk workers to bring their Jacquard machines.[10]

So it is not the prolific mulberry trees or the hundred-foot vine-trellises from which birds steal the fruit that will provide the community with wine and silk. Their useless vigor merely indicates that conditions are favorable for the labor that will create the plantations and industries of Icaria. The territory of Icaria is no longer Mother Nature offering its shelter and its fruits to orphans of the industrial world. Rather, it is the fertile desert where the pioneers will hew out the neatly arranged plantations,

9. Letter of Lévi, ibid., Aug. 20.
10. Letters of Boissonnet and Buisson, ibid., Aug. 13.

the straight roads, and the rectilinear cities, where the most perfect lodgings will stand beside the most magnificent workshops housing machines
ad infinitum. The endlessly repeated caution will punctuate the story of
Icaria: one doesn't come here to enjoy Icaria but to build it. As early as
the publication of the "Confidence" in *Le Populaire* of May 9, 1847, which
announced the approaching departure for an as yet unspecified Icaria, the
founder had well determined the profile of the pioneers:

> They will not be a mob of human beings without ideas, driven
> solely by poverty and the egotistical desire to improve their
> personal lot. They will be Workers full of courage, intelligence,
> and learning, élite men, examined and tested, admitted or chosen
> like the first Christians; who, like the first Christians, will have the
> same ideas, the same opinions, the same sentiments, one and the
> same heart and soul; and who, as one man, afire with dedication
> and enthusiasm, will go out to win happiness for their posterity,
> their country, and all of Humanity, even more than for themselves.

Not people driven by misery: this principle is already implemented in
the materiality of the conditions for admission. Besides a well-stocked
trousseau, each volunteer must make a personal contribution of 600 francs:
four to five months' wages for a worker comfortably making 5 to 6 francs
a day, a year's wages for an unskilled laborer making 2 francs a day. These
conditions are enough to close the door of paradise glimpsed on binder
Romégous and printer Lechapt:

> I deeply regret being enough of a proletarian not to be able to share
> in the common happiness of our brothers who have left, or are
> leaving, for Icaria, because I earn only a low day's wage to support
> my wife and two young children. . . . The darlings of Jesus believed
> that they had seen reborn in you their divine father, and their hearts
> bleed with despair at the idea that they could have been mistaken!
> They would like to conceal their unhappiness, but they cannot
> erase from their memory the words that were so heartrending for
> them: *we shall fix a minimum social contribution, which, for the first
> departure, may be six hundred francs per adult.* Hence they conclude
> that the doors of Icaria will be closed to them forever; and that
> they are losing not only their liberator but also all those of their
> brothers who, through the influence their fortune and talent give

them over the blind masses, have alone been able to pull them out of the abyss in which they sink every day.[11]

Bitter as it is, Lechapt's complaint confirms the principle of granting a pioneer role to proletarians already endowed with some fortune and talent: the young orphaned locksmith who possesses a sum of 5,000 francs and some properties that he offers to the Community; joiner Savariau de Niort, who is presently straitened by unexpected reverses but whose family expects to convert properties worth 50,000 francs into cash in order to go to Icaria; trunk-maker Gosse, who promises the price of his commercial stock, his personal property, and a rural property, and who immediately contributes twelve silver dinnerware pieces, two chains, a pair of earrings, a gold brooch, a wedding piece, and various little gold ornaments, to be used "in the best interests of the Society"; watchmaker Teyssier, who promises 80,000 francs to said Society; or the worker mechanic of Lyons, who is ready to contribute 12,000 francs for his brother and himself, a steam process for making bricks in large quantities, another to make raw wood immediately usable, and an idea for a machine to clear and plow an immense plain.[12]

This is also the disconcerting visage that the Icarian population offers to policemen and prosecutors pursuing these tatterdemalions who dream of the sharing of goods. Wherever the authorities send them to search or investigate—to last-maker Coëffé in Vienne, to weaver Butot or employee Lemoine in Reims, to joiner Popineau in Luçon, or to tilemaker Laurent in Sainte-Croix-de-Corbeny—they meet, not pillagers and incendiaries, but skilled workers, serious merchants, small entrepreneurs living comfortably, and, in general, citizens regarded highly enough to hold rank in the national guard or as firemen. How could these men, whose living conditions and lifestyles are so like those of decent people, dream of community property and want to leave everything for an unknown land? The argument could be turned around, of course. It is because they must change the world that Cabet has made them break with the ways of coffee-house revolutionaries, and it is to follow him to Icaria that they set about saving:

Says the prosecutor of Saint-Quentin to Lemoine: "From what I can see, you are a hard-working, intelligent man, even comfortable;

11. Letters of Romégous, March 19, 1848, and Lechapt, May 27, 1847, Fonds Cabet, Bibliothèque historique de la Ville de Paris.
12. *Le Populaire*, June 27 and Nov. 7, 1847.

and I don't see why you are abandoning this certain position for an uncertain one."

But it is the wrong way to pose the problem. Replies Lemoine: "I owe a part of what you call my comfortableness to M. Cabet. . . . As for intelligence, I get the best part of it from his newspaper and his writings. As for economy, it is because of his "Confidence" that I have imposed all sorts of privations on myself."[13]

His explanation would undoubtedly hold true for a certain number of Icarians in the great revolutionary cities (Paris, Lyons, Nantes, or Rouen): former militants of secret societies or communists close to materialism, whom the author of *Journey to Icaria* brought back to the paths of peaceable propaganda and moral and family order. But how can one be an Icarian in the innermost depths of the Champagne countryside? Even Champfleury, the pope of realism, come to inquire on the spot, must hide under circumstantial clichés his inability to comprehend the motivations of the tilemaker, the farmer, or the tobacconist:

> The people of Sainte-Croix have taken to communism like larks to a mirror.
> What is incomprehensible is the fact that they have amassed the goods they have with the heavy sweat of their brow. In cities like Saint-Quentin or Reims, it is understandable that men with no position would become the agents of such doctrines; they have everything to gain.
> But in a village where life is easy and sweet, when you have amassed a few little assets—to become a communist![14]

Asked about the same subject by the commandant of the constabulary, tilemaker Jean-Baptiste Laurent could only say that one day in 1844 when he went to Reims, he found in a bookstore the *Journey to Icaria*. Its ideas captivated him to the point where he eagerly subscribed, through the Reims correspondent, to the newspaper that was propagating this excellent doctrine.

What exactly was so admirable in the *Journey to Icaria*? Undoubtedly something akin to what enkindled the enthusiasm of Turgard, a specialist

13. Ibid., Jan. 30, 1848.
14. Champfleury, "Les communistes de Sainte Croix," in *Les Excentriques*, Paris, 1852, p. 189.

in artificial foliage, when he recognized it in the book: "Paradise on earth, men living as brothers, each sharing with the other according to need and capability, equality, unity, community—in short, one for all and all for one."[15] If the discovery of Icaria saved Turgard from the egotism into which he had been plunged by unemployment and his wife's illness, it is not destitution that propels him to depart, because he now has a prosperous line of work. The same holds true for shoemaker Vallet, recently raised to ownership by an inheritance but nevertheless taken with the idea he got from the book lent by a friend: "The theory was beautiful. Father, Mother, and boys soon became enthusiastic over the Idea of establishing a society where reason and conscience would rule. Without King or priests. No nobility but that of the heart. No poor, no rich. No tyranny, no oppression. A paradise on earth."[16]

To evoke this republican and lay image of the kingdom of Idomeneus, Cabet's *Voyage en Icarie* had to find already prepared minds and hearts. Such was Jacques-Pierre Vallet, a shoemaker who moved from Le Mans to Paris to seek a better living, and then from Paris to Orsay to flee the troubles of the city. He was an enterprising spirit. To his trade and his functions as mailman, town-crier, and drummer in the national guard, he added various profitable activities of a recreational and educational nature: raising rabbits for market, keeping a bathing house for the public, offering cheap boat rides on a rented pond, owning an assortment of masquerade costumes, and building himself a library of twelve hundred volumes. He had a sensitive heart, turning down well-endowed daughters to marry the youngest one, whose tears revealed her affection for him. A devotee of instruction and progress, he had been so enthused after July 30, 1832, by the *Journal des connaissances utiles* that he gave his second son the first name of its founder, Émile de Girardin. He was a freethinker content to worship God in his works, but also a moral reformer of popular amusements: he replaced the sorry customs of carnival days, in which the big amusement had been to fling excrement on houses and rare passers-by, with a superb festival including carts and people in procession, an orchestra, comic scenes, dialogues, and songs.

To this recognized originality of village philosophers—close to the capital, to be sure—correspond in negative terms the city sufferings of un-

15. Letter of Turgard, Feb. 8, 1848, Fonds Cabet, Bibliothèque historique de la Ville de Paris.

16. Émile Vallet, "Genealogical History of the Vallet Family," in H. Roger Grant (ed.), *An Icarian Communist in Nauvoo: Commentary by Émile Vallet* (Springfield: Illinois State Historical Society, 1971), p. 59.

recognized souls. Such is the young Lyons type-founder who evokes the discovery of his seventeen years: "Although still quite young, I had been bruised by this egotistical society and desired death as the only remedy for my anguish. You had just brought out the first issue of *Le Populaire* for 1841. I soaked in its doctrine. . . . It seemed to me that a new life was in me."[17] To grasp this disgust for society that can be surmounted only by the idea of a community of loving people, one need only see or read the accumulating "acts of social disorder," the enumeration of which in the weekly columns of *Le Populaire* for 1847 lengthens immeasurably with the effects of the crisis and the exigencies of propaganda. They are facts of misery but, even more, signs of a return to savagery, pictures of a humanity fallen back down into the animal state. In Mamers, a farmer notices a daily decrease in a pile of pomace that he had put in his courtyard. Keeping watch one night and surprising one of his neighbors, known as an honest man, he follows him home and discovers this pitiable spectacle: a whole starving family seated around a table and taking turns eating a formless mixture of flour and pomace out of a clay vessel. In Meurthe, there are families of four, six, and eight people who are living on beef blood alone; they go to the butcher shops of Phalsbourg for it so as to have it cooked. Near Le Havre, a young journeyman faints on the street for want of food. Kindly people carry him to a shop and give him a little nourishment. His sick stomach cannot keep it down, and the bystanders notice a mixture of straw and half-digested hay in his vomit. In Lille, for several days in a row, they pick up workers dying of hunger on the sidewalks. In Cambrai, a poor wretch who is a stranger to the city dies without means and is left unburied in the street for three days. The vestry and the relief committee refuse to defray the burial costs, so the inhabitants of the area have to assess themselves to get rid of the now rotting corpse.[18]

Atrocious misery is accompanied by accounts of savage behavior. In the Aube countryside, infested with bands of Alsatian or Ardenne beggars, a group trapped a rather large young dog, beat it to death, had it cooked, and ate it with relish. In Roubaix, it is a band of unemployed workers who come across a cow in a nearby field, kill it, dismember it, and eat it there and then, "in the manner of the Indians of the virgin forests." And everywhere there is a bit of the savagery of the food riots. Shopwindows are smashed in Tournai. There is a market riot in Roye. In Montignac, a riotous mob gathers to oppose the departure of corn. In Cambrai, the black

17. *Le Populaire*, Aug. 29, 1847.
18. *Le Populaire*, Jan., March, April 11, and May 23, 1847.

flag is paraded through the city with the cry: "Bread at twenty sous or death." In Châteauneuf-sur-Loir, the woodcutters attack the grain ships. In Tours, posters announce: "We want war." Everywhere fires break out and wreak destruction on something or other: in the Vosges, seventy hectares of communal woodland; in Saint-Louis (Alsace), a candle factory; near Château-sur-Loir, a spinning mill; in Sorlent (Haute-Loire), nine houses and four barns; in Bussière, near Clermont, almost the whole village. In Saint-Georges, near Saint-Malo, four vagabonds ranging from fifteen to eighteen years old show up and imperiously ask for alms. When they are refused by the villagers, because of their own poverty and the ability of the vagabonds to work, they are simply told that they will regret it; five minutes later, fires break out throughout the village.[19]

But there are equally full columns in *Le Populaire* about the ends of those who do not wait to return to animality, to collapse of hunger on the public road, to eat raw flesh, to utter savage cries of riot, or to wield firebrands. A Rouen worker throws himself into the Seine with his two little children roped to his body. An old servant of a great Parisian house, who does not want to die of starvation at seventy years of age, asphyxiates himself and his wife, after taking the trouble to bring his cat to the Market of the Innocents to give it a good master, and to kill his cherished old dog. An old man is arrested for begging in Amiens; the idea of appearing before a tribunal, after having lived seventy-two years with an unblemished reputation, steels his determination to stab himself twice in the stomach and straight through the heart the third time. A grocer, hounded by his landlord for unpaid rent, throws himself off the Column of July.

The list also includes those who suffer merely from the idea of famine or destitution and put an end to their lives. A farmer in Mans had been frightened by the drop in prices. A monomaniac in a village of Landes had gotten it into his head that he was bound to die of starvation: "No reasoning could triumph over this disastrous idea. And since the poor madman did not want to endure the horrible torments of hunger, he resolved to cut short his torment by cutting the thread of his days." Better still is the case of an honest young man who was quite rational. Foreman in a fine currier's shop, he committed suicide at 10:00 P.M. in a Parisian garret: "People swear that the young man, who was living comfortably and was highly recommended by his personal qualities, had been driven to this act of despair by his profound disgust at the state of commercial affairs."[20]

19. *Le Populaire*, April 18 and May 23, 1847.
20. Ibid., Feb., March, June 13, Sept. 5 and 26, 1847.

The epidemic of suicide, you see, levels classes, cultures, and ages. In Paris, it is a water-carrier driven to despair by poverty; in Châlons-sur-Marne, a discharged joiner; in Saint-Armand, a domestic afraid of being fired; in Semblançay, a notary seized with an insurmountable disgust for life; in Paris, the former secretary of the minister of agriculture who had sunk into destitution; in Villers-Cotterêts, a baker convicted for adulterating bread; a soldier of the seventh dragoons in Lille, a noncommissioned officer of the forty-eighth of the line in Paris, following unjust punishment. And there are others who kill themselves without anyone's bothering any more to indicate the reason. In Paris, a ministry employee hangs himself in his office. In Lyons, a surgeon–dentist shoots himself in the heart with a pistol. In Saint-Quentin, a tax employee asphyxiates himself with charcoal. In Mezières, an eighty-year-old man plunges into his pond. In Girolles, a child of eleven hangs himself behind his father's cellar door.

Among the victims who run afoul of the countless asperities of an egotistical society, a goodly number are the victims of some family constraint associated with the caste system and proprietary passion. On Rue Montorgueil a crockery dealer was forcing his daughter of eighteen to marry a man she did not love; on the morning of the wedding the girl went up to her chamber to dress, and her mother later found her lying on the floor in her wedding dress, near the classic charcoal heater. In Tourcoing, a young man of good family had made a mother out of a young servant girl and wanted to redeem his fault by marriage; he hanged himself in despair over the opposition of his parents. In the waters of the Seine boatmen fish up two corpses tied together; they had tied the girl's scarf around each other so that death would not separate them. In Corrèze, a beautiful peasant girl of sixteen, married barely three months, had been scolded by her father about damage done to a wheatfield by a flock of sheep. The girl went off and threw herself into a nearby pond. Her husband, who was madly in love with her, ran to the pond and threw himself in at the very spot where she had found death. Despite prompt help, rescuers could only fish two corpses out of the water.[21]

Close to these tragedies of love broken by paternal authority are to be placed the atrocities of certain family crimes. In Redon, a man starts a fight with his brother and kills him because the brother was bringing sheep to graze on his land. In Bourg-Saint-Andéol, M. Espouset is knifed to death by his wife, with the complicity of his twelve-year-old son. In

21. Ibid., March, April 11, May 23, June 6 and 13, Aug. 1, Sept. 26, 1847, Jan. 2, 1848.

Gréminy (the Meuse), a young man of twenty makes an attempt on his mother's life by slashing her neck with a razor.[22]

To complete the picture of a world in which paternal authority is merely oppression instead of providence, one must add those executed by machines. In Saint-Martin-de-Vivier, in a spinning mill, a young man is grabbed and turned twenty times around the motor drum before dropping off, his left arm broken and his two thighs crushed. In Darnétal, a foreman is carried off the same way, and a young worker is picked up by an axle-tree that makes sixty turns a minute. Given the unresponsiveness of employers, men of science, and local authorities, a joiner–mechanic of Darnétal used his spare time to study what was needed to invent a mechanism that could, in case of an accident, stop machines and the advance of the gears. But at the prefecture where he took his memorandum and his plans, no one took the trouble to read the former or look at the latter.[23]

Such is the haunting reality of an intolerable world. It is not that there are many Icarians in the murderous factories or in the cities of savage misery (Lille, Roubaix, Cambrai, etc.). And in Sainte-Croix-de-Corbeny, there are no reports of men who go out to eat the straw in the stables or dismember cows to eat them raw in the open field. But this second-hand reading is enough to upset the lives of men whose consciences cannot rest content with living impotently in a world where misery and oppression, prejudice and irrationality, are visible everywhere. Writes a merchant of Nancy, whose situation seems far from critical:

> Your idea of making Icaria a reality gives me new life. Death is preferable to life in the wretched society of today. Although my establishment is well-frequented and I have a large clientele, I long only for the moment when we can leave for Icaria. I had sought to insure my three children through an insurance company, where I deposited annuities of 1,300 francs. I am going to take out that sum immediately. It will serve as part of the contribution for my little family, and its existence will be much better guaranteed to the end of its days.[24]

Foresight is in vain in a society ruled by the arbitrariness of egotistical passions. From Périgueux, mirror-seller Pépin confirms that none of the satisfactions that success may bring are worth living for: "Here there are

22. Ibid., Aug. 1 and Dec. 5, 1847.
23. Ibid., June 13, 1847.
24. Ibid., Nov. 7, 1847.

several of us who are not alive. We languish to see so many absurd prejudices in the nineteenth century. But our courage revives us and gives us certainty of a better future. It is not that we are unsuccessful. On the contrary, we can consider ourselves to be among the privileged."[25] Illusory privileges, like the ornaments and trimmings one must use to hide from others the fact that one is already elsewhere: "With the full consent of my husband I am sending you my watch, my earrings, my wedding piece, a pair of my husband's studs as well as his watchkey. He would like to send you his watch if we were not forced to deceive the world with tinsel. But patience! The time is not far away when we shall no longer have need of our counterfeiting."[26]

But the time is even less far away when their enemies will try to create for these people, whose sufferings are much too intellectual and moral, living conditions consistent with the fancies that feed their disgust and their faith, and also try to make them like the image that pictures them as creatures without work or home. Such is the fate of those communists of Givors, whom their wives, influenced by relatives or confessors, have abandoned "solely for the reason that they are communists—in other words, *godless men, idlers, plunderers.*"[27] In Mirecourt, organ-maker Julien Chambry gives a detailed account of the vexations he has endured for having introduced communism into a region dedicated to musical harmonies by its industry:

> For four years communism has occupied all my leisure time. The first year I tried to enthrone it in Mirecourt, I was regarded as a madman or imbecile. The second, I was deprived of work, and I was even slapped by the brother of a rich man. The third year brought me a few proselytes, but no dedication. During this, the fourth year, I have been forced to learn the trade of sculptor. I am earning 1.50 francs a day during the whole winter, have two children, and must pay expenses for one of them whose eye was pierced by accident.[28]

The last organ-maker who was willing to employ this able and steady worker had to let him go; some "capitalists" forced his hand by threaten-

25. Ibid., June 6, 1847.
26. Ibid., Jan. 16, 1848.
27. Chapuis and Poncet to Cabet, Nov. 6, 1844, Fonds Cabet, Bibliothèque historique de la Ville de Paris.
28. *Le Populaire*, May 30, 1847.

ing to no longer discount his bills. To change his trade, Chambry became a student at the free school of design. There, again, his enemies pursued him, and his teacher needed the help of some leading citizens to prevent his exclusion. When the master employing him in his new trade came under persecution as well, Chambry had to leave for Nancy and give up "the great movement of ideas operative in the working class." But soon his employer will take back this apparently remarkable worker, and give him a raise; and the announcement of the departure for Icaria will create enough enthusiasm among the workers of Mirecourt that, despite the poverty, fathers of families will ask him to resume his apostolate and offer to pay him his daily wages if he is persecuted.

This respite does not last long, unfortunately. Soon the open confrontations of the republic will introduce these good workers and decent merchants to all the actual injuries of savagery, the mere idea of which prevented them from living. For a landlord of Falaise, a barber of Sartrouville, a tailor of Albi, and even in the village of Laonnais where the celebrated communists of Sainte-Croix have gone to hold a meeting, contact with the world of prejudice, ignorance, and animal fury is now direct:

> I recently received an anonymous letter, in which my wife is depicted as a prostitute and I am threatened with the gallows. As for my wife's fate, her head will be carried in triumph atop a pike. . . . After midnight, at long intervals, raucous, drunken voices cry out under my windows: Down with communists! Down with Guizot! Down with the barber! He should be hung on the Tree of Liberty. We will tether his head and drag him along like a muttonhead. . . . They have lain in ambush with knives, up to twenty or thirty of them. They have made so bold as to ask the deputy mayor of our township for permission to kill me. They have poisoned two goats in our meadow. . . . At 11:00 A.M. on Sunday they came to get me. A drum gave the signal to charge. They scaled the iron gate of our courtyard, which is locked with a chain, and threw a hailstorm of stones for half an hour. . . . A furious mob approached me, holding stools and benches. They threw me down into the orchestra—I didn't know where to flee. I was beaten unmercifully with a roulade of fists on the head, with stools and benches on my legs and back. . . . As we came out onto the street, we were assailed with stones, mud, and potatoes thrown by more than four hundred furious people. They gave the death signal, and only the mayor was able to save us. As for my carriage, these poor

misguided people threw it into the water. . . . They threaten my clients with all sorts of terrors. . . . In the afternoon several persons who came to do work at my place were stopped by our enemies and threatened with being thrown into the water. . . . They finally managed to make me lose almost all my work. Not long ago I was employing six workers, not counting my own work and that of my wife. Today I barely have enough for myself, and that only at the height of the season. . . . But my God! When will this long and painful martyrdom end for us. . . . Oh, how happy our brothers are to have left for Icaria![29]

Happy to have left for Icaria, but they did not leave for Icaria to be happy. Tailor Aron sums up well what the dispositions of the travelers ought to be: "It is the unanimous cry: since we cannot live here, let us set out for Icaria! Yes, brothers, let us all set out. But let us not have any illusions about our future joys. We shall have plenty of trouble in starting Icaria."[30]

This Icarian of the first hour has so few illusions about the future joys of Icaria that he will give up the idea of going to savor them himself. Perhaps he is aware of the contradiction in the all too clear inference of the invitation to Icarian dedication: "Since we cannot live here, let us set out for Icaria!" Don't people know already that those who are least able to live here are also those who are least able to set out for Icaria? But others also come across the countless shapes of the contradiction. There are those who do not leave for Icaria, thereby showing that they can live here and that Icaria for them was only an inconsistent dream giving color to the gray tones of their days under the monarchy of material interests. There are those who do leave, recognizing that they could no longer live here and that they are seeking a refuge from *their* unhappiness as much as an occasion to serve humanity. There are those who are prompted as much by instability as by dedication to abandon a situation in which they could live well enough, and who are always in danger of confusing the earthly merit of fraternal dedication with the vanity of being numbered in the ranks of the soldiers of humanity. Above all, there are those who combine all these motivations, more or less, sacrificing a social position that they certainly no longer had at the moment of departure, but that they might well still have had if they had not been Icarians; and those

29. Ibid., April 27, May 11 and 14, June 18, July 11, 1848.
30. Ibid., June 6, 1847.

who flee a country where they no longer find work and also sacrifice to the cause family properties sold cheap; and those who, in order to found Icaria in a land of fevers and savages, risk their lives but not necessarily their situation.

The paradoxical situations of these half-measure daredevils will be brought out in the fraud suit that some bring against Cabet after the debacle. Says jeweler Dubuisson: "I had been persuaded to become a part of the Icarian society because of the poor state of affairs in France and because it was my belief." That must also have been the twofold motivation of his colleague, jeweler Poiret. Asks the presiding judge: "What made you decide to return to France?" Replies Poiret: "It was the news of June 1848. I thought my house of business could suffer as a result of events." He is not upset by the judge's malicious question: "So you were living in community in Icaria but had separate interests in France? You withheld your house of business for yourself?" There is no contradiction in finding again, once Icaria is lost, the house of commerce that one had *left behind* in the land of commerce. Those with no business engaged in a similar division. Carpenter Bertrand sold all he possessed and gave 4,000 francs to Cabet. But in Le Havre he refused to hand over the family jewels: "I said that I had given 4,000 francs and that was quite enough." What he does not tell us is that the matter of the jewels was due to his wife's resistance which he had not acknowledged for fear of being excluded from the trip, since she was not an Icarian. It is the same story in the case of crystal-polisher Rousset, who again takes up his job at 10 francs a day when he returns from his Texas adventure. While demanding back from Cabet his contribution for the trip to an imaginary paradise and a trunk of linen his wife bought because she thought that she would not find "a shop with fancy articles" in the desert, he admits that his thirst for Icarian delights had made him lie about his wife, pretending that a woman so concerned about her toilette was a convinced Icarian. For such is the real substance of the suit at bottom. Behind the shabby effort to get back from the founder of an imaginary colony the money they had abandoned to the cause of humanity, these men are mainly seeking a settling of accounts for their lost hopes in a life other than that marked by the chicaneries of egotism. Says jeweler Chapron, who lost 2,000 francs in the bankruptcy: "I did not abandon Icaria, Icaria abandoned me. It threw us back into individual life. It owes us a settlement of accounts."[31]

31. *Gazette des tribunaux*, July 25, 1851. See Étienne Cabet, *Notre procès en escroquerie*, Paris, 1849, pp. 15–33; and *Procès et acquittement de Cabet . . .*, Paris, 1851, pp. 172–84.

In actual truth, the whole history of Icaria will be this interminable set-tling of accounts between travelers who did not find the Icaria promised by the writings of its founder, and a founder who, instead of the advertised Icarians, found this strange army of double beings influenced simultane-ously by the vanity of philanthropists and the avidity of the desperate, and caught up in the endless contradiction of discouraged dedication and im-patient enjoyment. It is certainly true that the Red River, on which Icarian prose had Icarian boats sailing, was not "perfectly navigable"; that the "national road" leading to Icaria was to be understood in the American sense of the term; and that instead of a million acres, there were only land grants to individual immigrants under the ordinary terms. But hadn't they made a commitment to found Icaria even before any cross was traced on any map, and shouldn't they have known that Icaria was a republic, not a territory? What mad impatience—for insatiable enjoyment or suicidal dedication—prompted them to abandon the verdant land of Sulphur Prai-rie, a stop on their journey, to traverse ravines, brushwood, and streams in order to reach the unhealthy confines of Cross Timber? For there, before they even had time to sow anything, they would be decimated by malaria after they had used their last ounces of energy to build thirty-two unin-habitable cabins giving them the ludicrous title to as many 100-acre plots carefully scattered by the grant of the Peters Real Estate Company. And what miracle prompted them, on arrival, to describe an enchanted land of hundred-foot trellises, miraculous dew, prodigious game and fish, whose looks would change so astonishingly in a few weeks?

> Up to now, fishing has been no more rewarding than hunting. We have fish in the Denton, but we have no nets to catch them. Turkeys, roe, and deer abound in the countryside, but the range of our guns is too weak to reach them. . . . Grapes are abundant, but they are eaten by birds. . . . The walnut trees produce almost no walnuts, and their fruit is hardly edible. . . . We have only four sheds and one American-style house in the center to lodge the sickest. The others live in the sheds, which are not big enough to protect us from the rain. In this area it almost always comes in squalls.[32]

On the whole, weren't they more at fault than their leader for wittingly embellishing a Promised Land, the reality of which was right before their

32. Collective letter of the first vanguard and letters of Therme, *Le Populaire*, Dec. 3 and 17, 1848.

eyes? And didn't they do it to lure their brothers more quickly to the soil of Icaria and enjoy the benefits of their labor?

The whole history of Icaria will resound with this crossfire of accusations: the pioneers saying that it is egotism that makes the newer arrivals delay so long in coming; the latter denouncing the egotism of the pioneers, who set a trap for them with specious images of the fraternal paradise. But in the summer of 1848 the soldiers of the first advance guard, felled by fever and the heat and waiting vainly for the relief column, have reason to put faith in the letter in which trunk-maker Gosse charitably informs them that they have been abandoned. It was on February 3, you see, that these former revolutionaries, converted to peaceful propagandizing only with difficulty, left Europe. Despite criticisms of their Father's prophecies, they had been convinced by them: "Here much time will elapse before the ruling authority is communist, or at least democratic and popular."[33] And it was on the twenty-fourth of the very same month that the editor of *Le Populaire*, master baker Robillard, and another longtime Icarian, file-cutter Montagne, were leading their comrades in an assault on the Tuileries and the conquest of the Republic. Writes Gosse: "So everything has changed. There was an unheard-of bustle at M. Cabet's. His house was transformed into an arsenal. . . . Then came the printing of newspapers and posters. My wife and I did nothing but fold newspapers. There was no time to eat. But for you, our poor brothers, nothing more."[34]

There is no real point in trying to find out whether it was out of spite at not having been given the editorship of *Le Populaire* that the disloyal Gosse wrote this "satanic" letter to his brothers in Texas. One thing is certain, at least: he is the only one who found time to write to them. This (Second) Republic, you see, needed only more hard work from Cabet to consolidate it—the very same Citizen Cabet who had not wanted it so soon, because he knew that the people were too ignorant and the republican leaders too ambitious for it to prosper. There was much to be done: pushing the enrollment *en masse* of workers in the national guard and ensuring the choice of republican officers in general and Icarians in particular; spreading the propaganda of *Le Populaire* and the Central Fraternal Society; ensuring the election to the National Assembly of thirty or forty solid communists and socialists (and who better than the founder of Icaria and his lieutenants?). In the energy he expended equally on the Luxembourg Commission, the

33. *Réalisation de la Communauté d'Icarie*, Paris, 1847, p. 37.
34. Gosse to Guillot, in *Réalisation d'Icarie: Nouvelles de Nauvoo*, Paris, 1849, p. 45.

provincial municipal commissions, and the association projects, we detect something more serious at bottom than the "ambition for power" denounced by Gosse: the feeling that the Republic could well be the true Promised Land of workers, the Icarian dream having merely served to sustain their wait for it. "I have often said that Communism and Republic were absolutely the same thing."[35] In truth, Citizen Cabet had never before uttered such a heresy. If he allows himself to utter it in the effusions of the Central Fraternal Society, the reason is that he is carried away by listeners who have always held this heresy as their true religion. It is for them especially that the Republic is the here-found land of a new fraternal world, tangible at this meeting where one proprietor, goldsmith Gentil, abdicates the privileges that the harshness of the world commanded him to exercise: "I am prepared to give back to the masses what I was withholding by force of circumstances, so long as I had to ensure my old age against disastrous eventualities. Today, now that society should be tending to situate itself in a different atmosphere and the material life of all human beings will be ensured, I am ready to divest myself of those things on behalf of all my brothers."[36]

A brief Parisian Icaria at the start of March: soon the Promised Land will again become the land of misery. In one sense, the total stoppage of business affairs comes down harder on the laborers of well-paid workdays and on the little employers who were ready to sell their belongings in order to pay for their own trip to Icaria and that of their less fortunate brothers. They will also be the ones most exposed to the persecution that will follow the reactionary demonstration of April 16, everywhere hitting the work, clientele, property, and persons of communists and forcing a goodly number of them into ruin, flight, and silence. Then it will again be time to dream of the distant Icaria, but it will no longer be the same dream. Most of those who were waiting impatiently to go will stay planted here: because increased poverty or sudden ruin devours their savings for the trip and imprisons them in worries about day-to-day survival; but also because their fraternal utopia is centered once again on the Republic of workers, and henceforth they will pursue it through political revenge (the coming elections) or economic revenge (worker associations). And those who do leave for Icaria in the autumn of the revolution, often without

35. Address of Cabet to the Central Fraternal Society, 8th session, April 10, 1848.

36. Central Fraternal Society, 4th session, March 6, 1848; and Gentil, *Organisation du travail*, Paris, 1848.

contributions and always without the little fortunes they had promised not long ago, will be not so much the "soldiers of humanity" as the exiles of the Republic seeking a refuge from the miseries and persecutions of the Promised Land in France to which they had sacrificed the other.

But the refuge does not exist. Well before they leave for it, their brothers in Texas, decimated by malaria and convinced that they have been abandoned, leave the territory where they were to have founded Icaria. When the debris of the Icarian avant-garde meets the defeated of the republican utopia in the commercial sewer of New Orleans, there is no longer a point on any map indicating an Icaria that has been founded or is to be founded. In *Le Populaire* the founder asks, with unaccustomed modesty: "Does Icaria exist? Where is it?" There are simple answers: "Icaria already exists, since we carry it in our hearts."[37] And there are equally peremptory retorts, such as that of shoemaker Decroq ("If Icaria exists everywhere, there is no point in making us travel through deserts like savages"),[38] or that of the Paris tribunal that sentences Cabet to pay back a soldier of the first advance guard:

> Whereas it appears from the discussions and documents of the trial that in issue 25 of the newspaper . . . Cabet set forth the bases of the social contract for his community of Icaria; that he stated in said newspaper that the general principles of this community had been indicated in his book entitled *Voyage en Icarie*;
> Whereas in this work . . . in Chapter One he depicts Icaria as a second Promised Land, an Eden, an Elysium, a new earthly paradise . . . in Chapter Thirteen he depicts childhood as happy and without work, manhood without care or fatigue, old age rich and without sorrow, living almost twice as long as human existence;
> Whereas . . . in Chapter Fifteen he declares the problem of social equality completely solved;
> Whereas in all the other parts of this work he devotes himself mainly to describing the wonders, magnificences, prodigies, and delights of Icaria;
> Whereas in presenting an imaginary enterprise as a reality and drawing such an alluring picture of chimerical advantages, Cabet's obvious aim was to entrap the trust of third parties, to persuade

37. *Le Populaire*, Jan. 21, 1849.
38. Cabet, *Notre procès en escroquerie*, p. 22.

them to become part of the Society formed by him and entrust their
capital to him . . . ;

Whereas it is under the sway of these maneuvers that Thorel
gave his consent and hence is well-founded in requesting its
voidance as null . . .[39]

It takes all the simplicity of men of the law, convinced in advance of
the naïveté of a people victimized by swindlers and ringleaders, to reach
such a conclusion as the obvious one, to include without further ado the
utopian no-place in the category of "fraudulent maneuvers" designed to
abuse the trust of little people. If they were not blinded by their compassion for the innocence of the common people, they could have noticed
some duplicity in the behavior of the plaintiffs. For shoemaker Decroq did
not journey through the desert, except to make the round trip from Le
Havre to New Orleans and back; the old Icarian Thorel, who went as far
as that desert of some little humidity and brushwood, has not yet returned;
and the most tenacious of the plaintiffs, crystal-polisher Rousset, admits
that only under constraint did he follow the order to leave the land of illusion, where he would have preferred to die. Dissident or loyal, the Icarian
proletarians have a slightly more dialectical conception of the relationship
of being to nonbeing; even if, to these accusations of fraud in which the
former submit the bitterness of their lost dreams to the pressure of family
interest, the latter respond by blaming the indefatigable Jesuit enemy who
is everywhere hard at work to lead the soldiers of progress astray. Underlying the "fraud" or "treason" is the mistake of making Icaria present and
localizing in some territory what is in truth a long-term trek: the foundation of the Icarian Republic, which presupposes the prior formation of an
Icarian people.

In March 1849, with Cabet leading them, 249 colonists will move to
Nauvoo, Illinois, on the banks of the Mississippi River. There they will
occupy the lodgings abandoned by the Mormons, who have left there to
establish their new Jerusalem in the desert. But these Icarians know that
they are not yet in Icaria, that they are at a stopping place needed to form
the material and moral elements for its foundation:

This outpost will be the laboratory where we shall mold all the
new brothers who join us. It will be the transition from the old

39. *Le Populaire*, Nov. 4, 1849.

world to the new, or, to put it better, from vice to virtue. Science, the arts, and industry will prepare the elements needed to build the Icarian State in the middle of the desert. Then we will have no problem sounding the profound wilderness around us to build the kingdom of Fraternity there.[40]

So Icaria will be founded in the desert only if it is already present, not only in the "heart," but also in the present organization and behavior of Icarians. This is the *good* anticipation of Icaria defined by one of Cabet's trustworthy men—jeweler, poet, and songwriter Prosper Bourg:

Brothers, the land where we have cast anchor is not the Promised Land where the wonders of Icaria are to be realized. Our modest labors are not yet even the rough draft, but Icaria nevertheless exists! Organic Icaria with its communitarian regime, its system of equality, its order, its harmony, its powerful concentration of each one's energies and aptitudes contributing to the welfare of all—finally it exists, with its incessant tension toward material, intellectual, and moral progress through the work, study, and practice of Fraternity.[41]

Organic Icaria: the organization of work is the first thing rendered to its subjects, the workers, and its goal, the common welfare. Such is the picture given to friends and especially relatives, who hardly share their enthusiasm, by wool-sorter Legros, employed in the kitchen, by founder Chicard, employed in the workshop of coopers, and by clerk Pech, who is in charge of the laundry:

Here there are no employers who try to make you produce as much as possible by using up your strength and your health. . . . Imagine a society of more than two hundred male and female workers from all trades, who are directed by directors chosen by themselves. Imagine all these workers organized in such a way that they spend their time usefully. . . . We all work with tireless zeal. And now that we are doing everything for love of humanity rather than love of money, there is no limit to our desire to work.[42]

40. Letter of Pech, *Le Populaire*, Sept. 2, 1849.
41. *Le Populaire*, April 7, 1850.
42. Letters of Chicard and Legros, *Réalisation d'Icarie*, pp. 98 and 100; and of Pech, *Le Populaire*, Sept. 2, 1849.

To be sure, the masons and carpenters of the community do not yet have the machines to ready the materials, the trolleys and portable tracks on which, in Icaria, the heaviest loads will glide effortlessly to platforms protected from the sun and rain. But already the entire community must take care to leave off work during the hot hours of daylight. It does not yet have the washing machine that would free its citizens from the age-old servitude to the lye-wash, its reaper is often under repair, and its threshing-machine sometimes catches a worker's leg, as it did in the work-shops of exploitation. But at least the risks and pains of these labors are shared by all. The boss of the joinery workshop participates in all the tasks of his "subordinates," and the professor of mathematics in charge of classes submits to the egalitarian division of tasks:

> The laborious jobs are shared by all. Is there sawing to be done? Each individual does it in turn. I take my turn as the others do. . . . For us the task is a duty bringing us only the esteem of our brothers. . . . The jobs regarded as proper for outcasts—kitchen duty, cleaning, etc.—are presently the lot of a goodly number of us, people of the most remarkable intelligence, moral value, and cultivated minds.[43]

For example, such is the situation of the "rewasher of plates and dishes," Montaldo the Spaniard. In one of those exemplary Icarian marriages where feeling shakes off the fetters of social prerogatives, he had married a gentlewoman, Mademoiselle Pigny, formerly head of a boarding school. Once a revolutionary in Barcelona, Montaldo is actually a teacher of mathematics and languages; and he will head the school and the com-munity before he is employed on the flatboat. In this redistribution of functions determined by the general interest, shoemaker Tabuteau enthu-siastically embraces the job of plowman; notary clerk Olinet is apprenticed in the bake-house; stationer Mahy moves from the kitchen to the wash-house and from the infirmary to woodworking; and Jacques-Pierre Vallet —shoemaker, mailman, drummer, and organizer of Orsay festivals—takes the job of cook before moving on to work in the garden. Only the founder of the community is exempted. But his privilege is largely "to get up first, go to bed last, work the most, and shoulder all the difficulties, cares, and privations."[44]

43. Letters of Savariau and Thibaut, *Le Populaire*, Sept. 2, 1849.
44. Prudent to Beluze, in *Réalisation d'Icarie*, p. 84.

And so fraternal—and paternal—solicitude replaces the all too frag-ile enthusiasm of pioneers. One must now speak a different language to Icarian candidates:

> I do not write letters like those of the first vanguard, letters with
> fine promises saying: Come, I am preparing a fine garden for you,
> good fruits, etc. None of that at all now. Our Society is a colony
> of Workers, who use their little corner of the earth to plant maize
> and potatoes to receive you. . . . Among us you will find fraternal
> love for you, for your wives and children the most tender affection
> that can derive from a doctrine as beautiful as ours. Come to be
> free. We do not say to share our privations—we have none; or our
> fatigues, since we work as hard as we can but no one drops from
> exhaustion among us. Our life is frugal, active, and that's it. . . . We
> are not rich, but we are not poor either.[45]

A family utopia quite different from that of the Saint-Simonian orphans. Even though Cabet did buy the ruins of the temple abandoned by the Mormons to rebuild it, the Sundays of the Icarian family scarcely evoke the fervor of Ménilmontant or Taitbout Hall; and the veneration of these people in their forties for a father in his sixties is far removed from the ambiguities that characterized the emotions of the young men and women of 1831. In the grammatically correct phrases and sprightly style of jeweler Bourg, undoubtedly more familiar with *Candide* than with Chateaubriand's *Les Natchez*, walks along the banks of the Mississippi take on a far less exotic complexion than do the garden of Ménilmontant or the banks of the Marne in the bombastic phrases of floor-tiler Bergier or the barbarisms of joiner Gauny. And the Icarian festivals of Fraternity resemble those family outings in the countryside that philanthropists deem suited to reminding proletarians of the antique simplicity of worker mores:

> In a country outing we had recently, I noted with pleasure the
> egalitarian variety of our outfits. No showy finery to be analyzed
> or envied, but no gloom-inducing rags either. Our dark velvet
> tunics highlighted our sisters' blue, rose-colored, and straw-colored
> dresses made of simple material. There were almost two hundred

45. Camus to his parents, Aug. 10, 1849, in *Réalisation d'Icarie*, p. 86; and col-lective letter of the Parisians in the community to their brothers in Paris, March 1851, Cabet Archives, International Institute of Social History, Amsterdam.

of us, and we all, from the children to the older adults, were dressed unpretentiously but nicely, neatly, and decently; each helping or being helped on the upward or downward slopes of our excursion; chats, friendly calls, and jokes springing up and being exchanged between all indiscriminately; and then our venerable and venerated Patriarch walking in our midst with a joyous air; all of us together offering the aspect of one big happy family. . . . And all emulating each other, without jealousy or care, full of a frank and expansive gaiety, we were, perhaps without noting it, under the influence—unknown alas! in the old world—of Liberty, Equality, and above all Fraternity.[46]

Without care: is *Sans-Souci* truly the name that suits the domain of the Icarian community? In the letters published in *Le Populaire*, we are astonished to keep coming across this theme. It seems hardly appropriate to describe the laboratory in which the foundations of the desert republic are being laid. Yet we are told again and again of the community's "soft, peaceful, and carefree life":

When we get up in the morning, a little glass of liqueur awaits us for our good health. We have three proper meals eaten with a fork. From about 11:00 A.M. to 3:00 P.M. we stop all forms of work to avoid the rays of the sun. . . . About six weeks ago, we felt the need to fill our mattresses again. So we scattered playfully in the nearby fields to gather corn leaves, and in a few days we all had top-notch mattresses. . . . If most tradesmen were aware of the tranquility we enjoy, they would truly envy our lot. Here we have no worries about the future, rents, bills due or about to come due, etc. . . . Meals, laundering, footwear, clothes—everything is made or done right here, and each person need only concern himself with those things put especially in his charge.[47]

There is very little distance between this ideal of the carefree community and the description of his solitary existence given by one of the first vanguard, tailor Bourgeois, who had remained on the lands of Icarian Texas. While "waiting for the community to be solidly established some-

46. Letter of Bourg, *Le Populaire*, Dec. 2, 1849.

47. Letters of Lafaix, *Le Populaire*, Sept. 2, 1849; of Legros, *Réalisation d'Icarie*, p. 100; and of Madame Chartre, ibid., p. 84.

where," he lets a troop of pigs who take care of themselves wander about his fields for weeks on end, raises chickens, and cultivates melons, watermelons, and sweet potatoes in the abundant leisure time afforded by his industry: "Where might one go to be happier when one restricts one's ambition to living freely and tranquilly?"[48] This life returned to "individualism" is equally the experience of a world where money becomes almost a forgotten item and where the prodigality of nature joins with human solidarity to offer everything a communist could dream about in Paris:

> Here payments are mostly made in kind. We exchange grains, pigs, cows, poultry, butter, eggs, etc., which means that I am more often paid in merchandise than in money. . . . I am not a hunter, but my closest neighbor gives me plenty of game meat, such as deer, turkeys, ducks, pigeons in winter. . . . Fishing also provides me with abundant resources. I need only travel half a league and fish for a couple of hours to get a good catch of fish every time. . . . Such is my position. Such is the life I lead. I go and come when and where I like. The little work I have for myself does not keep me from being free. Taking all things into account, in the whole course of the year I have only two days of work per week.[49]

Cabet certainly has his reasons for giving a good portion of space in his newspaper to the idyllic account of this solitary communist. The latter should prove to slanderers how nice life can be in the "deserts populated by savages" to which he is accused of having sent his disciples. But does he clearly perceive the fascination the solitary communist might exercise on his Nauvoo colonists, whose carefree existence nevertheless entails six days of hard work? For the images of the community as a peaceful refuge, where each need only be concerned about his or her moderate task, embellishes (just a bit!) the daily life of Icaria for the sake of old parents, farmers, and merchants, who are skeptical or incensed about the folly of their children. You cannot drag your feet at 4:00 A.M. in the summer when the trumpet sounds, if you want your share. The savor of three fork meals is fairly insipid "when one has lived a bit as a gourmet."[50] Although the community frees its members from worries about rent, bill payments, and laundry, it is powerless against the repeated blows of fate: hurricanes,

48. Letter of Bourgeois, *Le Populaire*, Dec. 2, 1849.
49. Bourgeois to his sister, *Le Populaire*, June 2, 1850.
50. Salarnier to Sarot, in *Lettres icariennes* Paris, 1859–1862, I, 324.

floods, accidents, epidemics. Before telling his parents about the carefree life of Icaria, Citizen Chartre waited until the end of the cholera epidemic, which killed twenty-three men, women, and children of the community. And when shoemaker Tabuteau, now an apprentice peasant, has his leg crushed by a machine, the community has only paternal love to offer to help him endure the pain: "Twice he asks to embrace the Father, who, repressing all untimely emotion, his figure pale but energetically calm, supports and excites the stoic strength of his worthy son."[51]

But these dramas—which the care of the good mother community for the security of her children was supposed to suppress—point up once more its superiority over an old world heedless of its maimed, its aged, and its invalids. A disabled young man of twenty-three draws the lesson himself: "It is in the face of such misfortunes that one sees and admires the advantages of the Association, of the community. . . . in the community one is employed according to one's strengths, and one has no uneasiness about the future."[52] The very harshness of Icarian life confirms the image of the sheltering community, protecting children, respecting women, welcoming orphans, and gently dealing with old people and the disabled. Its rhythm of births seems heedless of the restrictions that generally characterize the difficult beginnings of communities, and the arrivals continually include an excessive number of widowers and old Icarians. The widowers come to give their children a second mother; in the same contingent of August 1850 we find shoemaker Leclerc with five children ranging from three to thirteen, and Citizen Humbert with seven children ranging from five to eighteen. The old Icarians come from every corner of France (Coëffé from Vienne, Cadet from Troyes, Clèdes from Toulouse, Lavat from Marseille . . .) to relish the calm of old age in the bosom of the community: "We work as we can, without a concern for the morrow. We reap every day and our old age dies out surrounded by attentions and calm."[53] For there are no priests or solicitors to torment the repose of the dying: "One goes to sleep the long sleep in the midst of kind words and the most pleasant illusions. If in Icaria the times make life a bit hard for us, at least death here is light."[54]

Between the garden of Candide and the hospice for work's invalids, we get the whole gradation of images, sometimes playful, more often stoic,

51. "Revue de la semaine du 21 au 27 juillet," *Le Populaire*, Sept. 27, 1850.
52. Letter of Tabuteau, ibid., Nov. 8, 1850.
53. Lavat to Belvet, in *Lettres icariennes*, I, 310.
54. *Lettres icariennes*, II, 137.

that reflect Icarian satisfaction. It is an equivocal sentiment in which the dedication of the militant and the freedom of the philosopher meet with the enjoyment of "each for himself, the community for all." It is the presence, at the depths of the communist ideal, of an "individualism" that itself is composed of contradictory elements: the proletarian's request for assistance and the egalitarian ideal based on the exchange of work for wage; the dream of mastery associated with the colonial idea and the search for a refuge against the servitudes of industrialism. This contradiction in communist aspirations is further complicated by the ambiguous relationship of the New World to the Old World. For the characteristics that make America propitious for the realization of communism are also those that make it the blessed land of individualism. How can we not sense the ambiguity of the descriptions used by the new colonists to attract their brothers in France?

> How could one fulfill the prediction of death by want in this country where one is looking for people to fill these many fertile deserts, where the indolent American barely works three or four hours per day for six months of the year and takes it easy the other six months. . . . Wood costs nothing. Everyone goes out to cut it down in the forests when they feel like it, and they do not even bother to collect the shavings. Animals take care of themselves. In the morning you let out the cows, and they go off in the fields by themselves. They return in the evening to give their milk. . . . There are no beggars in America. Almost all Americans are property owners.[55]

The summons to community and the dream of property? Aren't these letters of professor Thibault and founder Chicard an invitation to "false Icarians," to "all those irresolute men who consider the realization of communism from only one viewpoint, that of their own future"?[56] Well, it is precisely these people, bound to leave the colony for the very same reasons that brought them there, whom Cabet's second-in-command, jeweler Prudent, would like to lock out of Icaria:

> Such people are constantly tossed about by uncertainty. Their sick imagination is always seeking a refuge from poverty, and they

55. Letters of Thibaut, *Le Populaire*, Sept. 2, 1849; and of Chicard, Sept. 23, 1849, in *Réalisation d'Icarie*, p. 99.
56. Prudent to Beluze, July 14, 1851, Cabet Archives, Amsterdam.

really latch onto any passing plank they see, quickly changing one for another. . . . America lends itself marvelously to this deceptive mirage of the dog who drops its prey for the shadow, until the moment when the sad reality wakes you up, more desperate than ever. Then you again take up your worker's chain as a lucky chance.

This explanation indicates clearly enough what feeling the most loyal and skeptical representative of the Icarian vanguard may have toward the mass of his brothers. But once again it fails to tell us precisely what the prey and the shadow, the mirage and the awakening, are. For these men driven by "poverty" do not pursue just any mirage. In this America where so many routes meet, those of Icaria never mingle with those of California's gold. It is a more complex sentiment that continually sends to Icaria about the same number of colonists as desert it. The America of Icarian dreams is the fertile desert, land of adventure and carefree living, of virginity and industry, of solitude and fraternity. The contradictory ideal presented here again can find momentary satisfaction in a period of rotation between the assured meals and the carefree routine of mediocre communitarian comfort and the first intoxication of the great expeditions, days or weeks long, to make hay, look for cattle, or cut down wood on the islands. But the monotony of Icarian meals and the mediocrity of work's results soon unite in a picture of monotone gray.

Too often the reports of colony activity resemble those of the spring and summer of 1851. In March the mill processed 2,200 pounds of flour a day and distilled 240 gallons of raw whiskey: an encouraging result, although the whiskey business is not really one of those preparing the foundations of the new moral order. And the Father, visiting one of the islands, found some zealous woodcutters who had already made up almost 300 cords of wood for burning and more than 300 oak or walnut logs for the sawmill. Unfortunately, the sawmill has had a breakdown, and the colony suffers from a chronic lack of mechanics; and the cooper's workshop, where two out of ten people are in the trade, had to hire a worker from outside to ensure the needed kegs (always whiskey) and learn the American way of working. For the "indolent" American works at a pace unknown to the colonists and especially likes to see work "promptly done." On March 30, the farmers went off happily under the direction of their chosen boss, joiner Cotteron. But the plowing was slowed by the snow and thwarted by the cutting of corn stalks. On the same date the masons and carpenters were at work building a new edifice; but between the end of April and

the beginning of May, a storm destroyed the carpenter shed. The report
of May 24 tells us that in one month 150 kegs of whiskey have been sent
to Saint Louis; but this production, quite modest, cannot count on Icarian
agriculture, still in its infancy, for its grain supply. So with some difficulty
they bought the needed wheat and corn and stockpiled them at the mill.
At the end of May, however, the mill was flooded; the grains are under
a meter of water. The island wood, of which there is no news, is probably lost; and the pigsty has been lifted by the storm. Aside from 55 kegs
of whiskey shipped to Saint Louis and a "considerable" quantity of flour
sold, July brought only disappointments: troubles with the mower, the
wheat too damp to be entrusted to the threshing machine, the blacksmith
inconvenienced by the bad quality of the charcoal, and the gardening impeded by the rain. The first half of August is just as disastrous: the wet
oats are impossible to thresh, the harvest of wheat is bad, that of the bar-
ley ruined, and the new wheel for the machine, which they had to have
cast in Keokuk, is defective.[57]

These difficulties and setbacks seem enough to sap the artificial enthusiasm of these unstable spirits; the very inability to satisfy their inconsistent
aspirations makes them communists in Individualism and individualists in
Communism. The loyal organizer of departures for the colony, cabinetmaker Beluze, points this out to Prudent, who is presiding over the uncertain destiny of the community while Cabet is away defending his case
before the court of appeal in Paris. Beluze notes that "triumph must be
assured" if dedication is to be "rekindled" in the French communists. And
the pessimistic jeweler is quick to extract the philosophy of this disclosure:

> It is a fact that dominates our era—everything has been material-
> ized: faith, hope, liberty, equality, fraternity, or love of neighbor.
> The direct relationship between one individual and another, the
> spirit of sociability, is coldly posed in consciences as a question of
> mathematics; we are caught up in individual sensual happiness
> and await the inoculation of collective happiness. Such are the
> encouragements we receive, when it is not hatred springing from
> a mistaken calculus.
>
> And it is only natural that the ideal has little appeal to stomachs
> that are crying out in hunger, to souls debased by the age-old
> organization of society, to slaves who break their chains and throw
> themselves on the disorder of the old world.[58]

57. *Le Populaire*, May 16, 23, and 30, July 4, Sept. 13 and 27, 1851.
58. Prudent to Beluze, Cabet Archives, Amsterdam.

The classic image of the unleashing of servile passions: Doesn't the Icarian balance-sheet validate the criticisms of those Catholic workers who challenge the communists to propose an ideal that will not be reduced to the egotistical satisfaction of interests by their adepts? But the simple inference leading from the difficulties of the task to the desertion of false apostles seems to be contradicted by the moral balance-sheet of the materially disastrous six months: "The six months just ended have not been kind to us in material terms, but, on the other hand, we have gained a great deal; and today more than ever before, as our adversaries themselves admit, the success of our enterprise is not in doubt."[59]

From the circumlocutions and reiterated negations of this reasoning it is evident, in any case, that Icarian enthusiasm does not depend on material success alone. During the six months of disappointments the colony has progressed in terms of dedication and fraternity, which have been confirmed after a disagreement and undoubtedly stimulated by the Father's absence. But Prudent's diagnosis does touch upon a sore point, nevertheless: the Icarian Republic, which is based on morality before being based on production and consumption, singularly lacks the proper means to fix the floating imaginations of its citizens on the majesty of the collective project. To be sure, the founder had had a vague daydream about rebuilding the Mormon temple for this purpose, but the heavens resolved the question of Icarian religion: the summer storms of 1850 brought the walls of the temple down at the feet of the workers in charge of rebuilding it. Much later, the spiritual heir of the Father, lawyer Mercadier, would again take up the question of diversions and Icarian "national festivals." He would see the organization of such festivals, "designed to maintain the moral barometer at a very high level," as a matter "far more serious than people might generally think."[60]

With or without theory, however, Icarian diversions would never manage to raise the barometer of community enthusiasm above the amiable lukewarmness of the entertainment offered one Sunday evening in winter and described by Bourg. There is a monologue by stationer Mahy in the guise of a janitor, and another by wool-sorter Legros on the "lamentations of a man of Champagne over the potato blight." Legros also sings a touching ballad (*Loin de sa mère*), and the *galop* from the ballet *Giselle* is danced. A vaudeville piece, "The Italian and the Bas-Breton," is presented in abridged form, shorn of anything that might "pervert or soil" the imaginations of little Icarians; in it Cabet's secretary, Lintilhac, and solicitor's

59. Collective letter of the Colony, *Le Populaire*, Sept. 13, 1851.
60. *Nouvelle Revue icarienne*, Feb. 1, 1860.

clerk Olinet give the cue to comic Mahy. This Icarian theater—purged in advance of those passions, those forms of "veritable sentimental gastritis," of which the young and chaste colony has no need to "live, prosper, and have plenty of children"—hardly offers the proper dramatic tension to introduce the final crescendo of the Icarian *Chant du Départ*, the verses of which are sung as a solo by the durable Mahy. The chorus of the *Seasons* sung by the little girls, the sol–fa rendition of the march of *Moses* by the little boys, and the report of the school surveillance committee surely augur for the next generation more worthy spectacles to accompany the march to the desert by the soldiers of Humanity.[61] For it is these pupils of the Icarian school whom one is counting on to establish Icaria, more than on the forty-year-olds, who are too deeply impregnated with the "habits of the old world" and daily exposed to the "Jesuitical" seductions of the individualistic world they traverse to reach the river, the mill, the fields, the wash-house, and elsewhere.

The task of the Icarian school involves correcting the children's first education, which is tainted with "the excessive indulgence parents habitually show toward their children." If the school is to be effective, its work must not be undone every Sunday by the counter-education of mothers. For one of the most radical contradictions of Icarian regeneration is to be found in the interplay between the moral formation of the Icarians of the future and the family morality of today's colonists. The entire first stage of this regeneration involved inculcating the regularity of family duties as a replacement for the ambiguities of a certain kind of fraternity: the male fraternity of revolutionary workers who were "pleasure-seekers" and "sensualists," philosophers of the billiard table, cabaret democrats, and conspirators in secret societies. Icarian fraternity is not the fraternity of the strong, the initiated, or the emancipated. Its underlying dedication is meant to link the concern of the strong for the weak with the decency of family ways: "The first duty incumbent on an Icarian is thoughtful dedication to the cause of Women, Children, the People, and Humanity."[62] This specific dedication to women and children and the banning of celibacy are present from the start in the "Requirements for Admission," stipulations and commentary on them growing with the passage of years and disillusionment. The male folly of the Texas vanguard and its brothers-in-arms seemed to be a practical verification of the basic principles of Icarian morality. But when the community of 260 members who had survived the

61. Bourg, "Une soirée de dimanche en Icarie," *Le Populaire*, March 3, 1850.
62. *Réalisation de la Communauté d'Icarie*, p. 235.

dissidence provoked by the Texas failure, and were just settling down in Nauvoo, became the victim of a new disagreement, a unanimous chorus of voices blamed the women for it: "Up to this very day the bachelors generally have proved themselves to be the most persevering. . . . The problem of desertions has come only from women in our midst who were not Icarians in dress, work, or food."[63] And after the third dissidence in autumn 1850, led by the young lady Naegelin whom Cabet's foresight had just married off to the ardent and melancholic Chevillon from Lyons, Cabet himself confirms the diagnosis: "Ninety percent of the disagreements have been caused by women who have come without conviction, without fixed ideas or with false ideas, and only to follow their husband, as if this were merely an outing in the country."[64]

From now on, throughout the course of Icaria's history, women will be accused of sapping the fraternal morality of the colony in two ways. First of all, they reintroduce the distinctions of station that were supposed to be eliminated by Icarian equality in dress, lodging, food, and work:

> They felt humiliated when they wore their silk dresses, their taffeta aprons, their ruffles, their flowery hats, and their parasols. They thought that in mid-summer, 7:00 A.M. was too early to begin the workday so as to finish at 6:00 P.M. They complained that we were always eating beef. They felt humiliated when they were with a hard-working sister who washed all our linen and was dressed more simply than they. . . . And when a holiday was coming and it was decided that all the men would wear tunics, the next day they would say ironically: how nice our men will look in tattered tunics.[65]

Even more than the guardian of social prerogatives, however, the female shows up as the driving force behind "individualism." The problem stems less than the comfortable habits of "rich" Icarians than from the very logic of marriages contracted with a view to family emancipation and social advancement. One widow willingly accepts living conditions to which she had not been accustomed: "Madame Lorieul, who not only is now without the care and cajolery of her maid but actually cajoles and cares for others, since she is the nurse . . . is quite surprised to find that she no longer suf-

63. Letters of Witzig, *Le Populaire*, Sept. 2, 1849; Madame Chartre, Sept. 23, 1849, in *Réalisation d'Icarie*, p. 85; and Camus, ibid., p. 86.

64. *Le Populaire*, Jan. 31, 1851.

65. Letter of Camus, in *Réalisation d'Icarie*, p. 86.

fers from the little indispositions that, for want of anything better, varied her ever so slightly lazy life in Beaune."[66] On the other hand, a former maid is quick to turn away from the community the new husband whose unstable disposition she was supposed to firm up. So, with great regret, Citizen Barelle had to leave the colony: "His wife, who had been a servant in a good house in France and left it to marry and get away, did not like either community life or work in the fields."[67]

In the long run, however, Icarian fraternity is even more threatened by those women who adapt to community life in their own way. Such are the women who bring little Icarians into the world all the more generously because pregnancy and nursing dispense them from communal labor in the workshop; who readily entrust their children to the Icarian school but take advantage of Sunday reunions to inculcate in them a family sense very different from that of the Father of the community. The mothers may offer their children toys made by their husbands with community wood. They may prepare their little girls for their future as wives by giving them a taste for "their toilette, corsets, and curls" and prompting them to dream of the future marriages that the rule commands but that need not be anticipated in imagination. Worst of all, they may foster in them the practice of secrecy, which is always associated with the taste for pleasures. Consider the mother whose daughter had been punished for an infraction at school. The girl had promised not to eat the Sunday fritters. The mother urges her to break her promise with these words: "Oh, you ninny, you simpleton, take one, eat one, no one will know a thing."[68] That is a fine lesson for a mother to teach her daughter, comments Cabet: "You can go far with one 'no one will know a thing.'" Indeed, they go so far as to destroy the glass house of community by taking opposite roads and ending up with the very principle that the moral and familial communism of Cabet was meant to serve as a bulwark against: the materialism of revolutionary communists, men of pleasure and secret societies.

Isn't that an inescapable consequence of the inconsistency that seeks to ground communism on the egotistical cell of the family? The contradiction certainly lies at the very core of the Icarian enterprise, but the reality cannot be reduced to this dialectical reversal or to the interpretation that turns feminine egotism into the solvent of community. It is certainly true that young Madame Chevillon was behind the dissidence of

66. "Extrait du journal de P. Bourg," in *Icarie*, Paris, 1849, p. 5.
67. *Le Populaire*, Oct. 18, 1850.
68. *Revue icarienne*, Jan. 1856.

1850, for example. And considerations of social station may well not have been alien to this daughter of an educated printer whose revolutionary and then Icarian choices were certainly never motivated by poverty. She did not marry her intelligent proletarian, son of a small manufacturer in Lyons, to be the companion of an Icarian wagoner. But she is also the one who had been put in charge of the Icarian education that, in a few months, had repaired the maternal damages done to the education of little girls. If she became a dissident, it was on behalf of the enlightened Icarian women who would like to force the president of Icaria to follow through with a logic that claims to promote women, and to declare them "voters and eligible for all public offices, even for the management."[69]

As for the dissidence of 1849, all the trouble allegedly stemming "from women alone," the explanation would seem to be less simplistic. The accusation brought against Cabet of confiscating trousseaus, separating households, and forbidding parents to talk to their children could be a more specific expression of female and family rancors. But the prohibition of Raspail's medicine, a popular medicine to which Cabet preferred "the meticulous system of homeopathy," was of equal concern to both sexes. And the protest raised against the "disarmament" of men deprived of the pleasure of the hunt well expresses the other "egotism" against which the founder wages his most dogged war: the male "sensualism" of revolutionaries steadfastly attached, even in the peaceful and hard-working framework of the community, to unproductive pleasures and secret adventures involving the real and symbolic possession of a gun. Finally, the most basic grievances have to do with the system of intellectual policing by means of which Cabet wages the struggle of the fraternal principle against both forms of "egotism": the "cellular system," which forbids them to talk to inhabitants of Nauvoo; the "collective" letters signed under "dictatorial pressure"; and the "reports made against one another" to ensure the "publicity" that is indispensable to Icarian transparency.[70]

The dynamics of Icarian conflict, of its shifting alliances, will become clear in the relationship between these three real and imaginary terms: the egotism of aristocratic distinctions, the sensualism of revolutionary workers, and the system of fraternal police. Every party, at every moment in the life of the community, will unfurl one and the same flag: that of the fight against egotism. But each time the whole problem will lie in

69. Cabet to Krolikowski, in Prudhommeaux, *Icarie et son fondateur Étienne Cabet*, Paris, 1907, p. 274.

70. *La Voix du peuple*, April 17, 1850.

recognizing the source and emblems of egotism. The long conflict leading in 1856 to the revolt of the majority and the exclusion of the Father
will be a conflict between two interpretations of egotism, two images of
the fight against individualism. The fight of Cabet's opponents will be
carried out in the name of a certain representation of the egotist menace:
the setting up of a new aristocracy of bureaucrats and bourgeoisie. Over
against that they will introduce the opposition of the producer to the idler,
choosing their emblems in the realm of dress and delighting in the pose
of the untidy worker and in denunciations of aristocratic toilettes. In this
display Cabet will recognize the very shape of egotism against which he
has waged war so long: that of the "sensualist" worker sacrificing the
sweet pleasures of fraternity to egotistical affirmation of his vanity as a
"free" worker, devotee of the individualistic pleasures of tobacco, whiskey, and the hunt. The whole rhetoric of Icarian conflicts is played out
as the representation of egotism slides back and forth between these two
poles. When, for example, the loyal Prudent has become the head of the
parricidal opposition, Cabet will strive in vain to remind him of his 1852
letters in which he pleaded with the Father of the community to come
back quickly to put an end to deviations; in vain will Cabet denounce
his alliance with the hardheads and the devotees of tobacco and the hunt,
with whom he had had a bone to pick not so long ago. A reply of the
anti-Cabet majority will set things straight about the famous "laxity" that
supposedly gave free rein to the sensualism of hunters and smokers while
Cabet was away: "But what and where exactly was this laxity? In toler-
ating scandalous vices? No. . . . It had to do specifically with a matter of
grooming."[71]

No confusion, then. In Prudent's tenacious defense of orthodoxy, in
his dietary economies that turned Icarian meals into "fasts," in his diatribes against the women who "wanted to resemble mares rigged out
in harness," and in his emulation of a general when he said he would
"not count the dead on the battlefield,"[72] we can already recognize the
rudiments of his future alliance with his one-time adversaries, the "partisans of unlimited liberty, absolute equality, and an independence to the
point of license."[73] Those partisans would be the "sensualist" workers:
cabinetmaker Mathieu, employed in making wheels and clapboard; tailor
Labrunerie, potter turned cooper and busy worker in the mobile work-

71. *Revue icarienne*, July 1856.
72. Ibid., April 1856.
73. Étienne Cabet, *Colonie icarienne aux États-Unis d'Amérique: sa constitution, ses
lois, sa situation matérielle et morale après le premier semestre de 1855*, Paris, 1856, p. 210.

shops of the woodcutters and clapboard-makers; his colleague Surbled, who also shifted from the peaceable trade of tailor to the rugged labors of the gardeners, woodcutters, and miners; and all those who, like them, abandon their sedentary trade to the weak, the "devoted," and the "stool pigeons" whose workshops adjoin the administration offices and the refectory from which one should not be too far away if one wants one's sure share of the community manna—all those who choose the rugged labors and adventurous life of the fields, the islands, or the flatboat to regain both the free air of individualism and the sense of communist solidarity. This choice already indicates the broad lines of the future alliance between their "sensualism" and the rigidness of the Icarian worker élite: serious and enterprising workers like joiner Gérard, an able farmer and good administrator, carpenter Ferrandon and wheelwright Cotteron, organizers of the rugged work of the crews in charge of cutting down and cleaving wood; the doctrinaires and bureaucrats of the Icarian old guard: jeweler Prudent, tailor Favard (brother of Cabet's deceased son-in-law), and teacher and Spanish revolutionary Montaldo.

The sentiment that they feel differently today, but that will unite them tomorrow, is that they are the "true Icarians." They are the ones who have burned their "boats" and "bridges" to the old world: cashing in their assets and giving them honestly to the community; abandoning a relatively satisfactory position in France; in America, changing the trade they had learned for the rugged works that ensure the material life of the community. They are the ones who feel that they embody Icarian faith and practice, like another old Icarian and old dissident, weaver Therme, who survived the first vanguard and shifted from the tranquillity of the pharmacy to the labors of the coopers and woodcutters: "I have reached the point where it would be impossible to work for myself personally. I am convinced that if I were to go back to the old world, even if I had every imaginable means to become rich, it would be impossible for me to do so. . . . I am a communist by nature and temperament. I could not be anything else."[74]

Above and beyond their conflicts, all those people are united against *the others:* the "false Icarians," driven by poverty and with nothing to lose, who came to enjoy rather than to build, and who left again clinging to who knows what plank of illusory salvation; the communists in their own imagination, who do not resolve to leave France and burn their boats but think that their propaganda work and their subscriptions for the colony

74. Therme, the eldest son, to his brothers, *Le Populaire*, Aug. 5, 1851.

give them the right to advise their brothers in Nauvoo; the amateurs and "aristocrats" who come to "give the community a try," all the more readily in that they are no longer asked to burn their boats. For the *Law of April 1850,* imposed by Cabet on a reticent community, permits the new arrivals, upon withdrawal, to take back 80 percent of their contribution; whereas the earlier members had surrendered their entire contribution to the society. The new rule encourages the coming of the irresolute people mentioned in Prudent's diatribe, where he bade the Parisian official in charge of departures to dissuade such people from seeking the American mirage. So the symbolic combat that will forge the first alliance between the guardians of orthodoxy and the ringleaders of dissidence will be the fight for the abrogation of the *April Law.* In their minds the law creates two classes in Icaria; and it transforms the old members, the soldiers of the vanguards and the great departures of 1848, who "burned their boats," into slaves or servants entrusted with the task of "washing the dirty linen" of the new arrivals (privileged people, bourgeois, aristocrats). The new arrivals come without burning their bridges behind them and enjoy the benefit of satisfying options: if they don't *like* it in the colony, they can take back most of their contribution; if they do like it, they can display all their finery and try to win a place in line with their capabilities.

So when President Cabet returns in 1852, he finds his lieutenants Prudent and Favard in agreement with the partisans of "unlimited liberty" and "absolute equality." But he has little trouble in unmasking the egotistical calculus behind their parade of communist orthodoxy. After all, what was the aim of the *April Law?* By easing the *material* conditions for admission, it sought to revitalize a propaganda adversely affected by the disappointments of the first two years and by the deteriorating situation in France itself, and thus to encourage contributions in the form of men and capital that would enable them to undertake the great project, the founding of Icaria in the desert. In asking for the abrogation of this law in the name of equality, the critics are doing nothing less than undermining promotional efforts and the means to build Icaria. And why should they want to kill Icaria in this way, if not out of an egotistical desire to divide its spoils?

It all fits together. The rigor with which the orthodox Prudent and Favard push for the departure of "hundreds" of Icarians, arguing that one must deal with the evil and "root out all the habits, all the defects, everything . . . incompatible with communitarian life,"[75] has the same objective as the demagogy that commands the "rich" to "burn their boats" and the

75. Prudent to Beluze, Cabet Archives, Amsterdam.

sensual appetite that, under the appearance of great community works, goes away to hide its vices and concoct its intrigues far from the gaze of the administration. The aim of refusing to refund contributions is to increase the community portion; and the aim of forcing as many colonists as possible to leave, especially the rich ones, is to reduce the number of those who have a right to a share. And what lies behind this desire for sharing if not appetites that have been whetted, in the Father's absence, by indulgence toward hunting, tobacco, and whiskey? Thus the unnatural alliance of rigorist bureaucrats, hard workers, and revolutionary pleasure-seekers avows its logic and its purpose: to dissolve the great community and keep the money of all those driven out; to get rid of the widows, orphans, old people, and disabled, who burden the colony with the weight of fraternity; to share out the spoils and "live in individualism or in small private associations."[76] The latter would be egotistical associations of workers laboring hard but on their own hours and for themselves alone, proscribing the hierarchy of directors and directed, the luxuries of bourgeois comfort, and aristocratic distinctions, but devoted to the coarse sensual pleasures of tobacco, whiskey, and the hunt; "individualistic communities" already prefigured in the little republics—the little secret societies—of the mobile workshops of the woodcutters and miners, on the fields several leagues away where the farmers spend the busy season together, on the flatboat that spends its week between Nauvoo, the islands, and Keokuk, and at the mill, the distillery, and the nearby house that had to be rented to lodge their workers during peak periods, when they work day and night.

So it all fits together. And the high-sounding words of Citizen Prudent ("burning one's boats," "burning one's bridges," "sword of Damocles," serfs, slaves, bourgeois, aristocrats, privileged . . .) are incapable of disguising the individualism that is contaminating the fraternal morality of communism through the roundabout pathways of worker pride or doctrinal purity. It is no accident then that between the battle over the *April Law* won by Cabet in 1852 and the great Icarian crisis of 1855–1856 lost by him, the essential battle in the life of the community centers on the "moral reform" of November 1853.[77]

The ensemble of thirty-seven points submitted to the general assembly by Cabet clearly brings out the link, and the order of priorities, between the productive progress of the colony—preparing to immigrate to the "desert" of Iowa, where it has just bought land and sent its first detach-

76. Cabet, *Colonie icarienne aux États-Unis*, p. 210.
77. *Colonie icarienne: Réforme icarienne du 21 nov. 1853*, Paris, 1853.

ments—and the reform of individual colonists. To be sure, Articles 34 and 35, calling for better-chosen workshop bosses to watch over, direct, and report more completely on the work done, are adopted unanimously. But one would be surprised to find them near the end of the list, coming after Article 33, which calls for the embellishment of the common room and the maintenance of the grass and flowers on the walkway, if one did not realize that these material improvements are strict consequences of the moral principles in preceding articles: affirmation of an Icarian religion (Article 29; six opposed); need for an Icarian course of lectures to teach Icarian principles, and obligatory attendance at the course (Article 24; unanimous); prohibition of criticisms outside the constitutional framework of the general assembly (Articles 25 and 26; unanimous out of respect for the Constitution); devotion to the women and children, and observation of the proprieties required to further respect for the former and the education of the latter (Articles 3 and 28). But the major matter and the core of the reform are Articles 9 to 22. Articles 9 to 11 prohibit the use of whiskey, except as strictly regulated by the general assembly (unanimous out of respect for the general assembly). Article 22 prohibits hunting and fishing *as pleasures* and meets the full complement of opponents (twenty-eight). And, above all, Articles 12 to 22, opposed by seventeen who cannot be swayed, lay down minute details about refusing admission to smokers and the circumstances of time and place when the pipe and chewing tobacco may be tolerated in the case of old members who claim that they "cannot break the habit." For the question of principle far outweighs the reckoning of the material damages imputed to hunting and tobacco:

> My opinion, my conviction is . . . that the use of tobacco is unnecessary . . . pointless, expensive, harmful to health, dangerous, senseless, etc.
>
> More serious still, I am convinced that it is detrimental, not only to work, but also to study, learning, moralization. . . . I am convinced that it fosters sensualism, materialism, egotism, and that it extinguishes the sentiments of dedication and fraternity as well as the ideas of duty and mission. I am convinced that tobacco, in its effects, is the destruction of our Icarian doctrine, that it paves the way for the violation of all our principles, that it is essentially and eminently anti-Icarian, and that it will lead our community to ruin without fail.
>
> For me, then, the issue of tobacco takes in all the other issues. . . . In our system of Icarian community, everything fits together,

is connected and complementary. All the indicated conditions are necessary. With the abuse of tobacco, all sorts of abuses will follow. With reform of tobacco, all the other reforms will become easy. Without that reform, no other reform is possible.[78]

It all fits together, of course, but how is it that the question of tobacco could be the keystone of the community arch? And how can we determine or appreciate what goes back to the analysis of "egotism" (tobacco, sensualist enjoyment within the worker's scope . . .), what follows from the principle of obedience to their Father (versus the defiance of his authority and the specific insult to him, since he is bothered by tobacco smoke, the noise of loud conversations, and the noise of slammed doors), and what has to do with the taste for secrecy, which needs to be forbidden to be practiced? But behind the paternal fancy linked to the question of tobacco, there is also a perfectly down-to-earth conception of the buildup of communism, even though the touchiness of his proletarian children obliges their Father to present it in ambiguous terms:

We need to increase our number, since we want to form a People. We need men who will bring us not only their arms, but also all sorts of talents and money! But how might we be able to propagandize effectively? There are rich men and women, sympathetic to the cause of the People and Progress, disposed to sacrifice everything to join up with sober and thrifty workers, imbued with the sentiment of human dignity, fraternal, refined, clean, etc., etc. But how can we induce them to leave their homeland, cross the ocean, brave dangers and hardships, to come into the midst of a sensualist and egotistical people, smoking and chewing tobacco, etc., etc.?[79]

Clearly it is not the unbridled sensualism embodied in the use of tobacco that threatens to repel these people "sympathetic to the cause of the People and Progress." Rather, it is the odor of the pipe and the dirty face and beard of tobacco-chewing workers, who are probably brawlers as well, ill-dressed, and lacking in manners toward ladies. That is also why the issue of tobacco is linked to the matter of embellishing the common house, planting grass on the esplanade, tending flowers, deco-

78. Étienne Cabet, *Tempérance*; cited in *Lettres icariennes*, I, 63–64.
79. Ibid., p. 63.

rating the refectory, putting oilcloths on its rough-hewn tables, and replacing the wrought-iron dinnerware ("which looks black even when it
is clean")[80] with crockery. For this flirtatious "propagandizing through
the eyes" should combine with the reform of proletarian habits to attract
abilities and capital sums "sympathetic to the Cause of the People" and
indispensable for the building of Icaria.

The battle over the definition of egotism is, in fact, a conflict over the
course of the Icarian political economy as well. The "hard" workers, led by
the industrious joiner, farmer, and administrator Gérard, challenge Cabet's
economic competence, denounce the burden imposed by incompetent and
unproductive people, propose the creation of new industrial enterprises,
and envisage forms of competition at work. But Cabet sticks to a simple
economic principle: capital is needed to create enterprises. And so, in the
face of disappointing results, the balance-sheets of community activity
published under Cabet's responsibility tend to put less and less emphasis
on persevering effort and solidarity in trying ordeals, and more and more
emphasis on the limits of what can be done without capital. Thus, the
account of workshop activities in September 1855 stresses that "almost all
the workshops are in their infancy."[81] Improvements at the mill and the
distillery would require large expenditures, and fairly large sums would be
needed for grain purchases. For Icarian agriculture continues to operate
under precarious conditions—rented lands far removed from headquarters
and habituating their workers to individual living. It would take money
to remedy that situation. As for livestock, the colony so far has been limited to what was "strictly necessary." It has only 14 horses and 25 oxen
for plowing and transport; 400 to 500 pigs providing menus that are a
bit monotonous; and some 20 fine cows, whose 80 to 140 liters of milk
obviously cannot feed the 500 community members and assure them milk
with their morning coffee, one of the main Icarian frustrations. The cow-
sheds leave much to be desired also, because they would require large
expenditures "of money or time." New sources of income would also have
to be found by establishing "some large and lucrative industry"; but "large
sums of capital are needed to create big industries." The Icarian desert in
Iowa is now inhabited by fifty-seven pioneers, and it is hoped that construction of the first Icarian town will begin in the spring. Its hygienic

80. *Progrès de la Colonie icarienne établie à Nauvoo: M. Cabet à Julien, Icarien disposé
à venir en Icarie*, Paris, 1854, p. 16.
81. *Revue icarienne*, Sept. 1855.

lodgings will be laid out diagonally vis-à-vis the cardinal points, but obviously "the complete and definitive transfer will necessarily take time and a great deal of money."

The conditions for building Icaria are clear, then. It is sheer folly or treacherous calculation on the part of the supposed guardians of communist doctrine and laborers in the major Icarian enterprises to want to create a new and ridiculous "aristocracy of strong arms," to set up a party of "strong men" or workers in opposition to "new people," "bourgeois people," "intellectuals," and "aristocrats."[82] The primacy of production can only mean the primacy of capital. But capital goes only where it finds disciplined and orderly work. And it must be put to work by talented men, such as those who gradually gather around Cabet and replace the proletarians of the old guard: the American Émile Baxter, son of a Saint-Quentin manufacturer and experienced in all sorts of business matters, who does his best to persuade one of his friends, a prosperous manufacturer and unwitting communist, to contribute his expertise and his capital to the colony;[83] farmer Haymart, once a soldier in Africa, who returned from military service to learn agronomy and transform his lands into a model estate; the Raynaud family (father Raynaud, a democratic proprietor victimized by repression, contributes properties worth 20,000 francs to the cause, his wife takes over the school for little girls that was the haunt of dissidents not long ago, and their son is the best hope of the school for boys); the accounting expert Dujardin; and lawyer Mercadier, a man of action as well as of learning and eloquence.

In the spelling out of the two preconditions for the project, time and money, the workers should readily recognize their portion. It is that of time—that is, hard work and patience. If capital is to come and be put to work, the colony must have decent, first-rate workers who do not repel persons sympathetic to the people's cause; Icarians who give up their vanity as proletarians or communist veterans to give a fraternal welcome to men of ability; disciplined workers who leave it to capital and talent to prepare the great project and contribute the effort that depends on them. And they will do this by allowing themselves to be organized as need and competence require; by devoting themselves to work without wasting time in chatting or criticizing; by husbanding materials, keeping tools in good

82. Cabet, *Colonie icarienne aux États-Unis*, p. 216.
83. Émile Baxter to Cabet, Sept. 17, 1854, *Icarian Studies Newsletter*, Macomb, Illinois, March 1979.

392 THE CHRISTIAN HERCULES

repair, and preserving their labor power from the perils of tobacco, whiskey, and hunting. So what is required of them is something very different from the disorder created in the workshops by the self-styled partisans of industrial enterprises: "Some have arranged their shops as they felt like it . . . placing men of the same opinions together. . . . A worker leaves his shop to go to another, refuses the assigned task, refuses to give back his tools, or breaks them to get out of a job he doesn't like."[84] Not to mention the peculiar practices of those strange partisans of industry who, like joiner Chartre, in charge of the sawmill, break their tools to force the management to modernize the plant.

So it all fits together in the building of Icaria and in the primacy of the "fraternity" that governs it. The preconditions for economic growth, the moralization of the workers, and the means of propaganda dovetail, as we learn from the task of embellishing the refectory that is prescribed in Article 33. They will have to wait a bit for the crockery. But already painter Schroeder, himself a bit of a dissident nonetheless, is at work decorating its walls with inscriptions that combine the esthetic requirements of "propaganda through the eyes" with lessons suited to reviving the communist morality and fraternal discipline of the Icarian workers:

You must plow and sow
before
you reap.

The era of foundation
of labor and fatigue
is not
the era of enjoyment and repose.

There is no fruitful work without organization
without order
without direction and discipline.

License and anarchy
are the enemies
of liberty.

The aristocracy of muscles
would not be fairer
than the aristocracy of birth.

84. *Revue icarienne*, Jan. 1856.

Man is not nourished
by bread alone,
but also by doctrine.

Don't say:
Let no one say anything
so that all ills may be hidden.
Say, rather:
Let everyone say everything
So that no ill may be unknown.[85]

But there may be a less winning reason why the maxims of the Icarian course of lectures must be painted in multicolored letters on all the walls of the common room. It is that the Icarian course is impossible to hold. This is not a new situation. From the very start, the very conditions that make the course indispensable also make it impracticable. The course of lessons is designed to teach the principles of Icarian fraternity to those not literate enough to read the works of the founder, and to recall them to those who are letting themselves be corrupted by habits inherited from the old world. And it has a very specific purpose: to promote the unity of thought required for unity of action, to ensure that all speak, write, and act "as one human being with one single heart." But for the course to produce this unanimity, there must already be unanimity on the principle that it be held and that attendance be obligatory: "Everyone must attend; otherwise, its purpose will not be achieved."[86] It is also necessary that no conflict in the community prevent the founder from devoting himself to the preparation of the course. But, alas, that is what has kept arising. Planned before the departure, the course could not be held in the first three years because of difficulties and disagreements. When it had just started, it was interrupted in January 1851 by Cabet's trip to France. Article 24 of the Reform of November 1853 called for the resumption of the course and obligatory attendance. Unfortunately, it had to be stopped at the end of three months because the opposing party had found ways to directly counter its whole purpose:

To those who asked them, "Aren't you going to the course?" they replied: "No, I prefer to smoke my pipe rather than go to hear a

85. Fernand Rude (ed.), *Voyage en Icarie de deux ouvriers viennois*, Paris, 1952, pp. 257–66.
86. *Revue icarienne*, Jan. 1856.

sermon." Or: "I have already heard that humbug a hundred times." When they attended, they assumed a mocking air and tried to distract the attention of those around them with coarse jokes.[87]

The attitude of these opponents lays bare the futility of a discourse on fraternity whose whole effect was played out in the staged unanimity surrounding endorsement of the idea. It does not even take hostile talk to ruin it. All it takes is the silent opposition of one of the "lost children" who "affects to read a newspaper" during a ceremony in which the president is laboring to give a talk on fraternity.[88]

And, indeed, what might these opponents learn about the subject that is new? These are men who now have behind them ten or fifteen years of communist militancy and Icarian teaching: former lieutenants Favard and Prudent; clerk Marchand, a survivor of the first vanguard; Busque, former editor of *Le Travail* in Lyons; glover Mourot and cabinetmaker Mousseron, who regularly attended meetings on Rue Jean-Jacques Rousseau; Montaldo the Spaniard, who was propagating the doctrine in Barcelona before 1848. The operative fraternity now is their fraternity, but of course it is a "false" fraternity of partisan hiring, of vices they agree to conceal, of conspiracies plotted in silence. It is the fraternity of materialist communists and secret societies that has found its leader in glover Mourot, who was undoubtedly sent by the enemy to ruin Icaria. In France he was a devoted reader of the individualistic and anarchistic Proudhon, although no one knows exactly where he "found time to study him so thoroughly," and he is always ready to outdo the master in using words "beyond the understanding of the workers."[89] An active, intelligent, and daring man, he could certainly have been a "distinguished man" if he had followed the path of duty; but he was "a pleasure-seeking sensualist and rake, with a passion for billiards, etc., hence not much of a worker . . . and therefore inclined to secret societies, riots, and insurrection."[90] He had thrown himself into the June insurrection and found himself (by chance?) at the Fontainebleau barrier where General Bréa was assassinated, a deed from which he was exonerated (again by chance?). Then he came to carry out his Jesuitical mission in this community, his first act being to ravish, before the eyes of his wife, the female companion of the friend who had paid for his passage.

87. *Lettres icariennes*, I, 65.
88. Cabet, *Colonie icarienne aux États-Unis*, p. 211.
89. Nadaud to Mourot, *Revue icarienne*, July 1856.
90. Étienne Cabet, *Guerre de l'opposition contre le citoyen Cabet*, Paris, 1856, p. 47.

Futile, too, are these shocking revelations, which the sole publisher and editor of the *Revue icarienne* uses to illustrate the principle of publicity that is the soul of communitarian life. They can only reinforce the alliance of workers and pleasure-seekers, of dissidents and orthodox, in the "little private associations" where the opposition maneuvers to isolate or exclude the "devoted" followers of M. Cabet. In the isolated shops of the mill, the distillery, and the sawmill, the former co-director of the community, Favard, and the former manager of *Le Populaire*, merchant Caudron from Rouen, have joined up with long-time dissident Chartre; there they all put up with the excessive drinking of former tailor Pfund and former shoemaker Sterck. In the coopering shop Prudent has joined up with long-time dissidents Therme and Labrunerie, the "sensualist" Biton, a determined opponent of the Reform, and the two sons of the former shoemaker and philosopher of Orsay, Vallet, who himself resolved to persevere in his vice of smoking after Cabet called smokers "pigs." On the flatboat former director Montaldo comes to an understanding with the dissidents and drinkers: tailor Borremans, weaver Richard, shoemaker Voiturier, and marble-cutter Riondel. In the mobile workshops carpenter Ferrandon and wheelwrights Mathieu and Cotteron first seek a handshake from cooper Biton, dissidents Therme, Surbled, and Labrunerie, and even the "Bohemian Jew" Katz, famous and despised not long ago for his laziness.

All of them are now beyond the reach of fraternal discourse and paternal admonitions, solidly encamped in the bastions where the party of the "strong," the "Hercules," the "reds," the "oldtimers," and the "revolutionaries" encircles and isolates—in a division as imaginary as it is real—the party of the "devoted" encamped at the center of the colony. That party includes the administrators and "aristocrats" Raynaud, Baxter, Haymart, and Dujardin; the fine talkers like Mercadier, lawyer and Gascon; the "stool pigeons" who, like pork-butcher Romanoff and weaver Bégou, report the refectory conversations and refrains of the opponents; the "weak" workers of the sedentary workshops (shoemakers, tailors, and joiners); the infirm, like tailor Wocquefen, a survivor on crutches of the first vanguard, now posted to the infirmary; the old men, like Clèdes from Toulouse, who is employed in the refectory, and Coëffé from Vienne, who is in charge of distribution; and other faithful who can no more be armed by the litany of lectures on morality and fraternity than can the opponents be disarmed by it.

So it is a closed circle of education from now on. Failing to give the course, the Father of the community can keep printing and commenting indefinitely on the forty-eight conditions for admission in the *Revue icari-*

enne and various brochures. He can show once again how the fraternal principles are being violated: by the men who smoke in the workshops, break their tools, voice criticisms outside the general assembly, use community wood to make toys for their children, consume sixteen liters of whiskey in six days to make peach salad, and go so far as to break window panes to get at their favorite beverage; by the women who refuse to turn in their jewels, squeeze the waists of their little daughters into corsets to the point of suffocating them, wage war on the school regulation forbidding the curling and braiding of hair, and sometimes go so far as to kill their children with indigestion while complaining about Icaria's meager fare; by the little boys who are determined to eat unripe fruit, the girls who write love letters and swallow them when one tries to take them away, the youngsters fresh out of school who talk disrespectfully to their elders; and by the old man who caused his own death by stuffing himself with melon during a cholera epidemic.[91] The very mixture of male, "revolutionary" forms of sensualism with female, "aristocratic" forms of egotism can only increase the dissident front and close the reformer, more than ever, in the circle of popular moralization:

> The more miserable the people are by virtue of their ignorance, inexperience, and blindness, the more resolved I am to persevere in my dedication; because I say to myself that the unhappiness of Humanity will be perpetual unless someone has the courage to dedicate himself to putting an end to it by a better organization of society.[92]

But to put an end to the ignorance and blindness of the Icarian people, one must eliminate the obstacles to the necessary education that are being placed by the people or, rather, by the "party" corrupting them. The last commentary on the forty-eight conditions for admission clearly points up the means to escape the circle. The first condition is that one be thoroughly acquainted with the Icarian system, which presupposes the reopening of the course of lectures: "But for that it is absolutely necessary that I have more authority and no opposition."[93] The seventh condition is respect for fraternity, which is the soul of the community: "But to give fraternal feelings the force and charm that are properly theirs will require efforts

91. *Revue icarienne*, Jan. 1856; and Cabet, *Colonie icarienne aux États-Unis*, pp. 170–203.

92. Cabet, *Colonie icarienne aux États-Unis*, p. 213.

93. *Revue icarienne*, Jan. 1856.

and means involving great power in the management of the Society."
The eighth condition forbids members to abuse one another: "But the old
habits of the old world could gravely trouble the Society if the guardian of
public peace did not have the authority needed to wipe out forever these
remnants of barbarism." In short, there must be a quick return to the principles of Icarian fraternity: "But how is this to be done? By combining
the persuasion of the Icarian course with the firmness and vigilance of a
more empowered administration." No fraternity without education, and
no education without the authority needed to compel the rebels to submit
or resign. What claims to be a republic of work must be brought back to
its true source: the paternal dictatorship of love. One must save this Icaria,
which does not belong to the shareholders of Nauvoo but to the cause of
Humanity: "Icaria no longer exists today; hence I must resurrect it."[94]

It is a call for the return of Icarian authority to the man who rightfully
incarnates its full legitimacy: its founder. In the 1847 *Charter of the Society*
he had written, in the interest of frankness, that the official manager for
the ten years of transition would be M. Cabet. But after the second dissidence he had thought it wise to propose the bastard government that
ever since has had the doctrinal legitimacy of the Father's authority existing alongside the democratic and formal republic of associated workers.
Under this multiple management, the president and his five co-directors
submit to the voting of the general assembly. The only difference, unwritten but obvious, is that the five other managers submit to the choice
of their brothers, whereas the president has the legitimacy of his paternal
authority confirmed by the unanimous acknowledgment of his children.
In December 1855 Cabet denounces this double authority. He asks for a
presidential term of four years. He wants "supreme authority over everything having to do with education, the distribution of accommodations,
the distribution of workers in the workshops, and the makeup of those
workshops." Workshop directors or administrators are to be appointed to
deal more specifically with financial matters. And committees are to be
appointed to oversee the fulfillment of the rules and regulations and ensure "decency, propriety, simplicity, order, carefulness, thriftiness . . . and
the health of the children at the time of their arrival."[95]

This is an attempted coup d'état by Cabet; and his opponents, used
to taking up arms against monarchical ordinances, rise up against it, all
the more successfully since he lacks the material means to carry it out.

94. Cabet, *Guerre de l'opposition*, p. 14.
95. Cabet, *Colonie icarienne aux États-Unis*, pp. 228-29.

Faced with an opposition arrayed in the insignia of the defense of the Constitution, Cabet's paternal authority has no recourse except to Icarian public opinion. But the latter is powerless because it has allowed its unanimity to be impaired by the scheming of one party. The "Cabet coup d'état" permits the two parties to mimic the great sessions of the revolutionary assemblies in their Nauvoo meetings between December 1855 and May 1856. But its main effect is to reveal the Father's authority in all its nakedness and bring its majesty down to the bourgeois level of the vaudevilles and dramas so dear to the unpolished Icarian theater. In the terrible nighttime session of May 12, 1856, that saw his dethronement, it is not surprising that Cabet should take particular note of the comment by Favard, the same man who once recommended that the workers be governed with an iron rod: "Our President no longer wants the Constitution! He wants to govern as an absolute Master, as a Papa, a veritable papa! . . . A patriarch is not what we need."[96] Cabet undoubtedly has some right to be astonished that the speaker should try to evoke ridicule "with the words *Papa* and *patriarch*," a tack all the more unbecoming in the mouth of the brother of his son-in-law. But in this parricide, which he will denounce from that night in May when the majority of his children strip him of his authority to the November night when he will die far from the colony with his still-loyal children around him, are we not to see something other than a mere settling of family accounts? Namely, the end of the time when worker dreams of another world could recognize themselves in the offer of love made by those men who sacrifice their fortune and social position to the cause of the people? The end of the time when the verse of Saint Matthew's Gospel bidding the master to be the servant of all implied a reciprocal acknowledgment accepted by the most ardent republicans and communists: that is, that authority belonged rightfully to those who had the most to lose and were therefore making the greatest sacrifice?

This logic was evident to all, once upon a time. Today Cabet breathlessly tries to recall it to engraver Lafaix, who had once been an apologist for the "carefree" life of the colony and co-author of a letter of homage to Cabet, "who, as theoretician, has merited the title *Father of the People*." His lost son now talks about the courage shown by sedentary workers grappling with the tough work of farming and about men "used to a certain degree of comfort in their lives as individuals who have seen their loved ones die for want of a doctor." Cabet has a ready response:

96. Cabet, *Guerre de l'opposition*, p. 25.

For seven years he has sacrificed himself. . . . But did he do it for me or for himself? Was it not, as he said in his toast of February 3, 1855, for the certainty that when he would be sick, the community would take care of him, his wife, and his children, giving him the means to go out walking, cane in hand, like a fine bourgeois gentleman? And I also recall that when he might well have taken the opportunity to address a word of thanks to the head, who was sacrificing himself to procure for him such an enviable lot, he spoke only of the community. He had not a single word for the man who had spent his nights and days organizing things, who had sacrificed everything, fortune and family, to cross the ocean, braving all sorts of fatigues and dangers to ensure the happiness of his brothers.[97]

All these demonstrations are now taken the wrong way. The nights of paternal devotion are now nothing more than the spare-time activities of a lazy man and the sleepless nights of a despot seeking to amass dossiers and reports on his opponents and right now to organize a guard to protect himself from the parricides. They, for their part, "are sleeping peacefully in their beds after a day of hard work."[98] What about the alleged inequality of the sacrifice made by workers materially interested in improving their working-class lot on the one hand, and the man who spends himself solely for the welfare of the cause on the other? That is simply the haughty conceit of the philanthropist, who disparages the material situation and moral aspirations of his companions to get across his own merits:

> When Monsieur Cabet criticizes what he calls the opposition for not being worth a damn as compared with what he calls the bourgeois people, the men of insight and intelligence, that means he supposedly dragged us out of the depths of poverty in order to cover us with the shame of a black ingratitude.
> Let Monsieur Cabet give an account of our contributions, of our subscriptions and others. We shall see whether or not we were hard workers capable of creating our independence by our work.[99]

97. *Revue icarienne*, June 1856.
98. *Revue icarienne*, Feb. 1857; in Prudhommeaux, *Icarie et son fondateur Étienne Cabet*, p. 401.
99. "Réponse de la Communauté," *Revue icarienne*, July 1856.

To the man who now is nothing more than Monsieur Cabet, the redis-covered vanity of the "good" worker announces that the ages of love are past and gone.

The workers bid farewell to the friends of the People; the repetition of the great revolutionary scenes and the show of callused hands are revived in the pioneer pride of these "self-made men." Should we see this produc-tion as the prefiguration of the chants that will teach workers tomorrow that there is no supreme savior, that they must save themselves? Or is it possible that the murder itself is merely a substitute, that hating the Father is merely a disguised way of living the failure of the communitarian idea, of taking disgust for doctrinal fidelity still? Theirs is a disgust born of an accumulation of "little things" that have rubbed away at fraternal faith and worn it to shreds: bitterness at one's table mates for emptying the butter dish before it gets to the end of the table, then anger at the cooks who come up with a solution fit for children and cut the butter into equal shares before serving it; the humiliation of presenting requests for clothes to the committee, of being reproached for negligence and told how to be thrifty as clothes are handed out, of having one's own requests turned down when those of less careful and deserving brothers are honored; the weari-ness of seeing fewer and fewer people volunteer to unload the flatboat on Sunday mornings, until one Sunday only one man volunteers.[100]

Perhaps this explains the ambiguity of those manifestations of commu-nitarian orthodoxy embodied in sabotage of community tools or activities, and the fury unleashed against a despotic Father whom they enjoy hang-ing or burning in effigy in order to avoid avowing openly and honestly that their faith is dead. This is the lie denounced by those who leave the battlefield and return to the old world—since there is no new world—so as not to participate in the hypocritical staging of the Icarian Republic's salvation:

> For it's either one of two things. Either you want the Community or you don't want it. In the first case, if you want the Community, if you admit that it is better than individualism . . . then how could you forget that its author is precisely the man who is the butt of your outrages, and that for this reason alone you owe him more regard and consideration, not to mention respect and thanks.
>
> If, on the other hand, after your actual experience with the

---

100. Vallet, "Communism: History of the Experiment in Nauvoo of the Icarian Settlement," in Grant (ed.), *An Icarian Communist in Nauvoo*, pp. 28–29.

system, you find it defective, impossible without lies for the outside world and espionage and tyranny within, then in the interest of truth, your family and your friends, why don't you speak your mind openly?[101]

What typographer Crétinon would like to see admitted frankly by his comrades is the robust truth that Émile Vallet, a son of the shoemaker–philosopher of Orsay who became the painter–philosopher of Nauvoo, would hammer home thirty years later. He would put it in the 1884 issue of the *Revue icarienne*, where the last colonists of the Iowa "desert" were debating with the former inhabitants of Nauvoo and representatives of the young "worker movement" over whether they ought to have gone there and whether it was the ship or the crew that had been the problem: "Why not be honest and admit frankly that we made a mistake; that we donned a habit that is much too long for us; that we did everything we could to behave decently, but we step on it because it is too big for us. . . . Human nature does not agree with the principles of communism, or the principles of communism do not agree with human nature."[102] In another account Émile Vallet again excuses both the Icarian workers and the founder: "The majority of the members composing the Icarian Society was a selection from the best laboring class of France. The most laborious, honest, economical, intelligent, and philanthropic. . . . Cabet, on his side, was determined to sacrifice his career, his family, happiness, even his life, out of love for the laboring class and to show the practicability of communism. They and he were in ernest [*sic*]. But they were human. The ego was too strong to be subdued by the will. They were under the influence of their sensations. . . . Human nature. The beast began to show itself, plainly upsetting all the beautiful dreams."[103]

One should not be taken in too much by the seeming simplicity of this moral. If philosopher–individualist Émile Vallet can converse in terms of human nature in the review of the last Icarian squadron, the reason is that human nature in 1885 Nauvoo is no longer what it was in 1845 Orsay: that is, the false nature produced by a bad societal organization and a faulty education that was to be corrected by the rational organization and "solid education" of the new city. Human nature, too, has stayed in step with

101. Letter of Crétinon, in *Voyage en Icarie de deux ouvriers viennois*, p. 244.
102. *Revue icarienne*, Aug. 1884.
103. Vallet, "Communism: History of the Experiment in Nauvoo of the Icarian Settlement," pp. 27–28.

the progress, science, industry, and education that have, for forty years, brought together in countless unforeseen ways the reasons of individualism and those of communism, the paths of big business and those of worker emancipation. Vallet is not inviting his communist adversaries and friends to take note of the immutability of human societies or to return to ancient values. He is inviting them to grasp and appreciate the evolution that is transforming both material conditions and human mentalities, that will unite the incompatibilities of an earlier day and make truly possible the dream that shipwrecked the Icarians in pursuit of it.

Vallet appeals to an experience shared by those who have returned to the battles of individualism without ceasing to be militants for progress, and by those who continued to pursue the Icarian dream after their Father's death. Of those who continued to pursue the dream of community, the rebellious majority left Nauvoo for the promised land of Iowa. Those who remained loyal to their Father gathered in Saint Louis and then in Cheltenham, Missouri: rest stops on a desert journey they will never resume. It is with the majority in Iowa that the philosopher of Nauvoo, Vallet, argues his case. But the history of the loyalists in Cheltenham would undoubtedly be the best illustration of his philosophy of Icarian history. For while the "strong" workers of the majority were at work paying off their debts in Nauvoo and clearing land in Corning, Iowa, the shoemakers, tailors, "weak" workers, good students, and fine talkers of the minority were at work laying down the laws and principles of their republic. The death of their Father now compelled every citizen to assume responsibility for a republic that would obviously be a new thing in history: "We are inaugurating something of which we find no examples. . . . We have seen warrior peoples, secret societies, industrial and artistic nations. We, for our part, want to be a REFORMER People, a PHILOSOPHER People."[104]

So this philosophic people takes Icarian doctrine and organization into its own hands. It sets about weighing each article of its new constitution and busies its printshop, for want of more remunerative work, in publishing its law bulletins: on the social contract (adopted after five meetings), on the organization of work, on tobacco, on taking inventory, on dealing with outsiders, and so on. It solemnly resumes an Icarian course of study. This is no longer the Father's course of sermons, but a mutual schooling: the young people fresh from the Icarian school learn by teaching others; and female citizens, who do not have the right to vote yet, now take the

104. Address of Mercadier, in *Inauguration du cours icarien*, Paris, 1858.

floor to teach. Citizen Grubert, the widow of Nauvoo's music teacher, gives lessons on "what constitutes true happiness," and her daughter Claudine is deemed experienced enough to analyze "the causes of evil." The former director of the girls' school in Nauvoo extols the virtues of "politeness," and her son Charles Raynaud extols those of "emulation." Jules Clèdes celebrates "fraternity," and Louis Gillet celebrates "good will." President Mercadier concerns himself especially with "public festivals," which should be part of the course of instruction and thus "form a complete system dovetailing with the social order we propose to establish."[105]

It is the social order of a worker people that rejects both the vanity of the new woodcutters, miners, and bargemen of Nauvoo and the family routine that takes labor power away from productive work and uses it up in useless mending and repairing. The law on the organization of work reforms the workshops, which must now bring in serious returns, and it imposes silence as "a matter of salvation."[106] The *Commission de détruit* eliminates "mending" and concentrates the efforts of dressmakers and tailors, who are beginning to be mechanized, on production and sales. And the transfer of the community to Cheltenham, in theory at least, opens the way for new remunerative industries: a spinning mill, a brewery, a nursing home, and several nursery gardens. For the nursery gardens the Icarians in France are asked to send seeds of ten varieties of cabbage, of forty other vegetables, several varieties of cherries, peaches, prunes, apricots, and currants, and sixty varieties of flowers to grow in open ground until greenhouses are built.

Reading the balance sheets of director Mercadier, however, one can only wonder about the future of this philosophic people. Its vocation is not to cultivate its garden but, more than ever, to accumulate material and moral forces for the building of Icaria in the desert. It is heartening to see that the colony, now at last precise in the accounting that was not Cabet's strong point, is beginning to show returns: "We are earning about 140 dollars a week—tailors, 100 dollars; shoemakers, 15; coopers, 15; miscellaneous, 10. . . . I estimate that this season we will produce an average of 180 dollars a week. I estimate that expenditures will rise to 75 dollars a week."[107] But there is reason for uneasiness also: given the pace of the community's economy and good will, how many years will it take to realize the primitive accumulation for Icaria? And how many articles

105. *Cheltenham*, Paris, 1858, p. 16.
106. *Notre situation à Saint Louis*, Paris, 1857, p. 9.
107. *Cheltenham*, p. 8.

must be added to the statutes on the organization of work to put an end
to the rebelliousness of mason Loire? He comes late to work, dawdles,
talks during work, says that no one would want to knock himself out
at spinning, refused to go on the mulberry detail and made fun of those
who did, stops during work to take a sort of English course with Citizen
Dazy, went to dine with a hostile dissident, causes trouble in the general
assembly, and criticizes everything.[108] But if one wants to reinforce Icarian
legislation, isn't one in danger of curing evil with evil? Is it not possible
that the lawmaking passion of the philosophic people only seems to be
opposed to disorder in production and actually goes back to the one and
only source of communitarian ills: the perversion of the Icarian spirit by
the revolutionary spirit? Reading reports of the sessions that the general
assembly devotes to review and revision of the Constitution, one is im-
pressed first and foremost by the serious tone and skill in difficult debates
that have been acquired by the former students of teacher Cabet. There
are long and detailed debates, projects posted in the refectory for the reflection of all, efforts by the committee of conciliation, and supplementary
discussions carried over to the workshop of the tailors after dinner. Unfortunately, the result of all that is a new schism, which, in March 1859,
deprives the colony of one-third of its members and the core of the old
guard of devoted followers.

But that is no longer surprising. For the old Icarians are obviously
the ones most infected with the original vice of the community: the confused mingling of the revolutionary spirit and the Icarian spirit. It was
combatted with difficulty by Cabet's preaching between 1840 and 1847,
reinscribed in their thinking and their behavior by the ill-fated Revolution
of February 1848, and confirmed by the great debates in Nauvoo. So there
is nothing astonishing about the apparent inconsistency of these veteran
communists. They all continued to view their spirit of revolutionary solidarity as the spirit of Icarian fraternity, and their republican passion for
laws and regulations as a sense of community order.

So director Mercadier, in Cheltenham, and Beluze, who is in charge
of the Paris office, are not distressed about what is not so much a dissidence as the end of an era: the tragic revolutionary decade that the former
combatants replayed as a farce, where they could. Rid of all those false
Icarians, all the falser in that they were longer in the movement, Icaria
can now finally begin: "It is only today that we are masters of ourselves

108. *Nouvelle Revue icarienne*, Nov. 15, 1858.

and are beginning to found Icaria."[109] Is some practical verification of this statement needed? During the three months of parliamentary debate, the average weekly intake of the colony had been 137 dollars. In May and June, with thirty-seven fewer workers and workshops in need of reorganization, the intake rose to 193 dollars. These figures are "more eloquent than any words we might say" to pass judgment on Icaria's prehistory, and they indicate the royal road of its history. With the young people who have learned true fraternity at the Icarian school, the new arrivals for whom Icarian courses are now organized in France, and the enlightened female citizens who are taking on new responsibilities, the little core of authentic Icarians will finally be able to undertake the building of Icaria. The new era, which was inaugurated on May 1, 1859, should reveal the principle of progress, work, in all its purity, a purity once stained by the revolutionary vanity of braggarts: "After the last crisis, debates have been put aside and the reign of production has been inaugurated."[110] To organize this reign and kingdom, director Mercadier has drawn up a ten-year plan: two years to settle the debts of the colony, two years of consolidation, and six years of high production to amass the capital for the founding of Icaria in the desert. That capital is the 500,000 dollars that Cabet, like all the reformers of his generation, was expecting from the generosity of people sympathetic to the cause of progress. The new era, the era of economy, must move beyond the duality of work and ownership in which it had been enclosed up to now:

> Let us practice the sort of economy and work that are based on properly understood self-interest and love of the Community; economy and work that come naturally, are ever present, constantly realize little gains, and produce considerable sums at the end of one year and the end of several years. Let us be diligent and punctual, showing the sort of initiative and relish that often double returns without any more effort or difficulty. Let us have the prudence dictated by the dangers involved in acclimation. Let us acquire the bold know-how so necessary for colonists. . . . Let us conform more and more each day to the promptness and facility of the Americans, thanks to which America is undergoing great and quick development.[111]

109. *Lettres icariennes*, I, 91.
110. Ibid., p. 268.
111. Ibid., p. 176.

But isn't this communist science of Poor Richard, reinvented by the producer and director of Cheltenham, really lagging behind on the march of economic progress it claims to embrace? One senses that it is torn between a pioneer conception of "bold know-how" and the "promptness" of great American enterprises on the one hand, and the old morality of saving on the other. The reason is that the productivity objective must be reconciled with the formation of Icarians who should be fraternal before being strong, thrifty before being enterprising. To launch the battle of Icarian accumulation, there is a need for individuals who measure up to the definition of the Icarian as one who is "honest, decent, hard-working, but, above all, good and fraternal."[112] That is the goal of the Icarian course of study. It is also the goal of the Sunday entertainments in which men and women, young and old, are to participate equally, and in which good will counts for more than does know-how.

Such is the evening entertainment of November 13, 1859.[113] Citizen Droussent, shoemaker and member of the entertainment committee, announced the start of the entertainment. The music of the students was a march, pretty rather than new, which left something to be desired as a harmonious whole. Then Citizen Defay, her voice slightly dimmed by the emotion of this first offering, sang the ballad "Marguerite, fermez les yeux." Citizen Bira, wife of the last soldier of the first vanguard, had a cold and proved only her good will by singing "Le petit mousse blanc." Another woman, Citizen Vinsot, did a fine job with "Balthazar," a song depicting the destitution of Lazarus at the rich man's door; and the daughter of deceased tailor Gluntz sang an appropriate song, "L'orpheline." The girls recited several poems, mingling elegy with social criticism: "L'Enfant du riche et l'enfant du pauvre, naître, croître et vieillir" by Joseph Déjacque, who himself cannot find too much sarcasm for the virtuous circle of the Icarian family, and "Le Ruisseau" of the young Charles Raynaud. The girls spoke naturally and with expression, but with wooden gestures and a diction too curt for pieces that call for ample gestures and a slow, accentuated pronunciation. Young Louis Gillet injected a less languid note with the loony disguise in which he sang "Le Fulmicoton." The public also forgave him for tripping up and having to start over. But if they had good-natured applause for all these manifestations of fraternal good will, it was a song memento of 1848 that managed to reawaken their enthusi-

112. Ibid., p. 304.
113. Ibid., pp. 229–32.

asm. In a burst of patriotism, the whole assembly joined Citizen Sainton
in repeating the refrain of Pierre Dupont's "Chant des soldats":

> Les peuples sont pour nous des frères (three times)
> Et les tyrans des ennemis.

> To us the peoples are our brothers
> And tyrants our enemies.

The evening ended with another memento, the Icarian "Chant du départ." So everyone could retire with "a joyous heart, a radiant soul, a
tranquil conscience, hence ready to take up tomorrow's work with new
energy and ardor." And Mercadier could underline with satisfaction the
difference between this entertainment and the recreations of individualism,
composed "of coarse farces, filthy masquerades, vile, disgusting, degrading hodgepodges."[114] The newly arriving men and women are certainly
aware of the progress in community mores resulting from the elimination
of tobacco from the Icarian course and its entertainments. The women, in
particular, take note of the improvement in male behavior. Writes Madame
Lavat: "You never hear coarse talk or swear words. You can go anywhere
with them at any time without having to blush, because all of them, from
the youngest to the oldest, treat us with the greatest respect."[115] Contrasting with these valuations of colony life are the shock and dismay of men
and women like Citizen Sauger and Citizen Claudine Mauvais, who for
family reasons have had to leave the colony permanently or temporarily
and now are back in the outside world:

> Here we are in the land of exile. . . . When one has tasted Icarian
> life and is even a bit of an Icarian, one can no longer live in this
> chaos. . . . The old world scares me. I cannot live here much longer.
> . . . It tore my heart to see wretched women, dirty and in tattered
> rags, using words which I usually did not understand but which I
> guessed to be very coarse. I also suffered a great deal in the shop
> where I worked. I could never have a sensible conversation with
> the women working alongside me. They were only concerned with
> trifles, or with speaking ill of one another.[116]

114. Ibid., p. 232.
115. Letter of Madame Lavat, ibid., p. 329.
116. Letters of Sauger and Claudine Mauvais, *Nouvelle Revue icarienne*, Dec. 15,
1859; and *Lettres icariennes*, I, 133.

Such is the paradox of the Icarian colony. It maintains the nostalgic memories of those who have left it much better than it retains those who live in it. Bidding farewell to the colony, Citizen Corne declares: "The prevailing decency and the elimination of the coarse remarks that existed in the workshops of individualism proved once more to me that the Community was making people moral."[117] But these compliments about morality cannot compensate for the laboring arms that disappear from the effort to carry out the ten-year plan of Icaria. And so the president's address of June 24, 1860, on "economy" presages a more combative conception of Icarian labor and economy for 1861. In 1861 the workshops will have to "manufacture on a large scale, work quickly, not waste a single moment in the year." At the same time, the colony will have to move away from its family routine and envisage the market for its production and consumption in a larger order—not that of shopkeeper exchanges, but rather that of a worldwide trade:

> In 1861 we shall have to concern ourselves with a matter that has been overly neglected: commerce. We say that our principles abolish commerce. But if we understand the point of this statement correctly, we will be convinced that commerce is not abolished for us insofar as it is useful. We propose to abolish fraud, the waste of time, avarice, and the hoarding of commodities: that is, the abuses and troublesome aspects of commerce. But commerce, understood as the exchange of products, should be encouraged and practiced by us. . . . Up to now it has been neglected too much in the Community, and that has been a big mistake. We must begin to correct it by familiarizing ourselves with the main products we consume, and with the countries that can provide us with them. We must be familiar with the commodities and raw materials provided by the markets of New York, England, France, Paris, Rio de Janeiro, Buenos Aires, etc. . . . In 1861 we must begin to familiarize ourselves with the idiom and habits of commerce.[118]

In prefiguring the problematic and rhetoric of the communist state capitalists of 1920, the communist economism of 1860 merely reveals its own ridiculousness. For it is in a situation where a reserve fund of two hundred dollars would be quite useful for unforeseen community expenses, and

117. *Lettres icariennes*, I, 214–15.
118. Ibid., pp. 341–43.

where, in the absence of capital or government, it does not even possess the "industrial army" described by the Icarian law on the organization of work. For if the arrivals of 1860 are no longer the badly reformed revolutionaries that the colony has finally rid itself of, it would be hard to say exactly who or what they are. Citizen Fortel was not serious enough, or enough of an Icarian, to be admitted at the end of his probationary period. The younger Sablier was not an Icarian at all, and his father, whose contribution was paid by the Paris bureau for his services as a propaganda veteran, was no more of an Icarian than he. Citizen Palis, a woman who said she was paving the way for the arrival of her husband, crossed the Atlantic only to flee him. Madame Michel had been presented as a person who knew nothing about the Icarian idea, and this opinion proved to be fully justified. As for Citizen Tesson, he concealed his money, criticized the lack of progress in Icaria, and ended his experiment by saying "that he had shown enough dedication and was sick of it."[119]

It is not surprising that director Mercadier asks himself and the Parisian official in charge of departures "if there will be many Icarians of this sort and if it is worth continuing Icaria." But what exactly is he complaining about? He did not want any more revolutionaries, and these people do not seem to suffer from barricade fever. He wanted good, decent, hard-working, fraternal people, and these people were probably that sort; but in France, "with their lives and habits and everything else fixed and regular for a long time," they simply lacked the virtue "they had not had the occasion to see so close up in France—perseverance at work in the face of drawbacks."[120] Moreover, these arrivals readily excuse themselves by admitting that they are not "combative men." They are not dissidents, revolutionaries, or "false Icarians." They are simply *non-Icarians,* a new variety of the inexhaustible family of people who come to enjoy Icaria rather than build it.

But what if this persistent mistake was the result of the false approach adopted by Icaria? Mercadier admits this himself, without taking heed, when he analyzes the thinking of these transient Icarians: "Rightly or wrongly, they miss the material position they left behind. And since no philosophical idea enters to fill the void that can be created by the loss of material satisfactions, they get discouraged."[121] But isn't the absence of a *philosophical idea* to be blamed on the colony rather than on the new ar-

119. Ibid., II, 6–7, 14–16.
120. Ibid., p. 292.
121. Ibid., p. 141.

rivals? Don't they complain about seeing "so little harmony . . . sympathy and fraternity among the members of the Society"? Don't they criticize the state of neglect in which Icarian education has been left? Upon their arrival they were astonished not to find the solemnities that once surrounded fraternal welcome.[122] To be sure, the community can answer that charge: if the colony has not been able to offer a solemn welcome to the most recent arrivals, the reason is that it has been too absorbed in its work. It is only imitating the example of its director, former law student Mercadier, who spends his days in wagon transport between Cheltenham and Saint Louis and then tends to his animals before plunging into his nighttime administrative work. But this good reason reveals the radical flaw in the course chosen, the flaw that Beluze vainly tried to combat in writing to Mercadier

> more than a hundred pages to prove to him that in choosing a
> president, the Society meant to provide itself with a guide as
> well as an administrator, not a wagoner and *commissionnaire;* that
> the functions of president were essentially and primarily those of
> surveillance and initiation; that he was to watch over all the parties
> and the social movement as a whole, in order to ensure observation
> of the rules and, above all, observation and practice of the very
> principle of the Society.[123]

In the approach based on work and production, which at first seemed to him to be stamped in the gold of the Icarian principle, the guardian of the Icarian heritage in Paris came to recognize too late the latest and most cunning corruption of Icarian doctrine by the revolutionary impatience that is connected with the spirit of pleasurable possession. The dedication of wagoner–president Mercadier is nothing but a reverse reproduction of the demagogy of Nauvoo's "strong workers" and "reds": "the application in our Colony of direct government by the people, that chimera invented by jealousy in the midst of our European discords and revolutions."[124] If you replace the Father, founder of a new moral world, with a shock-troop worker–intellectual and base the future of communism solely on increased productivity and apprenticeship in commerce, then you should not be surprised to see the arrival of people who judge the community in terms of

122. Ibid., p. 303.
123. Ibid., p. 304.
124. Ibid., p. 305.

the well-being it can provide them. For you are simply confirming the narrow, automatic view of the working class:

> Most of them see Icarian doctrine merely as a system of social organization that guarantees workers against poverty better than individualism does. . . . What they understand best is the organization of work in common, which, through the use of machines and the new forces that Science has made available to humanity, allows for a large enough production to satisfy the needs of all in large measure. . . . But, as we have seen already, that is only one side, one part, of our project: the system of social organization. There remains the moral side: our doctrine.[125]

So Icarian propaganda was duty-bound to reestablish the primacy of moral commandment over material organization. Instead of that,

> our publications generally contain nothing but reports on the operations of the Society, its laws and rules, in short, anything and everything having to do with the organization of the Icarian system. We find a considerable lacuna in our teaching, and the result is that we train incomplete Icarians. Moreover, in the letters of colony members and especially in the complaints of dissidents, we repeatedly come across these words: "I like it" or "I don't like it" here in the community. At the very least, these words are very strange on the lips of people who have taken the designation "soldiers of humanity," who have left home and family to go three thousand miles away and build a model society in order to regenerate the world.[126]

If the educators allow themselves to be educated by those they are supposed to teach, then failure is inevitable. And a pitiless logic governs this apparently paradoxical situation: from the material standpoint, the Cheltenham society "seems to be alive, its life more vibrant than ever"; but from the moral standpoint, it is "crumbling bit by bit."[127] No longer capable of correcting the flaw that is killing the colony, the man in Paris responsible for propaganda prefers to abandon it to its fate.

125. Ibid., pp. 308–9.
126. Ibid., p. 312.
127. Ibid., p. 303.

Many remarks would be in order with regard to the analysis of Citizen Beluze, especially with regard to the "vibrant material life" that he contrasts to the moral feebleness of the colony. The truth is that the colony is in the throes of death, not having been able to fulfill the first objective of its plan: paying off its debts. The reason is that the moment it chose for its economic takeoff coincided, unfortunately, with the general economic crisis, then with the Civil War, when half of its members headed elsewhere to defend the cause of right and liberty. Beluze's explanation links the egotism destroying the community with the persistence of the demagogic chimera. But isn't that explanation contradicted by the perseverance of the Nauvoo rebels, who alone will hold up the Icarian banner for three more decades at their farming retreat in Corning? But the crux of the matter does not lie there. It lies, rather, in the way in which Beluze, the guardian of Icarian doctrine, evades and then wriggles out of the questions one might rightly ask him. How should they go about—how should they have gone about—impressing on people's spirits the very simple doctrine that the master expounded in countless articles, pamphlets, lectures, and addresses without ever having been able to form a single true Icarian? What actions should be, should have been, manifestations of this communitarian fraternity that is not to be equated with revolutionary solidarity, constitutional strictness, or the collective tension of production? How is one to forge this Icarian faith that one must have before launching into its practice, but that never ceases to be corrupted by practice? Is Icaria bound to perish without ever having begun because they never knew what an Icarian was?

It is here that Citizen Beluze wriggles out of the problem, under the modest guise of offering a practical solution for the problem of Icarian formation. It is now pretty well established that no course in fraternity can possibly replace the period of transition between individualism and communism that the author of *Journey to Icaria* had envisioned to form the ideas, mores, and capabilities of Icarians, but that the founder of Icaria, persecuted by his enemies and pressed by his impatient disciples, had not been able to carry out in reality. But, says Beluze, right in the heart of the old world there is a transitional system capable of developing practical abilities, understanding, and a sense of fraternity at the same pace: the system of worker associations. Some might well argue that the experiment was tried in 1848 and that it hardly passed its material or moral tests. But, says Beluze: "These kinds of operations always go badly in the disorderly periods that naturally follow great social upheavals. To develop and grow, these institutions need calmness in human spirits and security in business and labor."[128] The prosperity of the file-cutters, armchair-joiners, chair-turners, piano-makers, masons, and others bears ample witness to the economic viability of this institution and its potential as a force for social education. So the thing to do is to get resolutely involved in the association movement, which is stirring with new life. These associations will then become "veritable nurseries rearing Icarians, people anxious to practice more completely the solidarity in which they have been formed by practice."[129]

Some might again retort that this approach is hardly more suitable than that of Mercadier for separating the Icarian idea from the surrounding succession of ideas about production and well-being. And they could remind Beluze of the scorn that the theoretician of Icaria had for these petty associations—just right for improving the individual material lot of their members, but incapable of serving the great cause of humanity. But that is precisely what distinguishes Beluze's new proposal from the false economistic approach of Cheltenham. The very limitations of worker association rule out the possibility of confusing, as the Cheltenham approach did, the paltriness of the organization of work with the new communist world: "Above all, let us have no fear that association ideas will absorb Icarian ideas. That is impossible. Does the pale brightness of a star eclipse the brilliant light of the sun? Does the rivulet absorb the river? No. Associations will become veritable nurseries of Icarians."[130]

But do the Icarians who talk like this assume that their brothers are so ignorant that they do not know that the ratio of star to sun is exactly the opposite in the realm of science, which now governs human progress? The apparent modesty of the provisional morality that keeps the dream of the Promised Land in reserve is there only to hide the fact that there is no Promised Land any more—that the great Idea was, in fact, one of those little rivulets that believed they would get there, only to end up disappearing in the great river of progress. Without too much heartbreak, one must get used to the idea that morality is incapable of begetting a new world for a rejuvenated humanity, that at most it can moderate the relationship between the education of individuals and the objective progress embodied in the new scientific and industrial achievements.

Worker association is no longer the result of a moral effort to redress the flaws of a false societal education; it is the "need of our time." Isn't it

128. Circular letter of Beluze, Jan. 1863, p. 3.
129. Ibid.
130. "Rapport de la Commission nommée pour vérifier la gestion du citoyen Beluze," Nov. 1862.

being forced even on those least sympathetic to it: "fortune's favorites"? To no avail would philosophers and moralists have preached union, solidarity, association, to those egotists. But the development of production forces has constrained them to create those stock companies in which the owner is associated with his janitor and the errand boy on the streetcorner: "What the philosopher would have been incapable of doing, the steam engine has accomplished."[131] It will ultimately be the same for those workers whose situation should have led them to association spontaneously. If propaganda work has had only modest success in bringing them to association, necessity is going to force it on them. For they are faced with machines that are competing with them today but could reduce their toil and increase their well-being tomorrow: "They are the instrument of their emancipation. It is they that will make them real citizens, free and independent human beings."[132] Provided, of course, that the workers are assured intellectual and material mastery over the machines; and association is their only chance for ensuring that. The combined power and objectified labor of the machine imposes association and gives it its model, a new identity of necessity and liberty that gives association the same attributes and effects the machine has: "It is the thing that will emancipate the worker, raise him to the dignity of a free human being, bring comfort and convenience to his family, and facilitate the intellectual and moral development of all its members."[133] So there is no point in quibbling over which liberates which, in debating whether association is liberative as a means of appropriating the machine or whether the machine is liberative insofar as it is the property of an association. One thing is certain. The effort, morality, and struggle of the worker, which formerly contrasted the pathways of progress with those of egotism, are meaningful today only on the basis of this objective movement that establishes the royalty of work only as the royalty of industry, hence outside the worker: "Work, which even yesterday was despised and abandoned by all those who could avoid it, is honored today. It prompts the most solemn ceremonies of nations. Splendid palaces are dedicated to it, and the highest rewards are given to the winners of the great competitions that the modern nations have instituted under the designation 'Exposition of Industrial Products.'"[134]

If the kingdom of work can be proclaimed today and tomorrow war-

131. Beluze, *Les Associations, conséquences du progrès*, Paris, 1863, p. 40.
132. Ibid., p. 28.
133. Ibid., p. 20.
134. Ibid.

rant the renewed parade of the glorious producer, the reason is that it is already objectified, outside the brains and hands of workers, in the palaces of the machine and the festivals of industry. This objectification allows escape from the vicious circle of community. Community is the only thing capable of turning the aspirations of the workers into reality, but they cannot undertake to turn it into reality without destroying its principle. The communist dream can be saved only by removing it from the contradiction that unceasingly reveals pleasurable possession at the heart of dedication, individualism at the heart of community, the old world at the heart of the new world. The objectification of the kingdom of work will henceforth prevent it from being mingled confusedly with the animal kingdom of egotistical enjoyment, the longing for which was disguised as producer pride and communist fraternity. It is not that the iron age of the machine has come along to put an end to the golden age of the communitarian dream. It is because community is impossible that the machine offers its promise to those who are willing to defer their dream and recognize that the only road to a new society finds its source and principle in this objective socialization of productive forces wherein liberty is making a new covenant with necessity, the principle of well-being with the principle of education.

Community must be set aside in order to open the way to communism, its way being the way of all. It is certainly true that there is no Icaria, and tailor Bourgeois will die in the desert named Dallas without having been able to pay his promised visit to his brothers in Corning. But perhaps it was fitting and necessary to get lost on the way in order to find the true way to happy tomorrows on the great river that the steamboat traverses from New Orleans to Nauvoo, passing by Saint Louis. There is no old and new world any longer, no roads of communism leading to lands other than those of individualism. Tomorrow's conflicts over the possible and the impossible, reform and revolution, presuppose common acknowledgment of the new geography of the pathways of the future. The scandalous phrase of a traitor of the future sums up nicely the inevitable certainty that presents itself to all: from now on, it is not the goal but the movement that counts, not the Promised Land but the river, not the river but the machine that tames and traverses it.

But this shared certainty can be expressed and practiced in two ways. One is the way of the philosopher of Nauvoo, Émile Vallet, who spells it out for the last veterans of Icaria and for the young, impatient anarchists of Europe in 1886. It is the slow way of the reforming, educating industrial republic:

The pear must grow and ripen before it falls. . . . But, you will say, we are tired of waiting; your evolutionary method is too long; if, by a bold stroke, we could make ourselves masters of the situation and put our ideas into practice, we would force the march of progress. Perhaps you are right. But to carry out a bold stroke, one must have the strength; and you do not. And the people, not being up to it, will turn against you at the first mistake you make. . . . The new economic situation, large-scale production, is going to impose a new social organization, just as the present one imposed itself on preceding ones. The machine is our savior.[135]

This wisdom promises salvation through the steam engine, but only at the cost of reducing its speed to the rhythm of maturing fruits. Over against this approach stands a second way. By way of anticipation, it sees in the steam engine and its speed all the characteristics of the energy that all revolutionaries sense to be the real energy of revolution— electric energy, whose simultaneousness solves the impossible problem of communism, the problem of getting the progress of production and the progress of human spirits to coincide in a flash. This is the future that was pointed out, back in 1850, by a communist without community. Tailor Gluntz, in charge of the Icarian warehouse in Saint Louis, puts it in a letter to his brother communists in Lyons:

To tell you in a single word what the state of America is today, I would say that it is absolutely the same as in Europe, insofar as workers are concerned. You find rich and poor, exploiters and exploited. So the social question is debated in all the big cities. . . . In our city there are meetings that communists attend to propagandize, and soon there will be more communists in America than in Europe. . . . The number of workers without work and even the number of beggars is increasing rapidly in the United States, but social progress moves ahead as quickly as the steamboat on its rivers.[136]

135. Letter of Émile Vallet, *Revue icarienne*, Jan.–Feb. 1886.
136. Gluntz to his friends in Lyons, *Le Populaire*, Aug. 1850.

Epilogue

The Night of October

EVENING OF LOST BATTLES, dawn of the new age? Fantasies that have vanished in the sunlight of science, or a once-solitary utterance that has become the flesh and blood of a socialist movement dovetailing with the law governing the universal evolution of beings? To be sure, there are those who can do sums without remainders, thanks to their long experience in keeping the books of worker associations. Such are the former barricademan Abel Davaud and the former man of *L'Atelier* Magloire Capron, whose *Moniteur des syndicats ouvriers* is celebrating this night in October 1891. For young and old workers are coming to take their place in line and put their hands on the fruits of what may well be the exemplary project of the century. Tomorrow, you see, the painting business *Le Travail* is going to divide up 250,000 francs among all those who have contributed to its success over the past fifty years. That sum will come from the enormous reserves of the house founded by the pioneer of participation, the former worker painter who became a philanthropic patron and militant Fourierist, Edme-Jean Leclaire:

> What happiness it is for working-class families to take in a rich harvest of coins, the fruits of bygone labor, in autumn, as winter approaches! There you saw handsome young men, frail old men, many fathers of families in their prime, widows of workers who died at work, and venerable workshop ruins crushed by the weight of age. The last, the white-bearded pensioners, were allowed free access as a favor, but the others lined up heroically. The first three arrived at 1:30 A.M. to take their place outside 11 Rue Saint-Georges. A huge group had joined them by 3:00 A.M. By the light of a lamppost, some of them made up numbers and put them

on their hats to verify their place in line. . . . A young scene-painter with a lively imagination, who was one of the first in line, told us that during his long vigil he had seen two apparitions hovering in the night sky above the houses on Rue Saint-Georges: one, glorious and radiant as a star, was the figure of the worker painter Leclaire looking down at his magnificent project; the other, contrite and humiliated, was the sad figure of the hapless police superintendent of this same district, who, back in 1842, by order of the ultraindividualist and ultrabourgeois government of Louis Philippe, had notified Leclaire that he was expressly forbidden . . . to assemble his workers in order to give them a share in his profits.[1]

Hours of expectant waiting very different from the night sweeter than day celebrated only about ten years ago by the nostalgic barcarolle of the *Tales of Hoffman?* Would today's worker painters give an example of realistic visions? Or is that the common fate of young people anxious for the enjoyments promised by the coming century and of apostles who now benefit from the comforting economies of their forced labor? By 1879, when he published his couplets under the title *La Forêt de Bondy*, even *rentier* Gauny seemed inclined to sacrifice the illusions of his metaphysical nights for the new sunshine of the worker's day:

> Le jour s'abat, bientôt une nuit vaporeuse
> Couvrira de chagrins le rêve que je creuse
> Dans la forêt encore, d'un regard enchanté
> Je vois, en m'en allant, marcher la liberté.
> Elle s'est retournée et son adieu me donne
> L'indice des erreurs qu'il faut que j'abandonne.
> Je la retrouverai plus large de poitrail
> Dans un beau jour doré par l'effort du travail.[2]

A new episode in his interminable farewell to old Dante. But our plebeian lion is in great danger of missing his latest rendezvous with the French Republic—the nursing, laboring Marianne. For a new hallucina-

1. *Moniteur des syndicats ouvriers*, Oct. 25–Nov. 8, 1891.
2. Louis Gabriel Gauny, *La Forêt de Bondy* (Paris, 1879), p. 59. "Day sinks, soon a misty night / will cover with regrets the dream I dig / in the forest again, with an enchanted gaze / I see liberty advancing as I leave. / She has turned back and her adieu is an indication / of the mistakes I must abandon. / I will find her again, her breastplate larger / on a fine day gilded with the exertion of work."

tion has stopped him before a freshly plastered wall of the proprietary order, and its whiteness invites him to a strange task. In it the work of a worker eager to catch up with his idol gets lost again in the lamentation of the proletarian and the pencil drawings of the rebellious child:

> J'atteins le mur d'un parc frais maçonné. Ce plâtre
> A vraiment dans ces lieux la blancheur de l'albâtre:
> Je ne sais quelle idée, avec un cri vivant,
> Apparaît sur ce mur et m'arrête devant.
> Mon coeur en retentit sous ma chair hérissée,
> Mon front porte le poids d'une foule insensée.
> Aux tons fuyants du soir, mêlés de clair-obscur,
> Je vais le crayonner sur l'enduit de ce mur;
> Le passant y lira nos douleurs et nos crimes
> Que la mort vient guetter en fouillant nos abîmes.
> D'une main d'ouvrier, à l'oeuvre, et charbonnons
> Des êtres bien connus en étouffant leur nom.[3]

But no passer-by will read the pencilings of the old joiner. Without any hope for their publication, he collects his thoughts of a half-century under the title *Le Belvédère*. Lacking a publisher sensitive to the "oddness" of his views, he undoubtedly could have paid for the cost of publication out of his investment revenues. But he was not one to forget the advice he had given the too thrifty philanthropist of the Bois-Colombes project, former tapestry-worker Julien Gallé: "Let us cast the revenues of our fortune to all the winds of human deliverance."[4] So Gauny placed a portion of his income in the service of the mutual-aid society of former Saint-Simonians, La Famille; as for the rest, the joiner resistant to the railway order succumbed to the charm of canals, investing it in the Panama Canal that was

3. Ibid., pp. 59–60. "I come to the freshly plastered wall of a park. / The plaster in these places truly has the whiteness of alabaster: / I know not what idea, with a vivid cry, / Appears on the wall and stops me before it. / My heart reverberates with it under my shaggy flesh, / My brow bears the weight of a senseless multitude. / In the fleeting tints of evening, mingled with chiaroscuro, / I will pencil it on the plaster of this wall; / There the passer-by will read our sorrows and our crimes / That death will waylay as it plumbs our abysses. / To work, with a worker's hand, and let us blacken with writing / creatures well-known as we wipe out their name."

4. Gauny to Gallé, 1878, Fonds Gauny, Bibliothèque municipale de Saint-Denis, Ms. 170; Reprinted in Jacques Rancière (ed.), *Louis Gabriel Gauny: Le philosophe plébéien* (Paris: La Découverte/Maspero, 1983), p. 178.

to be built by a French company in the 1880s. So Gauny no longer has the wherewithal to publish these meditations, even though they have to do with "the happiness of the human race": "My intellectual products are lost and gone. All their conscientious theorems, which I would have liked to communicate to human beings, have dried up and blown away, like the dead leaves of [the month of] Brumaire. My thoughts are scattered in the darkness and debris of myself. An octogenarian ruin, time blows on the gravel of my body as it crumbles on the edge of the grave. It is an existence to be begun again."[5]

Fortunately, Gauny believes in the transmigration of souls. For one can hardly count on the men of succeeding generations to embrace and pass on the transcendental "theorems" of the plebeian philosopher. The upcoming generations do not like the works of their elders except insofar as they can extract the rational core of their social criticism from its mystical gangue. The theoretician of "integral socialism," former shepherd Benoît Malon, puts it bluntly to the master of the generation now in its eighties, former Saint-Simonian missionary and theoretician of collectivism Constantin Pecqueur:

> From the standpoint of economics . . . it is in you that I found the most correct criticism of bourgeois individualism and the bases for the evolutionist communism that is my socialist creed.
>
> In philosophy or in religion, as you probably like to put it, we would be in less agreement. Neither the God of Rousseau nor the Jesus of the 1848 socialists has been able to establish my political faith. Diderot, Spinoza, Hegel, Schopenhauer, and the modern materialists are my favorites. My generation wants it thus, but I am not wholly with it; and my friends claim that I have preserved not a few mystical prejudices.[6]

The new suns of science and the advancing proletariat that some of the younger and more frivolous people would readily take back to the Argand lamps of singing societies and the outdated epicureanism of the *goguette* republic. Thus, typographer Marc Gilland has not done with celebrating the garrets where we make love at twenty and with rhyming *chanson* with *Lison*, *zéphyrs* with *soupirs, taille enchanteresse* with *volage maîtresse*, and *grâce*

5. Gauny, *Le Belvédère*, Fonds Gauny, Ms. 146. In Rancière (ed.), *Le philosophe plébéien*, p. 196.

6. Malon to Pecqueur, Fonds Pecqueur, International Institute of Social History, Amsterdam.

légère with *trace éphémère*. As the new century dawns, he undoubtedly continues to hail the morning star of the *République immortelle* as his father did. But is it his fault if he has retained, more than the Gospel of a father who disappeared prematurely, the simple and slightly skeptical pastoral of his grandfather Magu, the weaver–poet of Lizy-sur-Ourcq?

> Mais je n'ai pas d'illusion
> L'égalité n'est que chimère.[7]

> But I have no illusions
> Equality is mere chimera.

But the lilac season and the combatant month of the new "Labor Day," May, summon up somewhat less conventional souvenirs of love and more tenacious illusions for another patriarch. The former head of the phalanstery school had returned, disabused, from the banks of the Red River, to which he had been transported by the invariable loquacity of tailor Bourgeois. But in early May 1890, he received a curious love letter from a widow who was his contemporary:

> Does Victor Considérant remember Jeanne Désirée?
> If he does, let him write her a word. She has forgotten nothing, neither Fourier nor the youthful sentiments of 1832. And she lives calmly in voluntary solitude, her heart filled with memories of her whole impassioned life.[8]

If the Widow Gay, alias Jeanne-Désirée, alias Désirée Véret, writes from her retreat in Brussels to a lover lost fifty-three years earlier, it is not out of any senile attachment to memories and witnesses of the good old days. The seamstress who founded *La Femme libre* has an old doubt to clear up and a confession to make to the one-time editor of *La Phalange*. Among the brief loves that preceded his marriage to the daughter of an eminent Fourierist, hasn't he retained the memory of a "good girl, quick to give herself and easy to leave"?[9] But he should know that the same pride that today requires his acknowledgment defrauded him then of the reward

---

7. "Les lunettes de mon grand-père," in Marc Gilland, *Après l'atelier*, Paris, 1900, p. 45.

8. Désirée Véret to Victor Considérant, May 5, 1890, Archives nationales (A.N.), 10 As 42.

9. Ibid., June 21, 1890.

of his good fortune: "I loved you passionately. . . . But I never found a word of love to say to you, nor a caress to give you."[10] This double miscalculation, between the falsely facile loves of the male intellectual and the too proud sentiments of the proletarian woman, was undoubtedly necessary to shape the dominant passion of their two characters, which is also the essential force behind progress: social love. It was also necessary to complete the primary education wherein this woman, who never found happiness except in "the life of emotion and passionate love," found herself "drawn to the apostles of social ideas" even before being "responsive to sensual emotions."[11] And so she is not nostalgic about the disappointments of the free woman: "I dreamed of free love and I knew that your sentiments were engaged and that the line of your destiny was marked out; but I loved your apostle's soul, and I united my soul with yours in the social love that has been the dominant passion of my life."[12]

Quite aside from the abandonment of the female lover and the doctrinal disillusionment of the free woman, isn't this happy social love also doomed thereby to impotence? Doesn't the impossible love of the apostle and the seamstress point up the logic that left the phalanstery in a state of utopia by letting social love get lost in the too learned Fourierist schema of the cabalist, the butterfly, and the composite? This is the deeper import of the mistake in social physics underlying the manic and inapplicable rigorism of phalanstery organization: "The promoter of this social theory, the most diverse in its unity that has ever been elaborated, had the intention, so natural to complete geniuses, of asserting himself completely and consistently in the whole and in every detail. These geniuses do not take into account individual narrowness, or the fact that a molecule is not an entity."[13] The impossible synthesis of the one and the many is due to a failure to appreciate the "vital agent" required to link the social molecules: that is, the "universal soul," which is not to be found in the simple physics of atoms and combinations of social forces but which will come to be known as "the reward for the practice of universal solidarity." In this rekindled opposition between a learned physics of egotistical atoms and a popular physics of humanitarian waves and fluids, the original social stake comes out clearly: the rigidity of phalanstery combinations of the one and the many is at once cause and effect of the option taken, of the prejudice that sacrificed proletarian loves and popular aspirations to the quest for

10. Ibid.
11. Ibid., Aug. 15 and Sept. 7, 1890.
12. Ibid., June 21, 1890.
13. Ibid., Oct. 9, 1890.

capital investments and other forms of support that the powerful of the earth could contribute toward the realization of the phalanstery system. So the fate of the associative utopia was decided at the same time that the marriage of its spokesman was decided. And these individual findings prompt a broader examination of conscience about the proletarian adventures and bourgeois marriages of the social apostolate: "And you yourself, my dear old friend, are you not suffering from this rigidity? Haven't you suffered from it? Hasn't it sometimes driven away the tender sympathies that would have made you happy and that would have inspired what would have made you as great as the master, whose doctrine you would have applied by appealing to the sentiments of the disinherited rather than by appealing to the cupidity of the ambitious and the pleasure-seeking?"[14]

Another rendezvous that failed to take place between the bourgeois apostles and the dreams and aspirations of the common people? The blazing flame of a still-lively love that is, alas, powerless to shed light on the thoughts of the multitude and the pathways to the future? "I love you all the same, but fifty-eight years too late for you and me."[15] Isn't it regret over that lost opportunity that shows up clearly in the photograph Considerant sent her? The picture in which she delights to see the features of her friend and the visage of an apostle also saddens her for two reasons. First, instead of this stiff and somewhat outdated image, she would have preferred a photograph of him as he is now, "with no deliberate posing or planned coyness." Second, she would also have liked to recognize another image in it, that of "a fine, high-minded philosopher, as unskeptical as possible."[16] But looking at the photograph closely, she detects a very different expression: "Is it a hallucination of my eyes? It seems to me that your eyes are fraught with reproach for civilization, and that your mouth expresses a painful discouragement."[17] Désirée's sight, greatly enfeebled by progressive amaurosis, has not deceived her. That is how those who were eyewitnesses to his last years depict the old head of the Fourierist school: an odd old man who brought back from Texas an astonishing Mexican peasant outfit but few illusions; still faithful to the Fourierist cause, but convinced of the need for long preparatory studies; hence rushing about from the Museum to the Sorbonne, and from the Sorbonne to the Collège de France.

Over against these round trips of hope and bitterness between the me-

14. Ibid.
15. Ibid.
16. Ibid., Nov. 23, 1890.
17. Ibid., Oct. 2, 1890.

tropolis of science and the virgin lands of the American utopia, the female solitary of Place Sainte-Gudule in Brussels sets the confident lesson of her different course of travel, closer in space but farther ahead on the road to the new world. Her course was through the cities of exile for the democratic revolution that had become the metropolises of the international working-class movement and of the socialist revolution: London, Geneva, Brussels, and so on. She had traveled through Europe following her husband, Jules Gay, a communist by conviction and a bibliophile by trade, once a promoter of free unions and the trips around the world promised by *L'Humanitaire*. She had also done a great deal of collecting for the First International and headed its female branch for a time. Now she found herself again alone, and independent because of the "small fortune" left to her by her son and her husband. Her choice was to remain in this land of exile, which some today liked to regard as the exemplary locale of the social movement. If the Belgian capital was preparing to host the Congress of the Second International, it was perhaps because the land of César de Paëpe—given the Marxism of the Germans, the trade unionism of the English, and the theoretically "integral" but more often "municipal" socialism of the French—offered the best promise of resolving the contradictions of the socialist hope. It symbolized a union between the organization of the militant proletariat, offspring of the fight for democracy, and the sociability of associations and cooperatives, offspring of the utopian tradition. It symbolized the rooting of the thinking of the new world in the positivity of the fundamental people. And so, to observe "the social crisis that now confronts humanity and is of interest to her," the old woman chose to situate herself at the center of this microcosm where the needed density of popular sympathies was combining with the powerful passion of youth:

> This concentration of so many different individuals nurtures a down-to-earth sympathetic current. . . . The movement, seen up close here as a whole, is a curious thing to study insofar as it is a mixture of enthusiasm, sentiment, and, above all, the positivity that typifies the Belgian character. . . . Once upon a time I used to say jokingly that Belgium was a mere baby. Now it is entering its virile, passionate stage. Such must have been initiator peoples in moving from theory to practice.[18]

18. Ibid., Sept. 1 and Oct. 2, 1890.

This youthful power certainly imposes a difficult task on socialist educators. The Widow Gay, who dreamed sixty years ago of troops of "little apostles" and of urchins playing industrial armies, is now pained to see children escaping priestly indoctrination only to wander as pitiful beggars through the streets. On a different front, anarchist impatience threatens to degrade the utopia of the general strike. So the solitary woman cannot really stay in the modest place she assigns herself. She cannot remain a "mere spectator" of a social movement that she assists with her "little mite" and her "lively sympathy." In addressing herself once again to the apostle and lover, she is not simply trying to assure herself of his consideration or to exchange memories of love—albeit social love. She is also trying to renew this love in a new communion and a new project. It is certainly true that the opportunity was missed and that one must begin from the beginning again, but they can and should begin again in the brief interval between now and their deaths:

> Reread *Destinée sociale*, pick out what is applicable to today and immediate needs, make a little journal of scientific utopianism . . . and light will spring from this match. . . . If I were a great lady above the masculine point of honor, I would say to you: let us together found the school of scientific and social utopianism. Let us resuscitate the modern innovators. . . . It would be good . . . to do for the scientific utopia what Jean Macé, Verne, Flammarion, and Hetzel have done to popularize the experimental sciences. . . . In short, we must inject theory into action, starting with children and women.[19]

Now more than ever is the time to adopt the approach rejected fifty years ago, to commit the demonstrations and projections of utopia to an alliance with the passionate force and "down-to-earth sympathetic currents" of the multitude:

> We must address ourselves to the illiterate, to the crowd anxious to know what is wanted by these human beings who do not have their banners blessed, who do not enroll in church clubs, and who discipline themselves to march harmoniously to their moral and material uplifting. . . . Science must prove and reassure, and

19. Ibid., Sept. 1 and 7, 1890.

enlightenment must dispel phantoms. Strength and health are given
to elders to teach the young.[20]

The abortive failures of utopian hope are far from proving its sterility
or tempting human beings to abandon it for the certitudes of science:

> Utopia has been the mother of the exact sciences and, like many
> fertile mothers, she has often produced embryos that were sterile or
> too fragile, embryos born prematurely or under bad circumstances.
> Utopia is as old as the organized world. She is the vanguard of
> the new societies. And she will fashion society, harmony, when
> human genius makes it a reality through learned demonstrations
> that dissociate her from obscurities and temporary impossibilities.[21]

So a school of scientific utopianism would leave to utopias their "poetic
grandeur" and "legends of the future," subjecting to the scrutiny of reason
and experience "what could be gleaned from them in the way of practice
to move beyond old social follies."[22] For the new world is not beginning
on the distant sands of Egyptian deserts or in the woodlands of Texas.
It is taking shape every day before our eyes and in our heads: "The first
lineaments of phalanstery are visible already, greater than we dreamed,
and the materials are coming together from everywhere. Everyone in the
world is at work on it, whether they know it or not, and for those who
see these things from on high, the evolution is marvelous. . . . Though I
be taken for a visionary, in fancy I already live in this new world."[23]
How could she not be taken for a visionary when we read her own
description of the ecstasies she felt at the dawning of the October day that
marked the anniversary of Fourier's death?

> I opened my eyes in the midst of a gentle light and a sensation
> of tender calmness, as if I were hovering, moving without any
> awareness of movement. For some time I remained in this heavenly
> and earthly beatitude. The feeling remained with me as a persistent
> perfume. I recalled having heard Fourier describe a similar effect,

20. Ibid.
21. Ibid.
22. Ibid.
23. Ibid.

which he thought was the state of the souls who love us and thus hover around us in our atmosphere.[24]

The "skeptical friend and rigid reasoner" to whom she dedicates this vision would have every right to explain it in terms of the venerable physics of compensations. His old girlfriend is becoming blind. This "universal phalanstery," whose federations, groups, series, and industrial armies she already sees, may well have the same meaning as the illusions that, a half-century earlier, consoled a father afflicted with blindness:

> My father, who had lived to ninety in full possession of his strength and faculties, had been blind for several years. He believed that the fortifications of Paris under construction were the foundations of social palaces. A wicked practical joker told him the truth that kindly people were keeping from him. He suffered a brain stroke and died several days later of grief and disillusionment.[25]

Is it the age-old story of illusion lulling the peaceful dreams of the blind and of fatal returns to reality? The matter is complicated by the fact that octogenarian Désirée Véret suffers from two illnesses rather than one. Besides her amaurosis, she is afflicted with nerves. The latter seems to be a more benign affliction, which can be easily attended to. She herself indicates the remedy, calling to mind the household occupations of her old widower friend:

> I amuse myself thinking of all the little household chores that take up a good part of your time. I would like to have lots of little manias that become needs and feed little desires and impatiences. It is the active life of our age-period that is hygienic to cultivate with philosophy. Each age-period has its own. How calm and rested the brain becomes after these little exercises! . . .
>   Unfortunately for my nerves, I have always lived outside myself and for others insofar as the practical details of existence are concerned. After the struggle I used to fly off into the clouds of reverie, where I fashioned an ideal world for myself. *Real, earthly* life has always been painful for me.[26]

24. Ibid., Oct. 9, 1890.
25. Ibid., Sept. 1, 1890.
26. Ibid., July 1891.

But what about this hygiene and philosophy that calm the nerves and rest the brains of old people? Aren't they merely the theory and practice of the housekeeping servitude against which the first two young seamstresses, Marie-Reine and Jeanne-Désirée, revolted sixty years ago? They make old age gentle only for those who have lost their lives in that servitude. Such was little Sophie Béranger, of whom her mother was so proud. She could not escape the real, practical existence of proletarian and domestic servitudes: "My life is of no use, neither for me nor for others. And I really feel, you see, that it could have been otherwise. . . . If you only knew how much I suffer because I have come to know in marriage only what dogs, bears, and wolves know. . . . It is a harsh suffering . . . a life sacrificed without purpose, without enjoyment for others or oneself."[27] Living outside oneself, for others or in the ideal world of utopia, was the condition for experiencing the enjoyment of one who lives without a master. And the life of utopia, dreamed for oneself or for others, is neither opposed nor subject to the clear-eyed analysis of illusions: "Although I have lived more on dreams than on realities, I fear illusions. I destroy them by analyzing them, given that age has calmed my passions. But I have enough left to satisfy the optimism that colors my disappointments and sustains me."[28]

So we have here something very different from the identical symptoms of a hereditary malady. The incurable nervous troubles of utopia are not to be identified with the phantasms provoked by loss of sight. On the contrary, only blindness could bring our utopian back to earth, forcing on her the hygiene of the little needs and desires of real, practical life: "For more than eight years now, since I suddenly have become almost blind, I have been working on all sorts of little arrangements to get around with my eyes closed. And I may end up acquiring some physical manias that will replace the eccentricities of my brain."[29]

That is possible, but unlikely. But when she might have been able to tell us, she could no longer do so. To the chronicle of her loves she will now add only these few words, by way of an epitaph: "Be indulgent toward your constant girlfriend."

We will not learn how she went into her night.

27. Sophie Béranger to Enfantin, Dec. 23, 1860, and Dec. 1, 1855, Fonds Enfantin, Bibliothèque de l'Arsenal, Ms. 7695.

28. Désirée Véret to Victor Considérant, July 1891.

29. Ibid.

Outline Chronology

Outline Chronology

1830

July 27–29: Paris Revolution. Fall of Charles X.

August 1: Louis Philippe accepts lieutenant-generalship of the realm.

August–September: Worker agitations and strikes, particularly among the Paris typographers.

October: The Saint-Simonians transfer to Taitbout Hall the course of lectures begun in April at the Hôtel de Gesvres, Rue Monsigny.

December: Le Globe (editor: Pierre Leroux) becomes the *Journal de la doctrine saint-simonienne.*

1831

February 15: An antilegitimist and anticlerical riot leads to the sacking of the archbishop's residence. The first five Saint-Simonian workers meet on the evening of the riot.

April: The Russian army invades Poland in response to the revolution of November 30. Threat of European war. Louis Philippe chooses nonintervention.

July: "General Communion of the Saint-Simonian Family." Organization of propaganda work among the working class by neighborhoods.

September 7: Order restored in Warsaw.

November: A break takes place between the two supreme Fathers of the Saint-Simonian religion, Enfantin and Bazard, over the issues of the new morality and the "couple–priest." Enfantin issues his "Appeal" to woman and the proletarian and proclaims the organization of industry. Dissolution of the organization by neighborhoods.

November 21: Insurrection of the Lyons silk-weavers.

1832

January: Banning of Saint-Simonian courses of lectures and indictment of the Saint-Simonian leaders.

February: Cholera in Paris.

March–April: Financial bankruptcy of the Saint-Simonians. *Le Globe* halts publication. Enfantin announces his withdrawal to Ménilmontant with forty of his "sons" (April 20).

June 1: Publication of the newspaper *Phalanstère* by Victor Considérant. Some Saint-Simonian intellectuals and workers turn to Fourierism.

June 5–6: Republican insurrection (known as the Cloître Saint-Merri insurrection).

June 6: Saint-Simonians take the habit at Ménilmontant to the sound of cannonade in Paris.

July: Opening of the "Temple works." Banning of Sunday meetings at Ménilmontant, which had drawn as many as two thousand people. Désirée Véret and Reine Guindorff publish *La Femme libre.* It will change its name several times, and it will be picked up by Suzanne Voilquin and published until her departure for Egypt in 1834.

August: Enfantin, Chevalier, and Duveyrier, charged with immorality and violations of the laws governing associations, are sentenced to one year in prison. A second trial on charges of fraud will end in acquittal in October.

November–December: Five detachments of Saint-Simonian missionaries (a total of about forty people) leave Paris successively for Lyons, the center for the formation of the "peaceable army of workers."

Enfantin enters prison.

1833

April: Dissolution of the Saint-Simonian "family" in Lyons.

August: Freed from prison, Enfantin heads for Egypt. There the Companions of the Woman have prepared for his arrival.

September–November: Wave of strikes, often sparked by militants of the Society of the Rights of Man. Striking Paris tailors create a "national workshop." Many prosecutions and convictions.

Collapse of the Fourierist colony of Condé-sur-Vesgre.

Failure of a Saint-Simonian project envisioned in Louisiana.

Lamennais: *Paroles d'un croyant.*

1834

April: The law on associations provokes republican insurrections in Lyons and then in Paris (April 9–14).

Founding of the Association of Gilt Jewelers, inspired by the principles of Philippe Buchez.

1835

The Saint-Simonian enterprise in Egypt goes awry. Postponement of the dam on the Nile and plague. In France, Ménilmontant is sold.

Barbès and Blanqui create the secret Society of the Families.

Buchez resumes publication of *L'Européen: Journal de morale et de philosophie.*

1837

Return of Enfantin to France.

Suicide of Reine Guindorff.

Liaison between Désirée Véret and Victor Considérant. Marriage of Considérant to Clarisse Vigoureux.

Lamennais: *Le livre du peuple.*

1838

Ott: *Des associations d'ouvriers.*

1839

May: Suzanne Voilquin departs for Russia. Failure of the attempted insurrection organized by Barbès and Blanqui.

November: Saint-Simonian workers (Vinçard, Desplanches, Vannostal . . .) create *La Ruche populaire*, together with Fourierists (Lenoir, Fugère) and "democrats" (Lambert, Supernant, Gilland), who later withdraw. Publication is interrupted in 1842. It is followed by *L'Union* (1843–1846).

Perdiguier: *Le livre du compagnonnage.*

1840

July: International tension and a wave of nationalism in connection with the question of Egypt.

Communist banquet in Belleville.

July–September: Worker agitation and strikes. Gatherings of several thousand strikers on the plain of Bondy.

September: Publication of *L'Atelier*, founded by 150 workers of diverse tendencies but soon taken over by the Buchez party (chief collaborators: Corbon, Chevé, Leneveux, Danguy, Gilland . . .). It is published until July 1850.

October 15: Attempt on the king's life by Darmés. Prosecution of communists, especially in Paris and Lyons.

November: Troncin and Suireau, leaders of the "coalition" of tailors, are sentenced to five years in prison.

Louis Blanc: *Organisation du travail.*

Proudhon: *Qu'est-ce que la propriété?*

Pierre Leroux: *De l'Humanité.*

Cabet: *Voyage en Icarie.*

1841

March: Cabet publishes *Le Populaire de 1841.*

May: La Fraternité, managed by La Hautière, formerly associated with Cabet, then by "a group of communist workers" (editor: Benoît

Voisin). It disappears in 1843, then reappears in 1845 (collaborators include Savary, Malarmet, Stévenot, and P. Vinçard) and lasts until January 1848.

July: *L'Humanitaire*, a materialist communist journal (Gay, May, Page, Charavay . . .).

September 13: Attempt on the life of the Duc d'Aumale, a son of Louis Philippe, by Quénisset, followed by street agitations in Paris and the arrest of several "shareholders" of *L'Humanitaire*.

October: Suicide of Adolphe Boyer, typographer, following the failure of his book. Polemics about "worker writing and literature."

November: Trial of Quénisset. Trial of *L'Humanitaire*. Other trials of communist militants or publicists (Pillot, Seigneurgens, etc.) held throughout the autumn.

Olinde Rodrigues: *Poésies sociales des ouvriers.*

1842

The Fourierist painting entrepreneur Leclaire initiates worker participation in profits.

Fourierist colony in Brazil miscarries.

Chevé: *Catholicisme et Démocratie; ou: Le règne du Christ.*

1844

Pecqueur: *De la République de Dieu.*

1846

January: Solemn burial of Troncin, who had been freed as a dying man from the prison of Gaillon.

1846–1847

Economic crisis and food riots, notably in Buzançais in January 1847.

1847

May: Appeal in *Le Populaire*: "Let's go to Icaria!"

July: Start of the reformist "campaign of banquets."

1848

February 3: The first Icarian vanguard (sixty-nine persons) leaves Le Havre to found Icaria in Texas.

February 24: Insurrection in Paris. A republic is proclaimed.

March: Worker assemblies on the occasion of electing corporative delegates to the Luxembourg Commission, which was presided over by Louis Blanc.

March 16–17: Reactionary demonstrations by élite troops of the national guard and counter-demonstrations by the people.

March 19: Eugénie Niboyet publishes *La Voix des femmes.* Her collaborators include Jeanne Deroin, Désirée Gay (formerly Véret), and Pauline Roland.

April 16: The national guard, called out to restrain a gathering of workers, demonstrates to cries of: "Death to Cabet! Down with the communists!" Persecution of communists in the provinces.

The first Icarian vanguard docks in Shreveport and learns that before July 1 it must build one house on each lot it has been granted in the territory of Cross Timber.

April 23: Elections to the National Assembly. Success of the right. Election of Corbon. Failure of Cabet and the worker candidates proposed by the Luxembourg Commission and the clubs.

May 4: Meeting of the Assembly, presided over by Buchez.

May 15: The Assembly is invaded by a demonstration organized by the worker clubs. The protest fails. Proceedings against socialist republican leaders.

The first Icarian vanguard continues the journey, arriving in Icaria June 2.

June 3: Departure of the second Icarian vanguard from Le Havre.

June 21: Measures to dissolve the national workshops.

June 23–26: Paris insurrection put down by General Cavaignac.

July 5: The National Assembly accepts the proposal of vice president Corbon and votes a credit of three million francs for worker associations. The Committee for the Encouragement of Worker Associations begins its work on July 12.

In Texas the Icarians are hit with malaria and must stop all work.

September: The leader of the second vanguard, Favart, arrives in Icaria and decides that they should pull back to Shreveport and then New Orleans.

September 28: The third vanguard leaves Le Havre.

November: The men of *L'Atelier* resign from the Committee for the Encouragement of Worker Associations following the Remquet affair.

November–December: Four "big departures" of Icarians (300 persons).

December 10: Louis Napoleon Bonaparte is elected president of the Republic.

1849

January: Cabet joins up with the Icarians in New Orleans. They are afflicted with illness and dissidence.

March: The loyal Icarians settle in Nauvoo, Illinois. They are hit with cholera and, soon after, a second dissidence.

May 13: Election of the Legislative Assembly in France. A joint push by reactionaries and Montagnards. Failure of the moderates, including Corbon. Election of Gilland.

June 13: After France's military intervention against the Roman republic, the democratic Montagnards vainly urge the people to rebel against the French government and its violation of the constitution. Their failure permits a purge of the Legislative Assembly.

September: Cabet is convicted of fraud *in absentia.*

1850

L'almanach des associations ouvrières lists, for Paris and vicinity, 211 associations, including 28 associations of cooks and 47 associations of hairdressers.

April: The *April law* liberalizes the financial conditions for admission to Icaria.

April–May: The success of the Left in several legislative by-elections persuades the majority of the Legislative Assembly to pass the law of May 31, which puts restrictions on universal suffrage.

1851

January: Third big Icarian dissidence.

July: Cabet returns to France to plead his case and is acquitted on appeal.

September: Disappearance of *Le Populaire* and creation of an ephemeral *Républicain populaire et social.*

December 2: Louis Napoleon Bonaparte's coup d'état.

1852

July: Cabet returns to Icaria.

December 2: Reestablishment of the Empire in France.

1853

November: Vote on Icarian "Reform."

1854

Death of Gilland at the age of thirty-nine.

Perdiguier: *Mémoires d'un compagnon*; published in exile in Geneva.

1855

December: Establishment of the Fourierist colony of Réunion in Texas, headed by Victor Considérant.

Cabet proposes to modify the Icarian constitution and give more power to the president.

1856

February: Cabet is voted down by the Icarian general assembly; he and his loyalists become the minority.

May 12–13: The new Icarian "red" majority ousts Cabet. The Icarians are split in two for good.

September–October: Cabet, excluded from the community, leaves Nauvoo with his loyalists and settles in Saint Louis. He dies there on November 8.

1858

The Cabet loyalists of Saint Louis, led by lawyer Mercadier, settle in Cheltenham, Missouri.

1859

Corbon: *De l'enseignement professionel.*

1860

The remaining members of Nauvoo's "red" majority settle in Corning, Iowa.

1861

American Civil War. Some Icarians enlist in the Union Army.

1862

World Exposition in London. French worker delegations are sent under government sponsorship. Their reports appear in the *Cahiers populaires,* published by the Palais-Royal group, workers who have gone over to the regime.

1863

The Icarian representative in France, Beluze, resigns from his functions, publishes *Les associations, conséquence du progrès,* and founds the *Crédit au travail.*

Corbon: *Le Secret du peuple de Paris.*

1864

Dissolution of the Icarian community in Cheltenham.

Worker Manifesto in France, known as the Manifesto of the Sixty.

September 28: Creation of the International Workingmen's Association (the First International) in London.

1865

Meeting of the commission of inquiry that is to draw up a law on cooperative societies. It hears testimony from surviving members of the worker associations of 1848.

1867

World Exposition in Paris.

1869

Victor Considérant returns to France after the failure of Réunion.

1877

Death of Suzanne Voilquin at the age of seventy-five.

The Icarian community in Corning, Iowa, encounters dissidence from the "Young Icarians."

1879

Vinçard: *Mémoires épisodiques d'un vieux chansonnier saint-simonien.*

1889

Gabriel Gauny dies at the age of eighty-three.

1890–1891

Désirée Véret Gay, an exile in Brussels, writes to Victor Considérant.

1891

Corbon, senator for life since 1875, dies at the age of eighty-two.

1898

Dissolution of the Corning community of Icarians.